Rock Climbing Desert Rock IV

The Colorado Plateau Backcountry: Utah

Help Us Keep This Guide Up to Date

Every effort has been made by the author and editors to make this guide as accurate and useful as possible. However, many things can change after a guide is published—trails are rerouted, regulations change, techniques evolve, facilities come under new management, etc.

We would love to hear from you concerning your experiences with this guide and how you feel it could be improved and kept up to date. While we may not be able to respond to all comments and suggestions, we'll take them to heart and we'll also make certain to share them with the author. Please send your comments and suggestions to the following address:

The Globe Pequot Press
Reader Response/Editorial Department
P.O. Box 480
Guilford, CT 06437

Or you may e-mail us at:

editorial@globe-pequot.com

Thanks for your input, and happy travels!

A FALCON GUIDE®

Rock Climbing
Desert Rock IV

The Colorado Plateau Backcountry: Utah

Eric Bjørnstad

Maps and topos drawn by
Holly Sorenson, unless otherwise noted

FALCON®

HELENA, MONTANA
GUILFORD, CONNECTICUT
AN IMPRINT OF THE GLOBE PEQUOT PRESS

A FALCON GUIDE®

Front cover: Crow's Head Spires and Bird's View Butte. Photo by Joe Slansky

Back cover: Looking Glass Rock. Photo by Mike Baker

Maps by Sue Carey © The Globe Pequot Press

Quotations introducing and ending each chapter of this book are from John C. Van Dyke's *The Desert* (1901), one of the publications edited by Edward Lueders in The Peregrine Smith Literary Naturalists Series (Salt Lake City): Gibbs Smith, Publisher [Peregrine Smith Books], 1980.

Library of Congress Cataloging-in-Publication Data

Bjørnstad, Eric

Desert Rock IV : rock climbing the Colorado Plateau Backcountry, Utah / Eric Bjørnstad.—1st ed.

p. cm. — (Rock climbing series) (A Falcon guide)

Includes Index.

ISBN 0-7627-1145-0

1. Rock Climbing—Utah—Guidebooks. 2. Rock Climbing—Colorado Plateau—Guidebooks. I. Title: Desert rock 4. II. Title: Desert rock four. III. Title IV. Series: A Falcon Guide

GV199.42.U8 B57 2003

796.52′23′09792—dc21 2002032515

Manufactured in the United States of America

First Edition/First Printing

WARNING:
CLIMBING IS A SPORT WHERE YOU MAY BE SERIOUSLY INJURED OR DIE. READ THIS BEFORE YOU USE THIS BOOK.

This guidebook is a compilation of unverified information gathered from many different climbers. The author cannot assure the accuracy of any of the information in this book, including the topos and route descriptions, the difficulty ratings, and the protection ratings. These can be incorrect or misleading, as ratings of climbing difficulty and danger are always subjective and depend on the physical characteristics (for example, height), experience, technical ability, confidence, and physical fitness of the climber who supplied the rating. Additionally, climbers who achieve first ascents sometimes underrate the difficulty or danger of the climbing route. Therefore, be warned that you must exercise your own judgment on where a climbing route goes, its difficulty, and your ability to safely protect yourself from the risks of rock climbing. Examples of some of these risks are falling due to technical difficulty or due to natural hazards such as holds breaking, falling rock, climbing equipment dropped by other climbers, hazards of weather and lightning, your own equipment failure, and failure or absence of fixed protection.

You should not depend on any information gleaned from this book for your personal safety; your safety depends on your own good judgment, based on experience and a realistic assessment of your climbing ability. If you have any doubt as to your ability to safely climb a route described in this book, do not attempt it.

The following are some ways to make your use of this book safer:

1. Consultation. You should consult with other climbers about the difficulty and danger of a particular climb prior to attempting it. Most local climbers are glad to give advice on routes in their area; we suggest that you contact locals to confirm ratings and safety of particular routes and to obtain first-hand information about a route chosen from this book.

2. Instruction. Most climbing areas have local climbing instructors and guides available. We recommend that you engage an instructor or guide to learn safety techniques and to become familiar with the routes and hazards of the areas described in this book. Even after you are proficient in climbing safely, occasional use of a guide is a safe way to raise your climbing standard and learn advanced techniques.

3. Fixed Protection. Some of the routes in this book use bolts and pitons that are permanently placed in the rock. Because of variances in the manner of placement, weathering, metal fatigue, the quality of the metal used, and many other factors, these fixed protection pieces should always be considered suspect and should always be backed up by equipment that you place yourself. Never depend on a single piece of fixed protection for your safety, because you never can tell whether it will hold weight. In some cases, fixed protection might have been removed or is now missing. However, climbers should not always add new pieces of protection unless existing protection is faulty. Existing protection can be tested by an experienced climber and its strength determined. Climbers are strongly encouraged not to add bolts and drilled pitons to a route. They need to climb the route in the style of the first ascent party (or better) or choose a route within their ability—a route they do not have to add additional fixed anchors to.

Be aware of the following specific potential hazards that could arise in using this book:

1. Incorrect Descriptions of Routes. If you climb a route and you have a doubt as to where it goes, you should not continue unless you are sure that you can go that way safely. Route descriptions and topos in this book could be inaccurate or misleading.

2. Incorrect Difficulty Rating. A route might be more difficult than the rating indicates. Do not be lulled into a false sense of security by the difficulty rating.

3. Incorrect Protection Rating. If you climb a route and you are unable to arrange adequate protection from the risk of falling through the use of fixed pitons or bolts, or by placing your own protection devices, do not assume that there is adequate protection available higher just because the route protection rating indicates the route does not have an X or an R rating. Every route is potentially an X (a fall could be deadly), due to the inherent hazards of climbing, including, for example, failure or absence of fixed protection, your own equipment's failure, and improper use of climbing equipment.

THERE ARE NO WARRANTIES, WHETHER EXPRESS OR IMPLIED, THAT THIS GUIDEBOOK IS ACCURATE OR THAT THE INFORMATION CONTAINED IN IT IS RELIABLE. THERE ARE NO WARRANTIES OF FITNESS FOR A PARTICULAR PURPOSE OR THAT THIS GUIDE IS MERCHANTABLE. YOUR USE OF THIS BOOK INDICATES YOUR ASSUMPTION OF THE RISK THAT IT MAY CONTAIN ERRORS AND IS AN ACKNOWLEDGMENT OF YOUR OWN SOLE RESPONSIBILITY FOR YOUR CLIMBING SAFETY.

UTAH AREA LOCATOR MAP

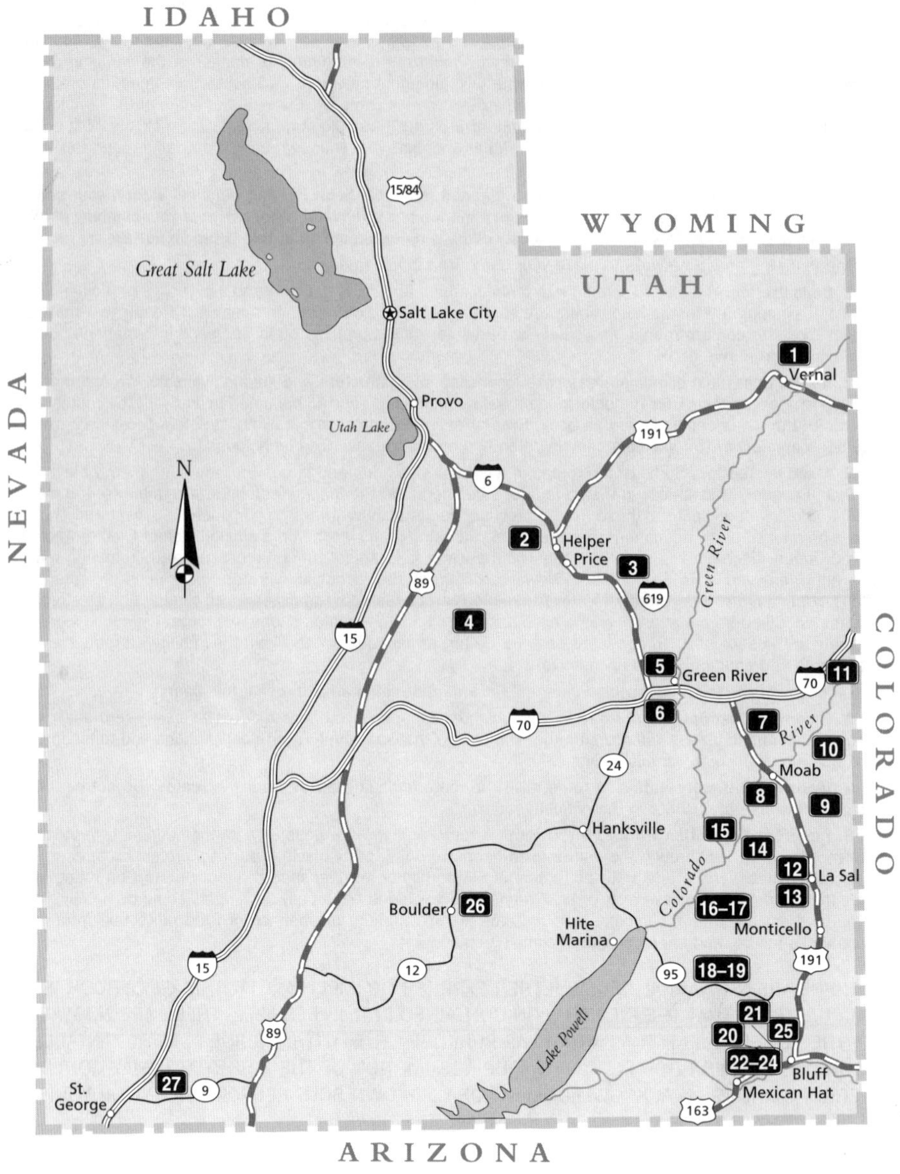

Contents

Photo: Bill Forrest

Lady in a Bathtub, Valley of the Gods.

A Tribute to George Hurley

Climbers spend an inordinate amount of time with their noses in guidebooks, planning the day's hit list or next season's road trip. But when we look past the grades and gear lists and take notice of the history and stories of first ascents, we experience the soul and flow of this peculiar thing we do, and appreciate more the pioneers who created the history from which all climbers eventually benefit. George Hurley's name crops up in guidebooks everywhere. His first ascents span the country, from New England to the Wind Rivers and Vedauwoo, to Lumpy Ridge and the Colorado Plateau.

Climbers in the golden years of the 1960s and 1970s are to be envied. Countless summits and huge expanses of rock were as yet untouched, and a sense of adventure permeated every facet of climbing. The door was open, and pioneers like George Hurley gathered new routes with an insatiable appetite. The routes that George and other hard men and women of the time left us are the foundation of modern rock climbing for all of us who followed. Just a partial list of George's climbs reveals his drive during these amazing years: Fugue (Cannon Cliff), China Shop (ice, Lake Willoughby), and numerous other first ascents in the White Mountains of New Hampshire; a new route on the north face of Flattop in the Wind Rivers; many new routes at Vedauwoo; first ascents of D7, the Obelisk, and Hypotenuse on the Diamond of Long's Peak; new routes on Mount Ypsilon; numerous first ascents on Lumpy Ridge; numerous desert first ascents, including Jacob's Chair, White Knight, Doric Column, the Titan, Gold Bar Tower, a new route on Argon Tower, and the east face of Baboquiari Peak in Arizona.

Nine years before I began climbing, I sat transfixed, reading the *National Geographic* account of the first ascent of the 900-foot Titan in southern Utah's Fisher Towers, by Layton Kor, George Hurley, and Huntley Ingalls. These men were near myths to young climbers, and their routes epitomized adventure. Years later, I climbed their Titan route, my partner and I loaded up with every modern device plus a hefty pin rack. We were amazed at the situations we faced—pin stacks in dirt holes, clusters of belay bolts on wild arêtes, scary traverses with psychpro—and even more amazed that such a bold and daring route was first done in 1962! What astounded me even more was that George Hurley went back just four years later to do it again for the second ascent.

Born in Mt. Vernon, Indiana, in 1935, George lived in the Midwest through his college (and early climbing) years, earning a master's degree in English and American literature from the University of Wisconsin. For more than a decade following, George balanced an English-teaching career with his passion for climbing. He taught at the University of Colorado, Namilyango College in Uganda, and Colorado Academy, working in the summers as a climbing guide for Colorado Outward Bound, Jackson Hole Mountain Guides, and Dick Powell's Gore Range School.

In 1974, George faced the choice that many climbers consider—whether to do it full time—and made the cut from traditional work to a climbing career. He never looked back, and has worked full time as a guide and instructor ever since. His resume is enviable: assistant director of the Fantasy Ridge climbing school, director of Bob Culp's climbing school in Boulder, chief guide for International Mountain Climbing School in New Hampshire, and one of the founders of Mountain Guides Alliance. George has also served with the Rocky Mountain Rescue Group in Colorado and the Mountain Rescue Service in North Conway, New Hampshire. He continues to guide and climb in the Alps, East Africa, Britain, and across the United States.

Perhaps George Hurley's love of climbing adventure is best measured by his time spent in the southwest desert. The Titan was only the beginning; his routes mark every corner of this vast area. Jacob's Chair, Gold Bar Tower, Doric Column, five towers in the Valley of the Gods—George did these amazing routes in the days when desert climbing trips were lonely, wild adventures, when awe-inspiring towers were just beginning to be explored, and when rudimentary gear demanded a bold and committed climbing style.

For years I scoped an amazing off-width and chimney line on Parriott Mesa near Moab, waiting for the skill and mind control it would clearly demand. While I waited, George and two other desert pioneers, Earl Wiggins and Katy Cassidy, climbed the route in 1988. *Ascended Yoga Masters* indeed is demanding—a 50-foot, 5.9 runout in a bottomless chimney—and I still aspire to it.

Desert climbing has become more familiar with time, and more desirable with modern gear and enticing photographs. Yet the spirit of climbing on the cracks and towers described in this book is alive and well, and for that we have the bold desert pioneers to thank.

George Hurley's craving for adventure is undiminished after more than forty years of hard climbing. It is to him—and to his spirit, which embodies the soul of desert climbing—that this volume of *Desert Rock* is dedicated.

Jeff Widen

George's climbing partners read like a Who's Who of pioneer and early climbers. To name a few: Andy Arnold, Bob Bliss, Dave Carlson, Katy Cassidy, Tom Condon, Mike Covington, Bob Culp, Larry Dalke, Dave Dornan, Bill Forrest, Phil Fowler, Walt Fricke, Jim Greig, Wayne Goss, Mike Hartrich, TM Herbert, Jonathan Hough, Huntley Ingalls, Ray Jardine, Steve Komito, Layton Kor, Peter Lev, Dave Rearick, Chris Reveley, Andy Ross, Paul Ross, Stan Shepard, Todd Swain, Jerry Sublet, Billy Westbay, Earl Wiggins, Prince Willmon, Kurt Winkler, and Dave Wright.

—EB

Foreword

Maybe you've seen some of these places from 30,000 feet in the sky, during a cross-country flight in a jetliner. They are the long dusk-time shadows of nameless stone totems cast across red soil and sagebrush. They are the mysterious canyons where rivers appear out of a shimmering nothingness and meander on, it seems, to nowhere. They are the mirror reflections of sun bouncing off desert varnish on an untouched buttress, sending Morse code invitations up to your plane and your imagination. You would have looked down, wondered Where the heck is that?, then noticed a lack of roads and towns. For this is the American outback.

The areas described in Eric Bjørnstad's fourth collection of southwest desert climbing routes reveal the remotest of the remote in the middle of nowhere. Yes, there are untapped Indian Creek–style Wingate mother lodes out there somewhere. Yes, there are full-pitch splitter cracks and slender towers awaiting first ascents. Seldom seen Anasazi dwellings. Unrecorded petroglyphs and pictographs. Creeks and pools untrampled by cattle, bikes, four-wheel drives, and boots. Lonely old shacks where settlers and miners lived lives of quiet desperation.

Photo: Eric Bjørnstad

Wilson Arch, US 191 South.

In the brief time I have spent climbing in southern Utah's red planet landscape, I've realized it is possible to find an equivalent sense of aloneness and foreverness as exists in wild realms like Baffin Island, Alaska, the Karakoram Range, or the dreamtime hinterlands of Australia. It's a sensation that is humbling, silent, terrible, and grand. By writing this book, Eric has handed its readers a key to a palace, and has given them an invisible, unwritten contract. Whether you know it or not, you sign this contract the moment you embark on a journey to any place in this book. Simply stated, the contract reads, "Don't wreck the place." Overlanding to anywhere in this remote landscape is an adventure; the climbs to be repeated or the first ascents that await are a privilege. To arrive there is a guaranteed epic—thank the gods—for these are the places of dead-end roads, the back of beyonds, the last resorts, the too-far-from-the-car, never-in-a-weekend lost crags of the desert rats. Get there if you can. Treat these places like priceless treasures you must. There ain't many of 'em left.

Greg Child

Castle Valley, Utah

Preface

This book is called a guide because it is intended to lead the reader to a richer experience while sandstone climbing in the great expanse of the Colorado Plateau in Utah. Most of the routes documented here have not previously appeared in print. It is hoped their discovery will encourage climbers to broaden their desert experience from often overcrowded areas, such as Wall Street, Castleton Tower, and Indian Creek, to the adventure of climbing in remote lands, reliving the magic of exploration that must have been a part of the climbing holiday for George Hurley, Layton Kor, Harvey T. Carter, and others in the early 1960s.

Climbing guides are inevitable, like it or not. It is my hope that the Desert Rock series might be more enjoyable to read—with climbers' quotes, anecdotes, background, and diversions—than the traditional climbing guides. I also hope this guide will lead you to challenging climbs within your ability, help you find worthwhile objectives with minimal effort and lost time, and encourage all climbers to tread lightly in this fragile desert. This guide is a repository of history, documenting the roots of a climb or climbing area. I am always saddened when I chance upon a young climber who has never heard of Layton Kor or Fred Beckey or other great pioneers of sandstone climbing. Their appreciation and enjoyment of the desert climb must be poorer for their ignorance of history. What a pleasure it is to know you are following in the footsteps of such legends as Charlie Fowler or Jimmy Dunn, or to read of Cameron Burns's or Mike Baker's epics on a soft-rock ascent.

There will always be climbers who prefer the climbing gym, where an audience is on hand to give praise and encouragement. This guide is not for them. Then there are the climbers whose enjoyment is diminished by continued and close familiarity with an area or route. This guide is also not for them. Those who object to a guide, for whatever reason, have the clear option not to read one. But the vast majority of climbers, both beginners and veterans, will welcome the guidance of a book such as this. The clock cannot be turned back. Guidebooks of all values have and will continue to appear. The days of nearly four decades ago when Fred Beckey, Harvey T. Carter, and I made only the third ascent in the Fisher Towers near Moab, spending five days establishing a route up Echo Tower, are relegated to history. But your climbs today will one day also be history. I hope this guide will be instrumental in the building of your scrapbook of desert memories, as precious for you in the years to come as the ascent of Echo was for me.

Eric Bjørnstad

Moab, Utah

January, 2002

Photo: Cameron E. Burns

Texas Tower and Lone Star, Texas Canyon.

Acknowledgments

This guide is the end product of two years of intense research involving thousands of miles of road trips, tens of dozens of bivouacs during field research, and hundreds of hours logged in telephone calls and visits with climbers familiar with the routes of these remote areas of the Colorado Plateau.

Charlie Fowler shared several road trips with me to the regions of western Colorado and eastern Utah. Tim Toula reviewed the text of Arch and Texas Canyons along with many other areas where he has climbed and, on several visits, administered healing acupuncture to an ailing sciatic nerve injury. Thanks to Wilson Goodrich and to Mike and Shar Baker for the comradery around the campfires at Hatch Wash and Comb Ridge and for the shelter and hospitality during visits to their homes at Cortez and St. George. Wilson contributed many photos and important route information. Mike and Shar shared their extensive collection of photos and topos and details of their many pioneering climbing routes. Paul Ross is an indomitable British hardman, guidebook writer, and former climbing partner of both Joe Brown and Don Whillans, now transplaced to the unlikely hamlet of Palisade, Colorado. Paul (and Marea) visited often and shared the incredible and sometimes unbelievable first-ascent details of their routes throughout the desert, most notably on the Kachina Towers, Bird's View Butte, and the Spring Point climbing areas. I have especially fond memories of our sojourn into the beautiful Escalante Canyon. Paul, who grew up in the Lake District of England, is now in his mid-sixties, yet, at that generally geriatric age, he remains the most prolific pioneer of soft-rock routes on the Colorado Plateau. James and Franziska Garrett, as always, gave me shelter at their beautiful home in the highlands of Salt Lake City. We shared many campfires in the San Rafael, Valley of the Gods, and Ibex (James recently published the latter's first climbing guide). He is an Air Med nurse, so if you crash in surburbia you are likely to be in his competent rock hands. Franziska is a physician. You may need to see her after James stops the bleeding. Both are world-class climbers and have been of invaluable help with all four volumes of this guidebook series. Greg Child, summiter of Everest and K2, has climbed worldwide. He is no Fred Beckey (too young) or Dean Potter (too old) but is the foremost spokesman for contemporary mountain sojourns, with numerous publications to his credit, including but not limited to travel and climbing magazines. I feel lucky to have Greg as my neighbor in nearby Castle Valley just east of my home in Moab. Greg's most recent writing project (eagerly anticipated) is a biography of Lynn Hill. Thanks to my dear friend Carolyn Ortenburger, who has been a great supporter of this guide and who photographed the Green River Towers on her yearly memorial visit and solo float down the Green River in memory of her father, Leigh Ortenburger, principle guidebook writer for the Tetons, who lost his life in the Oakland firestorm of 1991. Joe Slansky, a professional photographer and climbing guide who now makes Moab his home, gave expert help on the computer and took the cover photo of Bird's View Butte and Crow's Head Spires. Thanks to Holly Sorenson, who spent endless hours drawing maps and topos and commanding other miscellaneous duties toward the conclusion of this seemingly endless project. Credit is due Billy Snyder, manager of Pasta J's, for the countless hours of relaxing, writing, and watching tourists walk by from the restaurant's outdoor patio. Thanks, Billy, for the fermented grape, gourmet cooking, and encouragement. Fay MacDonald, when not trekking some exotic region of the planet, accompanied me on many road trips with pencil and paper, documenting mile markers, landmarks, and esoteric route information. Thanks Catrina Foster for your insight into Rockland Ranch. Doug McQueen has been a friend and supporter since the early days of this project. John Middendorf's visits have always provided clarity to the description of climbs and great encouragement. Now with his recent master's degree from Harvard in a field related to earth architecture, we will be hearing from John as he wears a new hat. Much appreciation to Brian Jonas of Pagan Mounteering in Moab and to Jose Knighton of Moab's Back and Beyond Books. Thanks to Dean Potter for the Crackhouse information. Keith Reynolds has always been a great source of new route material. Dan Langmate flew to Moab accompanied by Glen "LB" Rink (two of the original Banditos). We had lunch and reviewed route descriptions, then I returned them to their tiny plane at the airport, and they were soon airborn south to Flagstaff and Phoenix. It was one of the more pleasurable hours of research. A couple weeks later Ken Wyrick phoned to say he was thinking of flying to Moab for a visit. I had not seen Ken since 1975 when we climbed the Totem Pole in Monument Valley while working with Clint Eastwood on his film *The Eiger Sanction.* Ken and I reviewed desert climbs and old times before I drove him back to the airport, and he flew east to his home in Colorado. Steve "Crusher" Bartlett and Fran Bagenal on many occasions provided me with a good night's sleep at their home in Boulder, and Steve tirelessly contributed and reviewed miscellaneous route descriptions. Jimmy Dunn and Hellen Heaven made numerous visits while in Moab and have always been an inspiration. Bill Hatcher, the tireless climber's photographer, is thanked for his contributions. Steve Allen is acknowledged for his input and story of Utah's first rock climbers, the Ancestral Puebloans. Steve is *the* authority on canyoneering on the Colorado Plateau and author of three guides to the little-known reaches of this vast canyon country. Stewart Green and Cameron Burns both recently published climbing guides to canyon country, *Rock Climbing Utah* and *Selected Climbs of the Southwest* respectively. Both books were dedicated to me. They must think I'm not going to live much longer, or perhaps they feel disquietude for all the material they used from my files. Just kidding! Both are dedicated writers and excellent desert climbers and have been my friends for many years. I have lasting memories of the campfires shared with Cameron and Ann Robertson, who often provided lodging at their Basalt home during one or another of my field trips. Thanks to Stewart and Martha Morris for putting me up in Colorado Springs. Thanks to Myke Hughes at Adrift Adventures for the pleasure of several years as a backcountry 4-wheel-drive tour guide. Much appreciation to Jeff Widen, who wrote the biography at the back of the book, the profile of George Hurley, and the section on environmental considerations. Cris Coffey continues to correct my spelling, tend to my syntax, and pose pertinent questions, as she has done for me since the original *Desert Rock* in 1988. Last I wish to acknowledge my gratitude to my loving Australian shepherd, Rilke, who has shared the many road trips, campfires, long nights, and early mornings at the computer, usually accompanied by a Beethoven quartet or opera wafting from the magic of the Bose Wave Radio/CD player.

Much appreciation also to the following who contributed to this guide with slides, photos, topos, or in myriad other ways. You have all helped bring this volume to fruition. Jeff Achey, Jay Anderson, Steve Anderton, Chris Andrews, Doris Ann, Benny Bach, Jeff Baldwin, Fran Barnes, Lance Bateman, Scott Baxter, Mark Beardsey, Chris Becker, Fred Beckey, Jeff Blacker, Jim Bodenhamer, Brad Bond, George Bracksieck, Jon Burnham, Ralph E. Burns, John Butler, Keen Butterworth, Julie Calhoun, Kitty Calhoun, Harvey T. Carter, Kevin Chase, Dan Chure, Monette Clark, Tim Coats, Ed Cooper, Kyle Copeland, Marco Cornacchione, Katherine Corson, Tom Cosgriff, Jeff Cristol, John Culberson, Jersey Dave, Kim Davis, Steph Davis, Eric Decaria, Jim Detterline, Liz Devaney, Wendy Dickson, Carl Diedrich, Chris Donharl, Rick Donnelly, Andy Donson, Randy Donson, Chris Ducker, Glenn Dumire, Bill Duncan, Connie Engler, Brad Englund, Greg Epperson, Brian Fergison, Bryan Ferguson, Ralph Ferrara, Ben Folson, Bill Forrest, Paul Gagner, Bryan Gall, Paul Gardner, Chris Giles, Todd Gordon, Chuck Grossman, Jesse Harvey, Lisa Hathaway, Jorma Hayes, Leslie Henderson, Russel Hooper, Paul Horton, Jim Howe, Rodger "Strappo" Hughes, George Hurley, Jason Hurst, David Insley, Steve Johnson, Pete "Big Billy" Keane, Jason Keith, Tobin Kelley, Chris Kelly, Lianne Kelly, Sue Kemp, Max Kendall, Craig Kenyon, Luke Laeser, Mark Lassiter, David Littman, Craig Luebben, Karen Lupardus, Dougald MacDonald, Smith Maddrey, John Markel, Nathan Martin, Mike Maurer, Hollis McCord, Rob McKeracher, Dave Mealey, Dave Medara, Smith Meddrey, Stewart Middlemiss, Jay Miller, Michael A. Milne, Chris Moore, Matt Moore, James O'Hearn, Alison Osius, Bob Palais, Sonja Paspal, Mike Pennings, Andy Petefish, Jeff Pheasant, Cory Pincock, Andy Pitas, Linus Platt, Sean Plunket, Dave Pollari, Layne Potter, Duane Raleigh, Jason Repko, Keith Reynolds, Stu Ritchie, Gerry Roach, Andy Roberts, Andy Ross, Billy Rothstein, Chris Rowins, Bret Ruckman, Bill Russell, Jason Schroeder, Owen Schultz, Keith Sharp, John Sherman, Rob Slater, Jay Smith, Freddie Snalam, Kerby Spangler, Drew Spaulding, Bret Sutteer, Donnette Swain, Todd Swain, Jack Tackle, Pete Takeda, Eve Tallman, Al Torrisi, Robert H. Vreeland, Peter H. Walker, Robert Warren, Randall Weekly, Frosty Weller, Mark Whiton, Chad Wiggle, Ron Wiggle, Mark Wilford, Tony Wilson, Steve Wood.

The Desert Rock Series

The sandstone canyon walls, mesas, buttes, and spires of the Colorado Plateau are the focus of the Desert Rock series.

A technical rock climbing guide is, by necessity, an assemblage of material from a great many sources. This is especially true regarding the vast deserts of the Colorado Plateau. Unlike most areas, where routes are established mainly by resident climbers and route detail is easily accessible, here resident climbers are comparatively few and the majority of sources for route information are scattered across the country and overseas. Although the three years and 8,000 hours of research that went into the initial *Desert Rock* (1988) provided a solid foundation for the present series of guides, the past couple of years brought additional contacts with hundreds of climbers, and I racked up an astonishing number of research hours. I have climbed in the desert for more than thirty years; for thirty years I have made Moab my home. This series of guides is the product of a long love affair with the desert.

The Colorado Plateau is the physiographic province that lies north and east of the Basin and Range province and south and west of the Rocky Mountain province. It covers about 160,000 square miles (nearly the size of California) in Utah, Arizona, New Mexico, and Colorado. Within its vast reaches of sedimentary sandstone lies the greatest potential for crack climbing in the world. It is a sector of North America with thousands of miles of vertically fractured Wingate sandstone walls. Although thousands of climbs have been established, this is only a fraction of the potential on the plateau. The majority of routes lie within the higher register of difficulty, but there is a large selection of excellent climbs below the 5.10 level, all within the incomparable canyon country of the high southwest desert.

In *The Bright Edge*, Stephen Trimble writes, "Time ticks slowly for the Canyon Country. A year means nothing, a human lifetime sees arroyos deepened a bit, the collapse of an arch or cliff here and there, the creation of a new window or two. A millennium scarcely changes the landscape. Only in tens of thousands of years does the land see much change. And even then, a hundred thousand years is a fraction of an instant in the millions and billions of years of the earth's history. On this time scale the Plateau itself becomes a temporary phenomenon, a passing fancy of an earth with a restless skin of drifting, dynamic continents."

The plateau contains eight national parks—Zion, Bryce, Capitol Reef, Arches, and Canyonlands in Utah; Mesa Verde in Colorado; and Grand Canyon and Petrified Forest in Arizona. The plateau also contains nineteen other regions managed by the National Park Service—the greatest concentration of national parks and wilderness areas outside Alaska.

The Colorado River is the principle artery of the plateau, giving it its name and draining 90 percent of canyon country. Each year the river transports about three

Photo: Eric Bjørnstad

North Tower and Arrowhead Spire, Valley of the Gods.

cubic miles of sandstone sediment to the impounded waters behind Glen Canyon Dam. Like the branches of a tree, the Colorado is fed by a network of tributaries, with countless arroyos further contributing during storms. It is a land of haunting beauty, a region without parallel on earth, and its fragile ecosystem is in grave danger.

What has changed in the years since the original *Desert Rock* was first published, early in 1988, is the escalating number of people who are discovering and frequenting the desert. Each season, attendance records are broken at Canyonlands National Park, Natural Bridges National Monument, and Dead Horse Point State Park. Annual visitation at Zion National Park exceeds two million, and Arches National Park is approaching one million per year. Recreationists of every disposition now make the desert their vacation destination. The gamut runs from mountain bikers, river runners, climbers, and four-wheel drivers, to hikers, campers, artists, photographers, mystics, and nature enthusiasts. The challenge becomes balancing their enjoyment with preserving what they have come to enjoy.

It has long been assumed that the desert is a tough, indestructible land, indifferent to human impact. In other regions of the country, moisture promotes a bacterial breakdown. Trees rot, litter (with time) dissolves, new growth covers scars. But the desert is so dry and growth so slow that the land is like another planet, where time has stopped. Our appearance has been dramatic and caustic. The dry air mummifies our castaways. Orange peels, eggshells, and other material tossed to the land do not biodegrade. Discards become permanent monuments to our sloth.

Cryptobiotic soil is essential to the health of the desert. Without this vulnerable crust, the majority of indigenous flowers and other shrubs would simply not exist. Once the soil is impacted by tire or foot, such prints remain visible for decades. Recovery is estimated to take up to 250 years. If we are to preserve this island of earth, it is most important that we walk only on slickrock (rock devoid of soil or vegetation), in drainages, or on established trails. Direct cross-country travel is unconscionable.

The indelible print of our seemingly benign inroads into the desert is not readily apparent from our state-of-the-art vehicles, which are equipped with the emblems of our sybaritic society. With us we bring not only quick draws, spaceship alloy–light cams, freeze-dried foods, and satellite maps, but also an invincible confidence in our superiority as a species. We have a long history of annihilating the land as we reshape it to suit us. I implore all who visit the unique canyon country to be responsible not only for our present love of the desert, but for the generations yet to be thrilled by this magical place.

Perhaps now with the kindling of a new consciousness we are on the threshold of a new direction not previously traveled. We may now value and protect the wild regions of the planet not as a response to the short-term plunder of the past, but as the very root of our survival.

Please visit with prudence, responsibility, and love.

SERIES SUMMARY

Desert Rock I: Rock Climbs in the National Parks includes a subjective selection of routes in Arches and Zion National Parks and the known routes of Capitol Reef and Canyonlands National Parks. It also includes the adjacent Glen Canyon National Recreation Area and Green River area just outside the park boundary of Canyonlands.

Desert Rock II: Wall Street to the San Rafael Swell covers the region west of the Colorado River in the Moab area, and includes Wall Street, Day Canyon, Long Canyon, plus the majority of routes established in the San Rafael Swell.

Desert Rock III: Moab to Colorado National Monument covers climbs east of the Colorado River in the Moab area. Included are Kane Creek, Moab Valley, Sand Flats, the River Road (Scenic Byway 128), Castle Valley, Fisher Towers, Onion Creek, Mystery Towers, and Colorado National Monument.

Desert Rock IV: The Colorado Plateau Backcountry, Utah covers climbing routes on sandstone in isolated or remote lands managed by the Bureau of Land Management (BLM) or the National Park Service. Areas included are from Dinosaur

National Monument in the north to Valley of the Gods in the south, and west to St. George and east to the La Sal Mountains on the Utah/Colorado border.

Desert Rock V: Remote Areas of the Colorado Plateau, Colorado, Arizona, and New Mexico will include sandstone climbs in numerous other isolated regions of the Colorado Plateau.

Desert Rock VI: Indian Creek Climbs will offer definitive coverage of the Indian Creek and Cottonwood Canyon areas, with more than 1,200 routes identified on photographs.

ENVIRONMENTAL CONSIDERATIONS OF DESERT ROCK CLIMBING, by Jeff Widen

The Colorado Plateau is a stunning and magical arena in which to climb. After experiencing the desert world, many climbers have written about the need to slow down, take in the desert's aura and walk more slowly. Indeed, just being within this incredible landscape is a major part of any climbing trip. The starkness of the earth's bare bones, along with the extremes of heat, cold, wind, and weather, are all part of the desert climbing experience. As harsh as the desert may be in many ways, though, it is also an extremely fragile place. Plants and animals carry out a tentative existence and are easily disturbed. The visual scars left by careless activity are extremely slow to heal. The desert needs extra care, a lighter touch.

There is another compelling reason to tread lightly in the desert. The extractive industries of mining, timber cutting, ranching, and water development have long been criticized for their abuse of public lands. Damaging climbing practices threaten to put some climbers in the same category, at least in the eyes of environmental organizations if not the general public. Land management agencies increasingly view climbing as an activity with real impacts—one that can be dealt with fairly easily, meaning increased regulation. One has only to look at recent attempts at bolt bans by various agencies to understand the seriousness of the threat. Climbers can go a long way toward staving off overly harsh regulations by acting responsibly. Although the debates over climbing styles rage endlessly, nearly all climbers agree on the importance of protecting the climbing environment. The desert contains some of the most radical and outrageous crack climbs on Earth. It's up to everyone climbing there to help protect access to these climbs and to protect the rock and land itself.

Climbing impacts in the desert center around all aspects of a climb, from multiple trails to rock damage to trash. The desert environment requires extra care at each turn.

Approaches: Check out approach routes in advance. For the driving portion of the approach—a major part of many desert climbs—stay on established roads. If you are unlike most desert climbers and own some beefy four-wheel drive with real clearance, resist the urge to get a few hundred yards closer to the route by driving off road. On foot, follow established approach paths wherever possible.

Take an extra minute to see if there is a common route up to a climb. Take special care not to walk over areas of cryptobiotic soil (you can recognize this unique desert plant assemblage by its appearance as black, crusty soil). It is critical for prevention of erosion in the desert, takes hundreds of years to form, and is destroyed instantly when crushed. To avoid cryptobiotic soil and other plants and animals, walk in washes and over slickrock and boulders whenever possible. Approaching climbs in this way will also prevent the all-too-visible trashing of the desert's surface.

Protection: Using clean pro is perhaps the most important part of low-impact climbing in the desert—the rock simply can't take the abuse of piton placement. Free routes don't present much of a problem, since desert cracks are tailor-made for camming devices. On aid routes, however, there are too many examples where cracks have been nailed that could have been climbed with clean hardware (see "Pitons" section below). It's true that you need a huge stock of cam devices to climb desert routes, but that's part of the game. People often go in groups and pool their gear to do these routes. When retreating or rapping off, leave gear, webbing, etc., of neutral colors—brown, black, or tan are best.

Bolts: Nothing raises the ire of land managers more than over-bolting, whether real or perceived. If there is one thing climbers can do to prevent excessive regulation, it is to minimize bolt use. This doesn't mean bolt placement elimination, for indeed the nature of desert climbing—vertical walls and towers without natural rappel anchors—makes bolt placement a necessity. But climbers should keep the number to a minimum. The days of long bolt ladders in the desert are long gone. Short ladders are sometimes necessary to reach the crackless summits of towers, but when the route is a predominately bolt-clipping ascent, the formation is better left unclimbed.

Bolts placed next to cracks would seem anathema to most climbers, yet a disturbing number of bolts can be found next to bomber cam placements. If you don't have the gear, go hit up your friends and come back later. When bolts are placed, they should be placed well, whether to give you the extra courage to do a few more free moves or to prevent the eventual formation of an ugly and unusable hole when the bolt comes out.

The standard desert bolt has long been an angle piton pounded into a ⅜-inch hole drilled at a slight downward angle. Some of the newer expansion bolts are now being used—check out recent reviews in various climbing publications to see which ones are best for soft rock.

Power drills have no place in the desert. Not only can holes be quickly hand-drilled in sandstone, but a major part of the desert climbing experience is the feeling of quiet and vast open spaces, and the sense of high adventure. The use of power drills not only runs counter to this sense, but leads quickly to over-bolting.

Pitons: Climbers should adopt a minimalist attitude when nailing in the desert. Pin scars are more visible in sandstone, and nailing routes get beat out here faster than on any other rock type. Minimizing piton damage includes reducing the number of pin placements as much as possible, looking for alternative routes, and perhaps stopping to ask yourself whether a formation with existing routes really needs a new nail-up. Devices such as Lowe ball nuts and Tri-Cams, Rock and Rollers, and small camming devices can often substitute for pins down to Lost Arrow size. Using clean gear can also have the desirable effect of upping the fear factor of an aid route.

If you must nail, use constructive scarring techniques. This involves favoring upward blows to the pin when cleaning so the eventual hole will accept a nut or other clean pro.

Chipping/Gluing: These are destructive practices that are indefensible anywhere, especially in the desert.

Chalk: Many desert pioneers and early locals climbed without it, but most modern climbers use chalk. White chalk is especially visible and obnoxious on red rock. If you use chalk, use colored chalk—dark brown or dark red are the best colors. Most of the national parks already require colored chalk.

Archaeological Sites: The Colorado Plateau is rich in Native American archaeological resources. Special care must be taken to avoid these areas, whether ruins, rock art panels, or areas with pot shards, tool fragments, or other ancient artifacts. Stealing artifacts is a federal crime. Avoid climbing near any archaeological sites—you can bet there is another perfect crack around the corner.

Human Waste: Desert areas are booming in popularity, and human waste is becoming an increasing problem. It is critical to take the extra couple of minutes to do it right. Go at least 300 feet (91 m) from major washes and other watercourses. Although land managers are looking at the viability of surface disposal, the currently accepted method for dealing with excrement is still to dig a small hole 6- to 8-inches (15 to 20 cm) deep and bury the waste. Used toilet paper should be packed out in zip-locked bags and disposed of. There are also reports of increasing human waste near the bases of popular towers—climbers should treat the base of towers as a stream and go several hundred feet away to do their business.

Litter: The dry desert environment will preserve paper, cigarette butts, and other trash for years. Glass bottles, aluminum cans, and plastic containers will last for centuries. Pick up your trash and carry it out.

Wildlife: It is important to respect wildlife closures, usually imposed to protect nesting raptors or other species. Closures are posted at visitor centers or land managers' headquarters.

Attitude: No climbing is totally without impact. But in this desert land—with its special qualities of fragility, beauty, and silence—it is essential that we reduce our impact. We must walk and climb a bit more lightly. The self-interest issue of preventing over-regulation is crucial. But there is also a much bigger issue—it is the right thing to do and makes the incredible experience of climbing in this place all the richer.

GEOLOGY

Climbs east of the Colorado River are, with very few exceptions, up the eolian (windblown) Wingate sandstone that has made desert climbing famous. The Fisher Towers, Onion Creek, Mystery Towers, and River Tower are Cutler sandstone with a caprock of Moenkopi. River Road to Negro Bill Canyon (mile marker 3) is bordered by Navajo sandstone. Routes on the BLM Takeout Buttress near mile marker 10 on the River Road climb the Chinle Formation.

Mancos shale, Dakota sandstone, the Morrison Formation, and the Summerville Formation are the youngest layers of rock in the region but are not typically found on climbing formations. Entrada sandstone, the next youngest layer, is found on the formations in Arches National Park, which is included in *Desert Rock I: Rock Climbs in the National Parks.*

Navajo sandstone, the next layer, is a relatively soft rock found in Zion National Park and along Wall Street. Like the Wingate, it is of eolian (wind) deposition, fine grained, and often of whitish to buff color. It dominates River Road to Anasazi Buttress at mile marker 3.

Kayenta sandstone forms a bench between the two cliff-forming layers of Navajo and Wingate. It is the stream-deposited base rock of Dead Horse Point,

Photo: Eric Bjørnstad

Sand Island pictographs.

Island-in-the-Sky, Colorado National Monument, and the protective caprock of most desert towers.

Wingate sandstone is the predominant rock upon which climbs are established east of the Colorado River. It is also the stratum that comprises the well-known Castleton Tower, Moses, the walls of Indian Creek, and the climbs of Colorado National Monument. Wingate is unique in that it erodes slowly, fracturing along straight vertical planes. It is very angular in appearance, often with chimneys and crack systems remaining the same size for 100 feet (30 m) or more. Some Wingate rock—the Bride west of the Colorado River and the Coke Ovens in Colorado National Monument, for instance—is soft enough to be confused with Navajo sandstone. When erosion has removed its Kayenta sandstone caprock and its color has changed from russet to lighter-colored rounded domes, the rock is extremely soft, making it nearly impossible to place belay or rappel anchors.

Below Wingate sandstone are the slope-forming Chinle sandstone and the red/maroon Moenkopi sandstone, both of mudflat deposition. Moenkopi is the most recognizable stratum of rock on the Colorado Plateau. It resembles a chocolate layer cake and often appears with thin horizontal bands of light green (organic deposition). At the time of deposition, the Moenkopi Formation was a 200-mile (322 km), flat, expansive floodplain that stretched from present-day western Colorado to western Utah. Few climbs exist on Moenkopi, although it is the caprock of the Fisher Towers, Onion Creek, Mystery Towers, and River Tower.

The Cutler Formation rests below the Moenkopi, often a deep bright red in color and resembling Wingate in density. Because it tends to fracture horizontally and bears a soft stucco of decomposing mud, it is loose and relatively dangerous to climb. It is the dominant rock of the Fisher Towers, Onion Creek, Mystery Towers, and River Tower.

MEASURING AN ARCH

A greater concentration of arches are found in the United States than in any other country on earth, and approximately 60 percent of those are found on the Colorado Plateau. Observing the grace and beauty of a stone arc can be an awe-inspiring experience, bringing surprise and delight. The National Park Service, charged with protecting the scenic, scientific, and historical heritage of the country, has established a national park and two national monuments whose outstanding feature is their natural bridges or arches. In Arches, Canyonlands, Bryce Canyon, Zion, and Capitol Reef National Parks, natural arches are among the principal attractions. Recommended in the diversions section at the end of some chapters are outstanding arches worth a visit. To clarify the often confusing measurements of an arch made by geologists, scientists, and arch collectors, the following definitions are given: **Height** of an arch is the vertical distance between the bottom of the opening and the underside of the arc. The **span** (length) of an arch is the horizontal length of the arc of rock between its supports. **Width** and **thickness** is the mass size of the arc of rock. Width is a horizontal measurement of the arc of rock at its thinnest point. Thickness is a vertical measurement of the same arc of rock at its thinnest point. **Overall height** is the vertical distance from ground level to the top of the rock structure containing the arch opening.

ANCESTRAL PUEBLOANS—UTAH'S FIRST ROCK CLIMBERS, by Steve Allen

The route started with a long scramble up loose dirt to the base of a precipitous sandstone wall. A series of small, evenly spaced depressions on the otherwise smooth rock led upward for 75 feet to a thick flake. Awkward chimneying behind the flake took me to a small triangular-shaped hole that, after a heinous squeeze, provided access again to the outer wall. There, another row of small depressions led horizontally to the left before turning upward for 50 feet to the top of the buttress.

Difficult, exposed, 5.10 climbing on a remote wall sounds like a climber's desert dream. For me that climb was, but I knew I had not been the first on the intricate and interesting route. The depressions I had been smearing on and palming were actually Moqui steps, foot and handholds carved ladderlike up the wall by Ancestral Puebloan Indians between 700 and 1,700 years ago. The Ancestral Puebloans—often called Anasazi—were perhaps the first real rock climbers to venture up the vertical walls of southern Utah. Pecking steps by hand using either fire-hardened deer antlers or picks made with rock, the Ancestral Puebloans constructed routes into otherwise inaccessible areas. Steps are found going to cliff dwellings or granaries located high off the ground. Others descend into potholes. Most often, routes lead up canyon walls to the rim country where the Indians planted crops or hunted game.

For the climber, routes of most interest are those ascending steep walls that lead to high vantage points. Some of the routes are astonishing and, in several cases, mind-numbing. Envision an Indian on Comb Ridge, a hundred-mile-long escarpment immediately east of Cedar Mesa, working his way up a vertical 200-foot wall. Either barefoot or wearing deerskin moccasins, our athlete chips a small platform into the sandstone, just big enough for toes and the ball of a foot. Balancing, he now pecks a handhold, then another foothold. On and on he goes. Each hold takes up to an hour to fashion, and no rope holds him when his forearms pump out. Days pass and his compatriots watch him working the route, downclimbing at night, upclimbing early in the morning to start the work again. Finally he reaches the top. This route still exists and is plainly visible from the Comb Wash road.

But what is the significance of the route? A short, easy row of nearby Moqui steps goes to the top of the same cliff. In an Escalante River tributary, Harris Wash, a row of steps goes up a high wall while an adjacent sand dune can be more efficaciously used to gain the rim. At Fiftymile Spring at the foot of the Kaiparowits Plateau, several parallel rows of Moqui steps go up a wall. Again, an easy route to the top is nearby. There is no definitive answer why these functionally useless routes were installed. Those willing to speculate think that they were used in rituals, perhaps in the type that would show the elders that one was worthy of their respect. Maybe the steps were a form of punishment: "Son, you've been bad, now put a row of steps up that hundred-foot wall."

Many of the Moqui routes that exist today have been substantially changed by centuries of wind and water erosion. Big steps have faded and are sometimes just smears or shadow pockets visible only in perfect lighting. Later Indians—the Navajo, Paiute, or Ute—often reworked Moqui routes, as did miners and ranchers. These enhanced routes were the product of steel implements, and the telltale scarring is often visible. Good examples of these routes exist along the San Juan River and in several of the lower Escalante River tributaries.

Modern rock climbers can enjoy the work of the Ancestral Puebloans, but there are strict rules you MUST abide by before climbing Moqui routes. Unlike the bolting issue, which may have legitimate ethical sides, there are no ethical disputes with Moqui routes. These archaeological and historical sites are protected by law. Changing or enhancing steps in any way is illegal, simple as that. Placing bolts anywhere near a row of Moqui steps is not tolerable. Often "Moqui ladders," stairsteps of stacked rocks, or logs held in place by piles of rocks, are extant. These should be used with utmost caution or avoided completely if you deem them too unstable to use. Please remember that these sites belong to all. Some are sacred to present-day Native Americans. Luckily for poor climbers, catching those defacing Moqui routes can be a blessing: large rewards are available for those who turn in the miscreants. Report abuse to the appropriate land management office, whether it is the National Park Service or the Bureau of Land Management.

Recently, "climbers" drilled hooking holes up a short row of Moqui steps near the mouth of Escalante's East Moody Canyon. These canyon novices apparently did not realize that the route they defaced was an often-climbed V-2, or that there was an easy Class 5.4 route a hundred yards away, or a walk-up route to the top of the same cliff a quarter-mile downcanyon. They even had the audacity to leave their trash, the hooks, on the top of the climb.

Hardcore Moqui step climbers relish the idea of following the paths of the ancients and, perhaps like them, have the same gut-wrenching fear when the route is run out and the steps become thinner and more tenuous. Proper gear for climbing Moqui routes is a pair of climbing shoes, a sling for belay and rappel anchors on trees or bushes, and a rope to protect those seconding. Get the idea? These routes are not for sport climbers; they are for those who can safely climb routes that have not been rated and cannot be protected. If you rappel the route, always leave a sling around the tree or bush since the constant sawing of a pulled rope can kill them. Use complimentary or dark colors like tan, brown, or black. Make sure that old slings are cut out and make absolutely sure hikers cannot see the sling from nearby vantage points.

For the adventurous, the variety of routes are manifold. On Mancos Mesa, a row of Moqui steps leads to the top of a robust pinnacle, giving exceptional views of the surrounding landscape. In a canyon off Wilson Mesa, one must climb 50 feet up a cottonwood tree, then balance precariously along a thin branch before leaping for the lowest of the Moqui steps. A long vertical layback crack in a canyon off Dark Canyon Plateau is made much easier by the small fingertip-size dimples carved along the inside edge of the crack. Very thoughtful! High in the Poison Ivy Fork of Choprock Canyon, an implausible row of steps leads up a severe overhang; the toe and footholds have been protected from the elements and one can still pull through the route on holds that are in the same condition as when the Indians used them. The route, 30 feet long, would be a modern V-3 or 4; high bouldering for sure! My favorite route is in a small canyon that drops from the Waterpocket Fold. The route starts with foot-size steps. As one ascends, the steps get progressively smaller, until near the top hundreds of feet off the deck they disappear just as the angle of the rock recedes. It is that one move onto terra firma that still gives me nightmares.

Introduction

In his select guide *Rock Climbing Utah,* Stewart M. Green introduces the state:

> Utah is a magnificent landscape of startling diversity and beauty, filled with extreme contrasts, immense views, and a marvelous natural and geologic diversity that is unmatched anywhere else in the world. It is a land full of hidden places and undiscovered wonders. Dominated by the red-rock Colorado Plateau, roofed by the lofty Wasatch and Uinta mountain ranges, and edged by broad sagebrush-covered basins the size of Rhode Island, Utah is a land that always amazes and astounds. Every turn of the highway, every bend in the trail, every cliff-top view offers a secret glimpse into the hidden heart of Utah's natural soul.
>
> Numerous cliffs, crags, buttresses, and towers, composed of sandstone, limestone, granite, basalt, and metamorphic rock, scatter across the state's vastness. If all of Utah's cliff miles were added up, it could boast more exposed rock than any other state. Although much of Utah's rock is too soft and chossy to be climbable, only a step up from brown sugar, an abundant variety of high-quality stone offers world-class routes to challenge and tantalize climbers' skills and sensibilities.

Southern Utah epitomizes the sandstone of the Colorado Plateau, and it is here at the plateau's heart that sandstone climbing is most concentrated—a range of splitter cracks, chimneys, dihedrals, overhangs, and off-widths to tempt then challenge any appetite. Among the purple and blue-black varnished walls is the marrow of these sacred lands: its uniquely improbable freestanding edifices, the towers, spires, and the pinnacles.

Almost anyone thinking of sandstone climbs in the southwest desert first thinks of Indian Creek or Wall Street with its social scene or the freestanding towers of Castleton and Moses or Standing Rock isolated in Canyonland's Monument Basin. But there is so much more—the allure of the Wingate at Sunshine Wall north of Arches National Park or the remote Wingate of Hideout Wall, hidden on the north shoulder of the La Sal Mountains east of Moab. And so close yet so far are the Kachina Towers, isolated by an epic approach: a descent down a catwalklike narrow and exposed ramp, on your belly, into Hell Roaring Canyon. The approach by itself is worth five stars.

Beyond the trailhead of the Kachinas is the no-man's-land of the Tombstone and the Spring Canyon Point climbs at the distant north sector of the high Island-in-the-Sky Mesa, a little Sahara unto itself. For the intrepid backcountry hardman, there is Dabneyland, a distant zone of rugged red rock suggestive of a fragmented moonscape. The best of the best of these isolated areas is an unexplored narrow isthmus of land that connects Dead Horse Point State Park in the east with the Island-in-the-Sky District of Canyonlands National Park in the west. From the southern tip of the peninsula is a sweeping 360 degree view across the Needles District of the park, the Abajo Mountains more than 50 miles (80

Photo: Wilson Goodrich

Willis Tower, Moab area.

Photo: Paul Ross

Kachina Towers, Moab area.

km) distant, the soaring 13,000-foot (3,962 m) La Sal Mountains, and the Henrys, the last mountains to be mapped and named in the lower forty-eight. Below glistens a thin ribbon of the Colorado River and, separated from the rim by about a hundred yards, the needlelike Crow's Head Spires and Bird's View Butte.

These are but a few of the jewels in the treasure chest this volume may reveal, and only a scant number of the riches hidden in the tens of thousands of miles of Wingate walls within the domain of Utah's Colorado Plateau. The land beckons you to camp, climb, or otherwise venture into the hauntingly beautiful ancient home of the Anasazi, to feel their presence in rock art galleries, to hear their voices in the warm desert wind.

HISTORICAL BACKGROUND

Anasazi Indians (east of the Colorado River) and Fremont Indians (mostly west of the river) inhabited Utah from approximately A.D. 1 to 1300. It is estimated that at their peak, 500,000 lived in Utah. In the 1600s Ute and Navajo tribes roamed the state (which takes its name from the Ute tribe). In the mid-1770s Spanish explorers and New Mexico traders passed through Utah, the most notable being Fathers Dominguez and Escalante in 1776. In the 1820s fur trappers explored the state looking for beaver pelts. Best-known of the mountain men were Jedediah Smith, William Ashley, and Jim Bridger. Permanent settlement began in 1847, mostly with Mormon pioneers, and homesteading was greatly accelerated by the arrival of the railroad in 1869. Discoveries of rich minerals over the years, then cattle ranching and the long history of oil, coal, and uranium extraction continued to bring newcomers to Utah. Today it is tourism, skiing, mountain biking, and river running that attract people to the state.

HISTORIC TRAILS

From 1847 to 1869 approximately 70,000 Mormons traveled west from Nauvoo, Illinois, to Salt Lake City by covered wagon or handcart, a distance of 1,300 miles (2,093 km). The **Mormon Pioneer National Historic Trail** passes through Illinois, Iowa, Nebraska, and Wyoming, and ends at Salt Lake City.

The **Old Spanish Trail** between Santa Fe and Los Angeles is 1,200 miles (1,932 km) long. It passes through Utah, crossing the Colorado River at Moab. Negotiating the trail, a major trade route for more than twenty years, took longer than two months. It has been called the most arduous, longest, crookedest pack-mule route in the history of America.

More than 130 miles (209 km) of the original Pony Express Trail that passed through Utah is now the **Pony Express National Historic Trail** and can be followed on a BLM Back Country Byway.

GEOGRAPHY

Comprising 84,990 square miles, Utah is the eleventh largest state. Maine, Vermont, New Hampshire, Connecticut, Massachusetts, New Jersey, Maryland, and Rhode Island could fit within its borders. Three provinces cover Utah: the Basin and Range Province of the western part of the state, the Rocky Mountain Province, and the Colorado Plateau Province, which covers nearly half of the state, mostly at elevations between 3,000 and 6,000 feet (914 and 1,829 m).

Approximately 80 percent of Utah's land is administered by government agencies for public uses such as recreation, timber and wildlife management, mineral leasing, and livestock grazing. Deserts cover about 33 percent of the state.

Utah has five national parks, seven national monuments, two national recreation areas, and the Golden Spike National Historic Site. These occupy about 2.8 percent of the state's land.

Arches National Park is home to the largest concentration of natural stone spans in the world. There are seven national forests—Sawtooth, Wasatch-Cache, Ashley, Uinta, Fishlake, Manti-La Sal, and Dixie—totaling nine million acres, about 23 percent of the state's land. The BLM manages about 43 percent of Utah's land area, or about twenty-two million acres. The state manages about 9 percent, including forty-five state parks and numerous wilderness areas. About 4.6 percent, nearly two million acres, is controlled by the U.S. Department of Defense.

About 6 percent of Utah's land area, or three and a third million acres, is set aside for Indian reservations. Tribes include the Goshutes, Navajo, Shoshones, Southern Paiutes, Utes, and White Mesa Utes.

Utah's highest point is the 13,528-foot (4,123 m) King's Peak in the Ashley

National Forest of the south-central section of the Uinta Mountains. It was named for Clarence King, an early director of the U.S. Geological Survey. The **lowest point,** at 2,100 feet (640 m), is Beaver Wash Dam on the Utah-Arizona border. **Dark Canyon** is the deepest canyon in Utah, 1,800 feet (549 m) deep at its mouth on the Colorado River. Jan W. van Cott in *Utah Place Names:* "It is a deep, wild, rugged, isolated canyon."

The **Henry Mountains,** the last mountain range in the forty-eight contiguous states to be named, were originally called the Unknown Mountains by Major John Wesley Powell. He later renamed them in honor of Professor Joseph Henry of the Smithsonian Institution. Of Henry's five summits, the highest is Mount Ellen at 11,615 feet (3,540 m). The **Unita Mountains** are the only large mountain range in North America that runs east and west. Some of the best spelunking in the west is found in the caves of the Wasatch Range.

Utah has fourteen alpine ski areas and six cross-country areas. Resorts in Wasatch (Ute for "mountain pass" or "low place in a high mountain") average more than 500 inches (1,270 cm) of snow per year. In 1938 Utah's first ski chairlift opened at Alta—only the second chairlift in the country.

More than forty-five outfitters offer trips through Utah's 4,000 miles (6,440 km) of raftable rivers. The **Colorado River** is the second-longest river in the forty-eight contiguous states, after the Mississippi. It flows 1,400 (2,254 km) miles from the Colorado Rockies to the Gulf of California and drains parts of seven states. Its drainage basin is 900 miles (1,449 km) long and between 300 and 500 miles (483 and 805 km) wide. The Colorado River's name was changed from the Grand River in 1921.

Utah is a **dry state,** with evaporation exceeding precipitation. Among the fifty states, only Nevada receives less moisture annually than Utah's average of 13 inches (33 cm).

The **Great Salt Lake** is the largest inland saltwater lake in the country, covering 1,500 square miles. Its average depth is approximately 20 feet (6 m), and it has an extremely high salinity of 20 percent (seawater has 3.5 percent). With 80,000 California gulls nesting at the lake, it has been declared a World Heritage Bird Sanctuary.

UTAH FACTS

THE ARTS

Support for the arts began in 1899 when the Third Legislature authorized the nation's first publicly funded arts council to "advance the arts in all their phases," a legacy that includes the Utah Symphony, Ballet West, the Utah Opera company, Ririe-Woodbury Dance Company, Repertory Dance Theatre, and Children's Dance Theatre, among others. Cedar City has a nationally acclaimed Shakespearean Festival. Each January, Utah hosts the Sundance Film Festival, which premieres the works of independent filmmakers. Utah is also home to the Gina Bachauer International Piano Competition and the world-famous Mormon Tabernacle Choir.

State Symbol: Beehive, representing industry.

State Flower: Sego lily. The edible root was used by pioneers to stave off starvation.

State Grass: Indian ricegrass.

State Bird: California gull. The seagulls devoured the crickets that destroyed pioneer crops.

State Tree: Colorado blue spruce.

State Animal: Rocky Mountain elk.

State Fish: Rainbow trout.

State Fossil: Allosaurus.

State Gem: Topaz.

State Capital: Salt Lake City, elevation 4,330 feet (1,320 m).

Statehood: January 4, 1896 (forty-fifth state).

FAST FACTS

Mormons: Members of the church calls themselves LDS, Latter-day Saints, or "Saints" for short. More than 70 percent of Utah's population are members.

Utah Streets: The layout of streets in Utah was made to run true to the compass: east, west, north, and south. One block east of a designated main cross street is 100 East, 2 blocks east is 200 East, 1 block north is 100 North, and so on.

Medical: Scientists at the University of Utah in Salt Lake City have pioneered medical advances of international significance, including the first artificial human heart transplant in 1982.

Population: More than two million people (1996). Close to half of the population lives in the Salt Lake Valley. One of the most prosperous and fastest growing states in the Union, Utah is the thirty-fourth most populous state. Minorities make up less than 7 percent of the state's population: Hispanics 3.9 percent, American Indians 1.3 percent, Asians 0.9 percent, and blacks 0.6 percent.

Longevity: Utah is rated fourth in longevity at 75.76 years (third in the nation). The average age is 25.7 years, younger than the national average of 32.7. Utahns have the largest average household size of any state. Its population under eighteen years is 42 percent, the highest in the nation. Utah has one of the highest birthrates and lowest death rates in the country.

Suffrage: Utah was the fourth state in the Union to give women the right to vote.

Literacy Rate: 94 percent, first in the nation.

Time: The state is on Mountain Standard Time and goes on Daylight Saving Time (advanced one hour from May to October).

Area Code: Salt Lake, Utah, Davis, and Weber Counties, 801; all other counties, 435.

Copper: Brigham Canyon Copper Mine is the world's largest open-pit mine, and the largest excavation that humans have ever dug. It is 2.5 miles wide and a half mile deep.

Scenic Byways: There are twenty-seven paved scenic byways and fifty-eight unpaved backways in Utah.

About This Book

Each chapter in this book has the same format: The general location of the climbs are in shaded boxes; they are followed by a description of the area's location. Formation names and sub-areas are set between horizontal lines. Routes are listed from left to right on formations unless otherwise noted. Route names are followed by grade, free climbing difficulty, aid rating, number of pitches, length of route or height of the landform (measured from its longest side), and a star rating. First ascent particulars are followed by location of and access to the climb. Paraphernalia is followed by descent information.

MOAB AREA

KACHINA TOWERS

KACHINA TOWERS NORTH
III, 5.8, A0, 5 pitches, 380 feet (116 m) ★★★★★

The Kachina Towers are at the upper drainage of Hell Roaring Canyon.

First Ascent: Paul Ross, Paul Gardner, October 16, 1999.

Location and Access: From the descent into Hell Roaring Canyon, walk down-canyon past the Kachinas obvious in the skyline above. Approximately 500 yards (457 m) right of the towers, ascend a wash leading up slabs and rubble to a weakness in the left canyon wall. Locate a crack with holes that after 20 feet (6 m) turns into a ledge leading to the right.

Pitch 1: Climb the crack, then traverse right along a ledge to beneath an obvious short hand crack and belay from a tree, 5.5, 100 feet (30 m).

Pitch 2: Continue up a hand crack to a ledge and traverse left to a bowl, 5.6, 100 feet (30 m).

Pitch 3: Exit the bowl on the right with delicate moves up and left to the rim, 50 feet (15 m). Follow the ridge to the left and down to the left side of the tower to an obvious off-width crack.

Pitch 4: Climb the off-width (5.7) to the north base of the tower.

Pitch 5: Follow five drilled anchors to the summit (tie-offs are essential), 5.8, A0, 80 feet (24 m).

Paraphernalia: Friends (1) set; selection of stoppers; tie-offs; three 200-foot (60 m) ropes to be left anchored to trees on the approach to the base of the tower.

Descent: Rappel from double anchors atop the tower, then retrace the approach to the canyon floor and reverse the descent into the canyon.

Photo: Andy Ross

Paul Ross, first ascent of Golden Brown, *Lost World Butte.*

RATING SYSTEM

Each climb is given a grade of I through VI.

I	One to two hours of climbing
II	Less than half a day
III	Half-day climb
IV	Full-day climb
V	Two-day climb
VI	Multiday ascent

Climbing difficulty is broken down into six classes, with Class 5 (free climbing) broken down further into 5.0 through 5.13+, and Class 6 (aid climbing) broken down into A1 through A5.

1	Trail
2	Cross-country hiking
3	Scrambling
4	Exposed scrambling, usually with rope for protection
5	Free climbing
6	Aid climbing

Ratings of free climbs range from 5.0 to 5.13+. The easiest is 5.0 and 5.13+ the hardest. Beginning with 5.10, a subgrade of a, b, c, or d may be used. For example, 5.10a denotes the easiest 5.10 move, 5.10d the hardest 5.10 move. 5.10a or 5.10b may be designated 5.10-, and 5.10c or 5.10d designated 5.10+ where the finer gradations of a, b, c, d are unidentified. Throughout the guide - and + and a, b, c, and d are used. Some additional letter ratings denote the following:

R	runout
S	hurt on fall
X	killed on fall

Ratings of aid climbs range from A0 to A5:

A0	Aid points fixed
A1	Easy, secure placements
A2	More awkward placement that will hold less weight than A1
A3	Still more difficult placement and less secure; will hold only short fall
A4	Difficult placement, not secure enough for a fall; will hold body weight only
A5	Multiple A4 placements; a fall could result in injury or death

C1, C2, etc. are ratings for *clean*, hammerless aid.

STAR RATINGS

Star ratings are based on a scale of 1 to 5. With few exceptions, they are the general consensus of those who have climbed the routes. The absence of a star rating on a climb means that this information was not furnished.

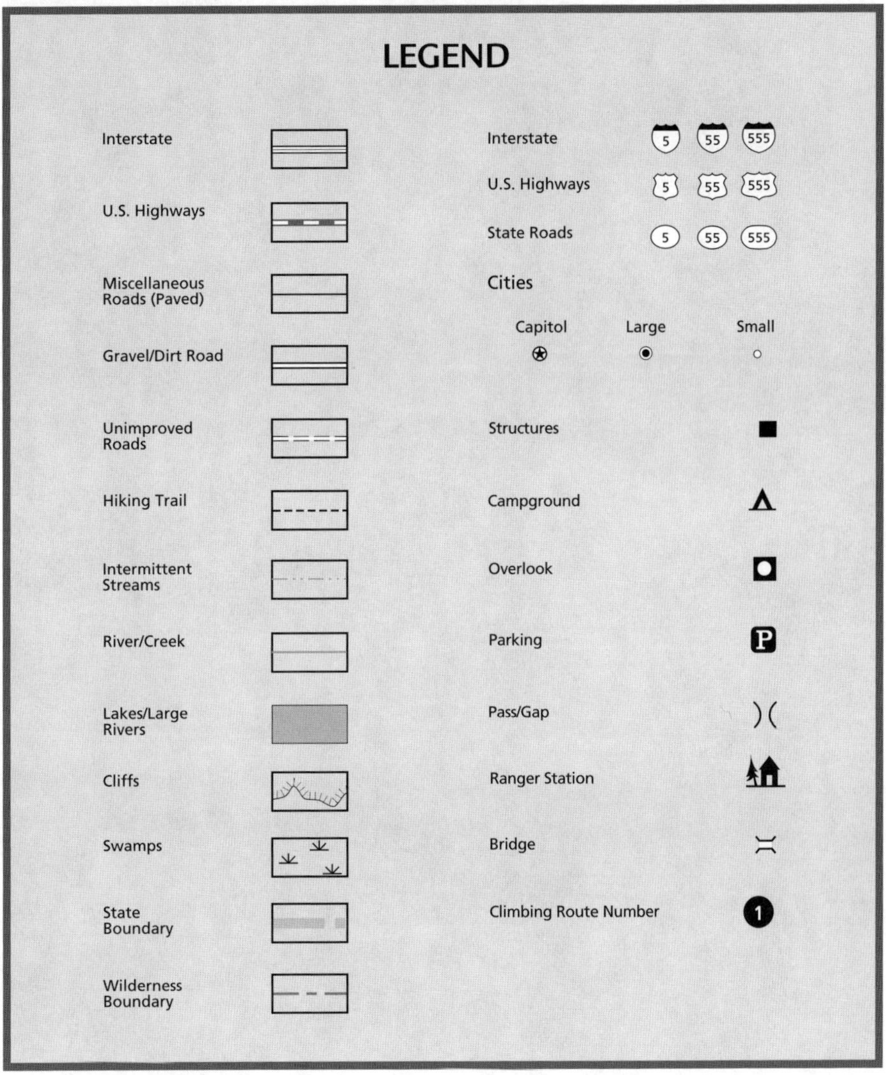

PARAPHERNALIA

A standard desert climbing rack for free climbs includes two sets of Friends, one set of TCUs, one set of stoppers, and quick draws with 25-inch slings for multiple-pitch climbs.

DIRT ROADS OF THE COLORADO PLATEAU

Dirt roads are generally referred to as trails, in keeping with such names as Shafer Trail, Burr Trail, and Long Canyon Trail, and are usually designated two-wheel drive or four-wheel drive.

Photo: James Garrett

Mark Synnott leading pitch 1, Steamboat Rock.

1
DINOSAUR NATIONAL MONUMENT

> What, for instance, could be more perplexing than the odd distortions in the forms and colors of the desert mountains! A range of these mountains may often look abnormally grand, even majestic in the early morning as they stand against the eastern sky. The outlines of the ridges and peaks may be clear cut, the light and shade of the canyons and barrancas well marked, the cool morning colors of the face-walls and foot-hills distinctly placed and holding their proper value in the scene. But by noon the whole range has apparently lost its lines and shrunken in size. Under the beating rays of the sun and surrounded by wavering heated atmosphere its shadow masses have been grayed down, neutralized, perhaps totally obliterated; and the long mountain surface appears as flat as a garden wall, as smooth as a row of sand-dunes. There is no indication of barranca or canyon. The air has a blue-steel glow that muffles light and completely wrecks color. Seen through it the escarpments show only dull blue and gray. All the reds, yellows, and pinks of the rocks are gone; the surfaces wear a burnt-out aspect as though fire had eaten into them and left behind only a comb of volcanic ash.
>
> –John C. Van Dyke, *The Desert*, 1901

Dinosaur National Monument, which straddles the Utah–Colorado border, is the site of the world's largest depository of fossil dinosaur bones. More than 2,300 bones from ten species of dinosaurs are exposed at the quarry site. Between 1909 and 1924, more than 350 tons of bones, including twenty-two complete skeletons, were quarried and transported to museums in the east.

Dinosaur National Monument encompasses more than 326 square miles (200,000 acres) of desolate, convoluted canyons with 1,000-foot (305 m)-high sandstone walls and pastoral valleys between high forested peaks at the eastern flank of the Uinta Mountains, named for the Ute Indians who lived there. Originally spelled Uintah, the *h* was omitted in Powell Expedition (1869) publications, being thought unnecessary to its pronunciation. The Uintas are the largest east-west trending range in the western hemisphere. Elevations in the park range from 4,750 feet (1,448 m) at the Green River near the dinosaur quarry to 9,006 feet (2,745 m) at Zenobia Peak on Douglas Mountain. The Green and Yampa Rivers converge in the heart of the park, both flowing 46 miles (74 km) through the monument. Ladore, Whirlpool, and Split Mountain Canyons of the Green River are among the deepest, most awesome, and beautiful of its 700-mile (1,126 km) length, and offer some of the most challenging rapids in Utah. Lodore, extending 19 miles (31 km) from the Gates of Lodore to the mouth of the Yampa, is the largest of the canyons, and is where the most dreadful rapids along the Green plunge over ancient Precambrian rock a billion years old, through a canyon more than 3,000 feet (914 m) deep. It was named by the Powell explorers for its resemblance to poet Robert Southey's "The Cataract of Lodore":

. . . And thumping and plumping and bumping and jumping,
And dashing and flashing and splashing and clashing;
And so never ending, but always descending,
Sounds and motions for ever and ever are blending
All at once and o'er, with a mighty uproar,
And this way the water comes down at Lodore.

Whirlpool Canyon, 14 miles (23 km) long and 3,000 feet (914 m) deep, passes through ancient Paleozoic rock. It was named by members of the 1869 Powell Expedition for its turbulent waters and gloomy ambience. The Green and Yampa Rivers enter Whirlpool Canyon just below their confluence at Echo Park.

The Yampa River, known earlier as the Bear, flows through colorful formations of red, pink, tan, brown, gray, and white rock. It is the last major undammed tributary of the Colorado River system. At its lower course its channel is sinuous, meandering at one stretch 7 river miles (11 km) over an air-line distance of 2 miles (3.2 km).

DINOSAUR QUARRY AREA

At the quarry, 7 miles (11 km) north of Jensen and US 40 via Utah 149, a visitor center encircles a rock face where dinosaur bones are in view in relief, as matrix rock is excavated to expose the 140-million-year-old graveyard. The visitor center was opened in 1958. The site is so popular that a mass transit system now ferries visitors from a parking area to the quarry during the summer season.

The quarry is the only location in the monument where dinosaur bones are in view. It is open daily all year except Thanksgiving, Christmas, and New Year's Day. The area receives an average of less than 9 inches (23 cm) of rain a year. *Utah: A Guide to the State* (1941 edition): "The region surrounding the quarry is the epitome of barrenness and desolation—a vast waste scarred by innumerable washes and strewn with dingy yellow-gray mounds of disintegrating stone. Isolated buttes rise abruptly out of the valleys, and naked hills hunch against the skyline like silhouettes of prehistoric monsters. South of the quarry the Green River creeps sluggishly across the desert floor toward Desolation Canyon, and to the east a series of broken upturned ledges in pastel shades of red, gray, and brown merge into the shattered pile of rocks that forms Split Mountain."

Dinosaur fossils were first discovered here in 1908 by Earl Douglass of the Carnegie (Natural History) Museum in Pittsburgh, Pennsylvania. The quarry contains in situ 1,600 fossil dinosaur bones that were deposited in a river 145 million years ago. It is considered the best Jurassic period dinosaur find in the world. Between 1909 and 1924, Douglass discovered ten species of dinosaurs, twenty complete skeletons, and rare juvenile skeletons and skulls, now on display in museums throughout the United States. In 1915 the quarry was designated a national monument. The park was expanded in 1938 to include the canyons of the Green and Yampa Rivers.

DINOSAUR NATIONAL MONUMENT ROUTE LOCATOR MAP

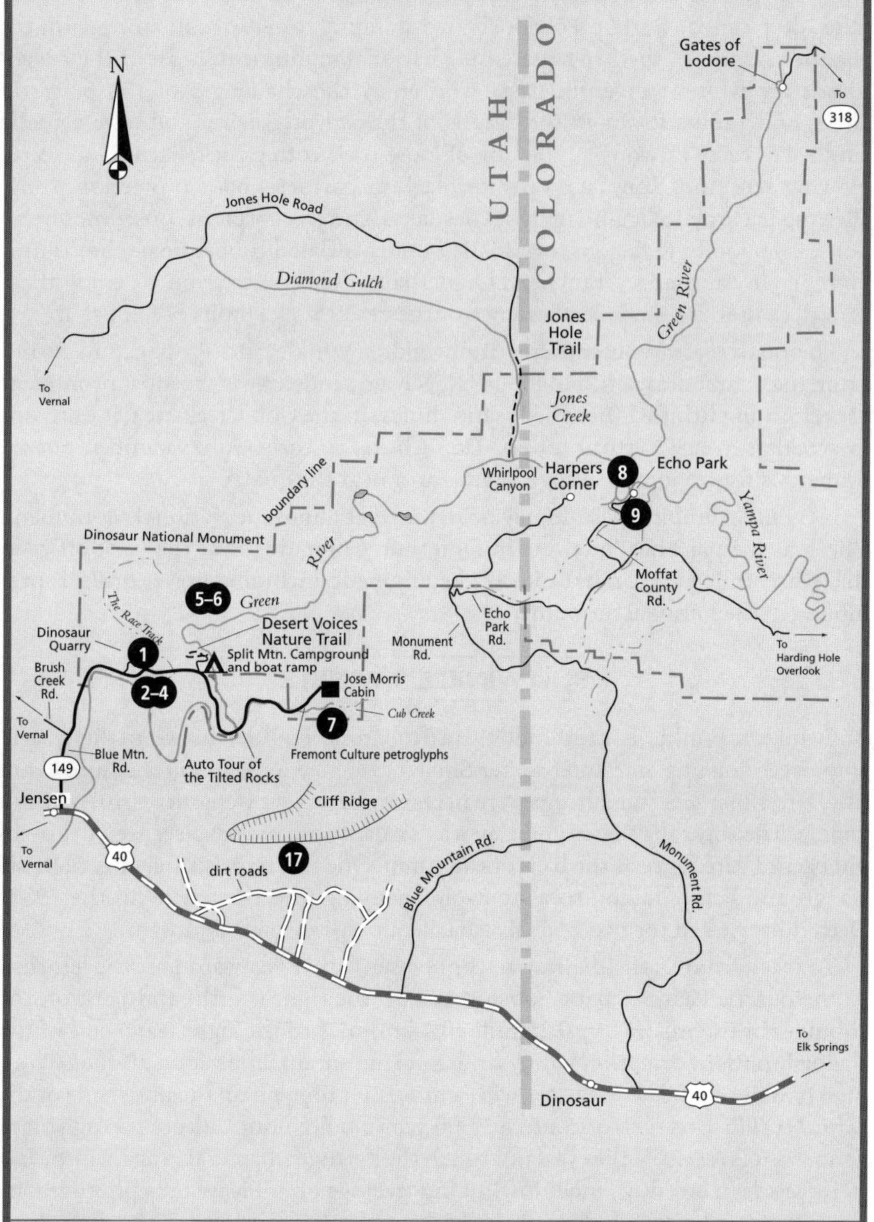

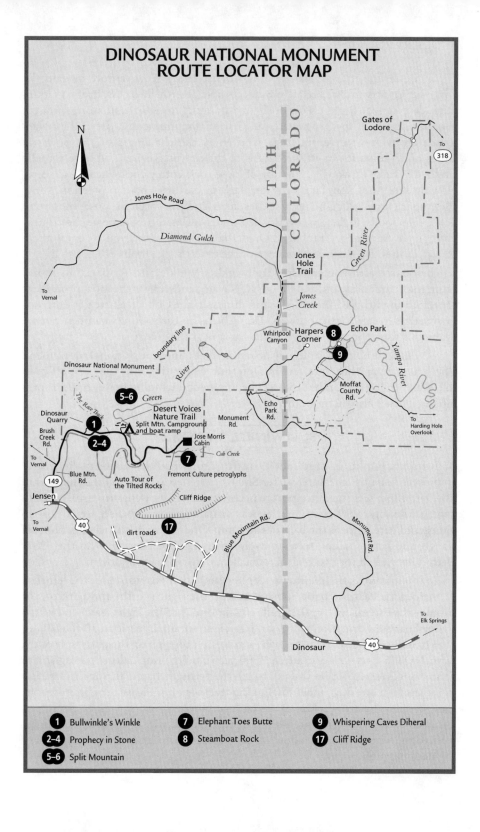

- **1** Bullwinkle's Winkle
- **2–4** Prophecy in Stone
- **5–6** Split Mountain
- **7** Elephant Toes Butte
- **8** Steamboat Rock
- **9** Whispering Caves Diheral
- **17** Cliff Ridge

Jim Detterline in *Rock and Ice*, July/August 1987: "Few venture beyond the Dinosaur Quarry into the relatively inaccessible desert wilderness. Broken mountains, deep canyons, and precariously free-standing towers of soft stone form the chaotic vastness of the 326-square-mile national monument. Most of the adventurer's are whitewater enthusiasts who enjoy the challenges of the powerful Green and Yampa Rivers in the depths of the canyons. Fewer still have actually climbed in these canyons. . . . Beware of loose rock, rotten rock, natural tar seeps, blowing sand, hot sun, lack of water, lack of partners, poor protection, sling-chewing packrats, ledge-hogging rattlesnakes, sneaky scorpions, upset mountain lions, dive-bombing falcons, overloaded under-inflated rubber boats, holds near petroglyphs, and angry ranchers. Or perhaps I should bid you to enjoy these things, as they are the special essence of the desert rock climbs of Dinosaur."

The quarry area encompasses Bullwinkle's Winkle and Prophecy in Stone. From the quarry area south to Plug Hat, Navajo sandstone is the most prominent rock, forming lithified (petrified) sand dunes. In the Cub Creek area, it outcrops in crackless, nearly vertical towers. Dan Chure, an early Gunks climber, put up numerous routes in the Swelter Shelter area near the quarry.

NOTE: A climbing permit may be required at Dinosaur National Monument. Check at the park headquarters in Dinosaur, Colorado, or at the park office at the quarry in Jensen, Utah. Motorized equipment, including power drills, is prohibited in the national monument.

BULLWINKLE'S WINKLE

Bullwinkle's Winkle is a 30-foot (9 m) top rope boulder between the quarry employees housing area and Swelter Shelter, a signed location on the Auto Tour. Jim Detterline: "Several outings were necessary before we were successful on Bullwinkle. The top rope's bottom belay was secured to the not-so-secure post of an old barbed wire fence at the base of the climb. One had to be sufficiently high off the ground before falling so as to avoid swinging into the fence." In the 1980s Detterline worked for two years as a backcountry ranger at Dinosaur.

To reach from Utah 149 (north from Jensen), drive eastward past the left turn to the quarry. Pass the park housing area to the right (north) and park on the shoulder of the road. Hike 0.25 mile (0.4 km) toward the right (east) end of the slabby Frontier Formation white sandstone mountain. Look for a 30-foot (9 m)-high boulder shaped like a wave, with a moose petroglyph on the underside of the wave. **NOTE:** This rock contains a 1,000-year-old Fremont Culture petroglyph of a moose. It is essential that you not touch the petroglyph; it is also against the law to molest it in any way—including taking tracings of it. Please take photographs only. Because the area is close to the park employees housing area, be discrete so as not to bother the residents. Do not disturb barbed wire in the area: A compromise to the wire fences may allow cattle to escape into the natural ecosystems of the national monument.

Photo: Jim Detterline

Dan Chure on Bullwinkle's Winkle.

1 BULLWINKLE'S WINKLE
I, 5.11 top rope, 1 pitch, 30 feet (9 m)

First Ascent: Jim Detterline, Dan Chure, summer 1982.

Location and access: On the overhanging face containing the moose petroglyph, face climb up the left side of the rock, completely avoiding any contact with the area of the petroglyph. Jim Detterline: "Dan and I took turns on the face. Rule number one was never touch the fragile petroglyph! The mere hint of a solution groove just to the left of the moose gradually faded as the wall arched inward. Finally I made the connection to thin holds on the outer edge of this ceiling and completed this most bizarre 5.11 problem." Bullwinkle's Winkle is weathered from Frontier Formation sandstone.

Paraphernalia: Top rope.

Descent: Rappel or lower off.

FRONTIER FORMATION AND MORRISON FORMATION BOULDERS

Numerous bouldering problems were solved by Dan Chure and Jim Detterline in the summer of 1982. To reach from Utah 149, drive past the left turn to the quarry and past the park housing area and park on the shoulder of the road. Hike 0.25 mile (0.4 km) right (east) to the end of the slabby Frontier Formation white sandstone mountain. There are many good established problems on the Frontier Formation boulders in the area. To reach the Morrison Formation boulders, pass through the gap of the Frontier Formation mountain and enter a small valley. On the Frontier Formation boulders are steep, soft, white and red sandstone problems. The Morrison Formation boulders are dark conglomerate boulders. The best of the Morrison Formation boulders is a fin with an overhung end. **NOTE:** The use of chalk in the monument is illegal. If necessary, use desert dirt.

PROPHECY IN STONE

Prophecy in Stone is right of Utah 149 (Blue Mountain Road) just south of the quarry (see locator map). Two routes and a variation have been established on the formation.

To reach from Utah 149, drive eastward past the left turn to the quarry. Continue to the signed Prophecy in Stone turnout and park. Hike north approximately 0.1 mile (0.16 km) to the obvious Prophecy In Stone formation.

2 EMILY'S CRACK
I, 5.7, 2 pitches, 300 feet (91 m) ★

First Ascent: Mikle Friedman, Pete Mills, late 1970s. Second Ascent: Jim Detterline, Doug Roberts, 1980s.

Location and Access: *Emily's Crack* is the right of two crack systems on the face of the formation.

Pitch 1: Climb up a sharp, detached flake left of a chimney, then traverse right on delicate holds to the base of the chimney and belay, 5.7, 150 feet (46 m).

Pitch 2: Begin with secure back and foot technique, changing to bridging near the top of the chimney. Jim Detterline: "Finally, lunge at a pile of broken rocks lying near the edge at the top of the formation." 5.7, 150 feet (46 m).

Paraphernalia: Standard desert rack.

Descent: Walk down the backside (north side) of the formation.

3 EMILY'S CRACK VARIATION
I, 5.7, 2 pitches, 300 feet (91 m) ★★

First Ascent: Jim Detterline, Doug Roberts, August 1982.

Location and Access: Begin left of *Emily's Crack.*

Pitch 1: Climb a crack system left of *Emily's Crack,* then traverse into the large chimney and belay, 5.7, 150 feet (46 m).

Pitch 2: Climb the chimney crack and pull over rotten rock onto the top of the formation, 5.7, 150 feet (46 m).

Paraphernalia: Standard desert rack.

Descent: Walk down the backside (north side) of the formation.

4 DOC'S CRACK
I, 5.10, 2 pitches, 300 feet (91 m) ★

First Ascent: Jim Detterline, solo, summer 1982.

Location and Access: *Doc's Crack* climbs the left of the two cracks on the face, left of *Emily's Crack* and variation.

Pitch 1: Climb a fist crack to a flared full-body off-width. Pull through a little overhung section and step into a large flared chimney to set up a belay, 5.10, 150 feet (46 m).

Pitch 2: Continue up, then out of the chimney system to the top of the formation, 5.10, 150 feet (46 m).

Paraphernalia: Standard desert rack; large units.

Descent: Walk down the backside (north side) of the formation.

SPLIT MOUNTAIN

Jim Detterline: "Split Mountain appears unclimbable to the RV inhabitants admiring the golden sunset on its walls from the campground across the Green River. But to those few willing to venture into its deep canyons and high slopes, Split is much more than just another difficult goal. During six years as a seasonal

Photo: Jim Detterline

Doc's Crack.

Photo: Jim Detterline

Penis Point on Split Mountain.

ranger at Dinosaur, Dan Lum had continually wondered what it would be like to stand on a certain prominent spire of the Split Mountain skyline. In the perverse imagination of this down-to-earth former oilworker from Oklahoma, the silhouette of Split resembled a sleeping but excited male. Dan called this phallic-shaped tower 'Penis Point.'"

To reach Penis Point from Utah 149, continue eastward past the quarry area. Turn off onto the signed Split Mountain boat ramp road. Park at the boat ramp parking lot. Use an unmotorized boat to cross the Green River and land at the first canyon downstream across from the boat ramp. Hike up the steep, narrow canyon, passing waterfalls, groves of ponderosa pine, and aspen to the top of Split's slickrock rim (approximately three to four hours from your car). Turn left on the summit plateau and hike an hour to the tower that stands alone. On the hike you will pass the unclimbed Chessman Towers. Penis Point is the tallest tower among several in the area. The route climbs a chimney visible from the other side of the river, to a bomb bay off-width.

5 PENIS POINT—SEMEN CHUTE
I, 5.5, A2, 1 pitch, 100 feet (30 m) ★★

First Ascent: Jim Detterline, Don Lum, October 25, 1983.

Location and Access: The route climbs a crack in the middle of the south face. Begin up a mostly wide crack, with an aid crux (2 bolts) in a small roof about halfway up. Continue with aid past three bolts to a 5.5 chimney, which is climbed to the 6,760-foot (2,060 m)-high summit. Jim Detterline: "This is a long adventure with much canyoneering, but can be done within a day." Penis Point is weathered from Weber Formation sandstone.

Paraphernalia: Standard desert rack; Camalots through #4; etriers, quick draws.

Descent: Rappel the route.

6 WHERE PEREGRINES DARE
II, 5.6, 3 pitches, 400 feet (122 m) ★

Location and Access: To reach *Where Peregrines Dare* from Utah 149, continue eastward past the quarry area. Turn off onto the signed Split Mountain boat ramp road and park at the boat ramp parking lot. Use an unmotorized boat to cross the Green River. The first ascent team crossed the river in a Sea Eagle inflatable kayak. Go slightly upstream and land where Split Mountain produces a 400-foot (122 m)-high bench. Ascend the scree slope to the base of the bench. The route climbs a prominent crack system in the center of the bench. The route was originally climbed by the park rangers to reach a ledge where a program to save peregrine falcons *(Falco peregrinus anatum)* was carried out. These beautiful raptors dive at speeds up to 200 miles per hour to snare swallows and other flying food. The area is no longer used for nesting. Where Peregrines Dare is weathered from Weber Formation sandstone.

Pitch 1: Begin up a solid hand crack to a belay stance, 5.6, 150 feet (46 m).

Pitch 2: Climb discontinuous cracks through ledge systems, 5.3, 150 feet (46 m)

Pitch 3: Climb broken cracks over ledges and small headwalls, ending with a 100-foot (30 m) scramble to the top, 5.2, 100 feet (30 m).

Paraphernalia: Standard desert rack with extra middle-size pieces.

Descent: Rappel the route.

ELEPHANT TOES BUTTE

Elephant Toes Butte (a.k.a. Brontosaurus Toes) is across Cub Creek and is reached from the Auto Tour of the Tilted Rocks road (see "Diversions" in this chapter). It is stop 12, 10.3 miles (16.6 km) from the beginning of the tour, 2 miles (3.2 km) from the monument drive. The rock art was created by the Fremont people about 1,000 years ago.

To reach from Utah 149, drive past the quarry area and continue eastward toward the Josie Morris Ranch. Park in view of the Elephant Toes Butte near the junction of the road to the ranch and the Blue Mountain Road. Hike five minutes across a wash to the west base of the formation with the toes.

Photo: Eric Bjørnstad

Elephant Toes Butte.

7 LICHEN RUN
I, 5.7, 1 pitch, 125 feet (38 m) ★★★

First Ascent: Jim Detterline, Eric Winicov, Richard Bennett, August 1983. Second Ascent: Eric Winicov, Tony Reed, Dana Reed, 1980s.

Location and Access: Scramble up a crumbly rock apron and across the base of the toes to the left, which is the northwest corner of the formation. Boulder up to the top of the second toe from the left and set up a belay. Make a tricky step onto a nearly vertical, holdless face and work up and left toward a small overhang. Look for four "desert bolts" (angle pitons inserted into drilled holes). Pull a small overhang (crux) to a ledge and friction climb over three more bulges to a crack system leading up the summit cap. Jim Detterline: "The challenge became 'four-wheeling' up the slick wall of ball-bearing sand grains and flaky lichens, passing three more bulges to reach the summit cracks. The view from the potholed but otherwise flat summit was stupendous! We looked down upon the lesser sandstone spires of Cub Creek, an area with numerous reminders of ancient Indian civilization. To the west rose the black-streaked white turrets of Split Mountain, and beyond, the snowcapped Uinta Mountains bathed in rosy alpenglow." A few weeks after the first ascent had been made, the second ascent team found the summit rappel sling shredded to pieces by rodents. Detterline suggests you bring a rappel sling as an offering to the pack rat god. Elephant Toes Butte is weathered from Navajo sandstone.

Paraphernalia: Friends, medium size; quick draws (4); 20 feet (6 m) webbing for the rappel.

Descent: Make one rappel with two 150 foot (46 m) ropes from an anchor around a summit chockstone.

STEAMBOAT ROCK AND WHISPERING CAVES DIHEDRAL

Layton Kor in *Beyond the Vertical:* "The bulk of my climbing in the desert was on the spires and pinnacles. Steamboat Rock in Dinosaur National Monument, with Mike Covington and Brian Marts in 1965, was an exception. Steamboat was no pinnacle—it was a wall. The climb followed a single straight crack system for some 700 overhanging feet."

Michael Covington writes of the climb in *Beyond the Vertical:* "The climbing on the lower section of the wall was hard direct aid, and Layton, who led the whole climb, used numerous knifeblades following a compact and incipient fracture. In the middle of the climb we came across a wonderful eagle's nest located dead center on a flat ledge. We admired the eagle that had built it for its remarkable craftsmanship. The roof of the eagle's nest alcove was a huge overhang, which

Photo: Cameron M. Burns

Steamboat Rock.

Photo: Mark Synnott

James Garrett leading above the Eagle's Nest Alcove on Kor-Covington-Marts Route.

Layton led, traversing right on direct aid for 75 feet. It was an enormous roof. Finally he disappeared over the lip and set up a belay higher up the wall. Brian went next on the haul line. It was an incredible situation when I lowered him out. He kept going out, and out, and out. Finally he was all the way out and used the Hiebelers (ascenders) to move up to Layton. I sent the haul sack out and then followed the aid with him belaying me on the other rope while I removed the pins."

In the late 1970s an unidentified party climbed the chimney system on the west (downstream) face of Steamboat Rock, and numerous routes have been established on the Echo Park side of the river.

From the town of Dinosaur, Colorado, drive 2 miles (3.2 km) east on US 40. Turn left onto Monument Road and continue approximately 27 miles (43 km), crossing into Utah. Turn right onto Echo Park Road and follow it for about 8 miles (12.8 km) back into Colorado. Turn left onto Moffat County Road 165 and continue approximately 4 miles (6.4 km) to Echo Park. Steamboat Rock is obvious across the Yampa River (north). Turn right and drive northeast, paralleling the river for 0.3 mile (0.48 km) to a parking area. Allow three to four hours for the approach from US 40.

Echo Park is named for the sounds that reverberate from the surrounding walls. The road into Echo Park descends more than 2,000 feet (610 m) in 13 miles (21 km).

8 KOR-COVINGTON-MARTS ROUTE
IV, 5.10+, A2+, 6 pitches, 700 feet (213 m) ★★★★★

First Ascent: Layton Kor, Michael Covington, Brian Marts, 1965. Probable Second Ascent: 1975 by an unidentified party.

Location and Access: The route climbs a southeast-facing wall obvious on the north side of the Yampa River.

Pitch 1: Climb with aid (pitons and nuts) up a right-facing dihedral past bolts to a small roof. Pass the roof (A2) to reach a 2- to 3-inch crack (5 to 7.6 cm). Belay at the bolts or at the wider section of the crack above.

Pitch 2: Continue up the widening crack with free climbing (5.10) or aid climbing (A1). Pass three bolts on the right wall and establish a hanging belay at a single anchor.

Pitch 3: Continue up the crack (5.10 or C1) to a prominent ledge (Eagle's Nest Alcove). Remnants of the abandoned nest are still on the ledge. The ledge is reached with hands/fists. Belay from double bolts.

Pitch 4: Aid climb (A2+) out the impressive 40-foot (12 m) cave roof pitch above the Eagle's Nest Alcove to a belay ledge.

Pitch 5: Continue up, passing smaller roofs and increasingly easy terrain to a belay (5.10, A1).

Pitch 6: Continue up the crack as it becomes gradually easier, then fourth class to the top (5.10+).

Paraphernalia: Friends (2) sets; Camalots (1) set through #4; TCUs (2) sets; pitons: a selection of knifeblades, Leeper-Zs, Lost Arrows, small angles.

Descent: Traverse east (right) approximately 500 feet (152 m) to a rappel station descending the north side of the mesa. Make two double-rope rappels, then fourth class to the southeast side of the landform and reverse the approach.

9 WHISPERING CAVES DIHEDRAL
I, 5.8+, 1 pitch, 75 feet (23 m) ★★★

First Ascent: KC Baum, Judy Baum, August 12, 1989.

Location and Access: The route is in Echo Park, 60 yards (55 m) downstream from Whispering Cave. Climb hands-to-fingers in a left-facing dihedral. Belay in an alcove.

Paraphernalia: Tri-Cams (1) #5; webbing, 5 feet for descent anchor.

Descent: Rappel the route.

DRY FORK CANYON

Dry Fork Canyon (a.k.a. Mountain Dell) is a ranching community 11 miles (18 km) northwest of Vernal. It is named for the fork, which is dry part of the year. Ward Roylance in *Utah: Guide to the State:* "Dry Fork Canyon was settled in the late

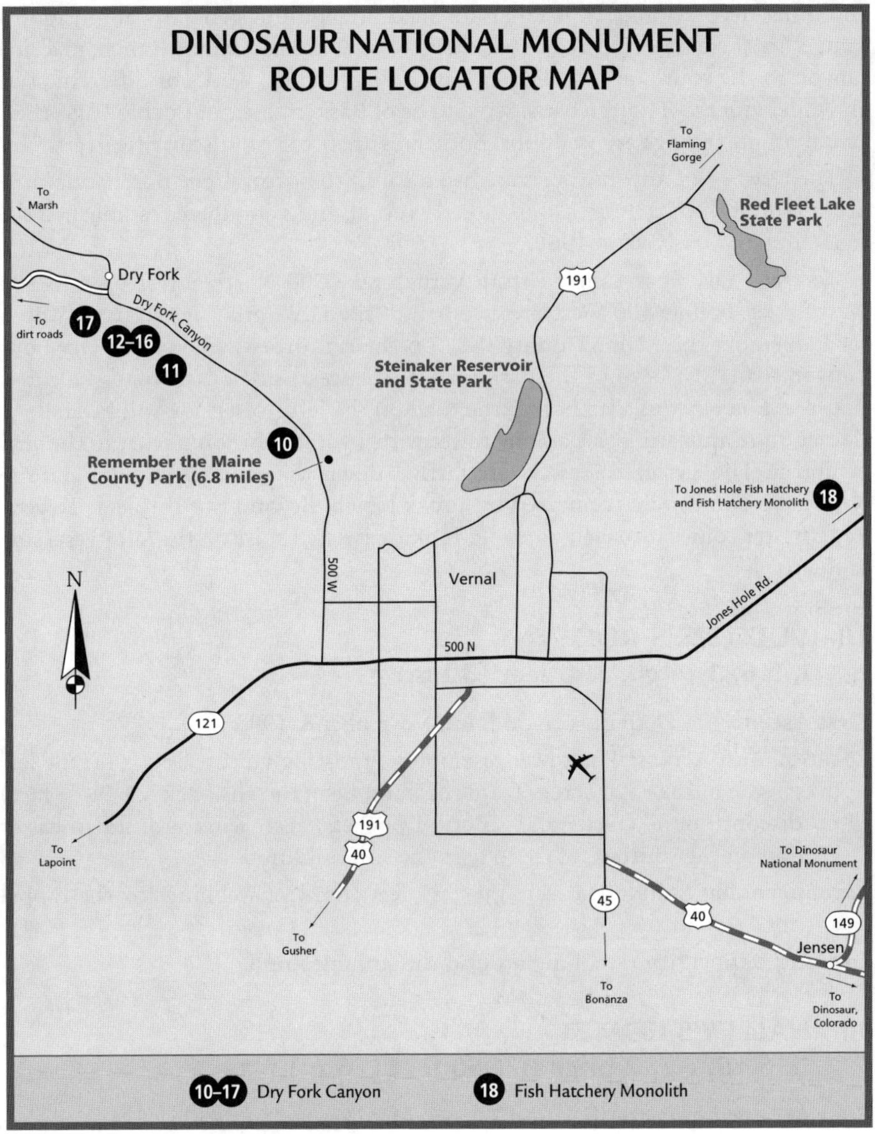

1870s. The canyon is more renowned as the site of the famed Dry Fork petroglyphs—hundreds of carved and painted pictures on the cliffs, apparently the work of more than one ancient Indian culture. The best-known panels are on the McConkie Ranch (private; permission must be obtained), where the glyphs are inscribed along the north cliffs for two miles. The McConkie site is a type site for the classic Vernal style. It is characterized by elaborate anthropomorphs (human figures), generally with trapezoidal bodies, head-dresses, necklaces, earrings, kilts, and other decorations. . . . Animals are also present, but generally are insignificant as are the occasional geometric designs. Near the McConkie Ranch, in a side canyon to the south, are the Peltier Ranch Petroglyphs, works of different style and older vintage. Though considered to be of Basketmaker or Pueblo I age, their actual origin and age are in doubt. Both sites are listed on historic registers."

The Dry Fork Canyon towers are listed south to north. Brent Boren, one-time proprietor of the Gateway Saloon outside Vernal, and Terry Pierce established the first climb in Dry Fork in 1969.

To reach Dry Fork Canyon from Vernal, take 500 North Street west to 500 West Street. Follow 500 West Street north to the Dry Fork Canyon road. Watch for Remember the Maine County Park on the right (east) side of the Dry Fork Canyon road. Just beyond the park on the left (west) side of the road, Vulture's Roost will be obvious. Farther up the road on the left (west) side will be Halley's Comet Spire appearing as a skinny tower with a giant solution pocket in the wall behind it. The Tyrolean Towers are farther down the road (west side) and are obvious as two towers connected by a rock bench. Beyond the Tyrolean Towers, Red Twister comes into view as a wild-looking twisted spire on the left (west) side of the road.

10 VULTURE'S ROOST
I, 5.6, 1 pitch, 100 feet (30 m) ★

First Ascent: Jim Detterline, Don Lum, November 8, 1983.

Location and Access: The tower resembles a roosting vulture and is on the left (west) side of the road across from the park. Begin on the backside (west face) up discontinuous cracks and solution pockets, then wind around to easier ground on the southeast face to gain the summit knob.

Paraphernalia: Standard desert rack; 20 feet (6 m) of webbing for the rappel anchor.

Descent: Rappel from webbing around the summit knob.

11 HALLEY'S COMET
II, 5.10, A2, 2 pitches, 250 feet (76 m) ★★

First Ascent: Jim Detterline, Rod Turner, Mike Keeley, September 3, 1985.

Location and Access: The route climbs a crack system in the middle of the wall facing the road (northeast).

Pitch 1: Climb an off-width crack to a ledge (poor protection). Belay near the base of the crack continuing above the ledge, 5.10, 100 feet (30 m).

Pitch 2: Free climb a steep hand and finger crack with some aid near the top, 5.10, A2, 150 feet (46 m).

Paraphernalia: Standard desert rack with off-width units.

Descent: Make two double-rope rappels from belay stations on the route.

TYROLEAN TOWERS (NORTH FACE)

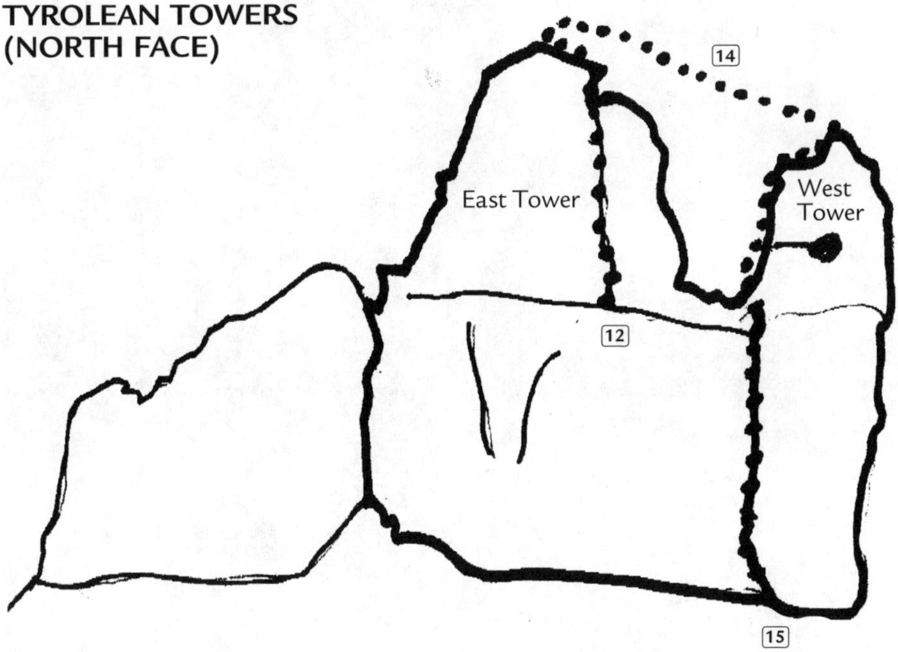

Topo: Jim Detterline

12 TYROLEAN TOWERS EAST—RAWHIDE
I, 5.9, 1 pitch, 100 feet (30 m) ★★

First Ascent: Jim Detterline, Tony Reed, Eric Winicov, August 29, 1983.

Location and Access: The tower is down the road from Halley's Comet, on the left (west) side of the canyon. Because one of the towers has a deep split in it, the Tyrolean Towers appear to be three when they are actually only two. When viewed as three, *Rawhide* climbs what appears to be the middle tower. The route ascends the north face up obvious cracks splitting the tower. A strenuous fist crack turns gradually into arm bars, off-width, and finally a wide chimney as it nears the top.

Paraphernalia: Standard desert rack with large units for the off-width.

Descent: Rappel 100 feet (30 m) from double summit bolts.

13 TYROLEAN TOWERS EAST—TEFLON CRACK
I, 5.10, 1 pitch, 150 feet (46 m) ★

First Ascent: Jim Detterline, Eric Werenskjold, October 18, 1983.

Location and Access: Climb the prominent crack on the south side of the tower. Begin up a sinuous fist-size jam crack that widens to a poorly protected off-width. The crux is a bulge about halfway up the tower. Continue up thin holds to an S-shaped off-width to the top.

Photo: Jim Detterline Collection

Jim Detterline leading first ascent on Teflon Crack, *belayed by Eric Werenskjold, 1983.*

TYROLEAN TOWERS (SOUTH FACE)

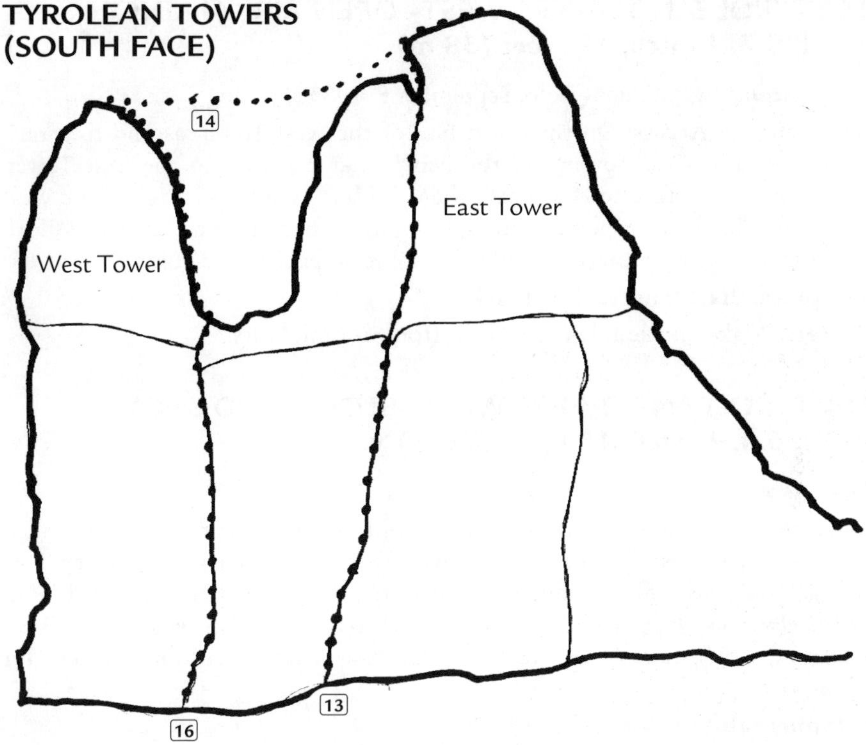

Topo: Jim Detterline

Paraphernalia: Standard desert rack; large units for the off-width.

Descent: One 100-foot (30 m) rappel down the north face from a 2-bolt summit anchor.

14 TYROLEAN TOWERS EAST AND WEST—JEEP PATROL TRAVERSE
II, A1, 5.9, 1 pitch, 100 feet (30 m) ★★

First Ascent: Jim Detterline, Uintah County Sheriff's Search and Rescue Jeep Patrol: Terry Shiner, Kevin Olson, Roy Wilkins, Eric Winicov, September 8, 1983.

Location and Access: Climb *Rawhide* to the top of the East Tower. Lasso the bulb on the top of the West Tower. Make a 50 foot (15 m) tyrolean to the West Tower.

Paraphernalia: Standard desert rack with large units for the off-width. First ascent team used one static 11mm rope, two dynamic 11mm ropes, and 20 feet (6 m) of sling material.

Descent: Make one double-rope rappel from summit bolts on the West Tower.

15 TYROLEAN TOWERS WEST—OPEN AIR CHIMNEY I, 5.7, 1 pitch, 125 feet (38 m)

First Ascent: Eric Winicov, solo, September 8, 1983.

Location and Access: On the north face of the West Tower, ascend the crack between the West Tower and the bench that connects to the East Tower. Chimney this crack to the bench, then climb the southeast edge of the West Tower. This is an exposed but slightly angled-back face that features horizontal cracks for protection and some solution pockets for holds.

Paraphernalia: Standard desert rack.

Descent: Make one double-rope rappel from summit bolts.

16 TYROLEAN TOWERS WEST—BLOOD AND SNOW I, 5.8, 1 pitch, 150 feet (46 m) ★

First Ascent: Jim Detterline, solo, November 19, 1983.

Location and Access: On the south face of the West Tower, ascend the crack between the West Tower and the bench that connects to the East Tower. This crack starts as off-width but soon turns into a hand crack to the bench. Join the *Open Air Chimney* route and continue up the southeast edge of the West Tower, using horizontal cracks for protection and solution pockets for holds.

Paraphernalia: Standard desert rack.

Descent: One double-rope rappel from summit bolts.

17 RED TWISTER SPIRE—WHO DUN IT? I, II, 5.8, A4, 2 pitches, 150 feet (46 m) ★★★

First Ascent: Jim Detterline, solo, September 20, 1983.

Location and Access: Jim Detterline: "A very thin 150-foot spire that is only about 5 feet wide on the edges and 10 feet wide on the faces. A really wild route in a really wild location." Start on the northwest corner of the spire. The route name comes from finding evidence of a previous attempt on the tower.

Pitch 1: Climb a discontinuous crack system, mostly aid on tenuous chock placements and old bolts to a small ledge, 75 feet (23 m). Traverse left 10 feet (3 m) and belay at the base of a bolt ladder, A4, 80 feet (24 m).

Pitch 2: Ascend the bolt ladder, using a cliffhanger move on some thin edges at a blank section, then make an exposed move on crumbly rock to reach the tiny summit, 5.8, 75 feet (23 m).

Paraphernalia: Standard desert rack; cliffhangers (2); etriers; quick draws.

Descent: Make one double-rope rappel from triple bolts on the summit.

Photo: Jim Detterline

Red Twister Spire.

FISH HATCHERY MONOLITH is a good-quality climb with only moderate difficulty in an area with potential for many other routes.

18 FISH HATCHERY MONOLITH—DIRECTISSIMA OF THE DESERT
II, 5.9, 3 pitches, 225 feet (69 m) ★★★

First Ascent: Jim Detterline, Duane Kitzis, August 22, 1986.

Location and Access: To reach from Vernal, drive east on 500 North Street to a signed left turn onto Jones Hole Road, then follow signs to the hatchery. Fish Hatchery Monolith is obvious behind the hatchery. Climb a prominent crack system in the middle of the face.

Pitch 1: Begin up a slot on the left side of a pillar. The crux is a finger crack with foot stems in the center of the pitch. Past the crux, climb the right fist crack to a comfortable ledge, 5.9-, 75 feet (23 m).

Pitch 2: Make a "tricky" traverse right 15 feet (4.5 m), which is protected by a fixed piton. Continuen over rotten rock up a gully to a good ledge with a three-pitons belay station, 5.7, 75 feet (23 m).

Pitch 3: Climb a dusty vertical hand crack on red rock. There is good protection with large stoppers and intermediate-size cams. Belay from a small ledge with a fixed piton, 5.9, 75 feet (23 m)

Paraphernalia: Standard desert rack.

Descent: Rappel the route.

CLIFF RIDGE

WHITE WALL

White Wall is at the base of Cliff Ridge northeast of Jensen. Approach from Utah 40 east of Jensen over obvious dirt trails. Several climbs have been established there, but further information is unknown.

DIVERSIONS

PLUG HAT BUTTE

Plug Hat Butte has various top-rope routes that may be accessed from the roadside. To reach from US 40 just east of the Colorado Welcome Center at Dinosaur (Utah/Colorado border), turn north onto Harper's Corner Road. Drive 6 miles (9.6 km); the butte will be obvious on the right (east) side of the road. There is a picnic area at 6.9 miles (11.1 km). Numerous ascents were made in 1983 by Jim Detterline, Jennifer Ertz, Robin Truitt, Elaine Adams, Jim McBrayer, and Russ Howe.

AUTO TOUR OF THE TILTED ROCKS

From the Dinosaur Quarry entrance to the monument, drive 2 miles (3.2 km) to the beginning of the auto tour, a highly recommended side trip. Fifteen numbered stops are posted beside the road as it travels east through Ashley Valley. The auto tour guide is for sale for 50 cents at the Dinosaur Quarry gift shop.

Stop 1, 1.0 mile (1.6 km): The "Swelter Shelter" is left of the road. Desert culture projectile points from 6,000 to 9,000 years ago were excavated here. The site was named by the paleontologists who excavated the site in the heat of summer. There are Fremont culture pictographs and petroglyphs on the walls of the shelter.

Stop 2, 2.3 miles (3.7 km): Prairie dog burrows are a common sight in the area. Prairie dogs can often be seen sitting upright or foraging for seeds, leaves, and insects. Also living in the area (but not frequently seen) are badgers, foxes, coyotes, and mule deer. Turn left on the road to Split Mountain Campground for stops 3 through 5.

Stop 3, 2.8 miles (4.5 km): View of Split Mountain where the Green River has created a deep canyon cutting through Weber sandstone, antedating the dinosaurs.

Stop 4, 3.1 miles (5.0 km): Steeply tilted rock, which suggests the river was present before Split Mountain made its upward warp. Split Mountain is considered a geological mystery because the geological evidence shows the upwarping took place before the river's presence.

Stop 5, 3.4 miles (5.5 km): Picturesque area with interpretive plaques and a boat ramp for river runners. Each year thousands of rafters run the white water of the Green River. To the right are a campground and picnic area with tables, campsites, rest rooms, fire grates, and trash collection; no potable water or firewood is available. Desert Voices Nature Trail begins across from the campground and is 2 miles (3.2 km) long, considered a moderately strenuous loop. For stop 6, return up the hill and drive to the stop sign, then turn left.

Stop 6, 5.8 miles (9.3 km): View of Cub Creek Valley, elevation 5,000 feet (1,524 m). The area gets less than10 inches of precipitation per year.

Stop 7, 6.5 miles (10.5 km): Hills ahead and to the right are of Morrison Formation in shades of gray, red, purple, and brown that have been likened to melting Neapolitan ice cream. The same sandstone found at the monument's quarry, it contains 140-million-year-old dinosaur fossils. The Morrison originated as mudflats laid down by ancient rivers.

Stop 8, 7.2 miles (11.6 km): Short side trail to Placer Point. In the 1930s there was a gold mining operation along the large bend in the river. The operation folded after it was found the gold was too powdery to be extracted profitably. Beyond Placer Point, before the bridge over the river, there are plaques explaining the role of fire in the desert.

Stop 9, 7.6 miles (12.2 km): For 2.5 miles (4 km) beyond the bridge over the Green River, the road passes through the private land of the Chew Ranch, where sheep, cattle, alfalfa, and corn are raised.

Stop 10, 9.4 miles (15.1 km): On the left is Turtle Rock (a.k.a. Skull Rock), weathered from Entrada sandstone.

Stop 11, 10.0 miles (16.1 km): Continue left and cross the spring-fed Cub Creek. The right fork leaves the monument; it is steep, rough, and requires four-wheel drive.

Stop 12, 10.3 miles (16.6 km): Right of the road is Elephant Toes Butte, weathered from Navajo sandstone. The stratum dates from the age of dinosaurs, 144 million to 208 million years ago.

Stop 13, 10.6 miles (17.1 km): Fremont Culture petroglyphs.

Stop 14, 10.8 miles (17.4 km): Fremont Culture petroglyphs on the left above a rock ledge. There are two lizards and a kokopelli flute player along with several smaller images. Another 0.3 mile (0.48 km) farther down the road on the left is the last rock art panel on the tour. Typical of the Fremont, the figures are trapezoidal in shape, with necklaces and headdresses. The figures are known as the Three Princesses.

Stop 15, 11.7 miles (18.8 km): Josephine Bassett Morris home at Cub Creek. Josie established a homestead in Cub Creek in 1914 and spent most of the next fifty years here. Although she had been married several times, she lived alone, raising livestock and crops without the aid of electricity or motor vehicles. Josie died in 1964, and her land eventually became part of Dinosaur National Monument.

FREMONT CULTURE PETROGLYPHS—DRY FORK CANYON

Native American petroglyphs are found all along the Navajo sandstone cliffs in Dry Fork Canyon. An auto tour guide to the petroglyphs is free at the visitor center in Vernal. The self-guided tour takes you through the town of Maeser to Dry Fork Canyon.

Along the way is Remember the Maine County Park. A sandstone cliff at the park is the canvas for an American flag and the words: "Remember the Maine." The original painting was done in 1898 in memory of the many Americans who were injured or died when the American battleship the *Maine* was bombed in Havana harbor.

The parking lot for the petroglyphs is located 0.75 mile (1.2 km) off the main canyon road and is accessible year-round. Contributions are accepted.

> At evening . . . the range seems to return to its majesty and magnitude. The peaks reach up, the bases broaden, the walls break into gashes, the ridges harden into profiles. The sun is westering, and the light falling more obliquely seems to bring out the shadows in the canyons and barrancas. Last of all the colors come slowly back to their normal condition, as the flush of life to one

recovering from a trance. One by one they begin to glow on chasm, wall, and needled summit. The air, too, changes from steel-blue to yellow, from yellow to pink, from pink to lilac, until at last with the sun on the rim of the earth, the mountains, the air, the clouds, and the sky are all glowing with the tints of ruby, topaz, rose-diamond—hues of splendor, of grandeur, of glory.

—John C. Van Dyke, *The Desert*, 1901

2

SPRING AND BOULDER CANYONS CRAGS

> You may spend days and weeks studying the make-up of these desert-floors—tiny blocks of jasper, carelian, agate—a pavement of pebbles so hard that a horse's hoof will make no impression upon it—wind-swept, clean, compact as though pressed down by a roller. One can imagine it made by the winds that have cut and drifted away the light sands and allowed the pebbles to settle close together until they have become wedged in a solid surface. For no known reason other portions of the desert are covered with blocks of red-incrusted sandstone—the incrustation being only above the sandline. In the lake-beds there is usually a surface of fine salt. It is not a hard surface though it often has a crust upon it that a wildcat can walk upon, but a horse or a man would pound through as easily as through crusted snow.
>
> —John C. Van Dyke, *The Desert*, 1901

Spring Canyon (a.k.a. Indian Rock) and Boulder Canyon Crags are approximately 6 miles (9.6 km) west of Helper, a historic railroad town 7 miles (11 km) north of Price. The Spring Canyon drains southeast into the Price River at Helper. The town was established in 1883 as Pratts Landing, and in 1892 was renamed for the coal-fired "helper engines" used to increase power for heavily loaded trains laboring up the steep grade to Soldier Summit. With improved railroad grades and more powerful diesel engines, the helper engines are a relic of the past.

Climbs in the area are concentrated on the 50-foot (15 m) cliffs above the junction of the two canyons. They lie 1 mile (1.6 km) northeast of Standardville (junction of Sowbelly Gulch and Spring Canyon). Jesse Knight established a community there in 1912 for coal miners working in his nearby mines. He named the place Storrs after George A. Storrs, his mine superintendent. The name was changed to Spring Canyon in 1924, after the demand for coal began to lessen. Miners moved away from the area, and the community soon became a ghost town. Remnants include a fading railroad bed, an old bridge, and a flagpole atop a high crag. Stewart Green: "A rough road shelves up above the north cliff to the pole, passing an old bed of blooming yellow roses."

At the junction of the two canyons, Boulder Canyon Crag is above the road on the right, Volkswagon wall above the road on the left. Collectively they are the Spring Canyon Crass. They consist of bolted sport routes intermingled with crack climbs. Difficulty ranges from 5.7 through 5.12. Stewart Green: "Most climbers will do all the routes they want in a three- to four-hour stopover." Miscellaneous boulder problems have been done on the large stones on the north side of the canyon.

The Boulder and Spring Canyon Crags are cliffs composed of rocks of the Mesa Verde Formation. Perhaps the most complex body of sediment in Utah, the formation is composed of a variety of rock types that interfinger with each other.

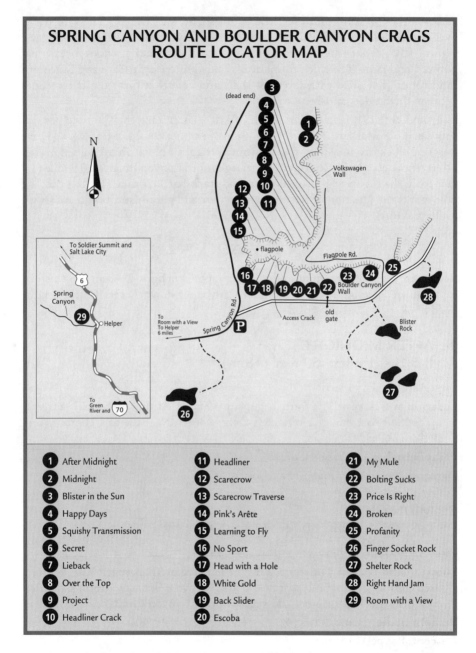

SPRING CANYON AND BOULDER CANYON CRAGS ROUTE LOCATOR MAP

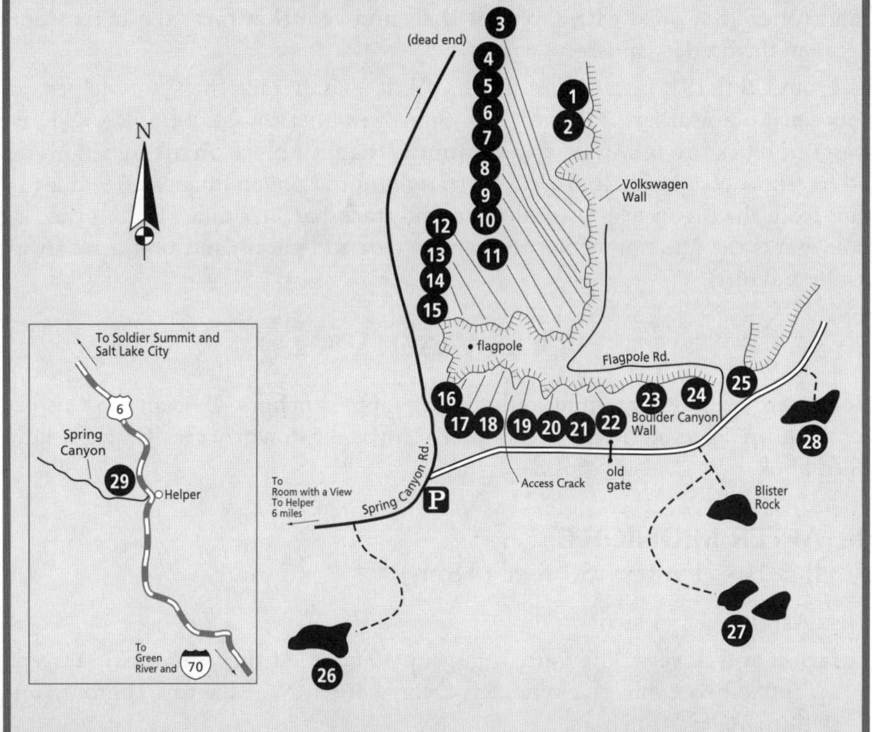

1 After Midnight
2 Midnight
3 Blister in the Sun
4 Happy Days
5 Squishy Transmission
6 Secret
7 Lieback
8 Over the Top
9 Project
10 Headliner Crack
11 Headliner
12 Scarecrow
13 Scarecrow Traverse
14 Pink's Arête
15 Learning to Fly
16 No Sport
17 Head with a Hole
18 White Gold
19 Back Slider
20 Escoba
21 My Mule
22 Bolting Sucks
23 Price Is Right
24 Broken
25 Profanity
26 Finger Socket Rock
27 Shelter Rock
28 Right Hand Jam
29 Room with a View

Its color includes red, green, gray, brown, and black and contains claystone, sandstone, carbonate beds, and deep water to marginal alluvial beds. The layer is more than 6,000 feet (1,829 m) thick along its southern margin.

The formation is regarded as the world's greatest repository of oil shale. Found in the formation are a variety of plants, nonmarine invertebrates, insects, lizard-skin impressions, bird feathers, and fish. Stewart Green: "The sandstone, part of the Mesa Verde Formation, is a compact layer that erodes into slabs and vertical faces broken by cracks and corners. Expect smears, edges, occasional pockets, and jams. The thick formation, divided into Castle Gate and Starpoint sandstones, is seamed with layers of shale and coal that form the talus slopes between the harder sandstone strata."

From US 6/191, seven miles north of Price, Utah, take the West Helper exit between Mile Markers 232 and 233. Sign: WEST HELPER—SPRING CANYON. Drive west one block to a four-way stop. Continue straight 1 block on the signed Bryner Street (through a residential area). Turn right onto Canyon Road. At 0.9 mile (1.4 km) from the highway, pass under railroad tracks; at 11.7 mile (19 km) the flag pole marks the junction of Spring Canyon (left and paved) and Boulder Canyon (right and dirt).

VOLKSWAGEN WALL

Routes are listed left to right and all have rappel anchors. Descent may also be made down Flagpole Road to Boulder Canyon or down Access Crack, a large open book.

1 AFTER MIDNIGHT
I, 5.10-, 1 pitch, 60 feet (18 m) ★★★

First Ascent: Cory Pincock.

Location and Access: The route begins up *Midnight*. At the second bolt, traverse up and left to a thin crack in a left-facing corner. Near the top, climb up and right to *Midnight* anchors.

Paraphernalia: TCUs; quick draws.

Descent: Rappel from *Midnight* anchors.

2 MIDNIGHT
I, 5.10c, 1 pitch, 60 feet (18 m) ★★★★★

First Ascent: Andrew Fry, Owen Fry, July 1993.

Location and Access: The route is on the left side of Volkswagen Wall, left of a deep chimney. Face climb past four bolts to a two-bolt belay station. Cory Pincock calls this "the original and classic Spring Canyon Climb."

Paraphernalia: Quick draws (4).

Descent: Rappel the route.

3 BLISTER IN THE SUN
I, 5.9, 1 pitch, 50 feet (15 m) ★★

First Ascent: Cory Pincock, Aimee Faucheux, summer 1994.

Location and Access: The route is left of a left-facing dihedral, approximately

VOLKSWAGEN WALL

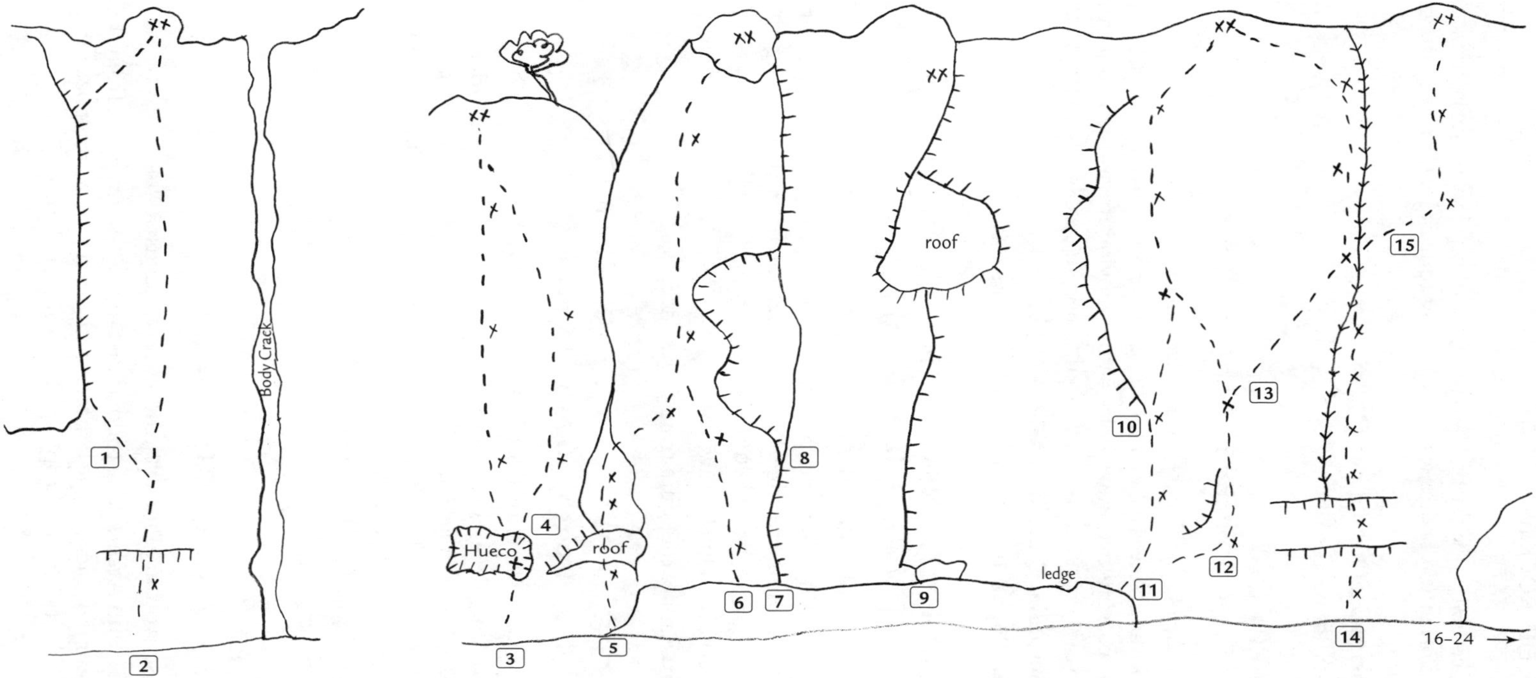

300 feet (91 m) right of *Midnight*. Climb over loose ledges/steps and pockets to a horizontal bedding seam, passing four bolts to a two-bolt belay/rappel station.

Paraphernalia: Quick draws (4).

Descent: Rappel the route.

4 HAPPY DAYS
I, 5.10 R, 1 pitch, 50 feet (15 m) ★★

First Ascent: Cory Pincock, Aimee Faucheux, July 1994.

Location and Access: Begin at *Blister in the Sun*. Pass a bolt and climb up and right, passing two more bolts before moving up and left to join *Blister in the Sun*. Cory Pincock: "Not led often, but is an excellent slab runout."

Paraphernalia: Quick draws (3).

Descent: Rappel from *Blister in the Sun* chain anchor.

5 SQUISHY TRANSMISSION
I, 5.9, 1 pitch, 50 feet (15 m)

First Ascent: John Howell, Andrew Fry, October 1996.

Location and Access: The route begins right of *Happy Days* up poor rock to the left of a prominent ledge. Pass a roof section before continuing up better rock. Three bolts are passed en route to the top.

Paraphernalia: Quick draws (3).

Descent: Rappel the route from *Secret* anchors.

6 SECRET
I, 5.11b, 1 pitch, 50 feet (15 m) ★★★★

First Ascent: Owen Fry, Cory Pincock, October 1994.

Location and Access: The route begins from a prominent ledge to the right of *Squishy Transmission* and climbs left of a large left-facing flake, passing four bolts to a double-bolt belay/rappel anchor. Cory Pincock: "Don't cheat by starting in the left crack."

Paraphernalia: Quick draws (4).

Descent: Rappel the route.

7 LIEBACK
I, 5.7, 1 pitch, 45 feet (14 m)

First Ascent: Cory Pincock, Andrew Fry, August 1994.

Location and Access: The route is just right of *Secret*. Begin from the prominent ledge and lieback a large left-facing dihedral to a two-bolt belay/rappel station. Cory Pincock: "Good top rope for beginner climbers."

Paraphernalia: Friends, small through medium.

Descent: Rappel the route.

8 OVER THE TOP
I, 5.9, 1 pitch, 45 feet (14 m) ★★★

First Ascent: Cory Pincock, Andrew Fry, August 1994.

Location and Access: Begin up *Lieback* and veer right, following a thin crack over a flake, then rejoin *Lieback* and continue up the left-facing dihedral to its two-bolt belay/rappel station.

Paraphernalia: Friends, medium; TCUs.

Descent: Rappel the route from *Lieback* anchors.

9 PROJECT (a.k.a. Unclimbable Crack)
I, 5.11+/5.12-, 1 pitch, 50 feet (15 m)

First Ascent: Cory Pincock, to within 10 feet (3 m) of the top, 1997.

Location and Access: The route begins from the prominent ledge and jams an overhanging crack to the right of *Over the Top*, then continues up a finger and thin hand crack, ending at a two-bolt belay/rappel station. The route is called *Unclimbable Crack* because, despite many tries, no one has been able to climb the final 10 feet and top out.

Paraphernalia: Friends, small through medium.

Descent: Rappel the route.

10 HEADLINER CRACK
I, 5.10a, 1 pitch, 45 feet (14 m) ★

First Ascent: Cory Pincock, solo, March 1994.

Location and Access: The route face climbs the wall below the flagpole area in view at the top of the cliff. Begin up *Headliner*. At the second bolt, follow the right-facing crack to the left, rejoining *Headliner* at its fifth bolt.

Paraphernalia: Friends #1, #1.5; TCUs (1) set; quick draws (3).

Descent: Rappel from *Headliner* anchors.

11 HEADLINER
I, 5.10a, 1 pitch, 45 feet (14 m) ★★★

First Ascent: Aimee Faucheux, April 1994. Bolted by Cory Pincock, Aimee Faucheux.

Location and Access: The route is right of *Project*. Begin at the right side of the prominent ledge and climb past five bolts to a belay/rappel station. The crux is at the third bolt.

Paraphernalia: Quick draws (5).

Descent: Rappel the route.

12 SCARECROW
I, 5.11a/b, 1 pitch, 45 feet (14 m) ★★

First Ascent: Cory Pincock, solo, May 1997.

Location and Access: The route face climbs up thin holds past two bolts, ascending a steep pocketed slab to the right of *Headliner*. It joins *Headliner* at its third bolt, and ends at a two-bolt belay/rappel station.

Paraphernalia: Quick draws (5).

Descent: Rappel from *Headliner* anchors.

13 SCARECROW TRAVERSE
I, 5.11d/5.12a, 1 pitch, 45 feet (14 m) ★★

First Ascent: Cory Pincock.

Location and Access: The route begins at *Scarecrow*. At the second bolt, traverse up and right, climb an overhang (crux) to join *Pink's Arête*, and end at *Headliner* anchors.

Paraphernalia: TCUs #0.5 (for tip of overhang); quick draws.

Descent: Rappel from *Headliner* anchors.

14 PINK'S ARÊTE
I, 5.12a, 1 pitch, 45 feet (14 m) ★★★★

First Ascent: Cory Pincock, July 1998. Bolted by Cory Pincock, Angie Pincock.

Location and Access: The route begins up an overhanging face right of *Scarecrow*. Climb the obvious arête, joining *Scarecrow Traverse* and finishing at *Headliner* anchors.

Paraphernalia: Quick draws (13).

Descent: Rappel from *Headliner* anchors.

15 LEARNING TO FLY (a.k.a. No Mo' Money Project)
I, 5.12a/b, 1 pitch, 75 feet (23 m)

First Ascent: Cory Pincock, solo, 1997.

Location and Access: The route begins up *Pink's Arête*, then traverses up and right. It continues over an overhang, passing two bolts to a belay/rappel station. Stewart Green: "Ran out of cash before all the bolts were in. Face climb the steep face creased with horizontal breaks below the flagpole. Look for a large Friend placement in the first 40 feet (12 m) to two-bolt upper slab. End at a two-bolt chain anchor."

Paraphernalia: Friends; TCUs (1) #0.5 (for upper slab); quick draws.

Descent: Rappel the route from double anchors.

BOULDER CANYON WALL

The wall is the cliff on the north side of the buttress. See Volkswagen Wall for descent information. Routes are listed left to right from the rock prow beneath the flagpole.

16 NO SPORT
I, 5.9, 1 pitch, 45 feet (14 m) ★

First Ascent: Cory Pincock, Kara Pincock, June 1997.

Location and Access: Climb easy rock to a belay ledge left of a large dihedral. Continue left on a ledge above a roof, then climb and work discontinuous cracks to a two-bolt belay/rappel station.

Paraphernalia: Friends (1) set; TCUs; long runners.

Descent: Rappel the route.

17 HEAD WITH A HOLE
I, 5.10a/b R, 1 pitch, 45 feet (14 m) ★

First Ascent: Cory Pincock, August 1994. Bolted by Cory Pincock, Aimee Faucheux.

Location and Access: Stewart Green: "Begin in trees right of a ledge and below a corner. Pull up around a flake to a bolt, then run it out to another bolt. Continue over striped, inverted black tongue." Pass three bolts to a two-bolt belay/rappel station.

Paraphernalia: Quick draws (3).

Descent: Rappel the route.

18 WHITE GOLD
I, 5.10b, 1 pitch, 45 feet (14 m) ★★★

First Ascent: Cory Pincock, Kara Pincock, July 1997.

Location and Access: Begin up *Head with a Hole* past a bulge, then face climb up and right, passing two bolts to a belay/rappel station.

Paraphernalia: Quick draws (4).

Descent: Rappel the route.

19 BACK SLIDER
I, 5.11b, 1 pitch, 45 feet (14 m) ★★★

First Ascent: Cory Pincock, Kara Pincock, August 1997.

BOULDER CANYON WALL

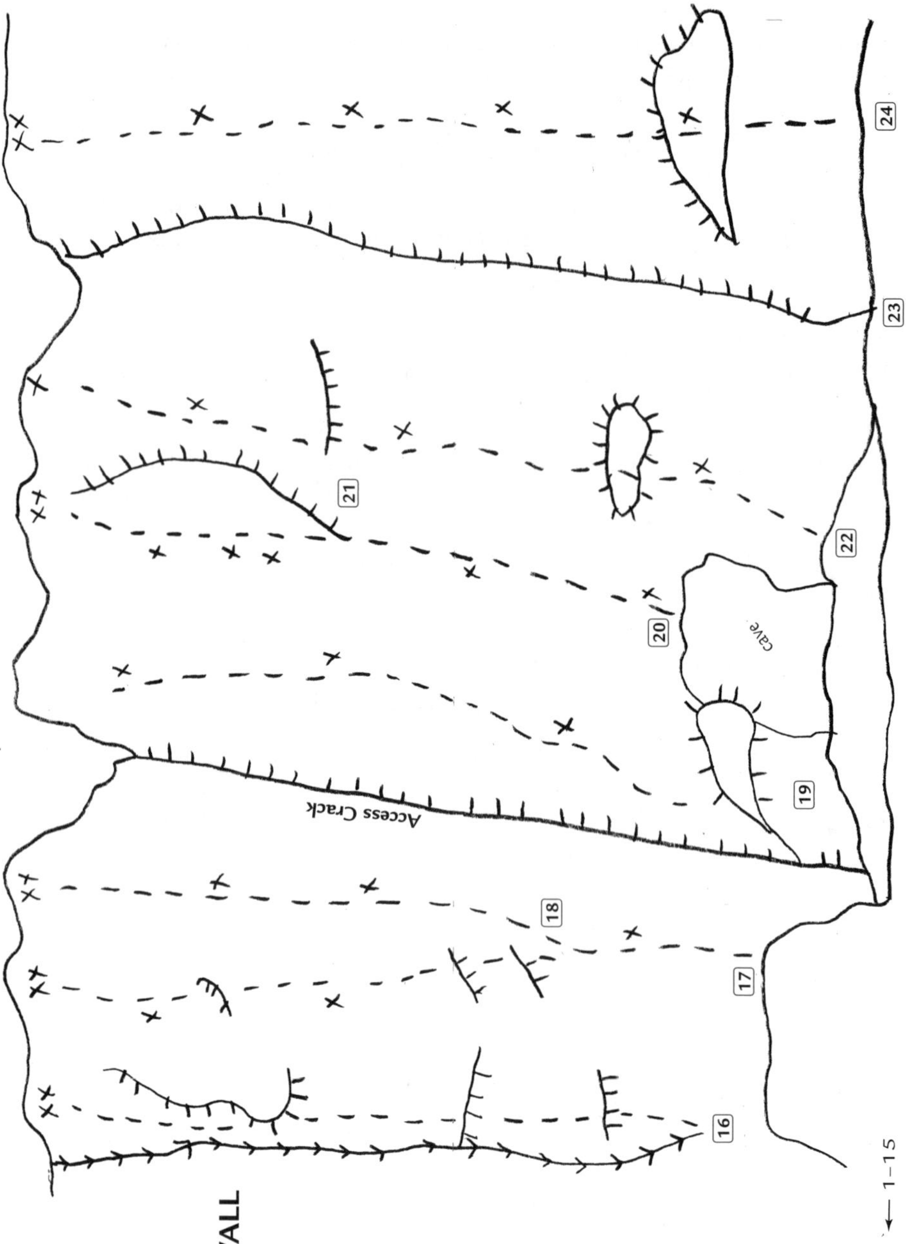

Location and Access: The route begins up a slab right of a large open book (Access Crack), right of *White Gold*. Climb rock with black streaks past three bolts to a double cold-shut belay/rappel anchor. Cory Pincock: "This is well worth an attempt or two. Seldom climbed."

Paraphernalia: Quick draws (3).

Descent: Rappel the route.

20 ESCOBA
I, 5.11+, 1 pitch, 45 feet (14 m) ★★★★

First Ascent: Cory Pincock, Kara Pincock, August 1999.

Location and Access: The route starts between a prominent roof to the left and a deep corner to the right. Climb a steep crack system past one bolt to a second bolt. Continue up and right to a right-facing corner, ending at a ledge with fixed anchors. *Escoba* is Spanish for broom, a necessary item for cleaning the route.

Paraphernalia: Friends, small through medium; quick draws.

Descent: Rappel the route.

21 MY MULE
I, 5.10-, 1 pitch, 45 feet (14 m)

First Ascent: Cory Pincock, Kara Pincock, August 1997.

Location and Access: The route begins up *Escoba* then climbs past bolts to the right of *Escoba* bolts, ending at *Escoba* anchors.

Paraphernalia: Camalots #2, #4; TCUs; quick draws.

Descent: Rappel from *Escoba* anchors.

22 BOLTING SUCKS
I, 5.9, 1 pitch, 45 feet (14 m) ★★

First Ascent: Cory Pincock, Aimee Faucheux, August 1994.

Location and Access: The route climbs the slab right of *My Mule*. Ascend dark rock to potholes and a bolt. Continue to a bedding seam, pass a roof, and end at a belay/rappel station.

Paraphernalia: Quick draws (3).

Descent: Rappel the route from a chain anchor.

23 PRICE IS RIGHT
I, 5.11a, 1 pitch, 45 feet (14 m) ★★★★★

First Ascent: Andrew Fry, solo, September 1994.

Location and Access: Stewart Green: "Quality. An excellent crack with a rating dependent on finger size. Easier for small fingers." The route begins right of

Bolting Sucks and climbs a left-facing lieback crack in a corner with hand jams and fingertip liebacking. No fixed anchor on the route. Belay is from trees.

Paraphernalia: Small Friends; TCUs; stoppers.

Descent: Rappel from trees.

24 BROKEN
I, 5.12a/b, 1 pitch, 35 feet (11 m) ★★★★★

First Ascent: Cory Pincock, October 1994. Bolted by Andrew Fry.

Location and Access: The route is at the right side of the buttress. Climb the cliff right of an overhanging prow, passing four bolts to a double-bolt belay/rappel station.

Paraphernalia: Quick draws (4).

Descent: Rappel the route.

25 PROFANITY
I, 5.10+, 1 pitch, height unknown

First Ascent: Cory Pincock, November 1994. Bolted by Andrew Fry.

Location and Access: The route is across the road from *Broken*. It climbs an unprotected face, which leads to a crack in a roof. Cory Pincock: "This one is a grunter, hence the name."

Paraphernalia: Undetermined.

Descent: Rappel the route.

BOULDER CANYON BOULDERS

Cory Pincock: "There are many boulders that line this canyon. You really have to search for the good ones, but when you find them they are Joe's Valley quality." Most boulders are approximately 20 feet (6 m) high with good landings and are not rated. See route locator map.

26 FINGER SOCKET ROCK

Classic undercling leads to a one-finger pocket on the east side of the rock. Good undercling problems on the north side.

27 SHELTER ROCK

Cory Pincock: "An underhung, clean, pocket test that will require powerful moves. Excellent."

28 RIGHT HAND JAM

Many problems, the most difficult being a full traverse left to right, then back to the left.

29 ROOM WITH A VIEW

Located approximately 2 miles toward Helper from the flagpole. Good quality boulders. Park on the right side of the road just past the last house on the Spring Canyon approach. Hike right, up through the cliff band to the boulders.

DIVERSIONS

WESTERN MINING AND RAILROAD MUSEUM

The Western Mining and Railroad Museum is at 296 South Main Street in Helper. The museum has a gift shop, an archive room for research on Carbon County, indoor displays, and two outdoor locations for exhibits of a 1917 railroad caboose and mining equipment from early to modern times. There are also re-creations of a mining company store and railroad office, schoolroom, beauty shop, blacksmith shop, doctor and dentist office, and World War I and II artifacts.

> The black dirt that lies a foot or more in depth upon the surface of the eastern prairies, showing the many years accumulations of decayed grasses and weeds, is not known anywhere on the desert. The slight vegetation that grows never has a chance to turn into mould. And besides, nothing ever rots or decays in these sands. Iron will not rust, nor tin tarnish, nor flesh mortify. The grass and the shrub wither and are finally cut into pieces by flying sands. Sometimes you may see small particles of grass or twigs heaped about an anthill, or find them a part of a bird's nest in a cholla; but usually they turn to dry dust and blow with the wind—at the wind's will.
>
> —John C. Van Dyke, *The Desert,* 1901

Continue up Spring Canyon from the flag pole to view numerous unclimbed crags—be wary of private property. It is a worth while drive just to view the ghostly remains of the once-thriving coal mining community. At 13.2 miles (21 km) from the highway (US 6/191), pass a cattle guard . At 15 miles (24 km) pavement ends. Sign: NO TRESPASSING—PRIVATE PROPERTY BOTH SIDES OF THE ROAD. DO NOT LEAVE THE ROADWAY. 100% PRIVATE PROPERTY.

3
NINE MILE CANYON

> Desert-birds look not very different from their cousins of the woods and streams except that they are thinner, more subdued in color, somewhat more alert. They are very pretty, very innocent-looking birds, but we may be sure that living here in the desert, enduring its hardships and participating in its incessant struggle for life and for the species, they have just the same savage instincts as the plants and the animals. The sprightliness and the color may suggest harmlessness; but the eye, the beak, the claw are designed for destruction.
>
> —John C. Van Dyke, *The Desert*, 1901

Home to the largest collection of petroglyphs and pictographs found in one place on the planet, Nine Mile Canyon has been called the world's longest art gallery. The canyon's name is misleading: It is actually 50 miles (80 km) long. It is famed for its prodigious assemblage of Fremont petroglyphs and pictographs, rock art that depicts both humans and animals. Human figures are horned and trapezoidal-shaped, and often have elaborate necklaces, earrings, shields, swords, loincloths, and headdresses. Animals are uniquely stylized. Although little recorded climbing has been done in the canyon, it is included for its remoteness yet accessibility, its beauty, and its potential for new routes.

To reach Nine Mile Canyon, turn north onto the Soldier Creek Road between mile markers 249 and 250 from US 6/191 south of Price (the Price, Green River highway) at Wellington. There is a sign on the left at the turn (northwest corner) and an information kiosk for the canyon. From the junction, it is 13.2 miles (21 km) to the Soldier Canyon Mine and the beginning of the dirt trail into Nine Mile Canyon. Three miles (4.8 km) farther the Tim Toula climb is obvious on the left of the roadway. There is much potential for top-rope climbing in the next several miles and seemingly endless potential for new routes up the Dakota sandstone in a pastoral setting. In 7.7 miles (12.3 km), pass a sign for Nine Mile Ranch. A half mile (0.8 km) farther is a sign: BUNK 'N BREAKFAST—CAMPGROUND—COUNTRY STORE—GUIDED TOURS. Beyond the campground there are numerous rock art panels and ample climbing opportunities for many miles.

HISTORY

The Fremont Culture lived in Nine Mile Canyon from approximately 1,700 to 700 years ago. The ancient peoples were named by Noel Morss of the Peabody Museum in 1928 because they lived in what is now known as the Fremont River drainage. The primitive peoples of the Fremont did not fashion rocks for tools as the ancient Anasazi or Pueblo Indians did. The Fremont were hunters and farmers, raising corn, beans, and squash and collecting seeds, nuts, and roots that they dried and stored in granaries built on rock cliffs. The Fremont's dwellings consisted of semisubterranean pit houses constructed of wood and mud, which

Photo: Fran Barnes

The canyon is famous for its many ancient petroglyphs and pictographs.

were entered through an opening in the roof. The Fremont moccasins made of hide and dewclaw hobnails were the precursor of today's crampons, especially the instep spikes that are worn on boots to prevent slipping on ice.

The 50-mile(80 km)-long canyon received its name from an 1869 government expedition through Utah led by John Wesley Powell. With him was a cartographer named Bishop, who found a small creek near his ninth-mile triangulation drawing. He named it Nine Mile Creek, and the canyon was subsequently referred to as Nine Mile Canyon. A more fanciful origin, although discounted by most historians, is of a family named Miles who reportedly lived in the canyon in the late 1800s. They had seven daughters and, with mother and father, totaled nine members, thus Nine Miles.

The canyon cuts through the Book Cliffs between Carbon Country and the Uintah Basin. In 1886 the U.S. Army upgraded a primitive trail through the canyon, creating a federal highway that linked the two regions. The U.S. 9th Cavalry, a regiment of African-American soldiers formed after the Civil War, built the road and telegraph line to support the military post at Fort Duchesne.

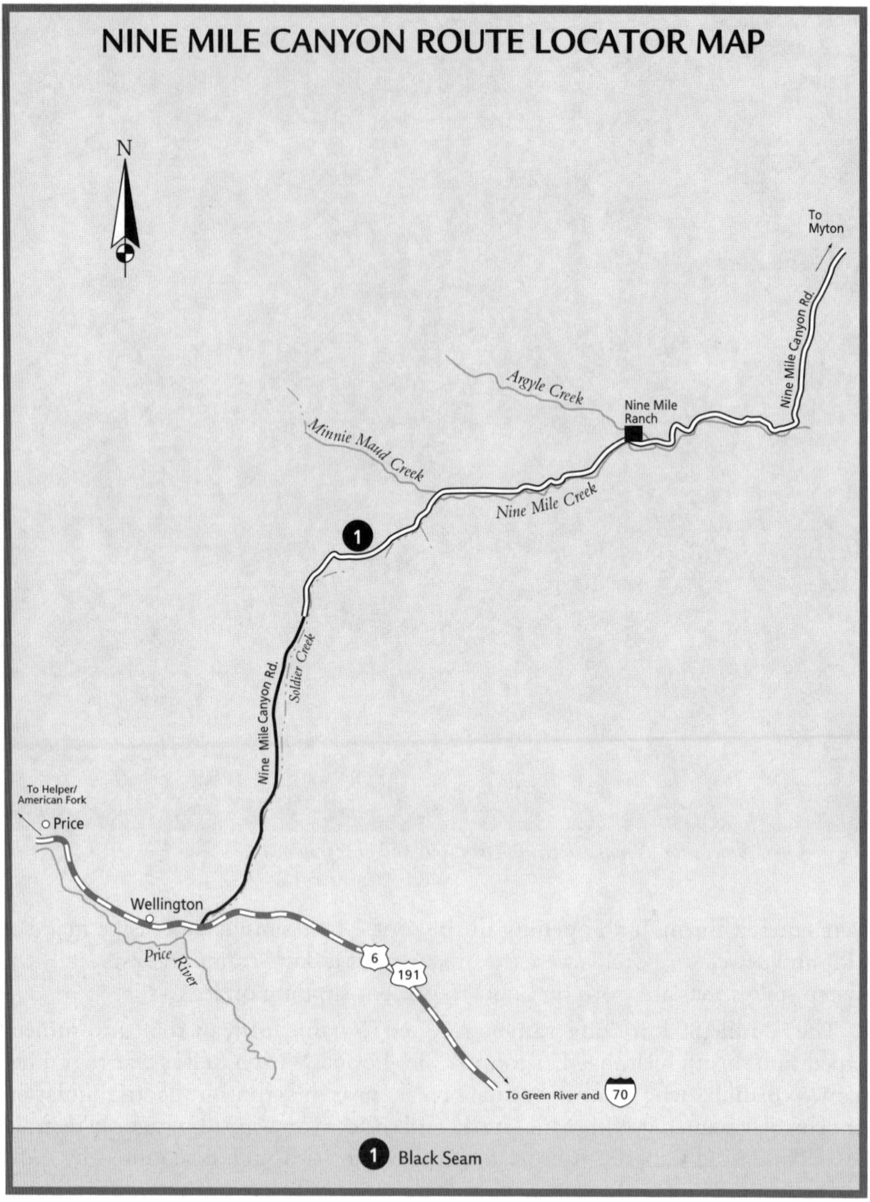

Because it was the departure point for homesteaders bound for the Uintah Basin, Price became the largest city in Carbon County. Homesteaders and their freight arrived by rail at Price, where the Nine Mile Canyon road originated. From 1886 through 1910, the road through Nine Mile Canyon was the most heavily traveled road in eastern Utah. Newspaper accounts estimate that horse-drawn wagons hauled as much as two million pounds of freight through the canyon each month and that fifty to one-hundred teams and wagons would be on the road at any given time. With the completion of US 40 and 191, Nine Mile became the road less traveled. The federal government turned it over to the state, and since 1990 it has been a national Back Country Byway.

TOULA WALL

1 BLACK SEAM
I, 5.10, 1 pitch, 30 feet (9 m) ★★★★

First Ascent: Tim Toula, solo, late 1980s.

Location and Access: Three miles (4.8 km) upcanyon from the beginning of the dirt trail, Toula Wall will be obvious on the left beside the road. The route climbs the best-looking line. It can be top roped by scrambling up the right side of the wall.

Paraphernalia: Top rope.

Descent: Walk off.

Photo: Eric Bjørnstad

Toula Wall: Black Seam *(left) and* Black Seam II *(right).*

DIVERSIONS

DINOSAUR MUSEUM

The College of Eastern Utah Dinosaur Museum in Price is a highly recommended stop. There are numerous displays relating to Nine Mile rock art, and its gift shop offers books and fliers about the canyon.

> Humanity at times has difficulty in withstanding this heat, for though it is not suffocating, it parches the mouth and dries up the blood so rapidly that if water is not attainable the effect is soon apparent. The animals—that is, the wild ones—are never fazed by it; but the domestic horse, dog, and cow yield to it almost as readily as a man.
>
> —John C. Van Dyke, *The Desert,* 1901

4
JOE'S VALLEY

> You cannot always see the wonderful quality of this sky-blue from the desert valley, because it is disturbed by reflections, by sand-storms, by lower air strata. The report it makes of itself when you begin to gain altitude on a mountain's side is quite different. At four thousand feet the blue is certainly more positive, more intense, than at sea-level; at six thousand feet it begins to darken and deepen, and it seems to fit in the saddles and notches of the mountains like a block of lapis lazuli; at eight thousand feet it has darkened still more and has a violet hue about it. The night sky at this altitude is almost weird in its purples. A deep violet fits up close to the rim of the moon, and the orb itself looks like a silver wafer pasted upon the sky.
>
> –John C. Van Dyke, *The Desert,* 1901

There are numerous bouldering areas near Ephraim, southwest of Price. The best-known is Joe's Valley. Also near Ephraim are many small sport crags, the most popular at Round Valley, 3 miles (5 km) south of Manti. There are small crags at New Canyon along the Nebo Loop Road north of Ephraim, and at Axhandle Canyon, Coal Canyon, and Dry Canyon. The best sources for information are Jason Stevens's guide to Round Valley, *Maple Canyon Rock Climbing,* available at stores in Ephraim and *A Bouldering Guide to Joe's Valley* by Jeff Baldwin.

Photo: Jeff Baldwin

Jared Roth on Super Sloper, rated V2.

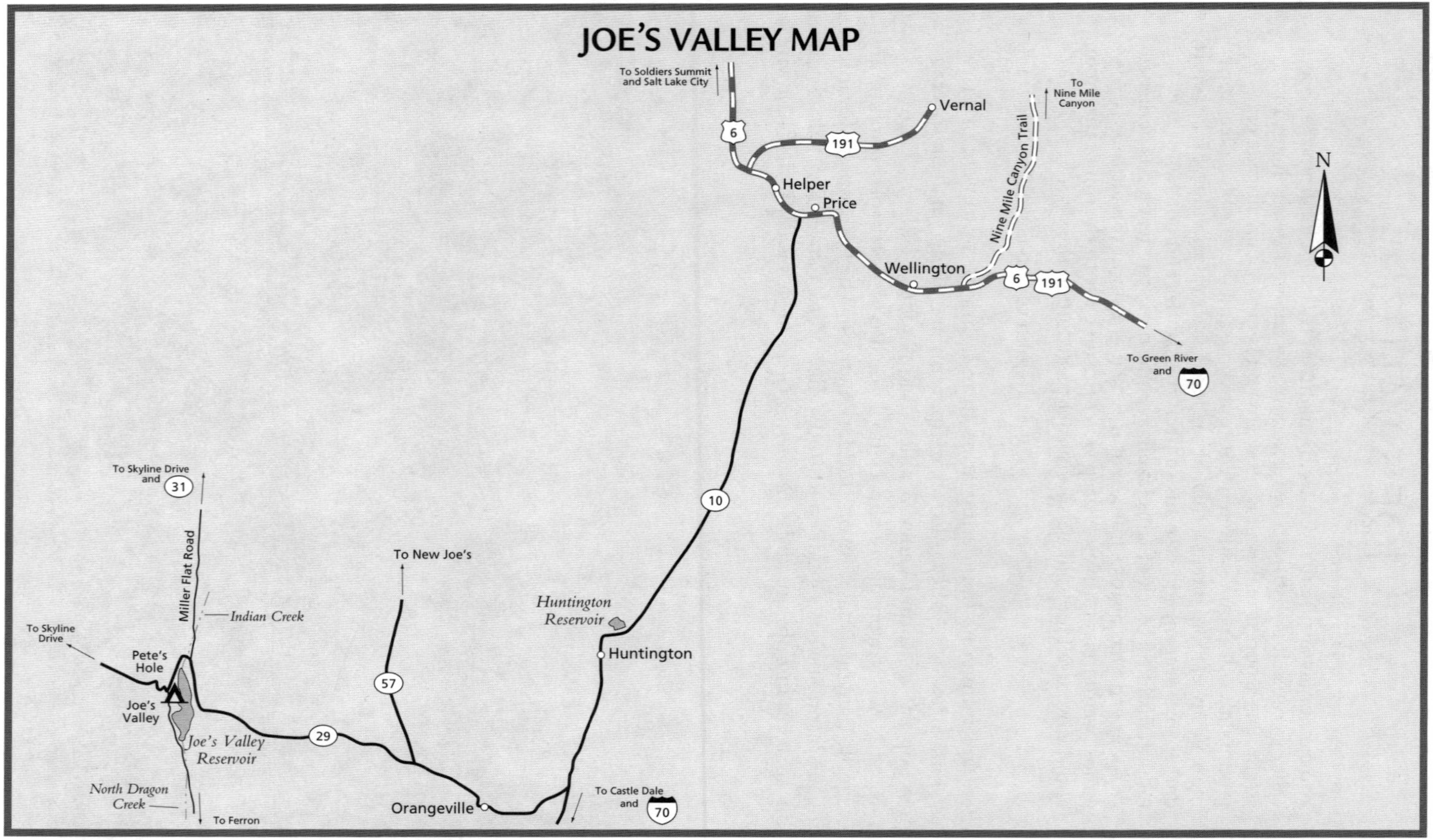
JOE'S VALLEY MAP
To Soldiers Summit and Salt Lake City
Vernal
To Nine Mile Canyon
Nine Mile Canyon Trail
6
191
Helper
Price
Wellington
N
To Green River and 70
10
To Skyline Drive and 31
Miller Flat Road
Indian Creek
To New Joe's
Huntington Reservoir
Huntington
To Skyline Drive
Pete's Hole
Joe's Valley
57
29
Joe's Valley Reservoir
North Dragon Creek
To Ferron
Orangeville
To Castle Dale and 70

Alison Osius: "Bouldering?—I can't ever do any of the problems. Bouldering is hard; it's meant to be. It is, after all, climbing distilled, and that means boiled down, to the gist. . . . No question, bouldering is good for anyone, and is the best way to get power (which I could use). You can work out sequences with friends, get used to trying moves that feel crazy. Getting just one problem can make your day. You can walk out to some lone granite outcrop in the woods near your house in the evening, bringing just shoes, a water bottle, and your dog; you can travel to Ibex or the Happy Boulders and find a whole like-minded community. These days, climbers are planning road-trip itineraries of ten bouldering spots, period. Bouldering may never be my end-all, but in recent years it's again become one of my climbing choices, a thing both easy and hard to do."

Stewart Green, speaking of Joe's Valley: "Stacks of problems on hundreds of sandstone boulders lie in the valley off Utah 29, west of Castle Dale."

Brian Mecham: "Bouldering is, in fact, one of the least expensive outdoor sports. You don't need to replace bike tires or worn-out hubs. And you don't need to retire expensive ropes and climbing hardware."

RATING SYSTEM

The original rating system for bouldering grew out of John Gill and Yvon Chouinard's bouldering in the late 1950s in the Tetons at Jenny Lake Boulders. They rated their problems on a B scale, with B1 being hard and B2 very hard. The B scale remained popular until the 1980s, when John Sherman, one of the leading boulderers at Hueco Tanks State Park near El Paso, Texas, created a new scale that uses V as the denominator. The V scale was named for its originator, who is known by the moniker Verm.

It runs V0- (5.8), V0 (5.9), V0+ (5.10a/b), V1 (5.10c/d), V2 (5.11a/b), V3 (5.11c/d), V4 (5.12-), V5 (5.12), V6 (5.12+), V7 (5.13-), V8 (5.13), V9 (5.13+), V10, 11, 12, 13, and V14 (5.14- through 5.14).

John Sherman: "Given the way they have spread, the *V* in V grades could stand for virus. It has become the dominant system in the United States and has even spread overseas, seeing use in South Africa, Australia, England (where they have substituted the prefix V for B), and other countries."

John Gill, in the foreword to John Sherman's *Stone Crusade, A Historical Guide to Bouldering in America:* "Each climber follows a unique vertical path, a sequence of steps determined both by choice and by fate that ultimately shapes his climbing history. Most new climbers discover the path where the lights are brightest: among the fashionable inclinations of the experienced many, joining a small army of jargon-spouting enthusiasts who march toward common goals, in perfect step with the media beat. But a few make a subtle turn and steal away on sojourns of a more eccentric character.

"What do I miss about bouldering? The first thing that comes to mind is the intensity of concentration, the focus on a single objective to the exclusion of all else. . . . I had an uncompromising zest for life that lasted for days after a good bouldering session. I felt serenely alive, floating above pedestrian travails. . . . I miss, also, the sense of dedication to an abstract ideal. The feeling that by

Photo: Jeff Baldwin

Kristian Merwin on Nerve Damage, rated V6.

engaging in this demanding and uncompromising activity I was filling a spiritual void in my life while advancing standards centimeter by centimeter. The purity of the sport from any commercial taint, its relative isolation, its benign character, its natural environment, its emphasis on personal development—all these gave bouldering a canonical significance. My friends and I were Quixote knights in search of an elusive grail: the perfect boulder problem."

John Sherman: "Utah might have more boulders than any other state in the nation. Unfortunately, these boulders are scattered far and wide. No one rock type provides consistently reliable bouldering.

"Bouldering—it's been called everything from 'instant suffering' to 'the poetry of mountaineering,' from 'low altitude siege climbing' to 'that most elegant and distilled of climbing games.' The boulders provide a venue for socializing, competing, solitary introspection, training, or pushing one's limits. The one constant in bouldering is the emphasis on adapting oneself to overcome a challenge presented by nature."

JOE'S VALLEY

The etymology of Joe's Valley is uncertain. One story suggests Joe was an early settler in the area. A second version is that early immigrants saw an Indian mistreat a fellow Indian named Joe. After being rescued, Joe became friends with the settlers and helped them in many ways.

Joe's Valley is the site of hundreds of sandstone boulders up to 40 feet (12 m) high in a remote setting. About 75 percent of the problems at Joe's Valley are rated V5 or easier. Gray or black boulders are the most solid; red is usually good rock, but brown stone is typically the most friable and unreliable. Many of the boulders are not in view from the road. *A Bouldering Guide to Joe's Valley* is divided into three sections: New Joe's, Left Fork, and Right Fork. It maps out twenty-eight different areas to climb and describes more than 350 problems.

Joe's Valley is 150 miles (241 km) from Salt Lake City. Drive south from Price through Huntington until you see the sign for Joe's Valley Reservoir and Orangeville, approximately 27 miles (43 km) south of Price. Drive through Orangeville and follow signs northwest on Utah 29 toward the reservoir (identified on Utah road maps). Utah 57 (going north) will lead you toward New Joe's. If you continue west, drive another few miles until you see an obvious fork in the road. The Left Fork continues up Straight Canyon to Joe's Valley Reservoir, while the Right Fork, a dirt trail, leads up Cottonwood Canyon to a coal mine.

It is approximately 5 miles (8 km) from Orangeville to the fork, and another 10 miles (16 km) farther to the reservoir, where signs give directions to the campground located on the west side of the reservoir.

CAMPING

There is good camping in Joe's Valley, with picnic tables, fire pits, rest rooms, and great views. Reservoir Campground charges only $8.00 a night. Free campsites are available if you drive up the Right Fork.

Photo: Jeff Baldwin

Steven Jeffrey on Resident Evil, rated V10.

DIVERSIONS

EPHRAIM

Ephraim, 5,500 feet (1,676 m) above sea level, is the home of Snow College. Its main street is listed as a Historic District on the National Register of Historic Places. The town's first settlers arrived in 1854 and named the area Pine Creek. The name was later changed to Cottonwood, then Fort Ephraim in honor of a tribe of Israel mentioned in the Book of Mormon.

THE GREAT WESTERN TRAIL—PETE'S HOLE

The Great Western Trail passes through the area and is recommended for mountain bikers. Pete's Hole is a 28-mile (45 km) singletrack, five-star-rated loop. See Gregg Bromka's *Mountain Biking Utah* for more information.

JOE'S VALLEY RESERVOIR

Joe's Valley Reservoir covers 1,170 acres at the upper end of Straight Canyon, 16 miles (26 km) from Castle Dale. North of the lake, a spur branches north to Upper Joe's Valley Campground, 9 miles (14 km), and Utah 31, 21 miles (34 km). The Upper Joe's Valley Campground, known as Indian Creek Campground, sits at an elevation of 9,000 feet (2,743 m).

JOE'S VALLEY CAMPGROUND AND MARINA

Joe's Valley Campground has two sections on the west shore of the reservoir, elevation 7,100 feet (2,164 m). Provided is a boat ramp; rental of fishing boats, rowboats, and paddleboats; and a cafe and store open mid-May to early November. It's posible to catch rainbow and cutthroat trout in the lake, and waterskiing is popular. The campground and marina are approximately 20 miles (32 km) west of Castle Dale. The pavement ends at the turnoff for Joe's Valley Campground, where a forest service trail continues west, climbing 13 miles (21 km) to Skyline Drive at an elevation of 10,200 feet (3,109 m) at the top of the Wasatch Plateau. The Castle Dale reservoir road is open in winter for ice fishing and snowmobiling.

NORTH DRAGON ROAD

North Dragon Road becomes a good dirt trail as it branches south between the two sections of Joe's Valley Campground and continues about 15 miles (24 km) to a dramatic overlook above Castle Dale, providing views of the San Rafael Swell and the Henry, La Sal, and Abajo Mountains.

SKYLINE DRIVE

Skyline Drive meets Utah 31 near the head of Fairview Canyon, where it extends north to Tucker on US 6 and south to Mayfield, Ferron, and Salina Canyon. The scenic drive traverses the Manti–La Sal National Forest for nearly its entire length as it serpentines along the Wasatch Plateau's summit at an elevation of 9,000 to 11,000 feet (2,743 to 3,353 m). The drive offers expansive views into the Sampete Valley and beyond into Nevada to the west, and east to Colorado.

From Ephraim, turn east on Utah 29, which climbs to the summit of Wasatch Plateau, where it intersects Skyline Drive at about 10,000 feet (3,048 m). East of Skyline Drive, the road descends through valleys and canyons past Joe's Valley Reservoir.

> The darkening of the sky continues as the height increases. If one could rise to, say, fifty thousand feet, he would probably see the sun only as a shining point of light, and the firmament merely as a blue-black background. The diffusion of light must decrease with the growing thinness of the atmospheric envelope. At what point it would cease and the sky become perfectly black would be difficult to say, but certainly the limit would be reached when our atmosphere practically ceased to exist. Space from necessity must be black except where the straight beams of light stream from the sun and the stars.
>
> —John C. Van Dyke, *The Desert,* 1901

5
GREEN RIVER AREA

> On the desert, perspective is always erratic. Bodies fail to detach themselves one from another, foreshortening is abnormal, the planes of landscape are flattened out of shape or telescoped, objects are huddled together or superimposed one upon another. The disturbance in aerial perspective is just as bad. Colors, lights, and shadows fall into contradictions and denials, they shirk and bear false witness, and confuse the judgment of the most experienced. No wonder amid this distortion of the natural, this wreck of perspective, that distance is such a proverbially unknown quantity. This is the one thing the desert dweller speaks about with caution.
>
> –John C. Van Dyke, *The Desert,* 1901

This area includes climbs in Black Dragon Canyon at the northeast edge of the San Rafael Reef 14 miles (23 km) west of Green River, and Battleship and Gunnison Buttes at the south edge of the Book and Roan Cliffs.

BLACK DRAGON CANYON

Black Dragon Canyon is named for its pictograph rock art panel that resembles a winged dragon shooting fire from its mouth, at the edge of the tilted Navajo sandstone of the San Rafael Reef. The canyon is home to many large panels of Barrier Canyon–style pictographs, making it one of the most popular destinations in the San Rafael Swell.

To reach Black Dragon Canyon, drive west from Green River on Interstate 70. Pass the Utah 24 turnoff, which is the route to Lake Powell and Capitol Reef National Park. Continue 2.7 miles (4.3 km) farther west on Interstate 70 and make a right (north) turn from the freeway onto an unmarked dirt trail between mile markers 144 and 145. Pass through a gate (which should be closed regardless of how it was found—its purpose is to keep cattle off the freeway). Drive 0.5 mile (0.8 km) to a sign: NOTICE: OLD MINES AND MINING CLAIMS MAY CONTAIN RADON, RADIOACTIVE MATERIAL, OR ABANDONED EXPLOSIVES. DO NOT TOUCH. REPORT FINDINGS TO THE NEAREST BLM OR SHERIFF'S OFFICE. A second sign declares NO CAMPING NEXT 2 MILES. Veer left and drive between the two signs. In approximately 1.2 miles (1.9 km) there is a sign for Black Dragon Wash. High clearance and/or four-wheel drive may be required to negotiate the canyon; otherwise, it is only a short hike into the canyon. A rail fence on the right (north) side of the canyon marks the location of the Black Dragon, which is actually red. On the same panel there are geometric glyphs of an anthropomorphic figure, and a dog composed entirely of short lines, an expressionist rendering. For a definitive guide to the climbs in the San Rafael, refer to *Desert Rock II: Wall Street to the San Rafael Swell.*

HISTORY

Interstate 70 is referred to as the "Main Street of America" by travel agencies and tour companies. It bisects the nation east to west from Washington, D.C. to Cove Fort, Utah. As it leaves Green River on its westward journey, a sign warns that there are no services for the next 110 miles (177 km).

The road up Black Dragon Canyon was built in 1918 to access a now defunct mining operation. Abandoned drill pipes throughout the canyon are the remains of a well that was drilled near the head of the mining road. Steve Allen notes in *Canyoneering the San Rafael Swell*, "Before Interstate 70 was forced through Spotted Wolf Canyon, this was the only road through the northern part of the Swell."

UNNAMED AND BEYOND HERE THERE BE DRAGONS

To reach these routes from the rail fence at the pictograph panel, return approximately 100 yards (91 m) down the canyon toward the freeway. On the left (north) wall, the routes ascend the first two right-facing dihedrals you come to and are about 50 yards (46 m) apart.

1 UNNAMED
I, not rated, 1 pitch, height unknown

First Ascent: Unknown.

Location and Access: The route climbs the first right-facing dihedral toward the freeway from the Black Dragon pictograph panel. Climb a fist-to-fingers crack to rappel anchors visible on the right wall of the dihedral.

Paraphernalia: Friends #1 through #3.5.

Descent: Rappel from anchors visible from below the climb.

2 BEYOND HERE THERE BE DRAGONS (a.k.a. Dragons Live Forever)
I, 5.10+, C1, 1 pitch, 140 feet (43 m) ★★★

First Ascent: Mike Baker, Leslie Henderson, March 15, 1998.

Location and Access: The route climbs the second right-facing dihedral from the Black Dragon pictograph panel. Climb a right-facing corner beginning with 5.9 face moves past a bolt. Continue with hands, then lieback, ending with 5.9 stemming. At a bolt, climb an off-width lieback at 5.10+. Continue with 5.6 fingers then 5.9+, ending with two moves of C1 up loose rock to double rappel bolts.

Paraphernalia: Camalots (2) each through #4, (1) #5; TCUs (1) each; Tri-Cams (1) #0.5, #1, #1.5.

Descent: Double-rope rappel from anchors visible from below the climb.

BEYOND HERE THERE BE DRAGONS

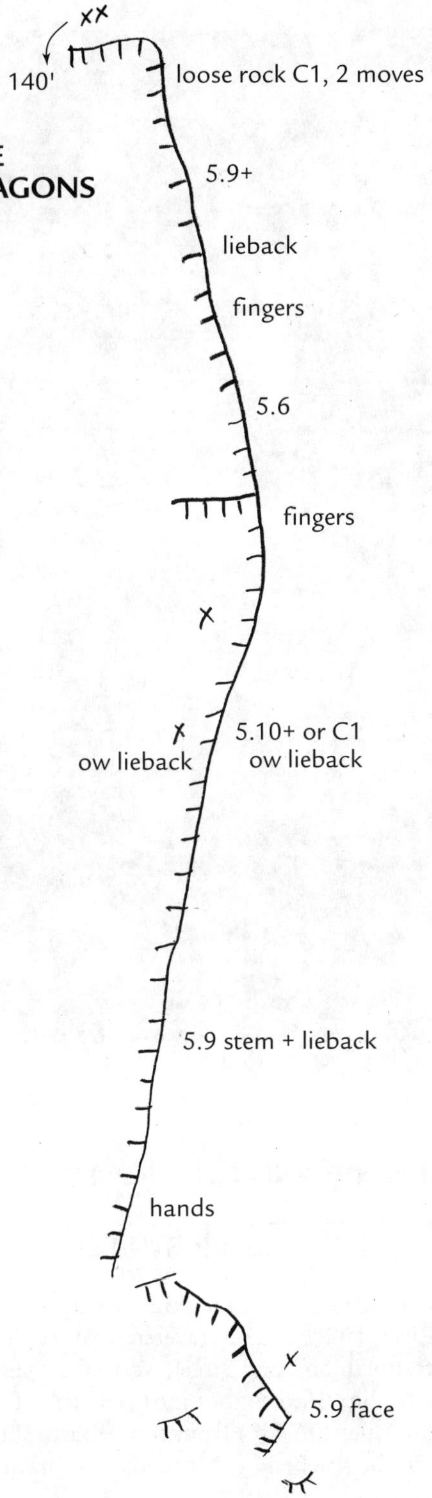

Photo: Mike Baker

Leslie Henderson on Beyond Here There Be Dragons.

BATTLESHIP AND GUNNISON BUTTES

BATTLESHIP BUTTE

Battleship Butte is the long dominant mesa in view approximately 4 miles (6.4 km) north of Green River, Utah, as one traverses east or west on Interstate 70. From Green River, turn north on Long Street, west of the Green River City Park. After a few blocks, Battleship Butte comes into view left of the road. When the pavement ends about 6 miles (9.7 km) from town, Battleship Butte—obvious 2 miles (3.2 km) away—can be reached by dirt roads that branch to the west. Both

Battleship Butte and Gunnison Butte are named on the 7.5-minute USGS Gunnison Butte, Utah, quadrangle. Both are composed of Mesa Verde sandstone above Mancos shale talus.

3 BATTLESHIP BUTTE
II, 5.5, pitches unknown, 1,000 feet (305 m)

First Ascent: Leo Dumas et al, 1968.

Location and Access: The route is climbed from the north side of the mesa. The first ascent team camped at Mushroom Rock, a prominent landform (and good camp) near the middle of the north face.

Paraphernalia: Belay rope.

Descent: Downclimb the route.

GUNNISON BUTTE

Gunnison Butte is at the mouth of Gray Canyon and is approximately 6 air miles (9.7 km) north of Green River. As viewed from the Green River area, it is right (east) of Battleship Butte and appears as a small angular formation with several notches along its summit ridge in the foreground of the Book Cliffs backdrop. Originally named Cathedral Butte, it was renamed by Major John Wesley Powell to honor Captain Gunnison, who crossed the Green River in the area of the town in 1853. Several days later, Gunnison and many of his men were massacred by Indians in the desert north of Sevier Lake. Gunnison Crossing was part of the Old Spanish Trail, first opened from Salt Lake to southern California in 1826 by Jedediah Smith of the Rocky Mountain Fur Company.

The Old Spanish Trail wound about the canyons and desert for more than 1,200 miles (193 km) and was the main route between Santa Fe and Los Angeles. First to travel the entire length of the trail was an American party led by William Wolfskill and George C. Yount during the winter of 1830–31. The Old Spanish Trail was long, but it traversed difficult Colorado canyons, avoiding hostile Apaches living south of the Grand Canyon, and made possible trading with the Ute tribe, who welcomed passing travelers. In 1883 the Denver and Rio Grande Railroad bridged the Green River at the Gunnison Crossing just east of the town by the same name.

Approach as for Battleship Butte up Long Street. Gunnison Butte will be right and ahead of the road, identified by a summit notch near its left (west) side. From the end of the pavement, the main dirt road zigzags 2.5 miles (4 km) farther before ending beneath Gunnison Butte. Traverse left around the landform to the route located near the notch on the north side.

4 GUNNISON BUTTE
II, 5.6, pitches unknown, 800 feet (244 m)

First Ascent: Leo Dumas et al, late 1960s.

Location and Access: The route climbs the butte from the northeast side to the prominent notch, then continues up obvious cracks to the summit.

Paraphernalia: A selection of pitons were used on the first ascent.

Descent: Downclimb the route.

DIVERSIONS

BARRIER CANYON–STYLE PICTOGRAPHS

This rock art panel is 5 miles (8 km) up Buckhorn Draw in the north San Rafael. Ward J. Roylance: "Buckhorn resembles numberless other gorges of Canyonlands, but it is more easily accessible than most, marvelous by any standards, a cameo masterpiece that more than repays visitation."

From Green River, drive 29 miles (47 km) west on Interstate 70 to Ranch exit 129. The exit road turns east and parallels the freeway for 3.6 miles (5.8 km), then makes a left (north) turn toward the San Rafael River and Buckhorn Draw. From the freeway exit, it is approximately 20 miles (32 km) to the river and the south entrance of Buckhorn Draw over a scenic, well-maintained dirt trail. At the river, a BLM-maintained campground has tables, toilets, fire grills, and an information kiosk. North across the river from the campground, the Mexican Mountain Road begins to the east. Straight ahead (north) is the beginning of the 10-mile (16 km)-long Buckhorn Draw. Five miles (8 km) up the wash is one of the Colorado Plateau's best Barrier Canyon culture pictograph panels. This rock canvas of haunting beauty is believed to be at least 2,000 years old. These ancient people were hunters and foragers. They did not have pottery, but used stone and bone tools with atlatls for hunting. In an intensive six-week effort (part of the 1996 Utah centennial celebration), the panel was restored, after being damaged by past carvings, paint, chalk, and bullet hole vandalism. The antiquities of Buckhorn Draw are listed on the National Register of Historic Places. Please respect this heritage for the generations yet to view it.

WEDGE OVERLOOK AT THE LITTLE GRAND CANYON

Wedge Overlook offers a breathtaking view 1,200 feet (366 m) into the Little Grand Canyon. Don't miss it. It is one of the most dramatic scenes on the Colorado Plateau and a great place to camp. There are BLM-designated campsites with established fire rings, a rest room, but no firewood is available in the area.

From Interstate 70, take exit 129 and drive north to Buckhorn Draw. From the north end of Buckhorn, turn left and drive to the next major intersection, where a sign will direct you to the overlook. For a scenic return to Price or Green River, take the Green River Cutoff (Old Spanish Trail) to US 6/191, then north to Price or south to Green River. The cutoff is the trail east from the north end of Buckhorn Draw and is passable with two-wheel-drive low-clearance vehicles.

CRYSTAL GEYSER

Crystal Geyser is on the bank of the Green River 10 miles (16 km) south of the town. It erupts only three or four times a day, but the spectacle is worth the wait. The geyser shoots approximately 60 feet (18 m) into the air for about seven minutes, discharging 4,350 cubic feet of cold salt water. In 1935 a 2,267-foot (690 km)-deep petroleum test well was drilled, concentrating the geyser's flow. Geologists suggest the thick layers of old travertine deposits at the site show mineral springs were active long before the test well was drilled. Green algae and orange and red minerals at the geyser make it an interesting stop even if the eruption is missed.

From Green River, drive east of town on the Interstate 70 business loop (Main Street). At mile marker 4, turn left onto a frontage road, drive 6 miles (9.7 km), and turn right just past a railroad overpass. Continue on the narrow paved road as it goes under Interstate 70 and continues unpaved for 4.5 miles (7.2 km). Keep right at a fork near power lines; the geyser site will be obvious. The buildings and antennas passed are remnants of the Pershing Utah Launch Complex of the White Sands Missile Range. Between 1963 and 1979 hundreds of Pershing and Athena rockets were launched at targets at White Sands, New Mexico, 400 miles (644 km) to the south.

JOHN WESLEY POWELL RIVER HISTORY MUSEUM

This museum is worth a visit. Although it emphasizes the adventures of Major Powell, it is also a hall of fame documenting the feats of other early river runners. On display are replicas of early river boats, including Powell's *Emma Dean*, along with high-tech boats and equipment used by today's sportsmen. A gift shop sells regional books, maps, T-shirts, cards, posters, film, and other souvenirs. An information center offers local travel and attraction information.

To reach the museum, drive east on Main Street in Green River. The museum is on the left (north) just past the bridge that crosses the Green River. Hours are from 9:00 A.M. to 9:00 P.M. daily, with reduced hours in the winter.

For additional attractions, see Sunshine Wall, Chapter 7.

> ". . . and in a shadow, look about you and see if there is not plenty of color there, too. The walls are dyed with it, the stones are stained with it—all sorts of colors from strata of rock, from clays and slates, from minerals, from lichens, from mosses.
>
> —John C. Van Dyke, *The Desert,* 1901

6
GREEN RIVER TOWERS

> You will not be surprised then if in speaking of desert, mesa and mountain I once more take you far beyond the wire fence of civilization to those places (unhappily few now) where the trail is unbroken and the mountain peak unblazed.
>
> —John C. Van Dyke, *The Desert,* 1901

The Green River Towers are spectacular Wingate sandstone spires on the west bank of the Green River. It is not known if they have been climbed, but they are among the most isolated and beautiful on the Colorado Plateau and are worth a visit. They can be reached only by a float trip (canoe, kayak, or raft) on the Green River through the calm Labyrinth Canyon, a highly recommended adventure that only requires a free BLM permit form be completed at the Green River or Ruby Ranch launch point.

Strata from the town of Green River to the takeout ramp at Mineral Bottom dip upstream, exposing progressively older layers of rock as you drift downstream. Numerous side canyons provide interesting hiking and climbing routes past Fremont and Anasazi petroglyphs, ruins, and remnants of the 1950s and 1960s uranium mining days. Among the many points of interest on the float trip are Crystal Geyser and two sites where the fur trapper D. Julien left his signature in 1836.

Photo: Carolyn Ortenberger

Green River Towers.

RIVER LOG—GREEN RIVER STATE PARK TO MINERAL CANYON

The following is a log of the geology and areas of note on a Green River float. Mileage on the river is measured upstream from the confluence of the Green and Colorado Rivers. The direction "left" or "right" presupposes that one is looking downstream.

Mile 120: Green River State Park (west bank) is built on a sandbar and lined on its river side with willow and tamarisk. A shady campground is located in a grove of cottonwood trees. There is a boat ramp for launching river trips through the calm waters of Labyrinth Canyon. Just upriver is the site of a historic fording point that was used by Indians, Spanish padres, mountain men, explorers, and settlers. On October 1, 1853, the Green River was crossed here by Captain John W. Gunnison of the U.S. Army; for a time after it was known as the Gunnison Crossing. Major Powell passed the crossing on his 1869 and 1871–72 expeditions down the Green and Colorado Rivers.

The town of Green River was founded in 1878 as a mail relay station. The Denver and Rio Grande Western Railway bridged the river at the ford in 1883. Mancos shale outcrops can be seen across the river (upstream). To the north, the Mesa Verde Group is visible in the Book Cliffs, the mouth of Gray Canyon, and Gunnison Butte.

Mile 119: Dakota sandstone is exposed at the mouth of a small stream entering on the right, and the Cedar Mountain Formation is in view river right. Cedar Mountain yields many of the gastroliths or "dinosaur gizzard stones" sold in souvenir shops on the Colorado Plateau.

Mile 118: The Saltwash member of the Morrison Formation, then varicolored cliffs of the Brushy Basin member, are in view at river level. The Morrison is the host rock for many uranium deposits in the area. The unit also yields dinosaur fossils and petrified wood.

Mile 116–115: Crystal Geyser at river left is Ruby No. 1 state well, an unsuccessful oil and gas test hole drilled to a depth of 2,267 feet (690 m) in 1935. For more information, see Green River Area Diversions, Chapter 5.

Mile 110: Morrison Formation is exposed at river level left and right.

Mile 104–103: Curtis Formation first appears at river right.

Mile 102–101: Entrada sandstone (beneath the Curtis Formation) is exposed as light orange cliffs at river right. River left is Dellenbaugh's Butte, named for Frederick S. Dellenbaugh, the seventeen-year-old artist and rower on the second Powell Expedition in 1871–72. The butte is known by locals as the Inkwell or the Anvil. Dellenbaugh is best remembered for his accounts of the Powell Expedition, writing *The Romance of the Colorado River* (1902) and *A Canyon Voyage* (1908), both highly recommended historical adventure narratives.

Mile 97: Ruby Ranch at river left. This is a popular put-in for river runners. It can be reached by taking Interstate 70 to exit 173 south, the only exit between

Green River and Crescent Junction. Take the scenic, good dirt trail and follow signs 14 miles (22.5 km) to the ranch. A small fee will be collected for the use of the launch ramp. This is a safe place to leave a shuttle vehicle, with a second one left at the Mineral Bottom takeout. At river right, the San Rafael River enters the Green.

Mile 97–96: The brown-red sandstones, shale, and siltstone at river right are the Carmel Formation. This is the same stratum as the Dewey Bridge in Arches National Park and the area south of Moab.

Mile 95–94: Navajo sandstone first appears at river left. This is also the true beginning of Labyrinth Canyon, named by the Powell Expedition for its complicated meandering.

KOLB BROTHERS

The Kolb brothers, Emery C. and Ellsworth, were famous Grand Canyon guides. The brothers, along with James Fagin, left Green River, Wyoming, in two flatboats in September 1911, and reached Bright Angel Trail in the Grand Canyon in November. They resumed their trip, arriving at Needles in January 1912. Ellsworth continued alone to the Gulf of California, reaching it in May 1913. An account of their trip, *Through the Grand Canyon from Wyoming to Mexico*, was written by Ellsworth Kolb.

Mile 90: Trin-Alcove Bend and Trin-Alcove (a.k.a. Three Canyons), also a Powell name, river right. It is the last remaining Navajo sandstone canyon on the Green River with undisturbed spur canyons. Others are now beneath Lake Powell.

Mile 89–88: Kayenta Formation first appears below the Navajo. Below it will be the Wingate. The Navajo-Kayenta-Wingate sequence is known as the Glen Canyon Group.

Mile 85: First exposures of Wingate sandstone at river left.

Mile 79–78: First exposure of Chinle Formation at river right.

Mile 78–77: Famous "River Register" on river left.

Mile 76–75: Hey Joe Canyon enters at river left. This is the location of the Hey Joe uranium mine in the Chinle Formation. There is a road beside the river (not passable in places) from Hey Joe Canyon to Mineral Bottom.

Mile 75–74: Inscription D. JULIEN, 16 MAI 1836 on left.

Mile 71–70: Moenkopi Formation first outcrops at river left.

Mile 70–69: Beginning of Bowknot Bend, a Powell name. A scramble reaches the notch on the skyline to the right, where the "post office river register" is located and river runners' names are recorded. At the west end of the saddle on a north-facing Wingate wall is a KOLB BROS 10-11 inscription. The bowknot cuts off 7.5 miles (12 km) of river.

Mile 68–67: Spring Canyon enters at river left.

Mile 56: Hell Roaring Canyon enters on river left. The best-preserved D. Julien inscription—1836 3 MAI—along with a boat and winged sun is on a low Moenkopi wall 200 yards (183 m) upcanyon on the right.

Mile 53–52: Mineral Canyon is on river left, and the Moenkopi Formation is exposed at river level. This is the location of the Mineral Bottom boat ramp, also the launch point for many Cataract Canyon float trips and the takeout for most Labyrinth Canyon river trips. The nearby Horsethief Trail climbs steeply to the mesa top, then east to Utah 313 and beyond to the junction of US 191 just 9 miles (14 km) north of Moab.

> The career of the Colorado, from its rise in the Wind River Mountains in Wyoming to its final disappearance in the Gulf of California, seems almost tragic in its swift transitions. It starts out so cheerily upon its course; it is so clear and pure, so sparkling with sunshine and spirit. It dashes down mountain valleys, gurgles under bowlders, swirls over waterfalls, flashes through ravines and gorges. With its sweep and glide and its silvery laugh it seems to lead a merry life. But too soon it plunges into precipitous canyons and enters upon its fierce struggle with the encompassing rock. Now it boils and foams, leaps and strikes, thunders and shatters.
>
> —John C. Van Dyke, *The Desert,* 1901

7
SUNSHINE WALL

> There is a war of elements and a struggle for existence going on here that for ferocity is unparalleled elsewhere in nature. Tones of color, shades of light, drifts of air. . . these are the most sensuous qualities in nature and in art. The weird solitude, the great silence, the grim desolation, are the very things with which every desert wanderer eventually falls in love. And wherever you go, by land or by sea, you shall not forget that which you saw not but rather felt—the desolation and the silence of the desert.
>
> —John C. Van Dyke, *The Desert,* 1901

Sunshine Wall is a Wingate sandstone buttress on the east side of the northern end of Salt Valley, north of Arches National Park. From US 191, turn east onto a good unmarked dirt road between mile markers 152 and 153. The turn is 4.5 miles (7.2 km) south of Interstate 70, approximately 26.5 miles (42.6 km) north of Moab, and drivable with low-clearance two-wheel-drive vehicles. The turn can also be identified as the first left (east) from US 191 south of the interstate. There is a stop sign for those entering US 191 from the east.

Immediately cross the railroad tracks, then pass the usually dry Valley City Reservoir on its left and take every major right turn to enter Salt Valley and the Sunshine Wall. Beyond a small bridge with white railings, turn right. Turn right

Photo: Eric Bjørnstad

Sunshine Wall.

SUNSHINE WALL ROUTE LOCATOR MAP

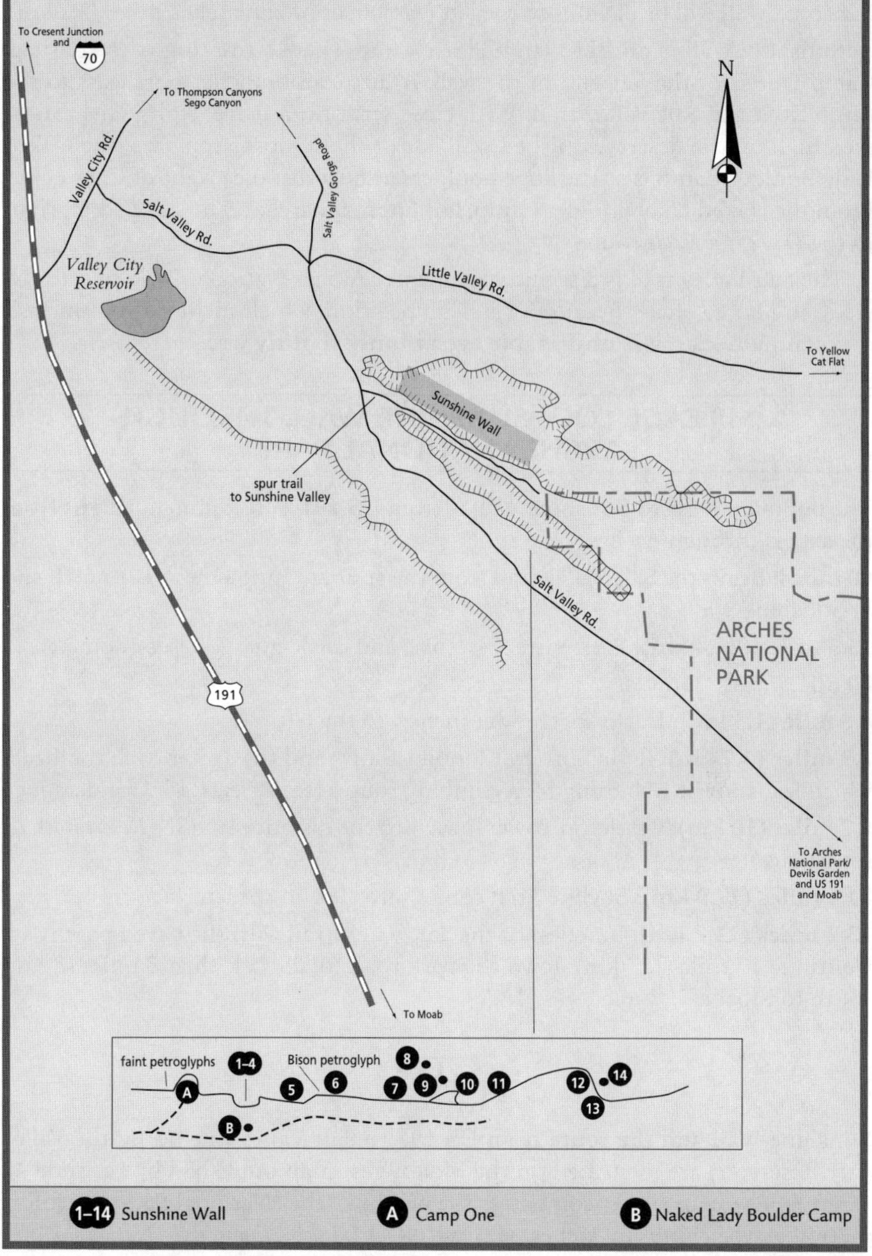

To Cresent Junction and
70
N
To Thompson Canyons Sego Canyon
Valley City Rd.
Salt Valley Rd.
Salt Valley Gorge Road
Valley City Reservoir
Little Valley Rd.
To Yellow Cat Flat
Sunshine Wall
spur trail to Sunshine Valley
Salt Valley Rd.
ARCHES NATIONAL PARK
191
To Arches National Park/ Devils Garden and US 191 and Moab
To Moab
faint petroglyphs
Bison petroglyph
1–4
5
6
7
8
9
10
11
12
13
14
A
B
1–14 Sunshine Wall
A Camp One
B Naked Lady Boulder Camp

again at the next major intersection (left goes to Thompson-Sego Canyons in the Book Cliffs north of Interstate 70). This is the beginning of the Salt Valley trail. Sunshine Wall will be obvious to the left (east) in approximately 2 miles (3.2 km).

Sunshine Wall is on BLM land. Please camp where a fire ring is established. Camp One is at the left end of the wall. A dirt trail branches northeast to the camp from the Salt Valley trail. With close scrutiny, a petroglyph panel can be seen high on the desert-varnished wall left of the camp. Camp Two, the Naked Lady Boulder Camp is at the large boulders a short distance right of Camp One. From the Naked Lady Boulder Camp, it is approximately 1.5 miles (2.4 km) right to the *Day of the Eagle* route.

The Salt Valley trail is a scenic way to enter Arches National Park, but it traverses on Manco shale. Because of its composition, which includes volcanic ash and bentonite clay, it is **undrivable even if only slightly wet.**

MILEAGE LOG—SUNSHINE WALL THROUGH ARCHES NATIONAL PARK

The popular access to Sunshine Wall is from US 191. A recommended exit from the area is through Arches.

00 miles: Begin the Salt Valley trail from the spur at Camp One at the north end of Sunshine Wall.

13.3 miles (21.4 km): Park entrance, fence, and cattle guard. Reset odometer.

00 miles: Park boundary.

0.8 mile (1.3 km): Dark Angel tower in view to the left.

2.9 miles (4.7 km): Right turn to Klondike Bluffs and the Tower Arch trailhead, which leads to the Marching Men climbing routes (see *Desert Rock I* for details).

6.2 miles (10 km): Castleton Tower in view to the distant east. (See *Desert Rock III* for details.)

11.1 miles (17.9 km): Skyline Arch comes into view to the left.

13.2 miles (21.2 km): Junction of the Salt Valley trail with the paved park road. Continue 17 miles (27 km) down the park road to US 191, then 5 miles (8 km) south to Moab.

MAPS

Sunshine Wall and the route from US 191 to Salt Valley (including the Valley City Reservoir) are identified on the Moab West map published by Latitude 40 Degrees. The map also encompasses the nearby Arches National Park. For information on the climbs in Arches, see *Desert Rock I: Rock Climbs in the National Parks.*

SUNSHINE WALL

Sunshine Wall climbing routes are listed left to right. *Mosquito Coast, Learning Curve, Love Hurts,* and *Lesson in Braille* are located about 20 feet (6 m) from each

Photo: Mike Baker

Sunshine Wall: 1. Mosquito Coast *2.* Learning Curve *3.* Love Hurts *4.* Lesson in Braille.

other and begin from a narrow 2- to 4-foot-wide (0.6 to 1.2 m) shelf above the Naked Lady Boulder Camp.

1 MOSQUITO COAST
I 5.8 R, 1 pitch, 120 feet (37 m) ★★

First Ascent: Andy Roberts, Liz Devaney, June 1998.

Location and Access: The route climbs the left side of the low-angled red and white slab above the Naked Lady Boulder Camp—right of Camp One. Face climb past two drilled pitons, then angle left to a prominent groove, which is followed past a drilled angle piton and a bolt to a double-bolt anchor on the right wall. The crux is the first two or three moves.

Paraphernalia: Camalots (1) #1; quick draws (5).

Descent: Double-rope rappel the route from double bolts.

2 LEARNING CURVE
I, 5.7, 1 pitch, 130 feet (40 m) ★★★★

First Ascent: Leslie Henderson, Mike Baker, May 2, 1998.

Location and Access: The route face climbs a sloping wall just right of *Mosquito Coast* to rappel anchors in view from below. There is an unnamed 5.9 crack/face climb just right of the route which is top roped from *Learning Curve* anchors.

Paraphernalia: Tri-Cams (1) #0.5, #1, #1.5; TCUs; quick draws (5).

Descent: Double-rope rappel the route.

3 LOVE HURTS
I, 5.9, 1 pitch, 135 feet (41 m) ★★★

First Ascent: Mike Baker, solo, February 1999. Second Ascent: Andy Roberts, 1999.

Location and Access: The route climbs the wall two cracks right of *Learning Curve* and shares anchors and belays. Climb a bolt-protected seam except for a #3 Camalot between the first and second bolt. There is a belay anchor at the start of the climb.

Paraphernalia: Camalots (1) #3; quick draws (8).

Descent: Rappel from drilled anchors atop *Learning Curve.*

4 LESSON IN BRAILLE
I, 5.10c, 1 pitch, 140 feet (43 m) ★★★★

First Ascent: Mike Baker, Leslie Henderson, June 1998.

Location and Access: Mike Baker: "I just returned from climbing in the Black Hills of South Dakota. After four good days of climbing, the weather took a turn for the worse so we headed for the Sunshine Wall. Amazingly the weather

Photo: Mike Baker

Science Friction: *Route starts at low point in center of face and at halfway point follows diagonal seam.*

there was not too hot! We established a new climb called *Lesson in Braille.* It is a face climb on bumps with an occasional edge." The route begins at the far right side of the approach shelf. Face climb on bumps with an occasional edge right of *Love Hurts*. Rappel anchors are in view from below the climb.

Paraphernalia: Camalots (1) #0.5; quick draws (12).

Descent: Double-rope rappel from bolts.

5 SCIENCE FRICTION
I, 5.9+, 1 pitch, 160 feet (49 m) ★★★★★

First Ascent: Mike Baker, solo, May 1, 1998.

Location and Access: The route is right of *Lesson in Braille*. Reach by hiking 0.25 mile (0.4 km) right (southeast) of Naked Lady Boulder Camp to the longest and highest section of Sunshine Wall. The route climbs the bolted face near the center of the wall. Rappel anchors are in view from below the route.

Paraphernalia: Quick draws (13).

Descent: Double-rope rappel the route.

6 WALKING ON SUNSHINE
I, 5.10+, 1 pitch, 80 feet (24 m) ★★★★

First Ascent: Mike Baker, Wilson Goodrich, November 30, 1998.

Location and Access: The route climbs the next slab/face approximately 100 yards (91 m) right (southeast) of the *Science Friction* buttress. Rappel anchors

Photo: Wilson Goodrich

Science Friction.

are visible below the climb. It can also be identified as 40 feet (12 m) right of a bison petroglyph. Face climb, passing ten bolts to a two-bolt rappel anchor. The crux is between the fourth and fifth bolts.

Paraphernalia: Quick draws (10).

Descent: Single-rope rappel the route.

7 MURPHY-NEWTON CONSPIRACY I, 5.9+, A2, 2 pitches, 160 feet (49 m) ★★★

First Ascent: Mike Baker, solo, May 1998. Second Ascent: Mike Baker, Leslie Henderson, 1998.

Location and Access: *Murphy/Newton Conspiracy* is approximately 0.25 mile (0.4 km) right of *Walking on Sunshine.* Pitch 1 climbs a left-facing corner to belay anchors, 75 feet (23 m). Pitch 2 climbs loose rock with aid (A2) but is not recommended because of the soft rock, 85 feet (26 m).

Paraphernalia: Standard desert rack; quick draws (1).

Descent: Rappel from bolts.

8 TEZCATLIPOCA I, 5.5, 1 pitch, 50 feet (15 m) ★★★

First Ascent: Mike Baker, solo by full moon, June 1998.

Location and Access: *Tezcatlipoca* sits atop Sunshine Wall. Mike Baker: "A fifty-minute hike from the far north end of Sunshine Wall—very easy and scenic." Reached by walking or driving to the far left (northwest) end of Sunshine Wall where a gentle grade climbs to the top of the buttress. At this point there are three sets of anchors established for unnamed

MURPHY-NEWTON CONSPIRACY

The name comes from a number of mishaps. First, my haul line getting hopelessly tangled in a bush, making it impossible to retrieve the gear I had left attached to it. Then after doing a hard mantel, I stood up and hit my head so hard I was seeing stars. After drilling a rap anchor at the top of the climb, I dropped the drill, and when preparing to rappel (from one bolt) I dropped my rappel device and had to make a carabiner brake. Needless to say, after Murphy and Newton ganged up on me, I was exceedingly grateful to be back on terra firma. Leslie and I went back to add another anchor, and the climb was much better than I remembered. I thought all had gone well on the second ascent until two days later when I discovered I only had one climbing shoe in my pack. I made another trip to the Sunshine Wall and, sure enough, there was my missing shoe at the bottom of the *Murphy/Newton Conspiracy.*

—Mike Baker

TEZCATLIPOCA

In Aztec and Toltec religions, Tezcatlipoca is the god of the night sky, the moon, and the stars. He is also known as Yaotl (the warrior). He was the protector of slaves, punishing anyone who mistreated them. Tezcatlipoca was also a wizard and master of black magic. He wore a mirror on his chest in which he could see all deeds and thoughts of mankind.

Photo: Mike Baker
Murphy/Newton Conspiracy.

top-rope ascents ranging in difficulty from 5.6 to 5.10. Continue about fifty minutes southeast along the ridge top to Tezcatlipoca pinnacle, which sits atop Sunshine Wall. Begin on the north side up a fist crack, then face climb to drilled anchors. Finish with a mantel onto the summit. An alternative start is 15 feet (4.5 m) left, which face climbs up 5.5 unprotected rock, meeting the original route where the crack ends and face climbing begins.

Paraphernalia: Camalots (1) #1, #2; TCUs (1) #2, #3; quick draws (1).

Descent: Single-rope rappel from bolts, then reverse approach.

9 TOWER 143—BURNING SHOES (a.k.a. Shattered Illusions of Love) III, 5.9, A2, 3 pitches, 250 feet (76 m) ★★★★

First Ascent: James Garrett, Pete "Big Billy" Keane, Brad England, October 14, 1998.

Location and Access: Tower 143 is the most prominent freestanding spire in the area where the northwest-to southeast-running Sunshine Wall angles a little more to the east. To reach from the Naked Lady Boulder Camp, hike right (southeast) about thirty minutes on the eroded four-wheel-drive trail to about 75 yards (69 m) left of *Golden Child*. The tower is at the left of a group of towers and is identified by a prominent backward "C" or sickle-shaped finger crack

Photo: Mike Baker

Tezcatlipoca.

Photo: Mike Baker

Tezcatlipoca.

TOWER 143—BURNING SHOES

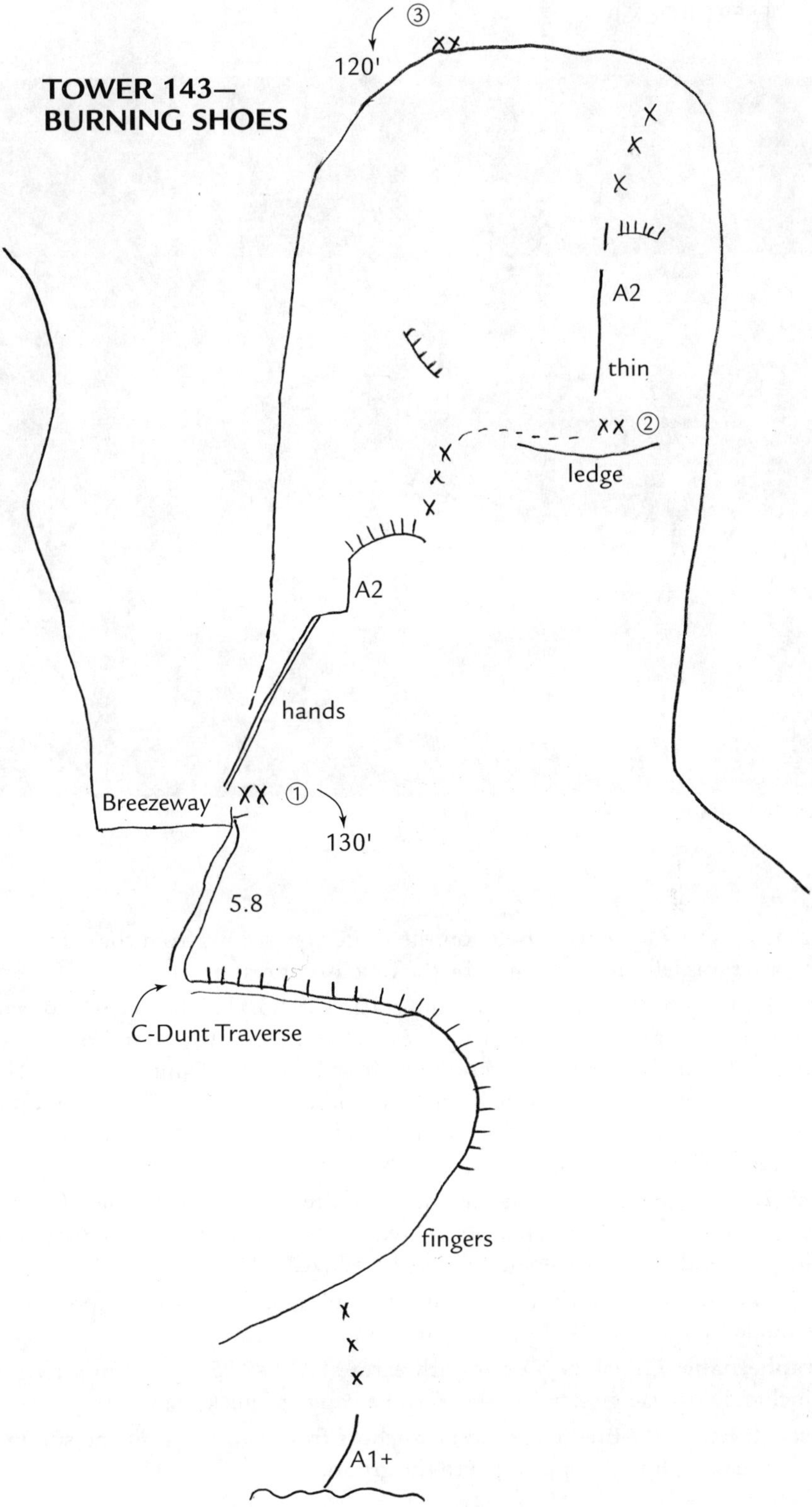

Photo: Brad Englund

Tower 143—Burning Shoes.

that goes to a large roof. Bolts on the route are obvious from the ground. A register was left on the summit by the first ascent team.

Pitch 1: Aid climb 20 feet (6 m) up a thin crack to a short bolt ladder, which takes you to a finger crack. Continue up the crack until it curves up and right, then back left, culminating in a section of off-width (the C-Dunt Traverse). This continues to a two-bolt belay ledge at a saddle (Breezeway). From the top of the bolt ladder, the crack widens from 1 inch to 5 inches (2.5 cm to 12.7 cm); 5.9, A1+, 130 feet (40 m).

Pitch 2: Climb a hand crack in the middle of Breezeway saddle, which leads to more thin aid and a bulging roof. Three bolts allow the roof to be passed on its right and reach a two-bolt belay ledge; 5.8, A2, 70 feet (21 m).

Pitch 3: Continue up a thin seam past one bolt and two drilled pitons to the rounded summit block; 5.8, A2, 50 feet (15 m).

Paraphernalia: Camalots (2) sets with extra #0.50, #0.75, #5; piton selection, including baby angles; birdbeaks; keyhole hangers; quick draws.

Descent: Rappel to Breezeway saddle anchors from two bolts on the summit, then make a double-rope rappel to the ground.

Photo: Brad Englund

Pete Keane approaching the summit of Tower 143 on pitch 3.

10 CONSOLATION CRACK
I, 5.10+, 1 pitch, 60 feet (18 m) ★

First Ascent: Andy Roberts, Dave Mealey, June 1998.

Location and Access: The route is halfway between Tower 143 and *Golden Child*. Ascend a 15-foot (4.5 m) bench to the start of the route, which climbs a wide right-facing corner to double rappel anchors in view from below.

Paraphernalia: Metolius cams #1 through #5; Camalots (1) #5.

Descent: No anchors; downclimb or a long walk-off to the left.

11 GOLDEN CHILD
I, 5.10d, 1 pitch, 90 feet (27 m) ★★★★

First Ascent: Mike Baker, solo, May 4, 1998.

Location and Access: The route is approached as for *Consolation Crack* up to the 15-foot (4.5 m) bench. Walk 50 feet (15 m) right on the bench to a left-facing dihedral located at the point where the northwest- to southeast-facing wall begins to angle slightly more to the east. Climb hands to fingers up a left-facing corner to double anchors in view from below the climb. Mike Baker: "*Golden Child* is the premier crack and by far the most striking feature on Sunshine Wall."

Paraphernalia: Camalots (2) #1, (4) #2, (1) #3; Metolius cams #3, #4, #5; quick draws (1).

Descent: Single-rope rappel from double anchors.

12 FAR EAST CRAG—THE GRADE
I, 5.10-, 1 pitch, 75 feet (23 m) ★★★★

First Ascent: Mike Baker, Wilson Goodrich, Leslie Henderson, May 3, 1998.

Location and Access: The route is located approximately 1.5 miles (2.4 km) right (southeast) of the Naked Lady Boulder Camp at a point right of where the west-facing Sunshine Wall curves to the west and becomes a north-facing wall. Climb a good finger crack with stemming. Rappel anchors are only visible when you walk away from the wall rather than directly below.

Paraphernalia: Camalots (1) set; TCUs (1) set; stoppers.

Descent: Rappel the route.

13 FAR EAST CRAG—DAY OF THE EAGLE
I, 5.10+, 1 pitch, 75 feet (23 m) ★★★

First Ascent: Mike Baker, Leslie Henderson, January 3, 1998. Second Ascent: Steve "Crusher" Bartlett, Brad Bond, Thanksgiving 1998.

Location and Access: The route is one crack right of *The Grade*. Rappel slings are not visible below the climb. Begin with 5.9 fingers up a right-facing dihedral. Pass a roof at 5.10+, then climb 5.9 hands, passing a bulge with 5.10 tight fists. Continue up a 5.7 chimney to double anchors on the left wall.

Photo: Leslie Henderson

Mike Baker on top of Day of the Eagle.

**FAR EAST CRAG—
DAY OF THE EAGLE**

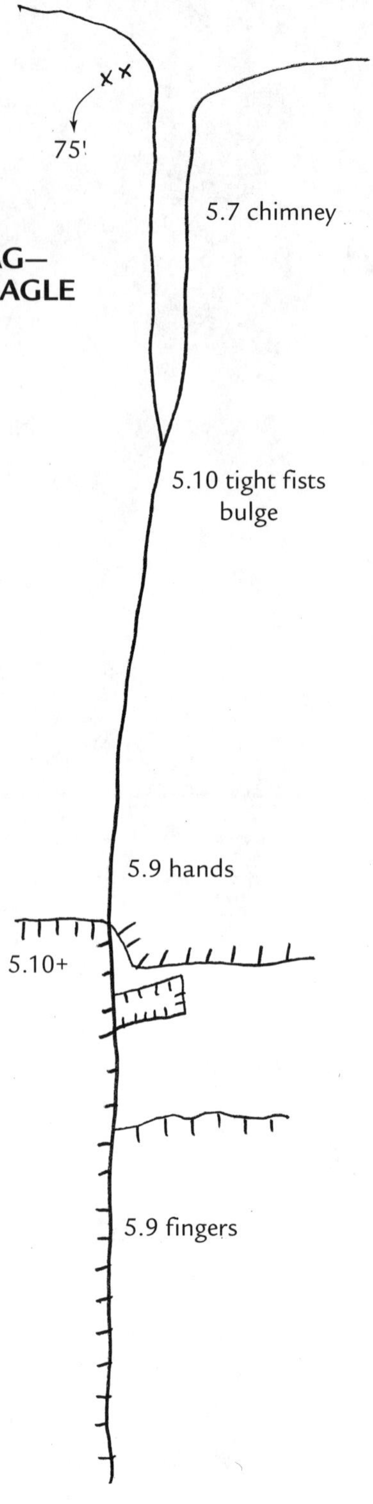

Paraphernalia: Camalots (1) #1, #2, (2) #3, (1) #4, #4.5; Aliens (1) set.

Descent: Rappel first crack left of route (*The Grade*) from double anchors.

14 DICK FOR
I, 5.9+, A2+, 2 pitches, 200 feet (60 m) ★★

First Ascent: Steve "Crusher" Bartlett, Brad Bond, Thanksgiving 1998.

Location and Access: *Dick For* is a prominent tower at the Far East Crag above *Day of the Eagle.* The route was originally climbed by a loose off-width 200 feet (60 m) right of the tower. It may be approached from Far East Crag—(*The Grade* or *Day of the Eagle*). Pitch 1 ascends an obvious crack system. Pitch 2 climbs with face and aid moves to the summit.

Pitch 1: Begin on the west face and climb past loose blocks in a right-facing corner, right of the tower; 5.9+, 100 feet (30 m).

Pitch 2: After moving the belay to the east side of the landform, climb the obvious thin cracks (angling left) to an awkward move onto the ledge on the east side. Traverse 20 feet (6 m) right, then ascend another crack to reach bolts and the summit; A2+, 100 feet (30 m).

Paraphernalia: Friends (2) sets #0.5 through #4; many wires; birdbeaks (1); Toucans (3); Bugaboos (3); Lost Arrows (6); ropes (2) to prevent rope drag on pitch 2.

Descent: Rappel the west face with double 200-foot (60 m) ropes.

DIVERSIONS

ARCHES NATIONAL PARK

Of the eight national parks within the desert lands of the Colorado Plateau, Arches and Capitol Reef were the last to be elevated to park status. Established in 1971, Arches is also the northernmost park and, along with Zion, the most frequently visited by climbers. Although more than 2,000 arches with 3- to 306-foot (0.9 to 93 km) spans have been documented, the spectacular hoodoos, towers, and fins are for many an equal attraction. Added to the magnificent landforms of the park is the spectacular backdrop of the nearly 13,000-foot (3,962 m) La Sal Mountains.

The park land ranges in elevation from 3,960 to 5,653 feet (1,207 to 1,723 m). Twenty-five percent is steppe covered by shrub, and 45 percent by a pygmy forest composed of juniper and piñon. The rest of the region is bare rock (but never barren!).

Be sure to stop at the visitor center located 5 miles (8 km) north of Moab. The center is open daily except Thanksgiving, Christmas, and New Year's Day. Winter hours are from 8:00 A.M. to 4:30 P.M., with extended hours in the summer. Weather forecasts, road conditions, closures, ranger-led hikes, nature walks, evening programs, and a variety of other useful information are available here. Every half hour, a fifteen-minute slide program is presented (a must-see introduction to the park). Also at the center are a geology museum and a history exhibit. Canyonlands Natural History Association, the nonprofit concessionaire, offers a good selection of books, maps, postcards, posters, slides, audiotapes, film, and water bottles. Water is available year-round at the visitor center, and in season at Devils Garden at the end of the 18-mile (29 km)-long park road.

For many, the highlight of visiting the park is a ranger-led hike through the Fiery Furnace. This dramatic three-hour tour covers a 2-mile (3.2 km) loop of moderately difficult terrain. Hikes are twice daily (morning and afternoon) and are limited to twenty-five persons. There is a nominal fee, and advance registration at the visitor center is required. Experiencing the hauntingly beautiful Fiery Furnace is highly recommended when visiting this unique region of the desert. To enter the Furnace without a ranger, it is necessary to obtain a permit and view a short slide show at the visitor center (violators are subject to a $50 fine), but exploring the fins of this labyrinthine maze independently is not recommended. There is little chance that you will experience much of this complicated place without a guide.

SEGO CANYON GHOST TOWN

Sego was a coal mining community established in 1910 up a scenic canyon in the Book Cliffs. It was the site of the first coal washer constructed west of the Mississippi. Sego was first known as Ballard, named for Harry Ballard, a local rancher who discovered high-quality coal in the area. Ballard sold the mine, and the town was then named Neslin, after Richard Neslin, the general manager of the American Fuel Company, purchaser of the mine. In 1915 Neslin was fired, and the community changed its name to Sego (the Utah state flower).

In its heyday, the town's population peaked at more than 500. Families lived in well-built houses, and bachelors stayed in a two-story boardinghouse.

In 1931 two large dinosaur tracks were found in one of the mines and sent to an eastern museum. One track measured 53½ by 32 inches, the other 44 by 32 inches. By 1950 railroad diesel engines had replaced the coal-driven steam engines, decreasing the need for coal. The mine was closed and owners sold their houses for salvage. Remaining are the walls of the company store, foundations, and other scattered ruins.

MILEAGE LOG—SUNSHINE WALL TO THOMPSON–SEGO CANYONS

00 miles: Camp One Sunshine Wall.

0.1 mile (0.16 km): Salt Valley trail.

0.2 mile (0.32 km): Bovine watering pond left (west) beside the trail.

0.5 mile (0.8 km): Colorful chert (flint) beds are up the dirt branch to the right (east).

1.1 miles (1.7 km): Cattle guard.

1.5 miles (2.4 km): Left branch to US 191; continue straight ahead. This is the beginning of the Salt Valley Gorge Road.

2.7 miles (4.3 km): Trail forks. Straight goes to the Yellowcat uranium mining area. Take the right (north) branch.

3.1 miles (5.0 km): Corral on the left (west). The trail climbs onto a high ridge from which there are expansive views to the desert, left and right of the trail. The La Sal Mountains are in full view to the east, the Henry Mountains to the southwest.

5.0 miles (8.0 km): Paved road begins. Left (west) is the Mid-American Pipeline Company Thompson Station.

5.7 miles (9.2 km): Pass under Interstate 70.

6.6 miles (10.6 km): Cross the railroad tracks in the nearly ghost town of Thompson Springs.

7.0 miles (11.2 km): A sign for Thompson Canyon (3 miles) and Sego Canyon (4 miles).

9.6 miles (15.4 km): Note the window in the rock cliff on the left.

10 miles (16.1 km): Cross a wash and turn left to the rock art panel. There are rest rooms, picnic tables, and fire rings. Signs give information about the history and geology of the area and describe the rock art found here. The pavement turns to dirt at the turn-in to the first rock art panels.

RESET ODOMETER AT THE FIRST ROCK ART PANELS.

0.1 mile (0.16 km): There is a rock art panel up the trail on the right approximately 500 feet (152 m) beyond these first canvases and a sign: PRIVATE PROPERTY. A cattle coral encloses the pictograph panel.

0.4 mile (0.64 km): Thompson Canyon ahead; turn right to Sego Canyon.

0.5 mile (8 km): Pioneer graveyard on the right.

0.6 mile (9.6 km): Fence and private property sign.

1.4 miles (2.3 km): Sego Canyon ghost town.

To reach the Thompson–Sego Canyons from US 191 at the Sunshine Wall turnoff, continue 4.5 miles (7.2 km) north to Crescent Junction and Interstate 70. Drive east on the interstate 5.4 miles (8.6 km) and take exit 185 between mile markers 184 and 185 (sign for eastbound travelers: NEXT SERVICE 56 MILES). At the freeway exit, take the Thompson Road 4.3 miles (6.9 km) to the first rock art panels, then follow the second part of the Sunshine Wall to Thompson–Sego Canyons Mileage Log to the canyons. This route is the less scenic approach; unless the trails are wet, the preferred route is the overland dirt trail described in the mileage log.

> That beam of light! Was there ever anything so beautiful! How it flashes its color through shadow, how it gilds the tops of the mountains and gleams white on the dunes of the desert! In any land what is there more glorious than sunlight! Even here in the desert, where it falls fierce and hot as a rain of meteors, it is the one supreme beauty to which all things pay allegiance.
>
> —John C. Van Dyke, *The Desert,* 1901

8

MOAB AREA

> The life, too, on the desert is peculiarly savage. It is a show of teeth in bush and beast and reptile. At every turn one feels the presence of the barb and thorn, the jaw and paw, the beak and talon, the sting and the poison thereof. Everything is at war with its neighbor, and the conflict is unceasing. Yet this conflict is not so obvious on the face of things. You hear no clash or crash or snarl. The desert is overwhelmingly silent. There is not a sound to be heard; and not a thing moves save the wind and the sands. . . . you look about at the wind-tossed, half-starved bushes; and, for all the silence, you know that there is a struggle for life, a war for place, going on day by day.
>
> —John C. Van Dyke, *The Desert,* 1901

Moab sits in a fertile valley bordered by high red rock walls. At 4,200 feet (1,280 m) it is one of the lowest points on the Colorado Plateau, and with an average of less than 10 inches (25.4 cm) of precipitation per year, it is considered high desert land. Some believe the name Moab comes from the Paiute word *Moapa* (mosquito) because the wetlands bordering the Colorado River along the northwest side of the valley are a rich breeding area for the pests. John F. Hoffman details the true origin of the name in *Arches National Park—An Illustrated Guide*: "Although Moab may look and sound as if it were of American Indian origin, it actually derives from the Bible. Moab, mentioned in the Book of Genesis, was the name of a biblical character, and also the place-name of a region east of the Dead Sea. The inhabitants of this ancient land were called Moabites. Moab's father was Lot, a nephew of Abraham. Lot, his wife, and two daughters lived in Sodom. According to the Bible, when God decided to destroy the wicked cities of Sodom and Gomorrah, Lot and his family were allowed to escape to Zoar, a small city near the southeastern end of the Dead Sea. Before fleeing from Sodom, Lot's wife, reluctant to leave the pleasures of the corrupt city, was warned not to look back. She defied the warning, and was instantly transformed into a pillar of salt. Lot was afraid to remain in Zoar, so he and his daughters fled into the nearby highland, where they dwelled in a cave. In the Old Testament account (Genesis 19:30–38), Lot's daughters plied him with wine and then lured him into incestuous relations. Moab was born to the elder daughter, and Ben-ammi to the younger. The descendants of Moab were called Moabites, descendants of Ben-ammi were known as Ammonites. The etymology of Moab first appeared in The Septuagint, a Greek version of the Old Testament, which dates from the third century B.C. In the English translation of The Septuagint by Charles Thornson, dated 1808, revised by C. A. Muses in 1954, Moab means '*From my father.*'"

Over the years the town has also been called Plainfield, Poverty Flats, Bueno, Spanish Valley, Grand Valley, and Mormon Fort. It once had a reputation as the "roughest, toughest town in Utah." The current population is approximately 9,000, diminishing in the winter and swelling in the summer. At the turn of the twentieth century, Moab was celebrated for it prize-winning fruit crops and was a sheep and cattle center.

Photo: Marea Ross

Paul Ross and Paul Gardener, first ascent of Kachina Towers, 1999.

In 1952, Charlie Steen discovered uranium 40 miles (64 km) south of town. This set off a mining boom that lasted for nearly two decades, bringing thousands of prospectors and miners into the area. In the 1980s, Moab gained popularity as a mountain biking and four-wheeler destination. For many years river runners have floated the white-water rapids of Cataract Canyon south of Moab and Westwater Canyon near the Colorado–Utah border east of Moab, as well as calm water floats just upriver. Since the early 1960s, rock climbers have visited the towers, buttes, and mesas of the area, but it wasn't until the mid-1970s, when Ray Jordine introduced his Friend camming device, that there was sound protection for the desert's countless parallel-sided cracks. Since then, rock climbing in the canyon country surrounding Moab has grown at an exponential rate, in part due to advances in technology and media coverage.

FLORA AND FAUNA

Desert wildflowers dominate from mid-April through the first two weeks of May. It is a time when the land is painted with all the hues of the rainbow, including the delicate yellow and pink prickly pear, purple fishhook, and claret cup cacti. Poison ivy is found in many canyons around Moab and along the cliffs of Wall Street (Scenic Byway 279, Potash Road). Remember the adage: "Leaves of three, let it be." Growing in disturbed soil beside roadways are the sweet-smelling, pearl white, bell-shaped blooms of the deadly jimsonweed (a.k.a. datura or moonflower), said to be a psychedelic drug used in the past by Indians as part of sacred ceremonies. The plant is pollinated by moths, blooms at night, and closes its petals in the early morning.

Throughout the spring, summer, and autumn, great blue herons are often seen fishing along the banks of the Colorado, and red-tailed hawks and turkey vultures are a common sight soaring on desert-heated updrafts. Mud-built swallows' nests can be seen along the banks of the river, and the sweet notes of the canyon wren and plaintive call of the mourning dove are frequently heard. The playful raven, said to have the intelligence of a canine, can be found throughout the mesas and canyons of the Moab area. Averaging 2 feet in length and with a wingspan of 4 feet or more, the raven is the largest member of the crow family. They mate for life and share in the raising of their nestlings. As they fly overhead, ravens can be distinguished from crows by their V-shaped tails; crows' tails are rounded.

Be wary of pygmy midget-faded and Great Basin rattlesnakes. Less common is the largest rattlesnake of the southwest, the 7-foot (2.1 m) diamondback. Lizards are ubiquitous, especially western fence, longnose leopard, desert spiny, plateau, sagebrush, side-blotched, tree, whiptail, and the amazing collared lizard (a member of the iguana family), distinguished by a prominent double black band around its neck and, on females in estrus, bright yellow-green and orange markings on their sides until eggs are laid. The collared lizard has been clocked at 17 mph, ranking it among the fastest of reptiles. It runs on four legs until reaching maximum speed, then stands upright and continues running on its hind legs, much like a miniature dinosaur. Be on the lookout for black widow spiders hidden in rock cracks or dead wood. Scorpions (the arachnid that gives live birth rather than laying eggs) live in the bark of trees or hide beneath clumps of dry wood (or sleeping bags).

The region surrounding Moab is home to desert bighorn sheep, and the Colorado River corridor is the home of golden and bald eagles. At the northwest side of the valley is the 875-acre Nature Conservancy–owned Scott M. Matheson Wetlands Preserve, where more than 180 species of birds live or stop over on their migratory flights. The desert slough is the only one of its kind on the banks of the Colorado River in Utah, the second driest state in the country.

CLIMATE

Throughout the Colorado Plateau, spring and autumn temperatures are the most pleasant for visits. In the spring, relentless winds are common. Summer temperatures during June, July, and August are sometimes in the 100s, but the heat is much more tolerable than in humid areas of the country.

Thundershowers can be expected in spring, summer, and fall and are especially dangerous. There have been a number of deaths from lightning strikes throughout the years, including a fatality to a climber on Castleton Tower in 1995, and a helicopter rescue after a second climber was struck later the same year. **WARNING:** If lightning occurs, avoid high ground, tall trees, and moist regions such as alcoves or drainages. If possible, stay in your vehicle until the storm passes, or crouch on the ground, preferably on something dry to insulate the body. Do not become a lightning rod by bunching together with your comrades. Trees, mountain bikes, and climbing hardware are natural lightning rods. If you are in an open area, crouch but do not sit—the goal is to get as low as you can with as little contact with the ground as possible.

Flash floods are another very real hazard in the Moab area. They can appear from nowhere and are frequently powerful enough to dislodge large boulders, uproot trees, and tumble vehicles like weightless toys. Avoid washes and dry arroyos, even if a storm seems distant. On a happier note, summer thunderstorms produce spectacular waterfalls cascading from slickrock canyon rims. Locals frequently jam the Colorado River Road (Scenic Byway 128 east of Moab) during cloudbursts to view more than a dozen major waterfalls within the first mile (1.6 km). Numerous waterfalls also add drama along the Potash Road on the west side of the Colorado River.

CALENDAR OF EVENTS

Moab Happenings, published monthly, is a free paper distributed throughout town. It includes current events, maps to dinosaur prints and petroglyphs, a restaurant guide, and other items of interest to visitors.

The following is a list of Moab's most popular annual events. For an updated calendar, visit the Travel Council in the Grand County Court House, one block east of Main on Center Street, or check current events in the local weekly *Times-Independent* newspaper.

January: "Bull Blast" bull riding and barrels at the Old Spanish Trail Arena south of town. Community Theatre at Star Hall.

February: Community Theatre. Chocolate Lovers Fling at the Moab Arts and Recreation Center. Art Walk, downtown Moab. Championship Team Roping at Old Spanish Trail Arena.

March: Art Walk. Half Marathon and 5K Run, Red Rock Roadrunners. High School Rodeo, Old Spanish Trail Arena.

April: Annual Canyonlands Film Festival. Annual Tour of Canyonlands Mountain Bike Race. Art Walk. Annual Jeep Safari. City of Moab Easter Egg Hunt, City Park. Red Rock Circuit Quarter Horse Show. Antique car rally.

May: Air Show and Fly In, Canyonlands Field/Moab Airport.

June: Art Walk. Butch Cassidy Days Parade. La Sal Mountain 5K Run. Moab Arts Festival. Rodeo, Old Spanish Trail Arena.

July: 4H Livestock Show. Art Walk. Dan O'Laurie Museum Ice Cream Social.

August: La Sal Mountain Summer Festival with music, food, lodging, camping. Art Walk. Grand County Fair.

September: Annual Moab Music Festival. Annual Labor Day Red Rock 4-Wheelers Campout. Art Walk. Moab Fall Quarter Horse Show.

October: Art Walk. Annual Points and Pebbles Gem and Mineral Show. Annual 24-Hour Moab Mountain Bike Race, behind the Rocks Area. Annual Fat Tire Mountain Bike Festival.

November: Chamber of Commerce Annual Banquet and Auction. Art Walk.

December: Tree Lighting. Electric Light Parade. Art Walk.

MAP

Identified on the Moab West map published by Latitude 40 Degrees are Crohn's Wall, Willis Tower, Utah 313, Crackhouse, Gemini Bridges Trail, Gemini Bridges, Surprise Overlook, Crow's Head Spires, Bird's View Butte, Spring Canyon Trail, Canyon Point Trail, Tombstone, Canyon Point Butte, Lost World Butte, Kachina Towers, Hell Roaring Canyon, Hell Roaring Canyon Pictographs, Hell Roaring Canyon Old Cattle Trail to the rim, the Goose Neck of the Colorado River, and Pyramid Butte. Future revisions of the map will include other isolated areas identified in this guide.

Moab has all the amenities of a big little city, including a climbing store, Pagan Mountaineering, 88 East Center. A good selection of gear is also available at Rim Cyclery, 94 West 100 North, and at Gearheads, 471 South Main. Moab Cliffs and Canyons, 63 East Center Street, is a guiding service offering canyoneering, rock climbing guiding, and climbing instruction.

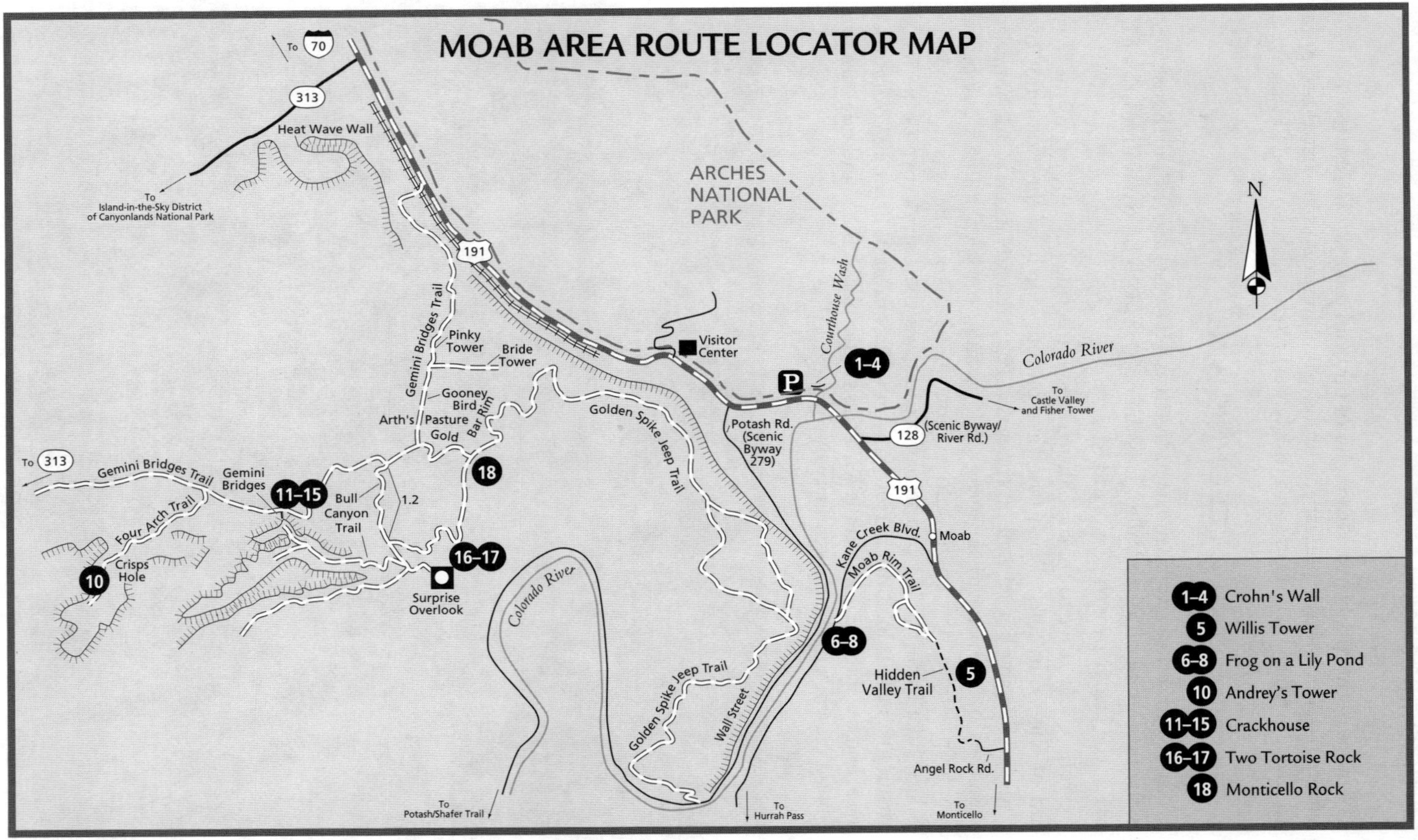
MOAB AREA ROUTE LOCATOR MAP
To 70
313
Heat Wave Wall
To Island-in-the-Sky District of Canyonlands National Park
ARCHES NATIONAL PARK
N
191
Gemini Bridges Trail
Pinky Tower
Bride Tower
Gooney Bird
Bar Rim
Arth's Pasture
Gold
Visitor Center
Courthouse Wash
P
1–4
Colorado River
To Castle Valley and Fisher Tower
128 (Scenic Byway/ River Rd.)
Potash Rd. (Scenic Byway 279)
Golden Spike Jeep Trail
To 313
Gemini Bridges
11–15
Bull Canyon Trail
1.2
18
Four Arch Trail
Crisps Hole
10
16–17
Surprise Overlook
Colorado River
Kane Creek Blvd.
Moab
Moab Rim Trail
6–8
Hidden Valley Trail
5
Wall Street
Angel Rock Rd.
To Potash/Shafer Trail
To Hurrah Pass
To Monticello
1–4 Crohn's Wall
5 Willis Tower
6–8 Frog on a Lily Pond
10 Andrey's Tower
11–15 Crackhouse
16–17 Two Tortoise Rock
18 Monticello Rock

Routes in the Moab area, although not far from town, are in isolated locations remote from previously published climbs. Climbing routes are listed beginning with Moab valley, then south, and finally west to the Island-in-the-Sky areas.

CROHN'S WALL

Crohn's Wall is the Navajo sandstone buttress left (west) above Courthouse Wash at the north end of Moab Valley. It is the only smooth brown wall north of US 191 at the bridge over the Colorado River.

From Moab, drive to the asphalt parking lot beside US 191, left of the lower end of the Courthouse Wash (the first pullout north of the Colorado River Bridge). Hike a well-used trail up the wash. The Arches National Park boundary is marked by a fence with a zigzag walk-through (to keep animals out but let people in) and a sign giving information about hiking the wash. The 5-mile (8 km) hike from US 191 to the park road gives the only "canyon experience" within the park. It includes narrow canyon walls, groves of Fremont cottonwood trees, and several small waterfalls with freshwater pools. Bikes and dogs are prohibited on trails in the backcountry of the park.

Photo: Eric Bjørnstad

Crohn's Wall: 1. Left Route *2.* Crohn's Odyssey.

A little less than 1 mile (1.6 km) up the wash, there is an 8-foot (2.4 km)-tall dull yellow water-depth measuring tower; 30 feet (9 m) south is a USGS bench mark. At the left edge of the buttress above (looking west), the right edge of Crohn's Wall is in view. The wall itself is just around the corner facing south. From the tower, walk to the cottonwood trees obvious left of upstream, then gain the middle tier of the three prominent Kayenta sandstone benches that border the wash to the west. Follow the upthrust (anticline) of the ramp up and left to the southern ramparts of the park and enjoy the great views into Moab Valley and the Colorado River. A short walk west will give access through the upper Kayenta steps to the south-facing Crohn's Wall. Routes are listed left to right.

1 LEFT ROUTE
I, 5.10, 1 pitch, 100 feet (30 m)

First Ascent: Kyle Copeland, Linus Platt, early 1990s.

Location and Access: Begin at a white chalky boulder at the base of the wall, two crack systems left of *Crohn's Odyssey*. Climb with fingers up a "V," passing a drilled angle piton on the left wall 10 feet (3 m) below an overhang. Pass the overhang on its left side and continue up a right-facing dihedral to double anchors on the right wall just below the lip of a shallow bench.

Paraphernalia: Friends #1 through #1.5; Camalot #3.

Descent: One rappel from double anchors visible from below the climb.

2 CROHN'S ODYSSEY
I, 5.11b, 1 pitch, 80 feet (24 m)

First Ascent: Kyle Copeland, Linus Platt, early 1990s.

Location and Access: *Crohn's Odyssey* is two crack systems right of *Left Route* or one crack left of a large right-facing dihedral with large boulders at its base. It can also be identified as three crack systems left of a lone 10-foot (3 m)-high juniper tree. Climb a splitter crack that ends on the face, then pass a roof at its left side. Continue with some off-width up a slightly overhanging left-facing crack, 5.11b. Finish with 5.11 fingers at a pod with double anchors on the right wall.

Paraphernalia: Friends #1 through #1.5 with off-width size units.

Descent: Rappel the route from fixed anchors visible from below the route.

3 PROJECT ONE
I, 5.9, 1 pitch, 30 feet (9 m)

First Ascent: Unknown.

Location and Access: *Project One* is one crack left of *Project Two* and climbs light-colored rock to a drilled angle piton on the left wall.

Paraphernalia: Friends #1, #1.5.

Descent: Rappel or lower from a single drilled angle piton visible from below.

4 PROJECT TWO
I, 5.10, 1 pitch, 30 feet (9 m)

First Ascent: Kyle Copeland, Linus Platt, early 1990s.

Location and Access: *Project Two* is one crack left of the right prow of the Crohn's Wall buttress. Climb a large right-facing dihedral hand-and-fist 25 feet (7.6 m) to a drilled angle piton on the left wall.

Paraphernalia: Friends #2.5, #3, #3.5.

Descent: Rappel from a drilled angle piton on the left wall visible from below the project.

DIVERSIONS

MOAB PICTOGRAPH PANEL (A.K.A. COURTHOUSE WASH PANEL)

The Moab Panel is rare for this area. There are hundreds of petroglyph sites, but few painted panels. This ancient Indian "canvas," only a few yards from the approach to Crohn's Wall, is worth a visit.

From Moab, drive to the asphalt parking lot beside US 191, left of the lower end of the wash (the first pullout north of the Colorado River Bridge). There is an information kiosk at the east end of the lot. A short trail leads over a bridge spanning Courthouse Wash, then up to the panel, which is in view on the smooth wall above US 191.

In the 1980s the pictographs were badly damaged when an unidentified party attempted to scrub the images from the wall. It is thought the vandalism took place because many of the anthropomorphic figures were anatomically correct, and offense was taken.

WILLIS TOWER

Willis Tower is in the west Moab cliffs high above the town. It is visible from US 191 as one drives south through the valley. Its location is close to the popular Hidden Valley mountain biking and hiking trail. Willis Tower was named for Andy Roberts's dog Willis, who insists on playing with a stick and barking unless he gets the command "get your stick and lie down."

From Moab, drive south on US 191 and turn west between mile markers 121 and 122 on Angel Rock Road. Drive 2 blocks and turn right onto Rimrock Lane. Follow it less than 0.5 mile (0.8 km) to its end, where there is a BLM register box and the posted Hidden Valley trailhead. Grunt up the steep switchbacks to Hidden Valley and follow the trail to its crest. Hike right (north) 10 minutes and the tower will come into view.

Photo: Wilson Goodrich

Willis Tower.

5 GET YOUR STICK AND LIE DOWN I, 5.8, 1 pitch, 95 feet (29 m) ★★★★

First Ascent: Mike Baker, Andy Roberts, Wilson Goodrich, March 13, 1999. Second Ascent: Jason Repko, Chris Giles, May 2000.

Location and Access: The route ascends the west side of the tower. Begin 5.7 and climb into 5.8 fingers before finishing with a 5.6 stem.

Paraphernalia: Camalots through #3; TCUs.

Descent: Double-rope rappel down the route from double bolts.

FROG ON A LILLY PAD (A.K.A. POINT OF MOAB, OLD LADY ON POT)

Frog on a Lilly Pad forms part of the Navajo rimrock bordering Poison Spider Mesa. From downtown Moab the monolith is obvious when looking west to the portal through which the Colorado River leaves Moab Valley. It is visible from Moab but not from the Potash Road. To reach from Moab, cross the bridge over the Colorado River at the north end of Moab and continue 2 miles (3.2 km) to the left turn onto Potash Road (Scenic Byway 279). Follow Potash Road 3.9 miles (6.2 km) to the Jaycee Campground (on the right). At the parking area is the Portal Overlook Trailhead. Hike the trail to the overlook, then on to the top. Contour back to the Lilly Pad (dome to the right of the Frog), walk to a point opposite the Frog, and look for three bolts with a chain in an alcove.

6 FROG TO LILLY PAD TYROLEAN III, 60-foot (18 m) tyrolean ★★

First Ascent: Chris Kelly, Lee Kelly, March 1, 2001.

Location and Access: From the Lilly Pad, loop two 200-foot (60 m) ropes through the anchor and rappel. Walk across to the base of the Frog and climb *Dead Sea* or *Another Wide One,* taking the two tyrolean ropes to the summit, which is climbed with a third 150-foot (46 m) rope. Secure the two 200-foot (60 m) ropes to the Frog's summit and tyrolean to the Lilly Pad, then back to the Frog. Pull the tyrolean ropes, then rappel from the Frog. The first ascent tyrolean team climbed the *Dead Sea* route.

Paraphernalia: Ropes (2) 200 foot (60 m), (1) 150 foot (46 m).

Descent: Rappel to the notch, then to the ground.

7 DEAD SEA III, 5.10, A1+, 4 pitches, 440 feet (134 m)

First Ascent: Harvey T. Carter, Tim Jennings, 5.8, A2, November 9, 1967. One bivouac, 19 bolts, 27 pitons.

Location and Access: Route ascends the tower from the southeast up a crack system directly below the right-hand saddle.

Pitch 1: Climb a bolt ladder to a rotten crack. Continue past a makeshift belay to a large ledge with bolt anchors, 150 feet (46 m).

Pitch 2: Free climb a thin corner to thin hands (5.10), then up to the notch, 70 feet (21 m).

Pitch 3: Walk around to the back (west) side, fourth class, and climb a crack through a roof (on clean aid) to a bolt ladder. Belay from a ledge at the top of the ladder, 150 feet (46 m).

Pitch 4: Climb a short pitch past two bolts to the top.

Paraphernalia: Friends through #3.5; TCUs; a few sawed-off 0.5", 1" angle pitons for pitch 1; quick draws.

Descent: Downclimb to solid rock, then double-rope rappel to the notch. Two more double-rope rappels reach the ground.

8 ANOTHER WIDE ONE
III, 5.11+, 3 pitches, 440 feet (134 m)

First Ascent: Earl Wiggins, Sonja Paspal, spring 1991.

Location and Access: Left of *Dead Sea*.

Pitch 1: Climb a right-facing (off-width) dihedral, which narrows to a hand crack and ends at a ledge.

Pitch 2: Traverse up and right over loose rock to the chimney of the original route, 25 feet (7.6 m).

Pitch 3: Follow *Dead Sea* to the summit.

Paraphernlia: Standard desert rack with units up to 6 inches; quick draws.

Descent: Rappel to the notch, then to the ground.

DIVERSIONS

HIDDEN VALLEY TRAIL AND PETROGLYPHS

Hidden Valley, just south of Willis Tower, is popular with hikers and mountain bikers. The moderately difficult trail climbs 680 feet (207 m) from Moab Valley over a series of switchbacks to a broad hanging valley. The path provides dramatic views east to the Sand Flats and the La Sal Mountains, and leads to Behind-the-Rocks Wilderness Study Area. At its northwest end (on the right) are two long buttresses of dark varnished rock, parallel in a generally east-west direction. Both walls are canvases for hundreds of Anasazi petroglyphs. The northern (second) wall ends at a high lookout where there are ruins of an ancient circular stone wall. South of the buttress, a four-wheel-drive trail extends from the head of Hidden Valley northwest to the difficult Moab Rim Trail, descending over rough terrain to Kane Creek Boulevard beside the Colorado River.

PYRAMID BUTTE

Pyramid Butte is the dominant isolated pyramidal landform above the west banks of the Colorado River at a geographic position just west of the Wind Caves (see Lockhart Basin Trail, Chapter 14). It borders the west side of the Colorado between river miles 21 and 23. The butte is in view from most of Lockhart Basin Trail as it descends from Hurrah Pass to the Wind Caves. Its summit is a very remote place, offering a spectacular vista of the river and the rugged red rock landscape in all directions.

The inner gorge of the Colorado River (at river level) is eroded from Hermosa sandstone. In ascending order above is the Elephant Canyon Formation, Halgaito shale, and finally the Organ Rock member of the Cutler Group from which Pyramid Butte was formed.

From the Potash Road (Scenic Byway 279) just north of the bridge over the Colorado River north of Moab, drive 15.7 miles (25.2 km) to the Potash Mine. Just beyond, the road becomes a dirt trail at the river runners' cement put-in ramp, and the road's name changes to the Shafer Trail. Continue 7.3 miles (11.7 km), pass the last Potash evaporation pond, park, and hike cross-country to the butte, which will be in view to the south.

9 PYRAMID BUTTE (See map on page 130.) II, easy fifth class, 500 feet (152 m)

First Ascent: Harvey T. Carter, early 1960s. Probable Second Ascent: Paul Horton, January 1997.

Location and Access: The summit is reached with scrambles over short rock bands between loose talus. The climb is exposed and offers little protection.

Paraphernalia: None required.

Descent: Careful downclimbing.

DIVERSIONS

THELMA AND LOUISE VIEWPOINT

Thelma and Louise Viewpoint was known as Pyramid Viewpoint until 1991, when it was renamed for the film *Thelma and Louise.* In the last scene, Thelma and Louise appear to drive off the rimrock into the Grand Canyon, but the filming actually took place at Pyramid Viewpoint, directly below Deadhorse Point State Park. Three motorless cars with Thelma and Louise dummies were catapulted from a ramp into the canyon to gain the desired shot. The cars were retrieved from the Colorado River by helicopter. Neither the National Park Service nor the Bureau of Land Management would grant permission to do the filming on their land. The site used for filming is owned by the state, which has fewer environmental damage restrictions than the BLM or the National Park System.

To reach the viewpoint, drive 10 miles (16 km) down the Shafer Trail from its junction with the Potash Road.

ANDREY'S TOWER

Andrey's Tower is in Crips Hole west of the Gemini Bridges. From Utah 313, turn left (east) onto the signed Gemini Bridges trail between mile markers 9 and 10. Follow signs to the Gemini Bridges, turning at the signed right spur 2.6 miles (4.2 km) from Utah 313. At 0.7 mile (1.1 km) from the right spur sign GEMINI BRIDGES LEFT, FOUR ARCH TRAIL RIGHT, CRIPS HOLE RIGHT, take the right spur. At 0.1 mile (0.16 km) from the sign, pass through a cattle control wire fence. A locked well is on the right at 0.7 mile (1.1 km), and at 1.9 miles (3 km) Andrey's Tower is in view ahead on the right side of the canyon.

Jimmy Dunn: "Andrey Barbashinov was a mountain guide from Kazakhstan, Russia. He was visiting the United States on the Anatoli Boukreev exchange program and was the first person to summit Denali in 2001. We climbed, played chess, and shared life together in Salt Lake City. We showed him pictures of climbing in Moab. He was very excited to climb in the desert, so he changed his flight to come with us. Just before we were to leave for Moab, Andrey was killed when a truck hit him as he was driving back from Wyoming on a motorcycle. We are honored to have known Andrey, and dedicate this tower to him."

10 THE RUSSIANS ARE COMING II, 5.10+, 3 pitches, 250 feet (76 m) ★★★★

First Ascent: Jimmy Dunn, Hellen Heaven, Billy Rothstein, Danny McCann, July 2, 2001.

Location and Access: Jimmy Dunn: "Thin, beautiful treat to be out there." Begin on the left side of the tower when viewed from the approach trail.

Pitch 1: Scramble up an unprotected (scary) gully to a chimney, fourth class, 60 feet (18 m).

Pitch 2: Begin from a ledge and stem, then face climb to a bush. Continue with thin hands to fingers (5.10+), then off-width through a 5.9 bulge. Follow the crack system up and right to a belay ledge, 180 feet (55 m).

Pitch 3: Climb out and right over loose rock to the summit, 10 feet (3 m).

Paraphernalia: Friends (1) set through #4; Camalots through #4.5; small wired stoppers #2, #3, #4, #5; 200-foot (60 m) ropes; several long slings.

Descent: Rappel the route.

CRACKHOUSE

Located near the Gemini Bridges, Crackhouse is the longest ceiling jamcrack in the United States. The popular 80-foot (24 m)-long Crackhouse One traverses the ceiling crack in a cave, which tapers from 6 feet to 8 feet (1.8 m to 2.4 m) aboveground. All combinations of the route have been climbed.

Crackhouse, Monticello Rock, and Two Tortoise Rock are identified on the Moab West map. To reach Crackhouse from Moab, use either of the following mileage logs.

ANDREY'S TOWER—THE RUSSIANS ARE COMING

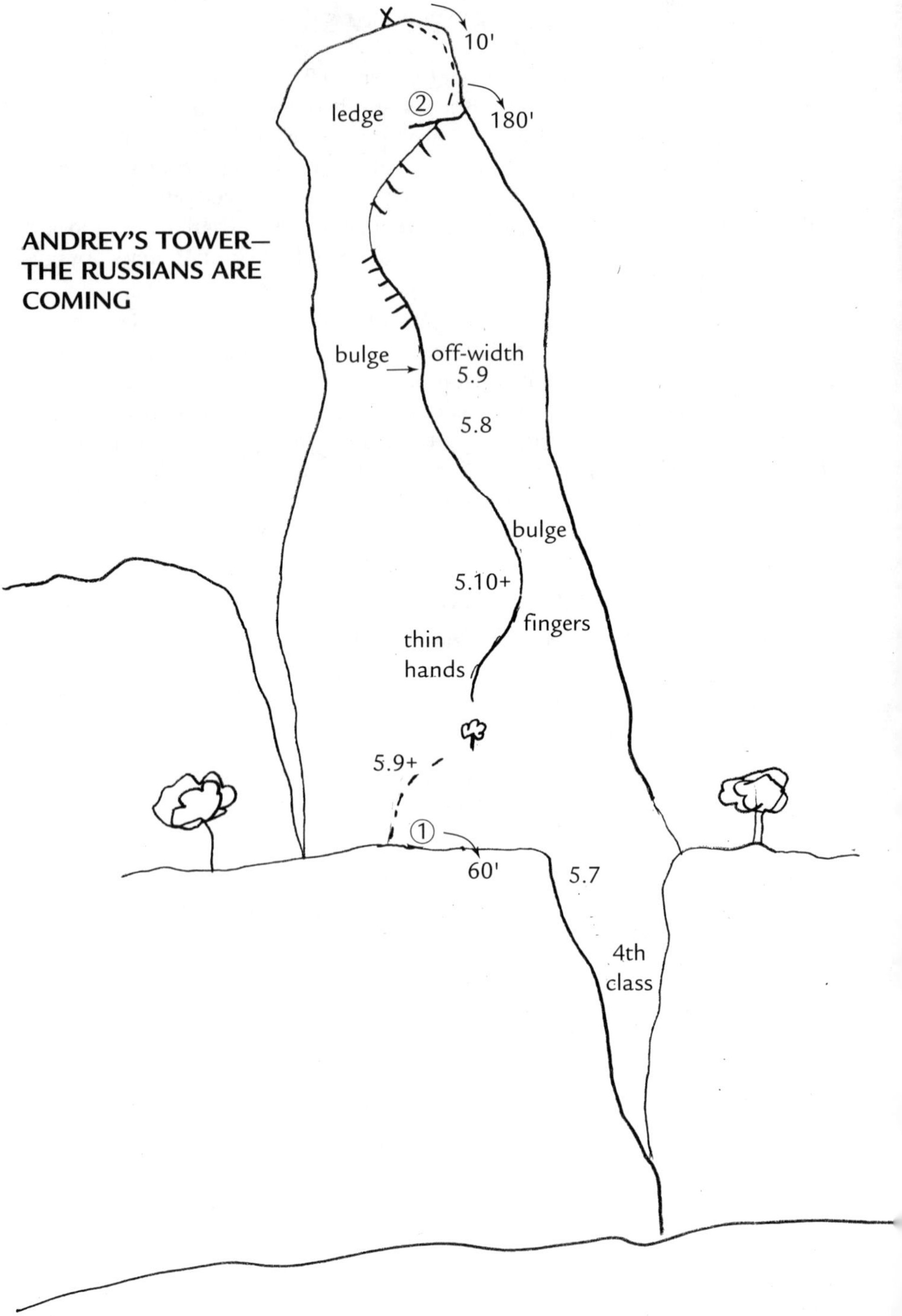

MILEAGE LOG—UPPER GEMINI BRIDGES TO CRACKHOUSE

This log begins at the junction of Utah 313 and Gemini Bridges Trail (between mile markers 9 and 10). Utah 313 is 9 miles (14.5 km) north of Moab on US 191. A high-clearance vehicle is essential.

0.6 mile (0.9 km): Sign: VEHICLES MUST STAY ON EXISTING ROADS.

2.2 miles (3.5 km): Cattle guard.

4.0 miles (6.4 km): Right spur. Sign: GEMINI BRIDGES. Continue straight for the quickest route to the Crackhouse.

4.5 miles (7.2 km): Power lines overhead go to Dead Horse Point State Park.

6.1 miles (9.8 km): T intersection; keep right.

6.9 miles (11.2 km): T intersection; keep right. Sign: GEMINI BRIDGES (RIGHT)—US 191 (LEFT).

7.6 miles (12.2 km): Crackhouse is on the right.

MILEAGE LOG—COLORADO RIVER BRIDGE TO CRACKHOUSE VIA LOWER GEMINI BRIDGES TRAIL

This is the longer but most scenic approach to the Crackhouse. It requires a high-clearance vehicle; the grade out of Arth's Pasture may require four-wheel drive.

00 miles: Bridge across the Colorado River at the north end of Moab Valley.

0.2 mile (0.3 km): Bridge across Courthouse Wash. US 191 follows the south then west border of Arches National Park for the next several miles.

0.5 mile (0.8 km): Right (north) of the highway is a paved parking area and information kiosk for the Courthouse Wash pictograph panel (a.k.a. Moab Panel) and is the approach to the Crohn's Wall climbs.

2.0 miles (3.2 km): Pickle Tower ahead, right of the road. Left turn onto the Potash Road (Scenic Byway 279). Approach to Wall Street, side canyons, Pyramid Butte, and lower (scenic) approach to Bird's View Butte.

2.3 miles (3.7 km): Entrance to Arches National Park on the right (north).

3.0 miles (4.8 km): Betty and Bert bouldering problems and the beginning of the old road to Moab and pre-1960 entrance to Arches.

5.5 miles (8.8 km): Right of the road are several grabens (German word for graves), created by faults or dropped areas sometimes formed when salt is solutioned out from beneath the earth's crust and the surface ground collapses, a geologic phenomenon found throughout the canyonland area.

5.6 miles (9.0 km): Railroad tracks enter 120-foot (37 m)-deep cut to level the grade out of Moab Valley.

7.2 miles (11.5 km): Turn left on the dirt spur (west) between mile markers 135 and 136. Gemini Bridges Trail information kiosk, register box, then a cattle guard. Sign for vehicles entering US 191: TO MOAB VIA OLD HIGHWAY (east across the highway).

7.3 miles (11.7 km): Left turn onto dike built from dirt taken from the railroad cut, constructed to divert water runoff from the tracks.

8.0 miles (12.8 km): Right turn off the dike.

8.2 miles (13.2 km): Beginning of the steep climb to Little Valley.

8.3 miles (13.3 km): Sign: OHVs PLEASE STAY ON EXISTING ROADS.

8.9 miles (14.3 km): Small hoodoo on the right.

9.2 miles (14.8 km): Top of the grade; begin descent to Little Valley. Great views of Arches National Park with North Window obvious in the Windows section of the park. With good lighting, Castleton Tower can be seen in the foreground of the La Sal Mountains far to the east and Moab Valley to the far right.

9.5 miles (15.2 km): Cattle guard. Enter Little Valley.

9.9 miles (15.9 km): Abandoned uranium mines in the Chinle slope right of the trail.

10.7 miles (17.2 km): Pinky Tower on the left.

11.0 miles (17.7 km): Gooney Bird in view ahead.

11.2 miles (18.0 km): Spur to the left goes to Bride Tower. Just beyond the spur, Bride Tower comes into view to the left (east).

11.4 miles (18.3 km): Gooney Bird Tower at the left (east) edge of the trail. Enter Arth's Pasture.

11.9 miles (19.1 km): Spur to the right goes to Crotch Arch, 300 feet (91 m) west.

12.0 miles (19.3 km): Sign: GOLD BAR RIM (LEFT)—US 191. This spur is the route to Monticello Rock. Climb a steep grade that might require high clearance and/or four-wheel drive.

12.1 miles (19.4 km): Cattle guard.

12.3 miles (19.8 km): Top of the steep grade out of Arth's Pasture.

12.7 miles (20.4 km): Left spur to Bull Canyon, Surprise Overlook, and Two Tortoise Rock. Keep right to the Crackhouse.

13.1 miles (21.0 km): Layered rock on the right looks like corrugated cardboard and is a textbook example of the stream-deposited horizontally stratified Kayenta sandstone.

13.3 miles (21.4 km): Left spur to Crackhouse and Gemini Bridges. Sign: GEMINI BRIDGES.

14.1 miles (22.7 km): Crackhouse is on the right.

11 CRACKHOUSE ONE
I, 5.13a, 1 pitch, 80 feet (24 m) ★★★★★

First Ascent: Dean Potter, solo, April 11, 1997.

Location and Access: This original line begins at the back right entrance of the cave (the Birth Canal), exits the cave at its left side, and climbs above an overhanging lip of rock to the top of the Kayenta sandstone bluff. Begin with a sitting start and traverse the ceiling with fist and foot jams. Follow the crack as it takes a 90 degree right turn. Continue to the left exit, then climb the cliff above the cave to the top.

Paraphernalia: Tape for hands, fingers, and forearms. A spotter is a good idea in the cave; an upper belay at the left cave exit will prevent a crash into boulders on the ground below.

Descent: Walk off.

12 HAND TRAVERSE
1, 5.13b, 1 pitch, 50 feet (15 m) ★★★★★

First Ascent: Dean Potter, solo, 1997.

Location and Access: The route begins 50 feet (15 m) right of the right cave entrance. Face traverse left with heel hooks to the cave's Birth Canal, then continue following *Crackhouse One.*

Paraphernalia: Same as *Crackhouse One.*

Descent: Walk off.

13 RIGHT SUMMIT
I, 5.12, 1 pitch, 30 feet (9 m) ★★★★★

First Ascent: Dean Potter, solo, 1997.

Photo: Eric Bjørnstad

Tim Toula in Crackhouse—Hand Traverse.

Location and Access: Begin at the back of the cave at its right entrance, the Birth Canal. Fist jam the ceiling crack out to the cave's right entrance, then to the top of the rock.

Paraphernalia: Same as *Crackhouse One.*

Descent: Walk off.

14 LEFT SUMMIT
I, 5.12, 1 pitch, 30 feet (9 m) ★★★★★

First Ascent: Dean Potter, solo, 1997.

Location and Access: Begin at the ceiling crack 15 feet (4.5 m) in the left entrance of the cave. Follow it out the entrance and to the top of the bluff.

Paraphernalia: Same as *Crackhouse One.*

Descent: Walk off.

15 RIGHT OF LEFT SUMMIT
I, 5.12, 1 pitch, 45 feet (14 m) ★★★★★

First Ascent: Dean Potter, solo, 1997.

Location and Access: The route begins at the back of a left spur ceiling crack of the *Crackhouse One* route when entering the cave at its left side. Traverse to *Crackhouse One* and follow it out and to the top of the bluff.

Paraphernalia: Same as *Crackhouse One.*

Descent: Walk off.

TWO TORTOISE ROCK AND MONTICELLO ROCK

To reach Two Tortoise Rock, drive to the intersection of the Gemini Bridges and Bull Canyon Trails following the Colorado River Bridge to Crackhouse via Lower Gemini Bridges Trail Mileage Log, page 95.

For an alternate approach from Utah 313, follow the Upper Gemini Bridges to Crackhouse Mileage Log, page 95. At 6.9 miles (11 km) from Utah 313 at the T intersection with the sign: GEMINI BRIDGES (RIGHT)—US 191 (LEFT), keep left and continue to the signed Bull Canyon spur forking to the right and follow: the Bull Canyon to Two Tortoise Rock Mileage Log, page 99.

The trail to Monticello Rock from this approach to Two Tortoise Rock requires difficult four-wheel driving the last quarter mile. For an easier approach to Monticello Rock, turn southeast from Arth's Pasture onto the signed Gold Bar Rim Trail. (To reach Arth's Pasture follow the Colorado River Bridge to Crackhouse via Lower Gemini Bridges Trail Mileage Log.) The Gold Bar Rim Trail turns southeast from Arth's Pasture 12 miles (19.3 km) from the junction of US 191 and the Lower Gemini Bridges Trail. Follow the most used trail and the landform will come into view. For the more difficult four-wheel-drive approach, branch north off the Two Tortoise Rock Trail approximately 0.7 mile (1.1 km)

Photo: Eric Bjørnstad

Two Tortoise Rock.

from its beginning at the Bull Canyon Trail and follow the most traveled branches in the direction of the rock soon in view ahead.

MILEAGE LOG—BULL CANYON TO TWO TORTOISE ROCK

00 miles: Bull Canyon and Gemini Bridges intersection. Take the faint left spur onto Bull Canyon Trail 1.2 miles (1.9 km) from the Bull Canyon and Gemini Bridges intersection. It appears at first to end at a campsite, but continues on to the climbs. High clearance required, four-wheel drive recommended. Route finding over difficult branches to the left will take you to Monticello Rock.

0.6 mile (0.9 km): Faint spur to the left; keep right. Two Tortoise Rock is in view ahead and Monticello Rock is in the distance to the left, with Gold Bar Tower between the two. (See *Desert Rock II: Wall Street to the San Rafael Swell* for Gold Bar Tower climb.)

0.7 mile (1.1 km): Spur to the left; keep straight.

0.9 mile (1.4 km): Spur to the right; keep left.

1.0 mile (1.6 km): Spur to the right; keep straight. The trail ends on the southwest side of Two Tortoise Rock.

16 TWO TORTOISE ROCK WEST—PUSHING THE TURTLE-HEAD
I, 5.10b, 1 pitch, 60 feet (18 m) ★★★

First Ascent: Stu Ritchie, Steve "Crusher" Bartlett, Tim Toula, March 13, 2000.

Location and Access: Begin under the steep slab on the north side of the summit. Steve "Crusher" Bartlett: "Climb gently past five drilled angles to the summit. Nice pitch, good summit."

Paraphernalia: Quick draws (5).

Descent: Rappel to the east from 10.5 millimeter rope wrapped around the summit or bring 30 to 40 feet (9 to 12 m) of webbing to replace the rope.

17 TWO TORTOISE ROCK EAST—GROSS MORAL TURTLE-TUDE
I, 5.7, A2, 1 pitch, 200 feet (60 m) ★

First Ascent: Steve "Crusher" Bartlett, Stu Ritchie, Tim Toula, March 13, 2000.

Location and Access: The technical pitch is 25 feet (7.6 m), the tower is 200 feet (61 m) on its longest side. Scramble to the high point below the east side of the

Photo: Eric Bjørnstad

Monticello Rock.

spire and belay at a Metolius bolt and an inscription, PETE IDIART 1929. Climb past a bolt and a drilled angle piton up a gently overhanging face. Tim Toula: "Exit onto potentially shifting dinner plates."

Paraphernalia: A selection of knifeblades and Lost Arrow pitons.

Descent: There are no summit anchors. Rappel/lower about 60 feet (18 m) down the west face.

18 MONTICELLO ROCK—THE FULL MONTICELLO II, 5.7, 2 pitches, 200 feet (60 m) ★★★★

First Ascent: Tim Toula, Stu Ritchie, Steve "Crusher" Bartlett, March 2000.

Location and Access: Steve "Crusher" Bartlett: "Monticello Rock is a truly moderate summit, a rarity for the desert. Great views." Begin on the north side of the rock at an obvious deep chimney.

Pitch 1: Start 150 feet (46 m) right of a brown left-facing dihedral and ascend a chimney, mostly easy, past a bulge near the top, to the prominent shoulder above, 5.7, 90 feet (27 m).

Pitch 2: Scramble up and left (east) to the main summit, 110 feet (34 m). Steve "Crusher" Bartlett: "For more fun, a scramble and a 5.5 move access the southwest summit."

Paraphernalia: Friends (1) #2.5, #3, #4, #5; 200-foot (60 m) ropes important for the descent.

Descent: Downclimb to a pine tree on the northwest side of the rock, then rappel 160 feet (49 m) to the ground. Tim Toula: "Classic overhanging rappel."

MILE MARKER LOG—UTAH 313 TO GEMINI BRIDGES TRAIL

Using the mile marker signs as reference points, this log begins at the junction of US 191 and Utah 313, 9 miles (14.5 km) north of Moab. Although not the shortest approach, it is the quickest to the bridges and the Crackhouse.

21–20: A dirt trail branches left to Heat Wave Wall climbing area. On the right, before the shallow Big Cave Valley, is a brass memorial plaque on the desert-varnished wall above the road. Left of the road are three clusters of Seven Mile Canyon campsites, each with an information kiosk.

15–14: Left (east) of the road is a paved parking area, rest rooms, an information kiosk, and expansive views east to Behind the Rocks southwest of Moab and the La Sal Mountains (snowcapped nine months of the year), and west to the San Rafael Swell. On the right beyond the viewpoint, the dirt Spring Canyon trail begins. This is the route to Kachina Towers, Roadside Fling Tower, and Hell Roaring and Spring Canyons, and the climbs at the Canyon Point area.

11–10: Horsethief Trail branches right. Sign: MINERAL CANYON BOAT RAMP 15 MILES. A second sign informs visitors that a backcountry permit is required for overnight travel in Canyonlands National Park. The trail descends to Green

River, Felony Tower, and the northwest beginning of the White Rim Trail (to Taylor Canyon and Moses and Zeus Towers).

10–9: Sign: GEMINI BRIDGES–6. Turn left on dirt trail.

MILEAGE LOG—BULL CANYON–GEMINI BRIDGES TO SURPRISE OVERLOOK

00 miles: Sign for Bull Canyon (left) and Gemini Bridges (right).

1.4 miles (2.2 km): Cattle guard.

1.5 miles (2.4 km): Sign for Bull Canyon (right); keep straight (the less used trail). The Bull Canyon right spur goes to the bottom of the Gemini Bridges, also a worthwhile venture.

1.7 miles (2.7 km): Right spur to uranium mine and Song of the Canyon Wren climb. Keep straight, down the obvious drainage.

1.8 miles (2.9 km): Walk to the right for a dramatic view into the right fork of Day Canyon.

1.9 miles (3 km): Just before a large sand dune, descend the sandy trail to the drainage on the left.

2.0 miles (3.2 km): Park in the drainage or on top at the large sand dune, then follow the directions below to visit Surprise Overlook. Four-wheel drive may be required to drive back out of the drainage. Walk ahead to see sculptured potholes and the pour-off.

DIVERSIONS

GEMINI BRIDGES

Gemini Bridges are two massive water-carved arches side by side in the north Island-in-the-Sky Mesa west of Moab. A difficult four-wheel-drive trail descends to the bridges, but most visitors park at the top and hike ten minutes down to the impressive spans.

The bridges were discovered by Lin Ottinger in the early 1960s. Lin, longtime owner of the Moab Rock Shop and Ottinger Tours, came to Moab from eastern Tennessee during the uranium boom of the 1950s and 1960s. While exploring the uncharted land west of Moab in his dune buggy, he became the first recorded person to happen upon the bridges. After taking a couple of photos, he made his way back to Moab. It took Lin eight years, searching every year, to find the bridges again. With a maze of mining roads established, the bridges are now a popular destination for four-wheelers and mountain bikers, and are one of the most frequently visited attractions in the Moab area.

The bridges can be reached from the bottom from US 191, or from the top from Utah 313 (Dead Horse Point and Island-in-the-Sky District of Canyonlands National Park road). The approach from the lower entrance could require four-wheel drive. There is an information kiosk at the lower entrance at the junction of the Gemini Bridges Trail and US 191, 8 miles (12.8 km) north of Moab. Two-wheel-drive vehicles with high clearance will have no trouble descending to within a ten-minute hike to the bridges from the upper trail.

To reach Gemini Bridges from the upper or lower trails, follow the Utah 313 to Gemini Bridges Trail Mileage Log on page 101, then the Upper Gemini Bridges to Crackhouse Mileage Log on page 95. For the lower approach, use the Colorado River Bridge to Crackhouse via Lower Gemini Bridges Trail Mileage Log, page 95. For further information visit the BLM office in Moab at 82 East Dogwood Avenue, or phone (435) 259-2100.

SURPRISE OVERLOOK

Surprise Overlook is a sudden and unexpected view into the north fork of Day Canyon. Follow the Colorado River Bridge to Crackhouse via Lower Gemini Bridges Trail Mileage Log, page 95. At 12.7 miles (20.4 km) on the log, take the left spur to Bull Canyon. At the next Bull Canyon sign and trail, keep straight; do not take the signed Bull Canyon spur. Continue to a large sand dune (end of trail) and park. Walk down to the drainage/pour-off ahead on the left. While standing at the edge of the pour-off, look down the narrow crack a few feet back from the rim to see daylight. Hike up (right) and around the point toward Day Canyon, then look back at the pour-off to discover you were standing on a very thin bridge—the surprise!

KACHINA TOWERS

The Kachina Towers are at the upper drainage of Hell Roaring Canyon. Although less than 20 air miles from Moab, the Kachinas are remote, and by any approach difficult to reach, demanding complicated route finding into Hell Roaring Canyon, then a multiple-pitch climb to reach the base of the towers.

Hell Roaring Canyon was named by Major John Wesley Powell when he came upon it in flood stage during the first descent of the Green and Colorado Rivers in 1869.

From Moab, drive 9 miles (14.5 km) north on US 191. Turn left (west) on Utah 313 at a sign for Island-in-the-Sky District and Dead Horse Point State Park. Drive 8.5 miles (13.6 km) to an unmarked dirt trail branching right (west) between mile markers 14 and 15. (A few yards before the trail, on the east side of Utah 313, is a paved parking area with rest rooms and a BLM information kiosk.) Drive west on the dirt Spring Canyon trail. At 1.5 miles (2.4 km) there is a spur to the right with a sign for Dubinky Well (right) and Spring Canyon Bottom (left). Keep left, continue 2.2 miles (3.5 km), and cross a cattle guard with a wire fence extending left and right. Just past the cattle guard, make a left turn down a dirt trail that parallels the fence on its west side. Continue 0.2 mile (0.3 km) and park at the eastern extension of Hell Roaring Canyon, a great place to camp. The Kachina Towers are in view ahead across the canyon, but they blend in with the background walls and are difficult to distinguish.

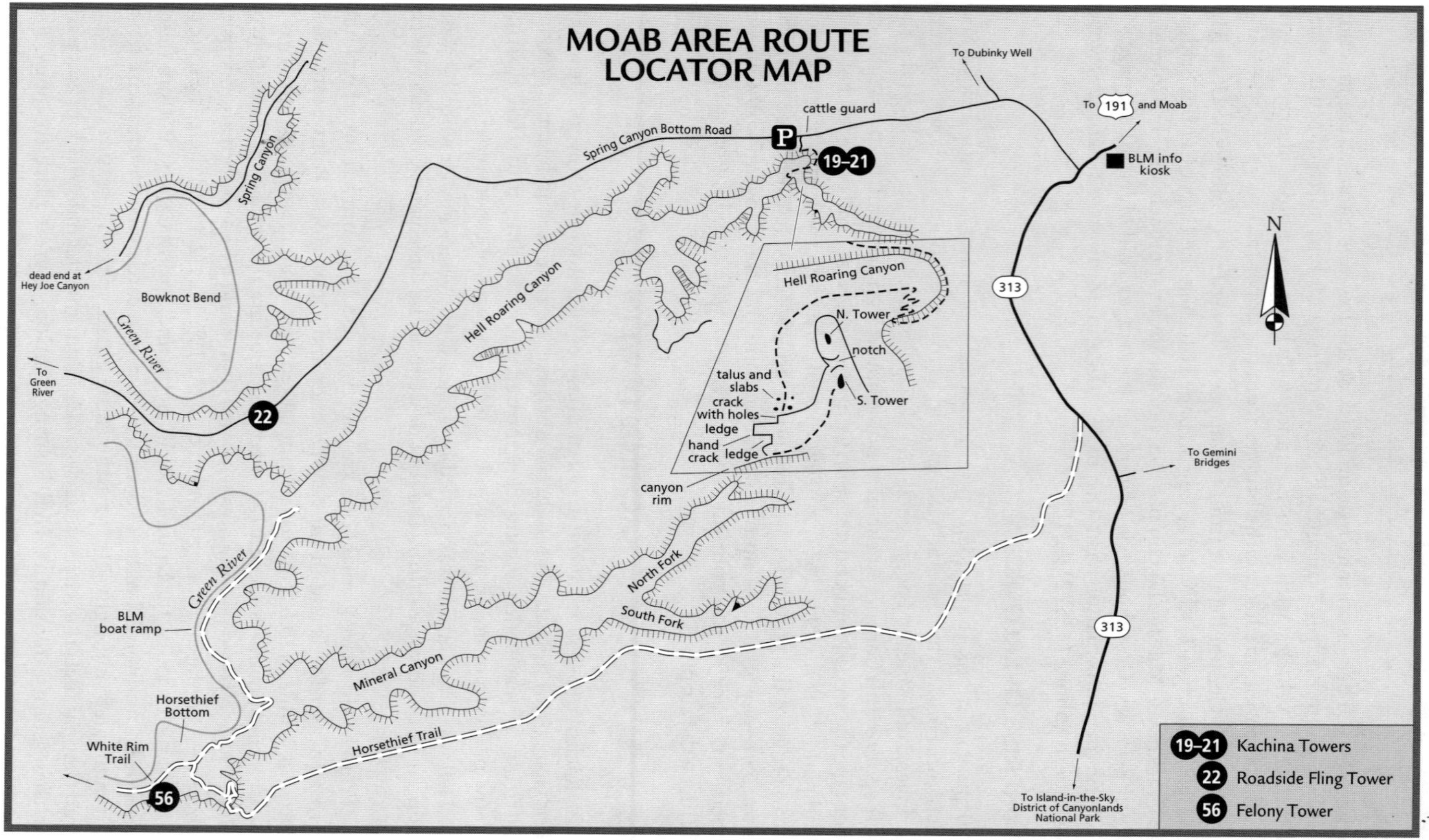
MOAB AREA ROUTE
LOCATOR MAP
To Dubinky Well
To 191 and Moab
BLM info kiosk
cattle guard
Spring Canyon Bottom Road
19–21
Spring Canyon
dead end at Hey Joe Canyon
Bowknot Bend
Green River
To Green River
22
Hell Roaring Canyon
Hell Roaring Canyon
N. Tower
notch
S. Tower
talus and slabs
crack with holes
ledge
hand crack
ledge
canyon rim
313
313
To Gemini Bridges
North Fork
South Fork
Mineral Canyon
Green River
BLM boat ramp
Horsethief Bottom
White Rim Trail
56
Horsethief Trail
To Island-in-the-Sky District of Canyonlands National Park
N
19–21 Kachina Towers
22 Roadside Fling Tower
56 Felony Tower

To reach the towers from the parking area, go around the wire fence where it ends at a drop-off into Hell Roaring Canyon. Contour around the rim of the canyon to its farthest southwest point, keeping on slickrock or in drainages to avoid trampling the fragile cryptobiotic topsoil. The Kachina Towers will be dominant in the skyline ahead across the canyon. Drop down two easy steps. The second step drops approximately 20 vertical feet (6 m), but there are stances and good handholds. Follow a narrow catwalk that requires hands, knees, and belly crawling down a ramp with overhanging rock above and a drop-off below. At the end of the ramp, route finding will be required to locate the easy traverse back and forth on ledges to complete the descent into the canyon. After reaching the canyon, hike cross-country to the right side of the Kachina Towers, obvious high on the rim above (south side of Hell Roaring Canyon). Paul Ross: "The approach alone is worth the trip."

19 KACHINA TOWER NORTH
III, 5.8, A0, 5 pitches, 380 feet (116 m) ★★★★★

First Ascent: Paul Ross, Paul Gardner, October 16, 1999.

Location and Access: From the descent into Hell Roaring Canyon, walk down-canyon past the Kachina Towers obvious in the skyline above. Approximately 500 yards (457 m) right of the towers, ascend a wash leading up slabs and rubble to a weakness in the left canyon wall. Locate a crack with holes that after 20 feet (6 m) turns into a ledge leading to the right.

Photo: Paul Ross

North and South Kachina Towers.

Pitch 1: Climb the crack, then traverse right along a ledge to beneath an obvious short hand crack and belay from a tree, 5.5, 100 feet (30 m).

Pitch 2: Continue up a hand crack to a ledge and traverse left to a bowl, 5.6, 100 feet (30 m).

Pitch 3: Exit the bowl on the right with delicate moves up and left to the rim, 50 feet (15 m). Follow the ridge to the left and down to the left side of the tower to an obvious off-width crack.

Pitch 4: Climb the off-width (5.7) to the north base of the tower.

Pitch 5: Follow five drilled anchors to the summit (tie-offs are essential), 5.8, A0, 80 feet (24 m).

Paraphernalia: Friends (1) set; selection of stoppers; tie-offs; three 200-foot (60 m) ropes to be left anchored to trees on the approach to the base of the tower.

Descent: Rappel from double anchors atop the tower, then retrace the approach across the canyon floor and reverse the descent into the canyon.

20 KACHINA TOWER SOUTH
III, 5.9, C1, 5 pitches, 100 feet (30 m) ★★★

First Ascent: Paul Ross, Andy Ross, May 1, 2000.

Location and Access: Approach as for Kachina Tower North. At the start of pitch 4, which climbs the South Tower, make an awkward traverse on the left or climb a 5.7 off-width on the South Tower pitch and descend the other side. Both reach the rappel slings on the south side of the notch between the towers. The awkward moves across the gap lead to two bolts, then up to a ledge and a single anchor (for the rappel back to the notch on the return). Climb the north side of the tower past about seven bolts, using Friend placements to the "excellent" summit, 100 feet (30 m).

Paraphernalia: Friends (1) set #2 through #5; quick draws, tie-offs (4); etriers.

Descent: Rappel the tower to the platform, 100 feet (30 m). From the platform make a short rappel into the notch between the North and South Towers. Make a 180-foot (55 m) rappel to the east, or do the rappel in two sections if not climbing with 200-foot (60 m) ropes.

21 KACHINA TOWER SOUTH—BEYOND THE 80TH MERIDIAN
5.7, A1, C1, 4 pitches, 230 feet (70 m) ★★★

First Ascent: Smith Maddrey, Wells Campbell, April 1–2, 2000.

Location and Access: Approach as for the north tower. Circle around the buttress system that jutts into the main canyon and watch for an obvious low-angle slab between the two towers leading to a large bowl. Above will be two soaring vertical crack systems leading up between the two towers. *Beyond the 80th Meridian* climbs the good-looking right-facing dihedral, which is the left of the two cracks (the right one turns to off-width).

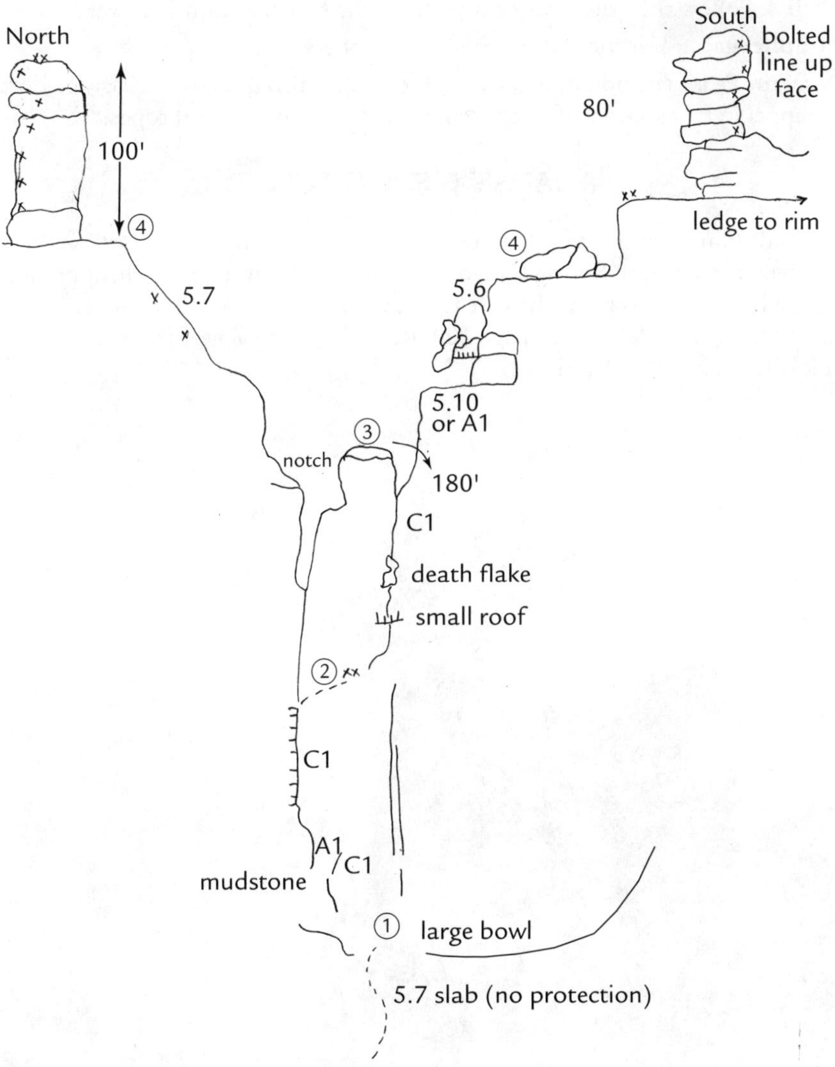

KACHINA TOWER NOTCH—
BEYOND THE 80TH MERIDIAN

Pitch 1: Ascend a 5.7 slab to a large bowl and belay.

Pitch 2: Begin up the mudstone (A1/C1) of the left crack and climb to a right-facing dihedral (protect with #00 TCUs). Move right at the top of the dihedral and belay from double anchors.

Pitch 3: Pass a small roof, then a loose death flake, and continue C1 to the notch between the two towers. Belay from the top of a small pedestal.

Pitch 4: Follow the original ascent pitch to the North or South Towers.

Paraphernalia: Selection of Friends and stoppers.

Descent: From the notch, make a 180-foot (55 m) rappel to the east, or do the rappel in two sections if not climbing with 200-foot (60 m) ropes.

ROADSIDE FLING TOWER

Roadside Fling Tower is at the left edge of the Spring Canyon trail just as it begins the steep descent into Spring Canyon and the Green River. To reach, approach as for the Kachina Towers. At the wire fence, follow the Utah 313 to Green River via Spring Canyon Mileage Log, page 109. Roadside Fling Tower is on the left, 11.3 miles (18.2 km) from Utah 313.

Photo: Andy Roberts

Roadside Fling Tower: The Things We Do for Love.

MILEAGE LOG—UTAH 313 TO GREEN RIVER VIA SPRING CANYON

00 miles: Junction of Utah 313 and Spring Canyon Bottom Road.

3.7 miles (5.9 km): Wire fence and cattle guard. Left turn is the approach to the Kachina Tower.

5.5 miles (8.9 km): Dubinky Wash is crossed.

7.5 miles (12 km): Spur to the right; keep straight.

8.2 miles (13.2 km): Oil tanks on the left.

8.9 miles (14.3 km): Spur to the left; keep straight.

11.0 miles (17.7 km): Spring Canyon.

11.3 miles (18.2 km): Roadside Fling Tower is on the left. The trail descends between the tower and the rimrock wall right of it.

12 miles (19.3 km): Cross the Spring Canyon drainage.

13.6 miles (21.9 km): Major Y intersection. Both branches reach the Green River. The left branch continues 3.6 miles (5.8 km) along the river before ending in a tamarisk thicket. The right branch also follows beside the river and at 0.6 mile (0.9 km), goes through a wire gate with a sign: PLEASE KEEP CLOSED. The trail continues for many miles along the Green, but requires a four-wheel-drive, high-clearance vehicle and possibly road building to continue very far.

22 THE THINGS WE DO FOR LOVE I, A2–C1, 2 pitches, 100 feet (30 m) ★

First Ascent: Andy Roberts, Jason Repko, March 19, 2000.

Location and Access: Begin on the downroad side of the tower.

Pitch 1: Climb C2, then A2 up the left profile of the formation to an obvious belay ledge.

Pitch 2: Continue above, passing a fixed anchor, then a birdbeak hole. Move right and climb C1, passing a fixed anchor to the summit.

Paraphernalia: Friends (1) #1, #1.5, #2, #2.5; Camalots (1) #1, #2, #3, #3.5, (2) #4, (1) #5; TCUs (2) #00 through #2; Lost Arrows (2) fat, medium length; baby angles (2); angles (1) #2; knifeblades (1) short, (1) long; Tri-Cams (1) #0.5 through #3; birdbeaks (2); selection of nuts; shoulder-length runners (6); quick draws (2); ropes (1) 200-foot (60 m) mandatory.

Descent: Rappel to the ground with a 200-foot (60 m) rope from fixed anchors.

DIVERSIONS

BARRIER CANYON–STYLE PICTOGRAPHS

This beautiful and rare art panel is across the Hell Roaring Canyon drainage from the Kachina Towers. Follow the directions for the approach to the Kachina

Photo: Jason Repko

Andy Roberts on The Things We Do for Love, *first ascent, March 2000.*

Towers, then hike downcanyon and watch for the pictographs in the first (giant) alcove reached on the right wall.

OLD CATTLE TRAIL TO THE RIM OF HELL ROARING CANYON

The Old Cattle Trail climbs to the rim of Hell Roaring Canyon. The trail was built by unknown persons who drilled holes in the rock, then pounded lead pipes into the holes. On these supports, they stacked logs, rock, and finally dirt. Although tenuous, it is passable on foot, but no longer with horse or cow.

To reach the trail from the top, drive approximately 2 miles (3.2 km) west on the Spring Canyon 2 two miles beyond the cattle guard turn to the Kachina Towers trailhead. At the obvious Dubinky Wash, park and hike less than a mile down the left side of the wash to Hell Roaring Canyon. The Old Cattle Trail will be easy to spot over the canyon's edge.

To reach the trail from the bottom, hike down Hell Roaring Canyon drainage approximately 2 miles (3.2 km), then up the first canyon on the right (north). It will be about 1 mile (1.6 km) from here up the Old Cattle Trail to Dubinky Wash and the Spring Canyon trail, and another 2 miles (3.2 km) back to the trailhead to the Kachina Towers. A good agenda is to leave one car where the Spring Canyon trail crosses Dubinky Wash. Descend into Hell Roaring Canyon by the Kachina Towers route, then hike downcanyon and up the Old Cattle Trail to the car.

CANYON POINT

Canyon Point is a remote region of the Island-in-the-Sky Mesa, north and west of Moab. Routes are listed left to right on Tombstone and Lost World Buttes. Several landforms in the area with established climbs are noted on the Moab West map, along with the approach trails.

From Moab, drive 9 miles (14.5 km) north on US 191. Turn left (west) on Utah 313 at a sign for Island-in-the-Sky District and Dead Horse Point State Park. Drive 8.5 miles (13.6 km) to an unmarked dirt trail branching right (west) between mile markers 14 and 15. (A few yards before the trail, on the east side of Utah 313, is a paved parking area with rest rooms and a BLM information kiosk.) Drive west on the dirt Spring Canyon trail. At 1.5 miles (2.4 km) there is a spur to the right with a sign for Dubinky Well and Spring Canyon Bottom; take the Dubinky Well Trail. After crossing the second cattle guard (before reaching Dubinky Well—a windmill and bovine watering pond are visible ahead) take the first left (Spring Canyon Point Trail), which will reach Tombstone Butte (a.k.a. High Rise), Cenotaph Spire, then the parking area and access to Dumpy Tower and the climbs on Lost World Butte. It is 9 miles (14.5 km) to the Tombstone from the Spring Canyon Point Trail turnoff. Canyon Point Butte is approximately 0.5 mile (0.8 km) northwest of the Tombstone.

An alternative approach, from Interstate 70 east of Green River, could require four-wheel drive. It was taken by the first ascent team of the Tombstone. Far less direct than the Utah 313 approach, it requires trial-and-error route finding. Take Ranch exit 173, the only exit between Green River and Crescent Junction, and

CANYON POINT (MOAB AREA) ROUTE LOCATOR MAP

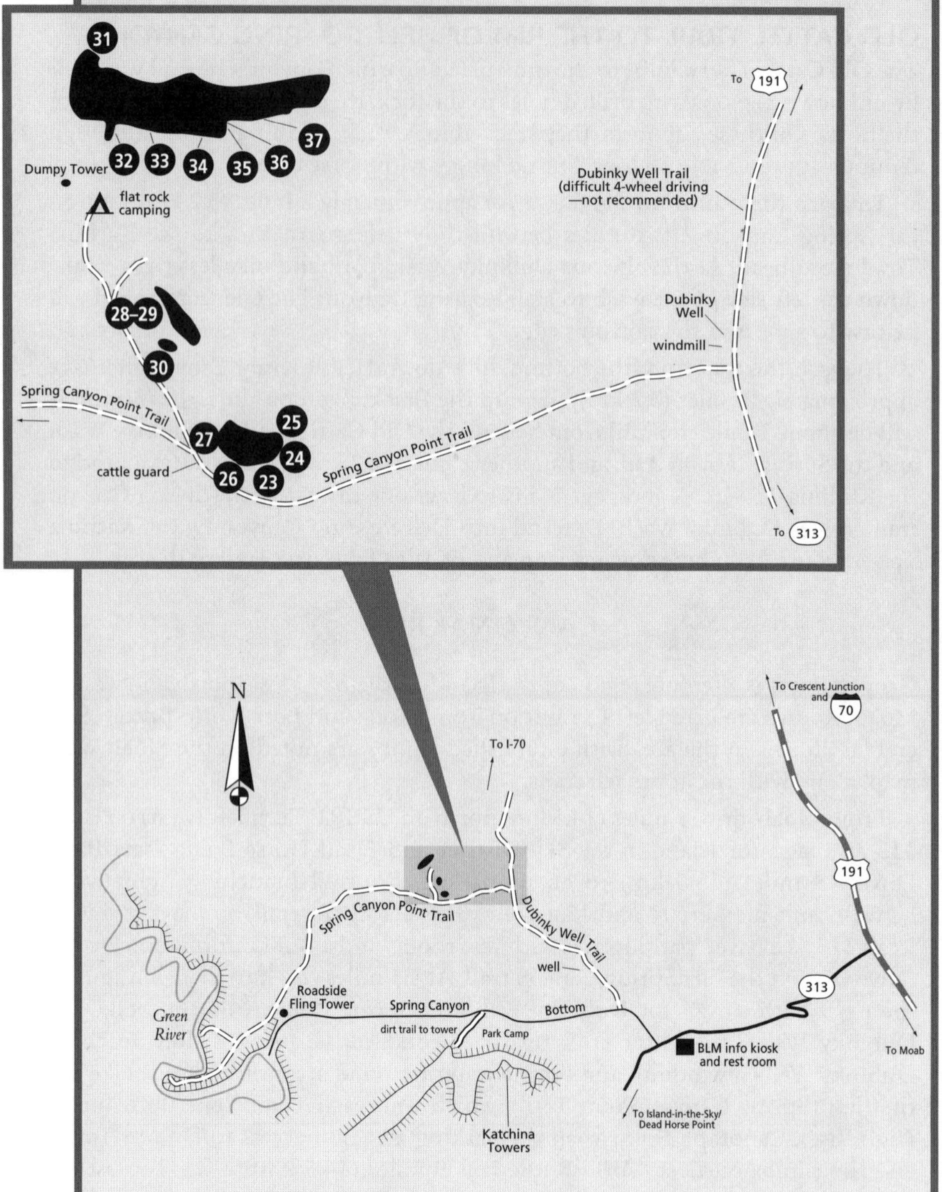

23–27 Tombstone

28–29 Canyon Point Butte

30 Cenotaph Spire

31–37 Lost World Butte

proceed north to Dubinky Well, then follow the directions for the Utah 313 approach.

TOMBSTONE

Keswick Lads Day Out was named for its first ascent team. Both climbers are from the town of Keswick in the English Lake District of Great Britain.

23 KESWICK LADS DAY OUT
III, 5.10, C3, 3 pitches, 280 feet (85 m) ★★★

First Ascent: Paul Ross, Colin Downer, June 1, 2001.

Location and Access: The route is one crack system left of *Family Plot* and climbs an obvious corner on the right-hand side of the east face of the Tombstone.

Pitch 1: Aid past old drilled angle pitons at 30 feet (9 m), a previous attempt by an unidentified party, and gain a 140-foot (42 m) corner. Use Leeper cam hooks and small regular cams to reach three bolts at the top of the corner where the crack closes. Belay from a three-bolt stance, C2, 140 feet (42 m).

Pitch 2: Move left to a crack system that leads to another bolt belay just left of a perfect hand crack, C3, 60 feet (18 m).

Pitch 3: Climb the hand crack to the summit, 5.10, 80 feet (24 m).

Paraphernalia: Friends (2) sets through #4; many TCUs; stoppers (1) set; Leeper cam hooks (2); ropes (2) 200-foot (60 m); etriers.

Descent: Rappel *Epitaph*.

24 FAMILY PLOT
III, 5.9, C1, 3 pitches, 280 feet (85 m) ★★★

First Ascent: Paul Ross, Andy Ross, October 5, 2000.

Location and Access: The route climbs a thin crack system on the northeast side of the tower, about 40 feet (12 m) left of *Epitaph*.

Pitch 1: Begin with a shoulder stand to reach the first bolt, then many small Friends with a few larger sizes are used for aid to a small ledge with belay bolts, 5.9, C1, 100 feet (30 m).

Pitch 2: Continue with Friends of various sizes. Pass a bolt and climb to a large ledge at the beginning of the last pitch of *Epitaph*, 5.7, C1, 100 feet (30 m).

Pitch 3: Follow pitch 3 of *Epitaph* to the summit, fourth class, 80 feet (24 m).

Paraphernalia: Friends, many small, with a few up through #4.

Descent: Rappel *Epitaph*. From the top of pitch 2, two 200-foot (60 m) ropes reach the ground.

25 EPITAPH
III, 5.10+, 3 pitches, 280 feet (85 m)

First Ascent: Brian Smoot, Jonathan Smoot, 1981. Second Ascent: Earl Wiggins, Katy Cassidy, December 20, 1987.

Photo: Paul Ross

Tombstone: 23. Keswick Lads Day Out *24.* Family Plot *25.* Epitaph.

Tombstone: Paul Ross, pitch 1, Keswick Lads Day Out, *first ascent, June 2001.*

Location and Access: The route follows a crack inside an oblique chimney on the extreme north ridge of the butte.

Pitch 1: Begin from a saddle on the north edge of the rock. The saddle can be reached by climbing a sand dune and traversing from the north end of a ledge level with the saddle, or by making a few bouldering moves up 15 feet (4.5 m) of overhanging rock. Climb a hand and fist crack 75 feet (23 m) to a bolt belay, 5.10+.

Pitch 2: Above the belay is an off-width and squeeze chimney that narrows to a hand crack. Ascend past an overhang, then continue to a good ledge with bolts. The lead begins 5.10 at the overhang and is 5.9 in the chimney.

Pitch 3: An 80-foot (24 m) fourth-class pitch leads to the top, which has a 10-foot (3 m) pit filled with sand. There is a cairn but no register left by the first ascent team.

Paraphernalia: Standard desert rack.

Descent: Double-rope rappels down the route.

26 TRES GATOS
II, 5.11, A0, 3 pitches, 370 feet (113 m)

First Ascent: Katy Cassidy, Earl Wiggins, March 13, 1988.

Location and Access: *Tres Gatos* (Three Cats) was the second route established on the Tombstone. The climb is at the far right side of the west face and climbs a shallow left-facing corner leading to a large roof.

Pitch 1: Approach through the Dewey Bridge member of Entrada sandstone, 5.9, 70 feet (21 m), then climb a left-facing corner, 5.11, 150 feet (46 m).

Pitch 2: Continue 20 feet (6 m) to a large roof that is turned on its right side (two points of A0). Climb a steep right-facing corner to a belay ledge on a ridge, 5.9, A0, 100 feet (30 m).

Pitch 3: Face climb to the top, 5.8, 120 feet (37 m).

Paraphernalia: Friends (2) sets through #3 with (1) #3.5, #4; small wires; quick draws.

Descent: Rappel *Epitaph*.

27 COFFIN DODGER
III, 5.10+, C1, 4 pitches, 330 feet (101 m) ★★★

First Ascent: Andy Ross, Paul Ross, October 16, 2000.

Location and Access: The route climbs the north end of the west face approximately 70 feet (21 m) left of *Tres Gatos*. From the ground, the bolt belay of pitch 1 is visible below an obvious chimney at about the 150-foot (46 m) level. Paul Ross: "Coffin dodger is a British slang term for an old guy who is avoiding death."

Pitch 1: Begin up the crack directly below a chimney to below an overhanging crack and right-facing corner, 90 feet (27 m). This is an optional belay point. Continue up a good-quality crack to a ledge below a chimney and a two-bolt belay, 5.10, C1, 150 feet (46 m).

Photo: Paul Ross

Tombstone: 27. Coffin Dodger *26.* Tres Gatos.

Pitch 2: Climb a strenuous chimney (passing three bolts) to a 4-inch (10 cm) crack in a corner and a roof. Pull the roof, then pass four bolts, moving right, up a light-colored cone to a natural belay at its top, 5.10+, C1, 80 feet (24 m).

Pitch 3: Climb the 4-inch (10 cm) crack to a wide chimney. Walk to the back of the chimney to the north side of the buttress and belay below a wide, overhanging undercling crack, 5.10, C1, 50 feet (15 m).

Pitch 4: Ascend the undercling crack, then the corner above to the summit, 5.10, C1, 50 feet (15 m).

Paraphernalia: Friends (2) sets through #6 with extra #3, #3.5; large stoppers.

Descent: Two double-rope rappels down the route.

CANYON POINT BUTTE

Canyon Point Butte is obvious 0.5 mile (0.8 km) northwest of the Tombstone.

28 REST IN PEACE
I, 5.10a, 1 pitch, 70 feet (21 m)

First Ascent: Dave Medara, Bob Novellino, Jorma Hayes, Bret Sutteer, May 1995.

Location and Access: The route climbs an obvious crack system at the northwest end of Canyon Point Butte at a location approximately 120 feet (37 m) left of *Shallow Burial*. Ascend hands to fist, reaching rappel anchors not easily seen from below.

Paraphernalia: Standard desert rack.

Descent: Rappel the route.

29 SHALLOW BURIAL
I, 5.10d, 1 pitch, 70 feet (21 m)

First Ascent: Dave Medara, Bob Novellino, Jorma Hayes, Brett Sutteer, May 1995.

Location and Access: The route is just left of the obvious Cenotaph Spire on the west face of Canyon Point Butte at a location approximately 120 feet (37 m) right of *Rest In Peace*. Climb thin fingers to hands to off-width. Rappel anchors are visible from below the route.

Paraphernalia: Standard desert rack.

Descent: Rappel the route.

CENOTAPH SPIRE

Cenotaph Spire is a satellite tower on the south side of a small mesa 0.3 mile (0.48 km) north of the Tombstone. To reach it, continue on the dirt trail north of the Tombstone where Cenotaph Spire will be in view, then walk across sand dunes to

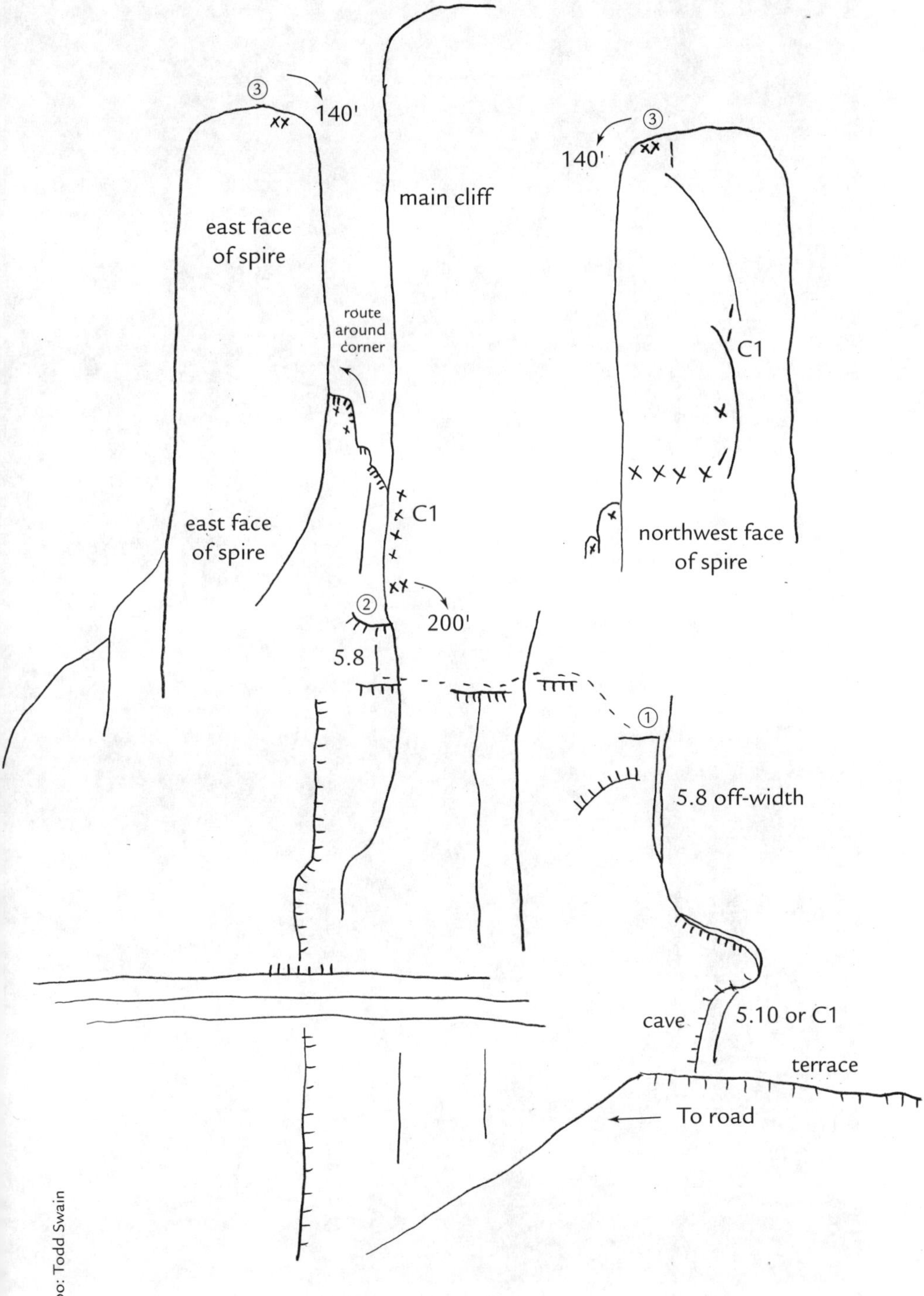
③
140'
main cliff
east face
of spire
③
140'
route
around
corner
C1
C1
east face
of spire
northwest face
of spire
②
200'
5.8
①
5.8 off-width
cave
5.10 or C1
terrace
To road
Topo: Todd Swain

CENOTAPH SPIRE

Photo: Donette Swain

Paul Ross on summit of Cenotaph Spire, first ascent, September 2000.

the right (south) side of the spire. Continue up a talus and dirt slope to a terrace at the base of the main wall right of the spire. A cenotaph, according to Webster's, is "a tomb or a monument erected in honor of a person or group of persons whose remains are elsewhere."

30 CENOTAPH SPIRE
III, 5.8, C1, 3 pitches, 340 feet (104 m) ★★★

First Ascent: Paul Ross, Todd Swain, Paul Gardner, September 28, 2000.

Location and Access: Begin at a cavelike area on the left edge of the terrace that runs along the base of the wall of the mesa.

Pitch 1: Climb with aid out a short crack in the cave to a sloping ledge. Continue up the off-width above to a belay stance on a ledge, 5.8, C1 (or 5.10), 90 feet (27 m).

Pitch 2: Traverse left (south) across ledges, then climb a sandy crack (5.8) to drilled anchors 30 feet (9 m) below the notch formed between the spire and the mesa behind (easy at first, then more difficult), 5.8, 110 feet (34 m).

Pitch 3: Climb with aid up four bolts left of loose, sugary white rock, then step left to a notch. Climb past two ledges, passing two bolts, then aid right around a corner on bolts to gain a crack/corner system on the northwest face of the spire. Free and aid climb the crack/corner system to the top, 5.7, C1, 140 feet (43 m). **NOTE:** The pitch may be split into two where the northwest face crack begins.

Paraphernalia: Friends #0 through #4; rivet hangers; small adjustable wrench useful; many long slings; 200-foot (60 m) ropes.

Descent: Rappel 140 feet (43 m) to the top of pitch 2, then 200 feet (60 m) to the ground.

LOST WORLD BUTTE

Lost World Butte is approximately 1.5 miles (2.4 km) north of the Tombstone. From Tombstone Butte, take the second right trail, then continue straight until it is possible to park at a flat rock just before Dumpy Tower. The hike to Lost World Butte is obvious ahead.

31 GOLDEN BROWN
II, 5.10, C1, 2 pitches, 170 feet (52 m) ★★★★

First Ascent: Andy Ross, Paul Ross, October 18, 2000.

Location and Access: Paul Ross: "Walk to the left end of the butte and look for an obvious brown splitter crack about 150 feet (46 m) up. This is the second pitch. The first pitch starts directly below, up a left-facing thin corner/crack."

Pitch 1: Climb a few feet up a thin crack behind a large block to a ledge, then up a corner, passing a bolt to a thin hand crack. Pass another bolt, then move left

Photo: Paul Ross

Lost World Butte: 31. Golden Brown *32.* If *33.* Road Not Taken *34.* Mirage Crack *35.* Paradise Lost *36.* Gateway to the Lost World *37.* Pearly Gates.

to a ledge. Finish up a chimney to double belay bolts, 5.10, C1, 100 feet (30 m). Ross: "The pitch was followed free at 5.12a."

Pitch 2: Move left up thin cracks to a roof. Pull the roof and jam a "beautiful" hand crack in a headwall to a double-bolt belay, 5.10, C1, 70 feet (21 m). Ross: "The pitch was followed at 5.11c with four points of aid."

Paraphernalia: Friends (2) sets #0 through #3.5 with extra #2, #2.5, #3, #5.

Descent: Rappel the route from fixed anchors.

32 IF
III, 5.9, C3, 3 pitches, 260 feet (79 m) ★★★★

First Ascent: Paul Ross, Layne Potter, November 16, 2001.

Location and Access: The route is approximately 600 feet (182 m) left of *Road Not Taken*. From the flat rock parking area, walk north directly to the butte. Paul Ross: "Walk to the small fat tower. Behind this the first ascent party fourth-classed up two short chimneys dragging a rope. When the ledge and slabs below the cliff proper are reached, traverse the ledges to the right for about 200 feet to the base of the impressive corner crack of the first pitch. The rope was anchored here, and gear and rest of party jumared directly from the ground. The route has excellent situations. Great views (as good as the view

Photo: Paul Ross

Lost World Butte—Golden Brown.

from Cleopatra's Chair) from the summit of the butte. Register on the west summit, about a ten-minute hike from the top of the route." Linear length of the route is approximately 300 feet (91m). The route is named after a poem by Rudyard Kipling.

Pitch 1: Begin with TCUs up an obvious crack, then up to #6 Friends to surmount the roof and on to a belay station, 5.9, C3, 100 feet (30 m).

Pitch 2: Continue up a wide crack with #3.5 through #4 Friends. Climb an overhanging crack to a good ledge and bolt belay, C2, 80 feet (24 m).

Pitch 3: A short bolt ladder leads up and right to reach a traverse line of slabs and pockets. Traverse approximately 40 feet (12 m) to a groove (some protection from camming units, one drilled angle piton, and one bolt). When an overhanging crack is reached just below the top, wiggle through a tight hole to the summit. Anchors for the belay and rappel are 60 feet (18 m) to the east (right), 5.7, C1, 120 feet (37 m).

Paraphernalia: Standard desert rack (2) with extra Friends #3.5 through #4, (2) #5, #6; wire hangers (4).

Descent: Rappel anchors are directly above the pitch 3 belay. Make one single-rope rappel to the chimney belay, then one double-rope rappel to a ledge at the start of pitch 1. More anchors for a final rappel are 50 feet (15 m) to the east.

33 ROAD NOT TAKEN
III, 5.10 (or 5.8, A1), 5 pitches, 300 feet (91 m) ★★★★★

First Ascent: Jeff Pheasant, Paul Ross, Layne Potter, October 11, 2001.

Location and Access: As one reaches the butte, the route is the very obvious system of ramps on the east face. The climb begins directly below the central spikey blocks in view midway up the ramp. The route is named after a Robert Frost poem. Linear length of the route is 520 feet (158 m).

Pitch 1: Traverse right across a flake to a short hand crack that leads to a long pebble-filled ledge and block belay at a bedding seam, 5.7, 60 feet (18 m).

Pitch 2: Traverse the bedding seam ledge left approximately 300 feet (91 m) to a two-bolt belay at the start of a massive right-diagonalling ramp. Belay from double bolts.

Pitch 3: Follow the ramp. At 20 feet (6 m) make 5.7 moves through a wide crack, which brings you to an easy scramble to a 5.6 step-down and a good ledge and two-bolt belay/rappel anchors, 190 feet (58 m).

Pitch 4: Climb up and through a 5.8 squeeze chimney and belay behind large blocks, 85 feet (26 m).

Pitch 5: Paul Ross: "A superb and unusual pitch, 'the ghoulie basher crack.'" Continue (5.7) to the final 20 feet (6 m), which is a 5.10 lieback into an off-width. The last part can be aided using two #6 Friends.

Paraphernalia: Friends with large units; webbing; 200-foot (60 m) ropes.

Descent: From the ledge just above the final belay, walk 300 feet (91 m) left to rappel anchors. Paul Ross: "It is essential that the first person to rappel takes ascenders and knots the ends of the rope, as one does not touch rock until about 40 feet (12 m) below rappel anchors." Swing in to double-bolt anchors and make a second rappel to the ground, or walk right, along the butte to the rappel anchors on *Pearly Gates*.

34 MIRAGE CRACK
I, 5.11+, 2 pitchs, 160 feet (49 m) ★★★★

First Ascent: Pitch 1, Andy Ross, Paul Ross, October 4, 2000. Pitch 2, Matt Lisenby, 2001.

Location and Access: The route can be seen from the flat rock parking/camping area, and is located right of *Road Not Taken*, left of *Gateway to the Lost World* (not in view from parking area). Paul Ross: "This crack is close to 300 feet [91 m] long and will in the near future be climbed in its entirety. The pitch 1 party stopped at 60 feet [18 m] and placed an anchor. Above, the crack widens to 4 inches [10 cm] and continues to widen to the summit—a magnificent project."

Paraphernalia: Friends (1) set.

Descent: Rappel the route.

35 PARADISE LOST (a.k.a. Kripling Groove)
IV, 5.7, C2, 4 pitches, 320 feet (98 m) ★★★★

First Ascent: Paul Ross, Layne Potter, October 20, 2001. To pitch 2, Jeff Pheasant, October 13, 2001.

Location and Access: The route follows a very steep and sometimes overhanging groove/crack system up the prominent buttress between *Mirage Crack* and *Gateway to the Lost World*. Paul Ross: "Kripling Groove is a pun on a famous English Lake District climb named Kripling Groove. On the first attempt on *Paradise Lost* on the 13th of October when the peyote moon was prominent, I took a fall near the top of the first pitch, tearing a muscle in his leg. At the start of the second pitch, Pheasant took a fall, hitting his foot on the descent and fracturing his heel bone, and was last seen hopping with his foot in plaster back to Hawaii. I took a week off to recuperate and returned with Layne Potter to complete the climb."

Pitch 1: Climb a corner crack to a two-bolt belay, C2, 110 feet (34 m).

Pitch 2: Follow a sandy crack until a move right to a ledge. Climb free past large blocks to a two-bolt belay below a good-looking 3.5-inch (8.9 cm) overhanging crack, 5.7, C1, 60 feet (18 m).

Pitch 3: Follow the overhanging crack, leap frogging #3 through #3.5 Friends to a two-bolt belay below a right-leaning overhanging flake, 5.7, C2, 90 feet (27 m).

Pitch 4: With large cams climb the flake and finish up a wide chimney to the top, 5.6, C1, 60 feet (18 m).

Paraphernalia: Friends, many #0.5 through #2 for pitch 1, (3) #3 through #3.5 for pitch 2; standard desert rack including (2) #5 and (1) #6; a few medium stoppers.

Photo: Paul Ross

Lost World Butte—Andy Ross climbing Mirage Crack.

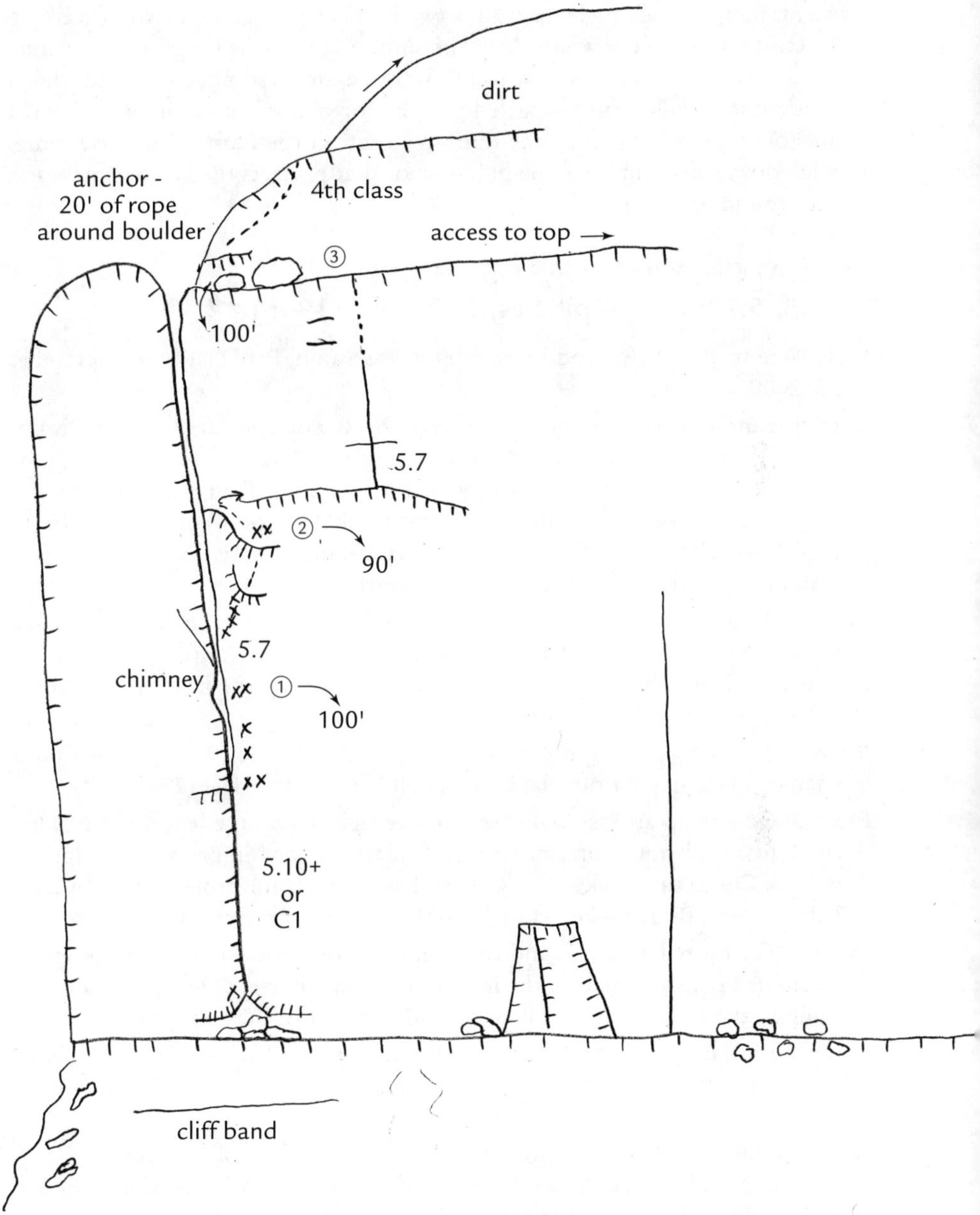

Topo: Todd Swain

LOST WORLD BUTTE—GATEWAY TO THE LOST WORLD

Descent: Rappel to a long ledge from a two-bolt belay station located by walking 100 feet (30 m) to the west side of the summit. From the long ledge continue the descent from *Gateway to the Lost World.* An easier descent can be made down *Pearly Gates.* Follow the long ledge right for about ten minutes to rappel anchors that bring you to the midway point on the *Pearly Gates* easy ramp. Walk down the ramp to a one-bolt anchor that protects the last few moves to the ground.

36 GATEWAY TO THE LOST WORLD
III, 5.10+, C1, 4 pitches, 390 feet (119 m) ★★★★

First Ascent: Paul Ross, Todd Swain, Donette Swain, Paul Gardner, September 26, 2000.

Location and Access: The route is just right of *Paradise Lost,* faces east, and is not in view from the flat rocks parking/camping area. Hike left to right along the butte. If a long ramp is reached, you have gone too far right. Todd Swain: "Begin below a beautiful corner to an anchor 80 feet (24 m) up (C1 or 5.10+)." Paul Ross: "The top of the butte is very beautiful and the views are outstanding. It is truly a journey into a lost world."

Pitch 1: Use #0.5 to #4 Friends to climb free and on aid to bolt anchors. The crack in the corner goes from 1 to 3 inches (2.5 to 7.6 cm). Continue up an overhanging off-width, passing two bolts to an anchor at the base of a chimney, 5.8, C1 (or 5.10+), 100 feet (30 m).

Pitch 2: Climbing an unprotected chimney (5.7) 30 feet (9 m) to four bolts enables an escape right to slabs and a bolt belay, 5.8, 90 feet (27 m).

Pitch 3: Go left up an easy flake, then move right to a large ledge and traverse right to an obvious intermittent vertical crack that improves as height is gained. Climb the crack (5.7, TCUs and small cams for protection) to a large ledge system. Belay on large blocks to the left, 5.8, 200 feet (60 m).

Pitch 4: The butte has a west and east summit. To gain the two summits, either scramble up a short slab to the left, fourth class, 40 feet (12 m), or follow the ramp to the right, which leads to the saddle between the two summits.

Paraphernalia: Friends #0.5 through #4 with many #2, #2.5, #3; TCUs; webbing, 20-plus feet (6 m), for the summit rappel from a large boulder; 200-foot (60 m) ropes.

Descent: Rappel 100 feet (30 m) to the top of pitch 2 from slings around a large summit boulder, then 90 feet (27 m) to the top of pitch 1. The final rappel is 100 feet (30 m) to the ground.

37 PEARLY GATES
I, 5.5, C1, 3 pitches, 250 feet (76 m) ★★★

First Ascent: Paul Ross, Jeff Pheasant, June 9, 2001.

Location and Access: The route climbs the obvious, easy-looking, right-slanting ramp. Paul Ross: "One of the easiest climbs in the desert, it takes you onto the

Photo: Paul Ross

Lost World Butte—Pearly Gates.

top of a beautiful butte with excellent views. The last pitch gives some real exposure!"

Pitch 1: Begin up the ramp, passing a 5.4 section at about 25 feet (7.6 m) to a cam belay below two large cracks, 140 feet (42 m).

Pitch 2: Continue with easy climbing between the cracks to a good ledge and a cam belay, 5.5, 60 feet (18 m).

Pitch 3: Follow six bolts over a headwall to a bolt belay, 50 feet (15 m). Walk right to the east summit and scramble to the top, C1.

Paraphernalia: Friends (2) #2.5, (1) #3; wire rivet hangers (3); ropes (2) 200-foot (60 m).

Descent: Rappel from a station approximately 80 feet (24 m) left of the top belay anchors (top of pitch 3). Make one 130-foot (40 m) rappel to the ramp, then descend the ramp to the ground.

BIRD'S VIEW BUTTE (A.K.A. BIRD'S EYE BUTTE)

Bird's View Butte is the southernmost landform dividing the Middle and East Forks of Shafer Canyon, which drains south from the extreme northeast corner of Canyonlands National Park and ends at a pour-off into the Colorado River at the Goose Neck below Dead Horse Point State Park. The massive butte can also be identified as the tower immediately south of the twin Crow's Head Spires.

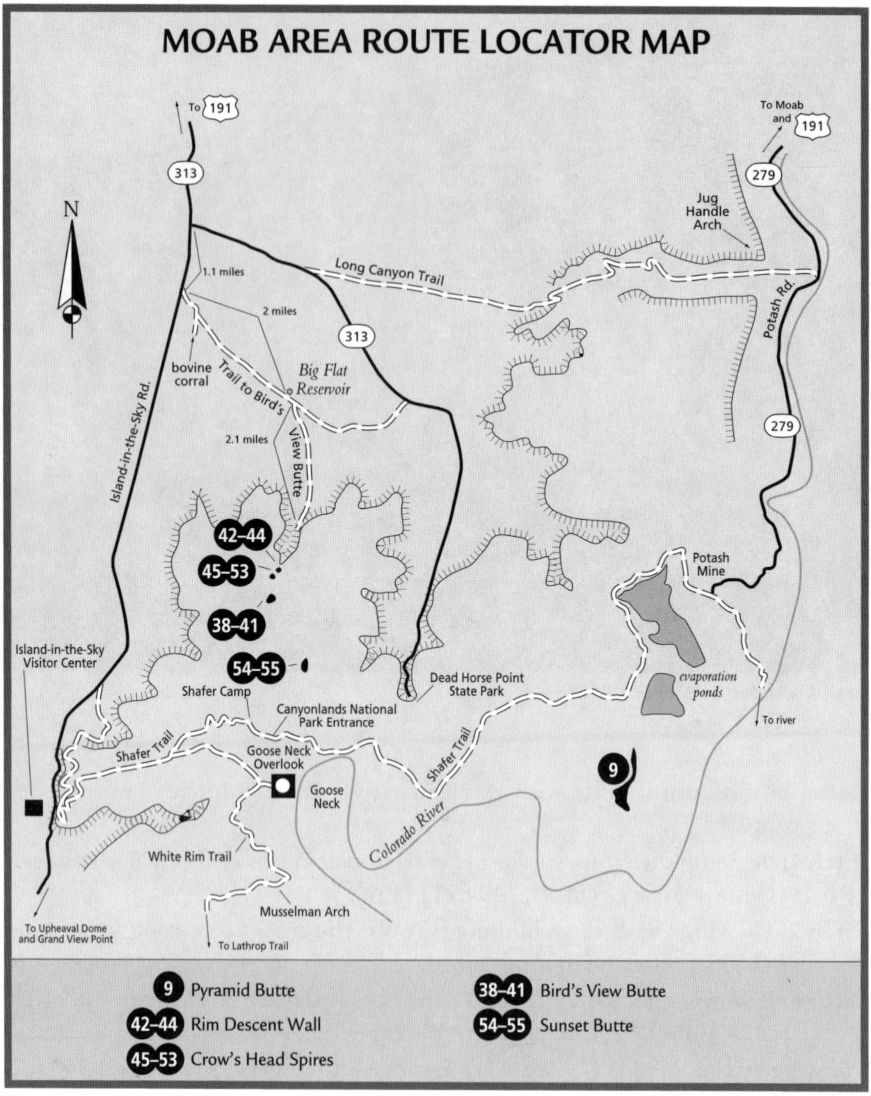

Crow's Head Spires and Bird's View Butte sit squarely on the Canyonlands National Park boundary line.

From the intersection of Utah 313 (east) and the Island-in-the-Sky Road (south), drive 1.1 miles (1.7 km) on the Island-in-the-Sky Road and turn left (east). This is the first dirt trail branching east as you drive south from the junction of the Dead Horse Point Road (Utah 313) and Island-in-the-Sky Road. Continue 4.1 miles (6.6 km), following the Island-in-the-Sky Road to Bird's View Butte and Crow's Head Spires Mileage Log.

MILEAGE LOG—ISLAND-IN-THE-SKY ROAD TO BIRD'S VIEW BUTTE AND CROW'S HEAD SPIRES

00 miles: Begin Bird's View Butte trail from Island-in-the-Sky Road.

0.4 mile (0.6 km): A right fork goes to a bovine corral visible to the south; continue straight.

2.0 miles (3.2 km): Big Flat Reservoir, a watering pond for cattle on the left; a fork in the trail to the right. (Several other forks straight ahead end at the fenced Dead Horse Point State Park boundary. Left forks will eventually come out onto Utah 313 before the park boundary is reached.) Take the right fork and continue on the most used trail, which becomes rocky and requires a high-clearance vehicle.

4.1 miles (6.6 km): The trail reaches the mesa's south edge at a dramatically exposed isthmus projecting south between the walls of the Middle and East Forks of the Shafer Canyon drainage. There is good camping in a spectacular setting. Please use existing fire rings.

Photo: Eric Bjørnstad

A. Bird's View Butte B. Don Juan Spire C. The Notch D. Luminous Being Spire.

MILEAGE LOG—POTASH ROAD TO SHAFER TRAIL

This alternative route to Bird's View Butte is longer, but it's a highly recommended scenic approach. The junction of US 191 and Potash Road (Scenic Byway 279) is 1.3 miles (2 km) north of the bridge over the Colorado River (north of Moab), or 1 mile (1.6 km) south of the entrance to Arches National Park. For information on climbing routes established along this route, see *Desert Rock II: Wall Street to the San Rafael Swell.*

SCENIC SIDE TRIP (NOT ON MAP)

On Island-in-the-Sky Road, 2.5 miles (4 km) south from the turn onto the Bird's View Butte trail, a dirt trail branches left (east). At 0.1 mile (0.16 km) take the right branch and drive 0.2 mile (0.32 km). There you'll find a good view to the southeast of Bird's View Butte and its Satellite Spire, a slender detached pinnacle located between the butte's northernmost projection and the *Unemployment Line* route on its east face. This is the only viewing area where you can see light between the detached pinnacle and the butte.

00 miles: Intersection of US 191 and Potash Road; go south on Potash Road.

2.7 miles (4.3 km): The Portal, where the Colorado River passes into the canyons from Moab Valley. High on the walls across the river are rounded domes of Navajo sandstone and a massive anticline where the strata tips sharply upward. In less than a mile the upper Navajo is at river level, and a short distance beyond, the Wall Street climbing area begins.

3.9 miles (6.2 km): Jaycee Campground, with rest rooms, tables, and campfire rings. A $5.00 nightly fee is charged for overnight stays. If not camping in a developed campground, you must carry a portable toilet system or be subject to a $50 fine. There is a sign at the campground for Portal Overlook and Poison Spider Mesa. A hiking trail leads to the top of the rimrock and is highly recommended for its views of Arches National Park, Moab Valley, and the land east and west of the Colorado River.

4.2 miles (6.7 km): Wall Street begins at a sign: PARK ONLY IN DESIGNATED AREAS. In the next 0.5 mile (0.8 km), there are 114 established crag routes, ranging in difficulty from 5.8 to 5.12+.

4.7 miles (7.5 km): Wall Street ends at one of the largest and best-preserved panels of petroglyphs in the Moab area. With the building of the road to the Potash Mine, several rock slopes extending to the river were cut away. As a result, a 100-foot (30 m)-long Fremont and Anasazi petroglyph panel is preserved high out of reach and free from mutilation or graffiti. Beyond, several spectacular canyons drain into the river from the right (west) as you continue downriver to the Potash Mine.

10.1 miles (16.2 km): Culvert Canyon is a popular hike with locals. About ten minutes up the drainage, a pool of water, a large cave/alcove, and lush growth are encountered year-round. On boulders on the right, upslope at the beginning of the canyon, there are canvases of Anasazi rock art.

11.3 miles (18.1 km): Day Canyon, approximately 3 miles (4.8 km) long and the home of a number of climbs. At its entrance there is a pedestrian gate (cows don't fit) and a sign: RROPERTY OF RRCO, NO TRESPASSING. The canyon is managed by the BLM, and access is not prohibited. If hiking the canyon, it is important to keep far left to avoid difficult bushwhacking. Approximately 0.5 mile (0.8 km) upcanyon, an old uranium mining road is reached and hiking becomes easier. On the left at the head of Day Canyon, an old cow trail climbs to the rimrock above.

15.0 miles (24.1 km): Long Canyon is the only drainage along the Potash Road that has a dirt trail up it, located right (west) 500 feet (152 m) beyond the signed Jug Handle Arch view pulloff. The canyon road climbs dramatically to the top of the 6,000-foot-high (1,828 m) Island-in-the-Sky Mesa, and will require high clearance and, in some seasons, a four-wheel-drive vehicle. Near the top of the grade, a large wedge of rock fell during the winter of 1995–96. Maintenance crews tunneled the road under the slide rather than blasting it away and chancing more rock fall.

POTASH ROAD AND MINE

The 16-mile (26 km)-long road to the Potash Mine was built in 1960 to service the plant at the site of the largest deposit of potash in North America. In 1964 an underground gas explosion at the mine killed eighteen people. Shortly after the disaster, the plant converted to "solution" mining, in which 480 gallons of water per minute are pumped from the Colorado River into the mine's 340 miles (547 km) of shafts and drifts, ranging in depth from 2,000 to 3,000 feet (610 to 914 m). After about a year, the water (now a solute of potash and salts) is pumped out of the mine and into one of twenty-three settling ponds covering 400 acres of ground. A blue dye is added to increase the speed of evaporation (the rate of solar heat absorption). In another year, when the water has evaporated, the white residues of potash and salts are bulldozed up and slurried through transmission pipes to the main plant, then submerged in a pond and aerated. As the salts float to the top, they are skimmed off, dried, bagged, and shipped throughout the United States to be sold as a water softener compound. The remaining potash is shipped in bulk by truck and rail to fertilizer markets from Canada to Mexico.

MILEAGE LOG—SHAFER TRAIL TO ISLAND-IN-THE-SKY

The Shafer Trail begins at the Potash Mine where Scenic Byway 279 (Potash Road) ends, 15.7 miles (25.2 km) south of US 191.

00 miles: Beginning of the dirt Shafer Trail.

1.5 miles (2.4 km): Dirt road ends at the BLM river put-in. Rest rooms and a cement boat ramp mark the departure point for river runners and daily commercial jet-boat tours.

2.6 miles (4.2 km): Faintly in view at the end of the long mesa in the distance left of the road is the shelter at Anticline Overlook in the Rims Recreation Area.

Southwest is Pyramid Butte, and between the two is the round Carousel Butte. Left of the trail is one of many capped gas or oil well pipes, standing about 5 feet (1.5 m) high. Numerous drill holes have been made, but there have been few finds large enough to be profitably mined.

3.7 miles (5.9 km): Continue straight as the right branch goes to Tangra'la (a.k.a. Caveman Ranch), a private resort owned by Richard "Bud" Tangren. Several motel units are blasted into the cliff above the river and will someday be open for tourist lodging.

3.8 miles (6.1 km): Stop sign before trail crosses the internal road system of the Potash Mine, which is posted private property.

4.4 miles (7.0 km): Balanced Rock on the right side of the trail.

4.7 miles (7.5 km): Potash Mine settling ponds on the left.

5.6 miles (9.0 km): Top of the hill is the most expansive view of the thirty-three ponds covering 400 acres.

6.6 miles (10.6 km): The slender semidetached Amazon Tower is in view to the south.

6.7 miles (10.7 km): The detached large boulder approximately 50 feet (15 m) west of the trail houses a hermit beehive. It is worth walking to and smelling the honey in the hive, but please do not disturb!

6.9 miles (11.1 km): Range cattle fence.

7.3 miles (11.7 km): Closest approach to Pyramid Butte (to the south).

8.6 miles (13.8 km): Bovine water pond to the north. One of the most photogenic views of Chimney Rock.

8.9 miles (14.3 km): The right trail goes to an abandoned uranium mine.

9.2 miles (14.8 km): Dramatic Rico limestone water pour-off, during thundershowers.

9.3 miles (14.9 km): View into the unnamed canyon (left) that the Shafer brothers used in the 1930s to reach the river as they herded their cattle from the 6,000-foot (1,828 m)-high Island-in-the-Sky summer grazing to the 4,000-foot (1,219 m)-high Kane Creek Valley winter grazing.

9.8 miles (15.7 km): Watering pond west of the trail. East are deep grabens (from the German word for graves), created by faults or dropped areas sometimes formed when salt is solutioned out from beneath the earth's crust and the surface ground collapses.

9.9 miles (15.9 km): Range cattle fence.

10.0 miles (16.1 km): Thelma and Louise Point. For more information see Diversions under Pyramid Butte, earlier in this chapter.

10.9 miles (17.5 km): First view down to the Goose Neck.

11.6 miles (18.6 km): Good view of the Goose Neck of the Colorado. The island rock formation ahead is Choo-choo Rock (a.k.a. Locomotive Rock).

11.9 miles (19.1 km): Last viewpoint for Goose Neck.

12.5 miles (20.1 km): Unknown climbing route on the right wall. Route climbs a finger crack up an open book up the Organ Rock member of Cutler sandstone. Rappel anchor is in view on the right wall.

12.6 miles (20.2 km): Rico limestone pour-off from Shafer Canyon.

12.7 miles (20.4 km): Canyonlands National Park entrance. Cattle guard, fence, and sign.

12.8 miles (20.5 km): Bird's View Butte comes into view to the right.

13.2 miles (21.2 km): "Nuts and Bolts" hoodoos high above the trail to the right. The formations are eroded from the Organ Rock member of Cutler sandstone capped with the seashore sand of the White Rim member of Cutler.

13.5 miles (21.7 km): Shafer Camp (rest room), one of several designated campsites within the park.

13.9 miles (22.3 km): Small pullout on the left for view of the Mushroom Rocks left of the trail. Bird's View Butte in full view to the north.

14.5 miles (23.3 km): Junction of White Rim Trail and Shafer Trail (rest rooms.) A sign gives distances to the visitor center, Musselman Arch, and Moab. Bird's View Butte is prominent to the north. Turn right (west) to climb the steep switchbacks of the Shafer Trail to the Island-in-the Sky Road.

19.8 miles (31.8 km): Junction of Shafer Trail and Island-in-the-Sky Road. Turn right to Bird's View Butte trail and follows the Island-in-the-Sky Road to Bird's View Butte and Crow's Head Spires Mileage Log.

To reach Bird's View Butte, which dominates the view to the south at the end of the approach trail, scramble down benches of Kayenta Formation and locate rappel anchors not visible from campsite level. The anchors are located at the southernmost tip of the rimrock opposite Crow's Head Spires. An alternative rappel point can be established from one of the several sturdy juniper trees 25 to 50 feet (7.6 to 15 m) from the edge of the canyon. Leave three ropes fixed for the 450 foot (137 m) return prusik. From the bottom rappel, hike south past the left (east) side of the Crow's Head Spires, then scramble up the Chinle slopes and steps to the northeast base of Bird's View Butte, a distance of approximately 0.75 mile (1.2 km). All routes in the area are listed left to right.

BIRD'S VIEW BUTTE—NORTHEAST FACE

38 UNEMPLOYMENT LINE III, 5.11a, 4 pitches, 450 feet (137 m) ★★★★

First Ascent: Mike Pennings, Drew Spaulding, September 1993.

Location and Access: *Unemployment Line* begins approximately 300 feet (91 m) left (east) of the northernmost projection of the butte, a point that is closest to the twin Crow's Head Spires.

Pitch 1: Begin 30 feet (9 m) left of a large triangular-shaped flake. Start up a V-slot, which leads to a 5.11a lieback. Protect with a #4 Camalot. Finish the pitch with a 5.8 runout that ends at the left edge of the flake. Continue up and left from the flake, beginning with 5.9. As the ramplike feature steepens, follow a 5.10 perfect hand crack that thins and becomes 5.11a. Belay from fixed Hexentrics at the beginning of an off-width crack.

Pitch 2: Continue 5.10+ up the off-width, then a right-facing V-slot (protect with #4 Camalots), passing loose blocks and ending with 5.9 fingers at a ledge. Traverse 15 feet (4.5 m) left around an arête and belay in a corner.

Pitch 3: Climb a left-facing finger crack at 5.10 (left of a pillar crack), which widens to a 5.10 hand crack. Begin 5.10 fist, then continue up a right-angling 5.9 corner 6 inches (15 cm), ending at a large ledge (with large boulders) formed at the bedding seam between the Wingate (below) and the Kayenta (above).

Pitch 4: Follow a 5.5 chimney to the summit at the top of the Kayenta Formation.

Paraphernalia: Friends (2) sets; Camalots through #4; TCUs (1) set; stoppers (1) set.

Descent: Four rappels. The first is to the bedding seam ledge from double anchors right of the route. The second is to double anchors above and right of the pitch 2 ledge. Rappel three is to fixed Hexentrics at the top of pitch 1. The last rappel is to the ground.

BIRD'S VIEW BUTTE—WEST FACE

39 SATELLITE SPIRE
IV, 5.9 R, C1, 5 pitches, 350 feet (107 m) ★★★★

First Ascent: Ralph Ferrara, John Rzycki, mid-1990s. Second Ascent: Todd Swain, Paul Ross, Donette Swain, Paul Gardner, September 22–23, 2000.

Location and Access: Approach as for *Unemployment Line.* Begin up an obvious crack system above a ledge approximately 100 feet (30 m) right (west) of the north end of the butte. The first ascent of Satellite Spire could have been made up the crack system on the east (left) side of the spire. Details of the route are unknown.

Pitch 1: Begin on the right (west) side of the spire. Climb a hand-and-fist crack to a ledge, 5.9, 90 feet (27 m).

Pitch 2: From the highest level of the ledge, climb a short corner to a saddle, then hand traverse down and right to an obvious overhanging fist crack. Aid (C1 or free) up the overhanging 3.5- to 4-inch (9 to 10 cm) crack until it widens. Chimney and jam up the crack system to a ledge on the right at a second notch, 5.9 R, C1, 110 feet (34 m).

Pitch 3: Scramble up and right on an easy ledge to a second ledge below an obvious varnished chimney, which is in view from the ground, fourth class, 40 feet (12 m).

Pitch 4: Continue up a squeeze chimney for 30 feet (9 m), 5.8, then climb a large

BIRD'S VIEW BUTTE, WEST FACE—SATELLITE SPIRE

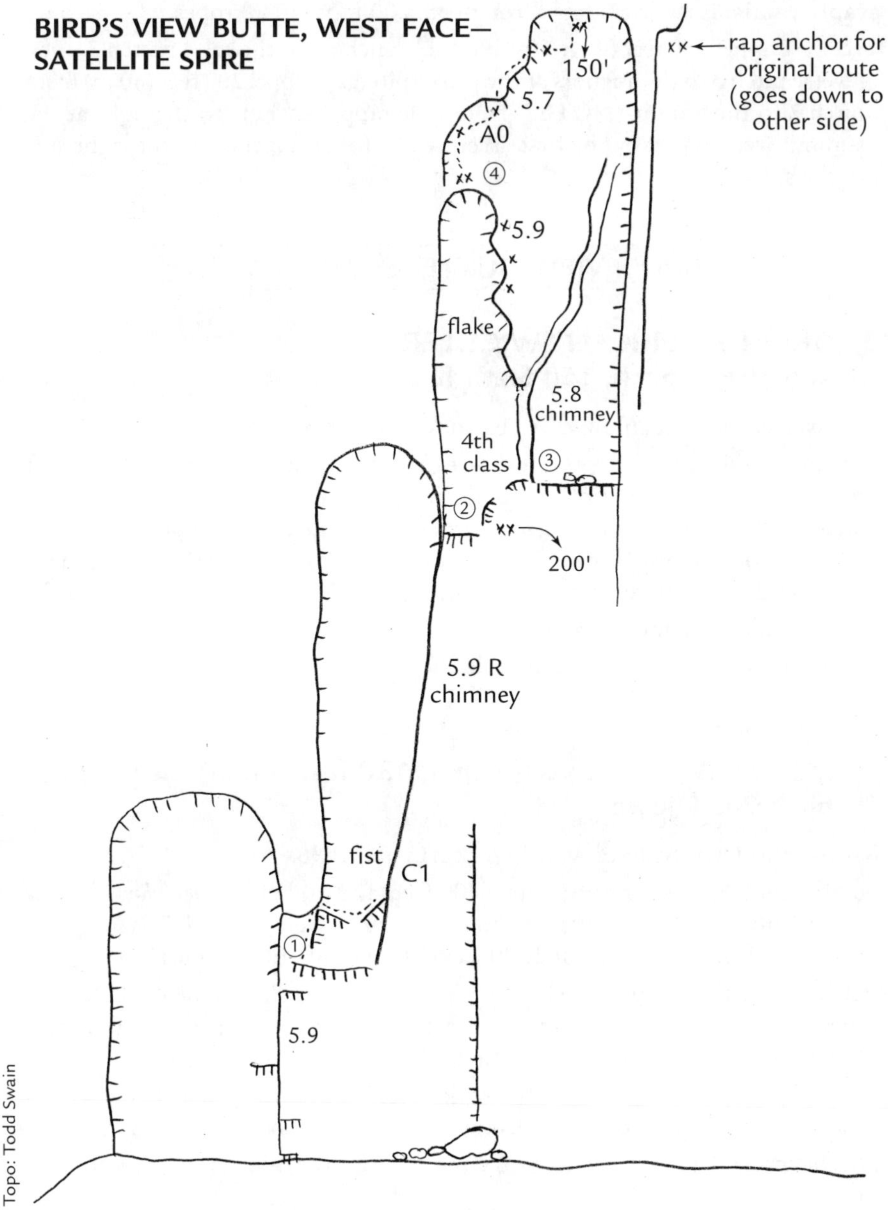

flake (Windstorm Flake) on the left, past three bolts near its top, to a belay stance with double bolts, 5.9, 90 feet (27 m). Paul Ross: "Three bolts were placed as the leader was caught in a violent windstorm."

Pitch 5: Move left to an arête, then pull past a bolt (A0) to lower angled terrain. Climb past a second bolt and a piton to a ledge. Move right and up to an anchor, which is just below the summit of the spire, 50 feet (15 m).

Paraphernalia: Friends (2) sets through #5; 200-foot (60 m) ropes.

Descent: Rappel 150 feet (46 m) from double anchors to the top of pitch 3, then reverse pitch 3 to the anchors at the top of pitch 2. Rappel 200 feet (60 m) from pitch 2 to the ground. **NOTE:** The double rappel anchors to the right at the summit were placed by the first ascent party for a rappel down the right side of the spire.

BIRD'S VIEW BUTTE—SOUTH FACE

40 GREAT AMERICAN SWIGGLER
1, 5.10+, 1 pitch, 150 feet (46 m).

First Ascent: Drew Spaulding, Ty Hydrusko, fall 1996.

Location and Access: *Great American Swiggler* is approximately 40 feet (12 m) left of *Happy Face*. Begin left of a large flaring squeeze system. Climb to a chocolate-colored, varnished left-facing corner. Continue 5.10 fists protected with #4 Camalots, ending at double anchors. Drew Spaulding: "Above is an awesome squiggly straight-in off-width, 5.10+, 4- to 5-inch [10 to 13 cm] crack."

Paraphernalia: Several Camalots #4.

Descent: Rappel the route from double anchors.

41 HAPPY FACE
I, 5.11a, A1, 2 pitches: pitch 1, 130 feet (40 m), height of pitch 2 unknown

First Ascent: Drew Spaulding, Jed Workman, fall 1996.

Location and Access: Approximately 400 feet (122 m) left of *Unemployment Line* on the south face of the butte. Begin up an obvious left-facing, left-leaning serrated hand crack approximately 40 feet (12 m) right of *Great American Swiggler*.

Pitch 1: From the top of the left-facing hand crack, angle left into a 5.11a slot, then continue with hands up a left-facing dihedral, then perfect feet moves (5.10+) to a belay ledge with a single anchor, 130 feet (40 m).

Pitch 2: Continue vertically up 5.10+ rock. Angle right up a 6-inch (15 cm) crack, then A1 past loose wedged blocks to a belay ledge with double anchors.

Paraphernalia: Hand-size cams with large units for the 6-inch (15 cm) section of pitch 2.

Descent: Rappel the route from double anchors.

RIM DESCENT WALL

The descent approach into the canyon to Crow's Head Spires, Bird's View Butte, and the return can be an epic in itself. Drew Spaulding has established two climbing lines from the canyon to the rim. He suggests: "*Titanic Corner* is a five-star route. The original method of descending/ascending the 450-foot canyonlands rim is to solo down 50 feet (15 m) from the rim by jumping onto a large boulder, which leads to a moderate chimney leading to a clean ledge. When soloing down, you are aiming toward the obvious arête of the rim wall closest to Crow's Head Spires. A three-bolt anchor is established below a 'clean crack ledge,' the closest point to the spires. Fix two ropes (tied together) and rappel, passing the knots as you go. At the end of the day, return to the fixed ropes and ascend the 450 feet (137 m) back to the rim, then solo to the canyon rim, returning to your car. I have established two three-pitch routes on the west face of the rim wall. They lead to the ledges soloed to the rappel anchors."

42 THINK YA SHOULD
III, 5.11c, 4 pitches, 380 feet (116 m) ★★★★★

First Ascent: Drew Spaulding, Mark Minor, Julie Peterson, September 1997.

Location and Access: *Think Ya Should* is approximately 150 feet (46 m) left of *Laser Crack*. Begin left of a large ramping gully. Drew Spaulding: "Pitches 2 and 3 are stellar splitter pitches."

Pitch 1: Begin up a right-facing dihedral with 5.9 fists. Angle right up a 5.10 squeeze, then a long 5.9 chimney ending with a tunnel to a belay ledge, 150 feet (46 m).

Pitch 2: Climb 5.11c straight in, thin hands for 90 feet (27 m). Left is a large ramping gully. Continue angling right with perfect hand jams at 5.10+ up a right-facing crack to a belay ledge with double anchors, 120 feet (37 m).

Pitch 3: Step left into an acute left-facing dihedral (5.10b), and climb through a triangular roof. Spaulding: "Chubby hands." Continue up a splitter face crack (5.10b), then move left and continue up a left-facing crack at 5.9+ to a large ledge with a two-bolt anchor, 140 feet (43 m).

Pitch 4: Traverse right, past the top of *Laser Crack* to an obvious exit to the top.

Paraphernalia: Standard desert rack.

Descent: This route is a climb back to the car after climbing Bird's View or Crow's Head. Rather than making the 450-foot (137 m) prusik back out, climbers can now climb out up this route.

43 LASER CRACK
III, 5.11a, C1, 4 pitches, 400 feet (122 m) ★★★

First Ascent: Drew Spaulding, Dan Hackett, Ty Hydrusko, Jed Workman, September 1997.

Location and Access: *Laser Crack* is approximately 150 feet (46 m) right of *Think Ya Should*. Drew Spaulding: "A three-star route, a bit circuitous, a bit of aid (clean), a few loose spots, overall great climbing, exciting!"

Pitch 1: Begin 5.9 up a clean right-facing chocolate corner, which climbs into a 5.10a off-width hand crack, ending at double anchors, 90 feet (27 m).

Pitch 2: Move left, then climb 5.10b up *Laser Crack*, which tapers from 2.5 inches to 1 inch (6.3 cm to 2.5 cm). There is about 15 feet (4.5 m) of C1 (with cams).

Move 5.8 right to a wedged block, then 5.9 up the right side of a flake to a good ledge with double anchors, 130 feet (40 m).

Pitch 3: Climb a 5.11a thin left-facing crack to a ledge, 140 feet (43 m).

Pitch 4: Traverse 15 feet (4.5 m) left, then up a short 5.9 left-facing corner to the top, 40 feet (12 m).

Paraphernalia: Standard desert rack.

Descent: This route is a climb back to the car after climbing Bird's View or Crow's Head. Rather than making the 450-foot (137 m) prusik back out, climbers can now climb out up this route.

44 TITANIC CORNER
II, 5.11a, 2 pitches, 230 feet (70 m) ★★★★★

First Ascent: Drew Spaulding, Mark Miner, September 1997.

Location and Access: *Titanic Corner* is approximately 200 feet (60 m) right of *Laser Crack* and approximately 300 feet (91 m) left of a leaning block against the buttress, which is the bottom of the standard rappel line.

Pitch 1: Climb a left-facing, right-angling corner with varnished wedged blocks to a large ledge with double anchors, 5.9, 90 feet (27 m).

Pitch 2: Continue up a left-facing dihedral with 5.10c thin hands (crux), to perfect hands, then 5.11a fingers to double anchors on the left wall, 140 feet (43 m).

Paraphernalia: Standard desert rack.

Descent: Rappel the route.

CROW'S HEAD SPIRES

Although the Crow's Head Spires were included in *Desert Rock II: Wall Street to the San Rafael Swell,* they are also included in this guide because of their proximity to Bird's View Butte. Since the publication of *Desert Rock II,* more detail on their approach is available, and there has been an additional route established on Luminous Being Spire.

LUMINOUS BEING SPIRE

Luminous Being Spire is the northern tower, right of Don Juan Spire when viewed from the edge of the mesa. To reach, see the approach for Bird's View Butte, page 135. Routes are listed right to left (north to south).

45 CROW'S BEAK
III, 5.10, A2+, 2, 250 (76 m) ★★★★

First Ascent: James Garrett, Chris Donharl, Ben Beezley, September 27, 1998.

LUMINOUS BEING SPIRE—CROW'S BEAK

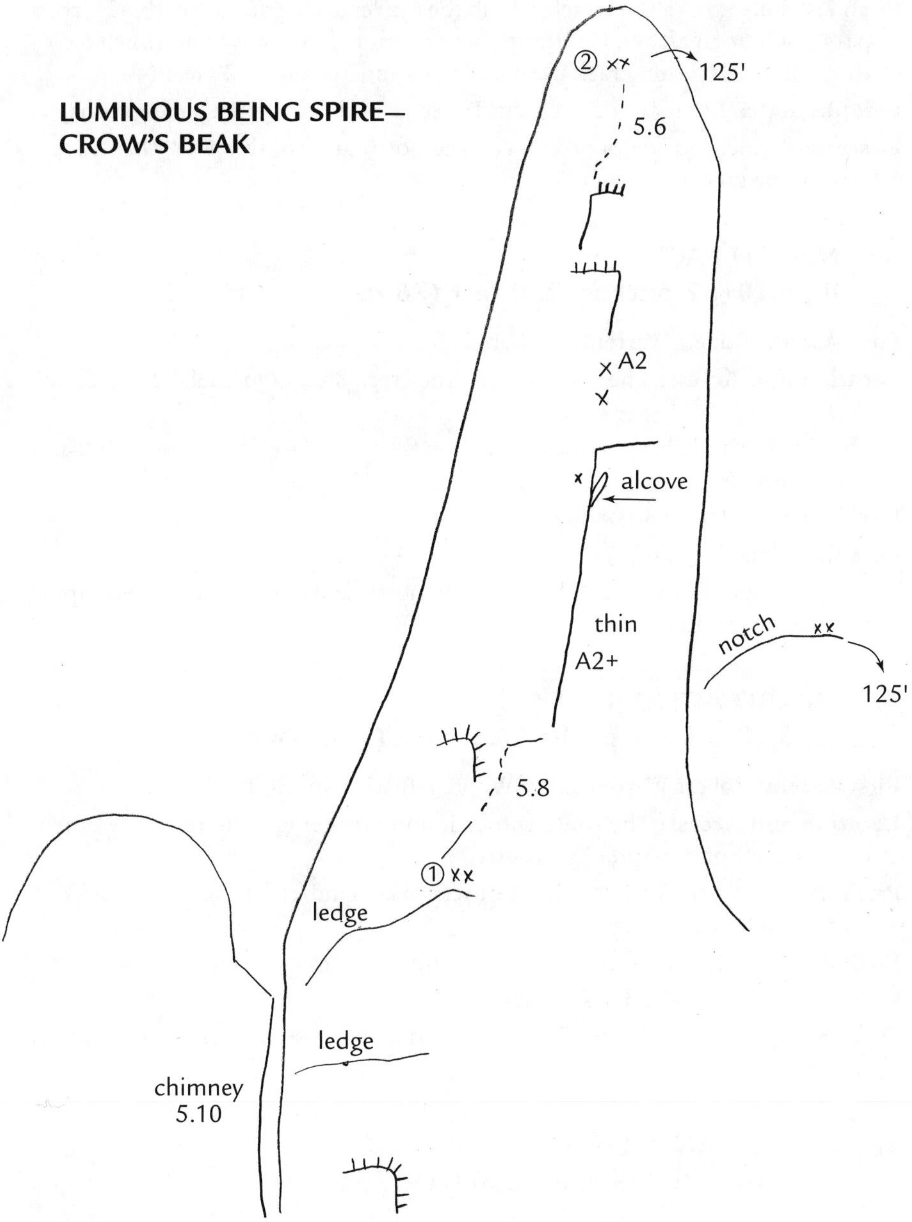

Location and Access: The route ascends the right skyline (northwest face) of Luminous Being Spire, when viewed from the rim rappel point.

Pitch 1: Begin at a loose chimney with good hand and finger cracks inside. Climb past a small ledge and on to a second ledge on the right, and belay from double anchors, 5.10, 120 feet (37 m).

Pitch 2: Climb 5.8 to a thin crack. Climb the thin crack, beginning with A2+, then pass a bolt at an alcove. Continue past two more bolts at A2 and finish 5.6 to the summit. The thin crack uses birdbeaks and Toucans, 130 feet (40 m).

Paraphernalia: Standard desert rack; Toucans; birdbeaks; extra small pitons.

Descent: Rappel to the notch between the north and south spires, then rappel west to the ground.

46 NORTH FACE
III, 5.10+, 2 pitches, 250 feet (76 m)

First Ascent: Robert Warren, Jeff Web, 1983.

Location and Access: The route climbs the crack system just left of the *Crow's Beak.*

Pitch 1: Ascend the obvious crack system on the north face, then traverse left and join *Lizard Action.*

Pitch 2: Follow *Lizard Action* to the summit.

Paraphernalia: Friends (1) set.

Descent: Rappel to the notch between the north and south spires, then rappel west to the ground.

47 LIZARD ACTION
III, 5.10+, A1, 2 pitches, 250 feet (76 m)★★

First Ascent: Robert Warren, Steve Wood, Jeff Web, spring 1983.

Location and Access: The route climbs Luminous Being Spire from the northeast, just left of the *North Face* route.

Pitch 1: Begin just north of the northern prow and climb obvious cracks to anchors at a belay stance.

Pitch 2: Move left a few feet and continue up the crack system to the top.

Paraphernalia: Standard desert rack.

Descent: Rappel to the notch between the north and south spires, then rappel west to the ground.

48 HECKLE AND JECKLE
III, 5.10, A1, 2 pitches, 250 feet (76 m)★★

First Ascent: Jason Keith, Greg Bimmesteffer, May 1993.

Location and Access: The route ascends the south ridge of Luminous Being Spire, left of *Lizard Action*, up obvious cracks. Further details are unknown.

Paraphernalia: Standard desert rack; selection of pitons.

Descent: Rappel to the notch between the north and south spires, then rappel west to the ground.

THE NOTCH

The Notch is the saddle between the north and south Crow's Head Spires.

49 THE NOTCH
II, 5.12, 1 pitch, 140 feet (43 m)

First Ascent: Robert Warren, Steve Wood, Jeff Web, spring 1983.

Location and Access: The route to the notch climbs the west side of the landform. The summit of the spires was not reached on the first ascent. Begin below the right side of the notch. Angle up and right, up thin cracks (5.12) to a left-facing corner, which is climbed 5.10 to the col between the two spires.

Paraphernalia: Friends (1) set; small wires.

Descent: Rappel the route.

DON JUAN SPIRE

Don Juan Spire is the southern (left) tower when viewed from the rappel point at the edge of the mesa. Routes are listed right to left.

50 LITTLE SMOKE
III, 5.9, 2 pitches, 250 feet (76 m)

First Ascent: Robert Warren, Steve Wood, Jeff Web, spring 1983.

Location and Access: The route climbs the southeast side of Don Juan Spire.

Paraphernalia: Friends (1) set.

Descent: Rappel to the notch between the north and south spires, then rappel west to the ground.

51 YESTERDAY'S NEWS
III, 5.9, A3, 4 pitches, 250 feet (76 m)

First Ascent: Bill Ellwood, Bryan Ferguson, May 26, 1984.

Location and Access: The route climbs the south ridge of Don Juan Spire, and is left of the left profile and out of sight when the spire is viewed from the mesa rim rappel point.

Pitch 1: Begin 5.7 up a left-facing corner, ending with 5.8 hands up broken rock to a belay stance.

Pitch 2: Move up and right (5.9) to a right-facing dihedral and belay.

Pitch 3: Continue up the dihedral, which becomes wide, and is climbed 5.9 to a fixed anchor. Climb with aid, angling up and left, then up a 5.7 face to a belay ledge.

Pitch 4: Follow cracks angling up and right to the top.

Paraphernalia: TCUs up through #3.5 Friends.

Descent: Rappel to the notch between the north and south spires, then rappel west to the ground.

52 YESTERDAY'S NEWS VARIATION III, 5.10-, A3, 4 pitches, 250 feet (76 m)

First Ascent: Jason Keith, Greg Bimmesteffer, May 1993.

Location and Access: This is a variation of the second and third pitches of *Yesterday's News*. From the top of pitch 1, veer left up a left-facing crack, ascending first on aid, then 5.9. Continue over the left side of a roof, 5.10-, up a wide crack system at 5.9, then to the top of pitch 3 of the original route.

Paraphernalia: Standard desert rack; small selection of pitons.

Descent: Rappel to the notch between the north and south spires, then rappel west to the ground.

53 DON JUAN II, 5.11+, 1 pitch, 250 feet (76 m)

First Ascent: Ken Trout et al., 1983. First Free Ascent: Jeff Web, Robert Warren.

Location and Access: The route climbs a left-facing corner up the left edge of the west face to the notch between the north and south spires, then to the summit from the notch.

Paraphernalia: Standard desert rack.

Descent: Rappel to the notch between the north and south spires, then rappel west to the ground.

DIVERSIONS

DEAD HORSE POINT STATE PARK

Dead Horse Point is 12 air miles (19 km) southwest of Moab at the southwest edge of the Island-in-the-Sky Mesa. It offers an exceptional view of the Colorado River 2,000 feet (610 m) below, as it bends back on itself in a great gooseneck. Beyond, the Needles District of Canyonlands National Park dominates the skyline as the point overlooks 5,000 square miles of canyons, mountains, and mesas of the Colorado Plateau. The breathtaking panorama sweeps east to the La Sal Mountains, south to the Abajo Mountains (a.k.a. Blue Mountains), southwest to the Henry Mountains, and west to the Aquarius Plateau. It is a must-see.

There are a number of tales of how Dead Horse Point received it name. The most convincing tells of how cowboys at the turn of the twentieth century rounded up wild mustangs and herded them across the narrow neck of land that separated the point from the mainland. The island peninsula forming the point was fenced off at the narrow neck, then young healthy ponies were culled and taken to market. The old or sick were left behind to return to the range. The legend says that the gate across the neck was accidentally left closed, and the sick and old died of thirst within view of the Colorado River 2,000 feet below.

I miss the old sign that once stood beside a gnarled old piñon pine near the neck at Dead Horse Point: STOP, LOOK, AND LISTEN. LISTEN TO THE SOUNDS OF THE NOT TOO DISTANT PAST. LISTEN FOR THE THUNDER OF HORSES' HOOVES RUNNING ACROSS THE MESA TOP AND THE SCREAMING COWBOYS BEHIND THEM RUNNING IN THE BLINDING AND CHOKING DUST. LOOK AT THE FLARING NOSTRILS AND RIPPLING MUSCLES ON THE POWERFUL MUSTANGS' LEGS AND SIDES AS THEY RUN PAST YOU HEADING FOR THE POINT.

To reach Dead Horse Point State Park from Moab, drive 9 miles (14.5 km) north of town on US 191 to Utah 313 and turn left (west) at a sign for Dead Horse Point State Park and Island-in-the-Sky. Continue on Utah 313 to a signed left branch to Dead Horse Point (still Utah 313). The state park boundary is 4 miles (6.4 km) from the intersection. Ahead (south) of the junction, the Island-in-the-Sky Road enters Canyonlands National Park. Four miles (6.4 km) farther and just past the entrance kiosk, a dirt trail goes to the left. It descends the steep switchbacked Shafer Trail 1,200 feet (366 m) in 4 miles (6.4 km) to the White Rim, a broad bench averaging 1,000 feet (305 m) below the Island-in-the-Sky Mesa and 1,000 feet above the Colorado River. For information on the climbing routes established in the area, see *Desert Rock I: Rock Climbs in the National Parks* and *Desert Rock II: Wall Street to the San Rafael Swell.*

MILE MARKER LOG—UTAH 313 TO DEAD HORSE POINT

Using the mile marker signs as reference points, this log begins at the intersection of Utah 313 and US 191, 9 miles (14.5 km) north of Moab.

21–20: A dirt trail branches left to the Heat Wave Wall climbing area. On the right just before the shallow Big Cave Valley, there is a brass memorial plaque on the desert-varnished wall above the road. Left of the road are three clusters of Seven Mile Canyon campsites, each with an information kiosk.

15–14: Left (east) of the road is a paved parking area, rest rooms, an information kiosk, and expansive views east to Behind the Rocks Wilderness Study Area southwest of Moab and the La Sal Mountains (snowcapped nine months of the year), and west to the San Rafael Swell. On the right beyond the viewpoint, the dirt Spring Canyon trail begins. This is the route to the Kachina Towers and Hell Roaring Canyon, the Tombstone (a.k.a. High Rise), Spring Canyon Point Trail, and the Green River.

11–10: Horsethief Trail branches right. Sign: MINERAL CANYON BOAT RAMP 15 MILES. A second sign informs visitors that a backcountry permit is required for overnight travel in Canyonlands National Park. The trail descends to the Green River, Felony Tower, the northwest beginning of the White Rim Trail, Taylor Canyon, and Moses and Zeus Towers.

10–9: Sign: GEMINI BRIDGES. (Turn left for Gemini Bridges.) Continue straight to Dead Horse Point.

SUNSET BUTTE

Sunset Butte is the small but prominent butte directly south of Bird's View Butte. It is identified as point 5726 on the Musselman Arch 7.5-minute USGS topographical quadrangle. To reach from Moab, follow the Shafer Trail to Island-in-the-Sky Mileage Log earlier in this chapter. When the butte is in view, park and hike cross-country up drainages to its south side.

54 SUNSET BUTTE—SOUTH FACE
I, 5.7, 2 pitches, 150 feet (46 m)

First Ascent: Paul Horton, Rob Mahoney, April 25, 1995.

Location and Access: Once the butte is reached from the Shafer Trail, hike the long talus slope to the south side of the butte. Begin with a shoulder stand and follow the line of least resistance.

Paraphernalia: Friends (1) set.

Descent: Rappel the *North Dihedral* from drilled angle pitons.

55 NORTH DIHEDRAL
I, 5.9/5.10, 1 pitch, 150 feet (46 m)

First Ascent: Unknown.

Location and Access: Approach as for *South Face*. Traverse to the north side and climb a prominent left-facing dihedral.

Paraphernalia: Friends.

Descent: Rappel the route.

FELONY TOWER

Felony Tower is a semidetached spire on the left at the far end of the Wingate buttress at the bottom of the Horsethief Trail switchbacks. From Moab, drive 9 miles (14.5 km) north of town on US 191. Turn left (west) onto Utah 313 at a sign for Island-in-the-Sky District and Dead Horse State Park. Just before mile marker 10, 12.3 miles (19.8 km) from US 191, turn right (west) onto a dirt trail, signed HORSETHIEF TRAIL. At 13.2 miles (21.2 km), the trail descends 2,000 feet (610 m) in 1.5 miles (2.4 km) down the spectacular switchbacks to Horsethief Bottom at the Green River and the northern beginning of the White Rim Trail. Felony Tower is high on the Wingate buttress left of the junction of the Horsethief and the White Rim Trails. (See route locator map, page 104.)

56 PONCHO COULDN'T COME
IV, 5.11a, A2, 5 pitches, 500 feet (152 m) ★★★★★

First Ascent: Pitch 1: Roger Schimmel, Chris Archers, Jim Bodenhamer, 1997. Pitches 2–5: Tom Cosgriff, Roger Schimmel, Jim Bodenhamer, 1997.

FELONY TOWER— PONCHO COULDN'T COME

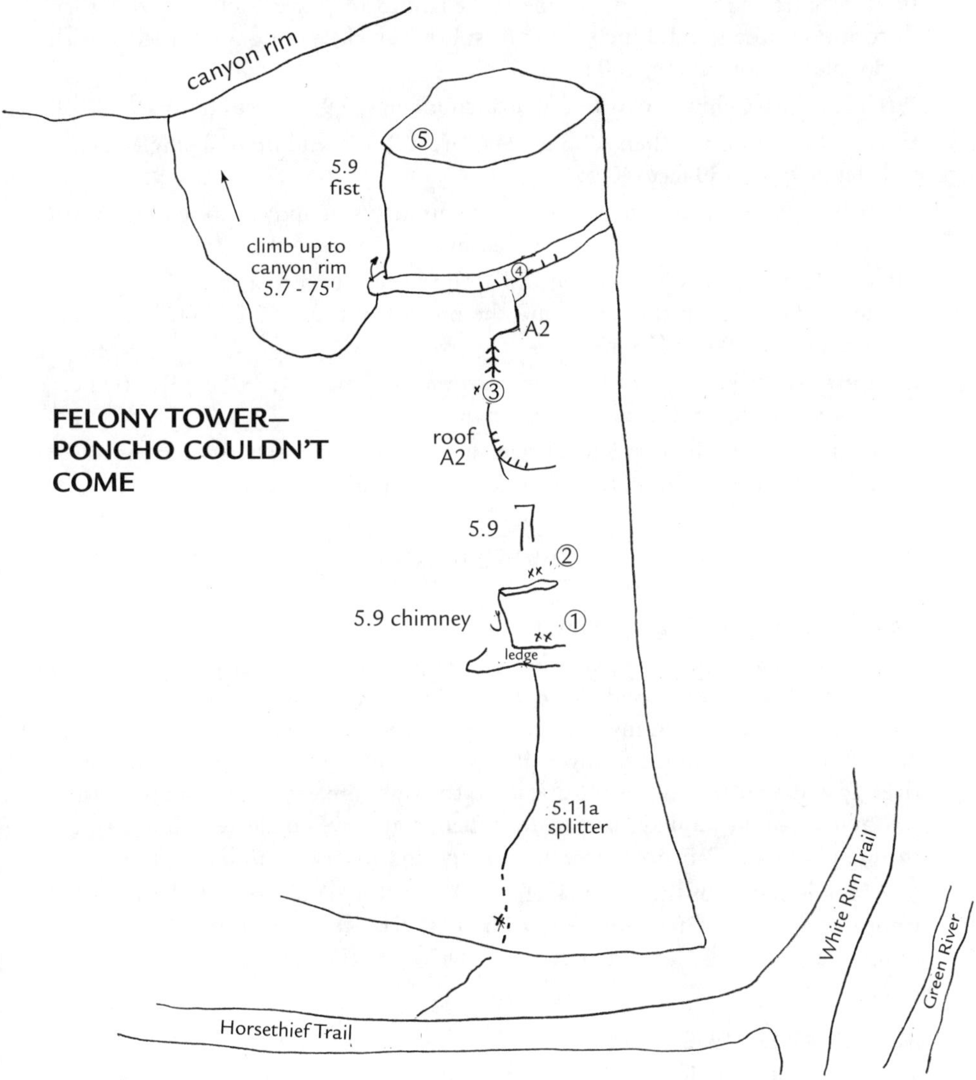

Location and Access: Rappel from the mesa to the notch behind the tower. (The first ascent team fixed a rope from the mesa top to the notch between the tower and the mesa, then left a car at the mesa top and drove a second car down Horsethief Trail to the beginning of the climb. Descent was made by a rappel to the notch between the tower and the mesa, then a prusik up the fixed rope to the mesa top.) Jim Bodenhamer: "Very helpful to leave a fixed line from the top of the mesa into the notch," 100 feet (30 m). Descend the Horsethief Trail and park at a pullout near the bottom of the switchbacks, then make a five-minute approach to the beginning of the climb.

Pitch 1: Start on the left (north) side of the landform, passing a fixed piton, then continue up a good 3-inch (7.6 cm) splitter crack, ending atop a ledge with double anchors, 5.11a, 180 feet (55 m).

Pitch 2: Climb a chimney to a double-anchor belay, 5.9, 60 feet (18 m).

Pitch 3: Continue 5.9, then A2 out "The Great Roof" and up to a single anchor belay, 5.9, A2, 130 feet (40 m).

Pitch 4: Traverse left on a ledge to a short chimney/slot and climb right, beneath a roof (A2), then to a ledge below the summit, 75 feet (23 m).

Pitch 5: Traverse left on the ledge and around the corner to a short fist crack at the saddle between the tower and the mesa. Continue 50 feet (15 m) to the summit, 5.9, 50 feet (15 m).

Paraphernalia: Friends (3) sets with extra #3 for pitch 1; TCUs (3) sets; Lost Arrows (5 or 6); knifeblades; small angles for pitch 3.

Descent: Downclimb pitch 5 to a ledge. Rappel into the notch between the tower and the buttress behind, then prusik to the top of the mesa.

DIVERSIONS

1836 D. JULIEN INSCRIPTION

D. Julien was a French-Canadian beaver trapper who left inscriptions on sandstone walls as he journeyed down the Green and Colorado Rivers. Near the mouth of Hell Roaring Canyon is the best-known and most accessible of his signatures. It is on the south-facing wall approximately 1,000 feet (305 m) from the river. Inscribed is D. JULIEN 1836 3 MAI. To the right are etchings of a boat with a sail and a round sunlike caricature. Julien may have made the first passage through Cataract Canyon, where his inscriptions are also found.

At the junction of the Horsethief and White Rim Trails, turn right and continue parallel to the Green River. At 3.5 miles (5.6 km) upriver from the BLM river ramp, Hell Roaring Canyon is reached. Drive up the canyon drainage to the inscription.

MOSES AND ZEUS TOWERS

Taylor Canyon and Moses and Zeus Towers are identified on the Moab West map. The two towers are at the head of Taylor Canyon just inside the northwest boundary of Canyonlands National Park. Overnight stays require a permit. Moses is second only to Castleton in tower climbing popularity. It soars 600 feet (183 m) above the isolated and remote Taylor Canyon, a true wilderness experience for all climbers, hikers, or campers who venture into its domain.

From the junction of the White Rim Trail and the Horsethief Trail, drive downriver to the park boundary, then continue 2.5 miles (4 km) to Taylor Canyon, which drains west into the Green River. Moses comes into view 2.3 miles (3.7 km) up the Taylor Canyon trail, which is generally passable by two-wheel-drive vehicles with high clearance. Five miles (8 km) up the canyon from the

Green River, the trail ends at a primitive campsite with a chemical toilet. A signed hiking trail leads 1 mile (1.6 km) to the base of Moses, then contours around the tower, giving exciting views in all directions.

> The shadows of foliage, the drift of clouds, the fall of rain upon leaves, the sound of running waters—all the gentler qualities of nature that minor poets love to juggle with—are missing on the desert. It is stern, harsh, and at first repellent. But what tongue shall tell the majesty of it, the eternal strength of it, the poetry of its wide-spread chaos, the sublimity of its lonely desolation! And who shall paint the splendor of its light; and from the rising up of the sun to the going down of the moon over the iron mountains, the glory of its wondrous coloring!
>
> —John C. Van Dyke, *The Desert,* 1901

9
HIDEOUT WALL

What a wilderness of fateful buffetings! All the elemental forces seem to have turned against it at different times. It has been swept by seas, shattered by earthquakes and volcanoes, beaten by winds and sands, and scorched by suns. Yet in spite of all it has endured. It remains a factor in Nature's plan. It maintains its types and out of its desolation it brings forth increase that the species may not perish from the face of the earth.

—John C. Van Dyke, *The Desert,* 1901

Hideout Wall is a delightful region high on the dwarf piñon pine and juniper woodland of the north shoulder of the 12,721-foot (3,877 m) La Sal Mountains east of Moab. Its approach is over an old four-wheel-drive, high-clearance uranium miners' trail, which meanders through wooded chaparral of squawberry, sage, and rabbitbrush. Wildlife includes coyotes, cougars, bears, and desert bighorn sheep. Climbs are on a Wingate sandstone buttress in a lonely and remote setting. A delightful place!

FLASH FLOODS

Todd Campbell in *Above and Beyond Slickrock:* "As you might suspect, Onion Creek sees some nasty flash floods. People often sense flash floods by the earthy, necrotic smell that precedes them. A slurry of piñon needles and juniper berries noses down the wash, first wrapping around, then flowing over boulders in its way. The flow crescendos rapidly, smashing the outer walls of each bend, spraying them high up with a silty deposit that will tell future travellers of its ferocity. Logs and whole trees carried down will become lodged in the narrowest corridors, sometimes causing tons of detritus to jackstraw up behind them. Days may pass before the creek flows clear again. Clay basins along the channel then dry up, shrink, and crack into fanciful geometric shapes, curling up at the edges to provide crackling accompaniment to the rare hiker."

FORMATION

The Mongoose, Sari, and Hindu Spires of Cutler sandstone tower above the Onion Creek–Fisher Valley Trail as it winds through multicolored gypsum beds and up Fisher Valley on the north shoulder of the La Sal Mountains. As the sinuous canyon cuts through the deep red rock, note the white crusty deposits in places near the creek. These are saline minerals dissolved from very old Paradox Formation salts. Squeezed from deep within the earth, gypsum (from the Greek *gypsos*, meaning "chalk") forms the hydrous calcium sulfate. Of Permian and Triassic age (208 to 286 million years old), it is now used as a retardant in portland cement and in making plaster of paris. Onion Creek's name derives from the malodorous springs that flow from above the salts of the gypsum upthrust. As

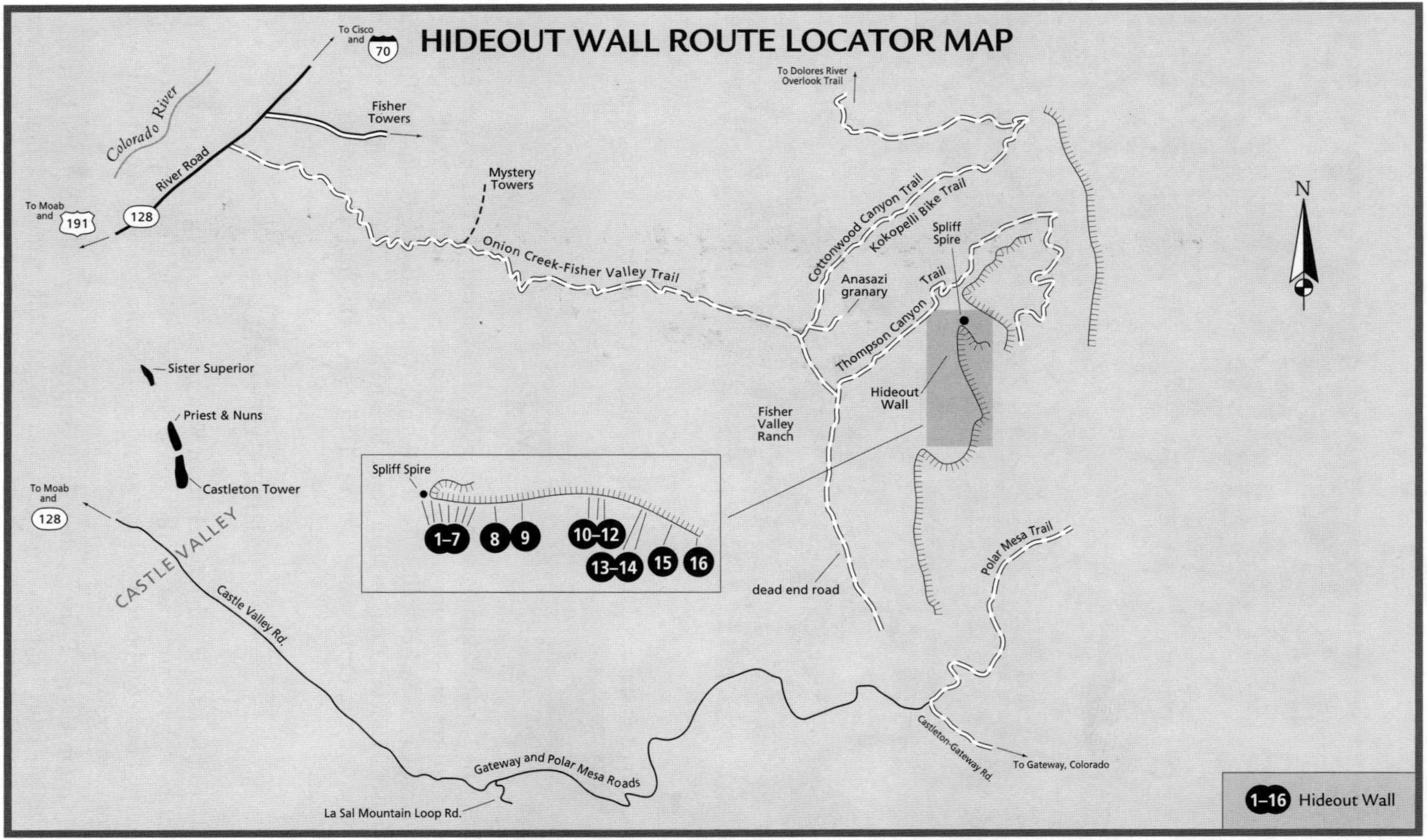
HIDEOUT WALL ROUTE LOCATOR MAP
To Cisco and 70
Colorado River
River Road
128
To Moab and 191
Fisher Towers
Mystery Towers
Onion Creek-Fisher Valley Trail
To Dolores River Overlook Trail
Cottonwood Canyon Trail
Kokopelli Bike Trail
Anasazi granary
Thompson Canyon Trail
Spliff Spire
Hideout Wall
Fisher Valley Ranch
dead end road
N
Sister Superior
Priest & Nuns
Castleton Tower
To Moab and 128
CASTLE VALLEY
Castle Valley Rd.
Spliff Spire
1–7
8
9
10–12
13–14
15
16
Polar Mesa Trail
Gateway and Polar Mesa Roads
La Sal Mountain Loop Rd.
Castleton-Gateway Rd.
To Gateway, Colorado
1–16 Hideout Wall

Photo: Chris Giles Photography

Hideout Wall.

you near the springs, Onion Creek becomes increasingly sulfurous with each of its thirty crossings.

MAP

Identified on the Moab East map (published by Latitude 40 Degrees) are many of the features on the upper and lower approaches to Hideout Wall, including Onion Creek–Fisher Valley Trail, Hideout Wall, Hideout Campsite, Hideout Canyon, Hideout Canyon Viewpoint, Spliff Spire, Bull Draw Campsite, Cottonwood Canyon, Cottonwood Canyon Trail, Kokopelli Trail, and Beaver and Polar Mesas.

HIDEOUT WALL

The climbs established in the Hideout Wall area are along the Wingate sandstone buttress above and east of the Forest Service's Hideout Campsite. It can be reached from the bottom off the River Road (Scenic Byway 128) or from the top from Beaver Mesa.

Onion Creek–Fisher Valley Trail Approach. To reach from the bottom, a 2,000-foot (610 m) elevation gain over rough trails requires a high-clearance vehicle with four-wheel drive. Turn east from the River Road onto the dirt Onion

Creek–Fisher Valley Trail between mile markers 20 and 21, signed FISHER VALLEY RANCH. After numerous crossings of the creek, cross a bridge over a deep, narrow gorge and continue the climb to Fisher Valley. Drive south up the valley to the second dirt spur branching left, signed THOMPSON CANYON TRAIL. Follow it through a pass, then down a steep grade. At a fork in the trail, branch right a few yards to the signed Hideout Camp. It is 10.4 miles (16.7 km) from the River Road to the Thompson Canyon Trail, and 1.8 miles (2.8 km) farther to Hideout Camp.

Beaver Mesa Approach. To reach from the top from Beaver Mesa, turn off the River Road between mile markers 15 and 16 and drive up the Castle Valley Road. At 11 miles (17.7 km) the La Sal Mountain Loop Road forks right (south). Continue straight as the paved road crests on the north shoulder of the La Sal Mountains and the road turns to dirt, 18.6 miles (30 km) from the River Road. In 2.2 miles (3.5 km) the dirt trail comes to a Y. The right fork is called the Castleton-Gateway Road. A sign gives distances to Gateway, Colorado (20 miles [32 km] to the right), North Beaver (4 miles [6.4 km] straight ahead), Polar Mesa (9 miles [14.5 km] straight ahead), and Fisher Valley (8 miles [12.8 km] straight ahead). At the Y take the North Beaver Mesa spur toward the mesa in view straight ahead. In 0.3 mile (0.48 km) the trail crosses a water diversion ditch that begins 5 miles (8 km) away at Don's Lake and was constructed to irrigate fields in Fisher Valley. A scramble down beneath the bridge gives a view of the top of the waterfall as it drops into Fisher Valley. In 4.2 miles (6.7 km) turn left onto the unsigned Thompson Canyon Trail and follow the most used trail as it descends steeply to the signed Hideout Camp. At 6.2 miles (10 km), views to the north reveal the Dolores River drainage rimmed with Wingate sandstone, beyond which is Uncompahgre Plateau (ancestral Rocky Mountains). At 7.9 miles (12.7 km) Hideout Canyon Viewpoint is to the left at an overhanging rock ledge. Beyond Hideout Canyon is the Fisher Valley and Onion Creek drainage with its deep red Cutler sandstone towers. Hideout Camp is reached at mile 13.4 (21.5 km).

To reach the climbs from the Hideout Campsite, bushwhack up the slopes to the Wingate buttress above the campsites. Routes are listed left to right.

1 SPLIFF SPIRE
I, 5.5, C2, 1 pitch, 70 feet (21 m) ★★

First Ascent: Andy Roberts, Jason Schroeder, August 1998.

Location and Access: Spliff Spire is at the left end of Hideout Wall. Hike to the notch on the left between the spire and the wall behind. Climb on hooks, passing five bolts to double belay/rappel anchors. Continue up boulders at the left side of the spire to the summit, 15 feet (4.5 m). Andy Roberts: "Will probably go free in the future."

Paraphernalia: Black Diamond Cliffhanger (1); Black Diamond Talon (1); quick draws (5).

Descent: Downclimb to double anchors, then make one single-rope rappel to the notch behind the spire.

SPLIFF SPIRE

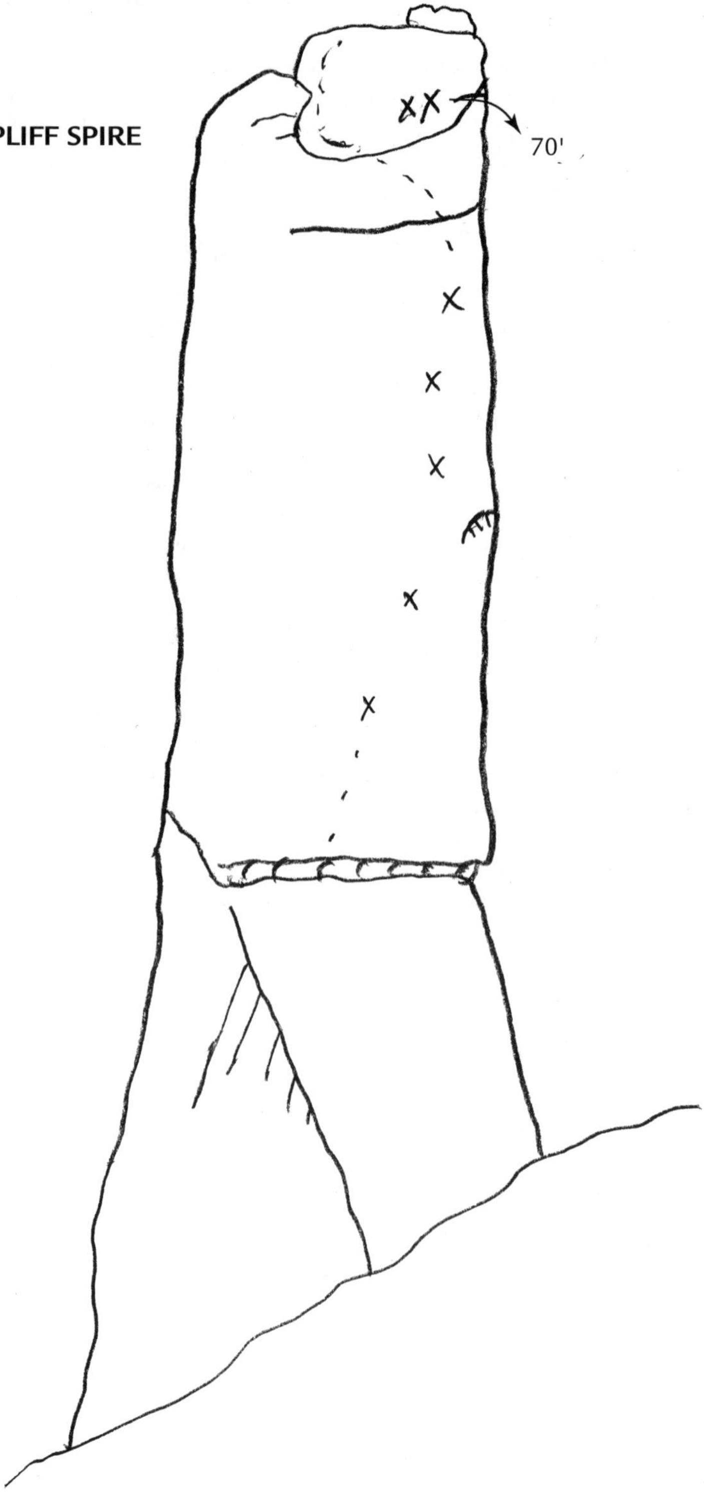

2 CONSTRICTER
I, 5.10+ R, A0, 1 pitch, 150 feet (46 m) ★★★

First Ascent: Dave Mealey, Andy Roberts, Jason Schroeder, October 1999.

Location and Access: The route is 40 feet (12 m) in from the far left end of Hideout Wall and climbs the prominent S-shaped chimney reaching from the bottom to the top of the buttress.

Pitch 1: Begin up a right-facing corner that quickly expands from hand size to off-width, 40 feet (12 m). Climb to where it is possible to traverse right to use twin cracks that split the right wall. Continue up 30 feet (9 m), trending left to reenter the chimney. Climb the squeeze chimney 50 feet (15 m) with no protection to a bolt on the right wall. Exit the chimney and follow three bolts to anchors on the right wall. Pitch 2 has been started but not finished.

Paraphernalia: Camalots (3) #3, #4, (1) #4.5, #5; Metolius cams (1) #3, #4, #5; quick draws (4).

Descent: Double-rope rappel from fixed anchors.

3 MOO'S UNIT
I, 5.10, 1 pitch, 100 feet (30 m) ★★

First Ascent: Dave Mealey, Matt Vansodell, October 1999.

Location and Access: *Moo's Unit* is at the left side of Hideout Wall, between *Constricter* (on left) and *Bionic Chronic* (on right). Climb a left-facing dihedral to double anchors on the left wall.

Paraphernalia: Friends through #3.5.

Descent: Rappel the route.

4 BIONIC CHRONIC
I, 5.10a, 1 pitch, 45 feet (14 m) ★★★

First Ascent: Andy Roberts, Jason Repko, April 7, 1999.

Location and Access: Climb the left side of Hideout Wall, two crack systems right of the long S-shaped *Constrictor*. Andy Roberts: "Nice hand crack that goes to small hands, then through a bulge on reachy hand jams."

Paraphernalia: Hand-size units.

Descent: Rappel from double fixed anchors on the left wall.

5 DYNAMO HUM
II, 5.10+, 2 points of aid, 3 pitches, 300 feet (91 m) ★★★

First Ascent: Andy Roberts, Dave Mealey, May 1999.

Location and Access: The route is two crack systems or approximately 50 feet (15 m) right of *Bionic Chronic*. Pitch 3 was led by Andy Roberts with two points of aid and followed free at 5.10+ by Dave Mealey.

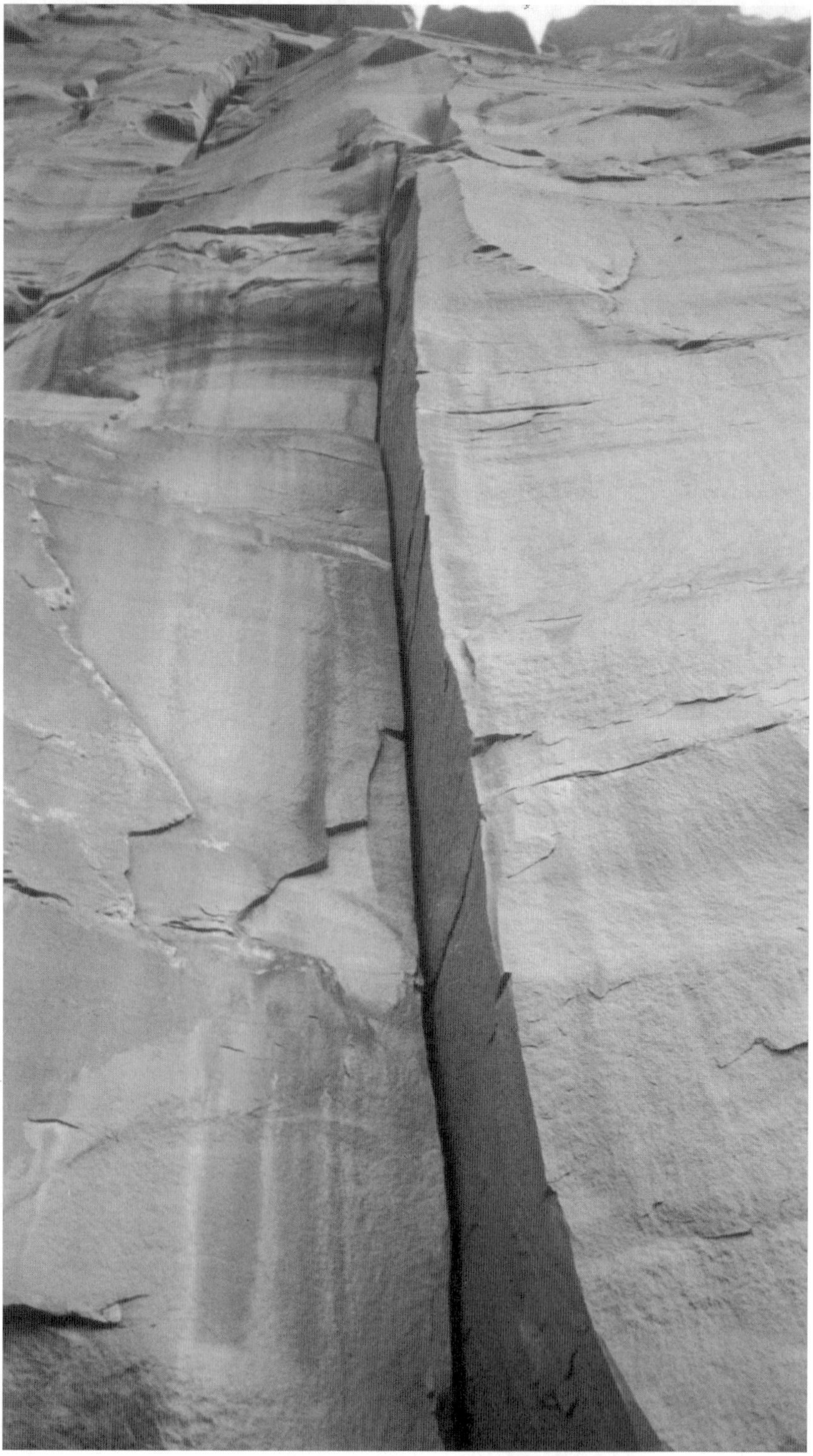

Photo: Andy Roberts

Bionic Chronic.

DYNAMO HUM

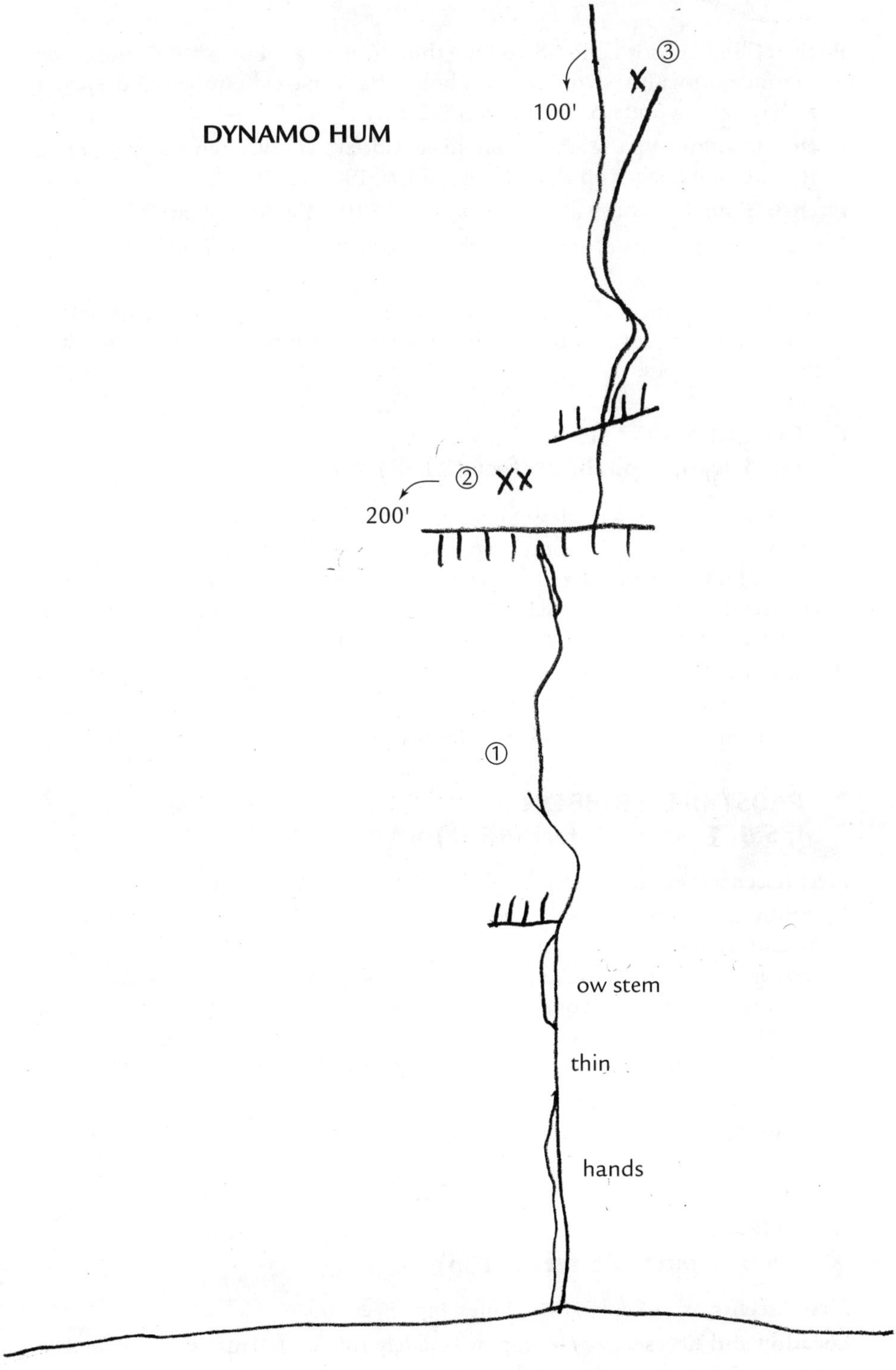

Pitch 1: Climb mostly hands, becoming thin through a short rotten section, then continue off-width, stemming to a bulge that is passed on the right. Anchor with camming units, 5.10a, 100 feet (30 m).

Pitch 2: Continue up the crack, climbing a wide system through a bulge, ending at a two-bolt anchor on a good ledge, 5.10a, 100 feet (30 m).

Pitch 3: Climb a mostly wide vertical splitter, 5.10+, 100 feet (30 m).

Paraphernalia: Camalots (2) sets with extra #3, #3.5, #4 and (1) #5; selection of nuts.

Descent: Rappel the route. The first ascent team rappelled from a single bolt to double anchors at the top of pitch 2, then rappelled to the ground with 200-foot (60 m) ropes.

6 CHICKEN LITTLE
I, 5.10c/d, 1 pitch, 70 feet (21 m) ★★

First Ascent: Dave Mealey, Jason Repko, June 4, 2000.

Location and Access: The route is approximately 60 feet (18 m) right of *Dynamo Hum*. Climb fingers to hands, finishing with fists. Begin up a radically zigzagging crack system left of a left-facing dihedral, 15+ feet (4.5+ m). Continue up a splitter crack to anchors visible below a large roof.

Paraphernalia: Fingers through hand-size Friends (2) sets, with (2–3) sets of fist-size Friends; Camalots (1) #5 or larger.

Descent: Rappel the route from double anchors.

7 PABST BLUE RIBBON
I, 5.8, 1 pitch, 50 feet (15 m) ★★★

First Ascent: Jason Repko, Chris Giles, Dave Mealey, June 4, 2000.

Location and Access: *Pabst Blue Ribbon* is 25 feet (7.6 m) right of *Chicken Little*. Ascend an obvious left-facing dihedral, hands to fists for 35 feet (10.6 m). Traverse left through 10 feet (3 m) of face climbing to a large ledge. Belay/rappel anchors are at the back of the ledge and not visible from below. Jason Repko: "Great little warm-up. Although anchors are not visible, the climb is easy to spot and is below an ominous-looking roof system high above."

Paraphernalia: Camalots (1) #2, (2) #3, (1) #4.

Descent: Rappel the route. Jason Repko: "Rope will run safely over the rounded edge."

8 ONE-HIT
I, 5.9, 1 pitch, 35 feet (11 m) ★

First Ascent: Jason Repko, Chris Giles, June 3, 2000.

Location and Access: *One-Hit* is approximately 130 feet (40 m) right of *Pabst Blue Ribbon* and climbs a short right-facing dihedral. Climb hands to fingers to a

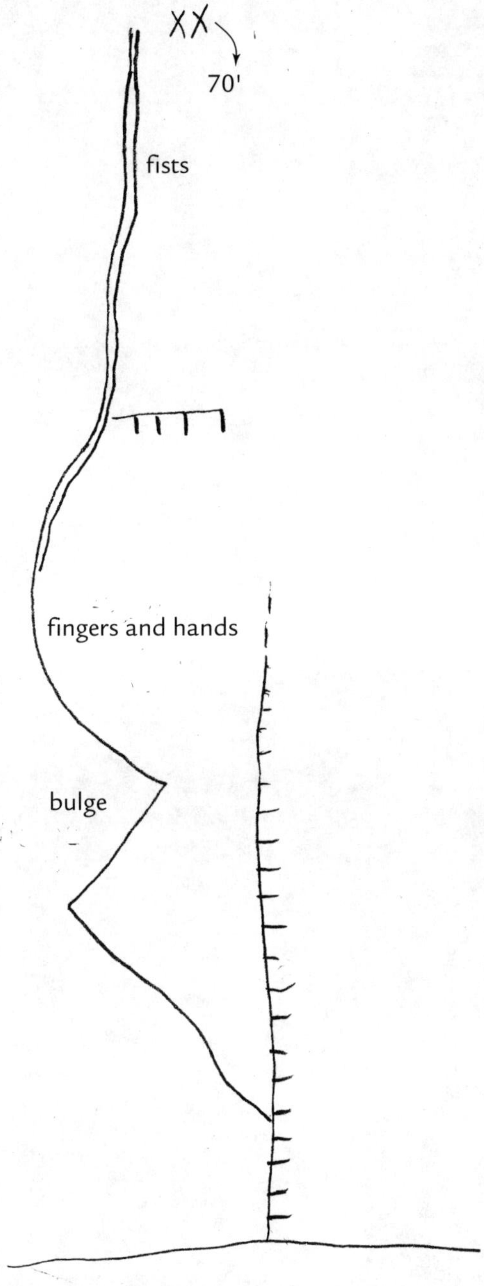

CHICKEN LITTLE

Photo: Chris Giles

Dave Mealy on Chicken Little, *first ascent, June 2000.*

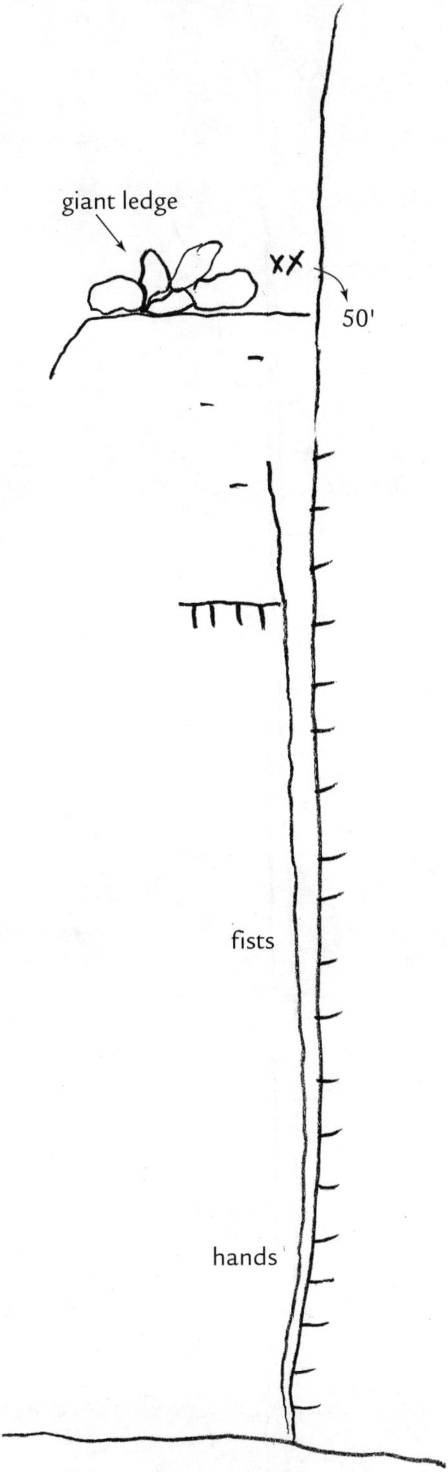

PABST BLUE RIBBON

ONE-HIT

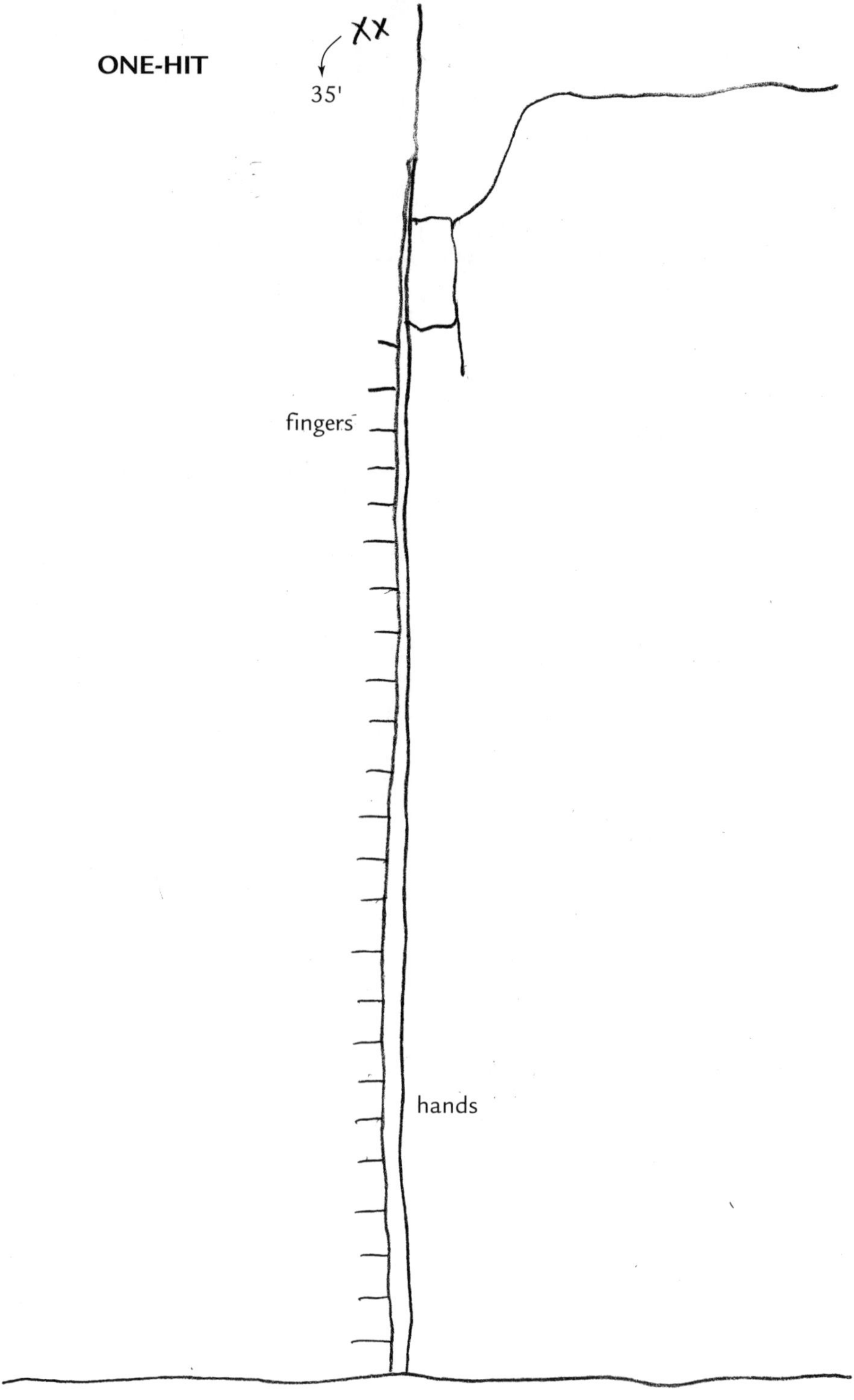

mantel onto a ledge with double anchors. Jason Repko: "Fun climb, although definitely the shortest route in the Hideout Wall area!"

Paraphernalia: Friends (1) #1, #1.5; Camalots (1) #2.

Descent: Rappel the route.

9 TWO MINUTES FOR ROUGHING
I, 5.9, 1 pitch, 45 feet (14 m) ★★

First Ascent: Andy Roberts, Jason Repko, April 7, 1999.

Location and Access: The route is approximately 200 feet (60 m) right of *One-Hit*. Climb a left-angling hand crack splitting a calcite-covered wall, to double anchors above a ledge.

Paraphernalia: Hand-size units.

Descent: Rappel the route from double-bolt anchors.

10 LUNG
I, 5.10, 1 pitch, 120 feet (37 m) ★★★

First Ascent: Lance Lemkau, Andy Roberts, April 23, 1999.

Location and Access: Climb a long crack approximately 500 feet (152 m) right of *Two Minutes for Roughing* and about 50 feet (15 m) left of *Bachelor Crack*. Begin up 20 feet (6 m) of soft rock, then continue into good hand jams that gradually become wide.

Paraphernalia: Camalots (3) #2, #3, #3.5, #4.

Descent: Rappel from double-bolt anchors on the left wall.

11 BACHELOR CRACK
I, 5.10 a/b, 1 pitch, 100 feet (30 m) ★★★

First Ascent: R. D. Pascoe, Andy Roberts, Frank Potempa, Scott Powers, Lance Lemkau, April 23, 1999. Andy Roberts: "Climbed during a joint bachelor party for R. D. and Andy."

Location and Access: *Bachelor Crack* ascends the right-facing dihedral opposite (left of) *Kister Twister*. Climb 40 feet (12 m) up soft rock to the beginning of a dihedral. Continue with mostly hands and some liebacking up a clean corner for another 60 feet (18 m) to a stance shared with the top of *Kister Twister*.

Paraphernalia: Standard desert rack.

Descent: One single 200-foot (60 m) rope rappel from anchors shared with *Kister Twister*.

12 KISTER TWISTER
I, 5.10a, 1 pitch, 100 feet (30 m) ★★★

First Ascent: Jason Repko, Andy Roberts, April 7, 1999.

Photo: Andy Roberts

Lung.

Photo: Andy Roberts

Bachelor Crack *(left) and* Kister Twister *(right)*.

Location and Access: *Kister Twister* climbs the left-facing dihedral opposite (right of) *Bachelor Crack*. Begin at the start of *Bachelor Crack* and climb 40 feet (12 m), then traverse right on an easy ledge to *Kister Twister*'s left-facing dihedral. Begin wide, then continue with small hands to double anchors shared with *Bachelor Crack*.

Paraphernalia: Standard desert rack; Camalots (3) #1.

Descent: A single 200-foot (60 m) rope rappel from anchors shared with *Bachelor Crack*.

13 KIAH CRACK
I, 5.10a, 1 pitch, 60 feet (18 m) ★★★★

First Ascent: Bill Kiah, Andy Roberts, Lance Lemkau, April 23, 1999.

Location and Access: *Kiah Crack* is 300 feet (91 m) right of *Kister Twister* and climbs a clean, good-looking, right-facing corner. Begin with 20 feet (6 m) of perfect hands, then continue with wide hands to a ledge with double anchors. Here it is possible to move right and continue 45 feet (14 m) to the top anchors of *Moab Flu* or rappel.

Paraphernalia: Camalots (1) #2, (3) #3, #3.5.

Descent: Rappel the route from double-bolt anchors.

14 MOAB FLU
I, 5.10b, 2 pitches, 105 feet (32 m) ★★★

First Ascent: Andy Roberts, Rob McKeracher, June 5, 1999.

Location and Access: The route climbs the splitter crack 10 feet (3 m) right of *Kiah Crack*. Andy Roberts: "Fun climbing with varied sizes. You can belay at *Kiah Crack's* anchors or continue on for another 40 feet (12 m) to another set of anchors above a ledge. The crack continues on for another 60 feet (18 m). The crack above is a perfect 1-inch (2.5 cm) splitter and looks very hard!"

Paraphernalia: Standard desert rack; extra Metolius cams #3, #4, #5.

Descent: Rappel with 200-foot (60 m) rope from double-bolt anchors. Andy Roberts: "One 200-foot (60 m) rope with stretch will get you down."

15 FIVE NINE FINGER CRACK
I, 5.11a, 1 pitch, 65 feet (20 m) ★★★★

First Ascent: Andy Roberts, Jason Schroeder, July 28, 1999.

Location and Access: *Five Nine Finger Crack* is 200 feet (60 m) right of *Moab Flu*, atop leaning rocks that form a cave against the buttress. Climb thin fingers up a left-facing corner to a stance with double anchors on the left wall.

Paraphernalia: Camalots (1) #2, #3.5; Metolius cams (1) #0, (4) #1.

Descent: Rappel the route from double-bolt anchors on the left wall.

Photo: Andy Roberts

Kiah Crack *(left) and* Moab Flu *(right)*.

Photo: Andy Roberts

Five Nine Finger Crack.

16 JENGA
I, 5.8, C1, 2 pitches, 170 feet (52 m) ★

First Ascent: Andy Roberts, Jason Schroeder, July 28, 1999.

Location and Access: *Jenga* is 150 feet (46 m) right of *Five Nine Finger Crack* on the far right side of Hideout Wall.

Pitch 1: Climb a chimney to a ledge with a tree, 5.6, 55 feet (17 m).

Pitch 2: Continue up the right side of stacked blocks, 5.8, 45 feet (14 m). With aid, ascend the splitter crack above to a two-bolt anchor on the left wall beneath a roof.

Paraphernalia: Standard desert rack; Metolius cams (1) #00, (3) #0, #1, (4) #2.

Descent: Rappel from double-bolt anchors to the ledge at the top of pitch 1, then from a tree to the ground. Double ropes are needed for the first rappel.

DIVERSIONS

ANASAZI GRANARY

The granary is identified by an Anasazi-built wall of rocks high on the west side of the small mesa at the northeast end of Fisher Valley. The mesa divides Cottonwood Canyon (left) from Hideout Canyon (right). From Fisher Valley, turn left onto the Cottonwood Canyon Trail (part of the Kokopelli Bike Trail), which is the first spur (left) reached in the valley from the Onion Creek–Fisher Valley Trail. Cross a deeply eroded wash, then turn right on a faint spur that ends at the nearby mesa's west edge. The granary is in view high on the wall above.

BULL DRAW FOREST SERVICE CAMPGROUND, DINOSAUR TRACKS

At 5.2 miles (8.3 km) beyond the La Sal Mountain Loop Road on the Beaver Mesa approach to the Hideout Wall, an inconspicuous unmarked dirt trail forks left (north) to the Bull Draw Forest Service public campground, which has a rest room and dramatic views hundreds of vertical feet into Fisher Valley. It is an excellent camp beneath large ponderosa pines. If the dirt trail is missed, drive to the crest of the road, approximately 500 feet or 0.1 mile (.16 km) before the pavement ends. Turn around and descend to a green cattle guard. The trail into the forest camp is about 0.3 mile (0.48 km) beyond the cattle guard. A high-clearance vehicle may be required to reach the campsite.

Dinosaur tracks and a stupendous view into Fisher Valley are reached from the crest of the hill approximately 0.3 mile (0.48 km) beyond the forest camp. Park at the pullout at the crest of the hill, just before the pavement ends. Go through a gate in the wire fence (please close it behind you) and walk approximately 50 feet (15 m) north. Watch for large three-toed tracks. Where possible, veer left through some bushes and view additional tracks. The view into Fisher Valley is about 100 yards (91 m) north of the dinosaur tracks.

> It is a gaunt land of splintered peaks, torn valleys, and hot skies. And at every step there is the suggestion of the fierce, the defiant, the defensive. Everything within its borders seems fighting to maintain itself against destroying forces. There is a war of elements and a struggle for existence going on here that for ferocity is unparalleled elsewhere in nature. The feeling of fierceness grows upon you as you come to know the desert better.
>
> —John C. Van Dyke, *The Desert,* 1901

10
TOP OF THE WORLD MESA

> [The Colorado River], for all its suggestion of blood it is not an unlovely color. On the contrary, that deep red contrasted with the green of the banks and the blue of the sky, makes a very beautiful color harmony. They are hues of depth and substance—hues that comport excellently well with the character of the river itself. And never a river had more character than the Colorado. You may not fancy the solitude of the stream nor its suggestive coloring, but you cannot deny its majesty and its nobility. It has not now the babble of the brook nor the swift rush of the canyon water; rather the quiet dignity that is above conflict, beyond gayety.
>
> —John C. Van Dyke, *The Desert,* 1901

Top of the World is a remote point overlooking Fisher Towers and Onion Creek's colorful gypsum outcrops. North and west is the Colorado River and Richardson Amphitheater. The La Sal Mountains dominate the eastern skyline. It is one of the most spectacular and dramatic overviews on the Colorado Plateau, a sight few have had the pleasure of experiencing.

COOLER THAN JESUS

Steve "Crusher" Bartlett: "A great climb, on great rock, easy approach, and a wild chimney that disappears way back into the hillside." To reach it, turn south off the River Road (Scenic Byway 128) just before the Dewey Bridge (an old suspension bridge) between mile markers 29 and 30. Follow Kokopelli Mountain Bike Trail signs up a graded dirt road. At approximately 3 miles (4.8 km) turn right, then immediately right again, and continue uphill with a high-clearance vehicle a couple of miles to the overlook. Hike about 50 feet (15 m) to the cliff edge and an obvious large dihedral topped with a large 150-foot (46 m) chimney.

1 COOLER THAN JESUS
I, 5.10-, 3 pitches, 300 feet (91 m) ★★★★

First Ascent: Steve "Crusher" Bartlett, Roger "Strappo" Hughes, May 26, 1991.

Location and Access: From a tree anchor, rappel 300 feet (91 m) with two ropes tied together or make two rappels, with the second from a stance 150 feet (46 m) down the route. The climb begins left of a large arête at a loose ledge approximately 50 feet (15 m) above the talus slope.

Pitch 1: Climb a right-facing corner to a good ledge, 5.10, 100 feet (30 m).

Pitch 2: Continue up a right-facing dihedral 5.9 into 5.10- to a belay at the base of a chimney, 100 feet (30 m).

Pitch 3: Climb the chimney to the top, either deep inside it or at its edge, 5.9, 100 feet (30 m).

TOP OF THE WORLD MESA ROUTE LOCATOR MAP

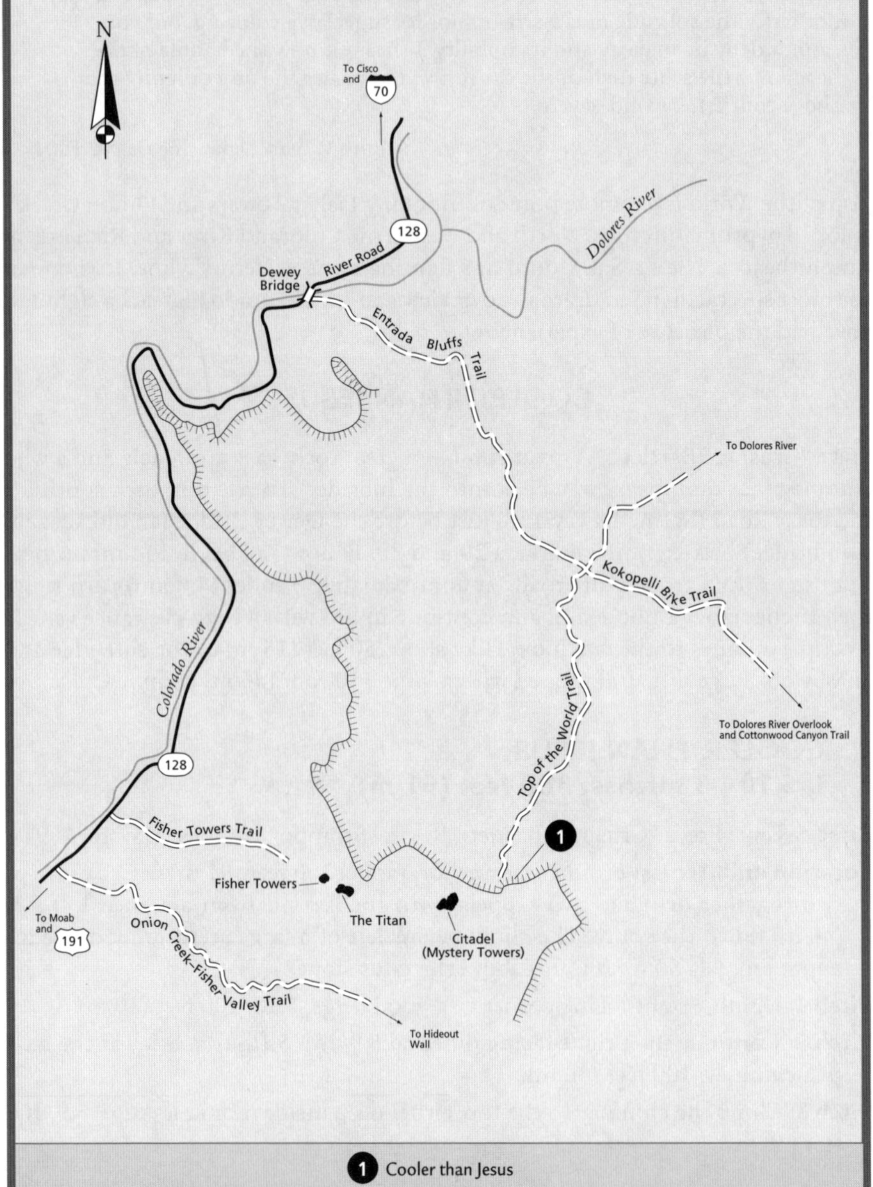

1 Cooler than Jesus

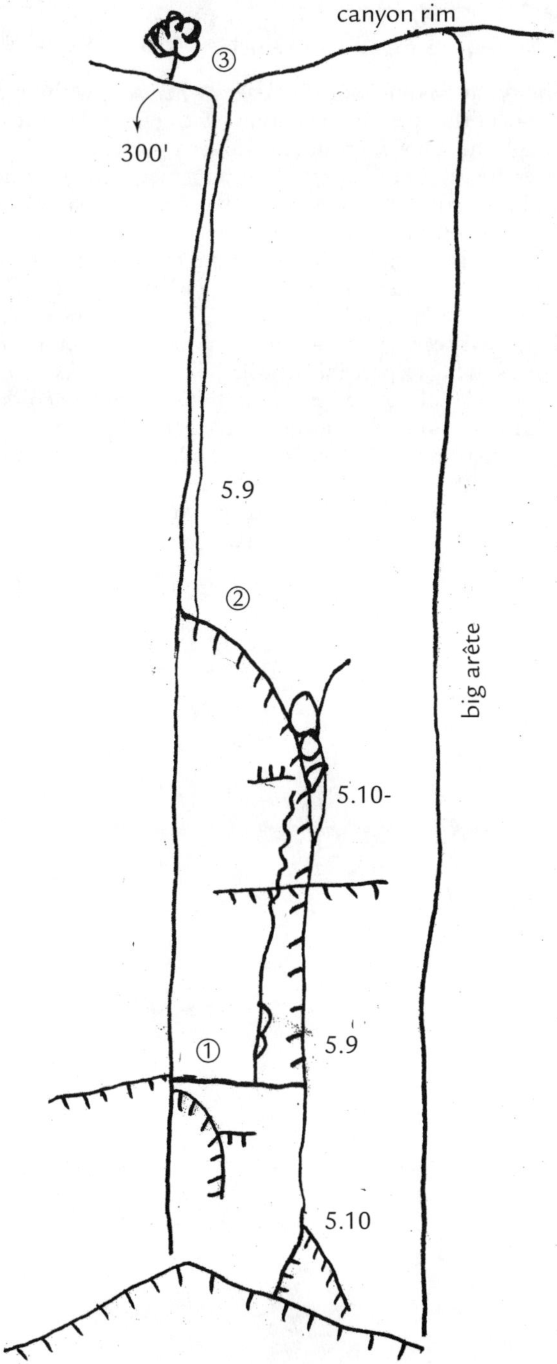

COOLER THAN JESUS

Paraphernalia: Friends (2) sets; wires.

Descent: Walk 50 feet (15 m) to your vehicle.

> Ordinarily the sky at evening over the desert, when seen without clouds, shows the colors of the spectrum beginning with red at the bottom and running through the yellows, greens, and blues up to the purple of the zenith. In cool weather, however, this spectrum arrangement seems swept out of existence by a broad band of yellow-green that stretches half way around the circle. It is a pale yellow fading into a pale green, which in turn melts into a pale blue. In hot weather this pallor is changed to something much richer and deeper. A band of orange takes its place. It is a flame-colored orange, and its hue is felt in reflection upon valley, plain, and mountain peak. This indeed is the orange light that converts the air in the mountain canyons into golden mist, and is measurably responsible for the yellow sunshafts that, streaming through the pinnacles of the western mountains, reach far across the upper sky in ever-widening bands. This great orange belt is lacking in that variety and vividness of coloring that comes with clouds, but it is not wanting in a splendor of its own. It is the broadest, the simplest, and in many respects the sublimest sunset imaginable—a golden dream with the sky enthroned in glory and the earth at its feet reflecting its lustre.
>
> —John C. Van Dyke, *The Desert,* 1901

11
WESTWATER CANYON

> The prevailing note of the sky, the one oftenest seen, is, of course, blue—a color we may not perhaps linger over because it is so common. And yet how seldom it is appreciated! Our attention is called to it in art—in a hawthorn jar as large as a sugar-bowl, made in a certain period, in a certain Oriental school. The aesthetic world is perhaps set agog by this ceramic blue. But what are its depth and purity compared to the ethereal blue! Yet the color is beautiful in the jar and infinitely more beautiful in the sky—that is beautiful in itself and merely as color. It is not necessary that it should mean anything. Line and tint do not always require significance to be beautiful. There is no tale or text or testimony to be tortured out of the blue sky. It is a splendid body of color; no more.
>
> —John C. Van Dyke, *The Desert,* 1901

The 17-mile (27 km)-long Westwater Canyon (a.k.a. Hades or Granite Canyon) begins just west of the Utah-Colorado border at Loma. It is approximately 25 river miles (40 km) from Loma to the Westwater ranger station. In Westwater Canyon, the Colorado River has carved through ancient Precambrian dark metamorphic gneiss and gneissic granites that are 1.7 billion years old. The canyon drew little attention from river rafters before 1970, but quickly became so popular that permits were soon required by the BLM. The canyon offers close to a dozen rapids, many second in size and turbulence only to the most dangerous found in Cataract Canyon downriver from Moab.

NOTE: River miles are counted upriver from the confluence of the Green and Colorado Rivers in the heart of Canyonlands National Park. The bridge over the Colorado at the north end of Moab Valley is river mile 64. The confluence of the Dolores with the Colorado is between river miles 96 and 97. Westwater ranger station is between river mile 127 and 128, and Loma put-in is river mile 152. River left and river right presuppose that you are looking downstream.

WESTWATER CANYON

RON'S TOWER

On Thanksgiving Day 1996, Bill Duncan, Steve Anderton, Mike Calacino, Ron Kirk, and Matt Simpson floated down the Colorado River from Loma, Colorado, to the "black rocks," a Precambrian igneous intrusion the river cuts through. Bill Duncan: "It forms nice beaches here, and Moore Canyon's mouth is nearby, as well as two or three sandstone towers of Wingate. We buried the turkey in the ground to cook Saturday morning, then went climbing on the very end of the towers, the most prominent one. The climbing was enjoyable, and we summited a couple of hours later.

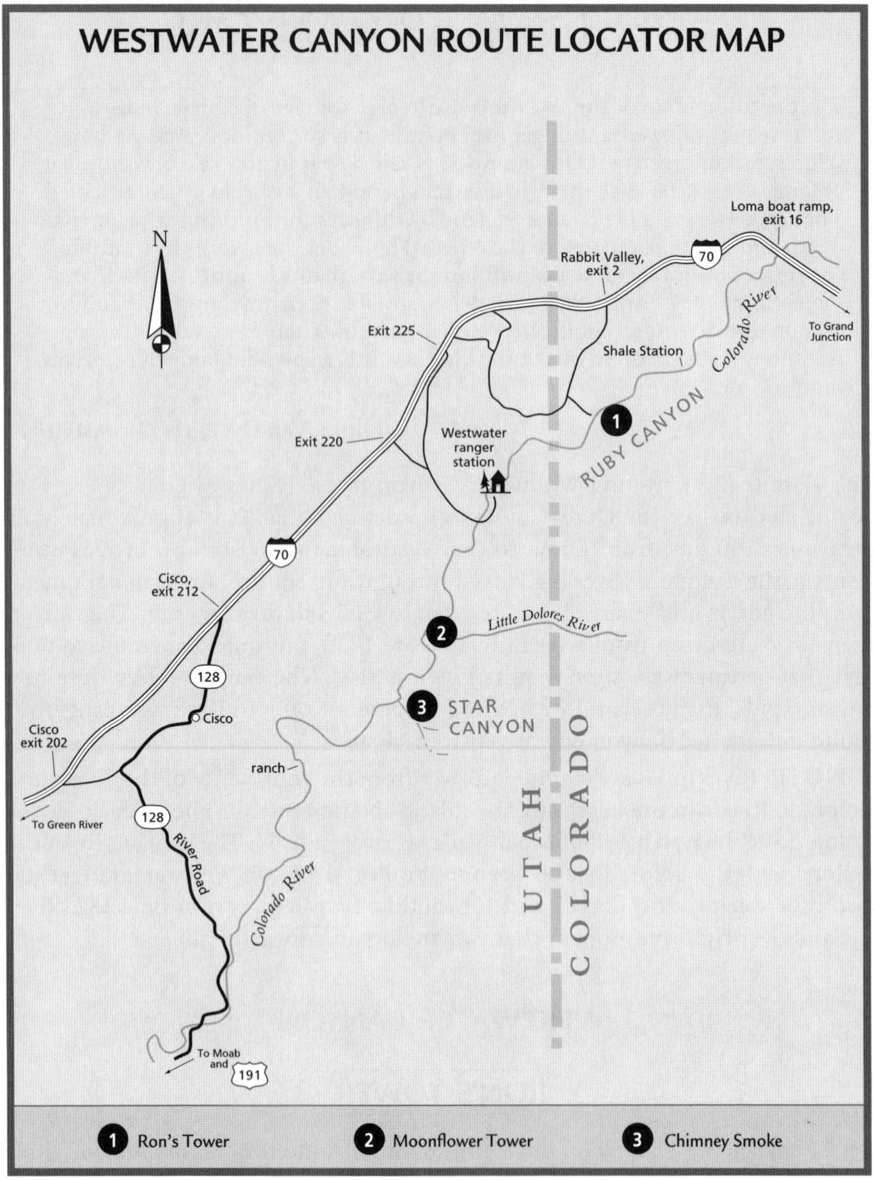

"We were basking in the sun on this remote desert tower, relishing the flavor of another fine first ascent, when we heard the most awful thundering of crashing boulders I have ever heard. In the midst of the crashing, I heard a blood-curdling scream. Now, this did not sound like just a few rocks coming down. The thundering crash had a bass to it that only comes from something big. My friend Ron Kirk was in the middle of all that rock. Apparently, his partner was standing on a large block that looked as if it was part of the firm ground, but it wasn't.

Westwater Canyon, view from river.

This block had been traveled on by me and two others; it appeared sound. But as Ron was downclimbing an easy section below it, it went flying down and crashed into an even larger flake, which gave way, bringing even more rock down—and Ron was in the middle.

"Miraculously, Ron survived the initial fall with all the rock. He managed to stay mostly on top of the blocks that were falling with him. He fell 20 feet and when he hit, the rock fell on his legs. He suffered a partial amputation of his right leg, and a complete and very serious compound fracture of his left, along with spinal injuries and numerous minor fractures."

The grueling and very complicated rescue is a very long story, best left for another time and place, but Ron's close call should be kept in mind whenever this tower is climbed.

To reach Ron's Tower, boat down Ruby Canyon from Loma, Colorado, to the ancient black rocks in Ruby Canyon. Near the black rocks, Ron's Tower is the most prominent spire on the east side of the river at the mouth of Moore Canyon (river left) between river miles 135 and 136.

It is possible to reach Ron's Tower by land by hiking down Moore Canyon from Glade Park to the south—a long approach, and not recommended. An alternative land approach is to exit Interstate 70 at mile marker 2, the Rabbit Valley exit. Drive south to the McClellan Canyon trailhead, then hike down the canyon to the river. Hike approximately 1 mile (1.6 km) upriver, then cross the river and hike to the tower at the mouth of Moore Canyon. Details of these alternative approaches are not given because they are not recommended.

1 RON'S TOWER—SOUTH FACE
II, 5.9, A1, 2 pitches, 160 feet (49 m) ★

First Ascent: Bill Duncan, Steve Anderton, Mike Calacino, Thanksgiving 1996.

Location and Access: The route climbs the south face of the tower. Bill Duncan: "Ron's Tower will go free at a 5.11 or more difficult free rating. Nice crack climbing."

Pitch 1: Begin up a 5.7 crack on the south face. Continue 5.9 to a good belay ledge.

Pitch 2: Climb a 5.9 right-facing dihedral into thin hands, then A1 to a squeeze chimney (5.8+) near the top.

Paraphernalia: Standard desert rack; Camalots (1) #5.

Descent: Double-rope rappel down the south face from fixed anchors.

MOONFLOWER TOWER

Moonflower Tower is reached by boat only, from the Westwater put-in to the popular Little D (Dolores) camp at the confluence of the Little Dolores River between river miles 120 and 121 (river left). Hike up Little Dolores Canyon approximately 3 miles (4.8 km) to the tower.

2 MOONFLOWER TOWER
III, 5.11, 3 pitches, 230 feet (70 m)

First Ascent: Dave Dawson, Kyle Copeland, May 1989.

Location and Access: Upcanyon from Little D (Dolores) camp.

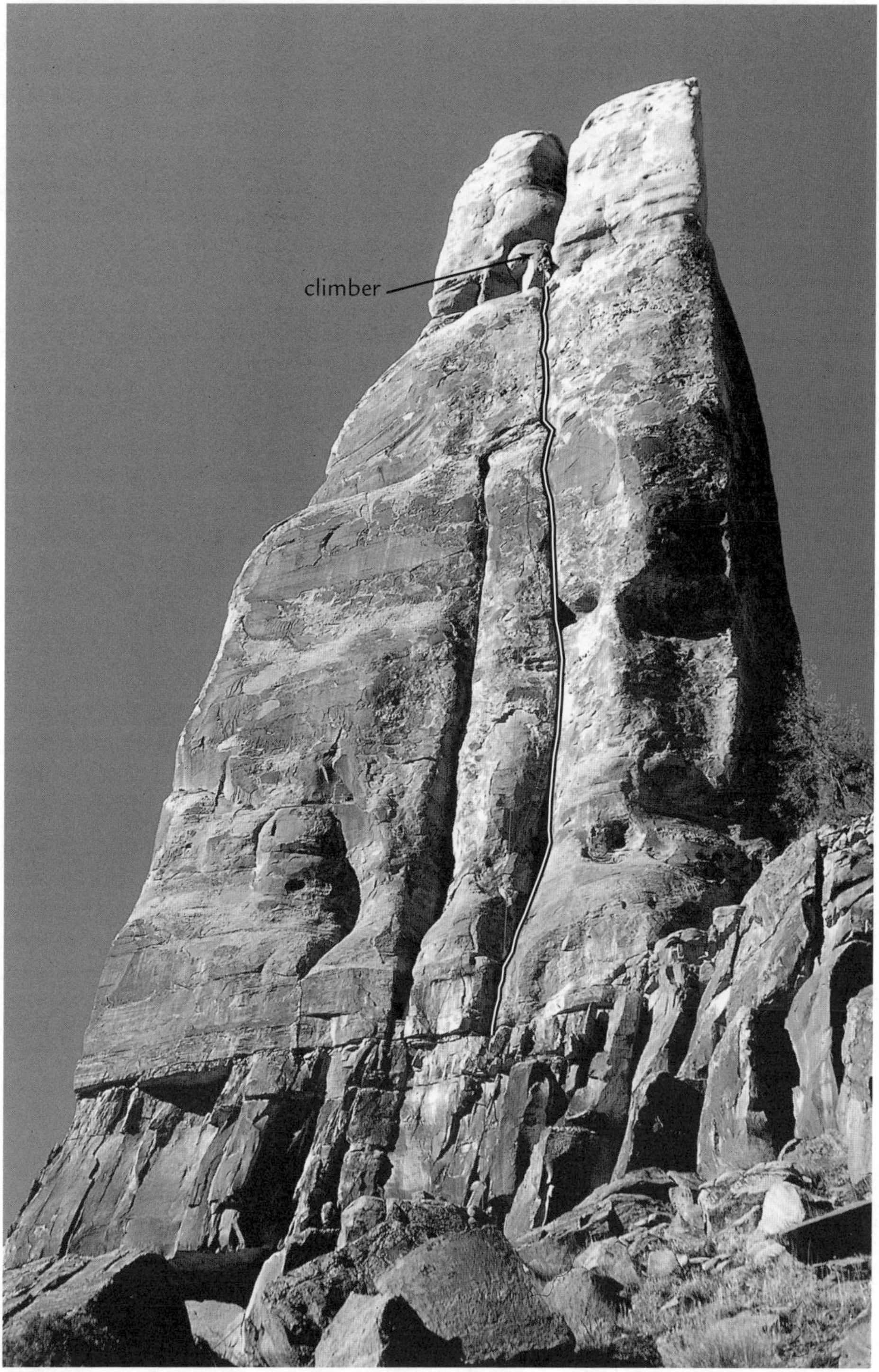

Photo: Bill Duncan

Mike Calacino on Ron's Tower, South Face.

RON'S TOWER—SOUTH FACE

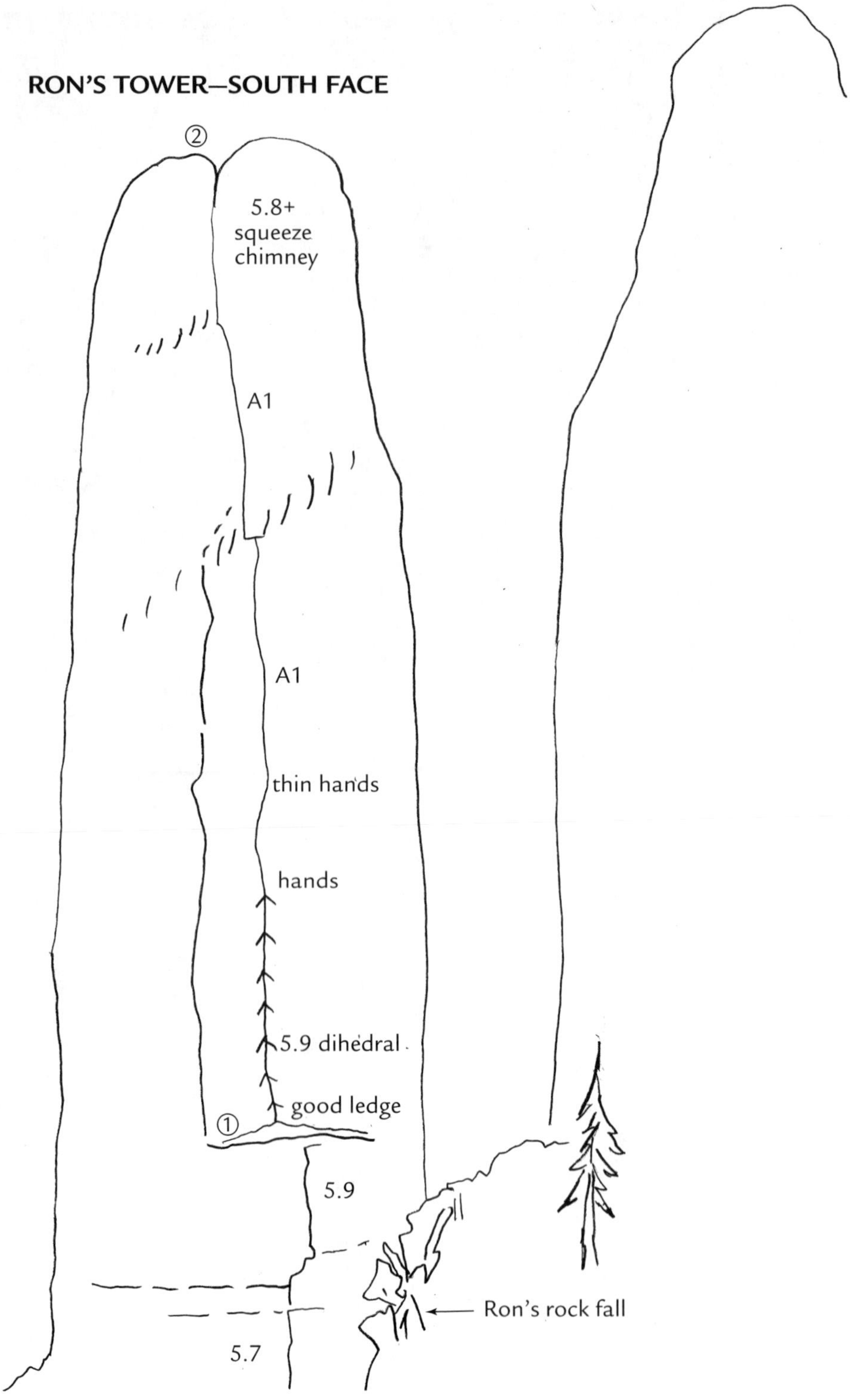

MOONFLOWER TOWER

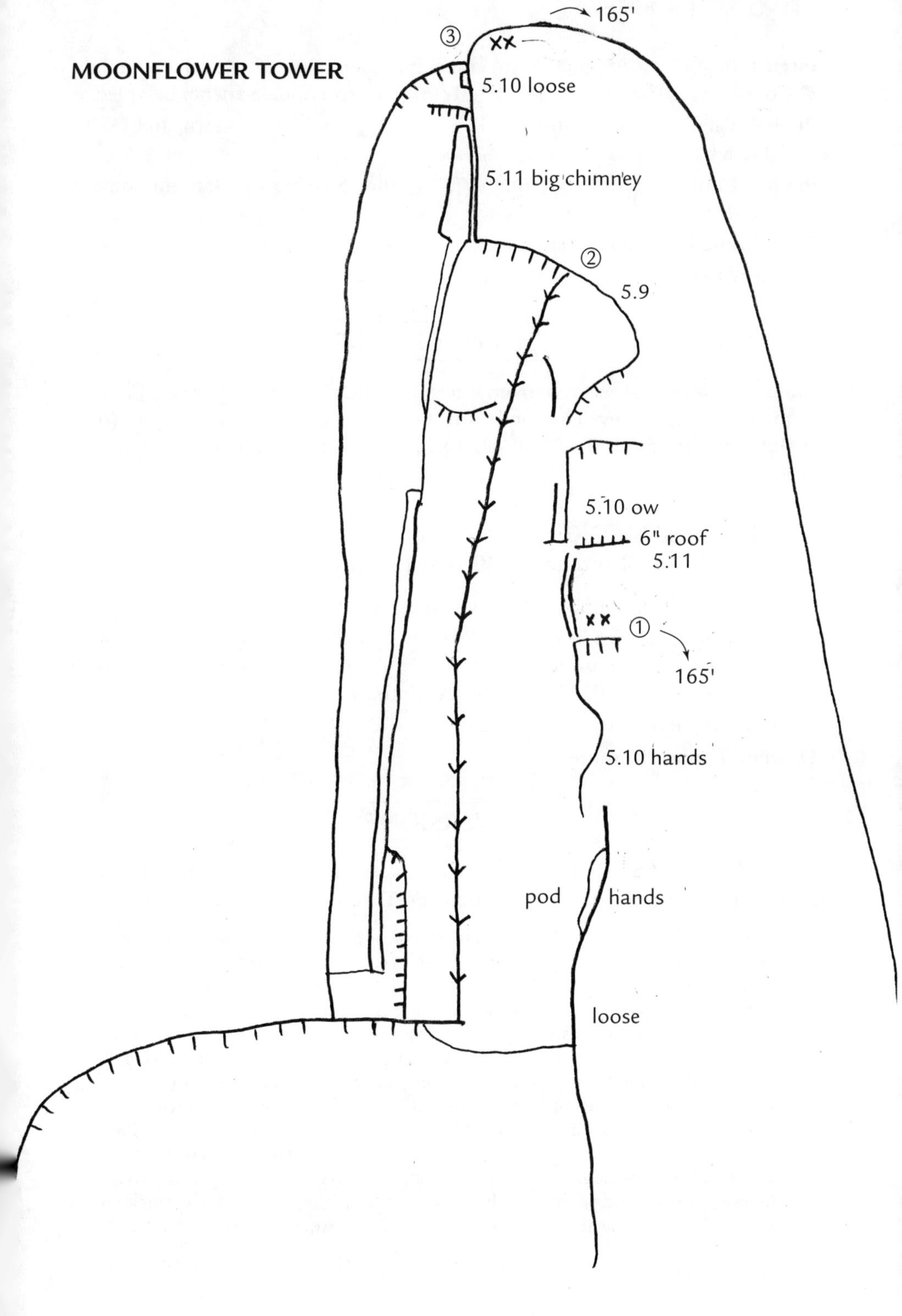

Pitch 1: Begin up a 2.5-inch (6 cm) crack. Pass loose rock and a pod with hands. Continue 5.10 hands up a 4-inch (10 cm) crack to a double-anchor belay ledge.

Pitch 2: Climb 5.11 past a 6-inch (15 cm) roof, then 5.10 off-width, and finally 5.9 to a belay stance.

Pitch 3: Continue up a large chimney (5.11), then 5.10 loose rock to the summit shoulder.

Paraphernalia: Standard desert rack.

Descent: Two double-rope rappels down the route.

CHIMNEY SMOKE

Chimney Smoke is between river miles 116 and 117 in Westwater Canyon. Approach by river only. The climb is reached after entering Star Canyon (river left). David Mondeau: "Red wall, big turn, first main crack on the first granite encountered."

3 CHIMNEY SMOKE
III, 5.8, A2, 2 pitches, 300 feet (91 m)

First Ascent: David Mondeau, Marty Barcus, July 1976.

Location and Access: Although *Chimney Smoke* climbs granite rock, it is included in this guide to sandstone due to its proximity to the climbs in Westwater Canyon. Further details are unknown.

Paraphernalia: Standard desert rack.

Descent: Rappel the route.

DIVERSIONS

Self-evident: the incredible rapids, scenery, side canyon hikes to historic sites, Anasazi ruins, pictographs, and petroglyphs. Take some time to explore the area.

> The bright sky-colors, the spectacular effects, are not to be found high up in the blue of the dome. The air in the zenith is too thin, too free from dust, to take deep colorings of red and orange. Those colors belong near the earth, along the horizons where the aerial envelope is dense. The lower strata of atmosphere are in fact responsible for the gorgeous sunsets, the tinted hazes, the Indian-summer skies, the hot September glows. These all appear in their splendor when the sun is near the horizon-line and its beams are falling through the many miles of hot, dust-laden air that lie along the surface of the earth. The air at sunset after a day of intense heat-radiation is usually so thick that only the long and strong waves of color can pass through it. The blues are almost lost, the neutral tints are missing, the greens are seen but faintly. The waves of red and yellow are the only ones that travel through the thick air with force. And these are the colors that tell us the story of the desert sunset.
>
> —John C. Van Dyke, *The Desert,* 1901

12
US 191 SOUTH

> One can almost fancy that behind each dome and rampart there are cloud-like Genii—spirits of the desert—keeping guard over this kingdom of the sun. And what far-reaching kingdom they watch! Plain upon plain leads up and out to the horizon—far as the eye can see—in undulations of gray and gold; ridge upon ridge melts into the blue of the distant sky in lines of lilac and purple; fold upon fold over the mesas the hot air drops its veilings of opal and topaz. Yes; it is the kingdom of sun-fire. For every color in the scale is attuned to the key of flame, every air-wave comes with the breath of flame, every sunbeam falls as a shaft of flame. There is no questioning who is sovereign in these dominions.
>
> —John C. Van Dyke, *The Desert,* 1901

US 191 is a major artery running from Interstate 70 south through Moab, Monticello, Blanding, and Bluff. It gives access to numerous climbing areas: Utah 46 east to Colorado's Unaweep Canyon, Dolores River Canyon, the numerous Dakota sandstone crags of the Lost World and Atomic Energy Crags area, and the Navajo sandstone crags of 16Z; Utah 95 east to Arch and Texas Canyons, Natural Bridges National Monument, Bear's Ears, Fry Canyon, and Lake Powell and the Hite Marina climbing areas; and US 163 south to Valley of the Gods, Mexican Hat, and Monument Valley; and eventually connecting with Flagstaff and Phoenix.

This chapter covers climbs established on Entrada sandstone, from south of Moab to Church Rock, located at the junction of US 191 and Utah 211 (gateway to Indian Creek). Routes are listed in order north to south.

FORMATION

The climbs in this chapter are on the Entrada rocks of the middle Jurassic period, 160 to 180 million years old. Few climbs have been established on Entrada sandstone, with the notable exceptions of Arches National Park and the area from Moab south to Church Rock. Entrada is not as dense as Wingate, but it is not far different. In a similar manner to the cliff-forming Navajo sandstone, Entrada fractures conchoidally, producing rounded arch forms—not the most desirable features to climb. Many areas do have vertical fracture lines, however, and this is one of the reasons for the rock's appeal in Arches and areas south of Moab.

MAP

The Moab West map published by Latitude 40 Degrees identifies US 191, La Sal Mountain Loop Road, Kane Springs (rest stop), Utah 46, Looking Glass Rock, Wilson Arch, and Joe Wilson Canyon. Future revisions of the map will include additional climbing areas south of Moab.

US 191 SOUTH ROUTE LOCATOR MAP

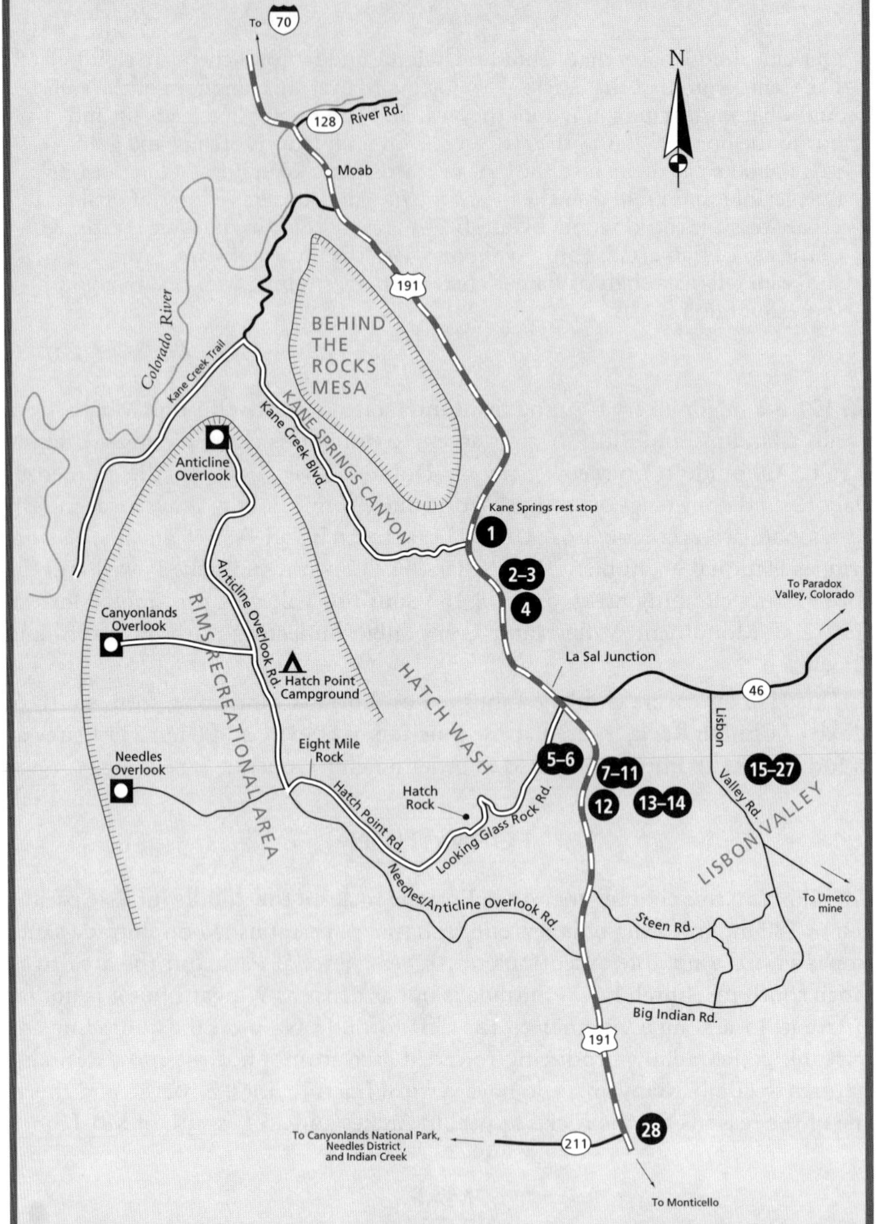

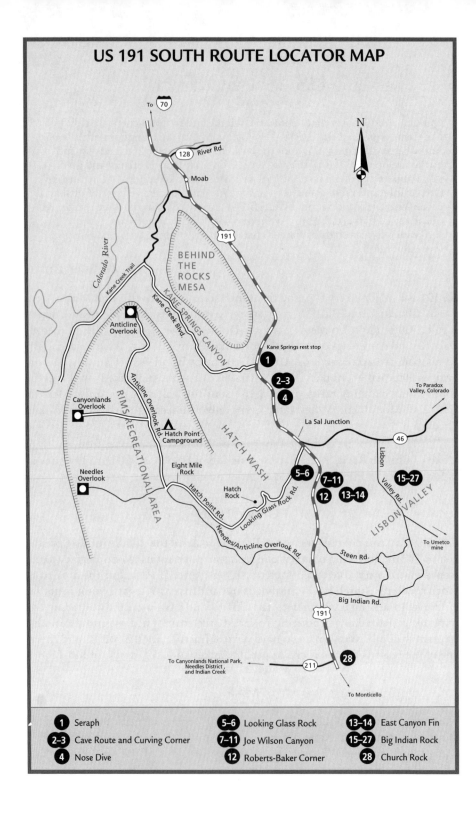

1 Seraph
2–3 Cave Route and Curving Corner
4 Nose Dive
5–6 Looking Glass Rock
7–11 Joe Wilson Canyon
12 Roberts-Baker Corner
13–14 East Canyon Fin
15–27 Big Indian Rock
28 Church Rock

MILE MARKER LOG—US 191 TO UTAH 211

This log begins at the south end of Moab Valley and ends at Church Rock at the junction of US 191 and Utah 211 (entrance to Indian Creek and the Needles District of Canyonlands National Park) using mile marker signs as reference points. To continue south to Bluff climbing areas, see the Monticello to Bluff Mile Marker Log in Chapter 20.

118: A paved road branches east, signed OLD AIRPORT ROAD. There is also a sign for San Juan County 194, and one giving distances to Pack Creek Picnic Area (9 miles), Oowah Lake (17 miles), Warner Lake and Campground (21 miles), Highway 128 (38 miles), Moab via Loop Road (57 miles), and Kens Lake (3 miles). From US 191, it's a 0.3-mile (0.48 km)-drive to the junction with Spanish Valley Drive and a sign for La Sal Mountain Loop Road (right) and Spanish Valley (left). Ahead on the left is the site of the old Moab airport during the uranium days of the 1950s. The La Sal Mountain Loop Road is a highly recommended two-hour all-vehicle road that gives expansive views of Moab Valley west to Canyonlands, Arches National Park, and Castle Valley. Continue south on US 191.

114–113: US 191 climbs Blue Hills as it leaves the southern reaches of Moab Valley.

111–110: Kane Springs is a rest area with rest rooms and a manicured grass picnic area beneath stately cottonwood trees. At the east (back) side of the rest stop is the Seraph, a 45-foot (14 m) Entrada sandstone tower. South of the stop is the Hole n" the Rock tourist extravaganza comprising a souvenir shop and guided tours of the "home" blasted into the rock by out-of-work uranium miners in the 1950s.

109–108: *Cave Route* and *Curving Corner* are above a pullout on the left side of the roadway.

108–107: *Nose Dive* is on the left side of the roadway.

104–103: The junction of Utah 46 East, which gives access to La Sal Creek Canyon Crag, Paradox Valley, and the numerous Dakota sandstone crags, including Lost World and Atomic Energy Crags, the Wingate of the Dolores River Canyon, and the Navajo sandstone of 16Z Crag. Sign: BLANDING 54—MONTICELLO 39 (continue ahead to the south).

101–100: Wilson Arch, east above the highway.

100–99: *Middendorf's Folly* is against the cliffs to the east. The dirt trail to Joe Wilson Canyon branches east from the highway.

98: Signed Lopez Arch view area pullout left (east) of the highway. The arch is a tiny, perfectly round window in an Entrada sandstone fin and is sometimes difficult to locate. It has a diameter of less than 2 feet (0.6 m). Named by Hardy Redd, of La Sal, for Fermin R. Lopez, a cowman who worked in the Dry Valley area for many years.

98–97: East Canyon Fin comes into view in the distant east.

96–95: Left (east) is the beginning of San Juan County 114, the Steen Road, which leads to copper and uranium mines and Big Indian Rock climbs. County 114 sign and REF 10 sign.

94–93: A paved road to the right (west) leads to Rims Recreation Area. The road is paved to the Needles Overlook, dirt to Anticline Overlook, and dirt and four-wheel drive to Canyonlands Overlook. All three overlooks give breathtaking vistas of canyon country. Canyonlands Overlook offers views of the Colorado River 2,000 feet (610 m) below the Rims' mesa top.

87–86: Church Rock is on the left (east). Utah 211 (west) leads to Newspaper Rock State Park, Indian Creek, and the Needles District of Canyonlands National Park.

SERAPH

Seraph is a diminutive tower with a celestial name. Seraph is one of the six-winged angels standing in the presence of God, according to *Webster's,* and is obvious at the back of the Kane Springs rest stop (a few yards north of the Hole n" the Rock tourist extravaganza). It is south of mile marker 111, approximately 14 miles (22.5 km) south of Moab. There is good camping on public land west of the rest stop, where a dirt trail descends to a wash with cottonwood trees. The trail eventually connects with Kane Creek Valley, but it is sandy and requires high clearance and difficult four-wheel driving.

1 SERAPH
I, 5.7, A2, 1 pitch, 60 feet (18 m)

First Ascent: Brian Smoot, Jonathan Smoot, 1981.

Location and Access: Begin on the north side of the tower between the spire and the buttress behind it. There is a 5-inch (12.7 cm) square steel post drilled into the back right col of the landform and much graffiti. Begin with 20 feet (6 m) of friction to gain an aid crack.

Paraphernalia: Small cams; Lowe Balls; selection of pitons.

Descent: Rappel the route, or rappel to the notch behind the tower then down-climb to steps chopped in the rock by an unknown party.

CAVE ROUTE AND CURVING CORNER

Cave Route and *Curving Corner* are between mile markers 118 and 119 on the left (east) side of US 191, opposite a 55 mph sign. There is a parking pullout on the (left) east side of the highway below the climbs.

2 CAVE ROUTE
I, not rated, 1 pitch, 130 feet (40 m)

First Ascent: Unknown.

Location and Access: The free climb ascends an obvious crack system below a

Photo: Eric Bjørnstad

Seraph.

large deep cave. Begin up an intermittent seam/face to a crack system. Climb 15 feet (4.5 m) up a face to the right, to an alcove and rappel slings that are visible from below the route.

Paraphernalia: Medium to small cams.

Descent: Double-rope rappel the route.

3 CURVING CORNER
I, 5.2, A2, 1 pitch, 55 feet (17 m)

First Ascent: Unknown.

Location and Access: *Curving Corner* is two crack systems right of *Cave Route.* Climb the obvious right-facing, right-curving corner. Begin up a vertical crack system to a right-facing dihedral. Continue past two fixed pitons and on to double-bolt rappel slings visible from below the climb.

Paraphernalia: Small cams; TCUs; small nuts; quick draws.

Descent: Rappel the route.

NOSE DIVE

At mile marker 118, *Nose Dive* (a.k.a. *Bridge Dihedral*) is right of a prominent buttress on the left side of the roadway. It can also be identified as east of the point

Photos: Eric Bjørnstad

Cave Route *(left)*, Curving Corner *(right)*.

Nose Dive.

where power lines cross the highway. Turn left (east) and go through a gate in the fence, then walk to the route in view on the nearby wall. Please leave the gate closed regardless of how you found it. It is there to keep cattle from entering the highway.

4 NOSE DIVE (a.k.a. Bridge Dihedral) I, 5.12, 1 pitch, 80 feet (24 m) ★★★★★

First Ascent: Steve Hong, Karen Budding, May 1982.

Location and Access: When viewed from the highway, *Nose Dive* is an obvious left-curving, left-facing overhanging dihedral. Climb a strenuous lieback crack to rappel slings visible on the wall at the top of the climb.

Paraphernalia: Friends (8) #4.

Descent: Rappel the route.

LOOKING GLASS ROCK

Looking Glass Rock is a rock shelter type natural arch eroded into a large rock dome. It has a span of 35 feet (10.6 m), a height of 34 feet (10.3 m), a thickness of 25 feet (7.6 m), and a width of 43 feet (13 m). The arch is approximately 2 miles (3.2 km) west of US 191.

The arch was named by John Silvey in 1889 because the sun shining through the opening creates an image on the wall of the deep cave, which reminded him of that created by a mirror or looking glass. It was also known in years past as Vulcan's Tomb.

To get there, drive west on the dirt trail between mile markers 113 and 114 (San Juan County 131/Looking Glass Rock Road). At a left fork where a sign identifies the rock, continue 500 feet (152 m) to a parking and camping area. If driving from Moab, Wilson Arch can be seen between mile markers 102 and 103, and Lopez Arch across from mile marker 98. San Juan County 131/Looking Glass Rock Road is also a scenic approach to the climbs in Hatch Wash (see Chapter 13).

5 ADVENTURE IN ENTRADALAND II, 5.8, C2, 1 pitch, 250 feet (76 m) ★★★★

First Ascent: Mike Baker, solo, December 1996. Second Ascent and First Free Ascent: Chris Ducker, James Bracken, March 28, 1998.

Location and Access: From the parking area at the west side of the rock, hike up and through the arch, then traverse left around a bench to the far end of the landform, where a two-bolt anchor marks the start of the climb. Ascend the thin crack above, then follow the underside of the arch-in-the-making, passing two drilled angles. The final moves climb straight up through a hole to a three-bolt belay/rappel anchor. Mike Baker: "This is the steepest pitch I've ever

Photo: Mike Baker

Adventure in Entradaland.

climbed! Major pucker factor. The route is climbed clean except for three pins to start the climb."

Paraphernalia: Camalots (2) #0.75, #1, #2, #3; TCUs (3) each.

Descent: Double-rope rappel from anchors at the top of the route.

6 EAST RIB
I, 5.7, 2 pitches, 290 feet (88 m)

First Ascent: Local cowboys. Second Ascent: Dave Medara, Brett Sutteer, August 1997.

Location and Access: From the parking area, traverse left or right around the rock to its east ridge.

Pitch 1: Climb the rib, starting at the lowest point, and continue for approximately 150 feet (46 m) to a natural belay, passing some fixed anchors on the way.

Pitch 2: Continue up the rock to the summit, passing fixed anchors, 140 feet (43 m).

Paraphernalia: Standard desert rack; quick draws.

Descent: Rappel out the hole from the top of *Adventure in Entradaland.* Dave Medara: "An incredibly exposed rappel. Scary." An alternative descent is to reverse the route.

JOE WILSON CANYON

Wilson Canyon is a hidden fortress of aesthetic slickrock Entrada sandstone that (except for a cowboy looking for a lost cow) is probably rarely visited. Paul Ross: "A very beautiful canyon." Five towers have been climbed in Wilson Canyon; all are reached within a short high-clearance drive (or hike) from US 191. There are two approaches: an easy 1.7-mile (2.7 km) high-clearance vehicle trail along the north buttress of the canyon, or a 2.4-mile (3.9 km) trail that follows along the canyon's southern edge. Climbs are listed left (north) to right (south).

To reach the northern trail, turn east between mile markers 99 and 100 onto a graveled road leading to a new housing development. To reach Tranquility Tower, turn right before reaching the first buildings and drive approximately 1.7 miles (2.7 km) to the end of the trail. Park (good campsite), then hike east to the obvious tower ahead across the canyon.

Queen's View and King Arthur's Seat are about 500 yards (457 m) beyond and to the right. King Arthur's Seat is the long ridged landform beside the tapered spire of Queen's View. The fastest approach to Queen's View and King Arthur's Seat is to hike across the white Navajo sandstone drainage 0.3 mile (0.48 km) before the end of the trail is reached, or 1.4 miles (2.2 km) into the canyon from US 191.

Moby Dick's Head and Tail landforms are in view to the east from US 191 between mile markers 99 and 100. Their easiest approach is from the south trail into Joe Wilson Canyon between mile markers 98 and 99, then a short hike. Turn east from US 191 0.2 mile (0.32 km) before the Lopez Arch view area. Go through a gate in the fence and, with high clearance, drive 2.3 miles (3.7 km). Park where the trail becomes four-wheel drive and will probably require shovel repair to continue. Moby Dick's Head and Tail can also be reached from the north trail with a twenty-five-minute hike past Tranquility Tower, then past Queen's View and King Arthur's Seat.

7 TRANQUILITY TOWER—FEEDING THE RAT
III, 5.7, C2, 3 pitches, 210 feet (64 m) ★★★

First Ascent: Paul Ross, Gene Vallee, June 13, 2000.

Location and Access: Scramble up the west end of the tower to a ledge. Paul Ross: "A superb line up a tower in very beautiful surroundings."

Pitch 1: Climb a pedestal to a horizontal crack. Continue left up the crack to a good belay. Protect the lead with Friends, 50 feet (15 m).

Pitch 2: Climb to a drilled angle with aid up a small crack using small cams or two #2 angle pitons. Move left to bolts and continue making #2 cam placements along a prominent bedding seam to a belay, 100 feet (30 m).

Pitch 3: Follow bolts past a large ledge, then to the summit, C2, 60 feet (18 m).

Paraphernalia: Friends (3) #00, (1) #1, (2) #2, #3, #3.5, (1) #5; tie-offs (10+), wire rivet type is best; very small camming units; 200-foot (60 m) ropes.

Descent: From bushes between the two summits, make one rappel down the east side of the tower with 200-foot (60 m) ropes.

8 QUEEN'S VIEW
II, 5.8, A2, 2 pitches, 120 feet (37 m) ★★★

First Ascent: Wilson Goodrich, Mike Baker, March 14, 1999.

Location and Access: The route climbs the right side of the tower.

Pitch 1: Begin at the left side of the east face (opposite the Joe Canyon Trail) and ascend 5.8, passing a fixed anchor, then angle right to a belay ledge with two fixed anchors, 5.8, 60 feet (18 m).

Pitch 2: Continue with A2 climbing, passing four fixed anchors and ending with 5.8 at the summit, 5.8, A2, 60 feet (18 m).

Paraphernalia: Camalots (1) #0.75, #2; Leeper Z (1); knifeblades (6); birdbeaks (1); quick draws (5).

Descent: Double-rope rappel from a bolt and drilled baby angle piton.

9 KING ARTHUR'S SEAT
II, 5.9, 3 pitches, 200 feet (60 m) ★★★★

First Ascent: Paul Ross, Gene Vallee, June 13, 2000.

Location and Access: The route begins at the obvious toe of a long ridge at the

Photo: Paul Ross

Tranquility Tower—Feeding the Rat.

Photo: Wilson Goodrich

Queen's View.

Photo: Paul Ross

King Arthur's Seat.

right (southwest) side of the dome. Paul Ross: "A good easy introduction to desert spires—well worth a visit due to its beautiful surroundings."

Pitch 1: Scramble onto a mound of rock below a slab and upper chimney, 5.7, 70 feet (21 m).

Pitch 2: Continue past two bolts on the right, then up slabs to a belay from Friends, 5.9, 60 feet (18 m).

Pitch 3: Follow the long narrow ridge to the top of a crownlike tower. The last 15 feet (4.5 m) are protected by a drilled angle piton, 5.7.

Paraphernalia: Friends (3); wire tie-offs; ropes (2).

Descent: Downclimb to the drilled angle piton, then descend 150 feet (46 m) to a natural bollard. From the bollard, make one double-rope rappel down the east side to the ground.

10 MOBY DICK'S TAIL—MIDDENDORF'S FOLLY I, 5.9, A2, 3 pitches, 150 feet (46 m)

First Ascent: John Middendorf et al., early 1990s.

Location and Access: Moby Dick's Tail is the tower left of Moby Dick's Head on the right (south) side of Joe Wilson Canyon and is visible from US 191. Summit anchors are visible from the slickrock on the north side of the tower. Begin with a scramble and friction up the slickrock Entrada sandstone.

Pitch 1: Approach the saddle below the climb from the north and belay.

Pitch 2: Climb to a red bench and belay.

Pitch 3: Continue to the summit.

Paraphernalia: Light desert rack emphasizing thin units.

Descent: Rappel the north face.

11 MOBY DICK'S HEAD
I, 5.8, A1, 2 pitches, 200 feet (60 m) ★★

First Ascent: Paul Ross, Jeff Pheasant, July 1, 2000.

Location and Access: Moby Dick's Head and Tail are visible from US 191 and are weathered from the slickrock member of Entrada sandstone. The route for the Head begins on the northwest side of the landform.

Pitch 1: Climb to a friction slab using a couple of Friend placements for protection at midheight, 5.8.

Pitch 2: Easy friction brings you to a group of holes (#3, #4 Friends). The two higher holes take a #6 Friend and a #2 angle piton. Continue to the top over soft rock (5.6, A1, but will probably be climbed free in the future).

Paraphernalia: Friends #3, #4, #6; angle piton #2.

Descent: Rappel the route.

ROBERTS-BAKER CORNER

The Roberts-Baker Corner is east of the highway, right (south) and beyond Lopez Arch, a tiny window less than 2 feet (0.6 m) in diameter. A signed viewing pullout for the arch is across from mile marker 98.

Photo: Paul Ross

Moby Dick's Tail (left), Moby Dick's Head (right).

To reach the Roberts-Baker Corner, continue south from the Lopez Arch pullout and turn left (east) onto the first dirt trail. When the trail ends, hike east to the mesa ahead. The route faces opposite the road and is in view only after hiking east past it and looking back to the west (toward US 191).

12 ROBERTS-BAKER CORNER
I, 5.9, 1 pitch, 110 feet (34 m) ★★★

First Ascent: Andy Roberts, Mike Baker, September 1998.

Location and Access: Climb a right-facing corner up Entrada sandstone. An unclimbed pitch 2 would be 5.9, C2.

Paraphernalia: Camalots (1) #1, #2, #3, #4, #4.5; TCUs (2) each.

Descent: Single-rope rappel from two drilled pitons.

EAST CANYON FIN

East Canyon Fin is approximately 25 miles (40 km) south of Moab, in the next (unnamed) canyon south of Joe Wilson Canyon, at a location just north of Hook and Ladder Gulch. The spire is in view from US 191 at the top of the hill between mile markers 97 and 98, looking to the northeast. It is identified by a prominent deep chimney system splitting the fin from top to bottom.

Turn east from US 191 onto a dirt trail between mile markers 96 and 97. Pass through a gate, leaving it closed to prevent cattle from entering the highway. The trail is passable for a short distance by a two-wheel-drive vehicle, but four-wheel drive is required to reach a point within a half hour hike to the tower. Begin the hike where the dirt trail makes a sharp, steep right turn into a large wash.

13 EAST CANYON FIN—NORTH FACE
II, 5.9 R, 3 pitches, 300 feet (91 m)

First Ascent: Ken Wyrick, Carol Harden, 5.5, A3, spring 1973. Second Ascent and to the summit: Mike Baker, Kenny Postle, October 12, 1998.

Location and Access: Begin the ascent from the north end of the fin. Three aid pitons were drilled in the soft Entrada sandstone during the first ascent.

Pitch 1: Climb 5.6 friction to a fixed piton, then 5.7 in an open book, passing two empty piton holes. Continue 5.8 up a right-facing corner to a belay at a slung block, 120 feet (37 m).

Pitch 2: Face climb past an empty piton hole (5.7) to a shoulder, then traverse to a rotten off-width that turns to a squeeze, passing two empty piton holes and an eye bolt (Wyrick/Harden original high point). Continue up an off-width/squeeze to a three-bolt rappel/belay station, 130 feet (40 m).

Pitch 3: Climb 5.3, making a 5.6 move near the summit. There are no fixed anchors on the pitch, 50 feet (15 m).

Photo: Mike Baker

Roberts-Baker Corner.

Photo: Mike Baker

East Canyon Fin—North Face.

Photo: Mike Baker

East Canyon Fin—West Chimney.

Paraphernalia: Camalots (2) #1, #2, #3, #4; TCUs (1) each size; webbing; quick draws (3).

Descent: Downclimb pitch 3, then make a double-rope rappel to three drilled anchors at the top of pitch 2. From here make a second double-rope rappel to the ground.

14 EAST CANYON FIN—WEST CHIMNEY II, 5.9, 1 pitch, 130 feet (40 m)

First Ascent: Mike Baker, Jay Miller, 1998.

Location and Access: Climb a prominent chimney in view from US 191 on the southwest side of the fin.

Paraphernalia: Friends #0.5, #1, #1.5; Tri-Cams; selection of angle pitons 0.5″ through 1″.

Descent: Rappel the route from double anchors.

DIVERSIONS

WILSON ARCH

Wilson Arch is obvious between mile markers 102 and 103. It was named for Joe Wilson, the son of Moab pioneers. Joe was shot through the foot, nose, and left eye by Indians on August 26, 1880, when he was a boy. The Indians left him for dead, but he recovered from these wounds with the help of two friendly Indian women, and later had a ranch in the area. The Utah Highway Department placed a sign at the viewpoint, calling the landform Window Arch. Pressure from local residents, particularly Sam Taylor, editor of Moab's *Times-Independent* newspaper, forced the Highway Department to restore the proper name in a ceremony at the arch on September 13, 1968, with the blessing of the U.S. Board of Geographic Names. The name Window Rock Arch was also used for a short time.

Robert H. Vreeland in *Nature's Bridges and Arches:* "Since it [Wilson Arch] is on a main highway, with plenty of room for parking on either side of the road, this may be the most photographed natural arch in the world." It has a span of 92 feet (28 m), a height of 46 feet (14 m), a thickness of 55 feet (17 m), and a width of 11 feet (3.3 m).

BIG INDIAN ROCK

Big Indian Rock is in view from US 191 at mile marker 93, approximately 30 miles (48 km) south of Moab. A nearby copper mine is named after the prominent Entrada sandstone landform, and although the mine's principal production is copper ore, it has also produced gem-quality malachite and specimen-quality azurite crystals. Routes on Big Indian Rock are listed right to left, beginning on the west face of the tower.

Photo: Eric Bjørnstad

Big Indian Rock (above) and Split Boulder (below).

For the most direct approach from US 191, turn east between mile markers 91 and 92 at a sign for Big Indian Road. A sign for Lisbon Valley Industrial Area (the site of Charlie Steen's famous Mi Vida uranium mine) is in view only from the east. This is 12.7 miles (20.4 km) south of the junction of US 191 South and Utah 46 East.

MILEAGE LOG—US 191 TO BIG INDIAN ROCK

00 miles: US 191 junction with Route 2448, Big Indian Road, between mile markers 91 and 92.

2.2 miles (3.5 km): Cattle guard.

3.2 miles (5.1 km): Two signs: ROUTE 2448 and REF 5. South of the road is a sign for Mid-American Pipeline Company, Lisbon Station.

4.0 miles (6.4 km): Cattle guard.

4.6 miles (7.4 km): To the right begins the signed Route 2447. Continue straight (west) at a sign for San Juan 106/Big Indian.

5.6 miles (9.0 km): Sign for Umetco Minerals Corporation, Valley Mine.

7.6 miles (12.2 km): Cattle guard.

7.7 miles (12.3 km): Split Boulder is on the right; above it is Big Indian Rock. High above the road on the left is Belagana.

MILEAGE LOG—STEEN ROAD TO BIG INDIAN ROCK

The Steen Road is an alternative and more scenic approach to Big Indian Rock. Turn east from US 191 on a paved road between mile markers 95 and 96 at a sign for Lisbon Valley Industrial Area, San Juan County 114, and Steen Road.

00 miles: Junction of US 191 and Steen Road. Cross cattle guard.

0.9 mile (1.4 km): Blue sign: ROUTE 2447. Green sign: REF 15.

4.1 miles (6.6 km): Blue sign: ROUTE 2447. Green sign: REF 10.

5.2 miles (8.3 km): Steen Road straight ahead at a sign for San Juan County 114/Big Indian Spur. Sign: UNION 76.

5.9 miles (9.5 km): Green sign: REF 5. Blue sign: ROUTE 2447. Southwest of the road is an expansive view of the Abajo Mountains, known locally as The Blues because of their unusual coloring.

7.3 miles (11.7 km): Cattle guard and T intersection. Left goes to a gas plant; keep right.

8.0 miles (12.8 km): The top of Big Indian Rock is in view to the left (east).

9.1 miles (14.6 km): Stop sign at a T intersection. Right goes to US 191, 4.6 miles (7.4 km). Turn left to Big Indian Rock. Two signs: END ROUTE 2447 and REF 0.1

10.0 miles (16.1 km): Dirt trail right. Signs for San Juan County 109/Little Valley and Umetco Minerals Corporation/Valley Mine.

11.1 miles (17.8 km): Cattle guard.

12.2 miles (19.6 km): Belagana route on the left, Split Boulder on the right.

12.3 miles (19.7 km): Across from Big Indian Rock are two signs: ROUTE 2448 and REF 10.

12.8 miles (20.6 km): Right turn from a curve (difficult to see when approaching from the south) leads to the east side of Big Indian.

12.9 miles (20.7 km): Pass through a wire fence and keep right at a fork in the trail. Continue approximately 0.6 mile (.9 km) to the east side of the rock and good campsites.

To reach Big Indian Rock from Colorado, drive east on Colorado 90 from its beginning at the edge of Naturita. The highway becomes Utah 46 at the border. Between mile markers 6 and 7, turn south on a paved road at a sign for Route 2430 and San Juan County 113/Lisbon Road. The south turn from Utah 46 to Big Indian Rock is 10 miles (16 km) east of US 191. At 6.4 miles (10.3 km) there is a Y; the right branch begins San Juan County 106 and the Big Indian Road, the left branch is a gravel road. Take the right branch. At 3.4 miles (5.4 km) from the Y is a sign: ROUTE 2448—REF 10. At mile 5.6 (9 km), a cattle guard is crossed and Big Indian Rock is in view ahead of the road. Continue 1.1 miles (1.7 km) farther to the rock, which is 11.5 miles (18.5 km) from Utah 46.

15 BELAGANA
I, 5.11a, 1 pitch, 70 feet (21 m) ★★

First Ascent: Bret Ruckman, Tim Coats, March 5, 1990.

Location and Access: Belagana is approximately 200 yards (183 m) across the road (west) from Big Indian Rock. The name translates to "white man" in Navajo. Begin up broken rock (#1 Friend placement), then climb a 5.11a splitter crack through a #0.75 flare to face climbing, ending on a ledge with double anchors. Rappel slings on the right wall are visible from the road.

Paraphernalia: Standard desert rack.

Descent: Rappel the route.

16 NO NAME
I, 5.10+, 1 pitch, 80 feet (24 m) ★★★

First Ascent: Charlie Fowler, Billy Mason, 1994.

Location and Access: The route climbs a steep hand crack up a left-facing corner at the far right buttress, right of Big Indian Rock.

Paraphernalia: Undetermined.

Descent: Rappel from a chain anchor at the top of the route.

Photo: Eric Bjørnstad

Belagana.

17 LEFT CORNER
I, 5.10, A1, 1 pitch, 60 feet (18 m)

First Ascent: Unknown, circa 1970. Second Ascent: Charlie Fowler, Billy Mason, 1994.

Location and Access: *Left Corner* is the right of two left-facing dihedrals on the buttress right of Big Indian. *Left Corner* climbs a left-facing dihedral 5.10 with fingers and hands and aid moves past a fixed anchor in view from below.

Paraphernalia: Selection of Friends.

Descent: Rappel *Analog Crack* from a chain anchor at the top of the buttress.

18 SWOLLEN KNUCKLES
I, 5.10b, 1 pitch, 50 feet (15m) ★★★

First Ascent: Charlie Fowler, Billy Mason, 1994.

Location and Access: The route is three quarters of the way to the right end of the mesa from *Left Corner*. Ascend a finger crack through a bulge to anchors visible from below the climb.

Paraphernalia: Friends #1; Camalots #0.75, #0.5.

Descent: Rappel the route from anchors visible from below or walk off to the right.

Photo: Eric Bjørnstad

No Name *(left) and* Left Corner *(right).*

Saint Slick *(left) and* Analog Crack *(right).*

19 ANALOG CRACK (a.k.a. Prize Fighter) I, 5.10, 1 pitch, 60 feet (18 m) ★★★★

First Ascent: Charlie Fowler, Billy Mason, 1994.

Location and Access: The route climbs an off-width on the opposite side (east) of *Left Corner* and is approached from the col between Big Indian Rock and the landform to its south. The climb may be identified by a cowboy etched in the rock near the base of the route. Ascend through a bulge with wide hands and arm-bars to a chain anchor. Billy Mason: "The climb makes you feel like you've been in a battle with someone."

Paraphernalia: Friends #4; Camalots #3.

Descent: Rappel the route from a chain anchor.

20 SPLIT BOULDER I, 5.9, 1 pitch, 25 feet (7.6 m)

First Ascent: Charlie Fowler, Billy Mason, 1994.

Location and Access: Split Boulder is obvious beside the east side of the road just before Big Indian Rock is reached from the south, approximately 200 feet (60 m) beyond *Belagana.* The route faces west. There is a four-star route on the right side of the boulder established by the same team. Climb fingers to hands, ending with arm-bars at the top.

Paraphernalia: None required.

Descent: In 1994, Charlie Fowler made a simul-rappel but left a two-bolt anchor for future descents.

21 SQUAW CRACK
I, 5.10, 1 pitch, 60 feet (18 m)

First Ascent: Jason Keith, Hollis McCord, early 1990s.

Location and Access: The route is at the western end of the mesa right of Big Indian Rock. Climb an obvious crack system to rappel anchors in view from below the route.

Paraphernalia: A selection of Friends.

Descent: Rappel the route.

22 SAINT SLICK
I, 5.10, 1 pitch, 60 feet (18 m) ★★

First Ascent: Jason Keith, Jennifer Johnstone, May 1993.

Location and Access: *Saint Slick* climbs the south end of the landform just south of Big Indian Rock. Ascend obvious wide cracks to rappel slings in view from below the climb.

Paraphernalia: Friends #3, #3.5, #4, large units.

Descent: Rappel the route.

23 FLAT TIRE ALE
II, 5.11, 2 pitches, 100 feet (30 m) ★

First Ascent: Marco Cornacchione, Steph Davis, 1997.

Location and Access: *Flat Tire Ale* is plaqued and climbs the left side of the north face of Big Indian Rock for one pitch. The first ascent of pitch 2 is unknown. Marco Cornacchione: "Could continue to the top via grungy rock." The letters JH are carved deep into the right wall.

Pitch 1: Ascend a right-facing corner on the right side of a pillar with triple rappel anchors visible from below the pitch, 100 feet (30 m).

Pitch 2: Continue up a right-angling rotten chimney to the top, 5.11.

Paraphernalia: Finger-size units to #4 Camalots.

Descent: Rappel the route, or rappel the south *Wyrick-Harden Route* from three summit bolts.

24 BANDITOS ROUTE
II, 5.9, A3, 3 pitches, 140 feet (43 m)

First Ascent: The Banditos: Stan Mish, Glen Rink, November 1988.

Photo: Eric Bjørnstad

Squaw Crack.

Location and Access: Begin on the left side of Big Indian Rock as viewed from the southeast.

Pitch 1: Climb fourth class up a widening chimney, 5.9. From a bolt, move right and continue to a double-bolt belay, 95 feet (29 m).

Pitch 2: Above the belay, make an off-width pendulum left and continue A3 to double anchors at the top of the lower summit.

Pitch 3: Climb A1, then fourth class to a ledge. Continue A1, passing a bolt to the top.

Paraphernalia: Friends (2) sets; quick draws.

Descent: Double-rope rappel from three summit bolts.

25 WYRICK-HARDEN ROUTE
II, 5.11a/b, 3 pitches, 140 feet (43 m) ★★★★

First Ascent: Ken Wyrick, Carol Harden, 5.7, A2, April 15, 1973. First Free Ascent: Bret Ruckman, Tim Coats, March 5, 1990.

Location and Access: This original ascent line climbs the first crack right of the south (left) end of the east face. The team placed fourteen bolts and seven drilled pitons. Pitch 1 is 5.11, and pitch 2 is rated 5.10.

Paraphernalia: Friends (1) set; many TCUs; quick draws.

Descent: Double-rope rappel from three summit bolts.

26 IT'S A GAS
II, 5.11b, 3 pitches, 140 feet (43 m) ★★★★

First Free Ascent: Bret Ruckman, Tim Coats, March 5, 1990. Second Free Ascent: Jim Howe, Keith Maas, May 6, 1991.

Location and Access: The route is the free ascent of the *Wyrick/Harden Route* with a variation to pitch 3. It was named by the second free ascent team in honor of the nasty smell permeating the valley from the nearby gas plant. Bret Ruckman: "Cool tips climbing first and second pitches. Three pitches but only 140 feet."

Pitch 1: Climb the first crack system on the left side of the east face, beginning with strenuous 5.11b, pass a fixed anchor and a pod, then continue up a left-facing corner to a belay ledge. Protect with TCUs.

Pitch 2: Continue past a fixed anchor, 5.11a, then climb a thin left-facing corner to a belay ledge.

Pitch 3: Move right on the belay ledge to avoid the original bolt ladder. Climb 5.10 hands, then a 5.7 thin crack to the summit.

Paraphernalia: Friends (1) set; TCUs (2) sets with several #2; keyhole hangers; quick draws.

Descent: Double-rope rappel from three summit bolts.

27 PALE FACE
II, 5.11, 2 pitches, 140 feet (43 m)

First Ascent: Robert Warren, Max Kendall, Steve Johnson, November 1988.

Location and Access: The route climbs the northeast corner of Big Indian Rock one crack right of *It's A Gas.* The route was the first free ascent of the tower.

Pitch 1: Climb a hand and finger crack to the notch at the left end of the west face, 5.11.

Pitch 2: Continue to the top with face moves past two fixed anchors, 5.10.

Paraphernalia: Friends, several #1, #1.5; quick draws (2).

Descent: Double-rope rappel from three summit bolts.

CHURCH ROCK

Church Rock is a prominent Entrada sandstone landmark on the east side of the junction of US 191 and Utah 211, approximately 40 miles (64 km) south of Moab and 14 miles (23 km) north of Monticello.

28 CHURCH ROCK
I, moderate fifth class, 1 pitch, 200 feet (60 m)

First Ascent: Unknown.

Location and Access: Church Rock is climbed by its north ridge.

Paraphernalia: Undetermined.

Descent: Reverse the route.

DIVERSIONS

BAIRD BRIDGE

Baird Bridge is weathered from Navajo sandstone of early Jurassic age, about 170 million years old. It has a span of 18.5 feet (5.6 m), a height of 3.5 feet (1 m), a thickness of 1 foot (0.3 m), and a width of 4 feet (1.2 m). Robert H. Vreeland in *Nature's Bridges and Arches:* "The bridge was probably first seen by the early traders who used this area as a campsite (the only dependable water for many miles) on the Old Spanish Trail, a pack trail from Santa Fe to Los Angeles, in use during the 1830s and 1840s."

To reach Baird Bridge, turn left (east) from US 191 onto the Steen Road between mile markers 95 and 96. Drive 3.6 miles (5.7 km) to a dirt trail branching to the right. A few yards farther is a second branch; keep left. Follow the trail to its end, then continue ahead to the rim of a canyon. Hike south along the rim to a faint trail descending into the canyon. Follow the canyon downstream for approximately 0.5 mile (0.8 km). The bridge will be on the left about 100 feet (30 m) from the main wash. It is not easy to see on the downcanyon hike.

Church Rock.

Nature knows very well that the attack will come and so she provides her plants with various different defenses. The most common weapon which she gives them is the spine or thorn. Almost everything that grows has it and its different forms are many. They are all of them sharp as a needle and some of them have saw-edges that rip anything with which they come in contact. The grasses, and those plants akin to them like the yucca and the maguey, are often both saw-edged and spine-pointed. All the cacti have thorns, some straight, some barbed like a harpoon, some curved like a hook. There are chollas that have a sheath covering the thorn—a scabbard to the sword—and when anything pushes against it the sheath is left sticking in the wound. The different forms of the bisnaga are little more than vegetable porcupines. They bristle with quills or have hook-shaped thorns that catch and hold the intruder. The sahuaro has not so many spines, but they are so arranged that you can hardly strike the cylinder without striking the thorns.

—John C. Van Dyke, *The Desert,* 1901

13

RIMS RECREATION AREA

> The morning is still and perfectly clear. The stars have gone out, the moon is looking pale, the deep blue is warming, the sky is lightening with the coming day. How cool and crystalline the air! In a few hours the great plain will be almost like a fiery furnace under the rays of the summer sun, but now it is chilly. And in a few hours there will be rings and bands and scarves of heat set wavering across the waste upon the opalescent wings of the mirage; but now the air is so clear that one can see the breaks in the rocky face of the mountain range, though it is fully 20 miles away. It may be further. Who of the desert has not spent his day riding at a mountain and never even reaching its base? This is a land of illusions and thin air. The vision is so cleared at times that the truth itself is deceptive.
>
> —John C. Van Dyke, *The Desert,* 1901

Rims Recreation Area is a seldom visited island region atop a 6,000-foot (1,829 m)-high plateau south of Moab. It is a wonderfully beautiful and lonely place where one is likely to encounter only the coyote or desert bighorn sheep. It borders Canyonlands National Park on its east, where it rises 2,000 feet (610 m) above the Colorado River. The Rims Recreation Area is divided into eight geographic districts whose present boundaries were set by the BLM in 1990. The only climbs established there are in the Hatch Point District, which is bordered on its west by the rimrock above the inner gorge of the Colorado River, north by Kane Creek Canyon, south by the paved Needles Overlook Road and east by Hatch Wash Canyon at the west border of Flat Iron Mesa. All climbs in this district are on Wingate sandstone.

As in much of the Colorado Plateau, there is a legacy from the 1950s and 1960s uranium days of four-wheel-drive trails crisscrossing the otherwise virgin land. The only paved road is the 22-mile (35 km) Needles Overlook Road, which extends west from US 191 to a breathtaking view of Indian Creek Valley and, beyond, the Needles District of Canyonlands National Park. There are two developed campsites with tables, fire rings, rest rooms, and drinking water: Wind Whistle and Hatch Point Campgrounds, both in the Hatch Point District.

Ward J. Roylance: "Hatch Point, a great peninsula with ragged edges, about 20 miles long but only a few miles wide. Circumscribed by precipitous cliffs up to 2,000 feet high, the Point is one among several 'islands' of the Junction Country rock platforms jutting from the 'mainland,' connected only by narrow causeways and surrounded by thin air. The Point's eastern rim overlooks Hatch Wash and Kane Creek Canyon, while its southern rim is formed by a chasm known as Hart's Draw. Its western edge, affording the grandest panorama, is a sinuous escarpment that serves as an outer wall of the Colorado's inner basin."

Geologist John Newberry, who accompanied the Macomb Expedition to the Rims area in 1859, wrote of the vistas to the west from Harts Draw: "From this point the view swept westward over a wide extent of country, in its general aspects a plain, but everywhere deeply cut by a tangled maze of cañons, and thickly set

RIMS RECREATION AREA ROUTE LOCATOR MAP

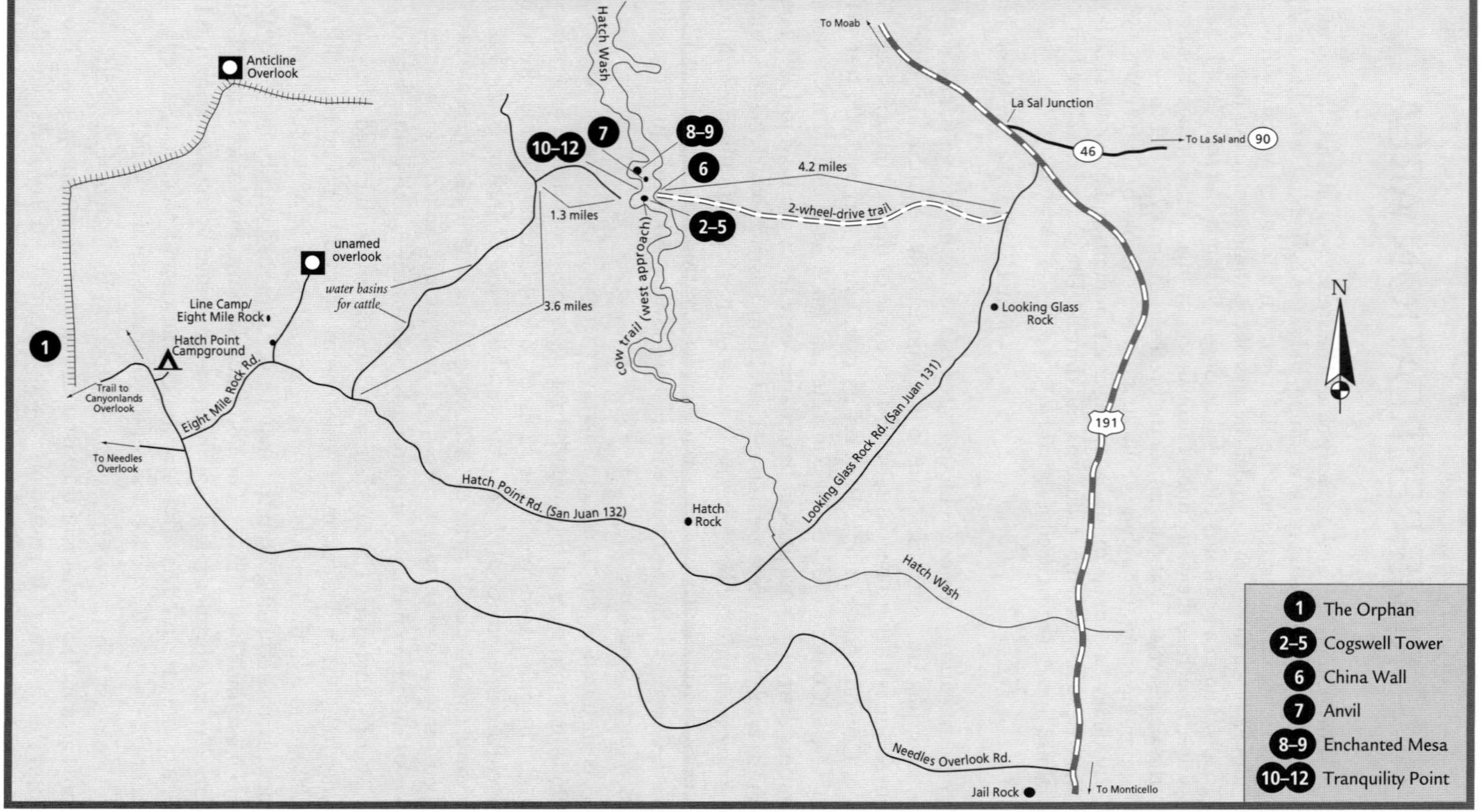

Hatch Wash
To Moab
Anticline Overlook
La Sal Junction
To La Sal and 90
46
10–12
7
8–9
6
4.2 miles
2-wheel-drive trail
1.3 miles
2–5
unamed overlook
water basins for cattle
3.6 miles
cow trail (west approach)
Line Camp/ Eight Mile Rock
Looking Glass Rock
N
1
Hatch Point Campground
Eight Mile Rock Rd.
Trail to Canyonlands Overlook
To Needles Overlook
191
Hatch Point Rd. (San Juan 132)
Hatch Rock
Looking Glass Rock Rd. (San Juan 131)
Hatch Wash
Needles Overlook Rd.
Jail Rock
To Monticello
1 The Orphan
2–5 Cogswell Tower
6 China Wall
7 Anvil
8–9 Enchanted Mesa
10–12 Tranquility Point

with towers, castles, and spires of most varied and striking forms; the most wonderful monuments of erosion which our eyes, already experienced in objects of this kind, had beheld. . . . Toward the west the view reached some 30 miles, there bounded by long lines and bold angles of mesa walls similar to those behind us, while in the intervening space the surface was diversified by columns, spires, castles, and battlemented towers of colossal but often beautiful proportions, closely resembling elaborate structures of art, but in effect far surpassing the most imposing monuments of human skill. In the southwest was a long line of spires of white stone, standing on red bases, thousands in number, but so slender as to recall the most delicate carving in ivory or the fairy architecture of some gothic cathedral; yet many, perhaps most, were over 500 feet in height, and thickly set in a narrow belt or series some miles in length. Their appearance was so strange and beautiful as to call out exclamations of delight from all our party."

THE ORPHAN

The Orphan is a detached spire off the Wingate buttress that borders the west reaches of the Rims Recreation Area. To reach it, turn west off US 191 at mile marker 93, 32 miles (51.5 km) south of Moab, at a sign for Canyon Rims Recreation Area. The paved road leads to the Needles Overlook of Canyonlands National Park and a dirt trail to Anticline Overlook. Follow the sign for Anticline Overlook. Pass a sign for Hatch Point Campground, continue ahead 1 mile (1.6 km), then turn left (west). This rough trail leads to the less visited Canyonlands Overlook and requires four-wheel drive and high clearance. At 1.3 miles (2 km) there is a post with an arrow. The main trail continues to the right. Drive straight down an unimproved trail for 1 mile (1.6 km) to a fire ring and a USGS marker. Hike approximately fifteen minutes to the mesa's edge, where the Orphan will be in view.

1 THE ORPHAN
III, 5.9, A2-, 2 pitches, 180 feet (55 m)

First Ascent: Brad Bond, solo, June 11, 1998.

Location and Access: Fix a 250-foot (76 m) rope at the rim for a rappel to the notch between the rim and the spire, and for a return prusik. Only four bolts were placed on the climb. A summit register was left on the first ascent.

Pitch 1: Begin up a 5.8 crack, which becomes 5.9 hands, then belay at a 3-inch (7.6 cm)-wide section.

Pitch 2: Continue with A1+, then A2- to a stance with a bolt. Move right, around a corner on a ledge and continue to the top, passing a second bolt.

Paraphernalia: Friends (3) #1 through #3, (2) #3.5, #4; TCUs (3) each; birdbeaks (2); knifeblades (4) long and thin; Lost Arrows (6) long; angles (1) each to 1"; Leeper-Z (1); quick draws (2); 200-foot (60 m) rope is mandatory.

Descent: Tyrolean to the buttress, then prusik the fixed rope to the rim.

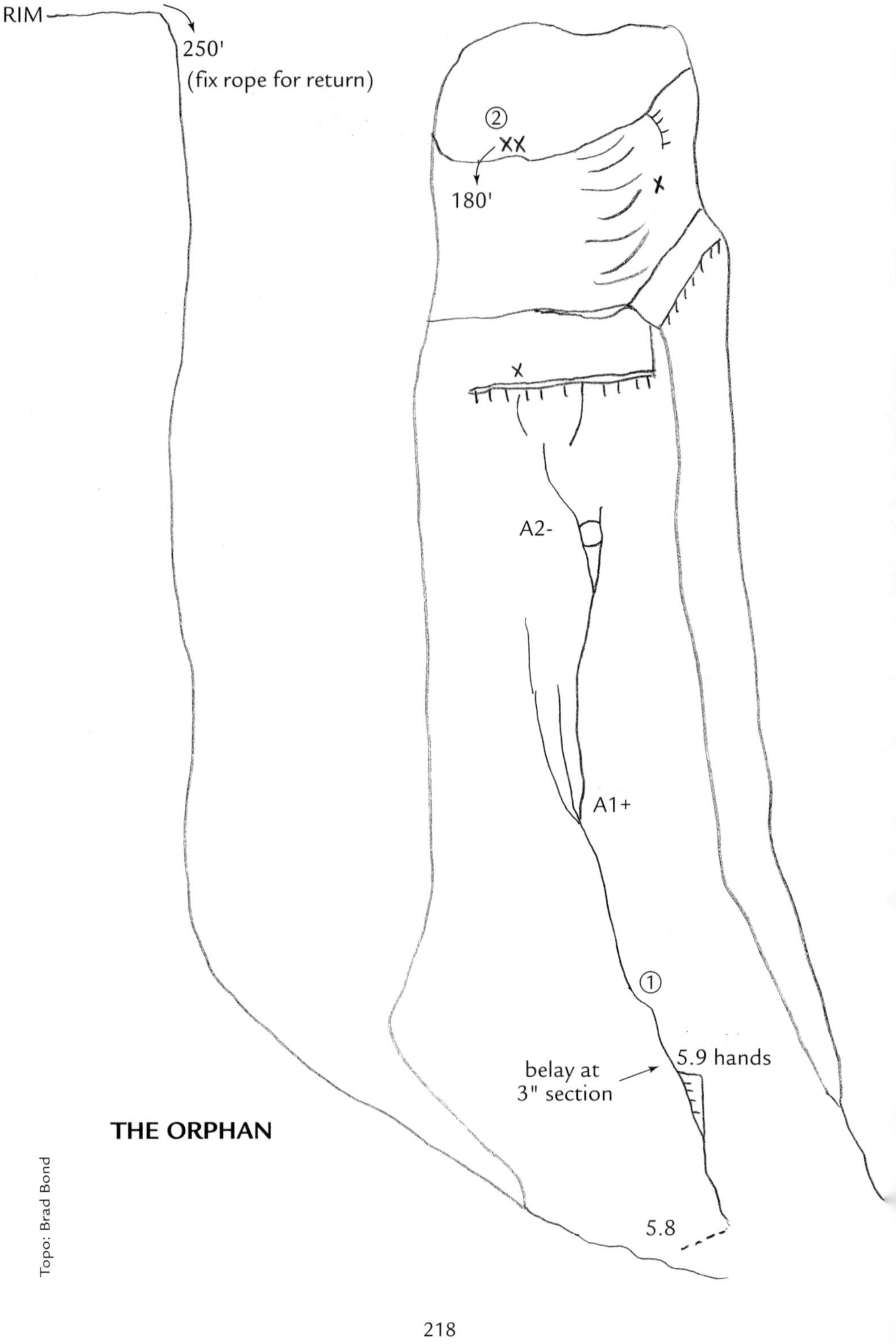

THE ORPHAN

Topo: Brad Bond

HATCH WASH

Hatch Wash is a deep Wingate sandstone-lined canyon that drains the Hatch Point District of Rims. Water flows year-round, but because of bovine pollution it should be treated before drinking. To reach the east rim of Hatch Wash, turn west from US 191 onto San Juan 131, the Looking Glass Rock Road, then take the first right branch (two-wheel drive) and continue on the most used trail 4.2 miles (6.7 km) to a point within 100 yards (91 m) of the east rim and the cairn-marked top of *Orient Express* on the China Wall. Make one short and two long double-rope rappels down the *Orient Express,* which is the point closest to Cogswell Tower obvious in the canyon. Two-bolt anchors are in place at each rappel/belay station.

To reach the east rim of Hatch Wash from US 191 and the Rims Recreation Road, a high-clearance vehicle is required. Turn west approximately 32 miles (51.5 km) south of Moab just north of mile marker 93. Follow the paved road 24.1 miles (38.8 km) to where it branches left to Needles Overlook and a dirt trail continues straight ahead. A sign for westbound traffic gives distances to Hatch Point Road and Needles Overlook. From the dirt trail just beyond the Needles Overlook intersection, turn right at a sign for Eight Mile Road. Drive 3 miles (4.8 km), then take the right (east) branch, signed SAN JUAN COUNTY 132 (Hatch Point Road). Drive 1.9 miles (3 km), turn left (north) on a faint branch, and set your odometer to zero. For many miles the road traverses the open Navajo meadowland. After 250 feet (76 m) take the right fork and at 500 feet (152 m) cross a cattle guard. In 1.1 miles (1.7 km) pass a water catchment basin for range cattle. At 2.2 miles (3.5 km) pass a second catchment basin. At 3.6 miles (5.7 km) veer right on a faint spur that is difficult to see. At 4.9 miles (7.8 km) reach Hatch Wash and an excellent campsite. A few yards ahead gives a bird's-eye view of Hatch Wash and Cogswell Tower. Hike the rim right (south) and locate cairns marking an old cow trail leading into the canyon. Cogswell Tower is obvious as you look into Hatch Wash from the east or west approaches.

ALONZO HATCH

Hatch Wash, Hatch Rock, and Hatch Point are named for Alonzo Hatch. In the fall of 1881, Hatch settled near a spring in a meadow in the northwestern end of Dry Valley, which borders the present-day Hatch Wash to its south. Before Alonzo's time, Hatch Wash was known as Hudson Wash, after "Spud" Hudson, a cattleman known for carrying a potato in his pocket to insure against hunger. Between 1830 and 1850, the famous Old Spanish Trail extending from Santa Fe to Los Angeles followed parts of Dry Valley before crossing the Colorado River at the north end of Moab Valley.

MILEAGE LOG—SAN JUAN COUNTY 131 (LOOKING GLASS ROCK ROAD) FROM US 191 TO EIGHT MILE ROCK

San Juan County 131, the Looking Glass Rock Road, becomes San Juan County 132, the Hatch Point Road. This is an alternative approach to the west rim.

miles: Junction of US 191 and Looking Glass Rock Road (between mile markers 103–102 on US 191).

5.0 miles (8.0 km): Looking Glass Rock Road and the junction of San Juan County 132, the Hatch Point Road.

5.8 miles (9.3 km): Homes carved into the rock buttress on the right.

6.1 miles (9.8 km): The trail crosses upper Hatch Wash where there are more cave homes.

8.1 miles (13.0 km): A dirt trail branches right to Rockland Motel. Sign: SAN JUAN COUNTY 116A.

9.3 miles (15.0 km): Spur trail left. Sign: SAN JUAN COUNTY 135—EAST SHORT CUT ROAD. Keep straight.

10.2 miles (16.4 km): Cattle guard.

15.1 miles (24.3 km): Right spur to Hatch Wash.

16.4 miles (26.4 km): Right spur to Line Camp at Eight Mile Rock.

16.6 miles (26.7 km): Cowboy Line Camp in the Eight Mile Rock, worth a look!

ROCKLAND MOTEL

The following description of the Rockland Motel in Hatch Rock is quoted from F. A. Barnes's *Canyon Country's Canyon Rims Recreation Area:* "Anyone traveling west from US 191 on Hatch Wash Road, the dirt road leading past Looking Glass Rock, will be entranced by the beauty of the dome of pink Entrada sandstone west of the road. . . . But what will capture attention is the anomalous series of large, square holes lined up all along a terrace on the south-facing side of the broad, smooth sandstone prominence—not the round or oval alcoves or softly sculptured natural arches usually associated with this colorful aeolian [sic] formation, but stark incongruities like great gaping cavities punched into the pillowy dome. . . .Hatch Rock is situated on a 'school section,' one of four tracts of land per township, given to Utah when it was granted statehood. Income from these is credited toward funding the operation of state schools. Far from any industrial center or even a small community, this school section seemed a poor candidate for any kind of income to the state via commercial means. So in 1974, when former teacher, logger, carpenter, and religious ex-communicant Bob

COGSWELL TOWER

Cogswell Tower is the name given by F. A. Barnes (a contemporary Moab writer) for the 300-foot (91 m) freestanding spire in Hatch Wash. Lieutenant Cogswell headed the military accompaniment of Captain John N. Macomb of the Corps of Topographical Engineers. The group set out July 12, 1859, from Santa Fe, New Mexico, to locate the confluence of the Green and Grand (Colorado) Rivers, map a route through the hostile Utah territory, determine its mineral potential, and survey the course of the San Juan River.

The tower was named Crows Foot Spire by the first ascent team, who apparently did not know it had long been called and identified on maps as Cogswell Tower. It is weathered from

Wingate sandstone with a thick caprock of Kayenta.

2 BOVINE II, 5.10+, A1, 2 pitches, 160 feet (49 m)

First Ascent: Robert Warren, Steve Johnson, March 27, 1988.

Location and Access: The route climbs the crack system below the notch on the left end of the south face between the mitten and thumb formation. The route does not reach the summit of the tower.

Pitch 1: Begin up a right-facing corner. Climb thin hands to a belay, 5.10+.

Pitch 2: Continue A1 up a thin crack to double-rappel anchors on the left wall.

Paraphernalia: Friends (2) sets from #2 up; Camalots (1) #4; Big Bro (1) #3.

Descent: Rappel the route.

3 RAVEN III, 5.11, C1, 3 pitches, 250 feet (76 m) ★★

First Ascent: Robert Warren, Steve Johnson, one point of aid, March 27, 1988. Second Ascent: Mike Baker, Chris Ducker, March 1998.

Location and Access: The route climbs the first crack system inside the right end of the southeast face.

Pitch 1: Begin with fists, then 5.9 hands, and finally a 5.8 move to a stance with double anchors, 100 feet (30 m).

Pitch 2: Climb a C1 off-width crack, then continue 5.10+, ending with fingers, then 5.11 hands at a double-bolt ledge.

Foster approached the State Land Board with a proposal to lease the rock for habitation purposes, his request was granted and a fifty-year renewable lease was signed. . . . With the help of two women, mothers of some of his many children, Foster proceeded to blast out holes for several complete living quarters, with laundry facilities, garages, and storage areas, and a room for the twenty horsepower diesel generator. He drilled two wells before obtaining enough flow to meet their needs, then installed a 1,000-gallon water tank high up on the rock, which, by gravity feed, furnishes all their culinary water and accommodates an automatic washer, flush toilets, and other amenities. Foster also constructed a 20,000-gallon waste disposal system, and a propane set-up to provide for cooking and hot water. . . . Woodburning stoves heat the living quarters, all of which are wired for lights, appliances, ventilators, and television. Four solar units generate additional electricity, with their storage batteries housed in the generator room. . . . Some of the rooms' walls have finished siding on them, while others have been left with their native bare rock showing. All the floors are lined with smooth cement. In addition, the dwellings are carpeted, while vinyl flooring suffices in the work areas. Furnishings include a collection of 300 videotapes and a library of 2,000 books. The children attend school through correspondence courses, but are also taught homemaking, gardening, carpentry, and many other skills."

Photo: Mike Baker

Cogswell Tower.

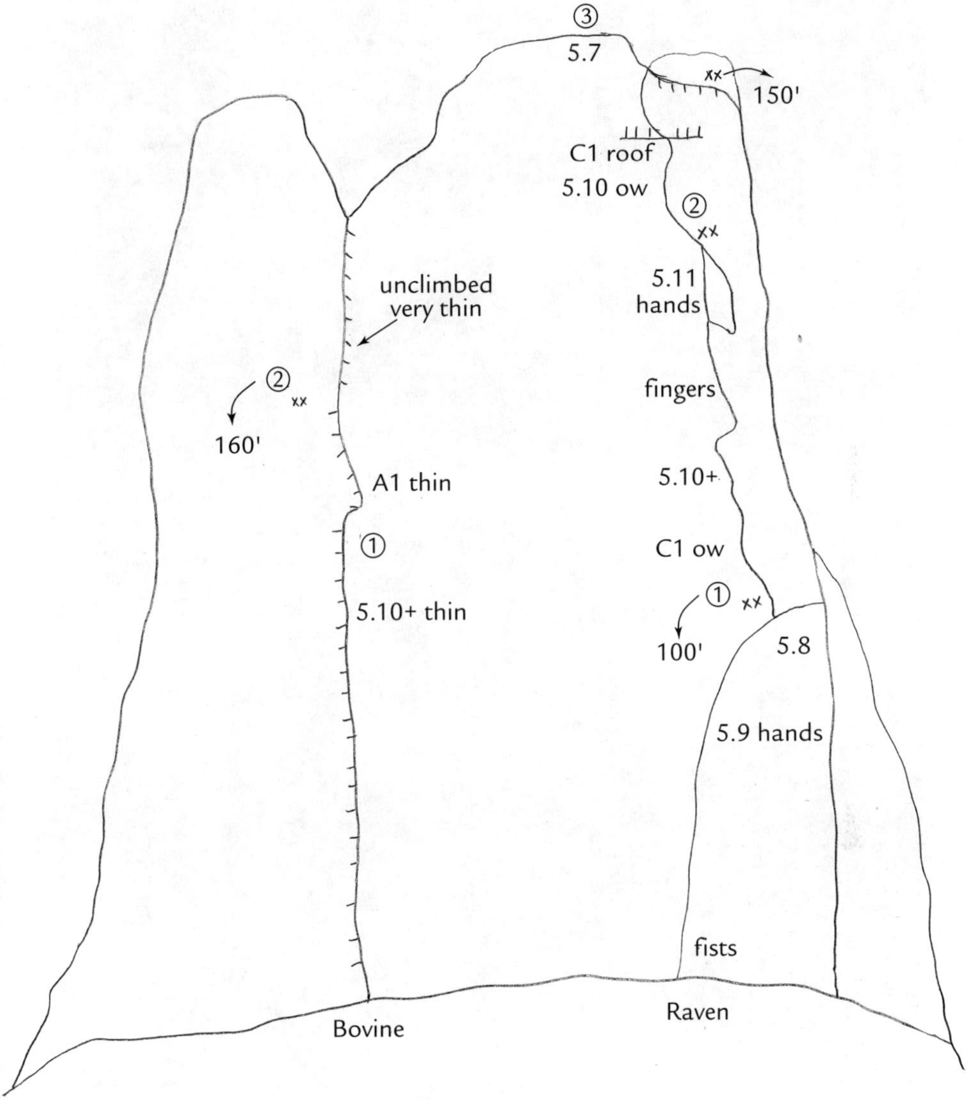

BOVINE AND RAVEN

Photo: Mike Baker

Cogswell Tower: Bovine *(left)* Raven *(right).*

Pitch 3: Continue up a 5.10 off-width, passing a roof with C1, and on to a 5.7 move that brings you to the summit.

Paraphernalia: Friends (2) sets from #2 up; Camalots (2) through #4.5; TCUs (1) set; stoppers (1) set.

Descent: Rappel 150 feet (46 m) from double bolts to the top of pitch 1, then 100 feet (30 m) to the ground.

4 COGSWELL TOWER—NORTH FACE III, 5.9, A2, C1, 3 pitches, 300 feet (91 m)

First Ascent: Kerby Spangler, solo, November 2, 1996.

Location and Access: Begin up broken cracks near the left side of the north face below a left-facing corner.

Pitch 1: Climb 5.9, C1 to a belay at a left-facing corner below a roof, 110 feet (34 m).

Pitch 2: One aid bolt negotiates the roof, then follow discontinuous cracks to the headwall splitter. Belay above the headwall on a ledge, A2, 140 feet (43 m).

Pitch 3: The final lead is an easy wide crack and a boulder problem to the top, 5.6, 50 feet (15 m).

Paraphernalia: Camalots (2) sets through #4; TCUs (2) sets; Lowe Balls; selection of nuts; cam hook (1); RPs; fat knifeblade (1); fat Lost Arrow (1).

Descent: Rappel *Raven*.

5 EMANCIPATION III, 5.11-, 3 pitches, 300 (91 m) ★★

First Ascent and First Free Ascent of tower: Mike Baker, Jay Miller, October 8, 1998.

Location and Access: The route climbs the west end of the north face between the mitten and thumb of the formation.

Paraphernalia: Standard desert rack.

Descent: Rappel *Raven*.

CHINA WALL

China Wall is directly east of Cogswell Tower. If approaching Hatch Wash from the east (Looking Glass Road), *Orient Express* on the China Wall is the rappel line into the canyon.

6 ORIENT EXPRESS IV, 5.10, A3+, 4 pitches, 355 feet (108 m) ★★★★

First Ascent: Mike Baker, Kirby Spangler, November 1996. Second Ascent: Chris Ducker, James Bracken, March 29, 1998.

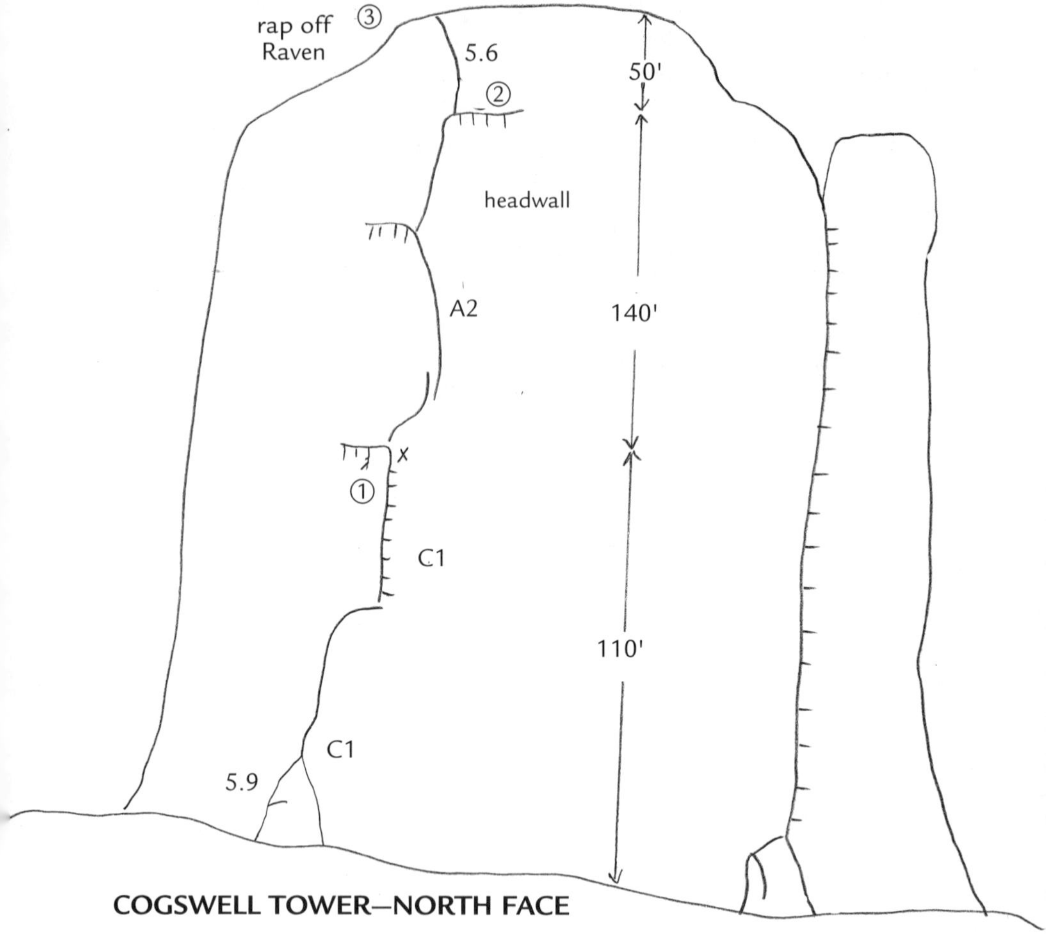

COGSWELL TOWER—NORTH FACE

Location and Access: The route is the most striking line on the China Wall; rock cairns mark the top and bottom of the route. At the top of pitches 1, 2, 3, and 4 are double-bolt anchors. No pitons are needed above pitch 2.

Pitch 1: Begin up a right-facing dihedral. Make a couple of cam hook moves (mandatory to avoid unnecessary aid), then continue A2+. Pass a roof on its right side with A3+ knifeblades to a double-bolt belay ledge, A3+, 70 feet (21 m).

Pitch 2: Climb A3 birdbeaks, then knifeblades, passing two bolts. Continue up a right-facing knifeblade crack, then A3+ thin to a bolted stance, 85 feet (26 m).

Pitch 3: Climb C1 for 8 feet (2.4 m) above the belay. Continue 5.8 up the right-facing corner. Hands then a 5.9 lieback bring you to double bolts below a roof, 5.9, C1, 150 feet, (46 m).

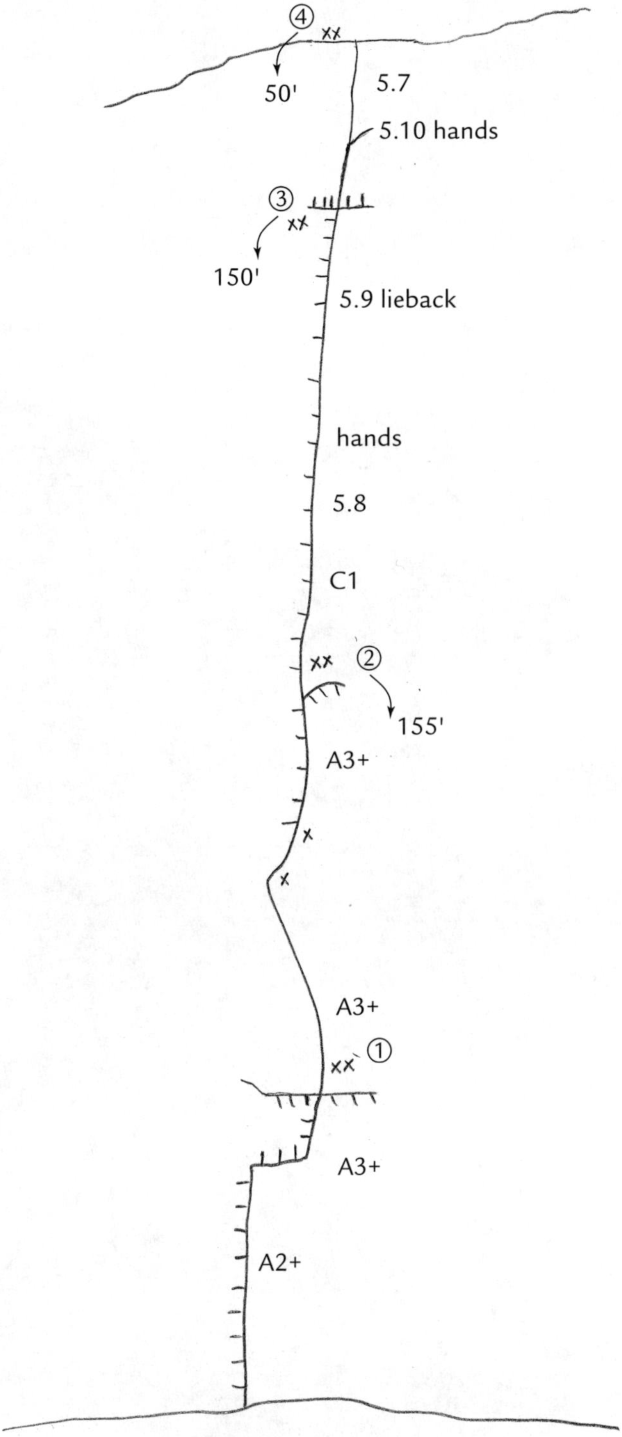

ORIENT EXPRESS

Photo: Mike Baker

Kirby Spangler on Orient Express, *pitch 1.*

Pitch 4: Continue with 5.10 hands, then 5.7 to double anchors at the top, 5.10, 50 feet (15 m).

Paraphernalia: Camalots (1) #0.5, #0.75, #1, (2) #2, #3, #4; TCUs (2) sets; Lowe Balls (2) sets; thin knifeblades (12); Lost Arrows (3); birdbeaks (6).

Descent: Rappel the route into Hatch Wash with one short and two long, or walk to your car, depending on whether the approach was from the east or west.

ANVIL

Anvil is approximately 0.25 mile (0.4 km) downstream from the China Wall. It can be identified as the first prominence encountered on the downcanyon hike.

7 BIG BOYS DON'T FLY
I, 5.10+, 1 pitch, 20 feet (6 m) ★★

First Ascent: Mike Baker, belayed by Leslie Henderson, 5.6, A0, July 1996. Second Ascent: Mike Baker, Sherob (full name unknown), 5.10+, November 1996.

Location and Access: Anvil is a spire detached from the rim. The first ascent used one point of aid. The route is approximately 20 feet (6 m) long and 60 feet (18 m) off the ground. Drop over the edge of the rim to a shelf, then make a full body stem (for a 5′ 10″ person) and climb past two bolts to the top.

Paraphernalia: For belay anchor, Camalots #2, #3, #4; Tri-Cams (1) #0.5 or #1.

Descent: One tricky rappel from two drilled anchors back to the belay.

ENCHANTED MESA

Enchanted Mesa is an island of Wingate sandstone in Hatch Wash, the result of an abandon meander (or rincon) created by the waters that carved the canyon. To view the mesa, walk north from the campsite on the west side of Hatch Wash. To reach it, walk north of Tranquility Point and locate a cairn, then follow an old cattle trail to the base of the mesa, or rappel the gully using a tree for an anchor.

8 SILENT DESTINY
I, 5.9+, 2 pitches, 175 feet (53 m) ★

First Ascent: Mike Baker, solo, September 1997. Second Ascent: Mike Baker, Wilson Goodrich, Kenny Postle, spring 1998.

Location and Access: The route climbs the northwest corner of the mesa (opposite the stream), following an obvious crack system to drilled anchors. The line of ascent is *Laughing Thunder*'s descent line. A register was left at the top of the mesa.

Pitch 1: Begin up a right-facing corner 5.8, then 5.9 hands to a 5.9 lieback. Pass

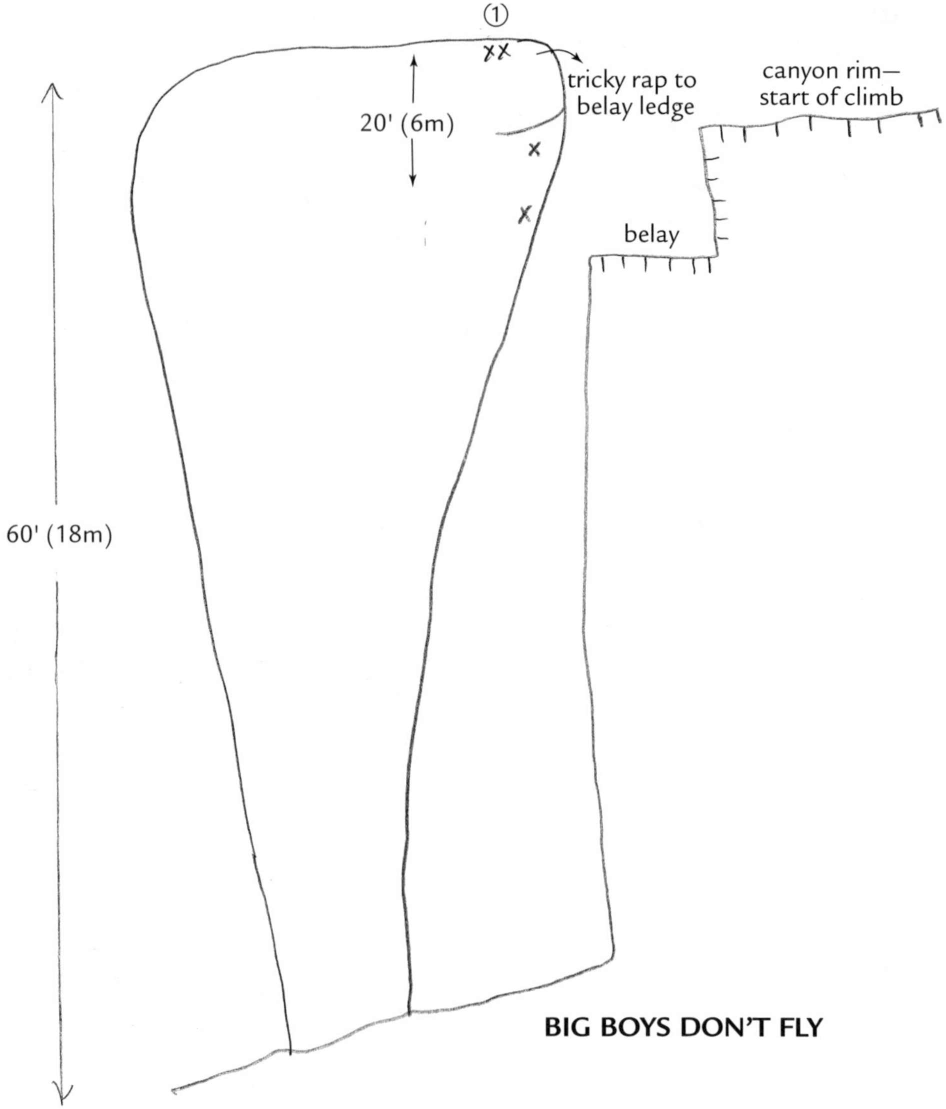

BIG BOYS DON'T FLY

huecos on the right with a lieback and stemming. Finish up the right-facing crack to double bolts, 5.8+, 75 feet (23 m).

Pitch 2: Climb 5.3 up and right to the top, 100 feet (30 m).

Paraphernalia: Camalots (1) #0.75, #1, #2, #3, #4; Tri-Cams (1) #0.5, #1, #1.5; TCUs (1) set; stoppers (1) set.

Descent: Walk to the northwest corner and downclimb a gulley 150 feet (46 m) to a two-bolt anchor, 5.2, then make a single-rope rappel to the ground.

Photo: Mike Baker

Enchanted Mesa.

SILENT DESTINY

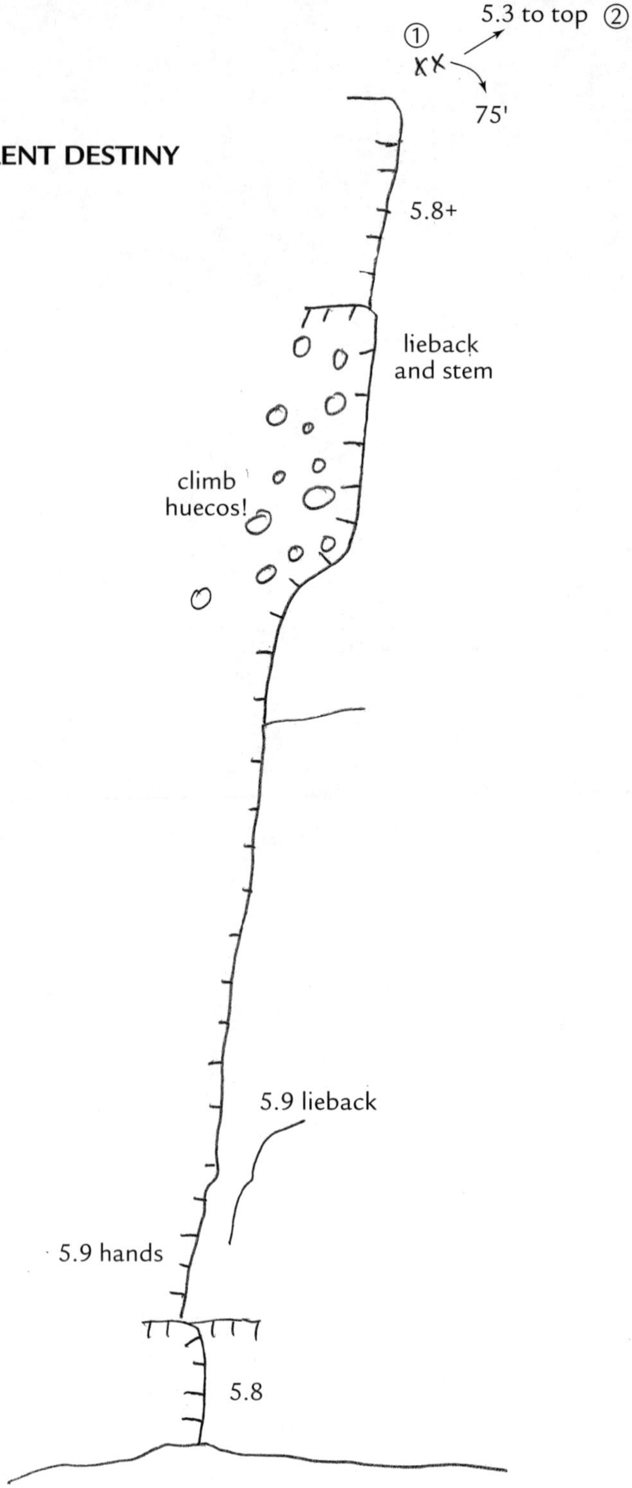

9 LAUGHING THUNDER
IV, 5.9, A2+, 4 pitches, 400 feet (122 m) ★★★★★

First Ascent: Mike Baker, solo, May 20, 1997.

Location and Access: The route is an obvious three-roofed crack and dihedral system on the stream side (northeast) of the mesa. It climbs through three progressively larger roofs. To reach from the west, hike to the end of Tranquility Point and locate a cairn, then follow an old trail down to the base of Enchanted Mesa. Contour north (left), passing *Silent Destiny*, then northeast. Mike Baker: "In late spring or early summer, the route gets morning sun then shade all day. It is possible to stay dry in rainstorms. Except for the last pitch, the route is completely sheltered by the large roofs."

Pitch 1: Begin with 5.9, then A2, passing a bolt up a left-facing corner. Pass a roof and a bolt and climb C2+, then 5.9, passing a second bolt, then C1 and 5.8 to a second roof, which is traversed right to left (A2+), passing two more bolts. Make a hook move to a single bolt and gear belay ledge.

Pitch 2: Climb A2+, then 5.9 to A2 up a left-facing corner. Continue up the left side of a flake (5.8) to a double-bolt belay at its top.

Pitch 3: Traverse left under the 50-foot (15 m) "Tsunami Roof," C1. Climb above to triple anchors, A2 then 5.9.

Pitch 4: Ascend a 5.4 chimney to the top.

Paraphernalia: Camalots (2) #0.5, #0.75, #1, #2, #3, (1) #4; TCUs or Allens (2) each smaller sizes; Lowe Balls (1) each size mandatory; knifeblades (3); angle pitons (3) 0.5; Chouinard hooks (1).

Descent: Walk to the northwest (right) corner and downclimb a gulley 150 feet (46 m) to a two-bolt anchor (5.2), then make one single-rope rappel to the ground, or rappel the gully using a tree for an anchor.

TRANQUILITY POINT

Tranquility Point is the land that juts from the west side of the canyon north of Cogswell Tower. Routes are listed north to south.

10 SPLITTER DECISION
I, 5.10, C2+, 3 pitches, 250 feet (76 m) ★★★★

First Ascent: Andy Roberts, Jay Miller, September 16, 1998.

Location and Access: The route is two crack systems right (north) of *Tranquility Crack.*

Pitch 1: Begin with 5.10 hand and fist jams, then delicate climbing to a stance and a two-bolt belay, 90 feet (27 m).

Pitch 2: Continue climbing a slightly overhanging 2-inch (5 cm) splitter crack (protected with a #1, then #2 Camalot), which widens to 3 inches (7.6 cm) for 70 feet (21 m), ending under a roof. Move left and protect with a natural

Photo: Mike Baker

Laughing Thunder.

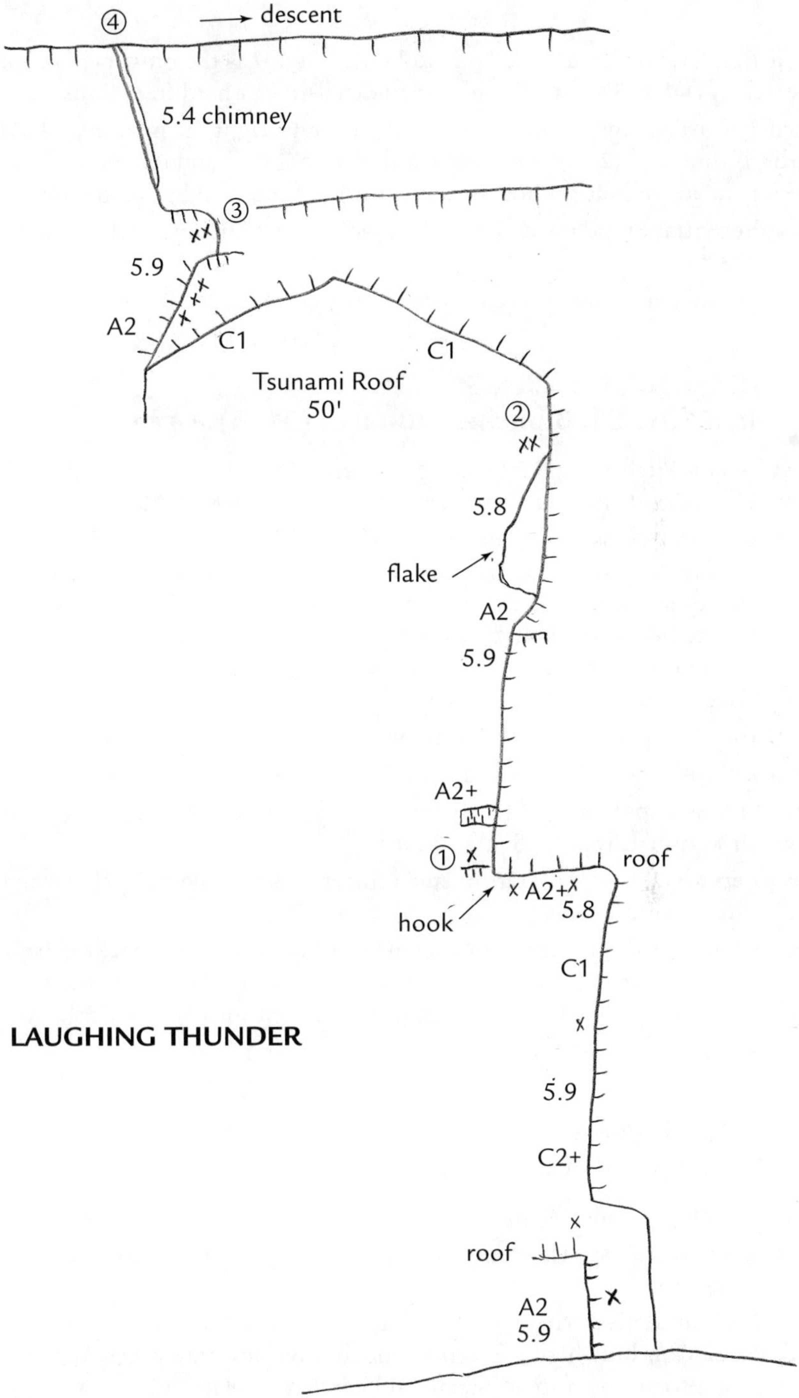

LAUGHING THUNDER

anchor, C1, 90 feet (27 m). Andy Roberts: "Pitch 2 is the most perfect splitter crack in Hatch Wash and would be an excellent but hard free climb."

Pitch 3: Traverse right under a roof (C2+) to gain a right-facing dihedral. Follow the 1- to 2-inch (2.5 to 5 cm) dihedral 60 feet (18 m) and end under a second roof and a two-bolt anchor, 70 feet (21 m). Pitches 2 and 3 can be combined.

Paraphernalia: Standard desert rack; selection of Camalots with extra #1, #2, and (1) #5.

Descent: Rappel to top of pitch 1, then to the ground.

11 TRANQUILITY CRACK
III, 5.10+, C1, 3 pitches, 300 feet (91 m) ★★★★

First Ascent: Pitches 1 and 2: Mike Baker, Kerby Spangler, November 1996. Pitch 3: Mike Baker, Chris Ducker, Sherob (full name unkown), May 13, 1997.

Location and Access: The route is just south of *Splitter Decision*, 15 feet (4.5 m) north of the north side of Tranquility Point. Cairns mark the top and bottom of the route. Approach as for *Orient Express*, or rappel the route, leaving anchors to be retrieved on the ascent. It is mostly a finger crack ascent and no pitons are needed on the route. Mike Baker: "This crack would make an awesome free climb at 5.12."

Pitch 1: Begin up a rotten slot to a belay ledge, 5.8, 25 feet (7.6 m).

Pitch 2: Climb a left-facing dihedral 5.9+, then 5.10+ to double bolts.

Pitch 3: Pass a roof with C1, then continue up a thin crack C1, passing an off-width section. Climb a 5.8 face to the top.

Paraphernalia: Friends (3) sets of small finger size; Camalots (2) #1 through #4. No pitons required.

Descent: Walk to your car if approach is from the east. If approaching from the west, rappel into the canyon (see east approach to Hatch Wash), then hike up the old cattle trail, which is the standard descent into Hatch Wash from the west.

12 BIG LIEBOWSKY
II, C2+, 4 pitches, 380 feet (116 m) ★★★

First Ascent: Jay Miller, Andy Roberts, October 1998.

Location and Access: The route is two crack systems south (toward camp) of *Tranquility Crack*.

Pitch 1: Climb 20 feet (6 m) up a loose crack system, then work into a right-facing dihedral. Continue high enough to enable a tension traverse right to a crack leading into an opposite left-facing dihedral and belay under a roof, 160 feet (49 m).

SPLITTER DECISION

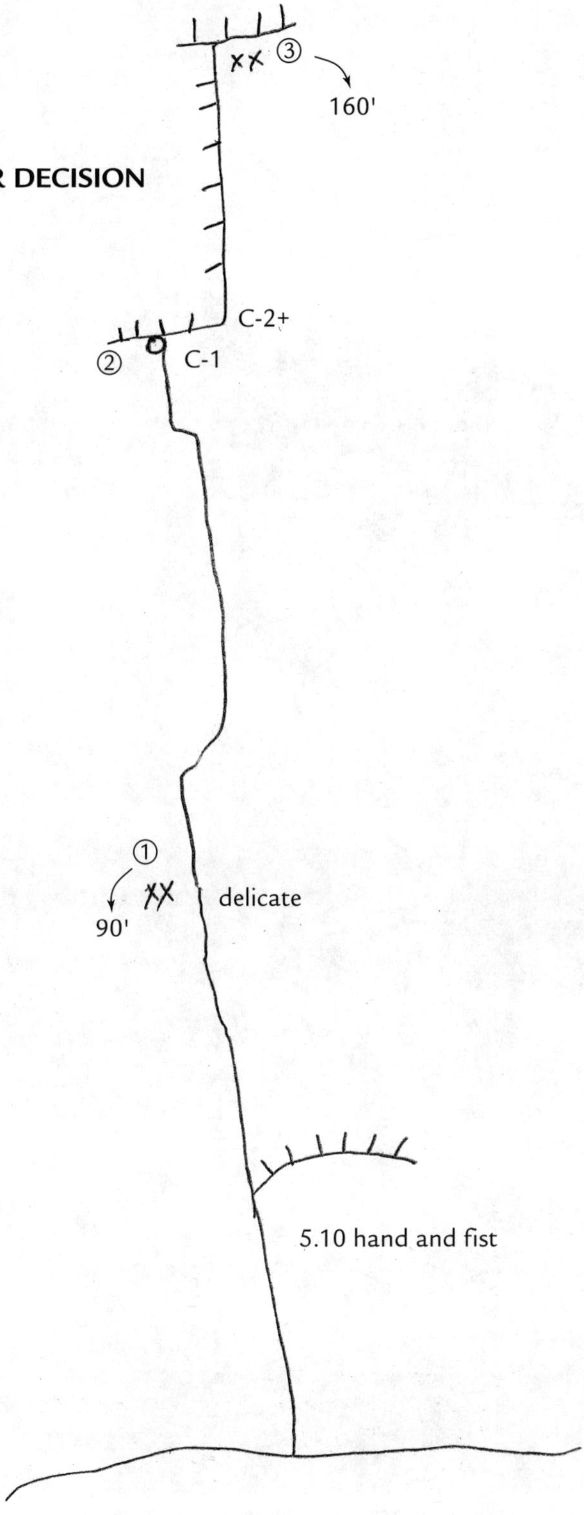

Photo: BMike Baker

Tranquility Point: Tranquility Crack *(left)*, Splitter Decision *(right)*.

TRANQUILITY CRACK

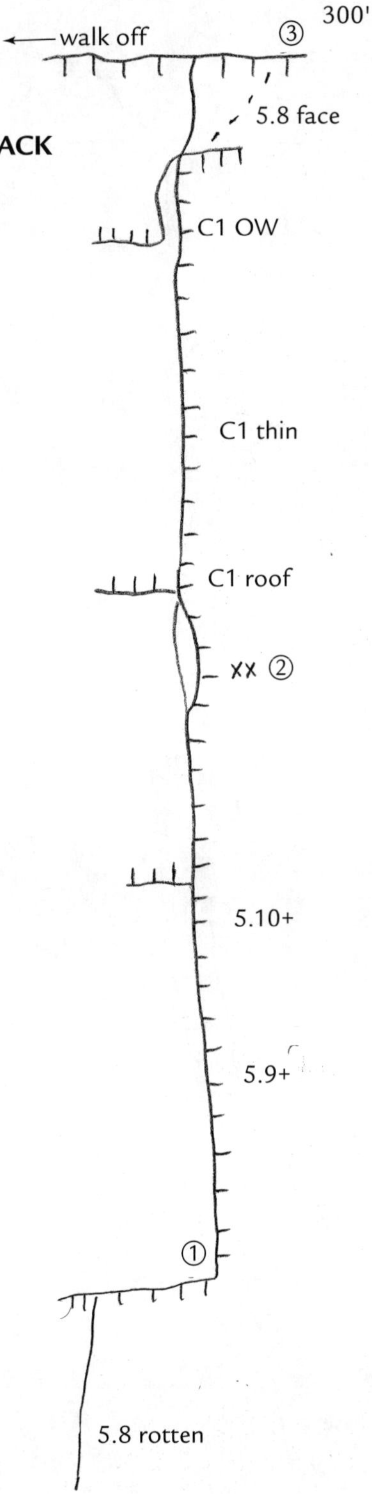

BIG LIEBOWSKY

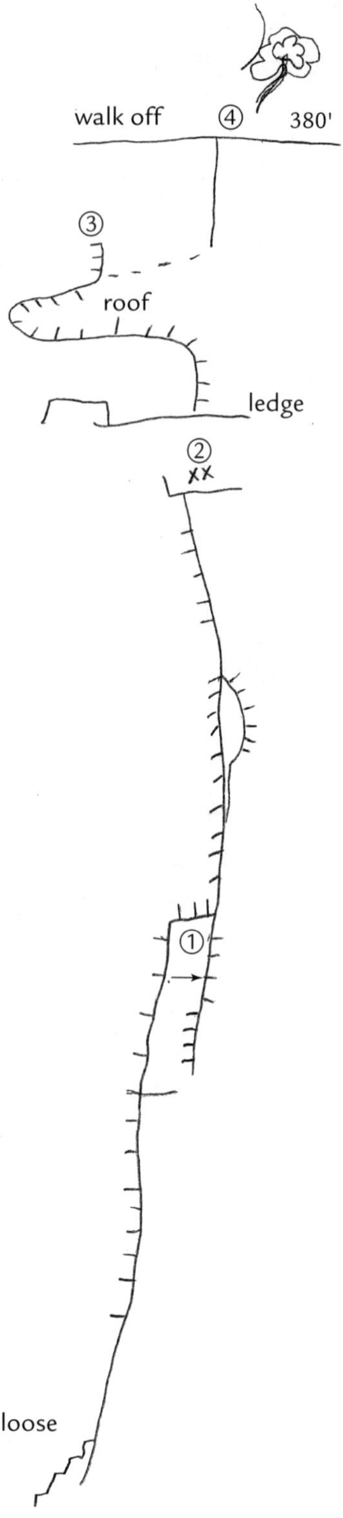

Pitch 2: Continue with aid up the right side of the roof (#1 Camalot) to gain a clean right-facing dihedral, which is followed past two short wide sections to a two-bolt belay, 150 feet (46 m). Andy Roberts: "This pitch is very free climbable."

Pitch 3: Gain the ledge above the anchors, then follow a widening crack left through a spectacular roof. Continue right, above the roof to a flat ledge, 45 feet (13.7 m).

Pitch 4: Traverse 15 feet (4.5 m) right, to a crack leading 25 feet (7.6 m) to flat ground. A tree 15 feet (4.5 m) back from the ledge is used for a natural summit anchor.

Paraphernalia: Camalots (2) sets with (1) #1, #5, and extra #0.75; TCUs (3) sets.

Descent: Walk to campsite if approach is from the west. If approach is from the east, descend the old cattle trail into the canyon and cross over to the fixed rope left for the prusik out.

DIVERSIONS

JAIL ROCK

Jail Rock is a pothole in a large Entrada sandstone dome. It was well known by early travelers between Moab and Monticello as an easy source of water. There are a number of stories of how it became known as Jail Rock. The most often told is that of the early 1900s rancher John Jackson, who would lower his wife into the 15-foot (4.5 m)-deep pothole for safekeeping whenever he had the urge to ride to Moab or Monticello for a drink.

F. A. Barnes gives a background on Jackson in his book *Canyon Country's Canyon Rims Recreation Area*: "After all, John Jackson did show up in this country, a Texas outlaw with a fresh bullet hole in him! He laid up at a spring under the rim of Wilson Mesa for several weeks until his wound healed. He apparently had provisions and there was sufficient water for himself and his horses. Then he '*went into the cattle business.*' As he told it, he started with two horses and an old steer. '*Within two months that old steer had 27 calves!*' Even though Jackson could neither read nor write, he eventually became very wealthy with such business acumen, and was known to loan large amounts of money to friends—providing they were good drinking buddies." Jackson Hole and Jackson Spring are named after John Jackson.

To reach Jail Rock, turn left from the Needles Overlook Road approximately 1 mile (1.6 km) from its junction with US 191. In 1 more mile (1.6 km) the trail crosses Dry Valley Road, the principal access trail into the Dry Valley District of Rims Recreation Area. At 1.5 miles (2.4 km) Jail Rock is reached. A spur trail gives scrambling access to the slickrock pothole. The land beyond Jail Rock is private and closed to public access.

LINE CAMP

This Cowboy Line Camp is still in use as a stopover during seasonal cattle drives. The Line Camp is in Eight Mile Rock and is reached by following the San Juan County 131 (Looking Glass Rock Road) from US 191 to Eight Mile Rock Mileage Log in this chapter.

> ". . . there is something very restful about the horizontal line. Things that lie flat are at peace and the mind grows peaceful with them. Furthermore, the waste places of the earth, the barren deserts, the tracts forsaken of men and given over to loneliness, have a peculiar attraction of their own. The weird solitude, the great silence, the grim desolation, are the very things with which every desert wanderer eventually falls in love.
>
> –John C. Van Dyke, *The Desert,* 1901

14
LOCKHART BASIN TRAIL

> Often the slope of the desert to the river is gradual for many miles—sometimes like the top of a huge table slightly tilted from the horizontal. When the edge of the table is reached the mesa begins to break into terraces (often cut through by small gullies), and the final descent is not unlike the steps of a Roman circus leading down into the arena. During cloud-bursts the waters pour down these steps with great fury and the river simply acts as a catch-basin for all the running color of the desert.
>
> —John C. Van Dyke, *The Desert,* 1901

The Lockhart Basin Trail, a designated Back Country Byway, offers exceptional views in a desolate setting as it traverses 57 miles (92 km) south from Hurrah Pass near Moab to Utah 211 at Indian Creek. Todd Campbell, in his mountain biking book *Above and Beyond Slickrock:* "Lockhart Basin is a vast, austere, and possibly fearsome place. It is not overmanaged by any agency, because it is a 'poor man's Canyonlands.' It is also no place to suffer an emergency, for even if you were to hike to the rim (possible in Lockhart Basin proper), there would be little if any traffic on the nearest dirt road. There are no obvious potholes to store rain water, although some stands of gauzy tamarisk shrubs have a tight affiliation with a couple of stock ponds. . . . From its trailhead on Highway 211 near the Needles, this easily followed ride crosses the archeologically rich Indian Creek to traverse a broad benchland, much like the White Rim Trail. But since the Lockhart Basin Trail is further removed from the river, it hasn't the gaping canyons cut to its very edge like the White Rim. Instead, it weaves through a wonderland of goblin rocks and shrieking effigies carved into the convoluted Cutler sandstone. These sometime appear as totem poles or balanced rocks, but mostly they are strange, transmogrified profiles, prominently splayed with white flecks or sulking in deep shades of purple, chocolate, or rust."

The trail is passable with two-wheel-drive vehicles with high clearance, except for a rough section at its north end a short distance from its right-angle (east) turn from the Chicken Corners Trail. Because of this rough section, the route is best traveled south to north with a four-wheel-drive high-clearance vehicle so that you descend the problem area.

It is possible to approach the climbing routes of the Lockhart Basin Trail with a two-wheel-drive high-clearance vehicle by descending from Hurrah Pass to the northern routes and approaching the southern routes from Utah 211 in Indian Creek. This chapter begins with the routes approached from the north reaches of the Lockhart Basin Trail, then those from the south end of the trail.

The Lockhart Basin Trail is named for L. B. Lockhart, who prospected in the area in the early 1900s. It was made passable by four-wheel-drive vehicles in the 1950s when uranium was discovered in the Chinle slopes the old trail traverses.

LOCKHART BASIN TRAIL ROUTE LOCATOR MAP

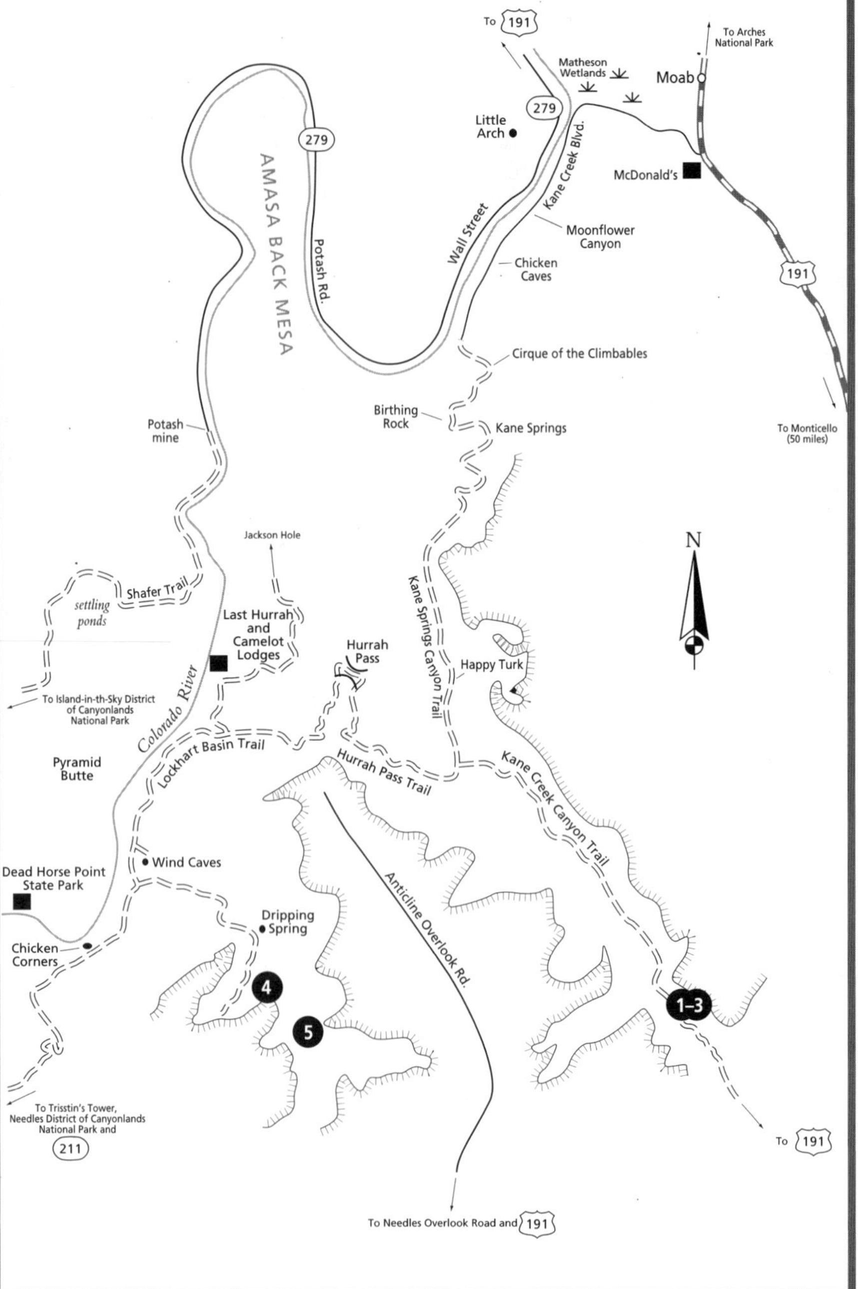

1–3 Nolan, Ella, and Broken Engagement

4 Soltice Tower

5 Amazon Tower

FORMATIONS

At 1.8 miles (2.8 km) from the junction of Main Street and Kane Creek Boulevard, the road turns left (south) at the portal, where the river enters the canyons from Moab Valley. At the portal, the walls on both sides of the Colorado rise dramatically as a result of the great Moab Valley salt anticline. The stratum beside the roadway is crossbedded stream-deposited Kayenta, which disappears below road level to reveal the eolian Navajo formation. As Kane Creek Boulevard turns east and enters Kane Springs Canyon, Kane Creek anticline is visible, and the layers of rock reverse themselves. The Navajo is uplifted, exposing first Kayenta, then Wingate, and eventually Chinle sandstone.

At Kane Springs Canyon, you pass through five distinct formations for an elevation gain of less than 100 feet (30 m). Just west on Amasa Back Mesa, as a result of the Kane Creek anticline, the Kayenta (deposited on the level by fresh water) spans a height differential of 1,000 feet (305 m) within 2 miles (3.2 km). The *Nolan*, *Ella*, and *Broken Engagement* routes in Kane Creek Valley are on Wingate sandstone. As the road climbs to Hurrah Pass, it traverses through first Cutler, then Moenkopi sandstone. Above the pass are the Chinle slopes, then the vertically fractured Wingate, which is capped by the Kayenta. Over the pass, the Lockhart Basin Trail begins descending to the Cutler sandstone Wind Caves. Amazon and Solstice Towers are high above to the east and are eroded from the dense Wingate sandstone.

MAP

Identified on the Moab West map published by Latitude 40 Degrees are (north to south) Scott M. Matheson Wetlands Preserve, several features in Kane Springs Canyon, the Hurrah Pass Trail, Lockhart Basin Trail, and the Wind Caves, identified as Catacomb Rock (a.k.a. The Grotto). They are an amazing structure of swiss cheese rock that was probably carved by water rather than wind. The caves are an excellent shelter from searing desert heat or summer thundershowers. They provide good campsites in a spectacular setting, but there is no firewood or water in the area. Also identified are Amazon and Solstice Towers, Dripping Spring, the difficult four-wheel-drive area of the trail, Chicken Corners, Pack-off Corner, and Lockhart Canyon. Future updated editions of the map will include additional climbing sites, including the *Nolan* and *Ella* area, Carousel Butte, and Trisstin's Tower.

LOCKHART BASIN TRAIL NORTH

Lockhart Basin Trail North is the approach to *Nolan, Ella, Broken Engagement,* Amazon Tower, and Solstice Tower. It can be reached with a high-clearance two-wheel-drive vehicle.

HISTORY

Hurrah Pass was originally called the Notch. In the 1930s, at winter's onset, the Shafer Brothers drove their cattle from the lush grassland of the 6,000-foot-high (1,829 m) Island-in-the-Sky mesa, across the Colorado River, and east to the 4,000-foot (1,219 m) Kane Creek Valley where the weather would be less severe. In the spring the drive was reversed. From the Island-in-the-Sky mesa top, the brothers improved an old Indian trail to one cow wide. Now called the Shafer Trail, it was widened further in the 1950s for vehicular travel by uranium miners. At the river the brothers kept the cattle in a "dry corral" until they were very thirsty, and therefore more willing to cross the river (cows are not too fond of swimming). On the other side of the river, they were herded up the steep narrow trail to the Notch. When the last cow was over the pass and on its way down to the Kane Creek Valley, the brothers would shout, "Hurrah!" The worst of their long journey was coming to an end, and the Notch has been called Hurrah Pass ever since.

To reach the Lockhart Basin Trail North from Moab, turn onto Kane Creek Boulevard from Main Street (US 191 at McDonald's). At 4.7 miles (7.5 km) the paved road ends and the boulevard becomes Kane Springs Canyon North. At 2.2 miles (3.5 km) pass Kane Springs gushing from the left wall, an excellent place to fill water jugs. At 4.3 miles (6.9 km) from Kane Springs, the Kane Creek Canyon Trail East branches left (east); ahead (south), the Hurrah Pass Trail begins. The left branch is the approach to *Nolan, Ella,* and *Broken Engagement.*

At 6.8 miles (10.9 km) from Kane Springs and 13.7 miles (22 km) from McDonald's, Hurrah Pass is reached. Continue south over the pass on what is now identified on the Moab West map as the Lockhart Basin Trail. At the bottom of the grade descending from Hurrah Pass, continue south on the most used trail to the Wind Caves. Watch for a low island of Cutler sandstone (Wind Caves) in a valley east of the road. A major spur branches left to the caves.

From Hurrah Pass south to the Wind Caves, Pyramid Butte lies across the Colorado River northwest of the Wind Caves. Above Pyramid Butte at the left point of the mesa in the backdrop is Dead Horse Point State Park. In view south of Dead Horse Point is a 12-mile (19 km)-long mesa, which is the 6,000-foot (1,829 m)-high Island-in-the-Sky District of Canyonlands National Park.

MILEAGE LOG—MOAB TO WIND CAVES

This log notes points of interest and climbing routes as one travels to the Wind Caves from McDonald's fast-food restaurant at the junction of US 191 (Main Street) and Kane Creek Boulevard. For a definitive guide to the Kane Springs camping and climbing area, refer to *Desert Rock III: Moab to Colorado National Monument.*

00 miles: US 191 junction with Kane Creek Boulevard (McDonald's).

0.8 mile (1.2 km): Fifth West and Kane Creek Boulevard intersection.

1.4 miles (2.2 km): Scott M. Matheson Wetlands Preserve right (north). Left is the tramway to the Moab Valley Rim. Frog on a Lily Pad Tower (a.k.a. Point of Moab) is straight ahead west of the river.

1.8 miles (2.9 km): The portal.

2.5 miles (4.0 km): Cattle guard with Little Arch in view west of the river.

2.7 miles (4.3 km): Moab Rim Trail.

3.0 miles (4.8 km): Kings Bottom campsites (7 sites, $4.00 per night).

3.1 miles (5 km): Moonflower Canyon campsites and petroglyphs (8 sites, $4.00 per night).

3.3 miles (5.3 km): Pit and Bear climbing route.

3.4 miles (5.4 km): Chicken Caves.

3.5 miles (5.6 km): Mastodon Petroglyph Road, which also leads to a bench with a great view of the Colorado River. Petroglyphs on Navajo sandstone wall east of the bench.

4.4 miles (7.0 km): Lone cottonwood tree and Charlie Fowler climbing routes.

4.6 miles (7.4 km): Pritchett Canyon.

4.7 miles (7.5 km): End of Kane Creek Boulevard and beginning of Kane Springs Canyon; cattle guard; dirt road begins. Pritchett Canyon opens on the left.

KANE SPRING CANYON

00 miles: Begin Kane Springs Canyon dirt road. Straight ahead is Amasa Back Mesa.

0.1 mile (0.16 km): BLM information kiosk and parking area on right.

0.3 mile (0.48 km): Petroglyphs are visible on the wall above the road (left). Others are viewed by hiking the base of the wall.

0.4 mile (0.64 km): First Tombstone of the Cirque of the Climbables, on the left.

0.5 mile (0.8 km): Third Tombstone and beginning of Surphase Tension Buttress, on the left.

0.7 mile (1.1 km): Large parking area on right. Trailhead on left is to the climbs *Burn Victim, Dark Star,* and *Driving While Asian,* as well as numerous petroglyphs and a good approach to the climbs on Surphase Tension Buttress. Sugar Walls is in view ahead and to the right (west).

1.0 mile (1.6 km): *The Farm* is on the left above a large boulder on the talus slope. There is no parking on the road below the climb. Abraxas Wall is in view to the right (west), right of the obvious arch in the making.

1.3 miles (2.0 km): Beginning of the signed Amasa Back four-wheel-drive trail, on the right. Arch in the making is in view to the west. Left of the arch are petroglyphs, right is an Anasazi granary.

1.4 miles (2.2 km): Birthing Rock with famous petroglyph, on the right.

1.5 miles (2.4 km): Upside-down rock with petroglyphs, on the right.

1.7 miles (2.7 km): Top of hill and trailhead to Funnel Arch, on the left.

2.0 miles (3.2 km): Second switchback and trailhead to *Archaic Revival* and *Kind, Other Kind* climbing routes, on the right.

2.2 miles (3.5 km): Kane Springs, excellent water source.

KANE SPRINGS

00 miles: Kane Springs gushes from the left wall.

0.1 mile (0.16 km): Spring campsite (4 sites, $4.00 per night).

0.9 mile (1.4 km): Stimulants Wall on the left is the site of Jim Beyer's routes up the overhanging hueco wall above the road.

1.0 mile (1.6 km): Hunters Canyon, on the left.

1.1 miles (1.7 km): *Grave* and *Unleashed* climbing routes on the left.

1.2 miles (1.9 km): Echo campsite (9 sites, $4.00 per night) on the right.

1.3 miles (2.0 km): Ice Cream Parlor climbing area on the left.

1.6 miles (2.5 km): Beginning of Kane Creek Valley. At the large boulder on the right is a sign: LEAVING RIVERWAY RECREATION AREA. This location is also the approach drainage to the grassy ledge leading to Scorched Earth Crag, on the right (west), and the approach to *Charlie's Sorry* and *Sorry Charlie* routes, on the left.

2.2 miles (3.5 km): Petroglyph of a bighorn sheep, anthropomorphic figure, and centipede-like creature, above the road on a large boulder, on the left. With the right kind of lighting, Predator Tower is in view to the far right.

3.2 miles (5.1 km): Note the improbable location of a large uranium loading dock high on the Chinle slope on the east (left) side of Kane Creek Valley.

3.4 miles (5.4 km): The Happy Turk hoodoo is left (east), and the *Pensive Putterman* climb is to the right.

4.2 miles (6.7 km): Cutler Towers on the left. *Shelbyville* on the right.

4.3 miles (6.9 km): The road crosses Kane Creek. Just beyond is the left branch (the Kane Creek Canyon Trail East) to *Nolan, Ella,* and *Broken Engagement.* Ahead is the beginning of the Hurrah Pass Trail.

7.8 miles (12.5 km): Hurrah Pass. High atop the rimrock (south), Anticline Overlook emerges. Beyond the pass (south) is the beginning of the Lockhart Basin Trail.

8.2 miles (13.2 km): The dramatic hoodoo left of the road is known to climbers as CB's Love Muscle; the route to its improbable summit is *Putterman Sex Machine.*

10.3 miles (16.5 km): Right turn down the wash leads to Camelot Lodge and the Last Hurrah Lodge.

10.5 miles (16.9 km): Just right of the trail is a rectangular opening to a natural bridge.

10.7 miles (17.2 km): At a T, take the right branch.

10.8 miles (17.3 km): Top of Hill. Sign: PRIVATE PROPERTY. Keep left on dirt trail.

12.1 miles (19.5 km): At a T, take the left branch to the Wind Caves. Cross a playa (dry lake bed), impassable if wet.

12.4 miles (20.0 km): Take the right fork at a Y and continue 0.1 mile (0.16 km) to the Wind Caves.

WIND CAVES

00 miles: Wind Caves east branch from the Lockhart Trail. For a scenic drive continue ahead (south). Sign: LOCKHART BASIN (STRAIGHT). DIPPING SPRING (LEFT).

1.1 miles (1.7 km): Viper Rock ahead on the left.

1.7 miles (2.7 km): The Rico limestone bridge a few feet right is not visible from the road, but a cairn beside the road usually marks its location. Good photo opportunity.

NOLAN, ELLA, AND BROKEN ENGAGEMENT

To reach *Nolan, Ella,* and *Broken Engagement,* drive 4.3 miles (6.9 km) past the crossing of Kane Creek in Kane Creek Valley (0.8 miles (1.2 km) past the Happy Turk). Just beyond the creek crossing, a left branch forks to Kane Springs rest stop 14 miles (22.5 km) south of Moab on US 191 (between mile markers 110 and 111). A difficult four-wheel drive is required to reach US 191 by this route. At the junction, the trail straight ahead goes to Hurrah Pass (the Hurrah Pass Trail) and the Wind Caves; this is the approach for Amazon and Solstice Towers. The left branch (to US 191) is the beginning of the Kane Creek Canyon Trail East. This branch is the approach to *Nolan, Ella,* and *Broken Engagement.* Drive 3.7 miles (6 km) from the junction (passable by two-wheel-drive vehicles). Park on the left at a boulder with petroglyphs, then scramble to the buttress above and the twin cracks of *Nolan* (left) and *Ella* (right). *Broken Engagement* is 100 feet (30 m) right of *Ella.* From the parking area, an old four-wheel-drive trail branches left toward the northwest buttress above.

> Nolan and Ella were two names Andy and Liz Roberts had picked for their unborn child. They had a girl and named her Ella.

1 NOLAN
I, 5.10a, 1 pitch, 100 feet (30m) ★★★★

First Ascent: Andy Roberts, Jason Repko, October 12, 1999.

Location and Access: Begin at a right-facing corner above a large boulder on the talus below the buttress. Climb 50 feet (15 m) up a perfect hand crack, past 5 feet (1.5 m) of broken rock, then continue another 50 feet (15 m) to a ledge on the right from a horn, or move right and belay from *Ella's* anchors.

Paraphernalia: Camalots (2) #1, (4) #2, (2) #3, (1) #3.5, (2) #4.

Descent: Rappel with a single 200-foot (60 m) rope from *Ella's* anchors.

2 ELLA
I, 5.10b, 1 pitch, 100 feet (30 m) ★★★

First Ascent: Andy Roberts, Jason Repko, October 12, 1999.

Location and Access: Climb the right-facing dihedral 12 feet (3.6 m) right of *Nolan*. Begin up loose rock, then continue up a good crack, alternating between fingers and hands to a two-bolt anchor on a ledge shared with *Nolan*.

Paraphernalia: Friends (2) sets.

Descent: Rappel from double bolts, 100 feet (30 m).

3 BROKEN ENGAGEMENT
I, 1 pitch, C1, 110 feet (34 m) ★★

First Ascent: Andy Roberts, Jason Repko, September 1999.

Location and Access: The route is 100 feet (30 m) right of *Ella*. Climb with clean aid up a right-facing dihedral of gritty, pocketed but good rock. Pass three bulges to a ledge on the left. The route has the potential to be climbed to the top, 300 feet (91 m).

Paraphernalia: Friends (3) sets.

Descent: Double-rope rappel from double bolts.

AMAZON AND SOLSTICE TOWERS

Amazon Tower is a thin, tall, detached spire with a pointed summit in view on the right wall of the Wingate buttress left (east) of the Wind Caves. Solstice Tower is the formation in the skyline southeast of the Wind Caves and comprises the back of a chairlike formation. Between Amazon Tower and Solstice Tower is the prominent round Carousel Butte.

From the Wind Caves, follow a dirt trail as it continues left (east) to Dripping Spring, an unreliable source of water. Farther east, the trail becomes increasingly difficult four-wheel drive and will eventually require a cross-country hike to Amazon Tower and a hike and a steep scree scramble to reach Solstice Tower.

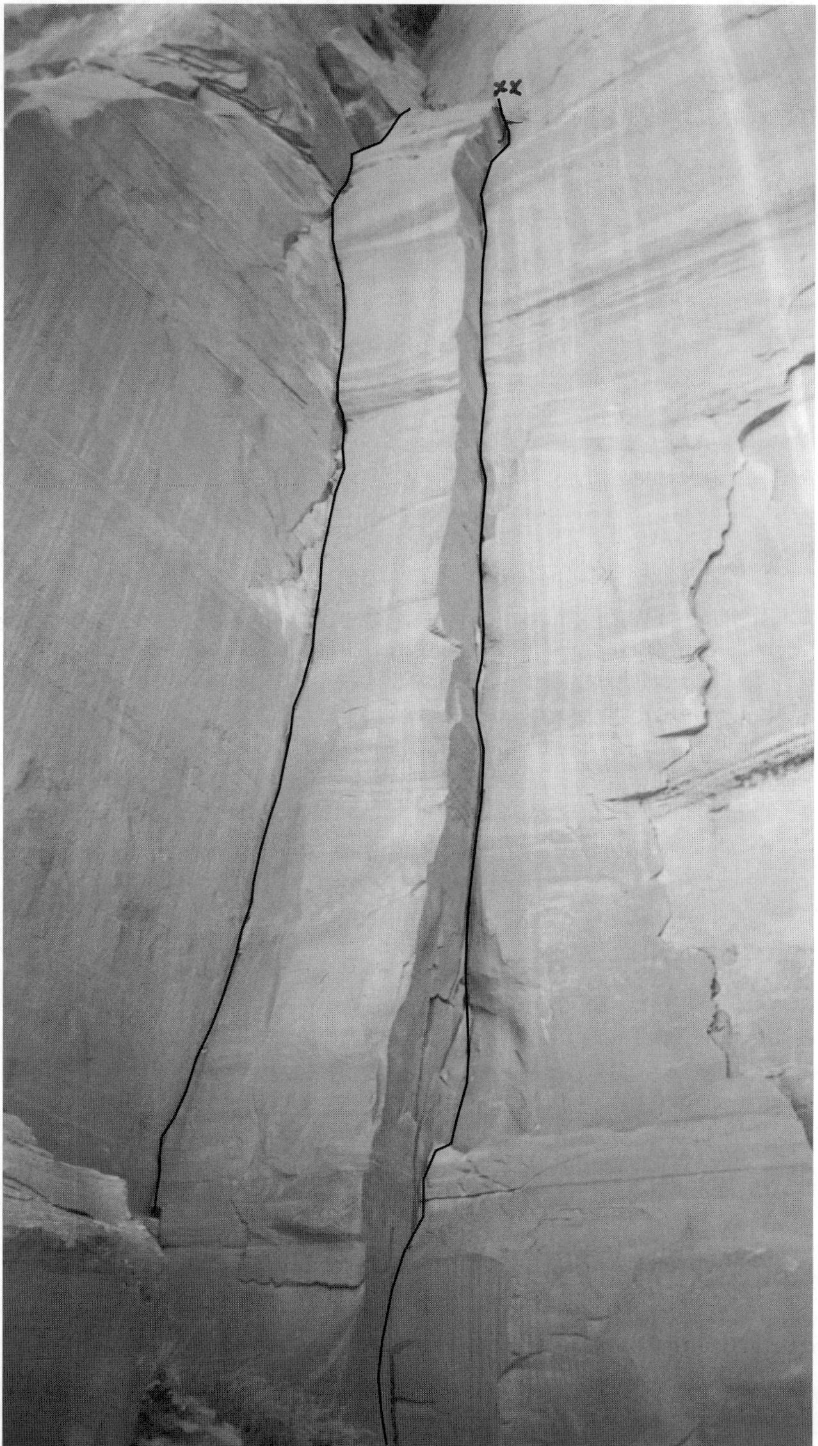

Photo: Andy Roberts

Nolan *(left) and* Ella *(right).*

Both landforms are in view from the road and are easily reached by foot from the point where four-wheel drive becomes necessary.

4 AMAZON TOWER
III, 5.11, A2, 4 pitches, 400 feet (122 m) ★★★

First Ascent: Andy Roberts, Dave Mealey, Matt Vanosdell, August 1998.

Location and Access: The ascent route climbs the west face of the spire.

Pitch 1: Begin up 10 feet (3 m) of a left-facing off-width chimney to gain a ledge. Traverse right and continue up a 0.75-inch (1.9 cm) crack for 15 feet (4.5 m), which then widens to hands and is followed to a hanging belay at a two-bolt station, 45 feet (14 m).

Pitch 2: Traverse left, then continue up 25 feet (7.6 m), passing a short wide section. Belay left of a wide crack, 90 feet (27 m).

Pitch 3: Climb a 4-inch (10 cm) crack (crux), passing a wide section with loose rock to "defecation ledge" and a double-bolt anchor, 135 feet (41 m).

Pitch 4: Squeeze through to the south face and traverse right to a rotten crack that after 5 feet (1.5 m) narrows and the rock quality improves. Clean aid up a #3 Metolius crack, which becomes wide before it ends. Continue, passing five bolts and three drilled holes for birdbeaks, to the summit and a two-bolt anchor station, A2, 130 feet (40 m).

Paraphernalia: Standard desert rack; Camalots (3) #3, (2) #4; Metolius cams (4) #3; knifeblades (2); Lost Arrows (1); angles (1) ½"; birdbeaks (3); talon hook (1).

Descent: Three double-rope rappels. Rappel to the right on the middle rappel to prevent the rope from getting stuck in the crack.

5 SOLSTICE TOWER
II, C2, 2 pitches, 190 feet (58 m) ★★★

First Ascent: Ted Rummings, Andy Roberts, June 21, 1999.

Location and Access: Ascend the splitter crack up the center of the east side of the tower (opposite side from the river).

Pitch 1: Climb a perfect splitter crack to a belay beneath a roof (mostly aid), C1, 110, feet (34 m).

Pitch 2: Angle up and left from the belay and continue through a steep headwall on marginal gear, C2, 80 feet (24 m). Andy Roberts: "Beautiful view from a perfectly flat rectangular summit."

Paraphernalia: Camming units (3) sets; Metolius cams (2) #00, #0, #1; blue Lowe Ball (1); birdbeak (1).

Descent: Double-rope rappel from double summit anchors.

AMAZON TOWER

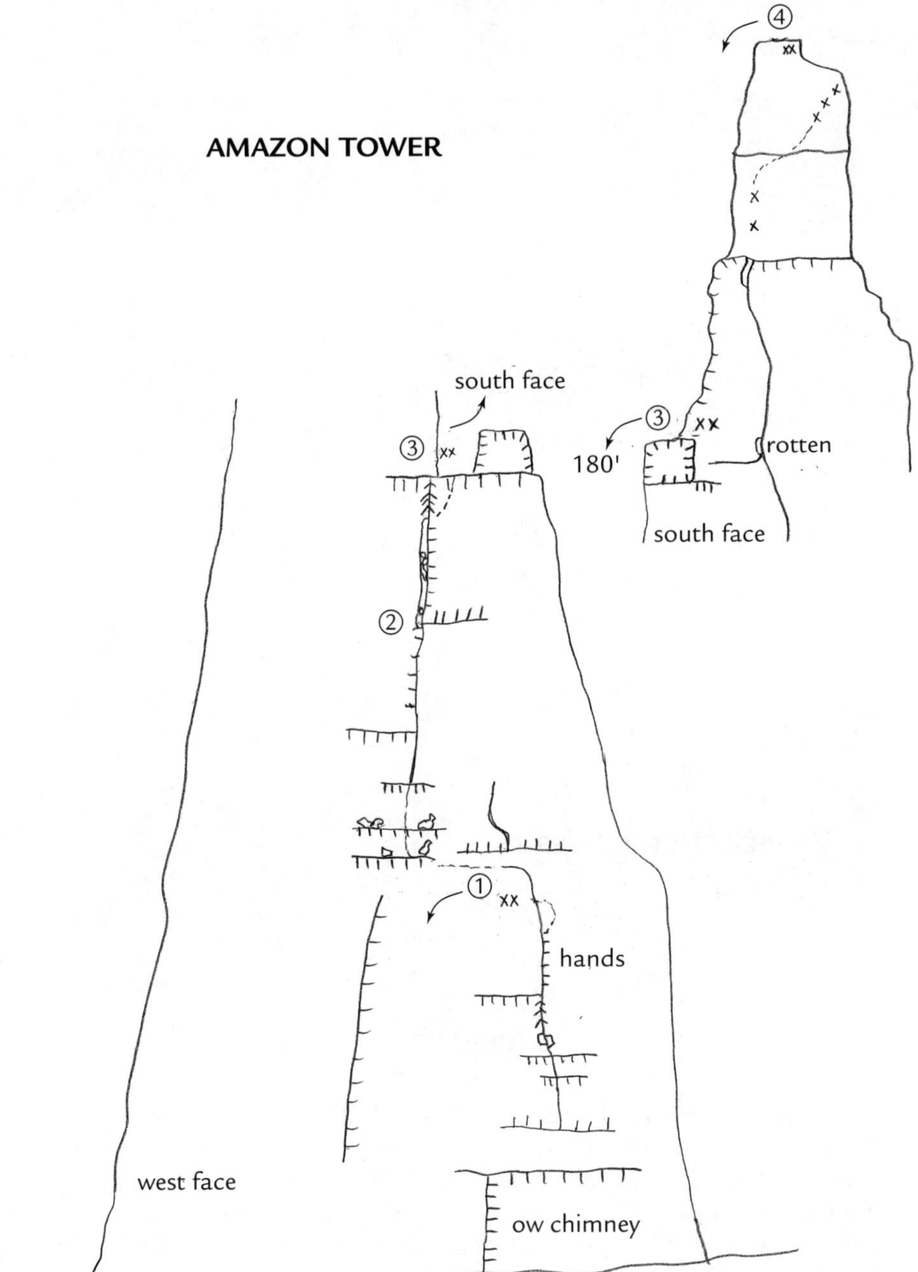

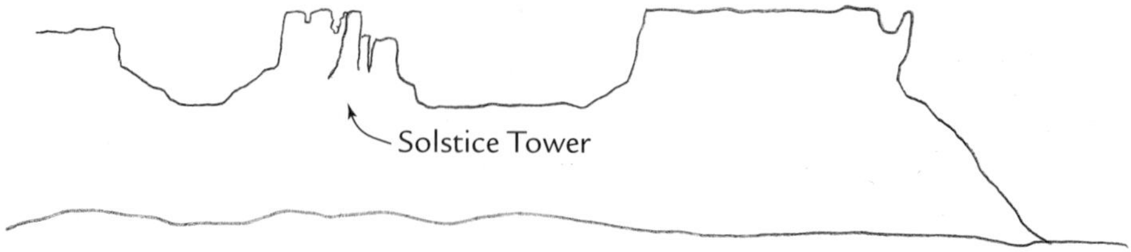

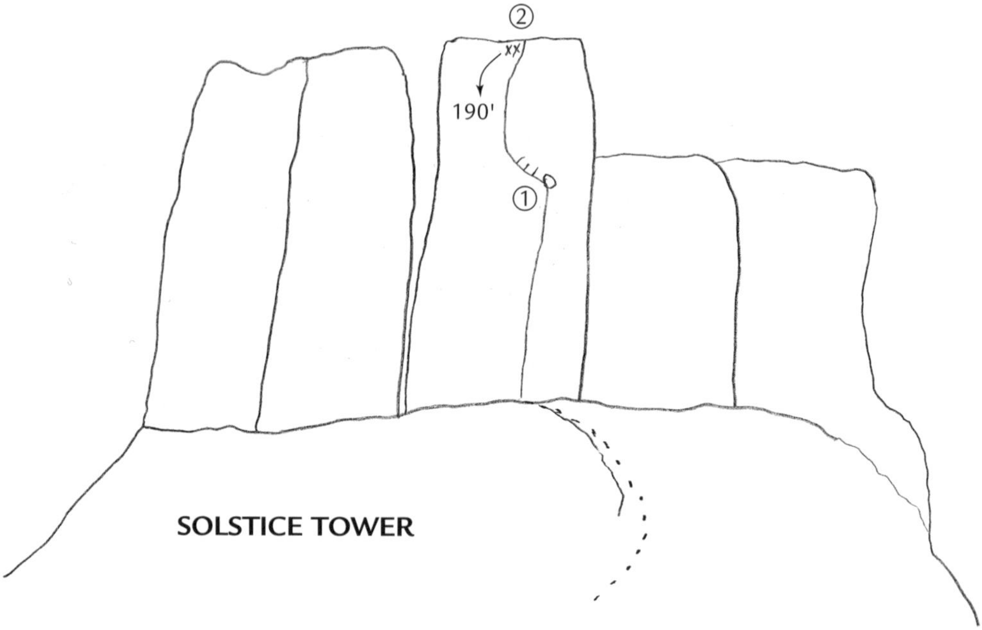

DIVERSIONS

SCOTT M. MATHESON WETLANDS PRESERVE

Worth visiting en route to the preceding climbing areas is the 875-acre Scott M. Matheson Wetlands Preserve, purchased in the early 1990s and managed by the Nature Conservancy and the Utah Division of Wildlife Resources. This unique desert slough is the only one of its kind on the banks of the Colorado River as it passes through Utah, the second driest state in the country.

The area has forests of cottonwood, willow, Russian olive, and tamarisk. According to the preserve's brochure, "It is an oasis in a desert where more than 180 species of birds have been identified, as well as frogs and mule deer." Those birds include bald eagles, peregrine falcons, northern harriers, red-tailed hawks, and golden eagles, and there is a great blue heron rookery at the lower edge of the wetlands. River otters and beavers also make their home here.

The entrance to the wetlands is on the right (north), 1.4 miles (2.2 km) down Kane Creek Boulevard from its junction with US 191 at McDonald's. There is an information kiosk at the parking area and passage to a scenic boardwalk that leads to viewing blinds and an observation tower. Naturalist-guided preserve walks are led Saturday mornings, April through September. For further information contact the Conservancy's Moab Project Office, (435) 259–4629.

LITTLE WINDOW

Little Window is in view high on the rimrock west of the Colorado from the cattle guard 2.5 miles (4 km) down Kane Creek Boulevard from McDonald's. Little Window is a misnomer, because it is a pothole-type arch (not a window) and is not little. It has a span of 40 feet (12 m), and is 20 feet (6 m) high, 25 feet (7.6 m) thick, and 15 feet (4.5 m) wide.

CHICKEN CAVES

As one descends downriver on Kane Creek Boulevard, several large man-made caves become obvious along the cliff line 3.4 miles (5.4 km) from McDonald's. The caves housed an egg farm in the 1960s and 1970s. Lights were turned on for eight hours, off for eight hours, then on for eight hours, tricking the hens into laying one-third more eggs than they would have under normal circumstances. The business was doomed when they found that the eggs produced were pale with more albumen and less taste than their competitors'.

KANE SPRINGS

Kane Springs is 2.2 miles (3.5 km) from the cattle guard at the beginning of the dirt road that marks the entrance to Kane Spring Canyon. Steep switchbacks descend to the canyon floor, where fresh water flows from the Kayenta Formation on the left side of the road. It is an aquifer that geologists suggest has its origin in the 12,721-foot (3,877 m) La Sal Mountains, more than 20 miles (32 km) to the east. At the spring, rich green mosses, maidenhair ferns, wild orchids (giant *Helleborine epipactis gigantes*), horsetail reeds, lush wet-site grasses and sedges, goldenrods, primroses, common reeds *(Phragmites australis),* squawberry bushes, cockleburs, fleabane daisies, virgin's bower (clematis), and thistles grow in lavish variations. At Spring Campground, 500 feet (152 m) downcanyon from Kane Springs, many other trees and shrubs grow in profusion, including hackberrys, cottonwoods, junipers, scrub oaks, poison ivy, greasewoods, rabbitbrush, Russian thistles, and the ubiquitous tamarisk.

LAST HURRAH AND CAMELOT LODGE

Camelot and the Last Hurrah are two very remote guest retreats. The Camelot Lodge brochure lists its amenities: five guest bedrooms each with private bath, five campsites with showers, a beachfront play area, a rustic living area with a spectacular view of the Colorado River, world-class hearty home-cooked meals, and camel treks. The Last Hurrah has a bicycle repair shop, sauna and hot tub, TV with satellite dish, laundry facilities, sand golf, horse rides, boat rides, and a corporate retreat conference hall. For further information contact the Last Hurrah and Camelot Adventure Lodges at P.O. Box 621, Moab, UT 84532, (435) 259-9721.

WIND CAVES

The Wind Caves are in an obvious large island of Cutler sandstone in the valley east of the trail approximately 4.6 miles (7.4 km) south of Hurrah Pass. Depending on road conditions, a two-wheel-drive vehicle with high clearance can usually reach the caves. From the end of the spur to the caves, you can enter the honeycombed rock and traverse north to southeast through tunnels that open to the east, framing the surrounding lands. Shades of rose and apricot light filter through the numerous openings in the ceiling and walls. It is a most amazing place of beauty and an excellent campsite.

RICO BRIDGE

The bridge is weathered from the Rico Limestone Formation of Permian age (245 to 286 million years old). It is beyond the Wind Caves on the right side of the trail along a flat open stretch and beyond the sharp left turn to Lockhart Basin. It is difficult to locate, but usually can be identified by a small rock cairn on the right side of the trail. Rico Bridge is approximately 50 feet (15 m) long and only a couple of feet thick. It spans the limestone bed a few feet lower than the road level. Great photos can be taken from the road looking down at the exposure beneath the bridge with someone walking across it.

LOCKHART BASIN TRAIL SOUTH

The Lockhart Basin Trail South is the high-clearance, two-wheel-drive approach to Trisstin's Tower and Attila's Thumb from Utah 211 at Indian Creek.

TRISSTIN'S TOWER

Trisstin's Tower is in Lockhart Basin on the east side of the Colorado River between Moab and Indian Creek. It is reached over the Lockhart Basin Back Country Byway, which follows a broad bench between the Colorado River and the soaring Wingate buttress bordering both the west flanks of 6,000-foot (1,829 m)-high Harts Point and Hatch Point in Rims Recreation Area. The complete traverse of the trail requires a four-wheel-drive high-clearance vehicle.

From Utah 211, the entrance to Indian Creek and the Needles District of Canyonlands National Park, turn right (north) 9.5 miles (15 km) beyond the Dugout Ranch obvious on the left (south). The turn is about 2.75 miles (4.4 km) before the boundary of Canyonlands National Park is reached. Drive 14 miles (22.5 km) to the middle of Lockhart Basin. Approximately 100 yards (91 m)

LOCKHART BASIN TRAIL ROUTE LOCATOR MAP

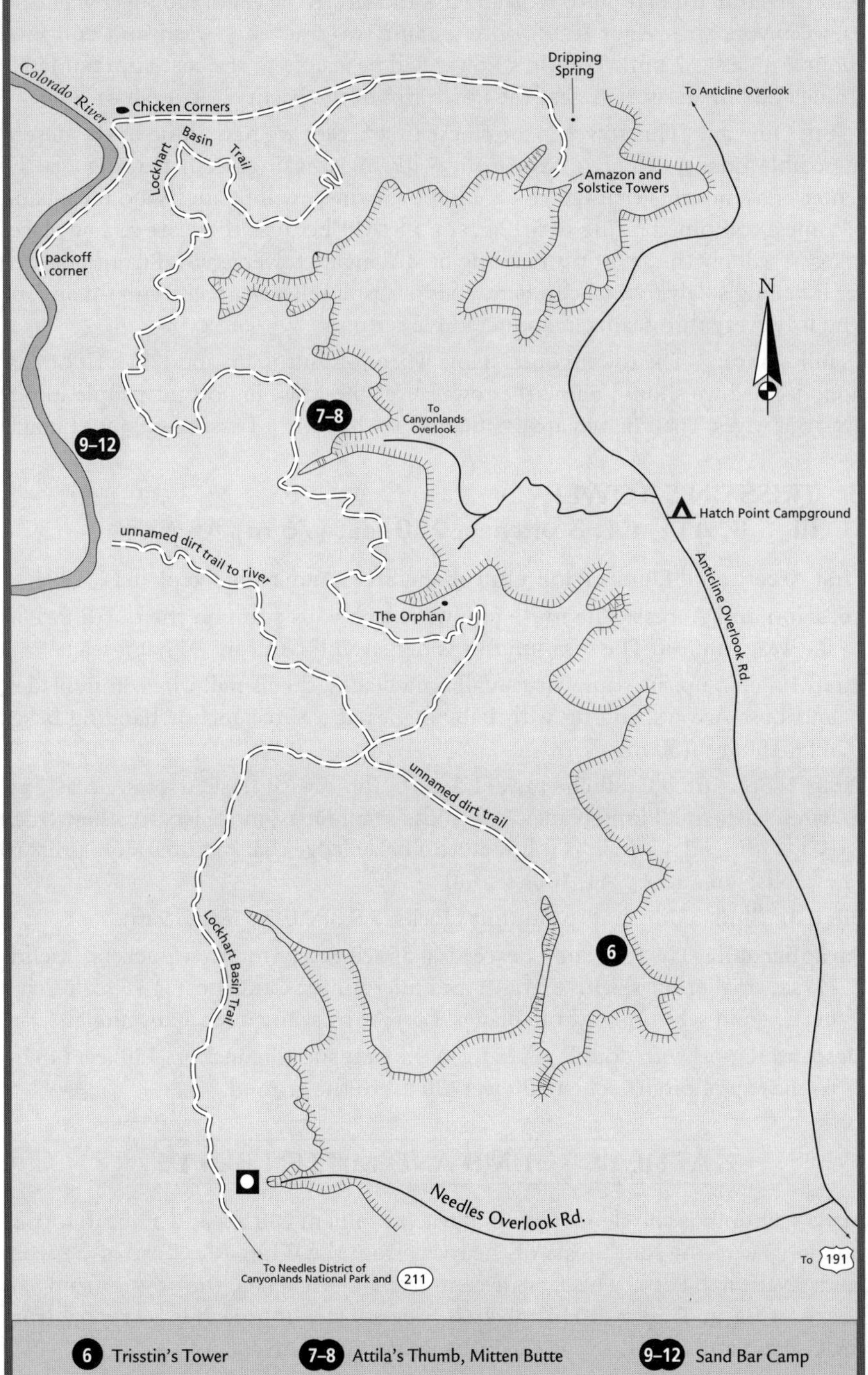
Colorado River
Chicken Corners
Dripping Spring
To Anticline Overlook
Lockhart Basin Trail
Amazon and Solstice Towers
packoff corner
N
7–8
To Canyonlands Overlook
9–12
Hatch Point Campground
unnamed dirt trail to river
Anticline Overlook Rd.
The Orphan
unnamed dirt trail
6
Lockhart Basin Trail
Needles Overlook Rd.
To 191
To Needles District of Canyonlands National Park and 211
6 Trisstin's Tower
7–8 Attila's Thumb, Mitten Butte
9–12 Sand Bar Camp

before the trail forks right to Hurrah Pass and left to the Colorado River via Lockhart Canyon, turn right (east) onto a faint two-track dry wash and continue about 2 miles (3.2 km). Trisstin's Tower will be visible to the east approximately 1 mile (1.6 km) away. It is near the north rim of the basin on its eastern side.

Bill Duncan: "This tower is the finest first ascent we have done in the desert. Incredible quality Wingate sandstone with an amazing seam flowing up the center of a smooth, vertical face. . . . I hope the tower will retain its aid rating and become a combined rating of 5.12a/b or 5.8, A1+ because there are so few places one can still ply the art of thin nailing on a Wingate tower *legally*. I would hate to see it belong solely to 5.12 climbers. This is absolutely a *must-do* climb for anyone who loves very thin seams in an incredible setting!"

Bill Duncan: "The tower got its name when Jon Burnham and I, in a fit of passion, decided we should name the tower after the most important people in our lives: our wives. Their names are Kristin and Trisha, hence Trisstin—sappy, I know!"

6 TRISSTIN'S TOWER
III, 5.8, A1+, C1, 3 pitches, 250 feet (76 m) ★★★★★

First Ascent: Bill Duncan, John Burnham, Steve Anderton, October 14, 1995.

Location and Access: The route follows the obvious seam on the north face to the west summit. The east summit is higher. Bill Duncan: "What a seam!"

Pitch 1: Begin up the seam with small knifeblades, then small wires, knifeblades, and Lost Arrows, ending with baby angles at a three-anchor hanging belay, A1+, 100 feet (30 m).

Pitch 2: Start up a 0.5-inch crack (1.2 cm). Climb with Lost Arrows, occasional wires, then small knifeblades. When the seam fades, move left to a new crack (C1, #1 Friends), which is followed to a belay ledge that requires large units to establish an anchor, A1, 100 feet (30 m).

Pitch 3: Climb a dihedral to summit blocks, 5.8 or A0, 50 feet (15 m).

Paraphernalia: The route never exceeds 0.5 inch except for a few pockets. Friends (1) set smaller sizes, with extra #1 and microunits; Camalots (1) #5 for pitch 2 belay; good selection of knifeblades, Lost Arrows, and a few baby angles.

Descent: Rappel with double ropes from the west summit anchors 150 feet (46 m) to the top of pitch 1, then 100 feet (30 m) to the ground.

ATTILA'S THUMB AND MITTEN BUTTE

Attila's Thumb is the slender spire of the prominent Mitten and Thumb formation in view to the south (east of the river) from the White Rim Trail of Canyonlands National Park. The first ascent team approached the tower from the Lockhart Basin Trail over Hurrah Pass. The shorter approach is by rappel from the Canyonlands Overlook at the Rims Recreational Area.

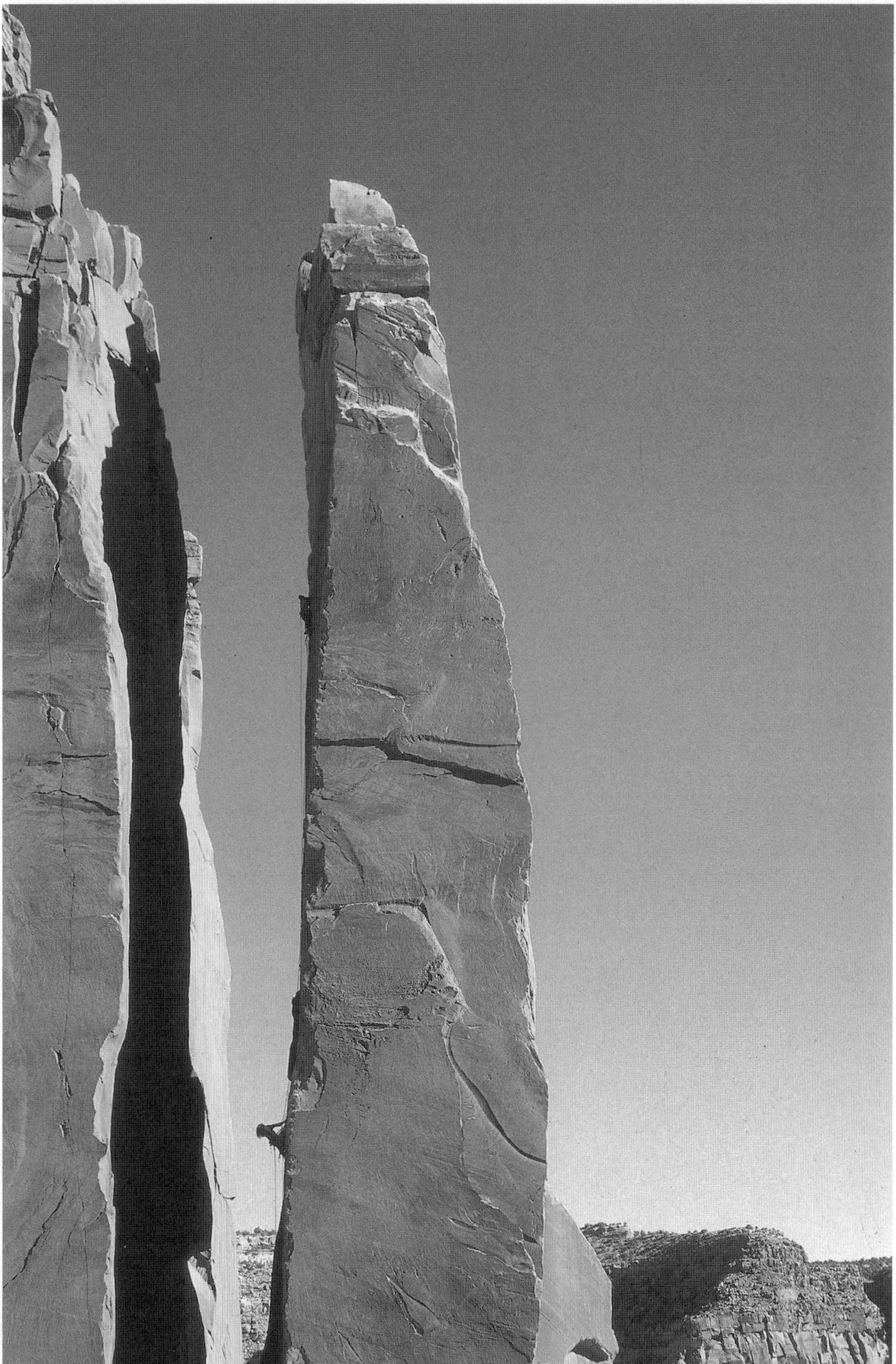

Photo: Bill Duncan

Climbers on the north face of Trisstin's Tower.

TRISSTIN'S TOWER

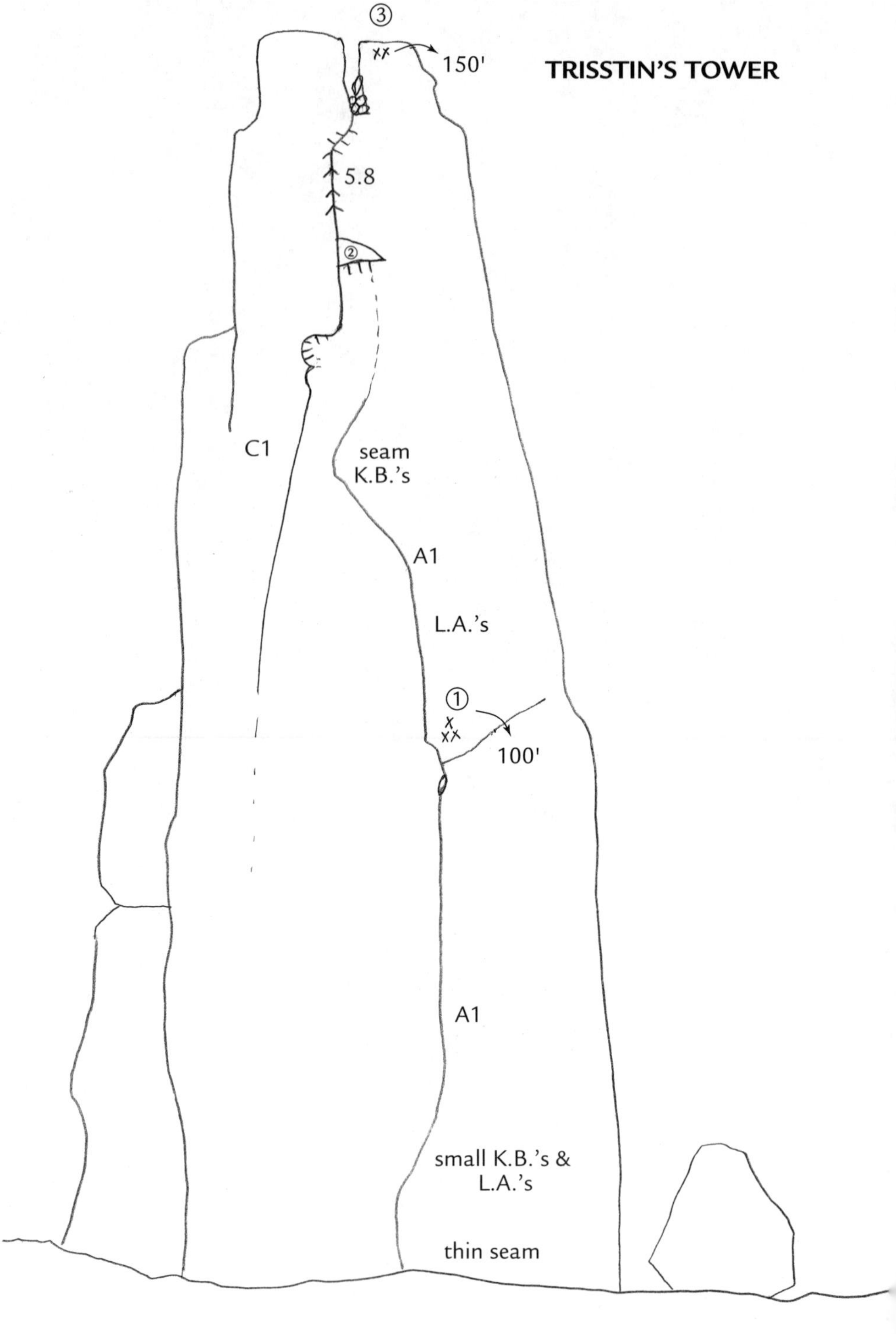

To reach from Utah 211 in Indian Creek (the two-wheel-drive approach), follow directions for Trisstin's Tower. Continue up the Lockhart Basin Trail until the Mitten and Thumb become obvious, then approach on foot up the southern talus slope to the tower.

To reach from Kane Creek, drive to Hurrah Pass and continue on the Lockhart Basin Trail with a four-wheel-drive high-clearance vehicle until the tower comes into view. Although more scenic, this approach is long and more difficult.

To reach by rappel, follow the approach directions for the Orphan in the Rims Recreation Area (Chapter 13), taking the most used trail to the Canyonlands Overlook, where the road ends at campsites identified by fire rings and a pit toilet. Make three rappels into the canyon, leaving fixed ropes for the return.

7 ATTILA'S THUMB—MOGUL EMPEROR IV, 5.11-, 3 pitches, 330 feet (100 m)

First Ascent: Robert Warren, Max Kendall, April 1988.

Location and Access: The route climbs the south face of the tower. Robert Warren: "The first ascent belay bolts were sound, but lead bolts were short and marginal. The climb is characterized by everything in the book." The overhang between the Thumb and the Mitten was named the Hang Nail.

Pitch 1: Begin up loose rock on the right side of the Thumb. Climb to a belay ledge with double bolts, 5.8.

Pitch 2: Climb a 5.11- roof with hands (crux). Pass two bolts, continuing with fingers, then hand-stacking-fist up a slot to a belay ledge with double drilled angles.

Pitch 3: Climb a left-facing corner, then 5.10+ face to double anchors on the summit.

Paraphernalia: Friends (1) set; wires (1) set; Hexentrics (1) set; tube chocks; quick draws (4).

Descent: Rappel the route.

8 MITTEN BUTTE SOUTH FACE—LYEPICK III, 5.11+, 5 pitches, 370 feet (113 m) ★★★★★

First Ascent: Nathan Clark, Cameron Tague, 1990s.

Location and Access: The route climbs the south face of Mitten Butte of the Thumb and Butte formation. Approach up the west talus from Lockhart Basin Trail.

Pitch 1: Begin up a hand crack/squeeze, then follow broken cracks, 5.9, 90 feet (27 m).

Pitch 2: Continue up a chimney and belay at a large terrace, 5.11, 60 feet (18 m).

Pitch 3: Ascend a left-facing dihedral to a splitter crack that cuts left at 30 feet (9 m). Move left and belay below a large roof, 5.11-, 120 feet (37 m).

Photo: Max Kendall

Robert Warren on the Hang Nail of Attila's Thumb.

ATTILA'S THUMB—MOGUL EMPEROR

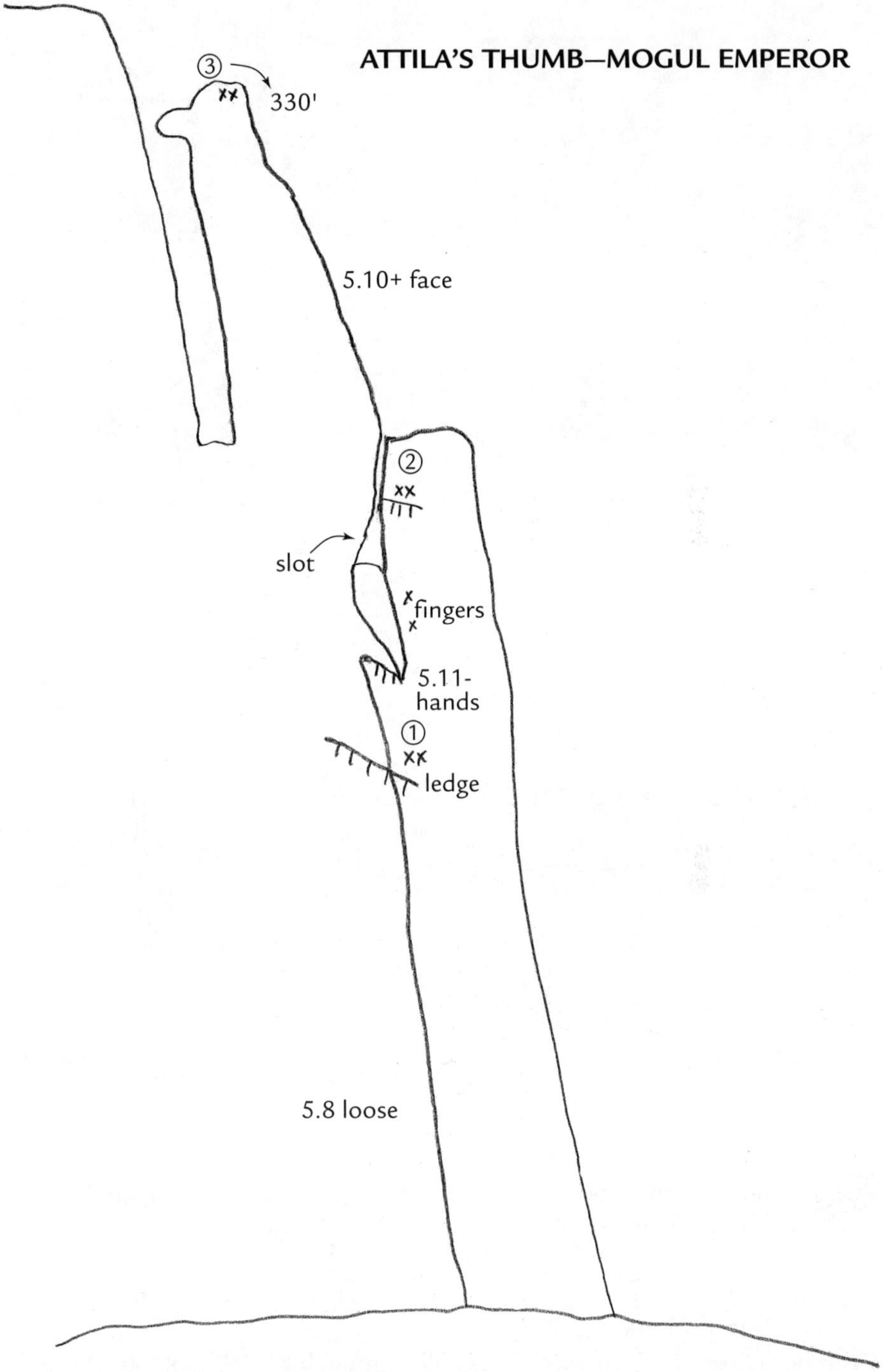

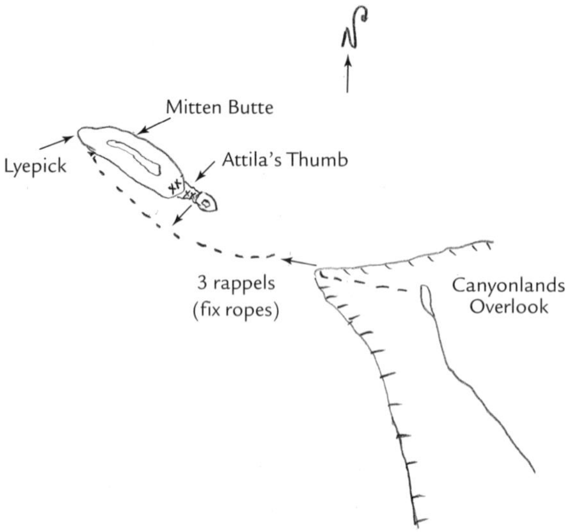

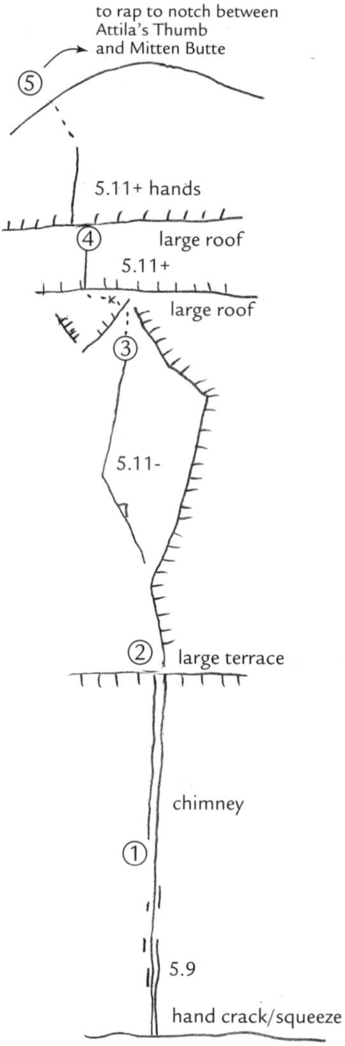

MITTEN BUTTE SOUTH FACE—LYEPICK

Pitch 4: The crux, protected by a bolt. Follow a hand crack left past a bolt, then climb through a large roof to a cramped belay below a second roof, 30 feet (9 m).

Pitch 5: Climb 5.11+ hands through the roof, then a hand crack to the summit, 5.11+, 70 feet (21 m).

Paraphernalia: Friends, hand-size; Camalots through #4; 200-foot (60 m) ropes.

Descent: With 200-foot (60 m) ropes, rappel to the notch between the Thumb and the Mitten, then down the south side to the ground.

SAND BAR CAMP

Lockhart Canyon Sand Bar Camp is the first stop on the Colorado River for those running Cataract Canyon. The site is the location of a large sandbar on the east side of the river, about 20 river miles (32 km) downriver from the standard put-in at the Potash Mine just beyond the end of Scenic Byway 279. Roughly 5 miles (8 km) east of Monster and Washerwoman Towers near river mile 29 and approximately 1 mile (1.6 km) downriver from Little Bridge Canyon, the area is known to river runners as Pumpkin Patch. The climbs are about 100 feet (30 m) away from the river.

From Lockhart Basin Trail South, hike about 1 mile (1.6 km) due east to the sandbar. Pass through a thick tamarisk growth, which is breached upriver at the right end of the sandbar. Begin from a large ledge system, also at the right end of the sandbar (fourth class).

9 FIST FIGHT
I, 5.10b, 1 pitch, 35 feet (10.6 m)

First Ascent: Mike Mayer, Brett Maurer, Christine Blackman, July 28, 1987.

Location and Access: Climb a right-facing corner up a 4- to 5-inch (10 to 12.7 cm) crack system at the far left side of the cliff face.

Paraphernalia: Friends (3) #4.

Descent: Rappel the route, then walk off to the right.

10 BEACH LAYBACK
I, 5.8, 1 pitch, 40 feet (12 m)

First Ascent: Mike Mayer, Brett Maurer, Christine Blackman, July 28, 1987.

Location and Access: The route ascends a right-facing corner just right of *Fist Fight* and left of a long, low overhang. Mike Mayer: "Fun layback with crack on face at finish."

Paraphernalia: Friends (1) #2, #3, #4.

Descent: Rappel the route, then walk off to the right.

11 DAWN DELIGHT
I, 5.10a, 1 pitch, 40 feet (12 m)

First Ascent: Mike Mayer, Brett Maurer, Christine Blackman, July 28, 1987.

Location and Access: The route is one crack right of *Beach Layback*. Begin with a 5.10 overhanging move, climb a perfect thin hand and finger crack to loose rock, then traverse left under the roof at the top.

Paraphernalia: Friends (1) #1, #2, #3.5.

Descent: Rappel from fixed anchors, then walk off to the right.

SAND BAR CAMP CLIMBS:
9. FIST FIGHT
10. BEACH LAYBACK
11. DAWN DELIGHT
12. FINGER FUN

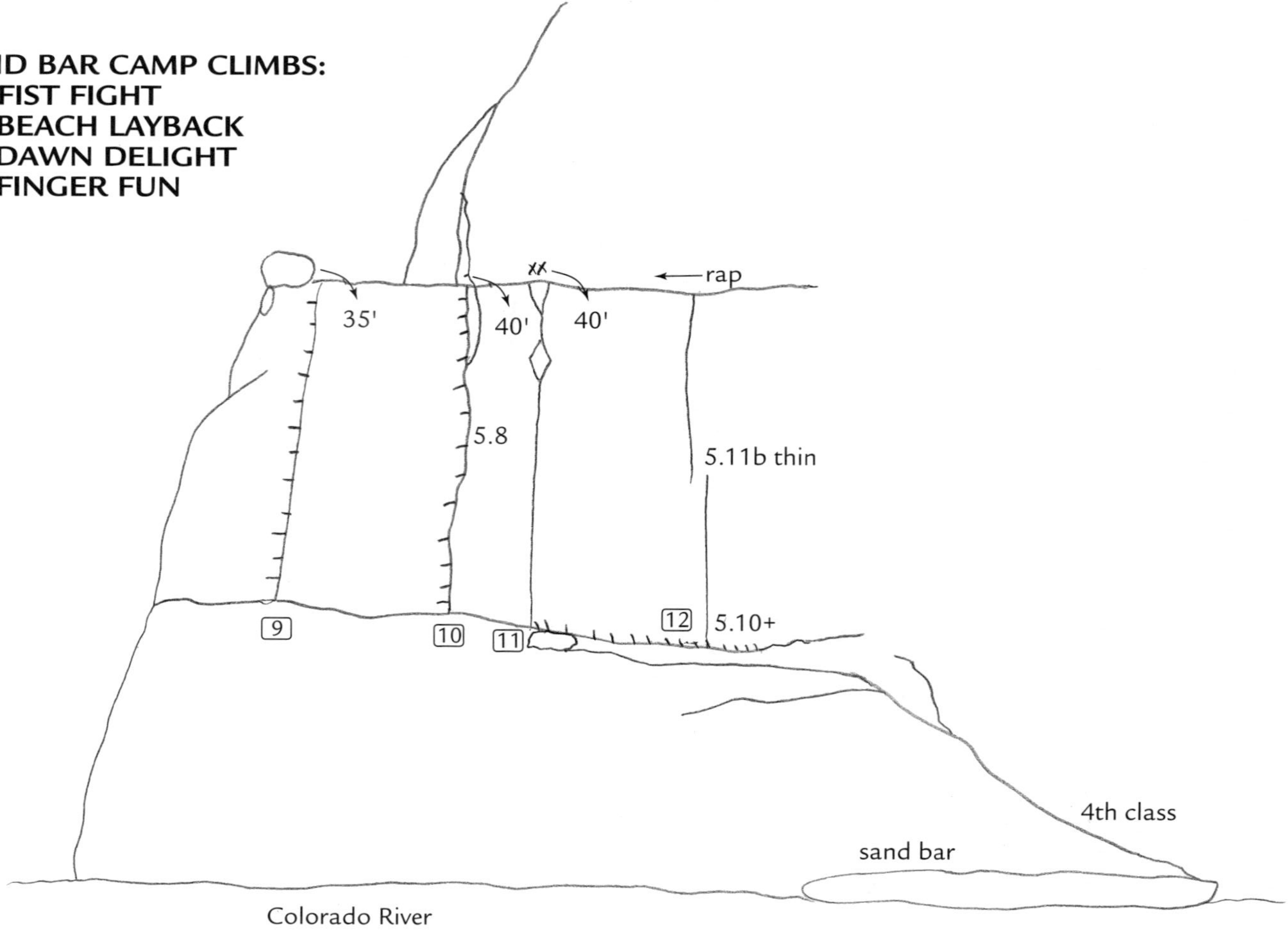

12 FINGER FUN
I, 5.11b, 1 pitch, 50 feet (15 m)

First Ascent: Mike Mayer, Brett Maurer, Christine Blackman, July 28, 1987.

Location and Access: The route is one crack right of *Dawn Delight.* Make a 5.10+ overhang move, then climb a 5.11b thin crack. Continue fingertip liebacking to an overhang and make an unprotected traverse left for 10 feet (3 m).

Paraphernalia: Friends (1) #1.5, #2; nuts.

Descent: Rappel from fixed anchors, then walk off to the right.

DIVERSIONS

LOCKHART CANYON TRAIL

The Lockhart Canyon Trail descends to the Colorado River, entering the Needles District of Canyonlands National Park at its lower end. On the descent are remnants of 1950s and 1960s uranium mining, and of oil drilling activity of the 1920s. At the lower end of the canyon are petroglyphs with historic inscriptions. The petroglyphs are on a south-facing wall to the right near where tamarisk growth begins. The historic inscriptions are on a wall to the north between the petroglyph panel and old shiplap-type board cabin near the end of the trail. Four-wheel-drive vehicles with high clearance are needed to negotiate the sandy areas of the trail.

TRAINING JET WRECKAGE

As the road curves at the north side of Lockhart Basin, the wreckage of an Air Force training jet crash can be seen. The Moab *Times-Independent* newspaper, September 11, 1952: "A T-33 Jet Trainer on routine flight from Larson Air Force Base, Washington, to Biggs Field, Texas, crashed and burned in the rugged canyon area southwest of Moab Saturday, killing the student and injuring the pilot. Both men jumped from the flaming plane, but evidence exists that one parachute failed to open, probably because the flyer was too close to the ground when he jumped. The accident occurred when one engine flamed out and the occupants of the plane were forced to jump."

The wreckage is on the inside of a sharp curve on the north side of Lockhart Basin beyond the left turn down Lockhart Canyon.

> It was not through paucity of imagination that the old Spaniards gave the name—Colorado. During the first fifty years after its discovery the river was christened many times, but the name that finally clung to it was the one that gave accurate and truthful description. You may see on the face of the globe numerous muddy Missouris, blue Rhones, and yellow Tibers; but there is only one red river and that the Colorado. It is not exactly an earthy red, not the color of shale and clay mixed; but the red of peroxide of iron and copper, the

sang-du-boeuf red of oriental ceramics, the deep insistent red of things time-worn beyond memory. And there is more than a veneer about the color. It has a depth that seems luminous and yet is sadly deceptive. You do not see below the surface no matter how long you gaze into it. As well try to see through a stratum of porphyry as through that water to the bottom of the river.

—John C. Van Dyke, *The Desert,* 1901

15

DABNEYLAND

> How delicately beautiful are the hills that seem to gather in little groups along the waste! . . . With surfaces that catch and reflect light, and little depressions that hold shadows, how very picturesque they are!
>
> –John C. Van Dyke, *The Desert,* 1901

Dabneyland is an area of towers skirting the cliffs under the White Rim just outside of and south of Monument Basin in Canyonlands National Park. Deathalonian Spire (mislocated in volume I of *Desert Rock*) is just inside Dabneyland. Pixie Stick is well inside the area. Steve "Crusher" Bartlett: "These towers are named after Park Superintendent Walt Dabney, who instigated the strict climbing regulations in Canyonlands in 1995. There are more towers around here, but the approaches are getting longer and longer."

Access the Dabneyland routes from an old road, now closed and marked with some logs, which leads off the White Rim Trail just south of Monument Basin. Hike the trail until the view to the east and south opens up, then locate a good rappel. Look for a bay to the north where the gully is obviously easy; the rappel is only about 60 feet (18 m) back from the cliff's edge. When viewed from the cliff top, Pixie Stick is obvious as a tiny, thin spire. Behind it are a line of four finlike towers. The farthest east (left) is Captain Pugwash. To the right are two adjacent towers: Captain Bird's Eye is on the left (one of the two "eye" holes can be seen from the cliff top); the other is which Captain Carbunkle has been climbed? Right again (west) is a separate tower that's a little larger, Captain Collywobble. Steve "Crusher" Bartlett: "Crack-climbing psychopaths are invited to attempt the striking 3- to 5-inch roof crack just northeast of the rappel. The Chocolate Starfish may surpass the Crackhouse as the longest horizontal roof crack in the United States. There is about 200 to 300 feet of air beneath."

1 DEATHALONIAN SPIRE
III, 5.10, A3+, 2 pitches, 200 feet (60 m)

First Ascent: Frosty Weller, Keen Butterworth, October 20, 1990.

Location and Access: The spire is climbed by its west face. Begin in a muddy groove on the north side. Aid and free climb up the groove about 40 feet (12 m), then free climb up and left to a 1-inch (2.5 cm) crack. Aid the crack and climb back right, to a belay ledge on the west shoulder, 5.10, A3, 80 feet (24 m). Continue up a corner and aid up a thin crack up and left under a short overhang to a ledge. Climb free and with aid to a 5-foot (1.5 m) headwall. A couple of aid moves using stacked pitons in solution pockets brings you to a ledge just below the summit and an easy move to the top, 5.8, A3+, 80 feet (24 m).

Paraphernalia: Standard desert rack; knifeblades and Bugaboo pitons (8), Lost Arrows (6), Leeper-Zs (2), angle pitons (3) 0.5″, 0.75″, 1.25″, (2) 1.5″, 2″.

DABNEYLAND AND SODA SPRINGS BASIN ROUTE LOCATOR MAP

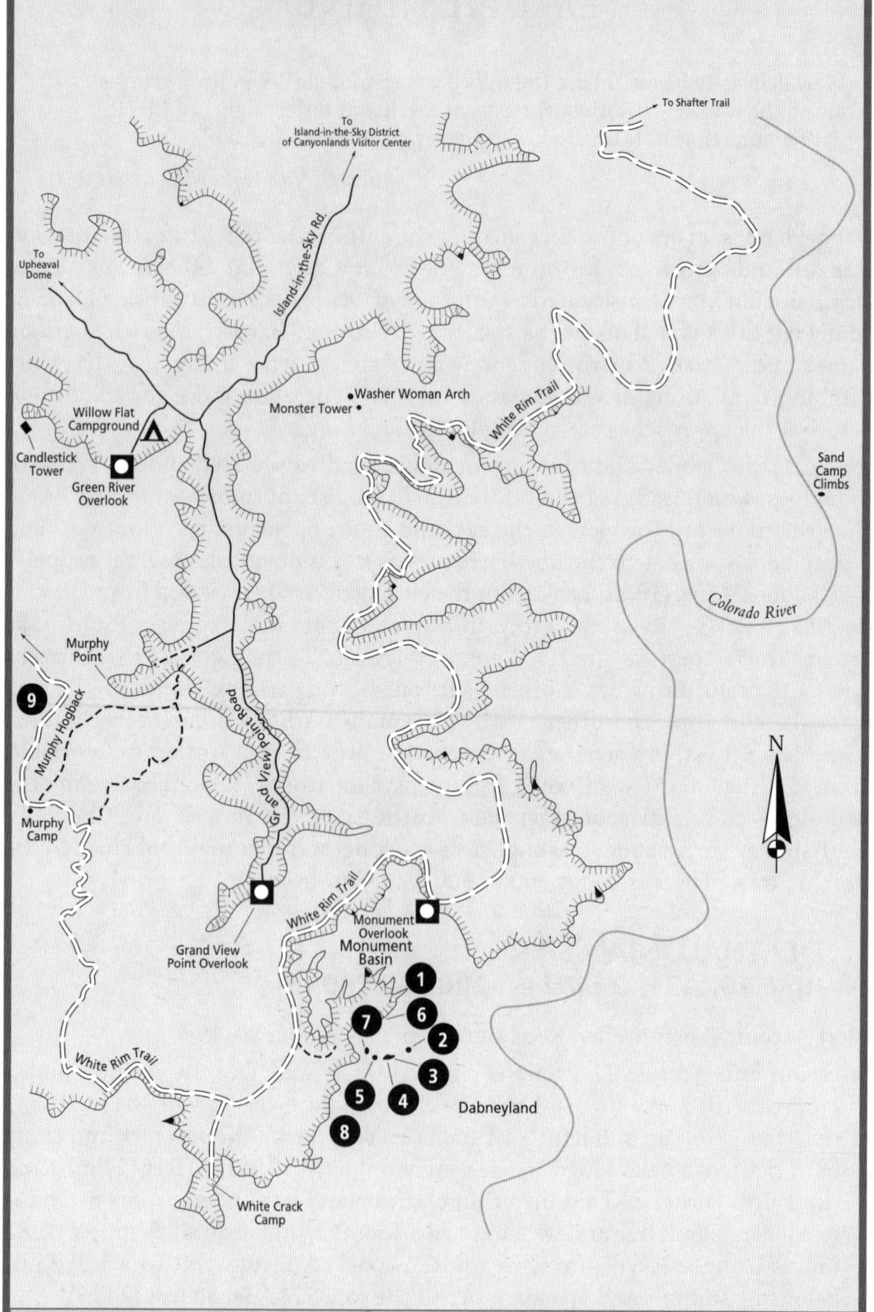

1–8 Dabneyland

9 Soda Springs Basin

Photo: Ralph E. Burns

Deathalonian Spire.

Photo: Steve "Crusher" Bartlett

Dabneyland: A. Captain Pugwash B. Captain Bird's Eye C. Captain Carbuncle D. Pixie Stick E. Captain Collywobble.

Descent: The first ascent party rappelled the west face 165 feet (50 m) to the base of the climb from 40 feet (12 m) of 9 mm rope tied around the summit. **WARNING:** Park regulations require all aid climbing on this route be clean aid. Traditional hammer aid is prohibited.

2 CAPTAIN PUGWASH—THE INTEMPERATE BASS IV, 5.11a, 2 pitches, 140 feet (43 m) ★★★

First Ascent: Kath Pyke, Steve "Crusher" Bartlett, February 1, 1999.

Location and Access: The tower is the easternmost of the towers in the area. The route begins up the west arête, then diagonals clockwise around the tower to the north side to finish.

Pitch 1: Climb to an obvious clean face with a finger crack onto a ledge. The thin crack is the crux. Continue right and up a corner to another awkward move onto a shoulder and belay, 5.11a.

Pitch 2: Move right to get over the initial overhang, then traverse right. Zigzag up and left until a mantel is made on the northeast side, which gains the summit, 5.9.

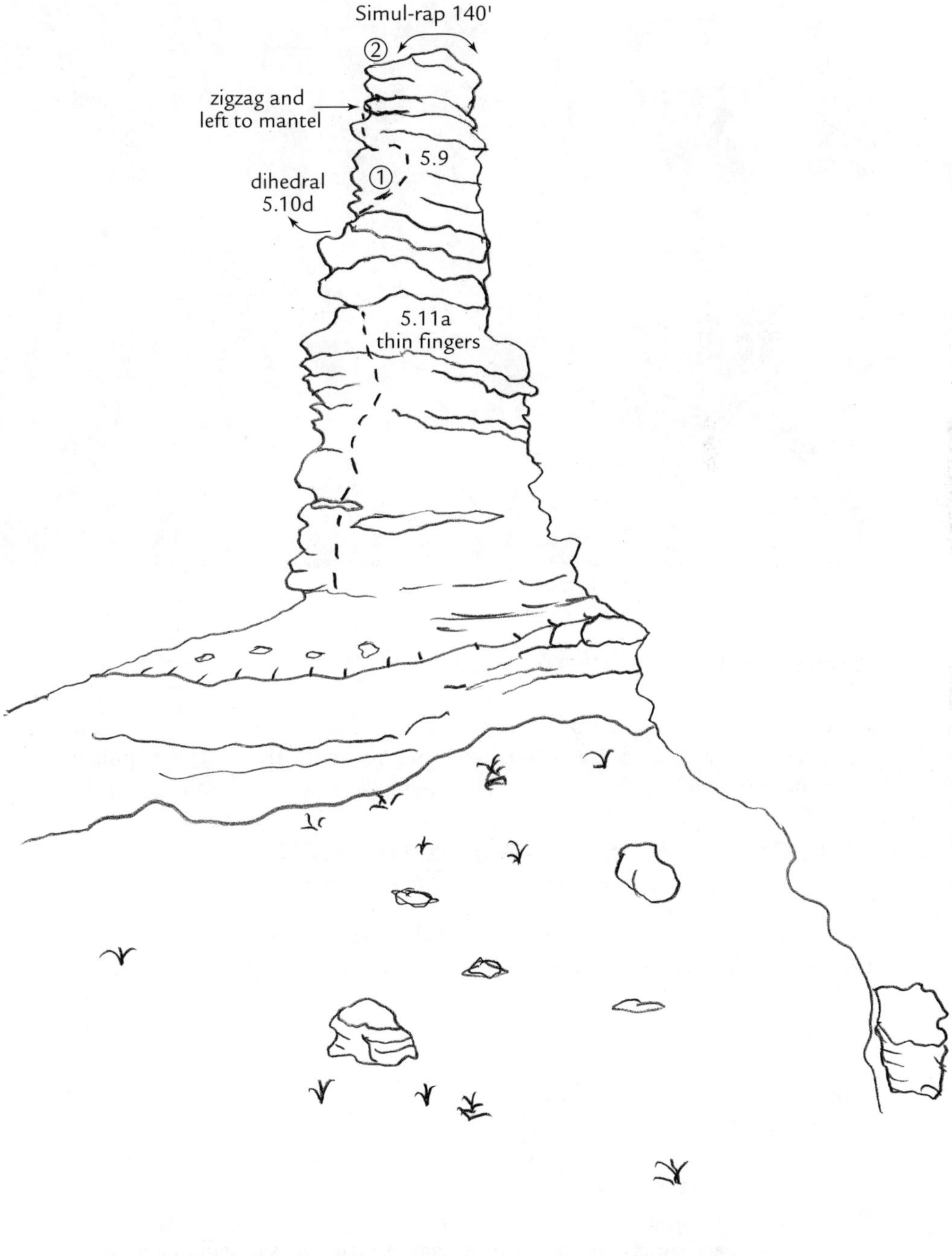

CAPTAIN PUGWASH—THE INTEMPERATE BASS

Photo: Kath Pyke

Steve "Crusher" Bartlett on top of Captain Pugwash.

Paraphernalia: Wide selection of camming units through 4″; wires; 9 mm ropes (2).

Descent: A 140-foot (43 m) simul-rappel gains the ground. Steve "Crusher" Bartlett: "Best to send one person down first to ensure that the ropes pull and are not tangled."

3 CAPTAIN BIRD'S EYE—THIS IS THE PLAICE IV, 5.10c, 3 pitches, 190 feet (58 m) ★★★★

First Ascent: Steve "Crusher" Bartlett, Nigel Gregory, October 1999.

Location and Access: Begin on the north side below a saddle between the two towers (Captain Bird's Eye and Captain Carbuncle). Steve "Crusher" Bartlett: "This is the best of the Dabneyland climbs." *Webster's* defines *plaice* as "any of various flatfishes, esp. a large European flounder."

Pitch 1: Climb to the saddle between the towers. Skirt a short slab on the left, then traverse right 12 feet (3.6 m) under large roofs and climb to a roomy belay ledge, 5.10c, 90 feet (27 m). Harder moves before the large roofs gain a crack/dihedral just right of the west arête.

Pitch 2: Move right and climb past a balanced block to another ledge. Mantel to a third ledge, then climb up and right, past short cracks to gain ledges on the south side. Traverse right 15 feet (4.5 m) to where a hard move gains a higher ledge system directly under a bulging headwall. Traverse back left to a thread belay at the "eye," 5.10c, 90 feet (27 m).

Pitch 3: Climb directly up the steep face just above the thread on the south side, 5.10c, 20 feet (6 m).

Paraphernalia: Friends (2 or 3) sets #2 through #3.5 with (1) #4; Camalots #4, #5; selection of wires; Aliens (2) sets; ropes (2).

Descent: Two 200-foot (60 m) ropes will allow a simul-rappel from the top. Steve "Crusher" Bartlett: "Best to first lower one person to the base to ensure that ropes are both down and ropes will pull, then have this person tie in to one rope at the base to act as anchor so the second person can rappel the other rope down the other side."

CAPTAIN BIRD'S EYE—THIS IS THE PLAICE

WEST ARÊTE

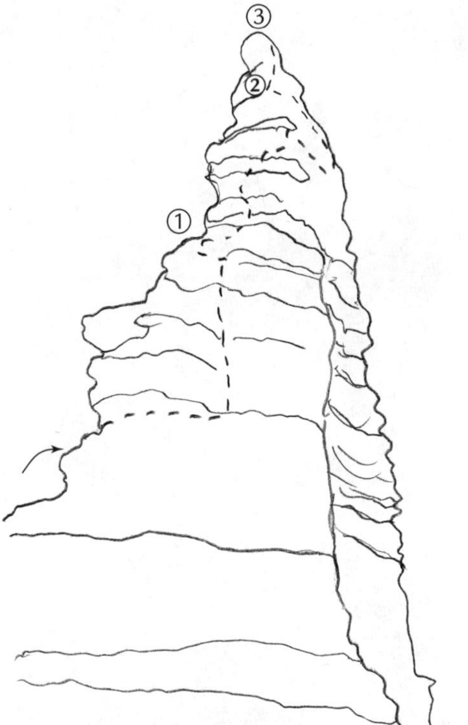

SOUTH FACE

Photo: Steve "Crusher" Bartlett

Stu Ritchie on Captain Carbuncle.

4 CAPTAIN CARBUNCLE—PERHAPS YOU SHOULD SEE A SPECIALIST
IV, 5.10d, 2 pitches, 190 feet (58 m) ★★

First Ascent: Steve "Crusher" Bartlett, Stu Ritchie, May 2000.

Location and Access: Captain Carbuncle is third from the left of the four fins behind the Pixie Stick, immediately west of Captain Bird's Eye. The route begins on the north face, 30 feet (9 m) from the west arête, and climbs directly up obvious weaknesses.

Pitch 1: Climb the left of two right-facing dihedrals to below the Shark's Head, an obvious right-pointing flake 30 feet (9 m) up. Lieback around the Shark's Head (5.10d) and continue up and slightly left, then up and slightly right (past a loose block) to gain a small stance on a large dinner plate and under a 3-foot (0.9 m) roof.

Pitch 2: Struggle over the roof (5.10c/d), then climb easier rock up through a 5.8 slot. Angle up and slightly left toward the top, over a couple more 5.10a bulges, to gain a ledge under a right-facing V slot in the final rock band. Hand traverse 15 feet (4.5 m) right, then squeeze through the Warm Compress (5.9+) to the summit. **NOTE:** On the first ascent, pitch 1 was led free with one hang, but followed free.

Paraphernalia: Friends (2 or 3) sets from #0.5 through #6; ropes (2) 200-foot (60 m).

Descent: A straightforward simul-rappel with two 200-foot (60 m) ropes from the obvious saddle just behind the west arête.

5 CAPTAIN COLLYWOBBLE—DOTTYBACK DEAMO DAY-DREAM
IV, 5.10b/c, 4 pitches, 200 feet (60 m) ★★★

First Ascent: Steve "Crusher" Bartlett, Ralph E. Burns, November 1, 1999.

Location and Access: The route ascends the north face, and after a steep, muddy start accesses a prominent clean crack in the upper middle of the face. Begin approximately 10 feet (3 m) right of the high point of the talus.

Pitch 1: Diagonal up and right to gain a shallow slot 15 feet (4.5 m) up by a reachy 5.10 move. Continue straight up, then slightly left through a finger crack in a small roof. Face climb left of a blocky crack above, to a ledge below the higher mud band. Traverse 15 feet (4.5 m) right, then up through another bulging finger crack. Belay on a cramped ledge, 5.10c, 60 feet (18 m).

Pitch 2: "Squirm" very carefully up a short chimney above, past loose stacked blocks to a slabby ledge (below another chimney). Traverse 30 feet (9 m) left on a superb hanging slab to gain the base of a good crack. Continue up 10 feet (3 m) and belay on a ledge, 5.9, 60 feet (18 m).

Pitch 3: Climb a crack system and belay on a ledge on the right, 5.9, 30 feet (9 m).

CAPTAIN COLLYWOBBLE—DOTTYBACK DEAMO DAY-DREAM

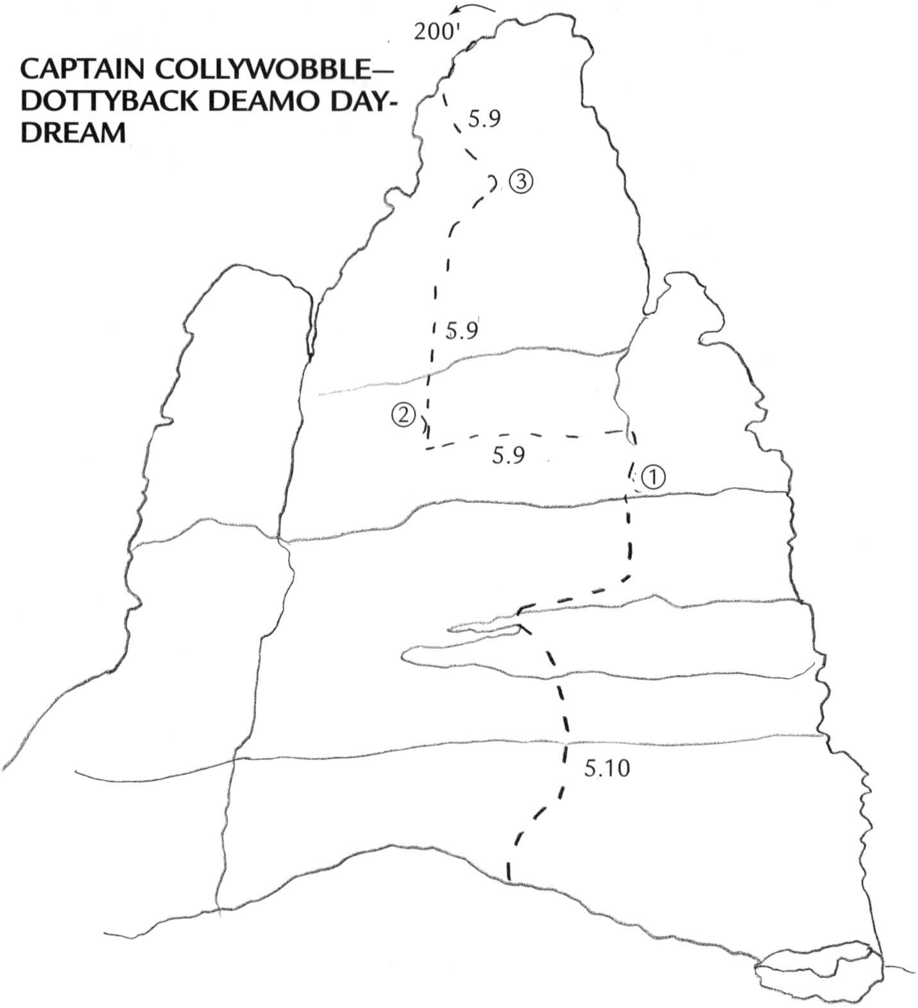

Pitch 4: Angle up and left, straight up over a small bulge, then left again to gain the east arête and the summit, 5.8, 35 feet (10.6 m).

Paraphernalia: Friends/Camalots through 4″; Aliens (2 or 3) sets; many quick draws; many wires, especially medium/large; runners; ropes (2) 200-foot (60 m) mandatory.

Descent: First ascent team used a 200-foot (60 m) rope and a 230-foot (70 m) rope for a long simul-rappel, but believe two 200-foot (60 m) ropes would work.

6 CHOCOLATE STARFISH
II, A1+, 1 pitch, 120 feet (37 m) long, 30 feet (9 m) vertical height

First Ascent: Steve "Crusher" Bartlett, solo, spring 2001.

Location and Access: Begin by fixing a rope from the top of the White Rim at the far end of the ceiling crack. From the rappel into Dabneyland, descend the rappel gully approximately 400 feet (122 m), then scramble up to the obvious ceiling crack. Bartlett: "This was climbed 'gladiator' style, at A1, with a short loop of rope preplaced at the fragile lip. Bring all your large Camalots. This may be the longest horizontal roof crack in the United States"

Paraphernalia: Friends #2 through #5; large Camalots; rope (fixed at the end of the ceiling crack).

Descent: Pull up over the lip of the crack to the top of the White Rim using the fixed rope.

7 PIXIE STICK
III, 5.10a R, 2 pitches, 175 feet (53 m) ★★★

First Ascent: Paul Gagner, Dougald MacDonald, Donna Raupp et al. 1996.

Location and Access: When viewed from the cliff top, the Pixie Stick is obvious as a tiny, thin spire (nearest the White Rim). Behind it are a line of four finlike towers. Dougald MacDonald: "The summit is the smallest I've ever been on, consisting of stacked discs of rock, like sandstone pancakes." *Webster's* defines *pixie* as "Fairy, a cheerful mischievous sprite."

Pitch 1: Begin on the southwest side of the tower and climb an obvious hand crack through bulges to a belay ledge, 5.9.

Pitch 2: From the right side of the belay ledge, climb a face/crack system free and with aid to the summit.

Paraphernalia: Standard desert rack, mostly cams; 200-foot (60 m) ropes.

Descent: One long rappel down the route.

8 NORTHERN FRIGHTS
III, 5.11, 2 pitches, 150 feet (46 m) ★★★

First Ascent: Steve "Crusher" Bartlett, Ralph Ferrara, Eve Tallman, March 31, 2001.

Location and Access: The spire is south of the various captains, approximately halfway between Monument Basin and White Crack Campground. Park at the turnoff to the closed road, just south of Monument Basin. Hike the closed road to the first large wash (with slickrock). Hike upstream and to another long-abandoned road laid in a southeast direction. Follow it to the rim then locate two long, easy gullies oriented south to north. Hike down the east gully and follow a terrace system north along the base of the cliffs about a quarter mile to the tower. Steve "Crusher" Bartlett: "The first ascent party, while bivied nearby on the night before the ascent, spent several hours watching a spectacular aurora display."

Photo: Steve "Crusher" Bartlett

Northern Frights.

Pitch 1: Climb a face and blocky crack to a ledge on the north side (5.10-), then traverse left easily to an arête. Some tricky moves gain another ledge on the north side, under a roof. Belay at the left end of the ledge.

Pitch 2: Continue up an obvious crack system to the top, 5.11.

Paraphernalia: Friends (2 or 3) sets #0.5 through #4; wires.

Descent: One 150-foot (46 m) simul-rappel.

SODA SPRINGS BASIN

Yum Kipper is below the White Rim Trial in Soda Springs Basin (south of Candlestick Tower) and is best viewed as you descend the north side of Murphy Hogback. It can also be glimpsed from the White Rim Trail as you drive around the south end of Candlestick Tower. *Webster's* defines kipper as "a male salmon or sea trout during or after the spawning season"; also, "to cure (split dressed fish) by salting and smoking."

To reach the tower from the White Rim Trial, park where the trail crosses a rocky area just as it veers away from the rim approaching Murphy Hogback. Depending on west or east approach, it may be after or before the hogback. From here a hike along the rim accesses a viewpoint overlooking the tower and a selection of rappel points. An 80- to 100-foot (24 to 30 m) rappel gains the basin floor near the tower.

An alternative approach is from the Murphy hiking trail, a signed right (west) turn from the Grand View Point Road between the right spur to Upheaval Dome and Grand View Point Overlook. Drive to the trailhead and hike a well-marked trail to the White Rim. The beginning of the trail is across a flat mesa top, then it descends in zig-zags down a rock slide. Near the bottom on the rock wall are old cowboy etchings dating from 1917. The trail soon forks. The left branch descends a dry creek bed; the right fork follows an old uranium miners' blaze to eventually rfeach the Murphy Hogback Camp. Both branches reach the White Rim Trial a two- to three-hour approach from the car.

HISTORY

Murphy Trial, Murphy Hogback, Murphy Point, Murphy Basin, and Murphy Camp are named for an early Moab family who ran the Murphy Brothers Land and Cattle Company. The winter range for Murphy cattle was below Grand View Point. Five of the Murphy brothers built the trail to the top of Grand View and also helped build the Shafer Trail, but rather than herding the cattle all the way north to the Shafer Trail, in 1917–1918 they built a trail from the winter range area directly to the top of the Island-in-the-Sky. Verona Murphy, born in 1905, first helped the senior Murphy herd the cattle up the trail when she was thirteen years old. She once commented, "When my father worked for other people, he was usually paid in cattle, normally two cows a month. That's how he built up his herd."

YUM KIPPER— TOAD RAGE

Photo: Steve "Crusher" Bartlett

Roger "Strappo" Hughes on Yum Kipper, rappelling off lumber.

9 YUM KIPPER—TOAD RAGE
III, 5.11c, 3 pitches, 250 feet (76 m) ★★★★

First Ascent: Steve "Crusher" Bartlett, Tony Herr, Roger "Strappo" Hughes, May 1999. Bartlett, Fran Bagenal on pitches 1 and 2, April 1999. Named for Strappo's canned Kipper bivouac snack. Yum Kipper (delicious fish) is a takeoff on Yom Kipper, the Hebrew day of atonement.

Location and Access: *Toad Rage* climbs the north side of the formation, beginning in an alcove at the left end of the north side.

Pitch 1: Climb the crack system straight to a shoulder, 5.9, 100 feet (30 m).

Pitch 2: Easy traversing right gains a short dihedral. Climb it to a small ledge, then another short, left-facing dihedral to a larger ledge at the base of an obvious final chimney, 5.10a, 70 feet (21 m).

Pitch 3: Climb the chimney, first on the north side (hands to off-width); then after gaining a good stance in a wider part of the chimney, continue up the south side. Continue up an off-width/flare and gain an easier final chimney section, 5.11c (free), 80 feet (24 m). Steve "Crusher" Bartlett: "On the first ascent this arduous pitch was sieged and was not led red-point style. Strappo and Crusher both pulled on a camming unit (though in two different locations!). Tony followed the pitch free. The onset of a big storm prevented further attempts and even prevented us driving out that evening."

Paraphernalia: Friends through #3; larger camming units through 7″ (3 or 4) sets; small selection of wires; lumber 4 x 4, 4′ 6″ long (1), 2 x 4, 3′ long (1).

Descent: Bartlett: "To descend this tower legally we had to leave no fixed anchor for the 250-foot rappel. Therefore we used a 4-foot, 6-inch 4 x 4 piece of lumber straddling the chimney top as a belay and rappel anchor. We duct-taped a second piece of lumber (a 3-foot-long 2 x 4) under one end, crucifix style. One end of the 2 x 4 protruded over the edge and was attached to enough rope to reach the ground. Rappel off the middle of the 4 x 4, down the chimney, then down the north face, using enough rope to reach the ground (this will likely require passing a knot). Then pull on the rope attached to the protruding end of the 2 x 4, and viola! Down comes the anchor."

> There is nothing remarkable about the desert clouds—that is nothing very different from the clouds of other countries—except in light, color and background. The colors, like everything else on the desert, are intense in their power, fierce in their glare. They vibrate, they scintillate, they penetrate and tinge everything with their hue. And then, as though heaping splendor upon splendor, what a wonderful background they are woven upon! Great bands of orange, green, and blue that all the melted and fused gems in the world could not match for translucent beauty. Taken as a whole, as a celestial tapestry, as a curtain of flame drawn between night and day, and what land or sky can rival it!
>
> —John C. Van Dyke, *The Desert,* 1901

16
CASTLE ARCH AND HORSE CANYON

> And it is not alone the bird of prey—not alone the road-runners, the eagles, the vultures, the hawks, and the owls that are savage of mood. Every little wisp of energy that carries a bunch of feathers is endowed with the same spirit. The downward swoop of the cactus wren upon a butterfly and the snip of his little scissors bill, the dash after insects of the fly-catchers, vireos, swallows, bats, and whippoor-wills are just as murderous in kind as the blow of the condor and the vice-like clutch of his talons as they sink into the back of a rabbit.
>
> —John C. Van Dyke, *The Desert,* 1901

Castle Arch is located in the southwestern region of Canyonlands National Park off Horse Canyon. Robert H. Vreeland, *Nature's Bridges and Arches,* Volume 3, Central Canyonlands National Park, Utah: "The third most interesting arch in the park, this one is the easiest of the three to reach. . . . It is a very old, rock shelter type natural arch eroded by weathering from both sides of a fin. The rock is in the Cedar Mesa Sandstone member of the Cutler Formation. It has a span of 165 feet (50 m), a height of 70 feet (21 m), a thickness of 12 feet (3.6 m), and a width of 16 feet (4.8 m). It was discovered in 1949 by photographers Ray and Virginia Garner, who were accompanied by ranger Merle Winbourne. They named it for its likeness, from one angle, to a castle, with the arch forming a flying buttress."

Horse Canyon, a major tributary of Salt Creek, is known for its windows, arches, and prehistoric ruins. It received its name from cowboys working for the Indian Creek Cattle Company. They built a fence across the mouth of the canyon and would leave their extra saddle horses corralled there.

From Moab, drive 40 miles (64 km) south on US 191 and turn right on Utah 211. Follow signs to Newspaper Rock and the Needles District of Canyonlands National Park.

From the Needles District Visitor Center, follow the paved park road west. At 0.7 mile (1.1 km) turn left (south), and at 1.4 miles (2.2 km) turn left again onto a gravel road. At 2.2 miles (3.5 km) turn right onto the Salt Wash four-wheel-drive road. At 4.9 miles (7.8 km) turn left into Horse Canyon. At 10.9 miles (17.5 km) park at a sign identifying the arch at the trailhead to a viewpoint of the arch. Because the park service might close the approach roads in the future, reaching the arch could require a long backpack. **NOTE** Check with park rangers for current climbing restrictions in the park and for updated approach directions.

1 CASTLE ARCH—SOUTH FACE
II, 5.6 R, X, 3 pitches, 200 feet (60 m)

First Ascent: Steve Anderton, Bill Duncan, Matt Kohlhaas, Pat Peddy, November 24, 1991.

CASTLE ARCH—SOUTH FACE

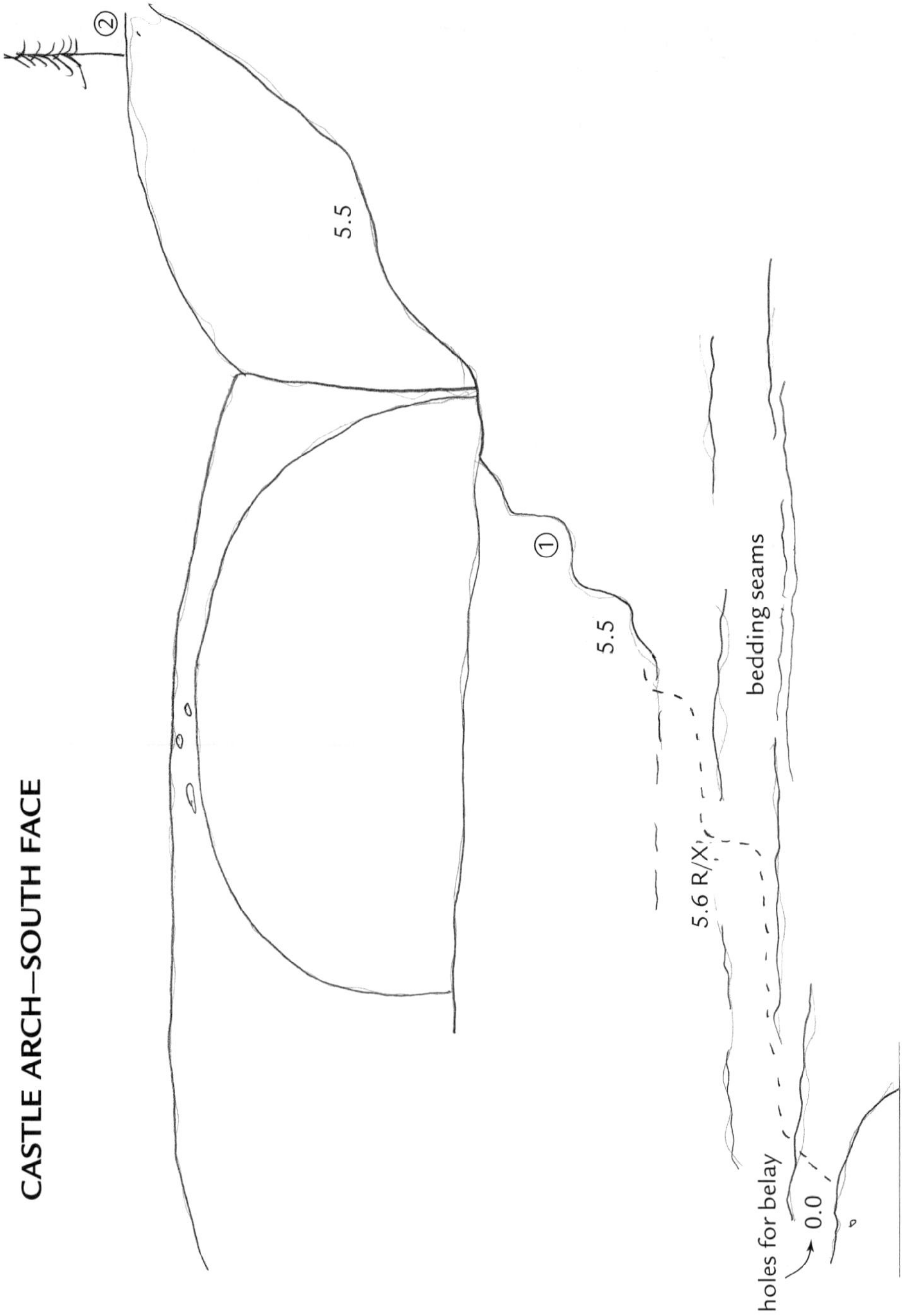

Location and Access: The route faces south. Bill Duncan: "This is a very aesthetic climb. There are three holes at the top of the span, which provide a view through the arch."

Pitch 1: From the base of the arch, climb through a bedding seam, up and right to a ledge below the arch, 5.6 R/X.

Pitch 2: Continue up an easy chimney to the rim above the arch.

Pitch 3: Fix a rope to a tree and lower into the arch.

Paraphernalia: Rope (1).

Descent: Downclimb the route.

DIVERSIONS

FORTRESS ARCH

Fortress Arch is in a side canyon of Horse Canyon 0.5 mile (0.8 km) beyond Castle Arch. It is eroded into a massive ridge of the Cedar Mesa sandstone member of the Cutler Formation. It has a span of 115 feet (35 m), a height of 52 feet (15.8 m), a thickness of 110 feet (33.5 m), and a width of 30 feet (9 m). The arch was named by a 1961 National Geographic Society expedition for its resemblance to a "crumbling mountain stronghold." The name was registered by the National Park Service in 1969. To reach Fortress Arch from Castle Arch, hike 0.6 mile (0.9 km) from the end of the road.

TOWER RUIN

Tower Ruin is 1 mile (1.6 km) past Paul Bunyan's Potty on the left (east) side of the canyon high in an alcove.

Other highlights of the area are Angel Arch, Peek-aboo Springs pictographs, Keyhole ruin, and Thirteen Faces. For locations and updated approach information, check at the Needles Visitor Center.

> At times it is a land of heavy cloud-bursts and wash-outs. In the summer months it frequently rains on the mesas in torrents. The bare surface of the country drains this water almost like the roof of a house because there are no grasses or bushes of consequence to check the water and allow it to soak into the ground.
>
> —John C. Van Dyke, *The Desert,* 1901

17
RING AND FISHEYE ARCHES

> The first going-down into the desert is always something of a surprise. The fancy has pictured one thing; the reality shows quite another thing. Where and how did we gain the idea that the desert was merely a sea of sand? Did it come from that geography of our youth with the illustration of the sand-storm, the flying camel, and the over-excited Bedouin? Or have we been reading strange tales told by travellers of perfervid imagination—the Marco Polos of today? There is, to be sure, some modicum of truth even in the statement that misleads. There are "seas" or lakes or ponds of sand on every desert; but they are not so vast, not so oceanic, that you ever lose sight of the land.
>
> —John C. Van Dyke, *The Desert,* 1901

Ring and Fisheye Arches are located in the Needles District of Canyonlands National Park. They are near the southern edge of the park in a remote area that is difficult to reach. It is advisable to visit with a park ranger at the Needles Ranger Station at Indian Creek for information on current regulations and road and trail conditions. A backcountry permit is required for all overnight stays.

From Moab, drive 40 miles (64 km) south on US 191 and turn right on Utah 211. Follow signs to Newspaper Rock and the Needles District of Canyonlands National Park. After visiting the Needles District visitor center, drive back toward Newspaper Rock and turn right at Dugout Ranch. Directions for the turn should be obtained at the visitor center because there might not be a sign. From the Dugout Ranch, drive 12 miles (19 km) to the Bright Angel Trail, which joins the two-wheel-drive dirt trail from the right (northwest). It will be at a point southwest of Cathedral Butte, a couple of miles beyond the southern tip of Bridger Jack Mesa, which the road has been paralleling since its beginning at the Dugout Ranch. Hike the Bright Angel Trail to the Salt Creek drainage at a fork about 1 mile (1.6 km) from the trailhead. Both arches are reached after about 2 miles (3.2 km) of hiking and are northwest of Cedar Mesa. Ring Arch will be obvious on the right side of the Salt Creek drainage. Fisheye Arch is past Ring Arch, down Salt Creek then up the first canyon on the right, high on the right walls near the head of the canyon.

RING ARCH

Ring Arch is eroded from the Cedar Mesa member of Cutler sandstone. It has a span of 100 feet (31 m), a height of 125 feet (38 m), a thickness of 8 feet (2.4 m), and a width of 15 feet (4.5 m). Robert H. Vreeland, *Nature's Bridges and Arches,* Volume 3, Central Canyonlands National Park, Utah: "It was named for its almost perfect symmetry. The NPS has shown this arch on its maps as Wedding Ring Arch and has even tried to register the name; however, the true Wedding Ring Arch is 2.5 miles to the south."

Photo: Fran Barnes

Ring Arch.

Ring Arch is named on the 1954 Mt. Linnaeus, Utah, and the 1968 Canyonlands National Park and Vicinity, Utah, 15-minute USGS topographic quadrangles. Ring Arch is also named on a 1969 Canyonlands National Park and Vicinity, Utah, quad, but a park border error puts the arch outside the park's boundary. To complicate matters, Ring Arch is mislocated on both maps. It is not on the 1954 Mt. Linnaeus quadrangle as designated, but in fact is on the 1954 Harts Point, Utah, quadrangle, where it is called "Natural Arch." This designation is at a point northwest of Fisheye Arch. On both the 1968 and 1969 Canyonlands National Park and Vicinity quadrangles, Ring Arch should again be located at the point designated Natural Arch, just northwest of Fisheye Arch.

1 RING ARCH
I, fourth class, 135 feet (38 m)

First Ascent: Gerry Roach, solo, November 1978.

Location and Access: Approach from the north, then cross on a ledge to a fin that then traverses back to the top of the arch.

Paraphernalia: None required.

Descent: Reverse the ascent.

FISHEYE ARCH

Fisheye Arch has a span of 30 feet (9 m), a height of 25 feet (7.6 m), a thickness of 5 feet (1.5 m), and a width of 8 feet (2.4 m). It was named for Frank E. Masland Jr. by Otis R. Marston in 1962 when they discovered it. Masland, a Pennsylvania business executive and a member of the advisory board of the park service, was nicknamed "Fisheyes" on a 1948 Colorado River trip.

2 FISHEYE ARCH
I, 5.8, 1 pitch, 30 feet (9 m)

First Ascent: Gerry Roach, John Ritchie, November 1978.

Location and Access: Approach from the north and climb to a fin that then allows access to the top of the arch. There is one 5.8 move. Gerry Roach: "The arch may also be climbed from the east fourth-class."

Paraphernalia: Rope for a belay optional.

Descent: Downclimb the route.

> The feeling of fierceness grows upon you as you come to know the desert better. The sun-shafts are falling in a burning shower upon rock and dune, the winds blowing with the breath of far-off fires are withering the bushes and the grasses, the sands drifting higher and higher are burying the trees and reaching up as though they would overwhelm the mountains, the cloud-bursts are rushing down the mountain's side and through the torn arroyos as though they would wash the earth into the sea.
>
> —John C. Van Dyke, *The Desert,* 1901

18
ARCH AND TEXAS CANYONS

> In our studies of landscape we are very frequently made the victims of either illusion or delusion. The eye or the mind deceives us, and sometimes the two may join forces to our complete confusion. We are not willing to admit different reports of an appearance. And how very shy people are about accepting a pink air, a blue shadow, or a field of yellow grass—sunlit lemon-yellow grass! They have been brought up from youth to believe that air is colorless, that shadows are brown or gray or sooty black, and that grass is green—bottle green. The preconceived impression of the mind refuses to make room for the actual impression of the eyes, and in consequence we are misled and deluded.
>
> —John C. Van Dyke, *The Desert,* 1901

Arch Canyon is home to three large natural stone arches and a small natural bridge. Angel Arch is the largest of the three, followed by Cathedral Arch and Keystone Arch. Climbs have been established on both Angel and Cathedral Arches. Keystone Arch is 11 miles (17.7 km) up Arch Canyon from Comb Wash, 3 miles (4.8 km) beyond the end of the 8-mile (12.8 km)-long Arch Canyon four-wheel-drive trail that ends near the junction of Arch and Texas Canyons. Keystone Arch has a span of 50 feet (15 m), a height of 35 feet (10.6 m), a thickness of 70 feet (21 m), and a width of 20 feet (6 m). Its name comes from the fact that the keystone of the arc of rock is missing, although the massive thickness above the opening will protect it from falling for years to come.

Cameron Burns: "Rock climbs in Texas Canyon are true wilderness experiences that require hard driving, long approaches, and difficult, sometimes scary climbing. But just a single visit to Texas Canyon will impress upon you just how isolated and beautiful portions of the Colorado Plateau can be." Texas and Arch Canyons are of Cedar Mesa sandstone and are north of Utah 95, between Natural Bridges National Monument and Blanding, Utah. A four-wheel-drive vehicle can drive up Arch Canyon to within 1 mile (1.6 km) of Texas Tower, but the original approach and the most popular is by rappel from the rim of the canyon.

From Blanding, drive south 4 miles (6.4 km) on US 191 to Utah 95 (at a Shell gas station). Turn west on Utah 95 and drive 14.4 miles (23 km) to an unmarked dirt road (San Juan County Road 235) branching to the right (north), a location just east of the signed Mule Canyon Indian Ruins. This trail climbs up Arch Canyon over very rough four-wheel-drive terrain.

To reach this point from the south, take US 163 (just north of Mexican Hat, Utah) to Utah 261 where signs direct to Natural Bridges National Monument. At the junction of Utah 261 and US 95, turn right (east), then left (north) on the unmarked trail (San Juan County Road 235).

To rappel into the canyon (the best way in), drive west on Utah 95 from US 191 to the unmarked dirt trail of Texas Flat Road (San Juan County 263). This intersection is approximately 1 mile (1.6 km) east of the Mule Canyon Ruins turnoff, and 19.4 miles (31 km) from the junction of US 191 and Utah 95. To rappel into

ARCH AND TEXAS CANYONS ROUTE LOCATOR MAP

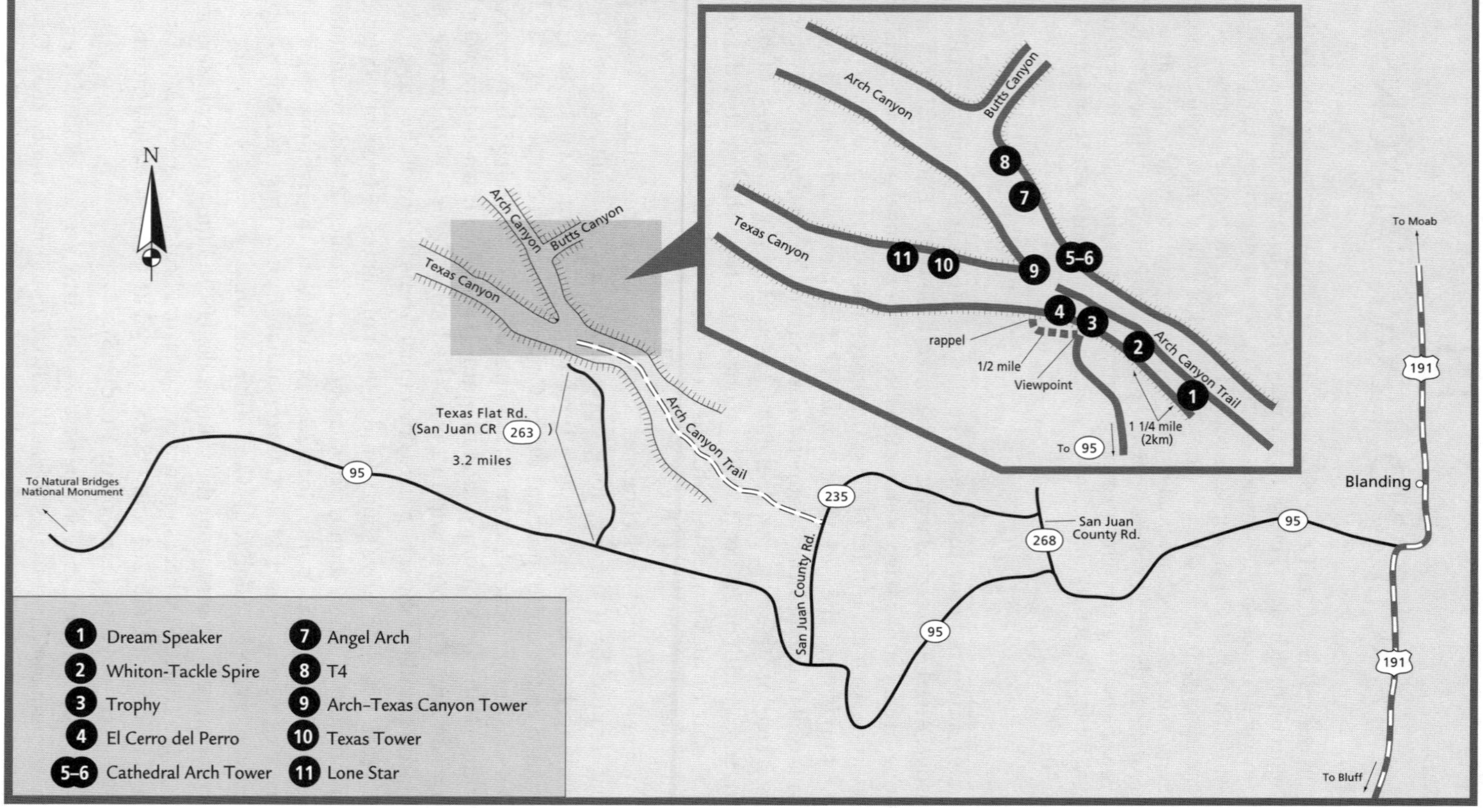

N
Arch Canyon
Butts Canyon
Texas Canyon
Arch Canyon Trail
Texas Flat Rd.
(San Juan CR 263)
3.2 miles
To Natural Bridges National Monument
95
235
San Juan County Rd.
268
San Juan County Rd.
Blanding
191
To Moab
To Bluff
rappel
1/2 mile
Viewpoint
To 95
1 1/4 mile (2km)
1 Dream Speaker
2 Whiton-Tackle Spire
3 Trophy
4 El Cerro del Perro
5–6 Cathedral Arch Tower
7 Angel Arch
8 T4
9 Arch–Texas Canyon Tower
10 Texas Tower
11 Lone Star

Photo: Freddie Snalam

Cathedral Arch in Arch Canyon.

Arch Canyon, continue 3.2 miles (5 km) to the canyon rim. On the north side of the road is an obvious white cliff band; just beyond is an overlook to Dream Speaker tower in Arch Canyon. Make one 160-foot (49 m) rappel.

To reach the usual approach into Texas Canyon, drive 6.8 miles (11 km) from US 95, paralleling the canyon rim, to a sign: END OF COUNTY MAINTENANCE. This is obviously the case. Backtrack 0.4 mile (0.6 km) to a short side road, which leads to the rim and a good camping site. Hike west along the rim 0.25 mile (0.4 km) to an inconspicuous USGS elevation marker. Two short rappels lead over rock bands and into a drainage that flows into the main streambed of Texas Canyon. This is north of the junction of Arch and Texas Canyons. Leave a marker for the return prusik back to the rim. Hike upcanyon forty-five minutes to Texas Tower (approximately 1.5 miles [2.4 km] from the rim). Paul Ross: "One actually only needs about 40 feet for the first rappel and 40 feet for the second–very easy angled rock. Jumars are not really needed; I just batmanned up. After the first rappel, near the camping area, walk left for about a qurter mile to find the second rappel down a brush-filled easy angled crack, then walk down a brush-filled talus slope."

From the bottom of the rappels, two canyons are in view to the west, Arch Canyon to the right and Texas Canyon to the left. There is a good campsite at the junction of the canyons. Routes are listed upcanyon beginning with Arch Canyon, then up Texas Canyon.

ARCH CANYON

DREAM SPEAKER

1 SOUTH FACE
II, 5.11b, 3 pitches, 250 feet (76 m) ★★★★

First Ascent: Tim Coats, Gary Rugerra, Scott Baxter, April 1984. Second Ascent: Tim Toula, John Middendorf, Kathy Zaiser, April 18, 1987.

Location and Access: Dream Speaker, like the Bride Tower near Moab, is very thin when viewed from the south profile. Scott Baxter: "This is a clean, straightforward route–four stars. Exhilarating." Dream Speaker is obvious as the first tower reached on the rough four-wheel-drive trail up Arch Canyon.

Pitch 1: Begin up soft 5.10 rock and continue up soft rock with 5.11b thin hands to a belay ledge with a fixed anchor.

Pitch 2: Traverse 20 feet (6 m) right and belay from a single anchor.

Pitch 3: Climb an "airy" 5.10b off-width, passing double anchors. Continue 5.9 off-width to the summit.

Paraphernalia: Friends (2) #0.5 through #3, (2) or (3) #3.5 through #7 for pitch 2; TCUs #0.5, #0.75; a small selection of Rocks or stoppers.

Descent: One 165-foot (50 m) rappel or two short rappels from the west edge of the tower.

Photo: Lin Ottinger

Dream Speaker.

WHITON-TACKLE SPIRE

2 WHITON-TACKLE
II, 5.10+, 2 pitches, 350 feet (107 m)

First Ascent: Mark Whiton, Jack Tackle, April 1989.

Location and Access: Whiton-Tackle Spire is 1.25 miles (20 km) up canyon from Dream Speaker.

Pitch 1: Climb an off-width crack system on the north side of the tower.

Pitch 2: Continue off-width up loose rock to summit anchors. A large person will be required to use face holds on the outside of the off-width.

Paraphernalia: Large Friends; Camalots #4; Big Bros. No pitons required.

Descent: Rappel the route from drilled angle pitons.

TROPHY

3 TROPHY
III, 5.11, A2, 4 pitches, 350 feet (107 m) ★

First Ascent: Tim Toula, Scott Baxter, Jim Thurmond, April 1995.

Location and Access: Trophy is an obvious needle on a pedestal located on the

Photo: Jon Butler

El Cerro del Perro.

west side of Arch Canyon south of the junction with Texas Canyon. Scott Baxter: "Thin, spectacular summit shaft. This is an unaesthetic, scary climb in a breathtaking setting. This is a one-star route in a five-star setting, but that may be generous!"

Pitch 1: Begin at the northeast side of the formation, the side facing the canyon wall. Climb a long, sustained 5.11 right-facing corner to a large ledge with an off-width toward the top of the pitch.

Pitch 2: Continue up a 40-foot face pitch, protectable with a birdbeak. A 5.10 move gets you to the base of the Trophy (needle).

Pitch 3: Make a short, easy traverse around either side to the downcanyon (south) side.

Pitch 4: Tim Toula: "On the south face, a scary bolt ladder (bolts pull out of soft, sugary sandstone) gets you to collect the trophy." Scott Baxter: "Desperate aid maneuvers in a trashy assortment of drilled holes to the top."

Paraphernalia: Gear through #5 Camalots; assortment of baby angle pitons.

Descent: Rappel the route.

EL CERRO DEL PERRO

4 EL CERRO DEL PERRO III, 5.10+ R, A3+, 2 pitches, 200 feet (60 m) ★★★★

First Ascent: Jon Butler, Jesse Harvey, November 18–19, 1995.

Location and Access: From the rappel into the canyon, the tower will be down the slope on the right side of the junction of Texas and Arch Canyons, uphill from two small towers. It is close to where the four-wheel-drive trail up Arch Canyon ends. The route ascends a dihedral on the southeast side of the tower (facing the rim). El Cerro del Perro translates to "the hill of the dog."

Pitch 1: Begin up a right-facing corner with 5.8 fingers. From a ledge, climb a 5.9+ squeeze past a fixed anchor, then 5.10 off-width past a second anchor. Continue up 5.10+ off-width, which ends with a 5.6 squeeze at a belay ledge with double anchors, 140 feet (43 m).

Pitch 2: Climb A3+ with birdbeaks and knifeblades. Jon Butler: "With a possible decking potential." Pass several hangerless bolts, then make a 5.6 mantel onto the summit and double-bolt anchors, 60 feet (18 m).

Paraphernalia: Friends (2) #1 through #2.5, (1) #3 through #4; Camalots (1) to (4) #4, #5 (if using a small number of large cams, leapfrogging will be necessary); thin knifeblades (4); long Lost Arrow (1); angles (6) ½", ⅝"; birdbeaks (6); ⅜" hangers (6); quick draws.

Descent: Rappel pitch 2 to pitch 1, then pitch 1 to the ground.

Photo: James Garrett

T4 in Arch Canyon.

CATHEDRAL ARCH

Cathedral Arch has a span of 50 feet (15 m), a height of 60 feet (18 m), a thickness of 50 feet (15 m), and a width of 20 feet (6 m). The name dates to the 1930s and comes from the appearance of the formation.

5 CATHEDRAL ARCH TOWER—SKIN WALKER IV, 5.7, A3, 5 pitches, 650 feet (198 m)

First Ascent: Bill Russell, Sean Plunket, April 4, 1995.

Location and Access: Cathedral Arch Tower soars above Cathedral Arch. Its location is opposite the mouth of Texas Canyon and is the first arch reached as one approaches up the 8-mile (12.8 km) Arch Canyon four-wheel-drive trail from Utah 95. Begin left of the arch.

Pitch 1: Begin right of a tree and climb A2 to double anchors on the shoulder of the tower.

Pitch 2: Continue 5.7, A1 to a belay ledge.

Pitch 3: Ascend with hooks and bolts to a right-facing corner, which is climbed A3, then move up and right past fixed anchors to a triple-anchor belay.

Pitch 4: Follow a bolt ladder to a belay at a shoulder of the tower.

Pitch 5: Continue fourth class+ to the summit.

Paraphernalia: Friends (1) each through #5; stoppers (12); Hexentrics #8 through #11; birdbeaks (4); Leeper Zs (4); angles (4) 0.5", 0.75", (3) 1" through 1.5", (1) 2", 3"; tie-offs.

Descent: Rappel the route.

6 CATHEDRAL ARCH TOWER—BATS IN THE BELFRY V, 5.10, A3, 8 pitches, 570 feet (174 m) ★★★

First Ascent: Jeff Lowe, Freddie Snalam, with Teri Ebel to pitch 2, June 29–30, July 11–13, 1999. One bivouac.

Location and Access: The first ascent team approached the route (two hours) over 8 miles (12.8 km) of four-wheel-drive, high-clearance trail up Arch Canyon. *Bats in the Belfry* climbs the prominent fracture system just right of the arch.

Pitch 1: Climb a hand and fist crack to double anchors and a hanging belay below a roof, 5.9/5.10, A1, 120 feet (37 m). Pitch 1 had previously been climbed by an unknown party. A couple of aid moves are used to pass a bat guano section 80 feet (24 m) up the lead.

Pitch 2: Pendulum left to a thin crack and double anchors, A2, 45 feet (14 m).

Pitch 3: Climb a thin crack through overhangs and loose rock, passing two bolts to triple belay anchors, 5.8, A3, 80 feet (24 m).

Pitch 4: Begin with A3, then climb A1/A2 and 5.8 and angle right, following the crack system to double belay bolts, 200 feet (60 m).

CATHEDRAL ARCH TOWER—BATS IN THE BELFRY

Watercolor topo: Freddie Snalam

Pitch 5: Continue to a belay bolt at a good bivouac ledge, 5.9, A3, 60 feet (18 m).

Pitch 6: Aid climb a thin crack with knifeblade pitons. Traverse right to a wide crack, which is climbed with free and aid techniques. Belay at a ledge band, 5.9, A2, 75 feet (23 m).

Pitch 7: Freddie Snalam: "A 25-foot shoulder-wide off-width with an ominous overhanging start led on upward." Belay from a drilled angle piton by a tree, 5.10, A1, 20 feet (6 m).

Pitch 8: Scramble 15 feet (4.5 m) to the summit.

Paraphernalia: Full desert rack, including Big Bros; 200-foot (60 m) ropes.

Descent: Rappel the route.

ANGEL ARCH

Robert H. Vreeland in *Nature's Bridges and Arches,* Volume 8, Southern Utah: "This is undoubtedly the original Angel Arch because the name was applied to this arch many years before it was given to the one in Canyonlands National Park or to the one on White Mesa." The arch has a span of 40 feet (12 m), a height of 100 feet (30 m), a thickness of 25 feet (7.6 m), and a width of 20 feet (6 m). The name dates to the 1930s and is derived from the shape of the landform.

7 ANGEL ARCH (a.k.a. Fallen Arch, Hell Bitch) V, 5.11, A3+, 8 pitches, 750 feet (229 m)

First Ascent: John Markel, Kevin Chase, June 1993.

Location and Access: Angel Arch is on the right beyond the junction of Texas Canyon and Arch Canyon.

Pitch 1: Begin 5.8, climbing left to right up the "Stairway to Heaven." Climb an expanding flake (A2) on its left side, then ledges to the "Chopping Block" and a belay at two bolts and a fixed piton.

Pitch 2: Climb A3+, passing a fixed bolt. Continue 5.11 up "Styx Crack" to a triple-bolt belay ledge.

Pitch 3: Continue 5.11, moving to the right crack, then 5.9 to a triple-bolt belay.

Pitch 4: Climb A3+ up the "Pearly Gates" to a triple-bolt belay.

Pitch 5: Climb 5.10 past two pitons (false belay), then up a 5.10+, 9-inch (23 cm) crack to a belay from two pitons and one bolt. Kevin Chase: "Good bivy ledge."

Pitch 6: Continue up a wide crack to a good ledge, 5.9.

Pitch 7: Climb A3+, passing bolts, "drilling fields." Move right to a belay.

Pitch 8: Climb A2, passing bolts to the summit.

Paraphernalia: Friends (3) sets with (2) #6, #7; Big Bros through #4; ball nuts; assorted angle pitons; knifeblades (10); quick draws.

Descent: Rappel the route.

8 T4—AIN'T NO STRANGER TO PAIN
III, 5.10, A2, 4 pitches, 425 feet (130 m) ★★★

T4's first ascent team considered the area so synonymous with Tim Toula that they named their spire for Texas Tower Tim Toula—the 4 Ts.

First Ascent: James Garrett, Chris Donharl, May 25, 2000.

Location and Access: T4 is in view from the overlook and the rappel point. From the rappel into the canyon, hike up Arch Canyon past Angel Arch, then 100 yards (91 m) uphill (east) to T4. Begin on the creek side (northeast face) at the lowest point of the prow and climb to right-facing dihedrals.

Pitch 1: Face climb steepening slabs past several bolts and holes to a good belay ledge, 5.10, A0, 130 feet (40 m).

Pitch 2: Climb 5.8 into A1 to a belay ledge with double anchors—Big Windy Ledge, 115 feet (35 m).

Pitch 3: Continue up an off-width chimney to a belay ledge, and anchor from natural gear—Golden Shower Cave, 100 feet (30 m). James Garrett: "Amazing bivy cave if you ever care to bivy there."

Pitch 4: Climb a right-facing dihedral (one move of A2) past a bolt to bolts at "Bat Dwellings," then 5.10 hands/off-width to the summit and double anchors, 80 feet (24 m).

Paraphernalia: Camalots (2) sets with (1) #4.5, #5; nuts (1) set; Leeper-Zs (2); Toucans (2); ¾" angles (2), ½" angles (2); keyhole hangers (4); ⅜" bolt hangers; 200-foot (60 m) ropes (2).

Descent: Rappel the route.

ARCH–TEXAS CANYON TOWER

9 BLOOD MERIDIAN
IV, 5.10 R, A3, C2+, 5 pitches, 550 feet (167 m) ★★★★

First Ascent: Tony Wilson, Russell Hooper, April 1995.

Location and Access: Arch–Texas Canyon Tower is the large tower near the junction of the canyons. When standing at the top of the canyon at the start of the rappels, the route follows the left (west) skyline. Tony Wilson: "The route is high quality with varied climbing. Helmets should be worn. There is loose rock, especially pitch 5." The name *Blood Meridian* comes from a novel about the West by Cormac McCarthy.

Pitch 1: Begin up loose rock, passing double fixed anchors, then A3 to a double-bolt belay, 5.7, R.

Pitch 2: Continue on aid past a fixed anchor to a double-bolt belay, A3.

Pitch 3: Climb C2 past a 5.10 R loose chimney to double belay anchors.

Pitch 4: Climb C2+ up a wide crack system past two anchors, then an A2 chimney, ending with 5.10 R up loose rock to a double-bolt belay station.

Pitch 5: Continue 5.9, C1 up a 0.25- to 3-inch (0.6 to 7.6 cm) crack to the summit.

Paraphernalia: Friends (2) sets; Camalots (1) #4, #5; TCUs (2) or (3) sets; nuts (1) set; Toucans (1); Lost Arrows (4) long, (2) short; angle pitons to 1" (2) each; Leeper Zs (2); ⅜" bolt hangers.

Descent: Rappel the route.

TEXAS CANYON

Texas Canyon is named for early Texans who drove herds of longhorn cattle into southeastern Utah Territory in the 1870s.

TEXAS TOWER

Texas Tower was first attempted in May 1986 by Tim Toula and Dave Hodson. Tim Toula: "A summit rivaling any in the Southwest, i.e. Spider Rock, Moses, etc. A very strenuous, long spire, combined with the approach from the rim, makes for a full day of wilderness climbing. Intermittent soft rock makes for scary free climbing. An adept off-width climber could probably free pitch 5, but I'm only brave enough to free the 5.10+ part. Pitches 7 and 8 comprise an incredible 200-foot (60 m) chimney. A scary 5.10+ move puts you on the magnifcent summit."

Photo: Paul Horton

Texas Tower.

10 TEXAS TOWER—SOUTH FACE
IV, 5.11c R, 8 pitches, 650 feet (198 m) ★★★★★

First Ascent: Tim Toula, Kathy Zaiser, 5.10+, A1, April 26, 1987. Second Ascent and First Free Ascent: Derek Hersey, Steve "Crusher" Bartlett, 1990. Second Free Ascent: Bret Ruckman, Tim Coats, October 29, 1991.

Location and Access: The *South Face* route ascends a splitter crack that splits the tower from bottom to top.

Pitch 1: Begin up a loose left-facing corner and climb to a belay ledge with double anchors, 5.9.

Pitch 2: Continue up an off-width chimney to a belay stance with double anchors, 5.9+ squeeze.

Pitch 3: Climb a chimney to a single-bolt belay anchor, 5.10.

Pitch 4: Continue up a short chimney and traverse right (5.10a face), passing a bolt and a piton, then past a death flake on its right, 5.10 R, and belay on a ledge from double anchors.

Pitch 5: The crux pitch. Continue up an 8-inch (20 cm) off-width. Pass three bolts on the way to an exposed belay stance with triple anchors, 5.11c, 140 feet (43 m). Bret Ruckman: "One hundred forty feet of wild climbin'."

Pitch 6: Begin with a 5.10 squeeze, then a chimney to a single-bolt belay.

Pitch 7: Continue up the chimney, passing a fixed piton and a bolt, to a good belay at the summit ridge and a fixed piton.

Pitch 8: Face climb the summit ridge to the top, 5.10d.

Paraphernalia: Friends (1) #1, (2) #1.5, #2, (1) #3, #3.5, (2) #4, #5, #7 (larger Friends very important); selection of wired stoppers; Hexentrics (1) #10, #11; tubes (1) 4.5″, 5″ (6″ optional but useful); (2) 200-foot (60 m) ropes; quick draws (8).

Descent: Four 165-foot (50 m) double-rope rappels on the back (west) side of the tower. To find the third rappel anchors, walk west along an exposed ramp until they appear. A belay might be comforting. The last rappel is to the end of the ropes to a small stance. It is necessary to downclimb 15 feet (4.5 m) to the floor of a tight chimney, which then leads west back to the start of the route.

11 LONE STAR—CREATURES FROM THE BLACK SALOON
IV, 5.7, A1/C1, 5 pitches, 445 feet (136 m) ★★★★

First Ascent: Jon Butler, Jesse Harvey, Cameron Burns, November 9–10, 1996.

Location and Access: Lone Star is 400 feet (122 m) northwest of Texas Tower in Texas Canyon, approximately 1 mile (1.6 km) from the junction of Texas and Arch Canyons. The 400-foot (122 m) spire is obvious when viewed from the south of Texas Tower. Fix a rope between pitches 3 and 4 to enable pulling into the pitch 3 belay on the descent. The route ascends a low-angle ramp over broken ledges on the south face, then finishes up a corner crack system on the east side of the spire.

Photo: Cameron M. Burns

Lone Star, first ascent, 1996.

Pitch 1: Begin A1 and climb past an expanding flake. Continue 5.7 to a belay ledge, 130 feet (40 m).

Pitch 2: Climb a 3-inch (7.6 cm) crack. Pass three bolts and climb A1/C1 up loose rock, passing a "death block" on its right. Continue to a double-bolt hanging belay on the left wall, 75 feet (23 m).

Pitch 3: Continue with C1 up the 3-inch (7.6 cm) crack, which widens to 4 inches (10 cm), then 5.6 to a double-bolt belay stance, 75 feet (23 m).

Pitch 4: Climb a bolt ladder, then a section of 0.5-inch width (1.2 cm) of A1/C1 before continuing up a bolt ladder to the summit shoulder and double-bolt anchors. Leave a fixed rope for the return pull into the belay anchors at the top of pitch 3, 165 feet (50 m).

Pitch 5: Fourth class to double anchors at the highest point.

Paraphernalia: Friends (2) sets with (4) #3.5; small Friends (1) set; Camalots (1) #4; wired stoppers (1) set; knifeblades (6); Lost Arrows (6) thin to medium; angles (8) ½" through 1"; birdbeaks; rivet hangers ¼" or ⅜" (30).

Descent: Three double-rope rappels down the route, skipping the second belay.

DIVERSIONS

See Diversions for the Natural Bridges National Monument, Chapter 19.

> Above the cumuli and often flung across them like bands of gauze, are the strati—clouds of the middle air region. This veil or sheet-cloud might be called a twilight cloud, giving out as it does its greatest splendor after the sun has disappeared below the verge. It then takes all colors and with singular vividness. At times it will overspread the whole west as a sheet of brilliant magenta, but more frequently it blares with scarlet, carmine, crimson, flushing up and then fading out, shifting from one color to another; and finally dying out in a beautiful ashes of roses. When these clouds and all their variations have faded into lilac and deep purples, there are still bright spots of color in the upper sky where the cirri are receiving the last rays of the sun.
>
> —John C. Van Dyke, *The Desert,* 1901

19

NATURAL BRIDGES NATIONAL MONUMENT

> In the fullness of time Nature designs that this waste and all of earth with it shall perish. Individual, type, and species, all shall pass away; and the globe itself become as desert sand blown hither and yon through space. She cares nothing for the individual man or bird or beast; can it be thought that she cares any more for the individual world? She continues the earth-life by the death of the old and the birth of the new. . . . Our outlook is limited indeed, but have we not proof in our own moon that worlds do die? Is it possible that its bleached body will never be disintegrated, will never dissolve and be resolved again into some new life? And how came it to die? What was the element that failed—fire, water, or atmosphere? Perhaps it was water. Perhaps it died through thousands of years with the slow evaporation of moisture and the slow growth of the desert.
>
> —John C. Van Dyke, *The Desert,* 1901

The high land of Cedar Mesa west to Lake Powell is one of the most desolate locales on the vast Colorado Plateau. It is remote and essentially unpopulated. The isolation of White Canyon and the three bridges carved in it, now Natural Bridges National Monument, can only be compared to the vast San Rafael and 527-square-mile Canyonlands National Park. Cedar Mesa is populated with hundreds of Anasazi sites. It is surprising and perhaps ironic that thousands more people populated the region in ancient times than today. Edward Abbey in *The Journey Home,* 1977, speaks of the land: "The canyon country does not always inspire love. To many it appears barren, hostile, repellent—a fearsome, mostly waterless land of rock and heat, sand dunes and quicksand, cactus, thornbush, scorpion, rattlesnake, and agoraphobic distances. To those who see our land in that manner, the best reply is, yes, you are right, it is a dangerous and terrible place. Enter at your own risk. Carry water. Avoid the noonday sun. Try to ignore the vultures. Pray frequently."

Included in the Natural Bridges National Monument area are the Bear's Ears, Mr. Potato Head, Needle, and Jacob's Chair. Routes are reached from Utah 95, which travels past Natural Bridges between Blanding and Hite Marina on Lake Powell.

MILE MARKER LOG—UTAH 95 FROM BLANDING TO HITE MARINA

Turn west from US 191 onto Utah 95, 4 miles (6.4 km) south of Blanding. Mile marker signs on Utah 95 are used as reference points.

119–118: Cross a cattle guard.

116–115: Cross another cattle guard.

NATURAL BRIDGES NATIONAL MONUMENT ROUTE LOCATOR MAP

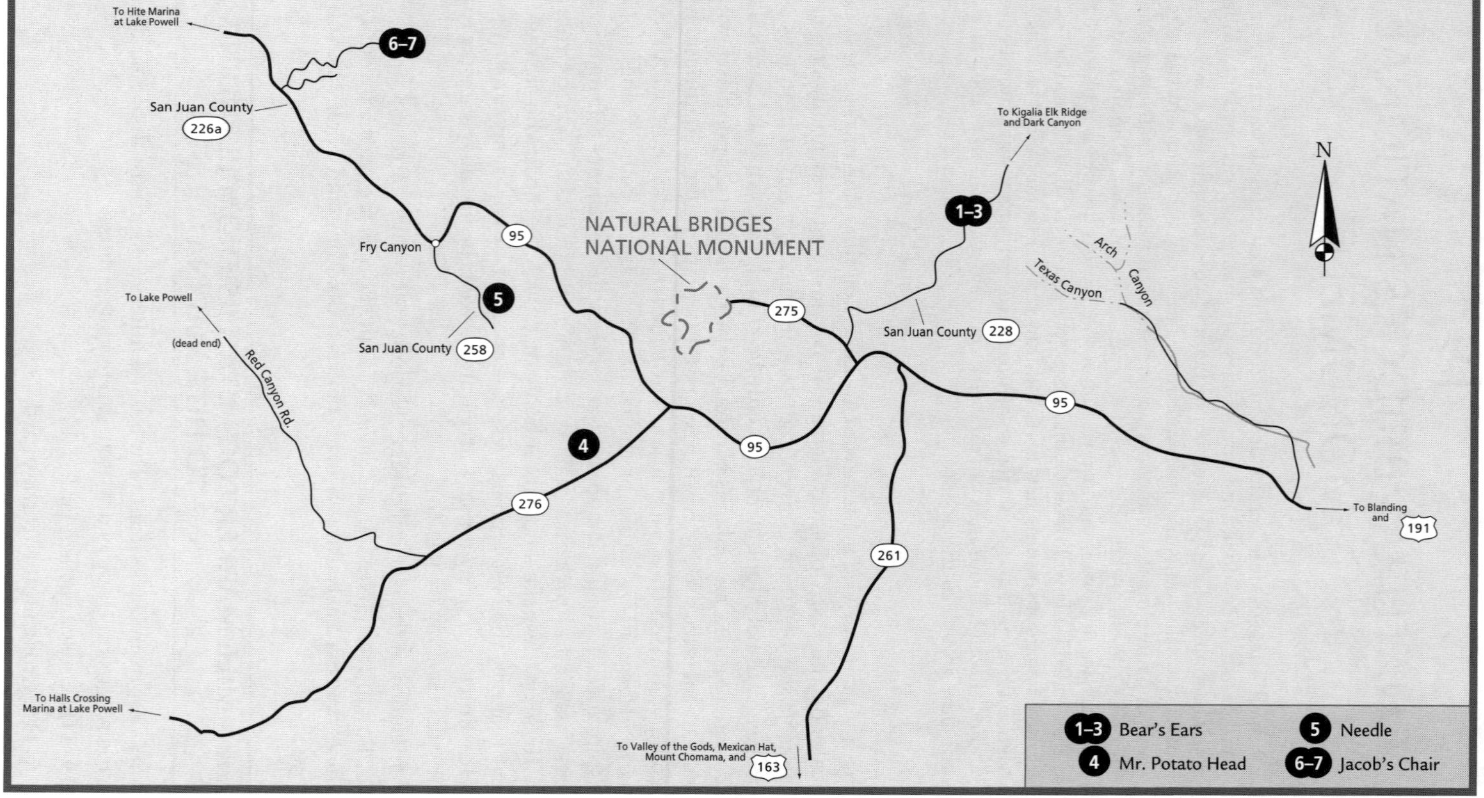

Photo: John Middendorf

Karen Lycett on summit of Mr. Potato Head.

112–111: Sign: BUTLER WASH INDIAN RUINS; arrow points right. Turn right on a paved road and drive 0.2 mile (0.3 km) to rest rooms and a trailhead to a viewpoint of Anasazi ruins.

108–107: Utah 95 passes through Comb Ridge via a dramatic deep cut in the Wingate sandstone. At the bottom of the hill below Comb Ridge, a dirt trail (San Juan County 235) branches left (south). A short distance ahead is a camping site beneath lush cottonwood trees, with tables, rest rooms, and an information kiosk. Just before mile marker 107, Indian ruins are in view beneath an overhang to the right (north) of the roadway.

103–102: Access to the 900-year-old Cave Towers (ancient Puebloan) in a tributary of Mule Canyon. Seven towers are precariously set high on the rim of the canyon. To reach the towers, turn south onto an unmarked dirt trail near mile marker 103, drive 0.5 mile (0.8 km) and park. A short hike reaches the ruin site. Unmarked dirt trail to the right leads to Arch Canyon

102–101: Mule Canyon Indian Ruins. Turn right on a paved road and drive 0.1 mile (0.16 km). There are rest rooms and a viewing area of 700-year-old Pueblo surface ruins, which include a kiva and tower and a block of rooms.

98–97: A sign details the history of Salvation Knoll. Note the tenuous hoodoo on the west side of the knoll.

97–95: Navajo Mountain is in view to the southwest. It is one of three mountains sacred to the Navajo People. A signed pullout marks a good viewing spot.

94–93: Junction Utah 261 and 95. A sign gives distances to Lake Powell, Natural Bridges National Monument, Fry Canyon, Mexican Hat, Grand Gulch Ranger Station, and Hanksville.

92–91: A sign for Manti-La Sal National Forest, Elk Ridge Access, Utah 275 North, and Natural Bridges National Monument.

89–88: Navajo Mountain comes into view ahead of the highway at eleven o'clock.

86–85: Henry Mountains in view at one o'clock.

84–83: Signs for Fry Canyon and Hanksville, and for Blanding, Mexican Hat, and Natural Bridges. This is the junction of Utah 95 West and Utah 276 South.

77–76: Sign: CHEESE BOX BUTTE.

72–71: Sign: FRY CANYON, GAS, FOOD, LODGING, EMERGENCY PHONE ONLY.

65–64: A sign indicates Jacob's Chair to the right (north). San Juan County 227A is a dirt trail to a soldier's grave.

55–54: Large color sign: GLEN CANYON NATIONAL RECREATION AREA.

55–54: A sign for White Canyon Access, Lake Powell.

54–53: Bridge over deep, narrow White Canyon. A spectacular view! Sign for Farley Canyon Access, Lake Powell. A view of Lake Powell.

50–49: Sewing Machine Needle in view to the right (north).

49–48: Left turn to Hite Marina. At mile marker 49, San Juan County 208A, Horse Tanks Road, goes right. This is the approach to the Ruminator Tower, Sundance Trailhead, and, more than 50 miles farther, Wooden Shoe Trailhead and the Bear's Ears. The route is complicated, with numerous branches and no signs indicating which ones lead to Bear's Ears. Maps are inaccurate. The drive should only be attempted with a high-clearance vehicle and a full tank of gas.

BEAR'S EARS

The Bear's Ears are twin buttes of Wingate sandstone at the southern end of Elk Ridge, west of the Abajo Mountains and east of Natural Bridges National Monument. The buttes were named *Orejas del Oso* (ears of the bear) by early Mexican travelers.

The two routes on the Bear's Ears climb the northwest end of the east butte. A 30-foot (9 m) project climbs the fracture system below the highest point of the east buttress of the east Bear's Ears. There is potential for several dozen routes up Wingate sandstone on both buttes, and excellent bouldering problems at their bases.

To reach the Bear's Ears, turn west onto Utah Bicentenial Highway 95, 4 miles (6.4 km) south of Blanding, approximately 75 miles (120 km) south of Moab. The scenic drive travels high up Cedar Mesa. Thirty-seven miles (60 km) west of Blanding, at the intersection of Utah 275, turn north at a sign for Natural Bridges National Monument. In a few hundred yards, make a right turn onto a dirt trail (San Juan County 228) at a sign indicating Kigalia and Elk Ridge Access to the right. In 3.2 miles (5 km) is a sign for Manti National Forest. At the col between the Bear's Ears, a sign gives the elevation of the left (west) butte at 8,929 feet (2,721 m) and the right (east) butte at 9,058 feet (2,760 m).

BEAR'S EARS EAST

1 BEAR'S EARS EAST—LEFT CRACK I, 5.8, 1 pitch, 100 feet (30 m)

First Ascent: Tobin Kelly, solo, summer 1979.

Location and Access: *Left Crack* climbs fingers-to-fist up the left of two cracks on the north/northwest face of the butte.

Paraphernalia: Finger- to fist-size units.

Descent: Rappel the route or walk off.

2 BEAR'S EARS EAST—RIGHT CRACK I, A1, 1 pitch, 100 feet (30 m)

First Ascent: Tobin Kelly, solo, summer 1979.

Location and Access: The route climbs a thin crack just right of *Left Crack*. No more information is known.

Paraphernalia: Selection of pitons.

Descent: Rappel the route or walk off.

3 BEAR'S EARS EAST—PROJECT
I, 5.9. 1 pitch, 30 feet (9 m)

First Ascent: Carl Diedrich et al, October 31, 1999.

Location and Access: Drive through the pass between the west and east Bear's Ears and turn right (east) at a sign: S. LONG PNT 4. Follow right branches 1 mile (1.6 km) to the nearest approach on the east buttress. A half-hour hike brings you to the base of the wall.The route begins up the longest crack system on the east side of the east butte, near its north end, and climbs to a tenuous death block at the start of a chimney.

Paraphernalia: Friends (1) set with extra #2.

Descent: Rappel the route from a sling around a boulder.

MR. POTATO HEAD

Mr. Potato Head is southwest of Natural Bridges National Monument. Turn south onto Utah 276 from Utah 95 between mile markers 83 and 84, just east of the Natural Bridges junction at a sign for Bull Frog-Halls Crossing. Utah 276 descends beside the Red House Cliffs on its 40-mile (64 km) journey to Halls Crossing Marina and toll ferry dock at Lake Powell. At 6.6 miles (10.6 km) south of Utah 95 on Utah 276, turn right (west) onto a dirt trail between mile markers

Photo: Eric Bjørnstad

Bear's Ears East.

84 and 85. Park at its end, approximately 1,000 feet (305 m), and hike to the left of two hoodoos obvious at the base of the mesa to the north.

4 MR. POTATO HEAD
I, 5.9, 1 pitch, 40 feet (12 m) ★

First Ascent: John Middendorf, Karen Lycett, October 1990.

Location and Access: Mr. Potato Head is climbed from its south side. Ascend an obvious straight-in crack system to the summit. Rappel the route from a single bolt.

Paraphernalia: Small selection of cams.

Descent: Rappel the route.

NEEDLE

Needle is in Fry Canyon, deep in the southeastern corner of Utah, approximately 130 miles (209 km) south of Moab. The canyon originates at the Red House Cliffs about 2 miles (3.2 km) southwest of Natural Bridges National Monument and drains northwest into White Canyon. Once a busy center for uranium mining, Fry Canyon is now a quiet resort site between Natural Bridges National Monument and Hite Marina. The Fry Canyon Lodge offers comfortable rooms, meals,

Photo: Eric Bjørnstad

Bear's Ear East: Project.

Photo: Michael Dudley

Needle, south face.

RV hookups, tent sites, a bathhouse, gasoline, propane, groceries, drinks, and souvenirs.

To reach Fry Canyon, drive 4 miles (6.4 km) south of Blanding, turn west onto Utah 95 and continue approximately 50 miles (80.5 km) to the Fry Canyon Store and Lodge and the entrance to Fry Canyon (between mile markers 71 and 72). The location is 21 miles (33.8 km) west of Natural Bridges National Monument.

Needle is reached by driving south on San Juan County 258–Radium King Road, left of the Fry Canyon Store. Within 200 yards (183 m) the trail angles left; continue straight for approximately 3 miles (4.8 km). The tower comes into view left of the roadway, just before the trail angles right. A faint trail heads toward Needle, which is approximately 1 mile (1.6 km) away.

5 NEEDLE
II, 5.11, A0, 2 pitches, 165 feet (50 m)

First Ascent: Michael Dudley, Brent Bringham, May 1985.

Location and Access: The route ascends the left end of the south face of the tower, just right of the west ridge.

Pitch 1: Begin up a left-to-right slope, ending with 5.7 climbing at a ledge. Continue up a left-facing corner, passing two fixed anchors and ending with 5.11 at a belay stance atop blocks.

Pitch 2: Drop down and to the right. Climb a right-facing corner at 5.8 to a vertical crack system climbed 5.7 up a loose chimney, ending at double anchors on the summit.

Paraphernalia: Friends (1) set; small nuts; quick draws (2).

Descent: Double-rope rappel from two drilled anchors in the chimney below the summit.

JACOB'S CHAIR

Jacob's Chair is the prominent Wingate sandstone butte in the area north of Fry and White Canyons. It is in view from Utah 95, 12 miles (19 km) northwest of Natural Bridges National Monument.

At mile marker 64 a sign identifies the tower. It is named for Jacob Adams, a cowboy and prospector who camped at a spring in the canyon and was later drowned while attempting to cross White Creek (near the butte) while it was in a flash flood stage.

From the Fry Canyon Store, continue northwest on Utah 95 to a mining trail (San Juan County 226A–Jacob's Chair Road) that begins on the right side of the highway at a point between Gravel and Long Canyons, between mile markers 66 and 67. The trail immediately crosses White Canyon (which is north of and parallel to Utah 95), then divides. Take the left fork past an old shack and continue up through red cliff bands. After approximately 5 miles (8 km), the talus cone below Jacob's Chair appears.

THE CHEESE BOX

The Cheese Box is a signed butte north of Utah 95 in view for several miles as you approach the Fry Canyon junction. It is reached by a circuitous cross-country hike from its nearest point to Utah 95. It was climbed by John Middendorf et al. in the early 1990s from the north (moderate fifth class). John gives the ascent two stars and says: "If it was a backyard crag, there would be a hundred routes on it." The Cheese Box is approximately 200 feet high (60 m). Climb the northeast side of the formation, working up loose slopes and rock bands to a summit with impressive views. To descend, downclimb the route.

6 JACOB'S CHAIR
II, 5.10, 3 pitches, 340 feet (104 m)

First Ascent: George Hurley, Bill Forrest, 5.7, A2, November 3, 1976. First Free Ascent: George Hurley, David Rearick, May 22, 1977.

Location and Access: The route begins on the west end of the formation, climbs the north face of the seat, then the north side of the back of the chair. Bill Forrest: "Ours was the first climbing ascent. A U.S. Coast and Geodetic Survey had helicoptered to the summit in 1952, leaving a bench mark and trash."

Photo: Eric Bjørnstad

Jacob's Chair—Critters in the Gallery.

Pitch 1: Scramble 15 feet (4.5 m) up the west end of the seat, then walk east along a bench on the north face. Start the first lead approximately 100 feet (30 m) from the west end of the formation at the first crack system heading to the seat. Climb 75 feet (23 m) at 5.7. Walk east along the level seat to the back of the chair. Skirt a small gendarme on the north and continue east on a bench about 50 feet (15 m) to the first free-climbing crack, 90 feet (27 m).

Pitch 2: Climb up and left to a narrow chimney. Begin by surmounting a bulge, then continue to a block that chocks the chimney entrance. Once over the block, chimney as high as possible and place protection in the blocks that cap the chimney. Chimney back down about 10 feet (3 m) and traverse out toward the face. Face holds and off-width cracks lead over a 5.9 crux to a good belay platform and a drilled-in angle and standard angle, 100 feet (30 m).

Pitch 3: Walk east, passing a large block on its left, then climb the crack above the upper right edge of the block to a 25-foot (7.6 m) A-shaped overhang (the second crux). Pass the overhang at 5.10 and continue 5.7 to the top, 150 feet (46 m).

Paraphernalia: Friends (1) set.

Descent: Rappel the route.

7 JACOB'S CHAIR—CRITTERS IN THE GALLERY III, 5.10, A2, 3 pitches, 370 feet (113 m) ★★

First Ascent: Carl Diedrich, Andy Pitas, Julie Calhoun, November 3, 1993.

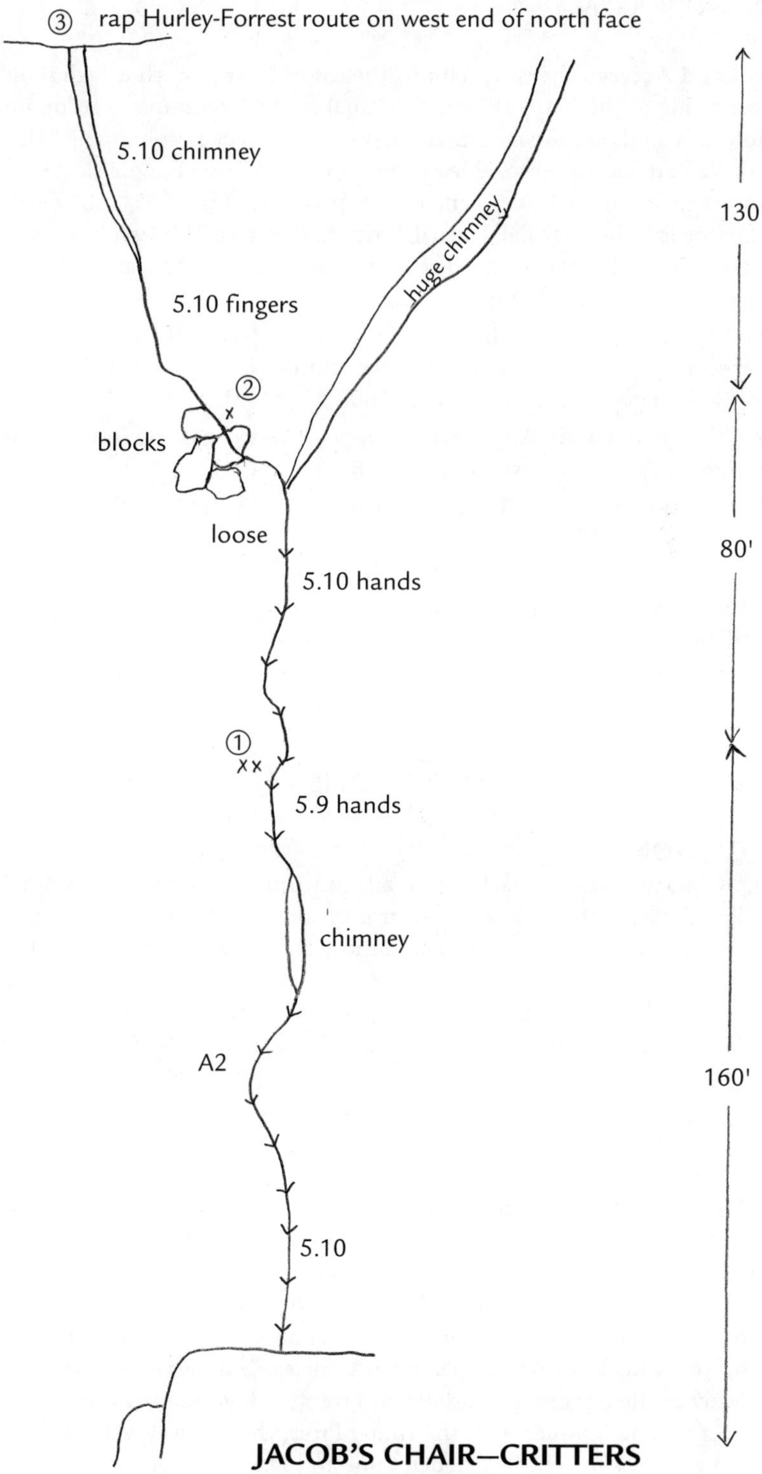

JACOB'S CHAIR—CRITTERS IN THE GALLERY

Location and Access: The route climbs the tower by the south dihedral on the opposite side of the Hurley/Forrest original route. Begin up the second most obvious dihedral on the west end of the south face. The first hanging belay has two drilled angles; the second ledge belay has one drilled angle. The summit has no register, but a USGS bench mark was placed in 1952. Carl Diedrich: "The name is in honor of all the wild critters that passed by while we were on the climb. Several bighorn sheep, a golden eagle, and the usual assorted creatures. Potential for many more routes."

Pitch 1: Begin up a 5.10 crack in a corner. Continue past three points of A2 in a corner seam (knifeblades), 15 feet (4.5 m). Climb a chimney, then 5.9 hands to double belay anchors on the left wall, 160 feet (49 m).

Pitch 2: Climb 5.10 hands. Angle left at a large chimney, passing loose blocks on their right, and belay at a single anchor, 80 feet (24 m).

Pitch 3: Continue with 5.10 fingers, then up a 5.10 off-width chimney to the summit, 130 feet (40 m).

Paraphernalia: Friends; Camalots (1) #4; TCUs (1) #1, #1.5, (2) #2, #2.5, (3) #3, (2) #3.5, #4; Big Dude (1) #5, #6; Big Bro (1) large unit for the chimney; several knifeblades.

Descent: Rappel the Hurley/Forrest original route on the west end of the north face.

DIVERSIONS

DARK CANYON

San Juan County 228, the Elk Ridge Trail, continues west past the Bear's Ears to Wooden Shoe Trailhead, a spectacular multiday backpack into the dramatic Dark Canyon Wilderness. Dark Canyon, more than 2,000 feet (610 m) deep, is one of the most imposing canyons on the Colorado Plateau, with many buttes and towers that hold great potential for quality climbing. Bighorn sheep, mule deer, mountain lions, bobcats, bears, and beavers have been identified there. Several varieties of snakes are found in the canyon, but poisonous species are rare. Both high mountain and desert birds nest in the area. Magpies, mourning doves, piñon jays, sage sparrows, canyon towhees, bluebirds, rock wrens, swallows, chickadees, ravens, and meadowlarks are the most plentiful; bald and golden eagles, cranes, finches, grouse, and water ouzels are sometimes seen in the canyon.

Approximately 50 miles (80 km) from Wooden Shoe Trailhead, the Elk Ridge Trail passes the Sundance Trailhead, a destination for many hikers, then intersects with Utah 95 close to Hite Marina at Lake Powell. The trail is generally drivable with two-wheel-drive high-clearance vehicles, but because of numerous major branches the traverse should not be attempted without directions from a BLM ranger or one familiar with the route. From the Elk Ridge Trail there are tantalizing glimpses into both Wooden Shoe and Dark Canyons.

NATURAL BRIDGES NATIONAL MONUMENT

In 1908 the three bridges—Sipapu, Owachomo, and Kachina—along with Mesa Verde were set aside as a national monument comprising 7,636 acres at an elevation ranging from 5,500 to 6,500 feet (1,676 to 1,981 m). In 1928 a rough road was built to the bridges from Blanding, over Elk Ridge and between the Bear's Ears Buttes. It was later replaced by the modern highway (Utah 95) at a lower level. The new road is known as the Bicentennial Highway because its hard-surfacing was completed in Utah's bicentennial year, 1976. The 133-mile (214 km) road links Blanding in the east with Hanksville to the west, a region previously considered one of the most remote sectors of the nation.

The three bridges, composed of Cedar Mesa sandstone approximately 260 million years old, rank among the largest natural bridges in the world. Long known to the Paiute Indians, they were called "under the horse's belly." From the visitor center, an 8-mile (12.8 km) one-way loop road reaches viewing areas and trailheads within a few hundred yards of each bridge.

Sipapu Bridge is the largest at 220 feet (67 m) high with a span of 268 feet (82 m), a width of 31 feet (9.4 m), and a thickness of 53 feet (16 m). The straightforward trail to the bridge involves steel stairs and wooden ladders and a descent of 600 feet (182 m). *Sipapu* is from Hopi legend and means "the gateway through which the souls of men come from the underworld and finally return to it."

Kachina Bridge is 210 feet (64 m) high with a span of 206 feet (63 m), a width of 44 feet (13 m), and a thickness of 93 feet (28 m). A 600-foot (183 m) trail with some handrails descends to the bridge, which was named by government officials during the proclamation establishing the monument. The prehistoric artwork on the bridge's abutment resembles Hopi masks worn by Kachina spirits. From the bridge, a trail leads approximately 200 yards (182 m) to a panel of pictographs and cliff dwellings.

Owachomo Bridge is 106 feet high (32 m) with a span of 180 feet (55 m), a width of 27 feet (8 m), and a thickness of 9 feet (2.7 m). The trail to the bridge descends a gentle 300 feet (91 m). The name *Owachomo* is a Hopi word for "flat-rock mound" and refers to a nearby landform. There are numerous pictographs and ruins in the area of the bridges. Further information is available at the visitor center.

In 1980 the world's largest solar-powered generating system at the time was built at the bridge's visitor center. It produces electricity for the center, ranger residences, and pump and water systems.

BLANDING

Blanding is a small community of a few thousand residents, but it's large enough to provide food, drink, gasoline, and motels. It is also home of the College of Eastern Utah–San Juan Center, and the Dinosaur Museum at 754 South 200 West. Museum exhibits of fossil bones, footprints, and skin of dinosaurs are featured. The museum also depicts animals that lived before dinosaurs and "a tree standing upright for the first time in 275 million years." There is also a special exhibition called *The Art and Science of Dinosaurs in the Movies*. Surely a must-see on a rest day or bad weather day.

The town of Blanding was settled in 1887 as White Mesa. Around 1908, the name was changed to Grayson after pioneer settler Nellie Lyman Grayson. In 1914 a wealthy easterner, Thomas W. Bicknell, offered a thousand-volume library to the Utah town willing to change its name to Bicknell. The pioneer communities of Thurber and Grayson became rivals for the prize. In the end a compromise was reached, with each town receiving half the library for the name change. Thurber became Bicknell, and Grayson became Blanding, the maiden name of Bicknell's wife.

EDGE OF THE CEDARS MUSEUM

Blanding's Edge of the Cedars museum and state park at 660 West 400 North is the site of an Anasazi Indian pueblo, with a ceremonial kiva built between 780 and 1,300 years ago. The ruin consists of six distinct habitation and ceremonial complexes, and the museum houses a gift shop, lecture hall, and excellent collection of Anasazi artifacts and pottery. For further information write P.O. Box 788, 660 West 400 North, Blanding, UT 84511, or call (435) 678-2238.

HUCK'S MUSEUM

Huck's Museum and Trading Post is on US 191 on the left (east) just south of Blanding. It is one of the best privately held collections of arrowheads, beads, pendants, and pottery of the Anasazi Culture. It's a very impressive collection, and is highly recommended.

> Nature never intended that we should fully understand. That we have stumbled upon some knowledge of her laws was more accident than design. We have by some strange chance groped our way to the Gate of the Garden, and there we stand, staring through the closed bars, with the wonder of little children. Alas! We shall always grope! And shall we ever cease to wonder?
>
> —John C. Van Dyke, *The Desert,* 1901

20
BLUFF

> Whatever the cause, there can be no doubt about the effect. The desert air is practically colored air. Several times from high mountains I have seen it lying below me like an enormous tinted cloud or veil. A similar veiling of pink, lilac, or pale yellow is to be seen in the gorges of the Grand Canyon. . . and it tinges the whole face of the Painted Desert in Arizona. . . . During the summer months its appearance is often startling. By that I do not mean that one looks through it as through a highly colored glass. The impression should not be gained that this air is so rose-colored or saffron-hued that one has to rub his eyes and wonder if he is awake. The average unobservant traveller looks through it and thinks it is not different from any other air. But it is different. In itself, and in its effect upon the landscape, it is perhaps responsible for the greater part of what everyone calls "The wonderful color"of the desert.
>
> —John C. Van Dyke, *The Desert,* 1901

FORMATION

Bluff sandstone and the Summerville Formation are of Jurassic age (144 to 208 million years old). Bluff sandstone is eolian (windblown) in origin and limited in its exposure from just north to south of the town. As with many rock names on the Colorado Plateau, it is also a place-name, named for the bluffs it forms on both sides of the San Juan River. The stratum sits atop the softer tide-flat-deposited Summerville Formation, which is widespread on the Colorado Plateau. The two strata of sandstone are characteristic of all of the plateau country, with cliffs that erode in a cliff-slope-cliff pattern. Geologists estimate that erosion in the Bluff area averages about ¼ inch every hundred years.

Bluff is one of Utah's most remote towns. It sits in a fertile valley at an elevation of 4,380 feet (1,335 m) at the confluence of Cottonwood Wash and the San Juan River and is watered by five artesian wells. The valley is bordered by imposing red rock cliffs of hard Bluff sandstone atop the softer Summerville Formation. To reach Bluff from Moab, drive 112 miles (180 km) south on US 191.

One of the most incredible stories of pioneer settlement is that of the Mormon San Juan Mission expedition of 1879–80. Sixty families—230 members of the Mormon Church—were "called" to colonize the Montezuma Creek region at the southeastern corner of the state. With 83 wagons and more than 1,000 head of livestock, they crossed some of the west's most rugged canyon country in an attempt to settle at Montezuma Creek on the San Juan River. The journey from the settlement of Escalante was expected to take six weeks, but turned into a six-month ordeal. The exhausted company arrived on the banks of the San Juan on April 5, 1880. Too tired to continue just 20 easy miles to Montezuma Creek, they stayed and founded the town of Bluff.

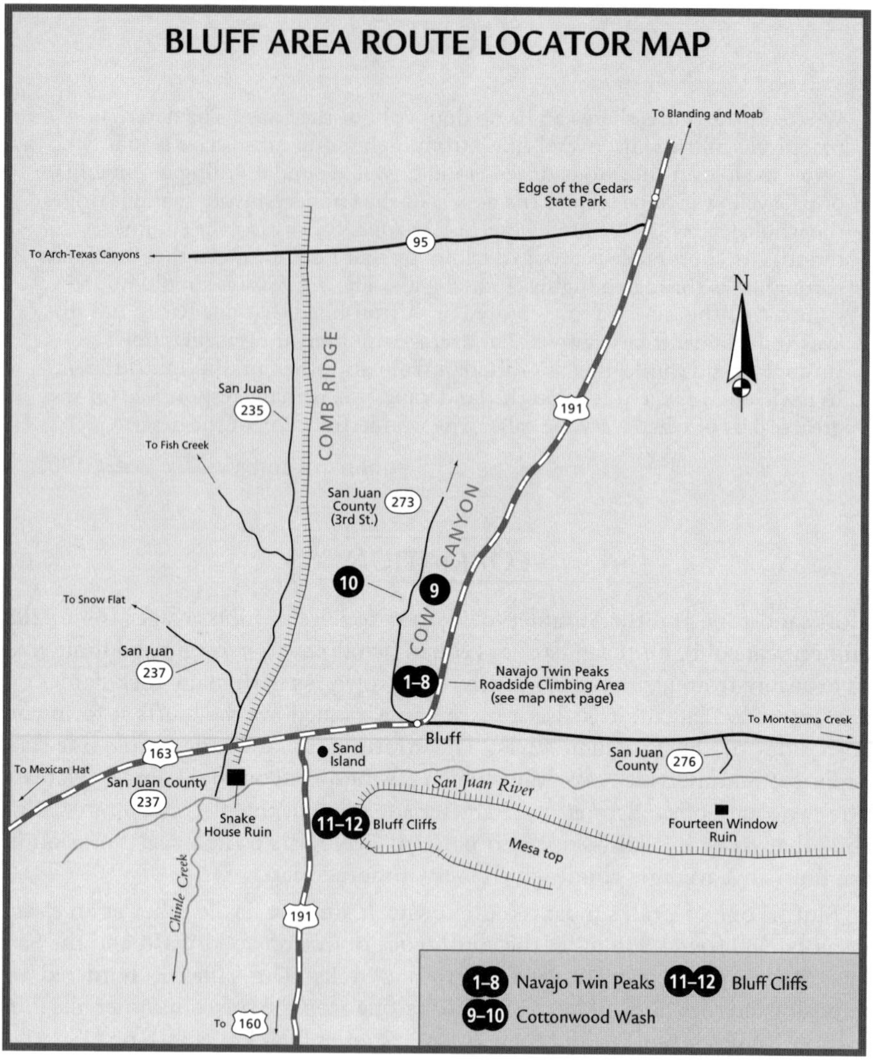

MILE MARKER LOG—MONTICELLO TO BLUFF

This log uses mile marker signs as reference points. To reach Monticello from Moab, see Chapter 12 for the US 191 to Utah 211 Mile Marker Log, which ends 14 miles (22.5 km) north of Monticello.

74–71: Monticello. A sign gives distances to Blanding (21 miles [34 km]) and Bluff (47 miles [75.6 km]).

66–65: Historical marker east of the roadway. On the west side of US 191 is an abandoned two-story Addams family–style gabled home.

61–60: Sign for Devil's Canyon Campground. To reach the campground, turn west and drive 0.6 mile (0.9 km) to the entrance kiosk. Thirty-three sites are located in a thick juniper and piñon pine woodland. There are rest rooms, tables, fire rings, and barbecue stands, but no water or garbage pickup. Day use is $3.00, overnight $8.00, and $4.00 for Golden Age card holders.

56–55: Recapture Recreation Area north of the dam; turn right on San Juan County 215 (Carrol Road), branch left in 0.1 mile (0.16 km), and descend to the lake. There is a camping site with a table and fire ring on the right; other sites are reached over dirt tracks to the left.

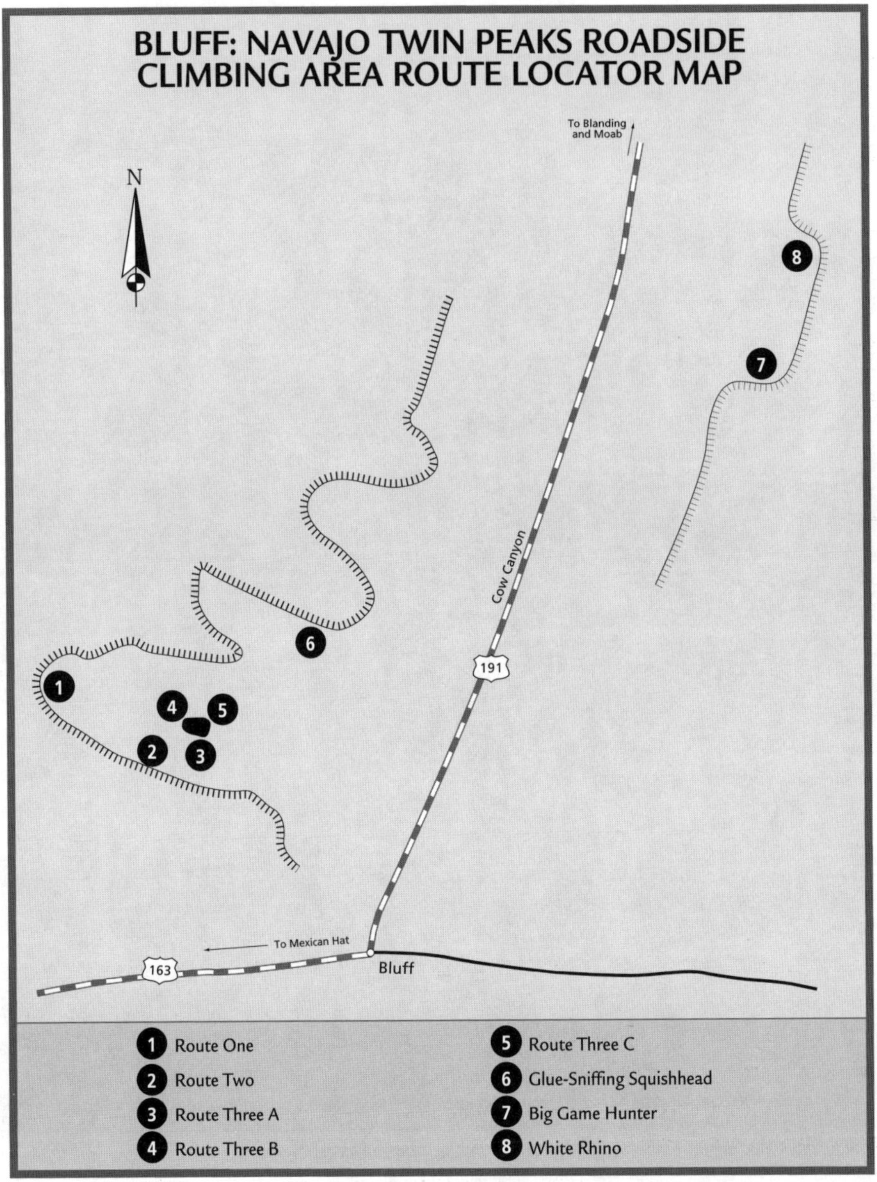

Photo: Leslie Henderson

Mike Baker leading on Million Dollar Baby *in Cottonwood Wash.*

55–54: Recapture Recreation Area west of dam: lake, rest rooms, picnic tables, and camping sites. The area provides boating in the summer and ice skating in the winter.

53–51: Town of Blanding, elevation 6,000 feet (1,829 m), population approximately 3,800. Blanding is home of the Edge of the Cedars State Park and Museum, the site of Puebloan ruins dating from A.D. 825 to 1220. At the museum is the largest display of Ancestral Puebloan (Anasazi) pottery in the four corners area—a worthwhile visit. Four miles (6.4 km) south of Blanding is a sign for Mexican Hat and Bluff. Branching to the right is the Scenic Byway Utah 95 (Bicentennial Highway) to Arch and Texas Canyons, the Bear's Ears, Natural Bridges National Monument, Fry Canyon, and Hite Marina at Lake Powell.

MONTICELLO

Monticello's elevation is 7,069 feet (2,155 m). The town's population is just over 2,500. Natural growth in the Abajos mountains just west of town forms the image of a blaze-faced horse on Horsehead Peak, and is easiest to identify after snow has fallen in late fall or early winter. The Horsehead can be identified through a view pipe in the City Park.

42–41: US 191 crosses the northern border of the Ute Indian Reservation.

38–37: Southern border of the Ute Indian Reservation.

37–36: Utah 262 East begins. Left to Hovenweep and Four-Corners Monument. Directional signs for Montezuma Creek, Aneth, Blanding, Monticello, Bluff, and Mexican Hat.

33–32: Comb Ridge is in view to the west.

28–27: Begin descent into Bluff Valley through Cow Canyon.

MILE MARKER LOG, US 163—BLUFF SOUTH TO MEXICAN HAT

27–26: Enter Bluff and the roadside climbing area. Elevation 4,380 feet (1,335 m), population approximately 300. Directional signs for Aneth, Montezuma Creek, Monument Valley, Navajo Twins, Sunbonnet Peak, Utah 163 East, and US 191-Utah 163. Turn right to Twin Rocks Trading Post and Cafe and an information kiosk for the Bluff Visitor and Business Directory Regional Map.

26–25: Sign for US 163 South and Mexican Hat.

23–22: East turn to rest area. Beginning of San Juan County 275/Sand Island Road. Sign for Sand Island Campground and Boat Launch, and Sand Island petroglyph panel (right branch). The glyphs cover a time span of 800 to 2,500 years. Campsite fee is $6.00 per night, river floaters $3.00. No fee required in winter. There are fire rings, tables, rest rooms, and an information kiosk with a bulletin board.

22–21: Sign for Mexican Hat, Mexican Water, Monument Valley, Utah 163 South, and US 191 South.

39–38: Descend through Comb Ridge. At the bottom of the grade, the dirt trail left (south) is San Juan County 237. A few yards beyond the south branch, San Juan County 235 branches north. There is an information kiosk for the Cedar Mesa Recreation Area.

35–34: Monument Valley towers come into view to the south: King on a Throne, Rabbit-Bear-Stagecoach, Shangri-la, Indian Chief, Eagle Rock Spire/Eagle Mesa.

34–33: Cedar Mesa in view to the west.

31–30: Valley of the Gods in view to the west with Cedar Mesa in the background.

29: Valley of the Gods 17-mile (27 km) loop road begins. Sign: VALLEY OF THE GODS—SAN JUAN COUNTY 242.

26–25: Signs for Lake Powell and Natural Bridges National Monument, Fry Canyon, Hanksville, Mexican Hat, and Goosenecks State Park.

25–24: Signs for Utah 261 North, Utah 163 South, Mexican Hat, and Kayenta.

24–23: Sign for Mexican Hat Rock (dirt trail to the left). The road to Mexican Hat Rock ends on the east shoulder of the hoodoo with a view of the San Juan River and the colorful Raplee Ridge, also known as the Navajo Tapestry.

22–21: Town of Mexican Hat. Elevation 4,244 feet (1,294 m), population approximately 150.

21: Bridge over the San Juan River (built in 1909) and the north border of the Navajo Indian Reservation.

NAVAJO TWIN PEAKS ROADSIDE CLIMBING AREA

Navajo Twin Peaks Roadside Climbing Area is in Cow Canyon, the narrow canyon through which US 191 gives access to Bluff from the north. The area is situated at the north edge of Bluff on the cliffs above US 191 between mile markers 26 and 27. To reach *Routes One, Two,* and *Three,* turn west onto a dirt track just north of the junction of US 191 and Utah 163 East. For northbound travelers, the turn is between a SPEED LIMIT 65 MPH sign and a yellow diamond sign with a serpentine arrow for the upcoming winding highway. The trail ends a few yards up a shallow alcove in view from the highway. *Route One* is at the far left end of the alcove. *Route Two* is at the left end of the buttress from *Route One* (toward the highway). *Routes Three A, B,* and *C* ascend three problems up a 50-foot (15 m)-high boulder obvious in the area. *Glue Sniffing Squishhead* climbs an improbable chimney a few yards farther up the highway on the west buttress. It is nearest US 191 at the right side of a shallow recess in the buttress. *Big Game Hunter* and *White Rhino* are farther up the highway on the east buttress, above a REDUCE SPEED AHEAD sign for southbound travelers. *Big Game Hunter* and *White Rhino* were named by the second ascent party.

1 ROUTE ONE
I, 5.11c, 1 pitch, 60 feet (18 m)

First Ascent: Mike Friedrichs, Jay Anderson, Manuel Rangel, Jean Rousch, October 1990.

Location and Access: *Route One* climbs a left-arching thin hands underclinging arch. Two drilled rappel anchors are visible behind a horn just below the top of the cliff.

Paraphernalia: Friends #2s.

Descent: Rappel the route.

2 ROUTE TWO
I, 5.10a, 1 pitch, 60 feet (18 m)

First Ascent: Manuel Rangel, et al., October 1990.

Location and Access: *Route Two* climbs a chimney with no fixed anchors.

Paraphernalia: Wide units.

Descent: Rappel the route.

3 ROUTE THREE A
I, 5.10, 1 pitch, 50 feet (15 m)

First Ascent: Unknown.

Location and Access: The problem ascends, with stacked hands, an off-width on the south side of a boulder.

Paraphernalia: None required, but an upper belay may be given from a rope thrown over the boulder from its north side.

Descent: Fix a rope on the boulder's north side and rappel the route.

4 ROUTE THREE B
I, 5.10, 1 pitch, 50 feet (15 m)

First Ascent: Unknown.

Location and Access: Climb the off-width on the north side of the boulder.

Paraphernalia: Same as *Route Three A*.

Descent: Same as *Route Three A*.

5 ROUTE THREE C
I, 5.11, 1 pitch, 50 feet (15 m)

First Ascent: Unknown.

Location and Access: *Route Three C* no longer exists. The route climbed the boulder up a fingers crack right of *Route Three A*. The mass of rubble on the east side of the boulder is all that remains of the route.

6 GLUE-SNIFFING SQUISHHEAD
I, 5.12a, 1 pitch, 40 feet (12 m)

First Ascent: Jay Anderson, Mike Friedrichs, October 1990.

Location and Access: The route ascends a buttress close to the road. Climb a

5.12a roof identified by a rope groove in the rock, and as the farthest left crack featuring a 5-inch (12.7 cm) fracture up very soft rock.

Paraphernalia: Medium to large units.

Descent: Rappel the route.

7 BIG GAME HUNTER
I, 5.11a, 1 pitch, 70 feet (21 m) ★★

First Ascent: Jay Anderson, Mike Friedrichs, Manuel Rangel, October 1990. Second Ascent: Mike Baker, Leslie Henderson, May 1997.

Location and Access: The route is right of *White Rhino*. Climb an off-width corner on the east side of the road. Begin up a left-facing dihedral. Pass a roof on its left (5.11a crux), then continue up a 5.10+ lieback. Angle right and follow a 5.9 crack, then lieback to a 5.10 off-width, and end with a squeeze to the top.

Paraphernalia: Camalots (2) #1, #2, #3, (3) #4, (1) #4.5, #5.

Descent: There are no anchors on top. Walk off to the left or rappel *White Rhino*.

8 WHITE RHINO
I, 5.10, 1 pitch, 70 feet (21 m) ★★★★

First Ascent: Mike Friedrichs et al., October 1990. Second Ascent: Mike Baker, Leslie Henderson, May 1997.

Location and Access: The route is on the left side of the east buttress. Begin up the "White Horn" (crux), then climb a right-facing dihedral 5.10 to 5.9, finishing with 5.10.

Paraphernalia: Camalots (3) #2, (2) #3, (1) #4.

Descent: Rappel the route from triple anchors or walk off to the left.

COTTONWOOD WASH

Cottonwood Wash extends north from Bluff Valley. Turn right from US 191 between mile markers 24 and 25 onto San Juan County Road 273 (Third Street West). One mile (1.6 km) from US 191, an illegally locked gate crosses the county road. The *Bant* is the small tower approximately 1 mile (1.6 km) farther along the cliffs to the right of the dirt trail (San Juan County 273). *Million Dollar Baby* is on the left wall of the valley.

9 THE BANT
I, 5.9+, 1 pitch, 75 feet (23 m) ★★★★★

First Ascent: Unknown, 5.8, C1. First Free Ascent and Fourth Overall Ascent: Mike Baker, Leslie Henderson, May 1997.

Location and Access: *The Bant* is climbed by its southeast corner. Begin up a left-facing corner with 5.9+ stemming, which leads to 5.9 liebacking. Continue 5.8

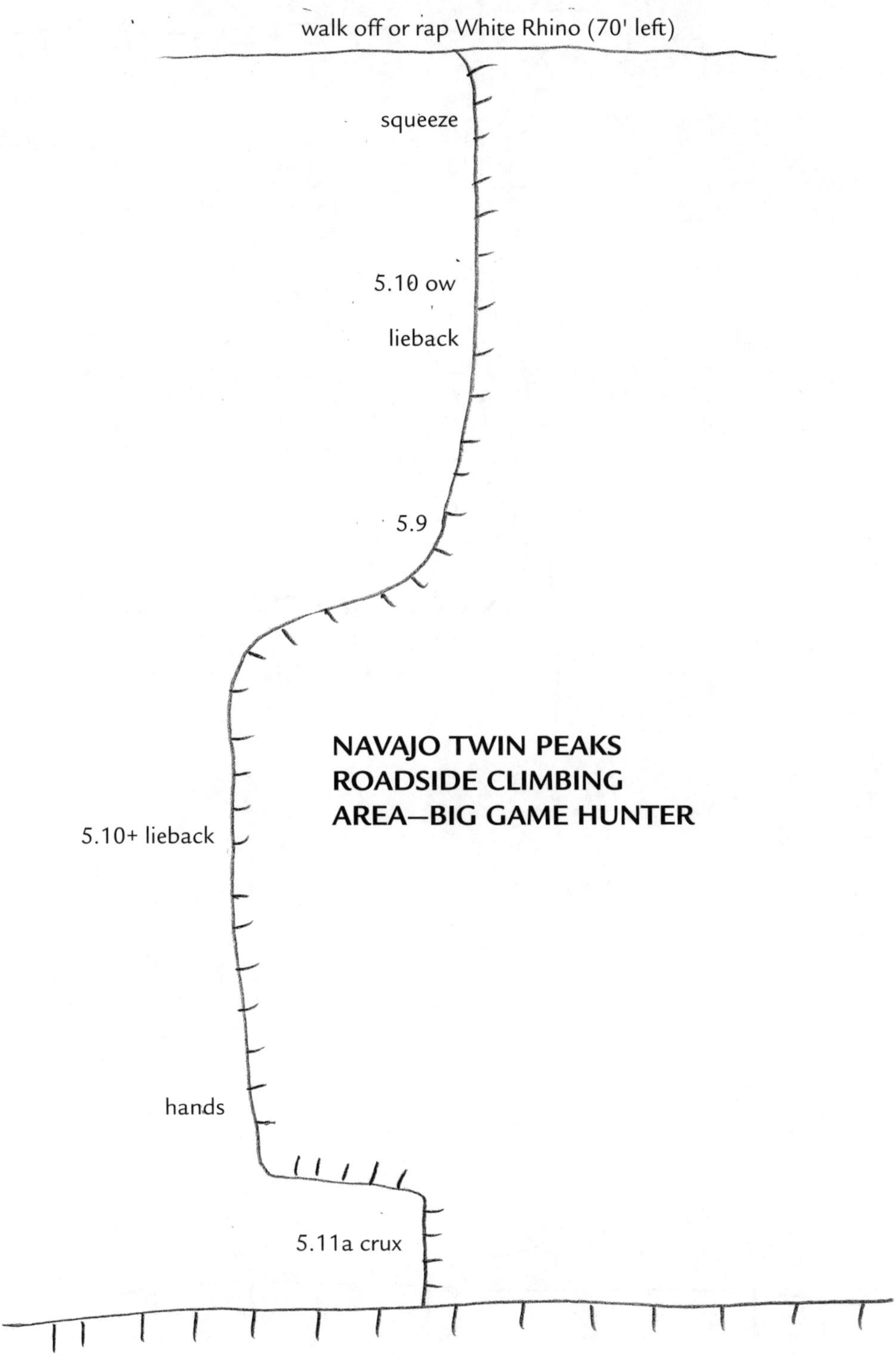

NAVAJO TWIN PEAKS ROADSIDE CLIMBING AREA—BIG GAME HUNTER

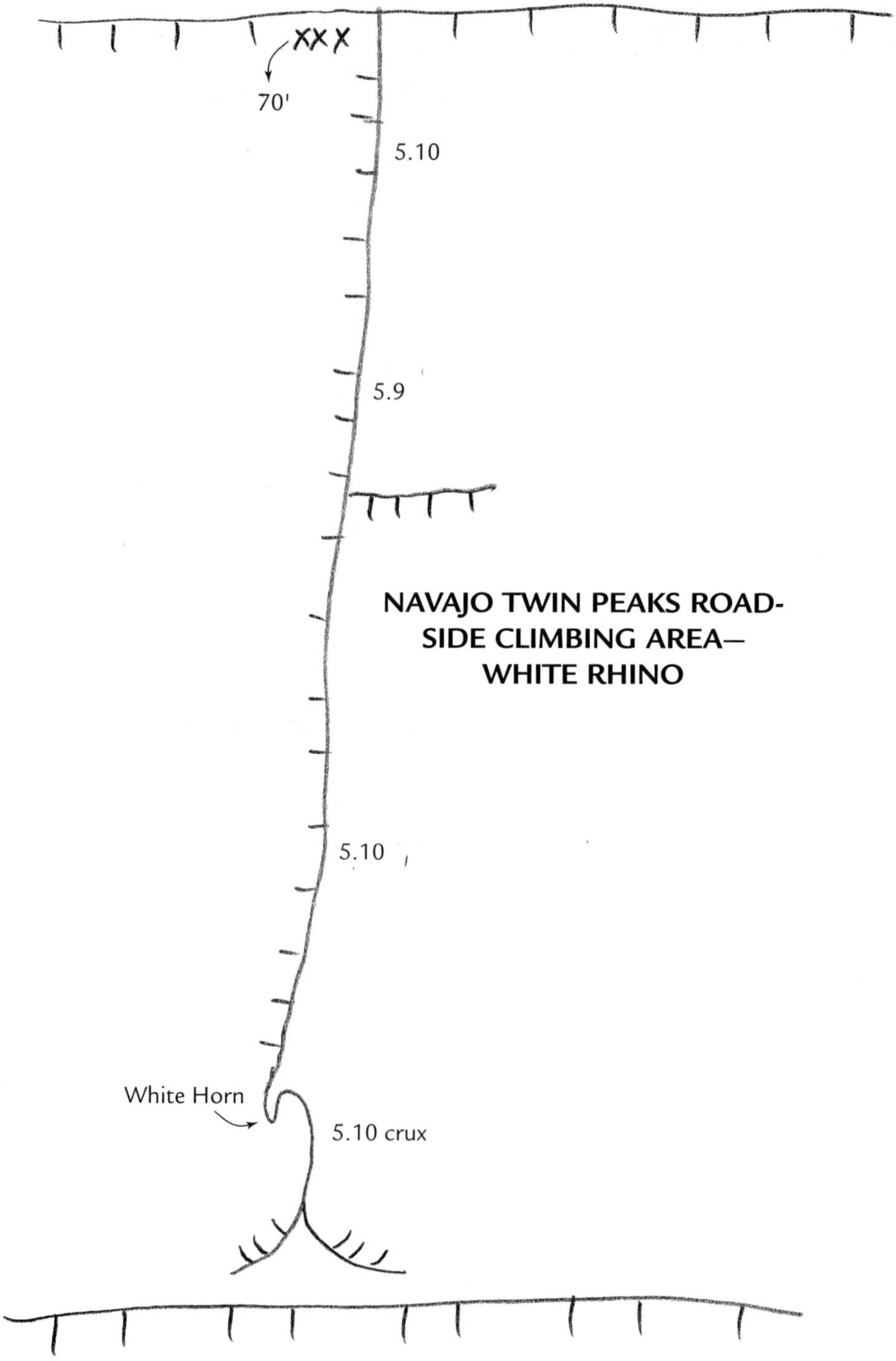

NAVAJO TWIN PEAKS ROAD-SIDE CLIMBING AREA— WHITE RHINO

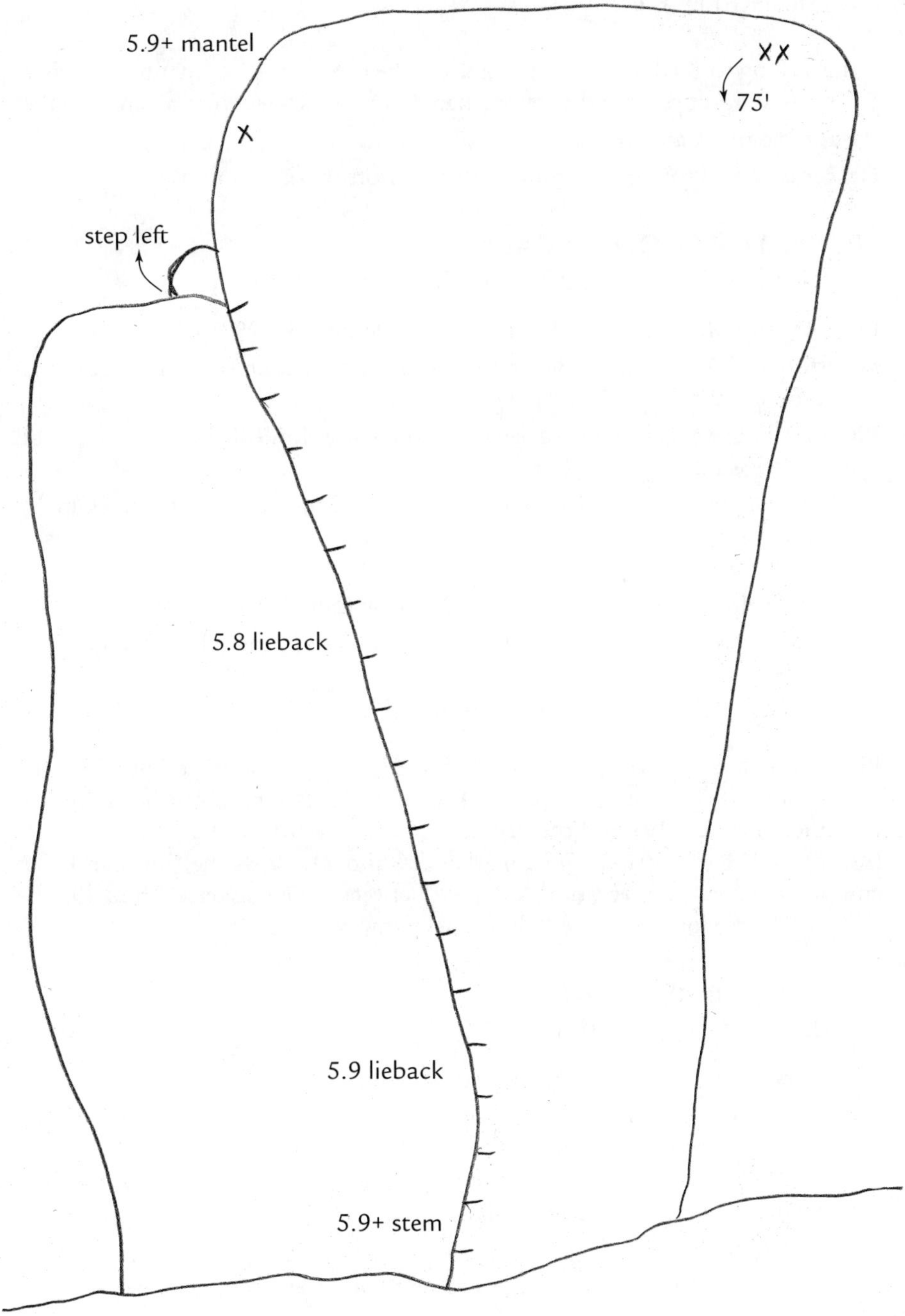

COTTONWOOD WASH—THE BANT

liebacking to a ledge. Step left and reach the top with a 5.9+ mantel. A register on the summit records the tower's name by an unknown first ascent party.

Paraphernalia: Camalots (1) #1, #2, #3; TCUs (2) each.

Descent: Rappel to the east from double anchors on the summit.

10 MILLION DOLLAR BABY
II, 5.9-, 2 pitches, 200 feet (60 m) ★★★★★

First Ascent: Mike Baker, Leslie Henderson, October 3, 1997.

Location and Access: Mike Baker: "The start of this climb is behind a beautiful 200-foot pinnacle on the main wall."

Pitch 1: Climb a 5.5 chimney 20 feet (6 m), then face climb 20 feet (6 m) to a good belay ledge, 5.6, 40 feet (12 m).

Pitch 2: The Amazing Hands Splitter pitch. Continue up a splitter crack (5.9-), beginning with fingers and going to fists. The pitch is 5.8 with two short sections of 5.9-, 160 feet (49 m).

Paraphernalia: Friends (2) #1, (3) #2, #3, (1) #4; Camalots (1) #0.75.

Descent: Rappel to the top of pitch 1, then double-rope rappel to the right.

BLUFF CLIFFS

Bluff Cliffs are an escarpment of Bluff sandstone just south of Bluff on the southeast side of the San Juan River. Drive 4.1 miles (6.6 km) west from Bluff to the junction of US 191 and the beginning of Scenic Byway Utah 163. Turn left (south) on US 191 between mile markers 20 and 21. Cross the San Juan River, entering the Navajo reservation, and park between mile markers 18 and 19. The cliffs will be obvious on the left above the highway.

11 BLUFF CLIFFS ONE
I, 5.9, 1 pitch, 100 feet (30 m)

First Ascent: Brian Povolny, Todd Gordon, January 1983.

Location and Access: *Bluff Cliffs One* is three cracks left of the right edge of the buttress. The route begins up a groove and climbs to a short 5.9 body chimney. Continue past a loose section, then up a hands/lieback on the right side of a flake to rappel anchors atop a pillar.

Paraphernalia: Friends (1) set.

Descent: Rappel the route from a drilled angle and fixed wired stopper.

12 CROW'S FEAT
I, 5.11, 1 pitch, 140 feet (43 m)

First Ascent: Bret Ruckman, Tim Coats, April 1989.

Location and Access: The route is four crack systems left of the right edge of

COTTONWOOD WASH—MILLION DOLLAR BABY

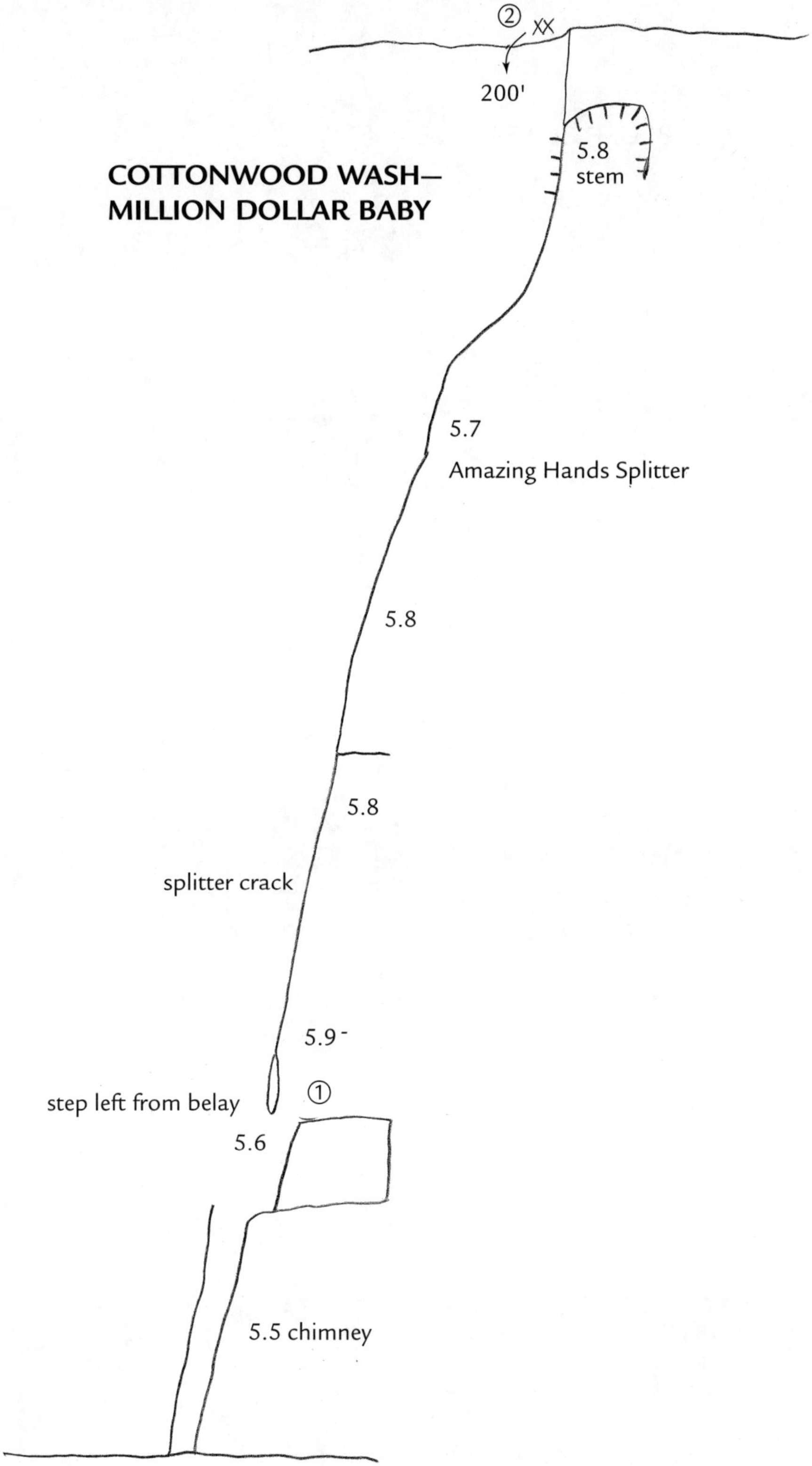

BLUFF CLIFFS ONE

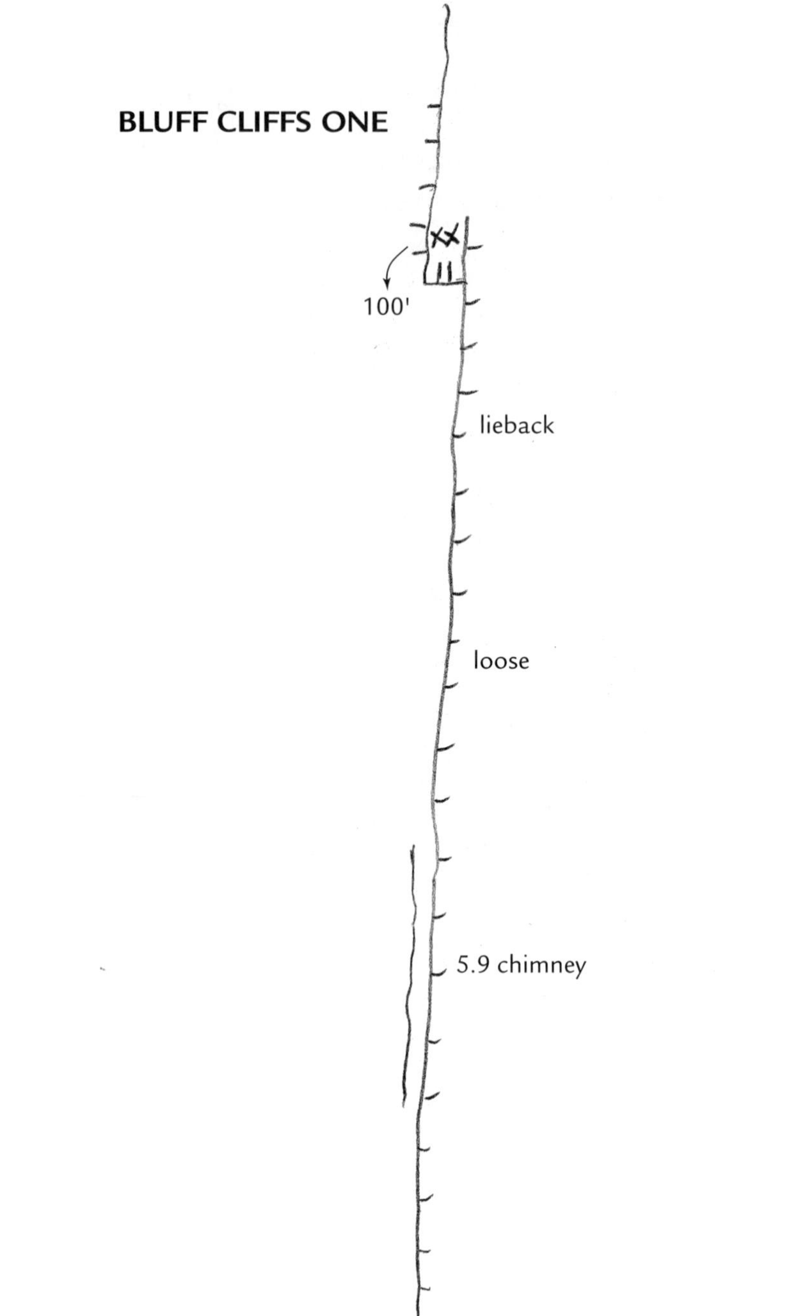

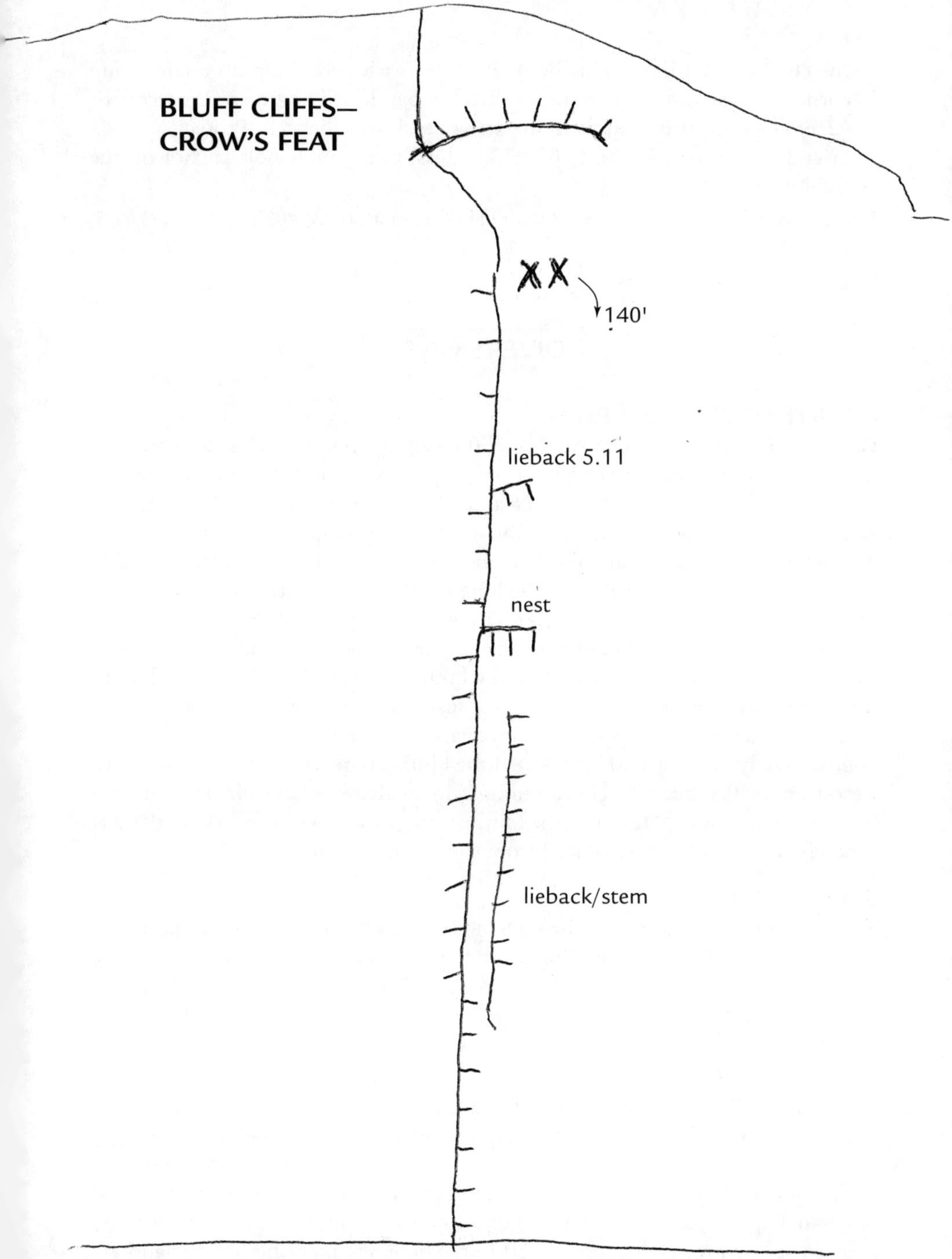
BLUFF CLIFFS—
CROW'S FEAT
140'
lieback 5.11
nest
lieback/stem

the cliff, above a large talus boulder. Begin with liebacking up a left-facing corner, then stemming to a stance with an abandoned nest on it. Protect with #2 Friends. Continue up a right-facing crack to a lieback. Protect with #2 Friends, then stem (#1 and #0.75 Camalots) to a double-bolt anchor on the right wall.

Paraphernalia: Friends, many #2 with (1) #4; Camalots (3) #0.75, (4) #1, (2) #1.5, #2.5, (1) #4.

Descent: Rappel the route.

DIVERSIONS

FOURTEEN WINDOW RUIN

Fourteen Window Ruin is an Anasazi cliff dwelling on the south side of the San Juan River. From Bluff, drive to the north end of town on US 191 and turn east on Utah 163 between mile markers 26 and 27 at a sign for Montezuma Creek and Aneth. At 1.7 miles (2.7 km) St. Christopher's Episcopal Mission is reached between mile markers 43 and 44. The mission was founded by Father Harold B. Liebler, known as the "priest with the long hair." Continue straight. At 2.1 miles (3.3 km) cross a cattle guard. At 2.9 miles (4.6 km) turn right on a dirt trail (San Juan County Road 276) between mile markers 44 and 45. In 0.5 mile (0.8 km) there is a Y in the trail. Take the most used track (right fork) 0.4 mile (0.6 km) to the trail's end at a picturesque hanging suspension footbridge across the San Juan River. Across the bridge follow dirt paths winding in a southeast direction approximately 0.5 mile (0.8 km). When the bluffs are reached, follow a dirt path west 0.5 mile (0.8 km). The cliff dwelling is in an alcove on the left. The ruin can be viewed with binoculars from the bluff north of the river by following the dirt fork left at the Y, 0.5 mile (0.8 km) from the south turn on Utah 163.

SAND ISLAND

Three miles (4.8 km) south of Bluff is Sand Island, a BLM-managed campground, and the principal boat launch for those floating the San Juan River. From the Sand Island junction, the road forks south to Sik-Is Bridge (Bridge of Friendship). Between the campground and the bridge, on a low bluff beside the river, is a large panel of petroglyphs with the famed kokopelli, the humpbacked flute player of ancient Pueblo mythology.

At Sand Island there are signs of beavers and tracks of raccoons and ringtailed cats. The Colorado squawfish, an endangered minnow species that weighs up to eighty pounds, is found in the river, along with catfish and the humpbacked sucker. In groves of cottonwood and tamarisk are mule deer, ring-necked pheasants, quail, partridges, wild turkeys, and porcupines. The canyon tree frog and red-spotted toad also make their home here. Frequenting Sand Island are bald and golden eagles, flickers, shrikes, finches, tanagers, and peregrine falcons, as well as the snowy egret, blue heron, black-crowned night heron, blue grosbeak, and mountain bluebird. On the bluffs above the river are cougars, desert bighorn sheep, and bobcats.

EDGE OF THE CEDARS STATE PARK

Edge of the Cedars was added to the National Register of Historic Places in 1971 and is worth a stop. The park, located on the site of an ancient Anasazi ruin that was occupied from A.D. 700 to 1300, has a self-guided trail through a ceremonial and living complex, and provides an excellent museum and Indian craft shop. The trail passes by a "great kiva," built for the whole community, as opposed to smaller kivas designed for single families, and is the northernmost of its type in Utah. Among the displays is a good collection of Anasazi pottery, and information about prehistoric sites on nearby Cedar Mesa is available.

To reach the park, drive to 660 West and 400 North at the northwest edge of Blanding. For further information contact the Superintendent, Edge of the Cedars State Park, Box 788, Blanding, UT 84511-0788.

> Occasionally one meets with a little stream where a fissure in the rock and a pressure from below forces up some of the water; but these springs are of very rare occurrence. And they always seem a little strange. A brook that ran on top of the ground would be an anomaly here; and after one lives many months on the desert and returns to a well-watered country, the last thing he becomes accustomed to is the sight of running water.
>
> —John C. Van Dyke, *The Desert,* 1901

21
COMB RIDGE

> The dark thunder-clouds that occasionally gather over the desert seem at times to reserve all their stores of rain for one place. The fall is usually short-lived but violent; and its greatest force is always on the mountains. There is no sod, no moss, to check or retard the flood; and the result is a great rush of water to the low places. In the canyons the swollen streams roll down boulders that weigh tons, and in the ravines many a huge barranca is formed in a single hour by these rushing waters.
>
> —John C. Van Dyke, *The Desert,* 1901

Comb Ridge is a dramatic, jagged wall stretching approximately 100 miles (161 km) from the southwest slopes of the Abajo Mountains (a.k.a. The Blues) south into Kayenta and the Monument Valley region of Arizona. It is a remote area rich in cultural history, including Anasazi petroglyph panels and cliff dwellings.

FORMATION

Comb Ridge is a narrow monoclinal uplift that gently slopes on the east. On its western escarpment, cliff faces plunge more than 800 feet (244 m) to Comb Wash. The sharp-toothed ridge is weathered from late Triassic Wingate sandstone 144 to 208 million years old. It is named for its resemblance to the comb of a rooster. In many respects, the ridge is similar to Capitol Reef's Waterpocket Fold and the San Rafael Reef.

Photo: Mike Baker

Comb Ridge.

HISTORY

In 1923 the West's last shoot-out between settlers and Indians took place in the Comb Ridge area. For dozens of years, conflicts between Ute Indians and ranchers festered as the white man took the Indian's land and the Indians took the white man's livestock. The shoot-out resulted in the surrender of the Ute tribe and drew national attention to their plight. Subsequently, the tribe was allotted White Mesa Indian Resevation, 12 miles (19 km) south of Blanding, puny compensation for what they lost. Comb Ridge was a formidable barrier to the 1879–80 San Juan Mormon Mission attempting to reach and settle the area of present-day Bluff on the San Juan River. They camped for four months while expedition members widened a narrow cleft so wagons, horses, and livestock could be lowered a quarter mile to the Colorado River. Today it is a registered historic landmark called Hole-in-the-Rock.

COMB RIDGE

San Juan County Road 235 is a good two-wheel-drive, low-clearance dirt trail extending approximately 18.8 miles (30 km) north/south between Utah 95 and US 163. Numerous Anasazi routes (Moki steps) reach the top of Comb Ridge. Seven contemporary climbing routes have also been established up the west-facing Wingate buttress.

From US 191 at Bluff, 100 miles (161 km) south of Moab, drive 4 miles (6.4 km) south of town and continue on US 163 (US 191 takes a sharp left turn to the east). At approximately 8 miles (13 km), Comb Ridge is obvious to the right. At 8.5 miles (13.6 km) turn north (right) onto San Juan County 235 (between mile markers 37 and 38). There is an information kiosk on the right.

MILEAGE LOG—SAN JUAN COUNTY ROAD 235 (US 163 NORTH TO UTAH 95)

This log may be useful in locating the climbing routes along Comb Ridge.

00 miles: Junction of US 163 and San Juan County Road 235; information kiosk.

0.5 mile (0.8 km): Park just beyond the wash crossing for the approach to *Sunshine Kids.*

2.3 miles (3.7 km): Fork in road. Left fork (San Juan County Road 237) goes to Snow Flat; keep right on San Juan County Road 235. Prayer Stick is obvious ahead and right.

2.6 miles (4.2 km): Cross wash and park on the right for approach to Prayer Stick.

3.7 miles (6 km): Bovine water pond on the right.

3.8 miles (6.1 km): Purple slopes on the right at the lower Chinle Formation contain petrified wood. Faint two-track branches right to the area.

5.4 miles (8.6 km): Cattle guard.

7.0 miles (11.2 km): *Vendetta* is above on the right.

7.8 miles (12.5 km): Cowboy line camp shack on the left.

8.4 miles (13.5 km): Boulder Camp; many petroglyphs on the boulders.

9.1 miles (14.6 km): Left branch goes to Fish Creek. Information kiosk; sign: FEE AREA.

9.5 miles (15.3 km): Ski Track Road. The name comes from the serpentine track, which looks like a slalom course.

10.3 miles (16.5 km): Spur track to boulders with petroglyphs. Camping and approach for *La Bonita* above and left of the parking area.

12.4 miles (20 km): Spur to the left goes to good Cottonwood Camp.

13.5 miles (21.7 km): *Positive Mental Attitude* and *Sweet Emotion* high on the right. Moki steps.

14.3 miles (23 km): Fence with wire gate. Please leave it closed for cattle control.

15.3 miles (24.6 km): Cross dry creek bed.

17.1 miles (27.5 km): Cross dry creek bed.

18.0 miles (29 km): Cross dry creek bed.

18.6 miles (29.9 km): Information kiosk and camping area, cattle guard, Utah 95. Left (west) to Natural Bridges National Monument, right (east) to Blanding.

SUNSHINE KIDS

Approach *Sunshine Kids* from San Juan County Road 235, reached between mile markers 37 and 38 on US 163. At 0.5 mile (0.8 km) up the county road, park just after crossing a wash, then hike up the drainage to the climb.

1 SUNSHINE KIDS I, 5.5, 1 pitch, 165 feet (50 m) ★★

First Ascent: Mike Baker, Leslie Henderson, November 1997.

Location and Access: Climb a right-facing dihedral 5.4, then 5.5 to a ledge. The corner above is rotten so move right to the face. Pass a bolt and face climb at 5.5, then pass a 0.5-inch (1.2 cm) crack to double anchors at the summit. Mike Baker: "Good beginner lead, good gear placements, although the approach may be harder than the climb."

Paraphernalia: Camalots (1) each through #3; quick draws (1).

Descent: Rappel 165 feet (50 m) from two drilled summit anchors.

PRAYER STICK

Prayer Stick is a pillar leaning against the Wingate buttress behind it. From US 163, turn north onto San Juan County Road 235 between mile markers 37 and

Photo: Leslie Henderson

Sunshine Kids.

COMB RIDGE—SUNSHINE KIDS

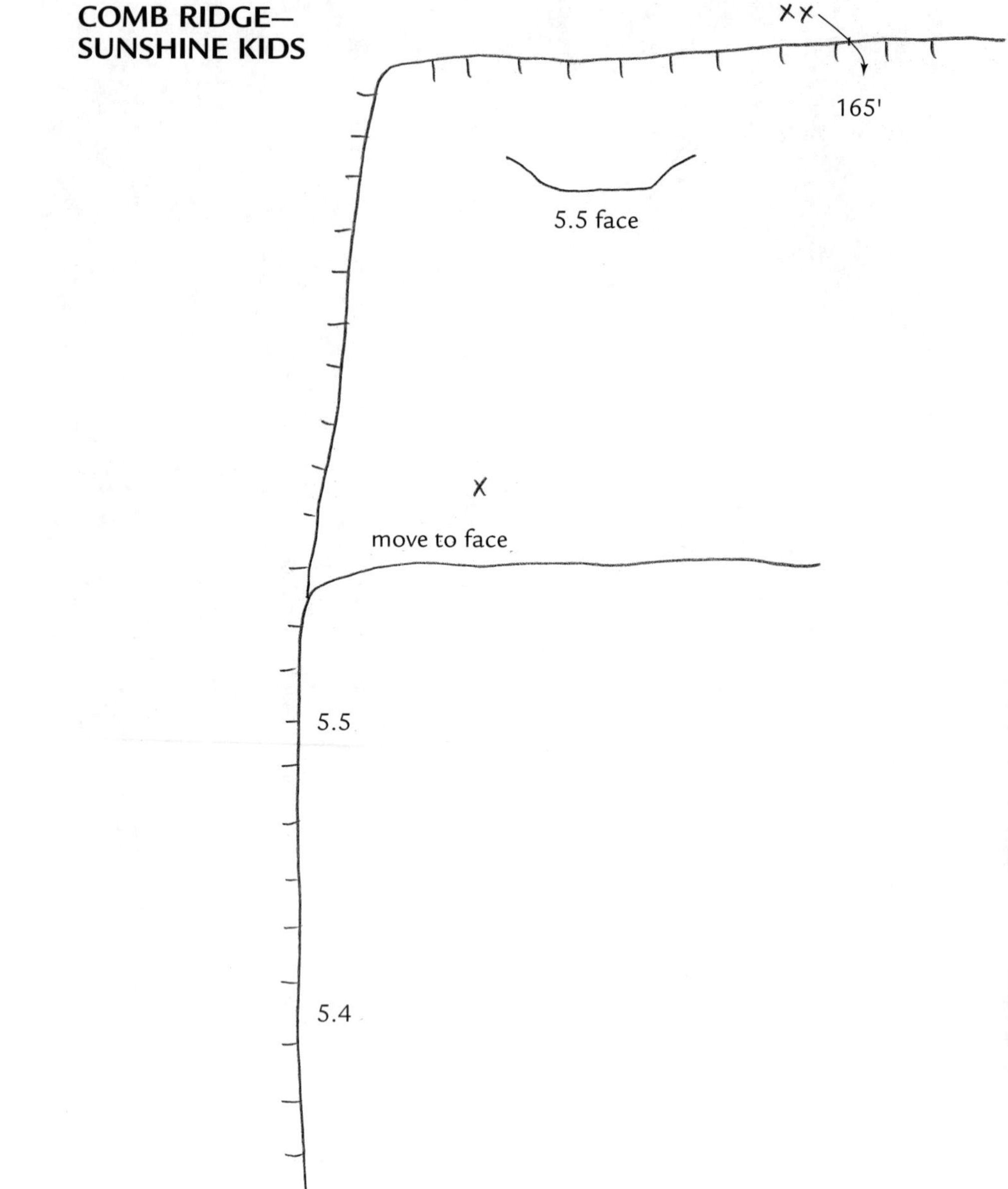

38. Drive 2.7 miles (4.3 km) and park in the field on the right just after crossing a wash. The hike up the wash to the talus below Prayer Stick takes about thirty minutes. Magic Man ascends the right side of the pillar.

2 MAGIC MAN (a.k.a. Dreaming Man) III, 5.10+, 5 pitches, 240 feet (73 m) ★★★★

First Ascent: Mike Baker, Leslie Henderson, March 1997. First Free Ascent: Mike Baker, Chris Ducker, April 1997.

Location and Access: The route climbs the right side of the pillar. The first ascent used five points of aid and 5.10+ free climbing. The second ascent climbed the route free after the bolts were in from the first ascent. A register was left on the first ascent.

Pitch 1: Begin up a loose right-facing corner to a double-bolt belay ledge, 5.7, 30 feet (9 m).

Pitch 2: Lieback at 5.10, then 5.10+, passing two bolts to a natural belay at a stance (no fixed anchors), 5.10+, 100 feet (30 m).

Pitch 3: Continue up the right-facing corner, passing a bolt (5.9) and a 5.8 roof on its right side, then pass a second bolt. Make a natural belay at a cave (no fixed anchors), 5.9, 50 feet (15 m).

Pitch 4: Continue up the corner system at 5.8, angling up and left at the top to double bolts, 5.8, 35 feet (10.6 m).

Pitch 5: Scramble to the summit, fourth class, 25 feet (7.6 m).

Paraphernalia: Camalots (1) #1, #2, (3) #3, (1) #3.5, (3) #4, (1) #4.5; stoppers (1) set; Aliens (1) set.

Descent: Downclimb to the top of pitch 4, then rappel the route with double ropes.

3 PERSONAL REALITY (a.k.a. The Dark Side) I, 5.9, 3 pitches, 240 feet (73 m) ★★

First Ascent: Mike Baker, solo, September 23, 1998.

Location and Access: The route climbs the left side of Prayer Stick. Approach as for *Magic Man*. Mike Baker: "This climb is on the north side/corner and stays shady most of the day."

Pitch 1: Begin 5.7 up loose rock to a stance, then move left around a flake after a bolt is reached. Continue 5.9 fingers, then 5.9 lieback, and belay at double anchors in a cave.

Pitch 2: Climb a 5.9 squeeze to double anchors at the shoulder of Prayer Stick.

Pitch 3: Scramble third class to the summit.

Paraphernalia: TCUs through #4; Camalots (2) #1, #2, #3. No pitons needed.

Descent: Rappel *Magic Man* (right side of Prayer Stick) or make two double-rope rappels down the route.

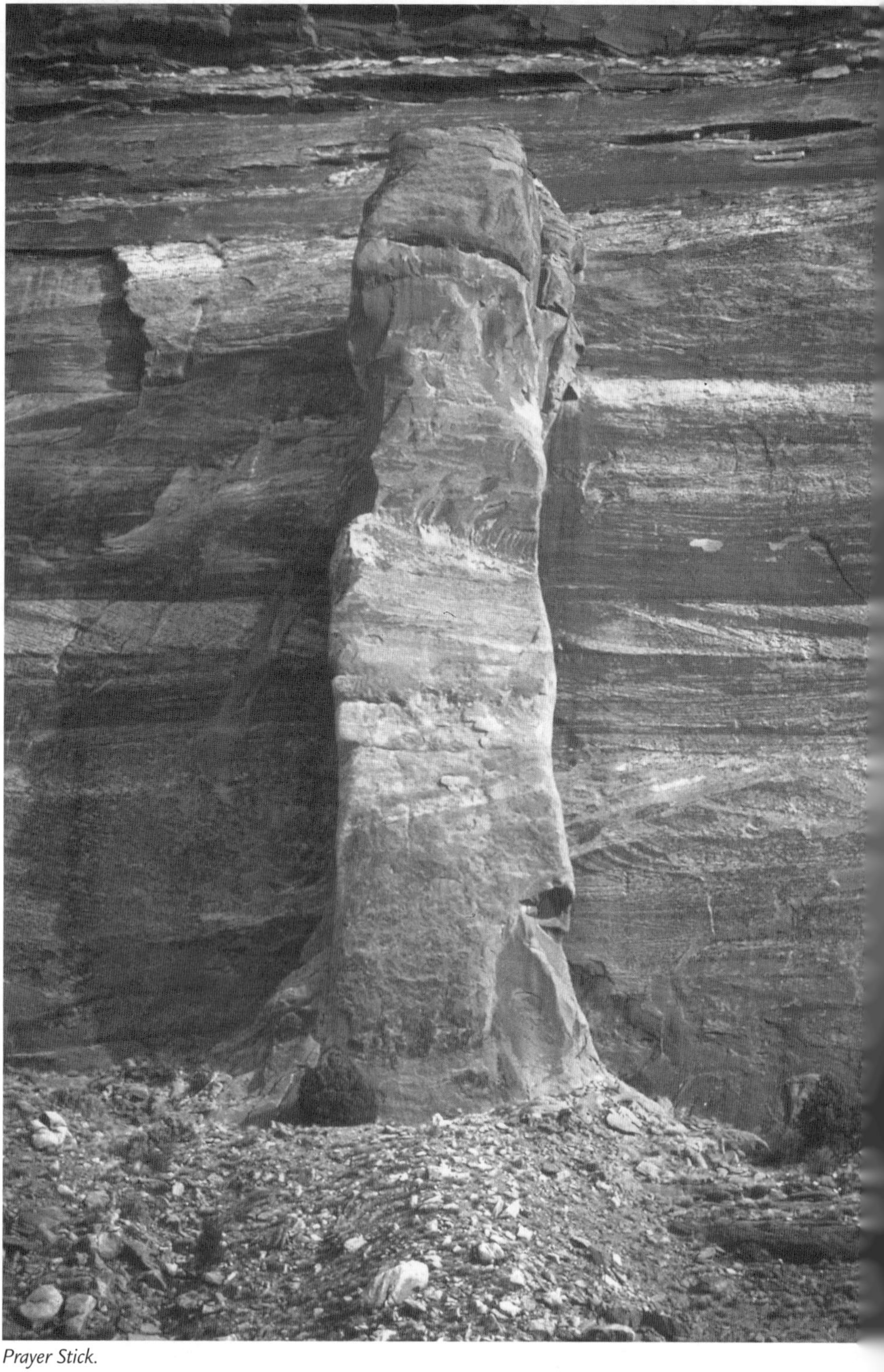

Photo: Cameron M. Burns

Prayer Stick.

PRAYER STICK—MAGIC MAN

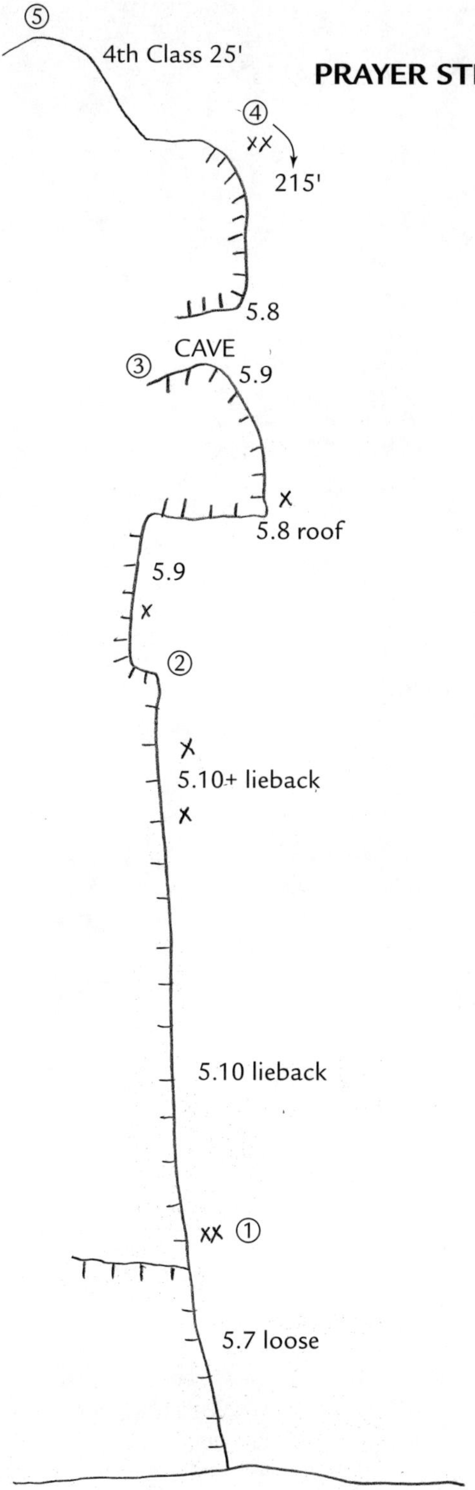

PRAYER STICK—PERSONAL REALITY

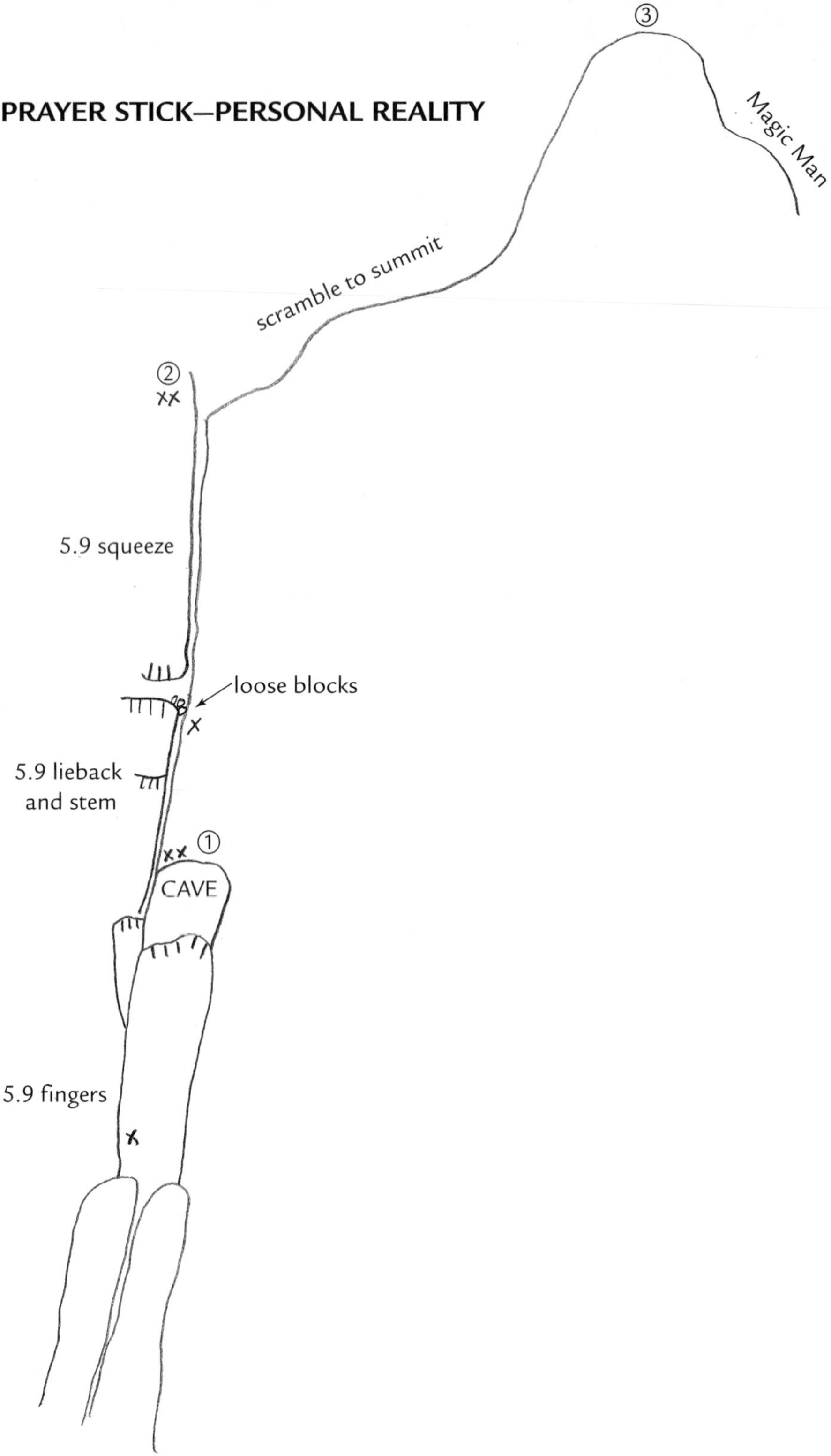

VENDETTA

Drive 7 miles (11 km) up San Juan County 235 from US 163. *Vendetta* climbs the left-facing dihedral obvious above on Comb Ridge. The left-facing dihedral is the second and third pitches of the route.

4 VENDETTA
II, 5.9+, 3 pitches, 210 feet (64 m) ★★★

First Ascent: Pitches 1–2: Mike Baker, Leslie Henderson, October 1996. Pitch 3: Mike Baker, Chris Ducker, April 1997.

Location and Access: While Mike Baker led pitch 2, a rock was dislodged, hitting Leslie Henderson in the eye. Baker returned with Chris Ducker to carry out a vendetta, thus the name.

Pitch 1: Begin up a 5.5 ramp to a belay ledge with triple anchors, 5.5, 60 feet (18 m).

Pitch 2: Climb a thin crack into 5.9+ lieback and fingers to a double-anchor belay ledge 150 feet (46 m) above the ground, 5.9+, 90 feet (27 m).

Pitch 3: Lieback 5.9 to a ledge to soft rock and double anchors, 5.9, 60 feet (18 m). Because of soft rock the route does not reach the top of the buttress.

Paraphernalia: Camalots (1) #1, #2, #3, #4; TCUs (2) each; stoppers (1) set.

Descent: From the high belay, make a 60-foot (18 m) rappel to the top of pitch 2, then a 150-foot (46 m) rappel to the ground.

LA BONITA

A short spur track to the right reaches the campsite and approach for La Bonita at 10.3 mile (16.5 km) up San Juan County 235 from US 163. The route ascends the right-facing corner obvious above on Comb Ridge.

5 LA BONITA
I, 5.8, 1 pitch, 75 feet (23 m) ★★★★

First Ascent: Mike Baker, Leslie Henderson, Chris Ducker, April 1997.

Location and Access: *La Bonita* means "the beautiful" or "little beauty." Climb a right-facing corner first with a 5.8 lieback, then lieback an off-width section to double anchors on the right wall.

Paraphernalia: Camalots (3) #3, #4, (1) #4.5 or #5.

Descent: Single-rope rappel the route.

VENDETTA

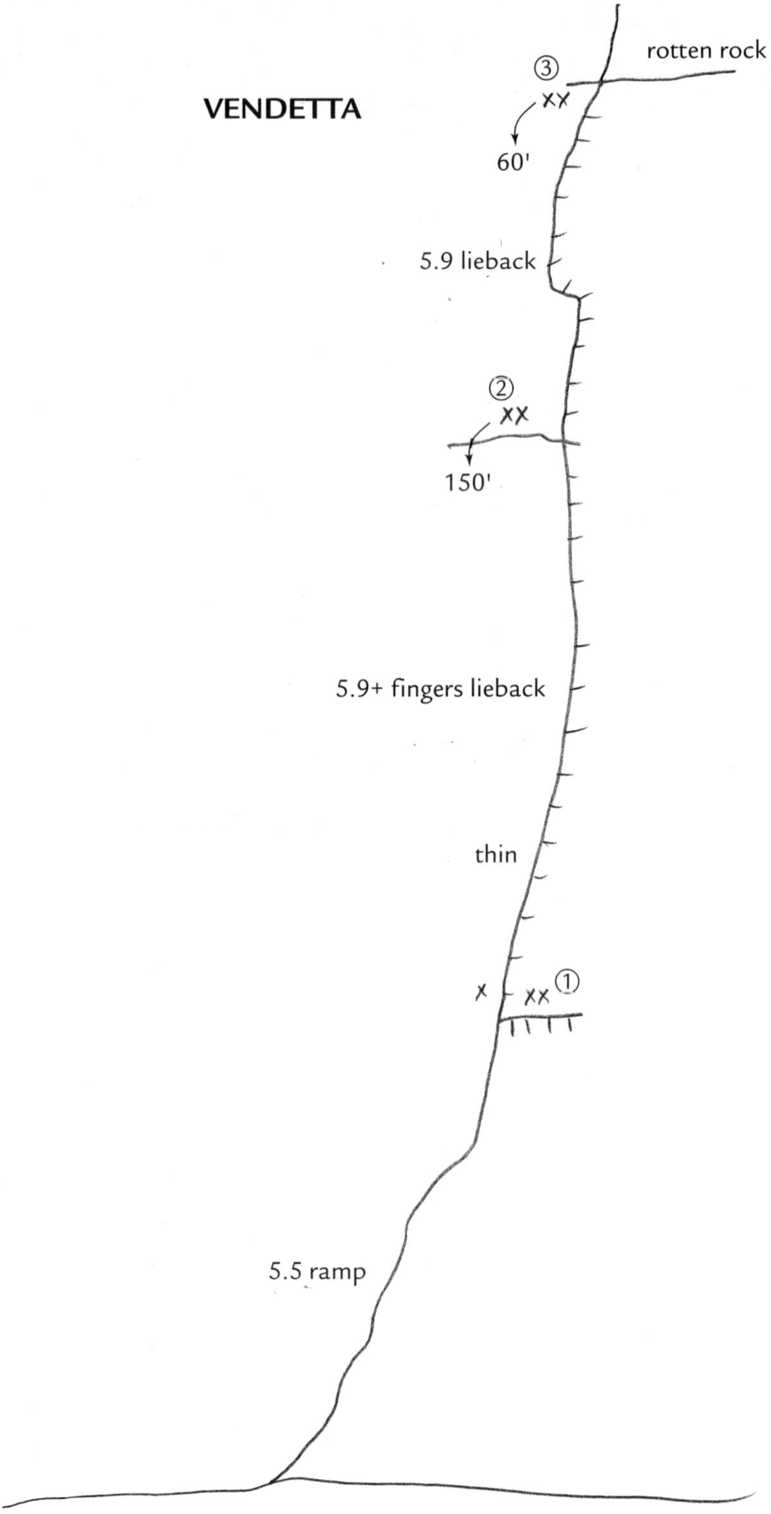
rotten rock
③
XX
60'
5.9 lieback
②
XX
150'
5.9+ fingers lieback
thin
X
XX ①
5.5 ramp

Photo: Cameron M. Burns

Mike Baker on La Bonita.

SWEET EMOTION AND POSITIVE MENTAL ATTITUDE

These two routes are reached 13.5 miles (22 km) up San Juan County Road 235. Mike Baker: "Left of *Positive Mental Attitude* are awesome Moki steps."

6 SWEET EMOTION
II, 5.9 R, 2 pitches, 180 feet (55 m) ★★

First Ascent: Mike Baker, Wilson Goodrich, October 11, 1997.

Location and Access: *Sweet Emotion* is approximately 60 feet (18 m) or one crack right of *Positive Mental Attitude.*

Pitch 1: Climb a left-facing dihedral beginning 5.7, then 5.8 past an 8-inch (20 cm) roof. Continue 5.9- past a fixed piton, then 5.8 to 5.6 R, ending on a belay ledge, 5.9, 150 feet (46 m).

Pitch 2: Continue to the top, 5.2, 30 feet (9 m).

Paraphernalia: Camalots (1) set; TCUs through #4.

Descent: Walk approximately 60 feet (18 m) left to rappel anchors for *Positive Mental Attitude* and make one double-rope rappel.

7 POSITIVE MENTAL ATTITUDE (a.k.a. PMA)
I, 5.6, 1 pitch, 150 feet (46 m) ★★★★★

First Ascent: Leslie Henderson, Mike Baker, October 2, 1997.

Location and Access: *Positive Mental Attitude* is approximately 60 feet (18 m) left of *Sweet Emotion* and climbs a prominent left-facing corner obvious when viewed from the approach road. Begin up a left-to-right ramp. Continue up a left-facing dihedral with a lieback, then 5.6 to stemming and liebacking. End with 5.5 face moves. The first ascent team left a register on the summit.

Paraphernalia: Camalots (1) each through #4; Aliens (1) each.

Descent: There are two fixed rappel pitons approximately 30 feet (9 m) left of the climb. Mike Baker: "One double-rope rappel over Moki steps."

DIVERSIONS

FISH CREEK AND DRY CANYON VIEW CAMPSITE

While climbing at Comb Ridge, a recommended campsite is on a wedge of land between Fish Creek (left/south) and Dry Canyon (right/north). Drive 9.5 miles (15 km) on San Juan County 235 from US 163. This is a point 0.4 mile (0.6 km) beyond a left branch and kiosk for the Fish Creek trail (fee area). Turn left (west) onto the Ski Track Road, named for its serpentine track, which looks like a slalom course. At 0.7 mile (1.1 km) keep right at a Y. At 0.8 mile (1.2 km) cross Comb Creek. At 1.7 miles (2.7 km) there is a capped drill pipe left of the trail; keep straight. At 2.3 miles (3.7 km), keep right at a Y. At 4.7 miles (7.5 km) keep left at a Y. At 4.8 miles (7.7 km) the end of the trail and the camp are reached. The location is as lonely and beautiful as any on the Colorado Plateau.

SWEET EMOTION

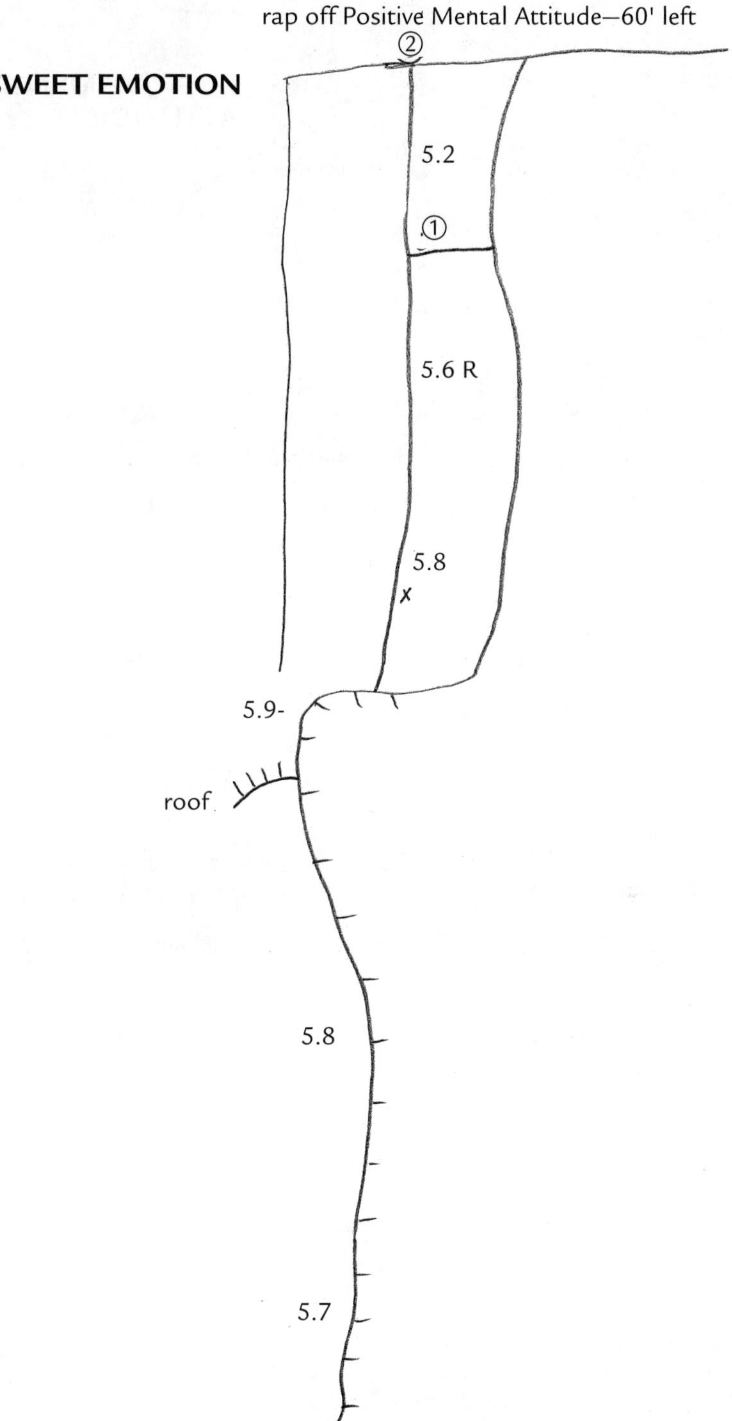

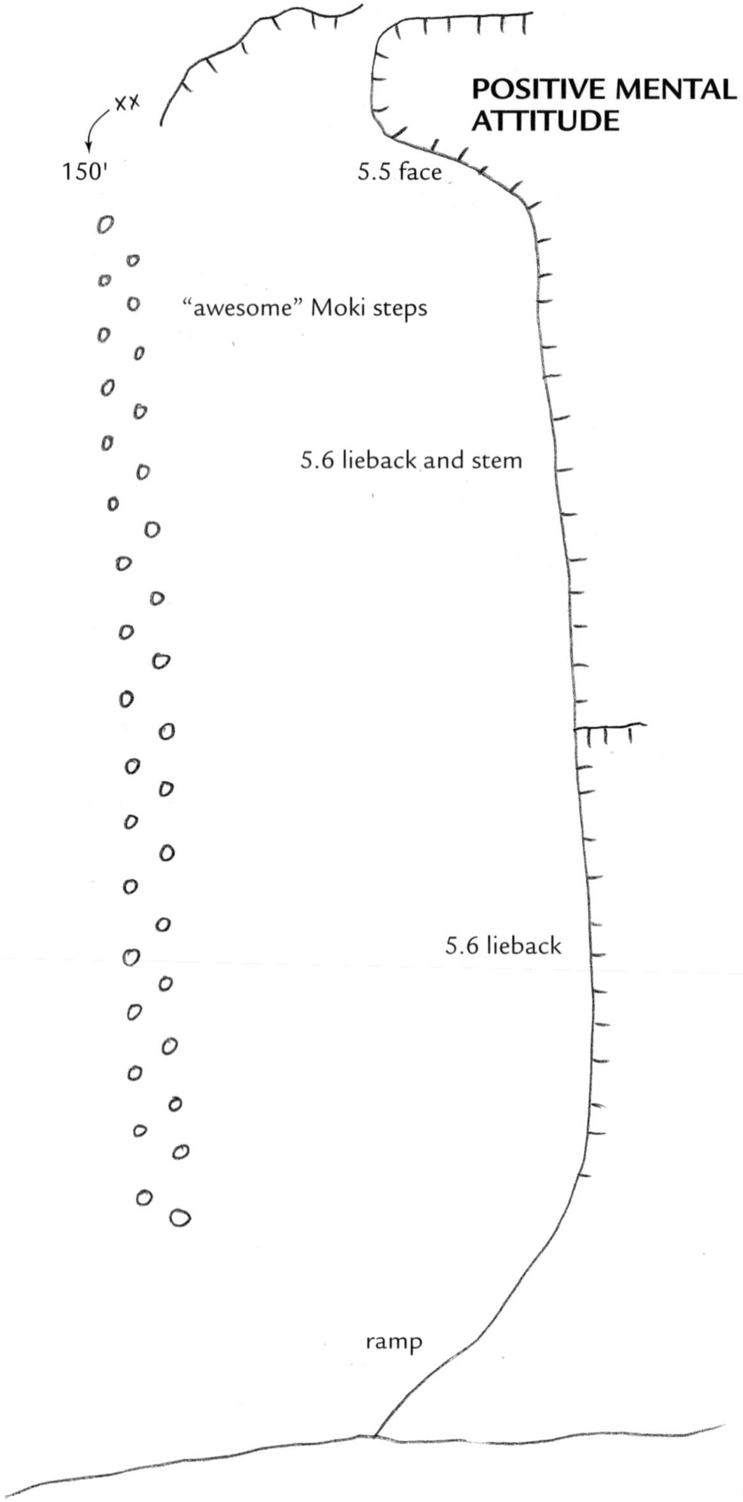

POSITIVE MENTAL ATTITUDE
XX
150'
5.5 face
"awesome" Moki steps
5.6 lieback and stem
5.6 lieback
ramp

Photo: Eric Bjørnstad

Anasazi Snake House Ruin (a.k.a. River House).

SNAKE HOUSE RUIN (A.K.A. RIVER HOUSE)

Snake House is a seldom-visited Anasazi ruin and an excellent area for camping along the San Juan River at the southern edge of Comb Ridge. To reach Snake House, turn south onto San Juan County 237 from US 163, between mile markers 37 and 38. The location is also identified by a diamond-shaped yellow FALLING ROCK sign. The prominent Mule's Ear peak/buttress is in view at the end of Comb Ridge across the San Juan River in Chinle Wash. At 1.8 miles (2.8 km) there is a cowboy line cabin on the right. At 4 miles (6.4 km) the trail branches. The trail straight ahead continues 0.6 mile (0.9 km) to the San Juan River and good camping. Take the steep trail uphill to the left. At 4.2 miles (6.7 km) cross a cattle guard. At 4.3 miles (6.9 km) a causeway is in view to the left, a remnant of the historic 1879–80 Mormon Hole-in-the-Rock expedition. Snake House is reached at 5 miles (8 km). It is named for a large snake pictograph in the ceiling of the ruin. Its second name, River House, comes from its location above the San Juan River. The ruin is a special place; please visit with respect.

Also see Bluff Diversions, Chapter 20.

> In the first stage of the talus the blocks are ragged-edged and as large as a barrel. Nothing whatever grows upon the slope. It is as bare as the side of a volcanic crater. And just as difficult to walk over. The talus is added to at the top by the falling rock of the face-wall, and it is losing at the bottom by the under blocks grinding away to stone and gravel.
>
> —John C. Van Dyke, *The Desert*, 1901

22
VALLEY OF THE GODS

> It is intensely hot on the desert at times, but the sun is not responsible for it precisely in the manner alleged. The heat that one feels is not direct sunlight so much as radiation from the receptive sands; and the glare is due not to preternatural brightness in the sunbeam, but to there being no relief for the eye in shadows, in dark colors, in heavy foliage. The vegetation of the desert is so slight that practically the whole surface of the sand acts as a reflector; and it is this, rather than the sun's intensity, that causes the great body of light.
>
> —John C. Van Dyke, *The Desert,* 1901

Valley of the Gods is a stark yet inviting land of freestanding spires, buttes, and broad vistas. The towers are as deities presiding over the hauntingly beautiful valley. It lies west of US 163, approximately 30 miles (48 km) north of the Arizona border and only 4 miles (6.4 km) north of the tiny hamlet of Mexican Hat. The valley's elevation is approximately 4,300 feet (1,311 m), bordered on the east by the San Juan River and the incredible and improbable Mexican Hat hoodoo, south by the Goosenecks of the San Juan River, and west by the Moki Dugway, Cedar Mesa, and the ancient Indian land of Grand Gulch. From US 163, a good 17-mile (27 km) dirt road loops through the valley, beginning at mile marker 29 where a sign points west to the Valley of the Gods and County Loop Road 242. The loop ends at Utah 261, about 5 miles (8 km) north of US 163.

Valley of the Gods has been called Utah's miniature Monument Valley. Ward J. Roylance in *Utah: A Guide to the State:* "Here in a basin between Cedar Mesa and the gorge of the San Juan is a red fairyland of blocky buttes and slender spires. In general these forms resemble those in the valley's more famous neighbor to the south, yet here they are more intricately sculptured and on a smaller, more intimate scale. Local guides apply such names as 'Lady in a Bathtub,' 'Seven Sailors,' 'Santa Claus and Rudolph,' 'The Turbaned Indian Prince,' and other fanciful terms. Others see visions such as 'The Southern Belle.'"

The region is remote and isolated, with its only resident living at the restored historic Lee Ranch, now the solar-powered Valley of the Gods Bed and Breakfast at the valley's southwest corner. It is the only home within the 360,000-acre Cedar Mesa Cultural and Recreational Management Area. The original ranch was built by Clarence and William "Buck" Lee in the 1920s. The rock mansion contained nine rooms, four with fireplaces, and water was piped into the house from a nearby spring. Buck Lee was an artist and teller of colorful tales who gave guided tours to area attractions.

To reach the Valley of the Gods from Moab, drive south on US 191. Just south of Bluff, US 191 makes a left turn to the east. Continue south on US 163 to mile marker 29, then turn west onto the signed Valley of the Gods dirt trail. See also the Bluff South to Mexican Hat Mile Marker Log in Chapter 20. For further information write the San Juan Resource Office—BLM, P.O. Box 7, Monticello, UT 84535, or phone (435) 587-2141.

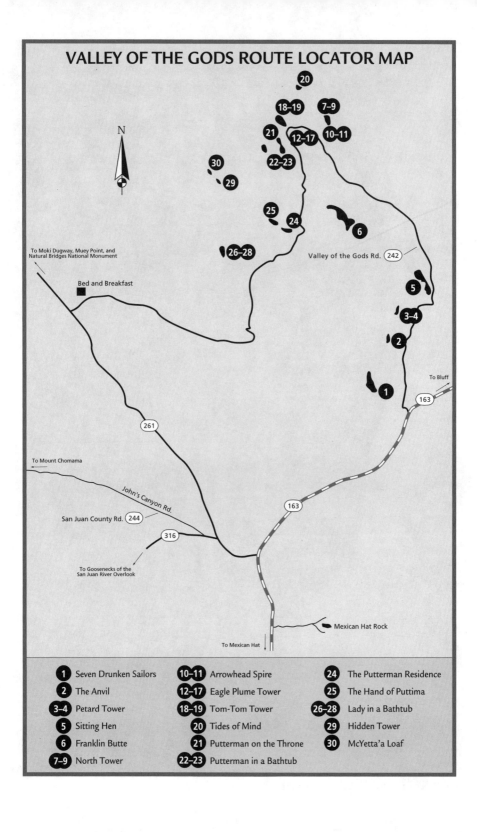

VALLEY OF THE GODS ROUTE LOCATOR MAP

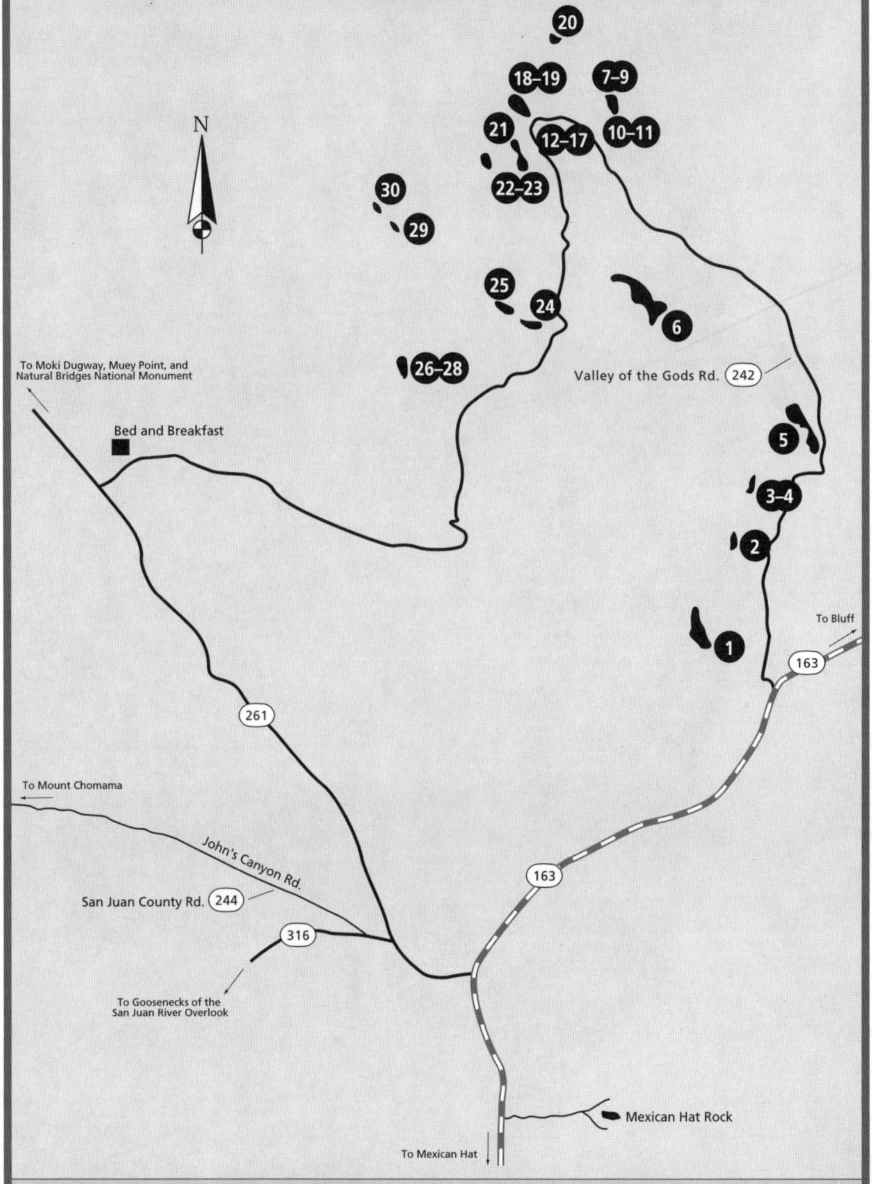

- 1 Seven Drunken Sailors
- 2 The Anvil
- 3–4 Petard Tower
- 5 Sitting Hen
- 6 Franklin Butte
- 7–9 North Tower
- 10–11 Arrowhead Spire
- 12–17 Eagle Plume Tower
- 18–19 Tom-Tom Tower
- 20 Tides of Mind
- 21 Putterman on the Throne
- 22–23 Putterman in a Bathtub
- 24 The Putterman Residence
- 25 The Hand of Puttima
- 26–28 Lady in a Bathtub
- 29 Hidden Tower
- 30 McYetta'a Loaf

Photo: Randall Weekly

Frosty Weller on first ascent of Arrowhead Spire.

FORMATION

The towers in the Valley of the Gods are weathered from Cedar Mesa sandstone atop Halgaito shale and are relatively soft and generally less enjoyable to climb than the Wingate, Entrada, or DeChelly sedimentary layers of the Colorado Plateau. Despite the softer rock, the towers have a great appeal for their statuesque beauty and remote setting.

CLIMBING HISTORY

Eric Bjørnstad: "It was not until 1974 that a climb was established in the valley, although its spires were clearly visible from US 163 as one traveled south toward Monument Valley. In October 1974, Ron Wiggle and I turned west at a lone wooden sign with an arrow pointing to the mysterious and unknown Valley of the Gods. A quick reconnaisance indicated the northernmost spire was the tallest, thinnest, and most aesthetic in the valley.

Ron and three companions had just completed my rock climbing course. Ron then hired me to take him up a "desert first ascent." I chose my long-kept secret, the Valley of the Gods, for the climb. Upon reaching the top of his first ascent spire, Ron was so nervous that he forgot his hard hat when he rappeled from the lofty summit. Todd Gordon, on the second ascent and first free ascent eight years later, found Ron's hat and noted in a *Climbing* magazine article: 'Such insane towers, and no people; just the coyote, spider, snake, and buzzard to watch the heroics on these crags.'"

George Hurley, author of numerous first ascents in the valley, writes about climbing there in a *Summit* magazine article titled "Breaking the Silence": "In the desert, climbers are usually serious. We look out at barren vistas and feel good but also apprehensive and small. The silence is weighty. The empty universe is harder to ignore and our activity seems only a bit more heroic and foolish than most other things we might be doing."

In *Rock Climbing Utah,* Stewart Green gives a somber warning to would-be visitors to the valley intent on a climbing holiday: "This is a place only extreme sandstone connoisseurs could love. Wear a helmet and expect loose rock, rubble-filled chimneys, scary protection, and bad bolts. Be aware that portions of formations as well as whole towers have collapsed within recent memory!"

Cameron Burns, writing in *Climber* magazine's "Postcards from the Trailer Park" column: "The towers and buttes sit atop these 500-foot talus cones, so that for every 400- to 500-foot tower you climb, you end up a good 800 to 900 feet off the valley floor. It's a pretty cool view." Burns also notes in *Selected Climbs in the Desert Southwest:* "It is one of the southwest's hidden climbing gems. Similar to the layout and feel of Monument Valley, Valley of the Gods lies just 20 miles north of the former. The land is managed by the Bureau of Land Management (BL M), and is thus open to climbing (unlike Monument Valley itself, where climbing is 'discouraged'). In essence, it is something of a 'white man's' Monument Valley. . . .

The climbs here vary from short, free routes to big aid affairs taking a full rack and a long day."

Pioneering the routes in the Valley of the Gods in the late 1970s were Bill Forrest, George Hurley, Frank Luptom, and Dave Rearick. In the 1980s new ascents were established by Steve "Crusher" Bartlett, Jeff Cristol, Bill Forrest, Todd Gordon, George Hurley, Craig Kenyon, Brian Povolny, Will Taylor, and Chip Wilson. Throughout the 1990s most towers experienced repeat ascents with new routes established, and most of the remaining buttes and towers were climbed. Active were George Arms, Benny Bach, Mike Baker, Steve "Crusher" Bartlett, Brad Bond, Cameron Burns, Jon Butler, Keen Butterworth, Marco Constant, Jeff Cristol, Chris Donharl, Mark Fleck, James Garrett, Jeff Gruber, Jessy Harvey, Leslie Henderson, George Hurley, Craig Kenyon, Mark Lassiter, Craig Luebben, Rich McDonald, John Middendorf, Stu Ritchie, Chris Rowins, Owen Schultz, Walt Shipley, Kendall Taylor, Randall Weekley, Frosty Weller, Jeff Widen, Chip Wilson, and Milissa Wruck.

MILEAGE LOG—VALLEY OF THE GODS

This guide follows the canyon country tradition of referring to dirt roads—two-wheel drive or four-wheel drive—as trails (Shafer Trail, Burr Trail, White Rim Trail), but because the 17-mile Valley of the Gods loop is designated a road, log references are to a road rather than a trail.

The Valley of the Gods 17-mile (27 km) loop road begins on the west side of US 163 across from mile marker 29. A sign reads, VALLEY OF THE GODS—SAN JUAN COUNTY 242. The square opening in the cliffs west of US 163 and the loop road intersection is the Devil's Window. South of Devil's Window is the Scotchman, but since the upper area of the formation collapsed a few years ago, it is not easily recognized. In a few feet the road crosses the shallow and rocky Lime Creek; drivable with two-wheel-drive low-clearance vehicles.

0.5 mile (0.8 km): Left (west) of the road is the Seven Drunken Sailors. Only six are visible; the seventh succumbed to the pull of gravity a few years ago. Mike Baker: "One sailor fell down, but there are still seven summits, although one is hidden from below." Unknown before the first ascent, there had actually been eight summits, with one fallen down!

0.9 mile (1.4 km): Looking ahead, Anvil appears to be on the right side of the road, but actually it is on the left side; left of the road is Petard Tower. The spur left is the best approach to the Seven Drunken Sailors. Park and/or camp at the wash with cottonwood trees.

2.1 miles (3.3 km): Old causeway in view to the right (east).

3.0 miles (4.8 km): The Anvil is left (south) of the road. Approach from a pullout on the left by large boulders.

3.4 miles (5.4 km): Petard Tower is left (south) of the road.

3.8 miles (6.1 km): Spur to the left ends under the west face of Petard Tower and is the best approach.

4.9 miles (7.8 km): Sitting Hen is left of the road. Franklin Butte is the mile-long mesa right of Sitting Hen.

5.2 miles (8.3 km): Spur to the left is the best approach to Sitting Hen.

7.3 miles (11.7 km): To the right of the valley's road, North Tower (left) and Arrowhead Spire (right) are obvious.

7.4 miles (11.9 km): Spur to the left leads to large boulders and camp for Eagle Plume Tower, looming above the road.

7.6 miles (12.2 km): The road climbs to a pass between Eagle Plume Tower (left) and Tom-Tom Tower (right). There is a spur to the right leading to parking for Tom-Tom Tower and a pullout on the left (south) for Eagle Plume Tower parking.

8.1 miles (13.0 km): Eagle Plume's south face is on the left. Right of the road are two towers connected by the same ridge base: Putterman on the Throne, right and higher, and Putterman in a Bathtub, left and lower. Beyond the two Putterman Towers are The Putterman Residence (nearest the road and with four distinct summits) and The Hand of Puttima.

9.1 miles (14.6 km): Pullout on the right for the approach to the Putterman Residence and The Hand of Puttima.

10.7 miles (17.2 km): Top of hill. Lady in a Bathtub ahead; to the right, Hidden Tower and McYetta's Loaf.

11.0 miles (17.7 km): Best approach to Lady in a Bathtub, Hidden Tower, and McYetta's Loaf: Hike the hard-surfaced blue-black Halgaito shale drainage.

16.2 miles (26.0 km): Valley of the Gods Bed and Breakfast on the right (west).

16.7 miles (26.8 km): The Valley of the Gods 17-mile (27 km) loop road meets Utah 261 East between mile markers 36 and 37. Turn left for Mexican Hat and the Goosenecks of the San Juan, right for Moki Dugway and Cedar Mesa.

SEVEN DRUNKEN SAILORS

At 0.9 mile (1.4 km) from the beginning of the 17-mile loop road, a spur track branching left gives the best approach to Seven Drunken Sailors. Park and/or camp at the wash with cottonwood trees and fire rings.

1 BARACHO GRANDE
II, 5.9, C1, 3 pitches, 100 feet (30 m) ★★

First Ascent: Mike Baker, Leslie Henderson, March 8, 1998.

Location and Access: A register was left on Sailor Six, the highest summit. *Baracho Grande* translates to "big drunk" in Spanish. Mike Baker: "Six summits reached—no bolts. All pitches free-soloed except the first!"

Pitch 1: Begin near the right side of the west face with a 5.9 stem and mantel to a left-facing corner. Move right and continue up a left-facing corner with a

Photo: Eric Bjørnstad

Seven Drunken Sailors—East face (routes are on west face).

couple of C1 moves, then 5.8 up loose rock. A 5.7 off-width is followed by more loose rock to a traverse ledge.

Pitch 2: On the ledge, third class left a few feet and climb 5.5 to the summit plateau on which the sailor summits sit.

Pitch 3: The far right tower is double summited (Sailors One and Two). One is climbed 5.2 and Two 5.0. Sailor Four is reached by a third-class traverse left, passing the unclimbed Sailor Three on the way. Climb Sailor Four with a 5.8 stem and chimney on the backside of the tower. The far left tower is double summited (Sailors Five and Six). Sailor Six is reached with a 5.8 jump from Sailor Four. Sailor Five is then summited with a downclimb from Sailor Six.

Paraphernalia: Camalots (1) #1, #2, #3, #4; Tri-Cams (1) #0.5, #1.

Descent: One 80-foot (24 m) single-rope rappel from double anchors at the base of Sailor One.

THE ANVIL

The Anvil is 3 miles (4.8 km) into the valley from US 163 on the left (south) side of the 17-mile loop road and appears anvil-shaped when viewed from far away.

2 POUNDING HERRADURRA
I, 5.7, A1, 1 pitch, 100 feet (30 m) ★★

First Ascent: James Garrett, solo, March 3, 2000.

Location and Access: *Pounding Herradurra* climbs the southwest face of the tower. Begin at the lowest point of the rock and climb past a bolt through ledges to the top, then third class (right) to a summit cairn. One bolt was placed low on the route for a self-belay. James Garrett: "The name implies drinking Herradurra tequila, and may also be translated to 'horseshoe,' which one works with on an anvil."

Paraphernalia: Camalots (1) set through #2; TCUs; knifeblades (1); angle pitons; keyhole hanger (1).

Descent: Rappel the route.

PETARD TOWER

Petard Tower is called Rooster Butte on the old 15-minute USGS Cedar Mesa topographic quadrangle, and to locals it is known as Prairie Dog on a Mound.

Photo: Eric Bjørnstad

The Anvil—Pounding Herradurra.

Photo: Eric Bjørnstad

Petard Tower: The Putterman Variation *(left)* and Hurley-Rearick Route *(right)*.

Because "petard" was an ancient explosive device used to break down a gate or breach a wall, and because this was the first climb reached in the area, the name fit well. George Hurley: "Petard Tower is just over 140 feet high and has three natural sections. It is about 200 yards from the road and can be climbed quickly as an introduction to the area. This was the shortest of the towers climbed in the Valley of the Gods."

Todd Gordon, writing of Petard Tower in *Climbing* magazine: "A cold wind picks up as I start up a radically loose chimney. Grunting like a soundtrack from a porno flick, I ascend the dirt-filled chimney on poor pro, dirt, rock, and bird spoo streaming down. Curt manages ten feet on jumars, spinning like a drunk marionette."

Petard Tower is 3.4 miles (5.4 km) from US 163. It is easily identified by a large overhang on the right side of the summit block when viewed from the road (north). Reach the tower and good campsite from a spur track beginning 0.4 mile (0.6 km) west of the tower. Take the spur left (south) 0.3 mile (0.48 km), then left 0.2 mile (0.32 km), ending at large boulders beneath the west face. An easy traverse takes you to the north (road) side of the tower and the *Hurley-Rearick Route*.

3 HURLEY-REARICK ROUTE
II, 5.10- R, 3 pitches, 140 feet (43 m) ★★

First Ascent: George Hurley, Dave Rearick, May 23, 1977.

Location and Access: The first two pitches are up a chimney and crack system. The final pitch requires three bolts, with the crux being a 5.10- mantel from the highest bolt.

Pitch 1: There are three crack systems at the base of the tower. Begin up the center system, following a loose chimney, 5.8, then 5.9 R, with no protection. End with a tunnel-through to a prominent ledge (bedding seam). Traverse right 40 feet (12 m) to belay the second pitch. There are no fixed anchors atop pitch 1.

Pitch 2: Climb the right side of a large block past flakes and a second bedding seam, and end with a squeeze to a belay at the top of the block, then move left to a fixed anchor, 5.8+.

Pitch 3: Move left and follow three bolts to the summit, finishing with a 5.10- mantel.

Paraphernalia: Friends (1) set; Camalots (1) #5 for pitch 2; TCUs (1) set; quick draws.

Descent: Rappel the route.

4 THE PUTTERMAN VARIATION
I, 5.9, C1, 1 pitch, 140 feet (43 m) to the summit ★

First Ascent: Cameron Burns, Jon Butler, Jesse Harvey, January 2, 1999.

Location and Access: The variation is to pitch 1 of the *Hurley-Rearick Route* first ascent line, and follows the obvious crack system about 40 feet (12 m) left of the original pitch 1 chimney. The crack system appears as an upside-down Y when viewed from the road. Climb a splitter crack that makes up the left branch of the Y over a bulge (5.9, C1) and into a squeeze chimney (5.7). The variation ends on the ledge where pitch 1 of the original route ends. Cameron Burns: "One point of clean aid was used while piles of rubble fell around me."

Paraphernalia: Camalots (2) sets through #4; quick draws.

Descent: Rappel the variation or, if the summit is reached, rappel the *Hurley-Rearick Route.*

SITTING HEN

Sitting Hen is the next landform north and west of Petard Tower and is in view as the solo tower south of the road 4.9 miles (7.8 km) into the valley's 17-mile loop road. At 5.2 miles (8.3 km) a spur track branches west of Petard Tower and is the closest vehicle approach to Sitting Hen.

5 MR. STUBBS
I, 5.9, A1, 3 pitches, 150 feet (46 m)

First Ascent: John Middendorf, Walt Shipley, 1989.

Location and Access: Climb three short pitches to reduce rope drag. Begin on the east side and traverse to the southwest, then climb 5.9 to the summit.

Paraphernalia: Selection of Friends.

Descent: Rappel the route.

FRANKLIN BUTTE

Franklin Butte is the mile-long mesa south of the valley's road, between Sitting Hen and Eagle Plume Tower.

6 FRANKLIN BUTTE
I, 5.8, 2 pitches, 150 feet (46 m)

First Ascent: John Middendorf, Milissa Wruck, 1990.

Location and Access: Franklin Butte is reached via a cross-country hike from Sitting Hen. The route of ascent is at the narrow east end of the mesa. Further information is unavailable.

Paraphernalia: Selection of Friends.

Descent: Rappel the route.

NORTH TOWER

North Tower is 7.3 miles (11.7 km) into the valley on the right (north) side of the serpentine dirt loop road at its northernmost point. The spur branching right and leading to the towers is closed to vehicles, because the land to the right of the road is now a wilderness study area, but it is a short hike to the landforms. The climb was the first route established in the Valley of the Gods. The first ascent team used a variety of chocks and pitons, in addition to bolts, over chunky, decaying white and red rock with often disappearing cracks. Todd Gordon, writing of North Tower in *Climbing* magazine: "We're on an unnamed tower on Halloween Day. The first pitch is so loose and off-width that I use my helmet as a chock when it gets too wide for my tube, knowing full well that if I blow, the helmet will flex, slings will rip off, and I'll be airborne as all the loose rock I'm sending into the abyss. In a tour-de-force, Brian frees a bolt ladder at 5.10 on a huge flake for the first free ascent (probably only the second ascent anyway). We rap off as it starts to hail, lightning striking the tiny summit minutes after we leave it. 'We almost died,' Brian froths, eyes as wide as an elephant's sphincter. Happy Halloween."

Photo: George Hurley

North Tower (left) and Arrowhead Spire (right).

7 SERENDIPITY
II, 5.10a, 3 pitches, 250 feet (76 m) ★★★

First Ascent: Eric Bjørnstad, Ron Wiggle, 5.7, A3, June 11, 1974. Second Ascent and First Free Ascent of the tower, Third Overall Ascent: Brian Povolny, Todd Gordon, October 31, 1982.

Location and Access: The route is on the northeast side of the tower, opposite the road. Approach from the right side of the landform.

Pitch 1: Begin 30 feet (9 m) right (west) of the right-hand notch and climb to a sloping belay shelf. Traverse 20 feet (6 m) left to the beginning of the second lead.

Pitch 2: Climb to the summit shoulder, passing bolts on the way.

Pitch 3: A short free climb leads to the highest point.

Paraphernalia: Friends (1) set; a selection of large units.

Descent: Rappel to the northeast 70 feet (21 m), then 100 feet (30 m) to the ground from bolt anchors.

8 NORTH TOWER—NORTHEAST
II, 5.10+, 2 pitches, 250 feet (76 m) ★★★★

First Ascent: Brian Povolny, Will Taylor, 1983.

Location and Access: The route ascends a Supercrack-like hand crack, followed by off-width and face climbing left of *Serendipity.*

Pitch 1: Scramble to the northeast base of the tower and begin up a hand crack to a left step-across, then belay.

Pitch 2: Climb to the east (lower) summit by a hand crack and off-width chimney. Traverse right to reach the higher summit.

Paraphernalia: Friends (2) sets with extra larger sizes; TCUs; stoppers.

Descent: Rappel *Serendipity* if the main summit is reached. If only the east summit is reached, rappel the route.

9 NORTH TOWER—SOUTHWEST
II, 5.10, 3 pitches, 250 feet (76 m)

First Ascent and Second Ascent of the tower: Bill Forrest, George Hurley, 5.9, A1, September 27, 1978.

Location and Access: Approach up the slope behind the tower as viewed from the road, then traverse onto the southwest face on a large ledge.

Pitch 1: Climb a 1-inch (2.5 cm) crack 10 feet (3 m), which leads to a 60-foot (18 m) -long wide crack, ending on a good belay ledge, 5.9.

Pitch 2: Continue up a chimney, which narrows considerably. There is a tunnel through to the opposite face just before the most difficult section of the pitch. The crux is a 4.5-inch (11 cm) crack, which overhangs for a short distance, 5.9. Traverse left 30 feet (9 m) on a good ledge and belay.

Pitch 3: Climb a thin-edged fin on the summit ridge, then go left to the obvious summit block. Three bolts were originally used for aid, but these can be bypassed free at 5.10.

Paraphernalia: Friends (1) set; a selection of larger units. The first ascent team used 4.5″, 6″, and 7″ Titons to protect the first pitch, and 4.5″ and 5″ nuts to protect the second pitch. (Titons were invented by Bill Forrest and are no longer available.)

Descent: Rappel the north face from the west end of the summit block using 25 feet (7.6 m) of webbing around a block for the first anchor. Rappel 70 feet (21 m) to a two-bolt second rappel anchor, then 100 feet (30 m) to the ground.

ARROWHEAD SPIRE

Arrowhead Spire is the freestanding tower off North Tower. The spire is climbed by its southwest face. From the road, approach by hiking right of North Tower and Arrowhead Spire. Come in to the west face from the north or backside of the

Photo: Eric Bjørnstad

Ron Wiggle on North Tower, first ascent, 1974.

landforms, traversing between the two formations. Traverse into the main crack system from the left to avoid an 8-foot (2.4 m) death flake.

10 ARROWHEAD SPIRE—SOUTHWEST FACE I, 5.9, A2, C2, 3 pitches, 120 feet (37 m)

First Ascent: Frosty Weller, Randall Weekley, March 20, 1993. Second Ascent: Jeff Widen, Rich McDonald, April 10, 1994.

Location and Access: Climb the obvious line on the south face, ascending a right-facing corner with a 10-foot (3 m) roof to its right. Cameron Burns: "This route should go clean on its next ascent, and will likely go free."

Pitch 1: Begin up thin cracks that become wide up a right-facing corner. Climb left out a large roof protected with #4 Friends (4 inches [10 cm] wide), then establish a hanging belay above the roof at double anchors, C2.

Pitch 2: Climb A2 past a fixed anchor, then A1, ending with 5.6 at a belay ledge with double anchors 30 feet (9 m) below the top.

Pitch 3: Continue from the right end of the belay ledge to double anchors on the summit.

Photo: Cameron M. Burns

Valley of the Gods: A. Putterman on the Throne B. Putterman in a Bathtub C. Tom-Tom Tower, and D. Eagle Plume Tower.

Paraphernalia: Friends (1) #1.5, (2) #2, #2.5, #3, (4) #3.5, (5) #4; Camalots (4) #4; knifeblades (2); quick draws.

Descent: Rappel 120 feet (37 m) to the col between North Tower and Arrowhead Spire, then reverse the approach.

11 ARROWHEAD SPIRE—NORTH BY NORTHEAST
I, C2, 2 pitches, 120 feet (37 m)

First Ascent and Third Ascent of the spire: Ralph E. Burns, Mary Ann Dornfeld, December 30, 1994.

Location and Access: The route climbs the crack opposite *Southeast Face*, which splits through the tower south to north. From the north (opposite the road) side of the landform, traverse left to the spire from the saddle between North Tower and Arrowhead Spire, using small cams and wires, before following a thin hand crack (#2 Friends) vertically to the soft top. Ralph E. Burns: "I think this line could be freed (5.11?) by a capable climber."

Paraphernalia: Friends #2; TCUs; wires.

Descent: Rappel to the col between North Tower and Arrowhead Spire, then reverse the approach.

EAGLE PLUME TOWER

Just beyond North Tower/Arrowhead Spire (500 feet, 152 m), the loop road continues along the north edge of Eagle Plume Tower, gently climbs to a pass between Eagle Plume and Tom-Tom Towers, then descends along the southwest side of Eagle Plume. Eagle Plume is a very popular tower, with five routes and one variation to its summit. Routes begin left to right on the north face, then right to left on the south face. In 1994 Robin "Black Death" Hyde BASE jumped from Eagle Plume and Tom-Tom Towers.

12 MILK CRATES FROM HELL
II, 5.4, A3, 3 pitches, 350 feet (107 m)

First Ascent and Second Ascent of the tower: Chip Wilson, Steve "Crusher" Bartlett, 5.4, A3, March 1987.

Location and Access: The route ascends the north face of the tower, directly opposite the south face's original ascent line. Steve "Crusher" Bartlett: "Imagine very tall stacks of red milk crates and you get the general idea—way kicks!"

Pitch 1: Begin up a 5.4 left-to-right crack and climb to the vertical system splitting the center of the tower.

Pitch 2: Climb A3, passing a bolt, then belay at a stance at a prominent bedding seam.

Photo: Eric Bjørnstad

Eagle Plume Tower: Milk Crates from Hell *(left),* Lola *(right).*

Pitch 3: Continue up a right-facing crack to the top, A3.

Paraphernalia: Friends (2) sets; angle pitons (2); Lost Arrows (2); quick draws (1).

Descent: Rappel the route with two 165-foot (50 m) rappels—the second rappel is from a prominent bedding seam 165 feet (50 m) above the ground—or rappel *Lola.*

13 LOLA
III, 5.10, A2, 3 pitches, 350 feet (107 m)

First Ascent: Jeff Gruber, solo, 1995.

Location and Access: The route climbs the far right crack system on the north face, right of *Milk Crates from Hell.* A summit register was left at the top anchors.

Pitch 1: Begin up the right-most crack system on the north face and climb to the first prominent bedding seam and belay.

Pitch 2: Follow the obvious crack system above to the uppermost bedding seam and double anchors.

Pitch 3: Climb the crack system above to the summit.

Paraphernalia: Standard desert rack.

Descent: Rappel the route, making three rappels or two long ones.

14 EAGLE PLUME TOWER—SOUTH FACE
III, 5.10, 4 pitches, 350 feet (107 m) ★★★★

First Ascent: Bill Forrest, Frank Luptom, 5.9, A3, spring 1976. Second Ascent: Jeff Cristol, solo, 1987. Third Ascent and First Free Ascent: Craig Kenyon, Jeff Cristol, December 1989.

Location and Access: The route follows obvious fracture lines near the center of the south face, directly opposite *Milk Crates from Hell.* Craig Kenyon: "Helmets are a good idea on this one." A register was left on the summit.

Pitch 1: Begin up loose blocky rock a little right of the route's upper crack system. Climb into a 5.8 crack, which leads into a 5.7 off-width, then onto a large ledge at a bedding seam.

Pitch 2: Continue up the crack above, passing three horizontal bedding seams, ending with 5.10 fingers at a stance with three fixed pitons. Pass two drilled pitons, which mark the second rappel station if rappelling the route.

Pitch 3: Climb the right-hand (south) crack, 5.9. Continue past a loose band of rock (bedding seam) to a belay stance.

Pitch 4: Move left over white calcite and climb a 5.9 right-facing hand crack (chocolate corner) to the summit, 30 feet (9 m).

Paraphernalia: Friends (2) sets through #4 with extra #2, #3; TCUs (1) set; medium to large wired stoppers (1) set; quick draws. No hammer required.

Descent: The recommended rappel is down *Lola* at the far right (west) crack system of the north face, or make two rappels down the Forrest-Luptom south face. The first off-slings between boulders (no bolts), 155 feet (47 m) to a two-bolt station in the middle of pitch 2, the second 140 feet (43 m) to ground.

15 EAGLE FEATHER
III, 5.10, 4 pitches, 350 feet (107 m) ★★★★

First Ascent: Craig Kenyon, Jeff Cristol, December 8, 1989.

Location and Access: The route is the free ascent of the original south face route (Forrest-Luptom), and the third overall ascent of the tower.

Pitch 1: Begin up a 5.8 crack, then climb a 5.7 off-width at the right side of the south face. Belay on a large ledge at a bedding seam.

Pitch 2: Climb loose 5.7 rock, ending in 5.10 fingers at a belay stance/slot with triple fixed pitons where two cracks begin.

Photo: Eric Bjørnstad

Eagle Plume Tower: Franziska's Foresight *(left),* Ritchie-Bond Variation *(center),* and Eagle Feather *(right)*

Pitch 3: Continue up the right crack, then up a ramp to a loose flake system (crux). Belay on a ledge at a loose bedding seam.

Pitch 4: Move left on a loose rock band and continue past a bolt up a right-facing hand crack (chocolate corner) that becomes 5.9 wide at the top.

Paraphernalia: Friends (2) sets through #4 with extra #1, #2.5, #3; Camalots (1) #4; medium to large stoppers; quick draws; webbing for summit rappel. No hammer needed.

Descent: Rappel *Lola* or move right and rappel from summit anchors to mid-pitch 2, 155 feet (47 m), then rappel from a double-bolt station 140 feet (43 m) to the ground.

16 RITCHIE-BOND VARIATION
I, 5.10, A2, 1 pitch, 350 feet (107 m) to the summit

First Ascent: Stu Ritchie, Brad Bond, 1994.

Location and Access: The variation ascends the first crack system left of the Forrest-Luptom original ascent line. Begin A2 and finish 5.10 up a 4-inch (10 cm) crack. At a prominent bedding seam (large ledge), traverse right and join the original south face route at the beginning of its second pitch.

Paraphernalia: Friends (1) set through #4; angle pitons through 1" for the variation. For the top three pitches: Friends (2) sets through #4 with extra #1, #2.5, #3; Camalots (1) #4; wired stoppers, medium to large (1) set; quick draws; webbing for summit rappel. Hammer not needed beyond the variation.

Descent: Rappel the variation or, if the summit is reached, rappel *Lola*.

17 FRANZISKA'S FORESIGHT (a.k.a. Chirachuaja Raiding Party)
IV, 5.8, A3+, 3 pitches, 350 feet (107 m) ★★★★

First Ascent: Chris Donharl, James Garrett, January 17–19, 2000.

Location and Access: The route ascends the far left crack system on the south face of Eagle Plume. James Garrett: "We loved this route—maybe the hardest aid in the Valley of the Gods?" The name was derived from James Garrett's wife, Franziska, who had hidden a key to their vehicle, a foresight that came in handy when the team returned from the climb to find their keys locked inside.

Pitch 1: Begin at the left edge of the south face and climb a 5.8 squeeze chimney to a large ledge at a bedding seam.

Pitch 2: Move left to the first crack system. At a bulge, start nailing an insipient seam. Pass a small overhang and continue up a crack system that becomes a seam. Pass several bolts over rotten rock, climbing A3+ to a small belay ledge with triple anchors. James Garrett: "Upper bolt ladder on pitch 2 due to multiple 30-foot leader falls by Chris on hooks, RURPs, and beaks."

Pitch 3: Continue A2 with thin nailing and stacked pitons, passing bolts to the summit. Belay at the top of *Lola* anchors.

Paraphernalia: Camalots (1) set; Toucans; thin pitons; rivet hangers; quick draws.

Descent: Rappel *Lola*.

TOM-TOM TOWER

Tom-Tom Tower looms above the right (northwest) side of the loop road directly northwest of Eagle Plume. In 1994 Robin "Black Death" Hyde BASE jumped from Tom-Tom and Eagle Plume Towers.

18 TOM-TOM TOWER—NORTH FACE III, 5.9, 5 pitches, 365 feet (111 m)

First Ascent: George Hurley, Bill Forrest, November 1, 1976. Second Ascent: Ralph E. Burns, Helgi Christensen, 1994.

Location and Access: The route climbs the center of the north face. Begin up very loose and dangerous rock, followed by relatively solid cracks and chimneys. Bill Forrest: "Seventy-five feet of rotten rock leads to a series of body-width cracks, which lead up the center of the north face to the summit."

Pitch 1: Climb up and right on loose and crumbling blocks, surmounting several short vertical sections. Continue to a platform at the base of the main crack system. Belay from a drilled-in angle piton, 75 feet (23 m).

Pitch 2: Use left arm locks and jams for the first 15 feet (4.5 m) to get inside a chimney. An average-size climber will have to climb without equipment because of the narrow structure of the crack. Continue up the tight chimney, encountering a bulge that forces you out to the lip of the crack. Once over the bulge, place the only protection on the lead. Continue up the difficult and sustained tight chimney to an easy walking section, which leads deeper into the rock. Chimney to near a large chock stone to a belay platform and two fixed angle pitons, 75 feet (23 m).

Pitch 3: Above the second belay, take the right hand crack. Chimney behind large blocks. The chimney narrows and becomes smooth (No Man's Land). Bear up and inward in No Man's Land to a chock stone in the back of the crack, which provides the only protection on the lead. Continue up and outward in this sustained and difficult chimney to a belay platform. Place an anchor at the chimney exit (large unit), and traverse 25 feet (7.6 m) east on the platform to two fixed angle pitons, 75 feet (23 m).

Pitch 4: Climb a large easier chimney, finally passing between two large blocks. Continue up an obvious crack on the south wall, above blocks to the summit terrace, 125 feet (38 m).

Pitch 5: Climb a 15-foot (4.5 m) summit block; no rope needed.

Photo: Eric Bjørnstad

Tom-Tom Tower–North Face: Tommy Knocker (left) and Tom-Tom Tower (right).

Paraphernalia: Friends (1) set; large units.

Descent: Rappel the route, the first from a large block on the summit, 115 feet (35 m), then from two angle pitons, 80 feet (24 m). Finally rappel from two angle pitons, 130 feet (40 m) to the ground.

19 TOMMY KNOCKER—SOUTH FACE III, 5.10, A2, 4 pitches, 360 feet (110 m) ★★★

First Ascent: James Garrett, Chris Donharl, January 22, 2000.

Location and Access: The route climbs a separate spire off and divided from the main tower by a 20-foot (6 m) cleft. James Garrett: "We knocked in a few pitons for sure." The first ascent team left a register on the summit.

Pitch 1: Begin below the main tower's south face. Climb up and right over loose rock, then up a 5.9 left-facing corner. Continue, angling right to a large ledge. Move right and belay at a left-facing dihedral, 5.9, 130 feet (40 m).

Pitch 2: Begin 5.9 up the left-facing dihedral and end over a short rotten section at the col between the main tower and its eastern satellite, 5.9, 80 feet (25 m).

Pitch 3: Continue up the left edge of the east peak, using hooks and passing four fixed anchors. Belay at a ledge at a bedding seam with double anchors, A2, 65 feet (20 m).

Pitch 4: Walk right, along the bedding seam ledge and climb first a left-facing groove, then a 5.10 off-width to the summit, 95 feet (29 m).

Paraphernalia: Hooks; keyhole hangers; quick draws.

Descent: Two rappels, first to the top of pitch 1, then to the ground.

TIDES OF MIND

Tides of Mind is a spire north-northeast and across a canyon from Tom-Tom Tower, and in view from the road when looking right of Tom-Tom. Park at a short spur on the right, which is gained at the pass between Tom-Tom and Eagle Plume Towers. Hike north up the broad valley between Tom-Tom and North Tower. Tides of Mind will be obvious at the far side of the drainage.

20 TIDES OF MIND—NORTH FACE I, 5.11c, 2 pitches, 60 feet (18 m) ★★★

First Ascent: Jeff Cristol, solo, December 26, 1989. First Free Ascent and Second Ascent of the tower: Keen Butterworth, George Arms, July 15, 1990.

Location and Access: The line of ascent faces northeast.

Pitch 1: Begin up a right-facing 5.11c crack, then angle left and climb 5.9 into 5.11 (angling right) to a good ledge.

Pitch 2: Third class to the summit.

Paraphernalia: Friends (1) set with (2) #1.5, (3) #2, (2) #2.5

Descent: Single-rope rappel the route from two drilled angle pitons.

PUTTERMAN ON THE THRONE

Putterman on the Throne is across the road (west) and directly south of Eagle Plume Tower where two towers are connected by the same ridge base. Putterman in a Bathtub is left (lower); Putterman on the Throne is right (higher). To reach the towers, drive 8.1 miles (13 km) into the valley on the loop road to just past the col between Eagle Plume and Tom-Tom Towers.

21 SUPERCALIFRAGILISTICEXPIALIPUTTERMAN III, 5.9, C1, 3 pitches, 400 feet (122 m) ★★★★

First Ascent: Cameron Burns, Jesse Harvey, January 9–11, 1999.

Photo: Ralph E. Burns

Tides of Mind.

Photo: Cameron M. Burns

Jesse Harvey on Putterman on the Throne.

Location and Access: Begin at the notch between the two towers. Start at the western end of the ridge on which the towers sit. Scramble fourth class onto the end of the ridge and walk east along a large ledge system on the north side of the landform, which leads to the notch between the two towers. Climb up and into the notch from the ledge (5.9 boulder move), then walk west to the first splitter crack (pitch 1) on the south face of Putterman on the Throne.

Pitch 1: Move around the corner to the south face and climb a splitter crack to a large ledge and a three-bolt anchor, 5.9, C1. Cameron Burns: "Will go free in the future."

Pitch 2: Follow the obvious line to a bulge on the ridge, then up a short bolt ladder through steep, soft rock, to a second large ledge with a double-bolt anchor, C1.

Pitch 3: Continue up the ridge, passing a 5.8 bulge, then a bolt, and finally a band of chocolate brown rock. Scramble to the top and a three-bolt anchor.

Paraphernalia: Friends (2) sets through #5 Camalot, with extra #2 through #4 Camalots; TCUs (1) set; quick draws.

Descent: Rappel the route.

PUTTERMAN IN A BATHTUB

Putterman in a Bathtub is left of Putterman on the Throne, and is the shorter of the two towers.

22 IT'S A MAD, MAD, MAD, MAD PUTTERMAN II, 5.9, C1, 2 pitches, 450 feet (137 m) ★★★★

First Ascent: Cameron Burns, Jesse Harvey, Jon Butler, Janaury 3, 1999.

Location and Access: Begin at the notch between the two towers. Start at the western end of the ridge on which the towers sit. Scramble fourth class onto the end of the ridge and walk east along a large ledge system on the north side of the tower, which leads to the notch between the two. From the notch, continue walking east to a prominent splitter crack with a bolt 50 feet (15 m) above. The splitter crack is pitch 1 of the route.

Pitch 1: Move past a loose band to the base of a splitter crack and follow it to a ledge, 5.9, C1. Cameron Burns: "Will go free at approximately 5.10+." Traverse left, then follow a thin crack that diagonals left to a large gravelly ledge on the crest of the ridge.

Pitch 2: Move right, around the tower onto the southwest side, and climb the obvious corner to the top, 5.8, C1.

Paraphernalia: Friends (2) sets through #5 Camalot; TCUs (1) set.

Descent: Rappel from webbing just below the rotten summit.

23 PU PLUX PUTTERCLAN PREJUDICE VARIATION (a.k.a. 4-Ps)
II, 5.10a, 3 pitches, 450 feet (137 m) to the summit ★★★★★

First Ascent and First Free Ascent of the tower: James Garrett, Chris Donharl, January 20, 2000.

Location and Access: This *Pu Plux Putterclan Prejudice Variation* was the second ascent of *It's a Mad, Mad, Mad, Mad Putterman*, and a direct start to the original ascent line. A register was left on the summit.

Pitch 1: Begin between *It's a Mad, Mad, Mad, Mad Putterman* and Putterman on the Throne. Climb loose rock to good hands (5.10) up a right-facing corner, then wide to the col between the two landforms.

Pitch 2: Move left over loose rock and ascend a left-facing corner, climbing 5.10a, then 5.9+ to the shoulder below the summit tower.

Pitch 3: Traverse around the right corner and ascend 5.8 to the top.

Paraphernalia: Friends (2) sets.

Descent: Two rappels, the first to the top of pitch 2, the second to the ground.

THE PUTTERMAN RESIDENCE

The Putterman Residence is closer to the road than its sister butte, The Hand of Puttima. It has four distinct summits, which are called (east to west) Point Ethan, Point Iris, Point Walden, and Point Talia. To reach The Putterman Residence, drive approximately 1 mile (1.6 km) from the twin buttes Putterman in a Bathtub and Putterman on the Throne and park near where the road crosses a wash. Hike to the right side of the north face.

24 THE PUTTERMAN RESIDENCE
II, 5.6, C1, 3 pitches, 300 feet (91 m) ★

First Ascent: Cameron Burns, Benny Bach, March 6, 1999.

Location and Access: Cameron Burns: "We did a pitch of free/clean aid on the right side of the north face, then traversed way left and scrambled up fourth-class ground to the bases of all the summit towers. All the summit towers went at easy fifth class." Rappel slings are on top of Point Ethan, Point Iris, Point Walden, and Point Talia. Point Talia was free-soloed on its first ascent.

Pitch 1: Begin C1 and pass a large roof on its left side. Continue 5.6 to a ledge with double anchors.

Pitch 2: Walk to the far left of the north face, then scramble diagonally up and right to a large ledge with double fixed anchors.

Pitch 3: Traverse the ledge to the left and climb Point Ethan to double summit anchors, 5.5. On the ledge, move right from Point Ethan and climb Point Iris to double summit anchors, 5.6. On the ledge again, move right and climb

Point Walden to double summit anchors, 5.5. Finally, from the ledge, move right and scramble fourth class to the summit of Point Talia.

Paraphernalia: Friends (2) sets through #5; TCUs (1) set.

Descent: There are rappel anchors on all summits.

THE HAND OF PUTTIMA

Cameron Burns: "The Hand of Puttima is a large formation west of The Putterman Residence. It has a large flat summit that one can easily walk around on." Approach from the same parking area as the Putterman Residence.

25 THE HAND OF PUTTIMA—JUST AN OLD FASHIONED PUTT-SONG II, 5.9, C1, A1, 2 pitches, 300 feet (91 m) ★★★

First Ascent: Cameron Burns, Benny Bach, March 7, 1999.

Location and Access: The route climbs a wide angling crack (beginning near the right edge of the north face) to a prominent ledge halfway up, then another wide angling crack to the summit. A summit register was left atop pitch 1 by mistake.

Photo: Cameron M. Burns

The Hand of Puttima (left), the Putterman Residence (right).

Pitch 1: Begin A1 and climb into a left-angling crack at 5.8, then C1 as it becomes 4 to 5 inches (10 to 13 cm) wide. Finish C1 to a ledge with double anchors. Walk left to the beginning of pitch 2.

Pitch 2: Climb a short corner to a ledge, then move right to a larger ledge and the start of the summit crack system, 5.9, C1. Begin 5.9 and pass two fixed anchors. Continue C1 up a 3- to 4-inch (7.6 to 10 cm) crack. Pass two more fixed anchors where the crack becomes a body squeeze. Climb up and to the right (5.7), then fourth class to the summit and two fixed rappel anchors.

Paraphernalia: Friends (2) sets with extra #3 through #5; TCUs; stoppers (1) set; selection of baby angles and Lost Arrows; quick draws (4).

Descent: Two double-rope rappels down the route.

LADY IN A BATHTUB

Lady in a Bathtub is called Balanced Rock on the USGS Cedar Mesa topographic quadrangle. George Hurley: "Angel's Fear is a 190-foot tower that looks like a totem pole when seen from the road a mile to the south. When seen from the east or west, however, it is a small mesa with a balanced column on its southern end." *Angel's Fear* ascends the west face of the tower, climbing a broken crack system that reaches the top of the butte north of the large summit block. The best approach is to drive 11 miles (17.7 km) on the loop road and park at a broad wash of hard-surfaced blue-black Halgaito shale. Hike up the drainage, then to the butte.

26 LADY IN A BATHTUB—ANGEL'S FEAR II, 5.9, C2, 2 pitches, 270 feet (82 m) ★★★

First Ascent: George Hurley, Bill Forrest, 5.9, A3, September 26, 1978. First Clean Ascent: Mike Baker, Kendal Taylor, April 1994.

Location and Access: Approach from the east and traverse to the left end of the west face, then ascend steep fourth-class talus to the beginning of the climb. Pitch 2 climbs cracks through the northwest corner of the summit block.

Pitch 1: Begin up a left-facing C2 crack and climb 25 feet (7.6 m) to a ledge and an intermediate belay (recommended, but not necessary). Continue C1, passing a large thin flake on its left, then C1 to double anchors at the top of the summit plateau, 5.9, C2, 120 feet (37 m).

Pitch 2: Traverse 200 feet (60 m) to the summit block at the south end of the butte and belay on the east side from obvious blocks. Climb the right (south) crack up the north face. Begin with fourth class to a fixed anchor, then climb C1, passing the right side of a detached block. Move left and continue up a 3-inch (7.6 cm) C1 crack, which becomes 5.6 wide before reaching the top, 5.6, C1, 70 feet (21 m).

Photo: Mark Lassiter

Lady in a Bathtub.

Photo: Mark Lassiter

Lady in a Bathtub—Angel's Fear.

Photo: Mark Lassiter

Lady in a Bathtub: geological contact between off-balance summit block and mesa.

Paraphernalia: Friends (2) sets; TCUs helpful; stoppers (2) sets; Lowe Balls useful on pitch 2.

Descent: Rappel 70 feet (21 m) to the east side of the summit block, then traverse north 200 feet (60 m) to double anchors at the top of pitch 1 and rappel 120 feet (37 m) to the ground.

27 CASHIERS VARIATION
II, 5.9, A2, 2 pitches, 270 feet (82 m) to the summit

First Ascent: Mark Lassiter, Owen Schultz, November 7, 1999.

Location and Access: *Cashiers Variation* climbs a crack system 50 feet (15 m) right of *Angel's Fear.* Mark Lassiter comments about his experience with this variation: "We dispatched approximately 750 pounds of loose rock off the tower, on both the new pitch and on the old Forrest/Hurley second pitch, including a 400-pound death rock at the base of the summit block . . . which rests precariously off-balanced on a layer of round claystone boulders. . . . This is an elegant and exposed tower and, with much of the loose rock dispatched, a great desert summit."

Pitch 1: Begin up loose rock, then a right-facing corner. Continue up the right side of a triangular roof block to the summit plateau.

Pitch 2: Traverse right and follow pitch 2 of *Angel's Fear.*

Paraphernalia: Friends (1) set through #5; wires (1) set; angle pitons (6) ½" with (1) long angle; Lost Arrows (3); knifeblades (2).

Descent: Rappel 70 feet (21 m) to the east side of the summit block, then to the ground from double anchors down the variation pitch, or traverse to the north and rappel pitch 1 of *Angel's Fear.*

28 CAPE TOWN CAPER
III, 5.8, A3, 3 pitches, 270 feet (82 m)

First Ascent: Chris Rowins, Mark Fleck, Marco Constant, February 1997.

Location and Access: The route climbs the south face of the tower.

Pitch 1: Begin up the left side of the south arête and climb to a ledge below a headwall, 5.8, 90 feet (27 m).

Pitch 2: Ascend a thin crack that splits the center of the headwall. Belay at a large blocky ledge, A2, 80 feet (24 m).

Pitch 3: Climb through overhangs and follow a thin crack up the center of the upper face. When the crack ends, a long reach up and right allows you to gain another crack system. Continue up the crack through an overhang to the summit, A3, 100 feet (30 m).

Paraphernalia: Friends through #3; long Lost Arrows; knifeblades.

Descent: Rappel *Angel's Fear.*

HIDDEN TOWER

Hidden Tower is behind and approximately 0.75 mile (1.2 km) northwest of Lady in a Bathtub. It is easily seen from many points along the Valley of the Gods loop road.

29 HIDDEN TOWER—NORTH FACE
II, 5.9, A1, 3 pitches, 300 feet (91 m)

First Ascent: George Hurley, Bill Forrest, November 21, 1977. Second Ascent: Rob Slater, Rodger Schimmel, 1994.

Location and Access: The route climbs a wide crack/chimney system that splits the western side of the landform.

Pitch 1: Climb broken rock to a difficult crack/chimney with a drilled angle piton. Climb the chimney, going behind large chock stones at the top. Continue to a rotten ledge, then hand traverse left to a two-nut anchor, 5.9, 140 feet (43 m). George Hurley: "Be careful; a loose block crushed Bill Forrest's finger while he was on this traverse."

Pitch 2: Continue over easy blocks to a wall. Use two points of aid up the wall and continue up an easy chimney.

Pitch 3: Traverse southeast, then climb to the summit.

Paraphernalia: Friends (1) set.

Descent: Rappel the route, skipping pitch 3. The first long rappel is from a drilled angle piton and the second long rappel is from a two-nut anchor at the top of the first lead.

MCYETTA'S LOAF

McYetta's Loaf is the butte behind (west of) Hidden Tower.

30 PLAID SKIRTED SCHOOL GIRLS II, 5.8, C1, 4 pitches, 300 feet (91 m) ★★★★

First Ascent: Cameron Burns, Jeff Widen, December 1999.

Location and Access: Begin up the right side of the north face of the butte.

Pitch 1: Climb a 5.8 face right of a 10-inch (25.4 cm) crack, then continue with hands 5.8 up a 6-inch (15 cm) crack to a belay ledge with no fixed anchors.

Pitch 2: Traverse left on the belay ledge, then fourth class to a higher ledge and traverse right to a belay at a 4-inch (10 cm) crack.

Pitch 3: Climb the narrowing 4-inch (10 cm) crack and up an overhanging splitter to a bolt ladder, ending on a belay ledge.

Pitch 4: Move left on the belay ledge and climb fourth class to the summit. Traverse right to the highest point and a double-anchor rappel station.

Paraphernalia: Camalots (2) sets through #4 with (1) #5; TCUs (3) sets.

Descent: Two double-rope rappels down the west face of the butte, first to the top of pitch 2, then to the ground.

DIVERSIONS

See Mount Chomama, Chapter 24.

> Dust is always present in the desert air in some degree, and when it is at its maximum with the heat and winds of July, we see the air as a blue, yellow, or pink haze. This haze is not seen so well at noonday as at evening when the sun's rays are streaming through canyons, or at dawn when it lies in the mountain shadows and reflects the blue sky . . . but it thickens the air perceptibly and decreases in measure the intensity of the light. Yet despite the

Photo: Jeff Widen

Cameron Burns on McYetta's Loaf.

fact that desert air is dust-laden and must be thickened somewhat, there is something almost inexplicable about it. It seems so thin, so rarefied; and it is so scentless—I had almost said breathless—that it is like no air at all. You breathe it without feeling it, you look through it without being conscious of its presence.

—John C. Van Dyke, *The Desert,* 1901

23
MEXICAN HAT AND ALHAMBRA ROCK

> You are always riding into the unexpected in these barren countries, stumbling upon strange phenomena, seeing strange sights.
>
> –John C. Van Dyke, *The Desert,* 1901

MEXICAN HAT

Mexican Hat (a.k.a. The Hat, Hat Rock) is a giant hoodoo of Cedar Mesa sandstone balanced atop a 25-foot (7.6 m) pedestal of Halgaito shale, which in turn rests upon a 300-foot (91 m) talus cone. An Indian legend tells of a handsome Mexican vaquero and a beautiful young woman falling in love near the river. Unfortunately, the woman was already married to a wicked old medicine man. When the medicine man learned of her indiscretions, he turned her lover into a stone sombrero. Wallace Stegner speaks of the town of Mexican Hat in his book *The Sound of Mountain Water:* "To start a trip at Mexican Hat, Utah, is to start off into empty space from the end of the world. The space that surrounds Mexican Hat is filled only with what the natives describe as 'a lot of rocks, a lot of sand, more rocks, more sand, and wind enough to blow it away.'"

Mexican Hat rock is 2.5 miles (4 km) north of the town of Mexican Hat, in southeastern Utah, a little more than 100 miles (161 km) south of Moab. It lies on BLM land and has no climbing restrictions. It is important to tread lightly, making as little impact as possible, to keep public lands open to climbing.

An early ascent of Mexican Hat was by helicopter, at which time a pipe was supported by a rock cairn to commemorate the event. According to Luther Risenhoover, the first people to scale the rock were river runner Norman Nevills and a local Navajo, Fred Yazzie. Nevills and Yazzie used a ladder and drilled a hole on top, into which they inserted a steel rod.

History was made on The Hat in March 1984 with a record attendance of seven climbers on the summit: Mike Brown, Reggie Thompson, Doug Smith, Todd Gordon, Jim Angione, Dave Evans, and Sam Hoffman. The 1984 record was shattered in 1988 when three West German climbers joined seven Boulder, Colorado, climbers for a ten-person gathering on the summit. Participants from Boulder: Stewart Sayah, Jean Hooper, Dirk Davorka, Bryan Brodeur, Melanie Pappas, Martha Goss, and Jay Belson; from West Germany: Joseph Zollner, Leo Reitzner, and Hubert Haass. On July 22, 1993, the record was again broken with twelve summiting the rock. Participants were Matt Moore, Claire Brown, and ten school children.

Todd Gordon writes of Mexican Hat rock in a *Climbing* magazine article: "A pancake, can't think of any other way to describe it; a pancake stacked on the apex of a talus cone . . . on the summit, a Coke bottle; inside is a Bill Forrest busi-

Photo: Eric Bjørnstad

Mexican Hat.

ness card and a picture from a biker magazine of a buxom topless female on a black Harley . . . somebody's got class." Rob Slater quotes Jim Bodenhamer: "It's not a spire, it's a hat!" Cameron Burns: "Mexican Hat is more an oddity than a climb. But it's a really cool oddity."

Stewart Green: "The rock, a famed landmark along US Highway 163, sits east of the highway above the tamarisk-lined west bank of the meandering San Juan River. The river, beginning far to the east in Colorado's San Juan Mountains, cuts through the Raplee Anticline and makes a bowknot bend just north of Mexican Hat. Below the hat, the river enters a spectacular, sinuous gorge aptly called The Goosenecks, where it twists back on itself in a series of entrenched meanders before emptying into the placid waters of Lake Powell. . . . The hat is somewhat notorious since it appeared in a fake ad for 'clear Lycra' in a spoof section of *Rock and Ice.*"

Fred Knapp: "In addition to a censored version of the biker mag, I found a host of other summit offerings, from illicit substances to fireworks. Always a surprise." Mark Lassiter: "In keeping with the Mexican Hat novelty tradition, we tethered a fifth of Jack Daniels to the summit with a [blank] grenade attached to it, complete with a note: 'Courtesy Cashiers Valley Vigilantes.'"

East of Mexican Hat across the San Juan River, Raplee Anticline (a.k.a. The Navajo Rug, Navajo Tapestry) dominates the landscape. Ward J. Roylance in *Utah:*

A Guide to the State: "This remarkable structure is an 'upfold or arch of stratified rock,' so symmetrical and picturesquely eroded that photographs of it are used in geology texts around the world. The anticline is 15 miles long and 1,500 feet high at its crest. . . . It is known to every geologist as a superb crustal flexure, displaying its classic, eroded curve in such clarity that even the most innocent layman cannot resist geologic enlightenment."

To reach Mexican Hat, turn east from US 163 onto a dirt trail between mile markers 23 and 24. At 0.2 mile (0.32 km) take the right branch and circle to the south shoulder of the hoodoo where there is an impressive view of the San Juan River and the colorful Raplee Anticline. **NOTE:** The left branch descends to the tamarisk-lined San Juan River and ends in 1.1 miles (1.7 km). The area provides good private camping in a spectacular setting at an elevation of approximately 4,300 feet (1,311 m). At the south shoulder of Mexican Hat, scramble fourth class up the line of least resistance to the base of the rock.

1 ROBBINS-TURNER ROUTE
I, A2, 2 pitches, 380 feet (116 m)

First Ascent: Royal Robbins, Jack Turner, May 1962.

Location and Access: The first ascent was rated A4. The route climbs the hoodoo from the river side of the tower. There are no fixed anchors on the route.

Paraphernalia: Friends (1) #3, #6; stoppers (1) #7; short Lost Arrows (5).

Descent: Rappel 80 feet (24 m) from two drilled pitons.

2 BANDITO ROUTE
I, C1, 2 pitches, 380 feet (116 m) ★★★

First Ascent: Banditos Stan Mish, Dan Langmade, A4, 1981. Second Ascent: John Matsen, Stan Mish, 1982.

Location and Access: The *Bandito Route* climbs the hoodoo from the southwest (highway) side of the tower. Five bolts and a fixed piton were placed on the first ascent. Rick Donnelly: "The *Bandito Route* was retrobolted in 1992–93 (first ¼" split shaft and second ½" angle sticking 60+ percent out were removed and replaced with ½" glued-in bolts w/Metolius hangers). In the spring of 1995 the first two bolts were chopped."

Paraphernalia: Rope; free carabiners (12); aid slings (2) sets; replacement bolts and hangers; clip-stick; quick draws (7).

Descent: Rappel 80 feet (24 m) from two drilled pitons.

3 FRITO ROUTE
I, 5.12, 1 pitch, 380 feet (116 m) ★★★★

First Ascent and First Free Ascent: Jeff Achey, Irene Boche, 1999.

Photo: Cameron M. Burns

Jesse Harvey and Jon Butler on Mexican Hat.

Location and Access: Begin 10 feet (3 m) left of the *Bandito Route*. Stick-clip the first two of three bolts in place, thus climbing the overhang with an upper belay.

Paraphernalia: Quick draws (3).

Descent: Rappel 80 feet (24 m) from two drilled pitons.

ALHAMBRA ROCK

Alhambra Rock is a prominent volcanic intrusive dike 3 miles (4.8 km) southwest of the town of Mexican Hat, south of the San Juan River. Its summit is 4,937 feet (1,505 m) above sea level. The rock was named by early Spaniards passing through the region. The contour of the monolith was thought to be a likeness of the medieval Moorish castle of Granada, Spain. To reach Alhambra Rock from US 163, turn west (right) between mile markers 19 and 20.

4 DICK OF DEATH—UNNAMED ROUTE I, 5.7, 1 pitch, 50 feet (15 m)

First Ascent: Tom Cotter, Rob Slater, Dan Langmade, 1986.

Location and Access: Alhambra Rock is obvious as you travel south from the town of Mexican Hat. Dick of Death is a small spire on the east side of the rock.

Paraphernalia: Undetermined.

Descent: Rappel the route.

DIVERSIONS

See Mount Chomama, Chapter 24.

> If we could but rid ourselves of the false ideas, which, taken en masse, are called education, we should know that there is nothing ugly under the sun, save that which comes from human distortion. Nature's work is all of it good, all of it purposeful, all of it wonderful, all of it beautiful. We like or dislike certain things which may be a way of expressing our prejudice or our limitation; but the work is always perfect of its kind irrespective of human appreciation. We may prefer the sunlight to the starlight, the evening primrose to the bisnaga, the antelope to the mountain-lion, the mocking-bird to the lizard; but to say that one is good and the other bad, that one is beautiful and the other ugly, is to accuse Nature herself of preference—something which she never knew.
>
> —John C. Van Dyke, *The Desert,* 1901

24
MOUNT CHOMAMA

> How delicately beautiful are the hills that seem to gather in little groups along the waste. . . . With surfaces that catch and reflect light, and little depressions that hold shadows, how very picturesque they are!
>
> —John C. Van Dyke, *The Desert,* 1901

Mount Chomama is a large pillar off the southeast edge of Cedar Mesa just south of Muley Point, where there is a breathtaking view down to the tower from the mesa top. Muley Point is also an alternative approach to the climb from a rappel to the bowl (notch) between the tower and the mesa behind. To reach Muley Point, take Utah 261 from its intersection with Utah 95. To get to the junction, see the Utah 95 from Blanding to Hite Marina Mile Marker Log in Chapter 19. Or reach Muley Point from Mexican Hat on Utah 261 from US 163 between mile markers 24 and 25.

FORMATION

Mount Chomama Tower is weathered from Cedar Mesa sandstone atop Halgaito shale, the same sedimentary layers that nearby Valley of the Gods and Mexican Hat are sculpted from. Ironically, there are no cedar trees on Cedar Mesa; cedar is a local name for the juniper tree that proliferates in the area. Halgaito shale is named for Halgaito Spring at Mexican Hat.

To reach Mount Chomama from US 163, drive 2.5 miles (4 km) north from the village of Mexican Hat. Turn left (west) on Utah 261 between mile markers 24 and 25 and continue 1 mile (1.6 km) to Utah 316, the signed Goosenecks State Park road. Drive 0.5 mile (0.8 km) to a dirt branch (right) and the beginning of San Juan County Road 244 (John's Canyon Trail). Continue 6.8 miles (10.9 km) and park at a pullout on the left (south) just before a gate. Mount Chomama is high on Cedar Mesa when looking east from the gate. The best camp for the climb is the pullout east from the gate on the south side of the road.

MOUNT CHOMAMA

1 REDNECKS, PISTOLS, AND WHISKEY IV, 5.9, A1, C1, 9 pitches, 600 feet (183 m) ★★

First Ascent: Cameron Burns, Bryan Gall, Smith Maddrey, Jeff Widen, March 12, 2000.

Location and Access: The ascent begins from John's Canyon Trail left of the tower and climbs to a large bowl between the tower and the mesa behind.

Pitch 1: Scramble fourth class to a belay ledge at a bedding seam left of the tower, 80 feet (24 m).

Photo: Eric Bjørnstad

Cameron Burns, Bryan Gall, Smith Maddrey, and Jeff Widen on Mount Chomama, first ascent, March 2000.

Pitch 2: Continue above over loose rock, a small overhang, then C1 to a belay stance with double anchors, 5.8+, C1, 100 feet (30 m).

Pitch 3: Angle right, passing a crack system, then climb a wide system to a belay at the base of the large bowl, 5.9, 60 feet (18 m).

Pitch 4: Scramble up the bowl 200 feet (61 m) to a belay at the base of a wide rotten section of rock.

Pitch 5: Continue up, making a short right traverse, then to the ledge above, 5.7, 70 feet (21 m).

Pitch 6: Traverse right, around to the southeast side of the tower.

Pitch 7: Climb a short section, passing a death block and belay at a ledge at the base of the tower, 5.8, C1, 30 feet (9 m).

Pitch 8: Climb past numerous bolts to a good ledge with double anchors below the summit block, A1, C1, 100 feet (30 m).

Pitch 9: Move left and free climb to the top, 5.7, 30 feet (9 m).

Paraphernalia: Camming units (3) sets through #5 Camalot; TCUs (3) sets; several small pitons; quick draws; 200-foot (60 m) ropes for the descent.

Descent: Rappel from double summit anchors to the ledge at the base of the summit block. Rappel to the base of the summit tower, then reverse the route.

DIVERSIONS

ANNUAL BLUFF INTERNATIONAL BALLOON FESTIVAL

The Bluff Balloon in Beauty Festival is a three-day event that includes workshops in mural painting and garden fountain building, a basket/rug seminar, an auction, band entertainment, dancing, a road race, and storytelling. Balloons from around the world soar above the Valley of the Gods, bringing it alive with color. It is a worthwhile diversion, held in January.

GOOSENECKS OVERLOOK BOULDERING AREA

Whether one is interested in bouldering or not, a visit to the Goosenecks State Park is a worthwhile side trip for climbers driving between Moab and Monument Valley. The park, established in 1962, is at an elevation of 4,500 feet (1,372 m). Managed by the Federal Bureau of Land Management, it was acquired for the grand sum of $50. Worthless land for some, invaluable for others!

The Gooseneck Overlook Bouldering Area is approximately 8 road miles (12.9 km) north of the town of Mexican Hat in southeastern Utah. The overlook views the San Juan River as it meanders more than 5 miles (8 km) through a series of sharp bends within a single square mile. The western end of the Goosenecks is only 5 miles (8 km) from the Colorado River, but the San Juan must travel 34 miles (54.7 km) before the two rivers converge. Along the edge of the overlook are numerous boulder problems on good-quality limestone, 1,200 feet (366 m) above the river.

Ward Roylance in *Utah: A Guide to the State:* "The reserve is . . . one of the world's most magnificent examples of an entrenched meander. . . . The river is viewed from the north rim as it flows north, then south, then north again, and finally south again, in a series of close-set curves. The center bend is 3 miles around, but the dividing ridge, at its narrowest point, is less than 100 yards wide. According to geologists, the San Juan once meandered over the surface of a level plain; a slow regional uplift forced the stream to cut deeper and deeper into the plain. Eventually, eons hence, the meanders may cut through, leaving a series of gigantic natural bridges. The canyon's rocks were formed in shallow waters some 300 million years ago in Pennsylvanian time, being laid down over a period of about 40 million years and consisting mainly of limestone, shale, and sandstone." The Goosenecks were previously known as The Twist.

To reach the park, turn west onto Utah 261 from US 163 between mile markers 24 and 25, 2.5 miles (4 km) north of Mexican Hat. In approximately 1 mile (1.6 km), turn left (south) onto Utah 316 and drive 3.5 miles (5.6 km). At the park there are rest rooms, sheltered tables, and an information kiosk. For further information write P.O. Box 660, West 400 North, Blanding, UT 84511, call (435) 678-2238, or visit on-line at parks.state.ut.us/parks/www1/goos.htm.

HONAKER TRAIL

There are two hiking trails from the canyon rim to the San Juan River. The Honaker Trail descends tight switchbacks and ramps at the deepest section of the canyon. Although only 1,235 feet (376 m) deep, the trail is so crooked that it is approximately 2.5 miles (4 km) long. It was laboriously constructed in 1904 by the intrepid gold prospector Augustus Honaker and was intended to be used by pack animals from placer deposits near the river. Don Baars: "[T]he only horse ever to attempt the descent fell off from a particularly steep, narrow stretch known as The Horn, and its bleached bones may still be seen lying at the base of the cliff."

From the approach to the Goosenecks State Park at the junction of Utah 261 and Utah 316, drive 0.5 mile (0.8 km) on Utah 316. Branch right on the dirt San Juan County Road 244 (John's Canyon Trail). Continue 2.6 miles (4.2 km) to a large pink water tank and cattle trough on the left and a welded sign: HONAKER. Fork left and drive to the trailhead, which will take route finding to locate. There are many excellent campsites in the area.

MENDENHALL TRAIL

The Mendenhall Trail is named for the gold prospector Walter E. Mendenhall, who explored the canyon in 1894 and 1895. He built a trail down the north rim of the canyon and a stone cabin in the notch of the gooseneck at river mile 29.8 (river mileage begins at the bridge over the San Juan River at Mexican Hat). He successfully processed gold dust into nuggets by adding a drop of mercury and baking the mixture in a hole cut into a potato. The mercury evaporated, leaving a nugget of gold.

The trail is reached with route finding by hiking overland west along the edge of the river gorge from the town of Mexican Hat.

MULEY POINT OVERLOOK

From 6,200-foot-high (1,890 m) Cedar Mesa, Muley Point Overlook gives a spectacular panorama south to the spires of Monument Valley, west to Navajo Mountain, and 2,400 feet (731 m) below to the Goosenecks of the San Juan River. Ward J. Roylance in *Utah: a Guide to the State:* "Muley Point offers a geological and scenic spectacle, a bird's-eye sweep across hundreds of millions of years of earth's crustal history, revealed in bare-bones stratigraphic clarity. Whereas the Canyonlands viewpoints are situated on middle-aged Mesozoic rocks (Jurassic-Triassic) looking down on older Permian rocks, Muley Point is situated on Permian rocks looking down onto even older Pennsylvanian rocks in the walls of the San Juan's canyons. In other words, Goosenecks State Park could be considered the lowest step in southeastern Utah's Grand Staircase; Muley Point the next higher step; and Canyon Rims, Dead Horse Point, and Grand View Point the third step. Suitable viewpoints on the summit of the Henry Mountains, Caineville mesas, or the Roan and Book Cliffs—overlooking relatively youthful Cretaceous formations—might well serve as the top of the Grand Staircase."

From the north, turn right (west) on a good dirt trail just before Utah 261 begins its descent down the Moki Dugway to the Valley of the Gods and Mexican Hat. Follow the trail 5.3 miles (8.5 km) to the viewpoint. From Mexican Hat, turn 2.5 miles (4 km) north of town from US 163 onto Utah 261 and climb the Moki Dugway to Cedar Mesa. At the crest of the steep grade, turn left (west) on an unmarked trail, then continue 5.3 miles (8.5 km) to the viewpoint.

NOTE: Moki (sometimes spelled Mokee or Moqui) translates to "small people" and is a name given by the Spanish to the peoples of the Hopi mesas to the south. Seeing the small storage cysts in the area led to the misconception that small people lived in the structures. It is thought to be a less than favorable slang term used by early Mormons in reference to the Anasazi and Fremont Culture Indians.

JOHN'S CANYON TRAIL

John's Canyon Trail, the approach for Mount Chomama, traverses 16.8 miles (27 km) along the rim above the San Juan River from near Goosenecks State Park northwest to a juncture with the southwest intersection of John's Canyon. The trail is a good low-clearance two-wheel-drive trail that begins on BLM-managed land. At 4.4 miles (7 km) it enters the Glen Canyon National Recreation Area.

John's Canyon originates on Cedar and Polly Mesas and drains southwest into the San Juan River. It was originally known as Douglas Canyon and, along with many locations on the Colorado Plateau, it has a colorful and often sordid history. It was named for James Douglas, a prospector in the early 1900s. In 1909, he discovered gold on the banks of the San Juan River just west of Mexican Hat. Soon after, the river flooded, covering his mine site. Douglas stayed in the area

REQUIRED READING

Wind in the Rock by Ann Zwinger is a must read for anyone visiting John's Canyon. Zwinger speaks of morning camp on one of her visits there: "Early mornings in the canyon have a distinct quality; they are a time I cherish. Out here there is time to watch the day begin, hear the small secret sounds that no one else is awake to hear, time to watch the light change, to anticipate the coming day, all the good hours stacked ahead. Cool dawn, in these dry canyons, is a time of rare perfection, fresh beginnings, infinite peace, total awareness unimpinged upon by the necessities of the day. . . . I lie on my back, arms behind my head, sleeping bag up to my chin, watching, watching the day begin."

until 1929, hoping to reclaim his gold bonanza, but he became increasingly discouraged and finally commited suicide by jumping off the San Juan River Bridge at Mexican Hat.

The canyon's present name comes from John Oliver and his brother Bill, who ran cattle in the area in the 1930s. Jimmy Palmer, who had murdered his father-in-law with whom he had run a cockfighting operation, rustled horses in the Blanding area and wanted to keep them in the canyon. When John Oliver would not move his cattle from the canyon, Palmer blasted Oliver in the face with a shotgun, then shot Oliver's grandson. He loaded the bodies into Oliver's truck and dropped them over the cliff into the San Juan River gorge, then fled south. He was captured and eventually died in a Texas jail.

John's Canyon is a remote and isolated location, easily rivaling any on the 160,000-square-mile Colorado Plateau for its desolation and beauty. It is a very special place well worth the visit.

MILEAGE LOG—JOHN'S CANYON TRAIL (SAN JUAN COUNTY ROAD 244)

From the junction of Utah 316 and Utah 261, the approach to Goosenecks State Park, drive 0.5 mile (0.8 km) on Utah 316 toward the park and branch right on the dirt San Juan County Road 244. See the Valley of the Gods locator map, Chapter 22.

00 miles: Utah 316 and San Juan County 244.

0.2 mile (0.32 km): United States Geologic Survey bench mark left beside a tall rock cairn.

2.6 miles (4.2 km): Pink water tank (left), a bovine water trough, and a welded sign: HONAKER. A dirt trail branches to the left; keep straight (right).

4.5 miles (7.2 km): Sign for Glen Canyon National Recreation Area.

6.9 miles (11.1 km): Pass through a gate. Mount Chomama Tower is high above, looking east from the gate. Good campsite and beginning of the climb.

7.3 miles (11.7 km): Petroglyph panel etched into a boulder right of the road.

While driving west, watch for glyphs of deer footprints. Pass the boulder and view the west face to see more etchings in the black desert varnish, including two suns, a snake, and anthropomorphic figures.

8.7 miles (14 km): Petroglyphs etched onto a black desert-varnished rock right of the road.

10.5 miles (16.9 km): USGS bench mark 50 feet (15 m) left of the road with a 4-foot (1.2 m)-high rock cairn marking the location.

11.0 miles (17.7 km): Hoodoo with a large caprock right of the road, which is difficult to see on the return (east) drive.

11.6 miles (18.7 km): Take the spur to the left, drive 0.2 mile (0.32 km), and park. Hike five minutes to the canyon's edge for a breathtaking view of the San Juan River 1,200 feet (366 m) below.

12.0 miles (19.3 km): Enter John's Canyon.

14.8 miles (23.8 km): John's Canyon and a creek crossing over the blue-gray Halgaito shale. This is a good turnaround point.

14.9 miles (24.0 km): Fork in the trail. Right branch continues up John's Canyon 1.8 miles (3 km) and ends at an impassable drainage crossing. The left fork crosses a pour-off at 1 mile (1.6 km), then continues along the rim of John's Canyon with several hundred-foot exposures into the canyon. At 2.2 miles (3.5 km) the trail deteriorates to marginal four-wheel drive and eventually ends at a fence and wilderness study area.

I never tired of the beauty of the desert. Its fiery dawns and orange sunsets, and opalescent air with the grim grandeur of its tall mountains never paled.

—John C. Van Dyke, *The Desert,* 1901

25
GRAND GULCH

> It has been said that our atmosphere breaks, checks, and diffuses the falling sunlight like the globe of a lamp. It does something more. It acts as a prism and breaks the beam of sunlight into the colors of the spectrum. Some of these colors it deals with more harshly than others because of their shortness and their weakness. The blue rays, for instance, are the greatest in number; but they are the shortest in length, the weakest in travelling power of any of them. Because of their weakness, and because of their affinity (as regards size) with the small dust particles of the higher air region, great quantities of these rays are caught, refracted, and practically held in check in the upper strata of the atmosphere. We see them massed together overhead and call them the "blue sky."
>
> –John C. Van Dyke, *The Desert,* 1901

Grand Gulch is the principal drainage of the 1,000-square-mile Grand Gulch Plateau. The canyon, more than 50 miles (80 km) long, is the geographic center of a complex maze of tributary canyons, including Kane Gulch, Bullet Canyon, Collins Canyon, Coyote Wash, Pine Canyon, and Dripping Canyon. Grand Gulch begins at an elevation of approximately 6,400 feet (1,950 m), about 6 miles (9.6 km) southwest of Natural Bridges National Monument, and cuts a twisting swath through the plateau to its junction with the San Juan River 2,700 feet (823 m) lower. Annual precipitation averages 10 inches (25 cm), but generally comes in sudden cloudbursts during July and August, flash flood season.

CULTURAL HISTORY

Grand Gulch's cultural history covers a tremendous span of time, from approximately 2,000 to 700 years ago. The vast area contains the largest concentration of prehistoric Basketmaker and Pueblo cliff dwellings outside of Mesa Verde. The Anasazi left behind hundreds of ruins and thousands of petroglyphs and pictographs.

FLORA AND FAUNA

Wildlife in Grand Gulch includes mule deer, mountain lion, black bear, coyote, bobcat, fox, ringtailed cat, spotted skunk, cottontail rabbit, white-tailed antelope squirrel, white-throated wood rat, Ord kangaroo rat, piñon mouse, Great Basin gopher snake, Hopi rattlesnake, and midget faded rattlesnake. Birds in the area include red-tailed hawk, great horned owl, mourning dove, titmouse, rock wren, and the bright blue piñon jay.

The vegetation found in Grand Gulch includes piñon pine, juniper, cottonwood, Gambel oak, single leaf ash, willow, sagebrush, blackbrush, rabbitbrush,

Photo: Bill Hatcher

Grand Gulch Spire.

prickly pear cactus, and a variety of flowering annuals. Ann Zwinger's excellent book *Wind in the Rock* is a highly recommended account of the beauty and mystique of Grand Gulch.

Utah 261 links Utah 95 (near Natural Bridges National Monument) with Utah 163 (just north of Mexican Hat), giving access to the Grand Gulch Primitive Area. The drainage is the largest of the San Juan River canyon tributaries, dropping 2,700 feet (823 m) in its 52 miles (84 km). Grand Gulch was named in 1879 by Mormon mission members of the Hole-in-the-Rock expedition, who scouted the region for a way around the 600-foot (183 m)-deep canyon.

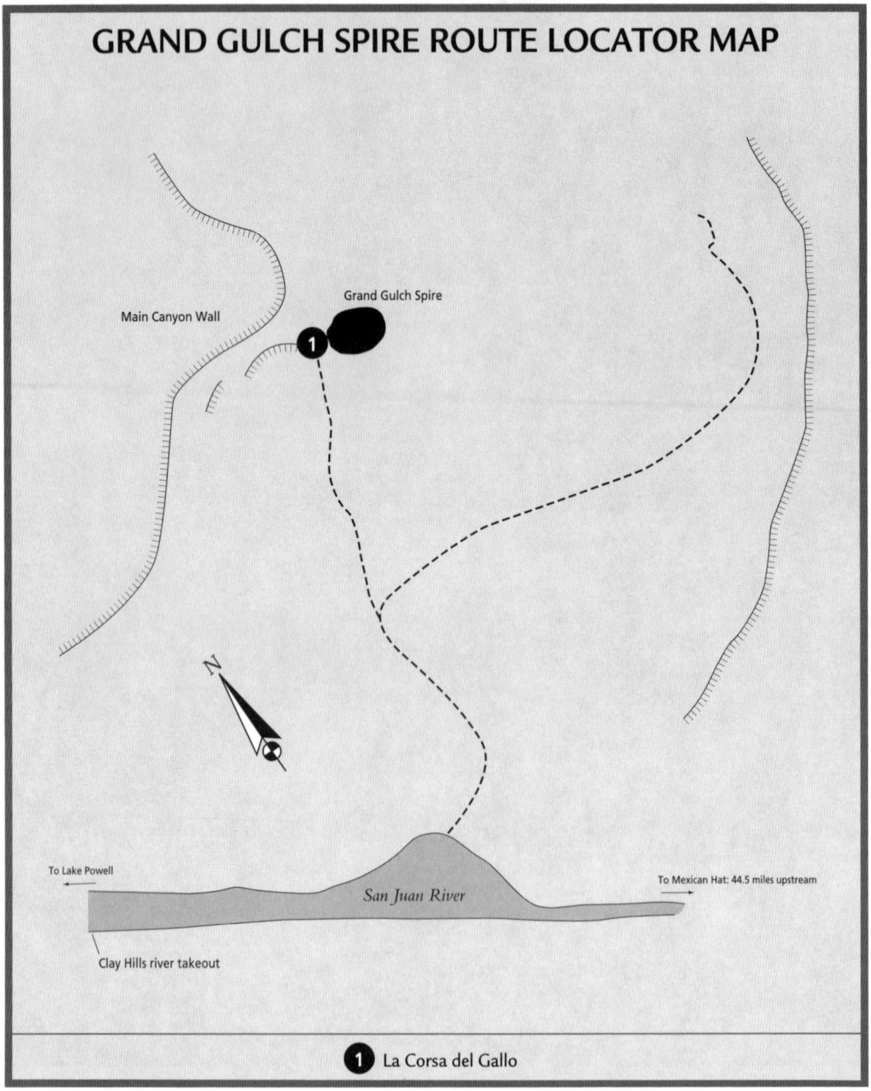

GRAND GULCH SPIRE

Grand Gulch Spire, a.k.a. Shima Sani (Navajo for Grandmother), is a semidetached pinnacle in lower Grand Gulch approximately 0.5 mile (0.8 km) from the San Juan River. It is accessed by floating down the San Juan.

The San Juan River originates in the San Juan Mountains of southern Colorado. In the Mexican Hat area it descends through limestone canyons to the stagnant waters of Lake Powell. The float is remote, with numerous side canyon hikes to petroglyphs and Anasazi ruins. Unlike floats trips through the Green River and Colorado River Canyons, the varied and colorful layers are missing in the limestone.

Grand Gulch is the largest of the San Juan River tributary canyons. It was named in 1879 by George B. Hobbs, Lemuel Reed, George Sevy, and George Morrill while they scouted the region for a way around the gulch.

To reach Grand Gulch Spire, put in at the Mexican Hat boat ramp. Float to the mouth of Grand Gulch, approximately 44.5 river miles (71.6 km). To exit, float approximately 12.5 river miles (20.1 km) to the Clay Hills Crossing takeout, where a second vehicle is left for the shuttle back to Mexican Hat. **NOTE:** BLM allows river users only one day (twenty-four hours) at Grand Gulch.

1 LA CORSA DEL GALLO
III, 5.10+, 6 pitches, 495 feet (151 m) ★★★★

First Ascent: Tim Toula, Dave Insley, Bill Hatcher, June 14, 1992.

Location and Access: Approach with a 0.5-mile (0.8 km) hike upcanyon, forty-five minutes from the river at Grand Gulch. The spire is obvious on the left (west) side of the gulch. The route begins at the notch between the main canyon wall and the west face of the tower. The first ascent team left a summit register.

Pitch 1: Begin up an easy fifth-class chimney on the river side of the tower, 80 feet (24 m).

Pitch 2: Continue with hands up the northwest face, passing two bulges (5.10+), then climb a 5.10+ off-width to a belay ledge, 140 feet (43 m).

Pitch 3: Climb 5.6, then a squeeze chimney to a belay ledge, 60 feet (18 m).

Pitch 4: Traverse left 70 feet (21 m) at 5.5, passing an off-width crack system. The traverse takes you from the northwest to the east face of the tower.

Pitch 5: From a third-class ledge, ascend 5.8, then 5.10+ off-width. Face climb to a ledge, then angle up and left to a ledge and belay, 165 feet (50 m). Death flakes and loose blocks are left of the pitch.

Pitch 6: Continue 5.10- to the summit, 50 feet (15 m).

Paraphernalia: Friends (3) sets #1 through #5 with a few #7; wired stoppers.

Descent: Two airy rappels off the southwest side of the tower. The first rappel is overhanging, the second is from a hanging station.

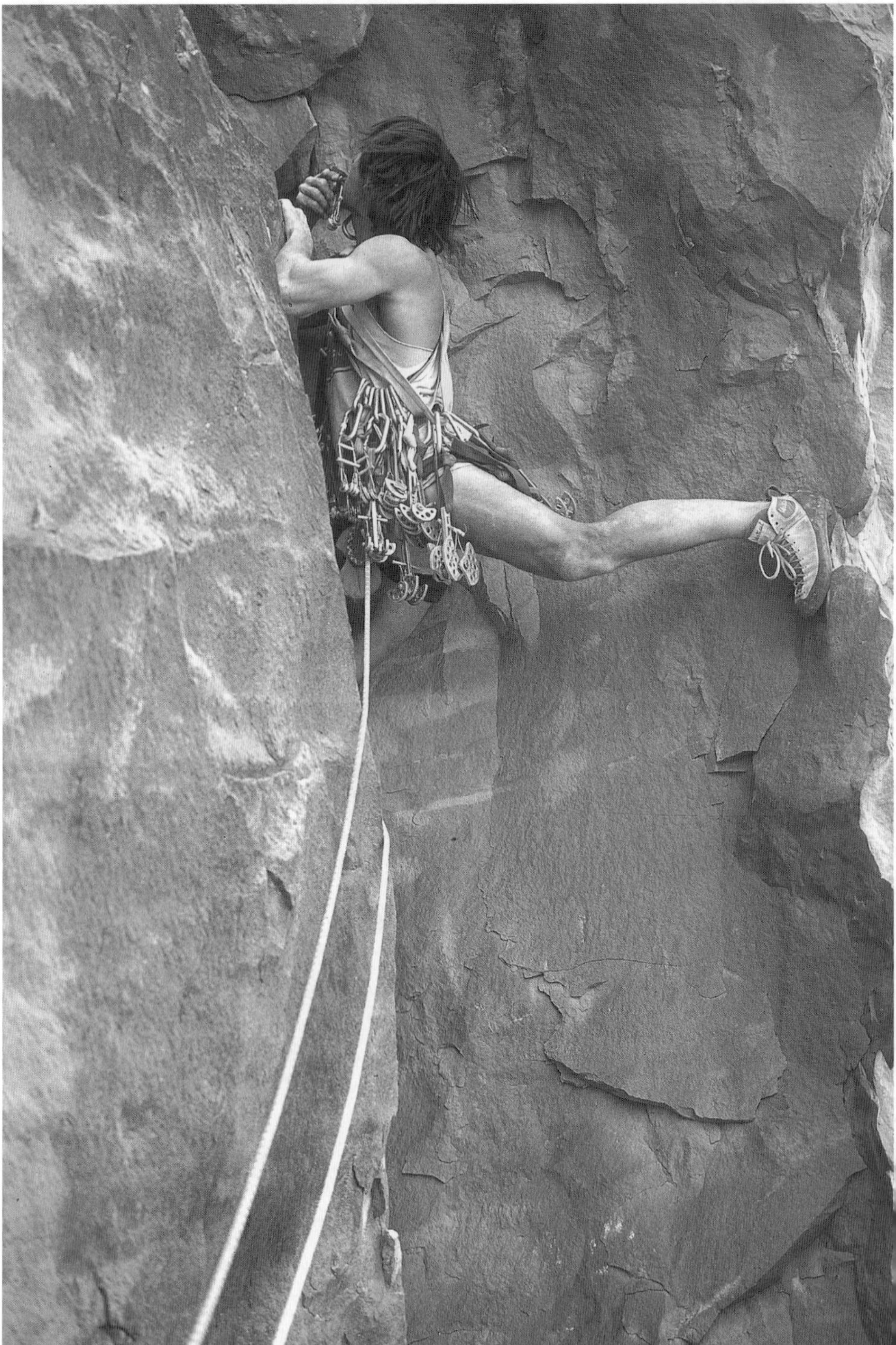

Photo: Bill Hatcher

Tim Toula on pitch 3, La Corsa del Gallo.

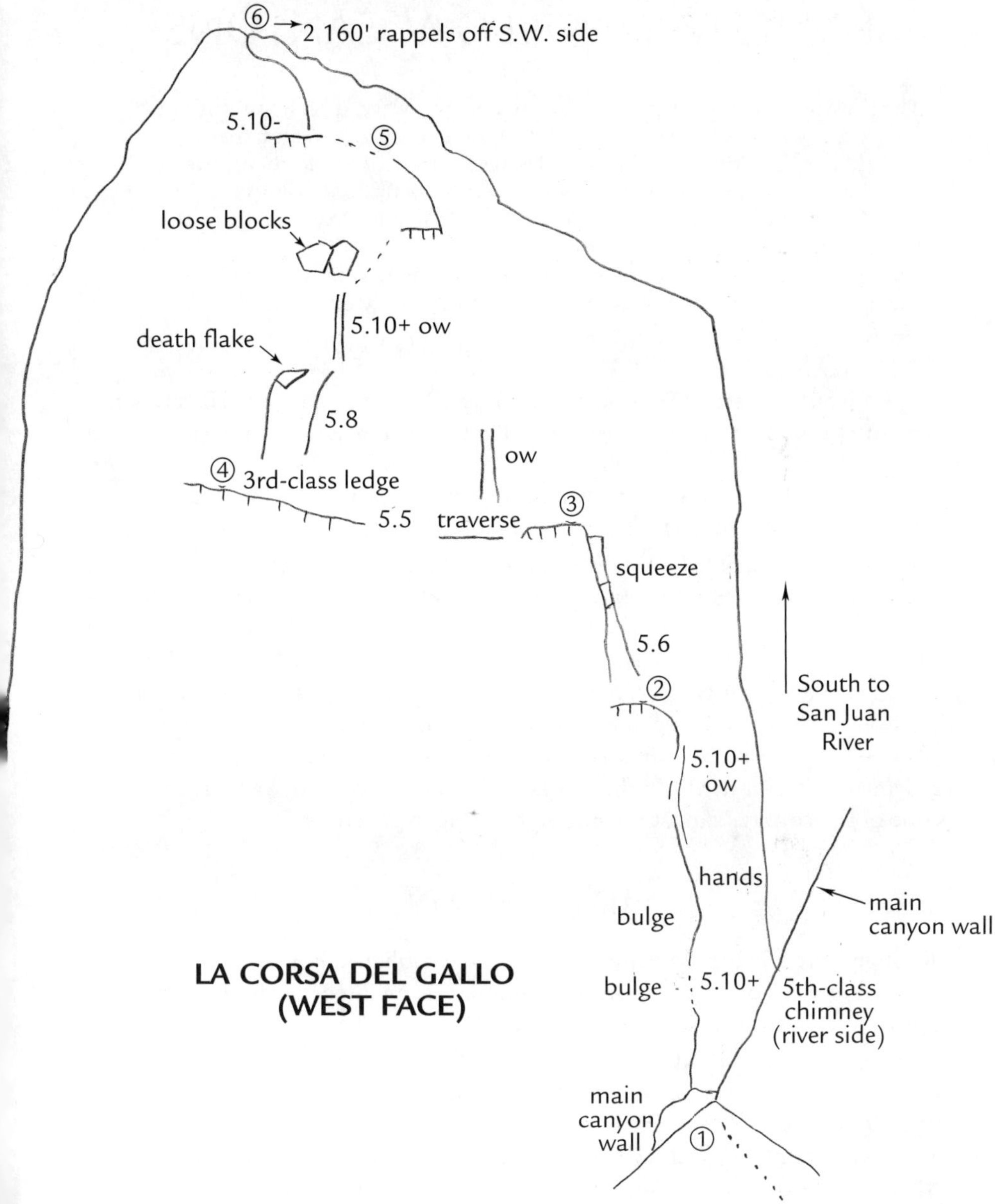

LA CORSA DEL GALLO (WEST FACE)

If there are clouds stretched across the west the ending is usually one of exceptional brilliancy. The reds are all scarlet, the yellows are like burnished brass, the oranges like shining gold.

—John C. Van Dyke, *The Desert,* 1901

26
LONG AND WILLOW CANYONS

> The shifting sands! Slowly they move, wave upon wave, drift upon drift; but by day and by night they gather, gather, gather. They overwhelm, they bury, they destroy, and then a spirit of restlessness seizes them and they move off elsewhere, swirl upon swirl, line upon line, in serpentine windings that enfold some new growth or fill in some new valley in the waste. So it happens that the surface of the desert is far from being a permanent affair. There is hardly enough vegetation to hold the sand in place. With little or no restraint upon them they are transported hither and yon at the mercy of the winds.
>
> —John C. Van Dyke, *The Desert,* 1901

Long Canyon is a narrow 500-foot (152 m)-deep chasm lined with Wingate sandstone. It is traversed by the famed Burr Trail, which extends 66 miles (106 km) from Boulder, Utah, into the Grand Staircase-Escalante National Monument, through Capitol Reef's Waterpocket Fold, then down to Lake Powell at Ticaboo and Bullfrog Resort and Marina in the Glen Canyon National Recreation Area.

The trail was established by Mormon ranchers to herd their cattle between summer grazing on Boulder Mountain and winter fodder at the lower Waterpocket Fold area of Capitol Reef. The trail is a graded dirt and gravel road, which in good weather can be traveled with two-wheel-drive vehicles, but high clearance and/or four-wheel drive is recommended. As the trail descends in a southeast direction from the Waterpocket Fold, it drops more than 800 feet (244 m) in 1 mile (1.6 km). For more than a hundred years, the Burr Trail has been in use by cattlemen and their herds. In the words of the state's Scenic Byways brochure, "It is one of the country's most moving sightseeing experiences."

LONG CANYON

Although only a handful of routes have been established in the canyon, there is potential for tens of dozens more, with numerous unclimbed splitter cracks. The approach from the car is about five minutes.

From Boulder, descend the Burr Trail into Long Canyon and cross Deer Gulch at the bottom of the grade. Three or four routes have been climbed at 5.9/5.10/5.11 on the south-facing wall above the trail by Jason Keith, John Patton, Chris McIntosh, Jeanne Korn, Tony Cosky, Pete Luketi, and Alan Hunt. Other routes have been established by Mike Baker, Leslie Henderson, and Wilson Goodrich. Further details are unavailable.

MILEAGE LOG—BURR TRAIL IN LONG CANYON

This log identifies the locations of climbs established in Long Canyon, but further information is unknown.

LONG AND WILLOW CANYONS ROUTE LOCATOR MAP

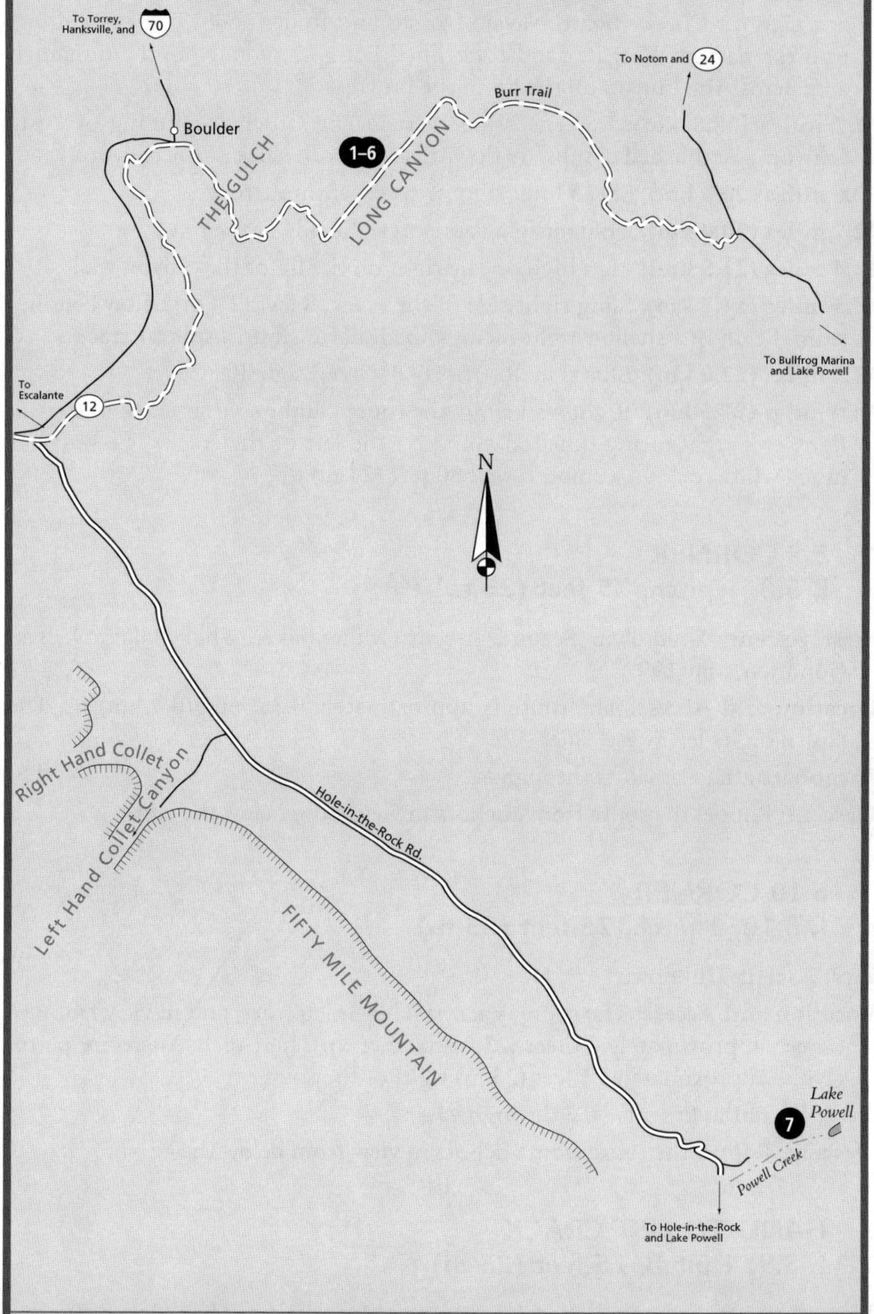

1–6 Long Canyon

7 Willow Canyon

00 miles: Begin at the junction of Utah 12 and the Burr Trail in Boulder, Utah, at a sign for Checkerboard Navajo Domes and Route 1668. The grade drops into the narrow Wingate sandstone-lined Long Canyon. Note the unnamed arch across the canyon on the lip of the buttress.

11.7 miles (18.8 km): Cement bridge across The Gulch (beginning of Long Canyon); established climbs are downriver on both sides of the canyon.

12.6 miles (20.3 km): Speed limit sign with serpentine arrow.

12.7 miles (20.4 km): Unidentified route on right side of the road.

13.4 miles (21.5 km): Arch high on the right on the lip of the canyon wall.

13.5 miles (21.7 km): Sling right side of the crack, 8 feet (2.4 m) below bedding seam. Begin in a shallow right-facing dihedral, finish up a splitter crack.

13.7 miles (22.0 km): Blue sign: ROUTE 1668. Green sign: REF 20.

14.0 miles (22.5 km): Right wall sling; the route climbs splitter crack one crack right of a right-facing dihedral. Sling on the left of the crack. The wall has much white rock on a smooth wall 80 feet (24 m) up.

1 5.8 CORNER
I, 5.8, 1 pitch, 75 feet (23 m) ★★★

First Ascent: Unknown. Second Ascent: Mike Baker, Shar Baker, Wilson Goodrich, May 1999.

Location and Access: The route is approximately 0.25 mile (0.4 km) up The Gulch on its left (west) side.

Paraphernalia: Camalots through #2.

Descent: Rappel the route from anchors in view from below the climb.

2 5.10 CORNER
I, 5.10, 1 pitch, 75 feet (23 m)

First Ascent: Unknown.

Location and Access: The route is across The Gulch (east) and in view from *5.8 Corner,* approximately 75 feet (23 m) farther up The Gulch. There are petroglyphs approximately 75 feet (23 m) right of the route.

Paraphernalia: Friends #0.5 through #1.5.

Descent: Rappel the route from anchors in view from below the climb.

3 HAND TO FIST CRACK
I, 5.9, 1 pitch, 75 feet (23 m) ★

First Ascent: Unknown. Second Ascent: Mike Baker, Shar Baker, Wilson Goodrich, May 31, 2000.

Location and Access: The route is about 10 feet (3 m) left of *Cactus Fall.* Climb a

Photo: Mike Baker
5.8 Corner.

Photo: Mike Baker

5.10 Corner.

hand to fist crack to rappel slings around a bush, barely visible from below the route.

Paraphernalia: Friends #2 through #3.

Descent: Rappel the route.

4 CACTUS FALL
I, 5.9, 1 pitch, 75 feet (23 m) ★★★

First Ascent: Mike Baker, Shar Baker, Wilson Goodrich, May 31, 2000.

Location and Access: The route is 150 feet (46 m) right of *5.8 Corner* on the same (west) side of The Gulch. Climb an off-width crack, with the crux at a bulge one-third up the route. Wilson Goodrich: "The name comes from my farming out dead cactus on the route. I asked Mike to move my pack at the bottom of the route. He did, but when I threw the cactus out from the wall, it landed in my open pack anyway."

Paraphernalia: Friends through #4; Camalots through #4.

Descent: Rappel the route from anchors visible from below the climb.

5 PATTON'S PUMP
I, 5.10, 1 pitch, 100 feet (30 m) ★★

First Ascent: Jason Keith, John Patton, early 1990s.

Location and Access: The route is on the left as you drive south down the Burr Trail and is identified by rappel slings. Climb an obvious lieback/jam crack. Further information is unavailable.

Paraphernalia: Standard desert rack.

Descent: Rappel the route from anchors visible from below the climb.

6 THANKSGIVING CRACK
I, 5.11, 1 pitch, 100 feet (30 m)

First Ascent: Jason Keith, Tony Cosby, Chris McIntosh, early 1990s.

Location and Access: Climb a splitter crack right of *Patton's Pump*.

Paraphernalia: Friends, several #1.5.

Descent: Rappel the route from anchors visible from below the climb.

DIVERSIONS

SCENIC BYWAY UTAH 12—BOULDER/ESCALANTE

The picturesque small towns of Boulder and Escalante, 29 miles (46 km) apart, are situated at the north edge of the Grand Staircase-Escalante National Monument, a 1.7-million-acre preserve designated on September 18, 1996, by then-President Bill Clinton. The east approach to Boulder passes through ponderosa pine, aspen, piñon, and juniper of the Dixie National Forest, giving expansive vistas of the vast, breathtaking desert canyon country to the east and south. Boulder and Escalante are the principle communities for approach and information to the region and are accessed by the magnificent Utah 12.

For about 122 miles (196 km), Utah 12 traverses between Capitol Reef and Bryce National Parks and is one of the most scenic stretches of highway anywhere on the Colorado Plateau. It was named one of the top ten scenic roads in America by *Car and Driver* magazine. It is a recommended route, regardless of climbing destination.

Boulder is on the sloping shoulder of Boulder Mountain at an altitude of 6,000 feet (1,829 m). It was settled in 1894 and named for the dark volcanic boulders on the slopes of the nearby lava-capped 11,000-foot (3,353 m) Boulder Mountain (Aquarius Plateau). It was the last town in the United States to receive mail by mules, and was the last incorporated town in Utah to have its main street paved. A park brochure warns: "Bears, ranging in color from blond to dark, dark brown, roam freely in the Escalante–Boulder area. Rarely seen, they are, however, wild and dangerous animals and should be avoided."

Utah: A Guide to the State offers a colorful picture of Boulder's past: "For years after settlement the tiny town was isolated from the world by towering walls of solid rock, 35 miles by pack train from Escalante. A man packed in a pick-up truck, in pieces, reassembled it, and ran it eight years without a license; gasoline, also 'imported' on pack horses cost seventy-five cents a gallon. In 1923, President Harding set aside 130 acres of public domain for a townsite, but a survey was neglected, and for nearly ten years residents were legally squatters, immune from taxation."

Boulder, Utah, does not have a chamber of commerce. Please contact Grand Staircase–Escalante National Monument (see p. 414).

Escalante, 5,300 feet (1,615 m) in elevation, was settled in 1875 by Mormon pioneers and was originally called Potato Valley for a type of wild potato found in the area. It was renamed for the river, which received its name from the second Powell Expedition in honor of Francisco Silvestre Velez de Escalante, a Spanish Catholic priest who explored portions of Utah in 1776. Anglos first visited Escalante in 1866 when Captain James Andrus and his military ensemble camped there while en route from St. George to Green River during the Indian Uprising of 1866. They harvested, cooked, and ate the wild potatoes that grew in the valley.

For a brochure and further information on the Escalante area, contact the Escalante Chamber of Commerce at P.O. Box 326, Escalante, UT 84726, or call (435) 826-4810.

ANASAZI INDIAN VILLAGE STATE PARK

The Anasazi Indian Village State Park in Boulder was home to one of the largest Ancestral Puebloan communities west of the Colorado River. The location is known as the Coombs Site and was occupied from about A.D. 1050 to about 1200. Two hundred people lived in about fifty dwellings, growing beans, corn, and squash. Arrow points, axe heads, pottery, and other artifacts excavated in the area are on display at the visitor's museum center. A superb diorama shows how the village is thought to have looked at the height of its occupation, with replicas of a pit house and storage rooms. The visitor's center sells books, videos, film, T-shirts, postcards, and other souvenirs. On the grounds are self-guided trails through the ruins. For more information write to P.O. Box 1429, Boulder, UT 84716-1429, call (435) 335-7308, or visit on-line at www.ut.blm.gov/monument.

LOWER CALF CREEK FALLS

Lower Calf Creek Falls drops 126 feet (38 m) over a Navajo sandstone canyon wall. The hike is over a flat canyon floor beneath towering walls streaked with desert varnish. Beaver ponds, arches, Indian ruins, pictographs, and inviting swimming holes entice the visitor. An old fence is a reminder of the early pioneers.

To reach the falls, take Utah 12 east from Escalante 12.5 miles (20 km) or south from Boulder 12 miles (19 km) to the Calf Creek Recreation Area and trailhead. The round-trip hike to the base of the dramatic waterfall is approximately 5.5 miles (9 km). Although the falls are the main attraction, the entire 8-mile (13 km) length of the scenic Calf Creek drainage (including the upper falls) attracts many visitors each year.

ESCALANTE PETRIFIED FOREST STATE PARK

During the late Cretaceous period of about 140 million years ago, rivers carried trees to the area of Escalante and, over time, buried them, preventing their decay. Wood cells were slowly replaced with silicone dioxide crystals and other minerals, coloring the lithified wood (turned to stone) with rainbow hues. Dinosaur bones from the Morrison Formation of the Jurassic period (144 to 208 million years ago) represent creatures trapped in marshy areas, whose bones were preserved when they were buried with the trees. Nature trails winding through the petrified forest include Wide Hollow, Bailey Wash, and Rainbow Loop Trails.

To reach the park, drive 1.5 miles (2.4 km) west of Escalante on Utah 12 (Scenic Byway). The state park has a visitor's center, a 22-unit campground, rest rooms, showers, and a sanitary disposal station.

AQUARIUS PLATEAU

Known as Boulder Top, the relatively flat summit of the Aquarius Plateau (Boulder Mountain) is a rolling tableland of approximately 50 square miles (80 km). Most of the area exceeds 10,000 feet (3,000 m) in elevation, with summits above 11,000 feet (3,353 m). Forests of Engelmann spruce and fir cover much of Boulder Top, along with meadows of arctic tundra and numerous small lakes and ponds. The heavy evergreen growth is very rare for such an altitude, and is thought to be one of the highest forests in the world. The unique region has more than 300 archaeological sites, as well as dramatic displays of metamorphosed rocks, the result of ancient coal fires. Utah 12 crosses the plateau as it traverses the mountain from the hamlet of Boulder to Torrey.

GRAND STAIRCASE–ESCALANTE NATIONAL MONUMENT

The 1.7-million-acre monument was designated on September 18, 1996, by then-President Bill Clinton, and is the largest combined national park land in the lower forty-eight states, contiguous as it is with Canyonlands, Capitol Reef, and Bryce National Parks, and Rims and Glen Canyon National Recreation Areas, totaling approximately five million acres. It is the only national monument to be managed by the Bureau of Land Management.

A diverse land, it offers exciting backcountry hiking, technical rock climbing, canyoneering, and unsurpassed beauty for the photographer, camper, and hiker. Attractions in the monument include the Escalante River (the last major river to be discovered and named in the continental United States), Calf Creek Falls, the Burr Trail, Hole-in-the-Rock, Straight Cliffs, Fifty Mile Mountain, Grosvenor Arch, the Cockscomb, and numerous arches, bridges, and slot canyons, as well as more than 300 archaeological and Native American rock art sites. Traveling the Burr Trail from the junction of Utah 12 at Boulder, the Grand Staircase–Escalante National Monument begins as the trail descends into Long Canyon. For further information write P.O. Box 246, Escalante, UT 84726, call (435) 826–5499, or visit on-line at www.ut.blm.gov/monument.

WILLOW CANYON

BROKEN BOW ARCH

Willow Canyon, a drainage to the Escalante River, lies just south of the boundary of the Grand Staircase–Escalante National Monument.

Broken Bow Arch is in the Glen Canyon National Recreation Area on the north wall of the canyon. Robert H. Vreeland in *Nature's Bridges and Arches, the Escalante River Basin, Utah:* "Broken Bow Arch is one of the most beautiful in the country, and is in a very pretty setting."

From the Escalante post office in the 400 block of Main Street (Utah 12), drive east on Utah 12 (Scenic Byway). At 5.2 miles (8.3 km) turn right onto Hole-in-the-Rock Road. Drive south for approximately 43.5 miles (70 km), then take a two-track trail southeast 1 mile (1.6 km) to Sooner Bench. Hike southeast into Willow Canyon for about 1.5 miles (2.4 km) to the arch. An alternative approach is a hike down Sooner Gulch to the south of Sooner Bench, but this approach is approximately 1 mile (1.6 km) longer. Bill Duncan: "Very lush and green; pools of water, and the lake is thirty minutes away. Good canyon hiking."

When Lake Powell is at high pool level, the arch can be reached with a 1.5-mile (2.4 km) hike up Willow Gulch. There is a narrow point with a 3-foot (0.9 m)-deep pothole just above Forty Mile Creek, which usually must be crossed.

Broken Bow was named by Alvey Edson when he found a broken Indian bow under the arch. A buttress-type natural arch eroded into the lower Navajo sandstone, it has a span of 94 feet (29 m), a height of 100 feet (30 m), a thickness of

Photo: Bill Duncan

Broken Bow Arch.

70 feet (21 m), and a width of 25 feet (7.6 m). Its summit is more than 200 feet (61 m) above the stream at its base, which has undercut the platform that the arch rests on.

7 BROKEN BOW ARCH
I, 5.8+ R, 2 pitches, 200 feet (61 m) ★★★

First Ascent: Jon Burnham, Bill Duncan, June 11, 1994.

Location and Access: Begin at the south prow of the arch.

Pitch 1: Face climb 5.7 R to a ledge, then 5.8+ past a second stance. Continue 5.6 past a small bush and on to a belay ledge with drilled piton anchors, 100 feet (30 m).

Pitch 2: Follow a large chimney past a constriction, then a 5.8 off-width to the summit, 100 feet (30 m).

Paraphernalia: Friends (1) set with extra large units; Camalot #5; Big Bros #3, #4 for the chimney.

Descent: Downclimb the wide chimney to anchors at the top of pitch 1, then rappel 100 feet (30 m) to the ground.

DIVERSIONS

HOLE-IN-THE-ROCK

The Hole-in-the-Rock is a narrow cleft in the wall of Glen Canyon through which Mormon pioneers in 1879 and 1880 lowered their wagons to the Colorado River. The 230 pioneers had been "called" by the Mormon Church to colonize the area near Bluff, Utah, in the southeastern corner of the state. Their journey began in November 1879 with 1,000 head of cattle and horses and 83 wagons containing survival paraphernalia, tools, farm implements, and a few personal items. Lashed to the wagons were water barrels and cages for chickens, ducks, and rabbits. The average age of the missionaries, including children, was eighteen years. The median age of adults was twenty-eight.

The caravan stretched over 2 miles (3.2 km). By the time the pioneers reached the walls of Glen Canyon, winter snows prevented them from turning back, so they chose to continue. At a narrow slot in the canyon's wall, they blasted, picked, and chiseled the cleft wide enough for their wagons to fit through. The 45 degree slope beyond to the river was prepared by driving wooden pegs into holes drilled into the cliff, then piling brush and rocks on the pegs to create a steep dugway. The wagons were prepared by "rough-locking" the rear wheels. Ropes and chains were attached to the rear axle and a dozen or more men hung on behind the wagon to help slow its descent. The livestock were then herded through the Hole-in-the-Rock and down the treacherous descent to the river. Nine horses lost their footing and fell to their deaths. A boat was built to ferry the wagons and pioneers across the river; cattle and horses swam the crossing.

Drive 4.5 miles (7.2 km) east of Escalante on Utah 12. Turn right onto the Hole-in-the-Rock Road, which extends to Lake Powell. The 57-mile (92 km) route

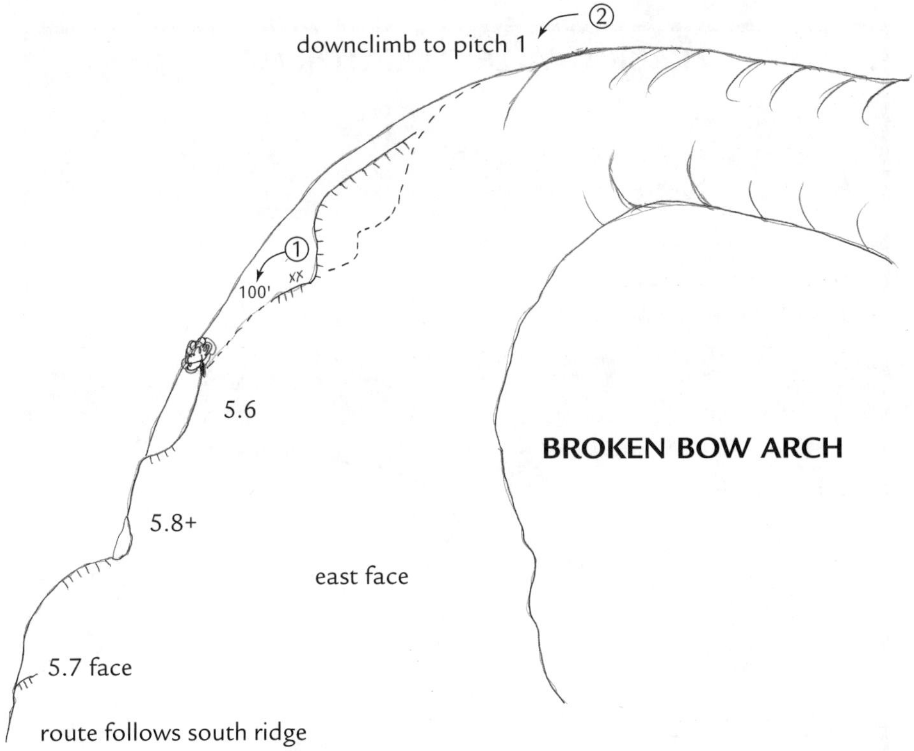

is gravel surfaced and passable by two-wheel-drive low-clearance vehicles. The last 6 miles (9.6 km) require four-wheel drive and high clearance.

SPOOKY AND PEEK-A-BOO GULCH SLOT CANYONS

Grand Staircase–Escalante National Monument is the home of many exciting slot canyons. Spooky and Peek-a-Boo Gulch are a good introduction, and are among the narrowest on the Colorado Plateau. Steve Allen: "This is the premier and most popular short slot loop on the Colorado Plateau. Claustrophobically tight narrows, a host of natural bridges, and sensuous curves of cross-stratified sandstone combine to provide a magnificent experience. Exceptionally rotund hikers cannot squeeze through Spooky Gulch." For further information on these and other slot canyons, refer to Steve Allen's excellent Canyoneering books published by the University of Utah Press.

RABBIT VALLEY BOULDERING

Rabbit Valley, Utah, is an excellent bouldering area. Bob Van Belle, past park manager at Capitol Reef: ". . . really good andesite, lots of extremely high, steep, technical pocket pulling and edging problems in a wild beautiful setting." Andesite is a fine-grained, dark-colored volcanic rock, named for the Andes Mountains of South America.

Rabbit Valley, a circular basin, sits at an altitude of 7,000 feet (2,134 m) between Fishlake and Awapa Plateaus. The community there was settled in the

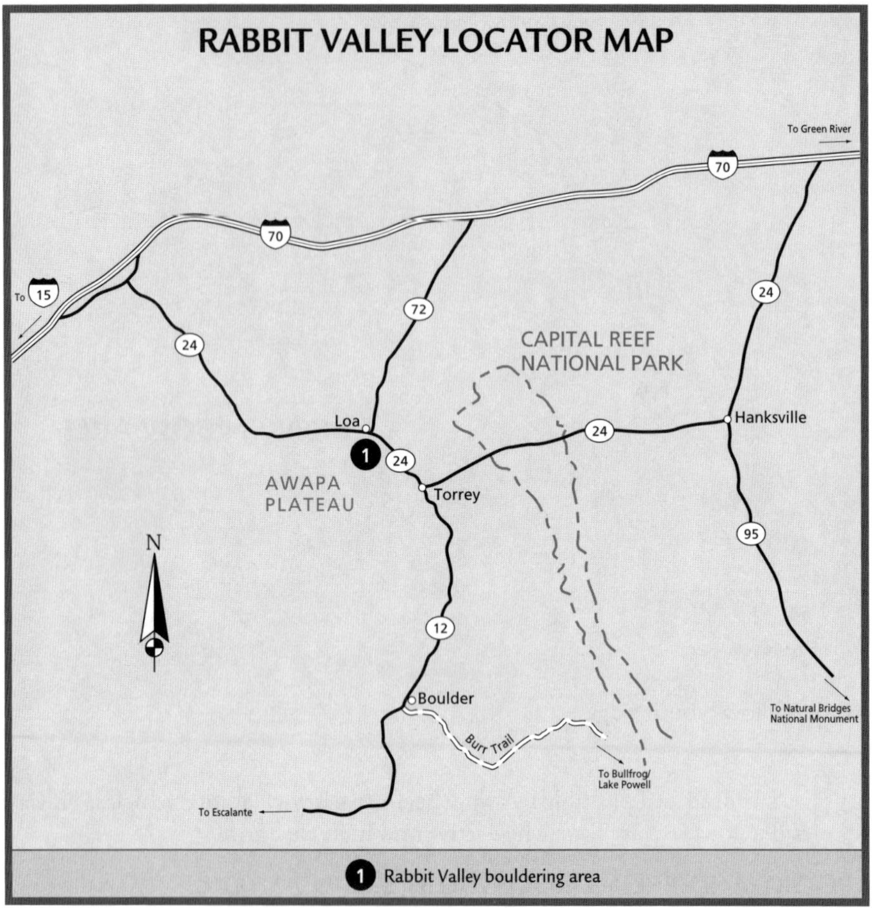

1870s. Both the Fremont River and Utah 24 pass through the valley, which was named by General William B. Pace as he and his men passed through the region following the Indian-white Battle of Red Lake.

To reach Rabbit Valley from Boulder, drive north on Utah 12 to Torrey, then northwest on Utah 24 to Loa. If approaching from the east, drive west on Utah 24 from Capitol Reef National Park to Loa. Rabbit Valley is south of the town at the edge of the Awapa Plateau.

> . . . the little stream running away from its lowest part is pure; and it dashes through the canyons, tumbles into little pools, and slips over shelving precipices like a thing of life.
>
> —John C. Van Dyke, *The Desert,* 1901

27

ST. GEORGE AREA

> The long line of dunes at the north are just as desolate, yet they are wonderfully beautiful. The desert sand is finer than snow, and its curves and arches, as it builds its succession of drifts out and over an arroyo, are as graceful as the lines of running water. The dunes are always rhythmical and flowing in their forms; and for color the desert has nothing that surpasses them. In the early morning, before the sun is up, they are air-blue, reflecting the sky overhead; at noon they are pale lines of dazzling orange-colored light, waving and undulating in the heated air; at sunset they are often flooded with a rose or mauve color; under a blue moonlight they shine white as icebergs in the northern seas.
>
> —John C. Van Dyke, *The Desert,* 1901

St. George is southern Utah's largest and fastest-growing town. In 1861, 300 Mormon families in the Salt Lake City region were "called" by the church to take part in the Cotton Mission to southwest Utah. St. George became the center of the new settlement. Brigham Young chose its name in honor of George A. Smith, who had served as the head of the Iron Mission during the 1850s. (The title "Saint" simply means he was a member of the Church of Jesus Christ of Latter-day Saints.) Visitor's centers boast that St. George is where Utah's summer sun spends the winter. The Hilton Inn's slogan for St. George is "The *other* Palm Springs."

PIONEER STATE PARK

The park is reached in a few minutes from downtown and offers excellent bouldering. From Skyline Drive, which runs along the north side of the city, drive 2.6 miles (4 km) from the junction of Snow Canyon Parkway and Utah 18 to a left turn at park signs, and follow a one-way loop through the park. The low foot-high fence on each side of Skyline Drive serves to protect endangered turtles from crossing the highway and being killed. At the far end of the loop, park and hike the obvious trail for about one minute to the bouldering/climbing wall. In the Narrows of the park, there is a 5.9+ tower with top-rope anchors.

BLUFF CLIFFS

The area offers some of the best crack climbing in the St. George region. Approach from a climbers' use trail at the end of 400 West on the right side of the Navajo sandstone bluff (about five minutes). Reach 400 West from Diagonal Street off Bluff Highway. Routes are listed right to left as they are reached from the approach trail.

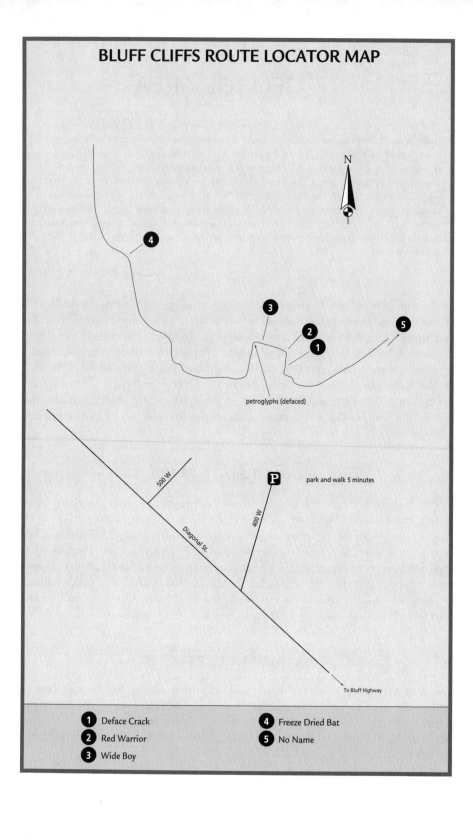

BLUFF CLIFFS ROUTE LOCATOR MAP

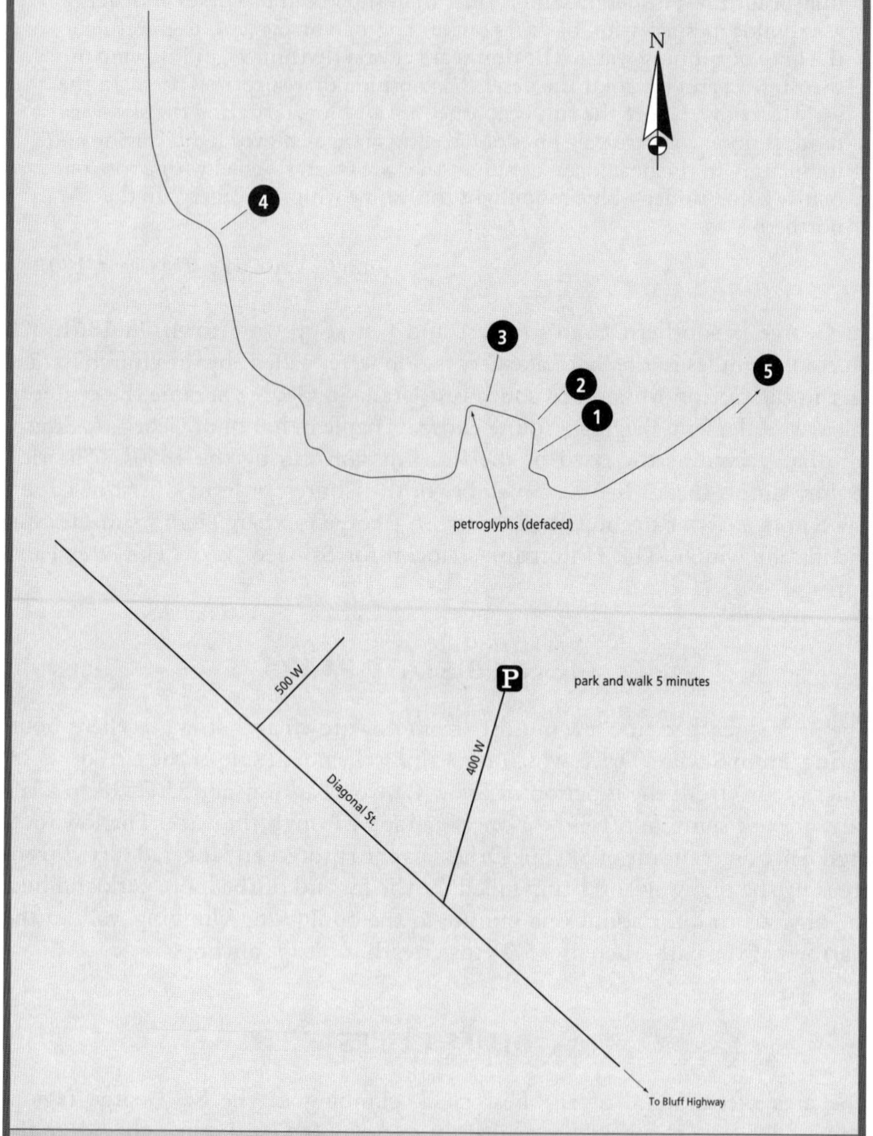

1 Deface Crack
2 Red Warrior
3 Wide Boy
4 Freeze Dried Bat
5 No Name

1 DEFACE CRACK
I, 5.10a, 1 pitch, 60 feet (18 m) ★★★★★

First Ascent: Bo Beck, Wayne Harding, Jorge Visher, Mat Kindred, 1991.

Location and Access: The route is one crack right of *Red Warrior* or three cracks right of the petroglyphs. Climb a splitter hand crack, ending with fist and knees at the top. The climb is named for the defaced petroglyphs left of the route.

Paraphernalia: Friends #3.5 and larger.

Descent: Rappel the route from a chain anchor shared with *Red Warrior*.

2 RED WARRIOR
I, 5.9+, 1 pitch, 60 feet (18 m) ★★★

First Ascent: Unknown.

Location and Access: The route is one crack left of *Deface Crack* or two cracks right of the petroglyphs. Climb a thin crack to anchors shared with *Deface Crack*.

Paraphernalia: Friends #0.5, #1.

Descent: Rappel the route.

3 WIDE BOY
I, 5.10a, 1 pitch, 60 feet (18 m) ★★★

First Ascent: Jorge Visher, Mat Kindred, early 1990s.

Location and Access: The route is one crack right of the petroglyphs and climbs hands to off-width, ending at a two-bolt belay/rappel station.

Paraphernalia: Friends #2.5, #3, #3.5; large units.

Descent: Rappel the route.

4 FREEZE DRIED BAT
I, 5.10c, 1 pitch, 60 feet (18 m) ★★★

First Ascent: Bo Beck, Wayne Harding, early 1990s.

Location and Access: The route is left of the petroglyphs and climbs a loose right-facing corner to a crystal-studded wall, ending at a sling anchor.

Paraphernalia: Selection of Friends.

Descent: Rappel the route from double anchors.

5 NO NAME
I, 5.11, 1 pitch, 60 feet (18 m)

First Ascent: Glen Griscom et al., early 1990s.

Location and Access: Right of *Deface Crack*. Climb an off-width crack up a west-facing wall to anchors at the shoulder of an arête.

Paraphernalia: Large units.

Descent: Rappel the route.

Photo: Jason Hurst

Bluff Cliffs: 1. Deface Crack *2.* Red Warrior *3.* Wide Boy.

Photo: Jason Hurst

Bluff Cliffs: 5. No Name.

SNOW CANYON

Snow Canyon is approximately 12 miles (19 km) north of St. George. A park brochure has a map of the canyon with the activities offered, which include geology, nature studies, wildlife viewing, photography, camping, ranger talks, and junior ranger programs. There are more than 15 miles (24 km)of hiking trails, a 3.5-mile (5.6 km) bike trail, and more than 5 miles (8 km) of equestrian trails. The park is open year-round and is especially appealing in the early spring and fall.

GUIDE BOOK

Todd Goss has done an excellent job documenting Snow Canyon climbing routes in *Rock Climbs of Southwest Utah & the Arizona Strip* (Sharp End Publishing).

From Interstate 15 at St. George, take exit 8 and turn right onto St. George Boulevard. Drive west to Bluff Street (a stoplight at a T intersection); turn right. At a stoplight at mile marker 4, continue straight onto Utah 18 North, then turn left (west) onto Snow Canyon Drive (Utah 300) at the Snow Canyon sign between

Photo: Eric Bjørnstad

Snow Canyon.

mile markers 11 and 12. A sign identifies the Red Cliffs Desert Reserve. The drive is 3.7 miles (5.9 km).

For further information, contact Snow Canyon State Park, P.O. Box 140, Santa Clara, UT 84765-1040, or phone (800) 322-3770.

WILDLIFE

The canyon is part of the 60,000-acre Desert Tortoise Habitat Conservation Plan. Wildlife in the park includes bobcats, coyotes, ringtailed cats, kit foxes, bats, ravens, quail, roadrunners, diamondback and sidewinder rattlesnakes, raptors, peregrine falcons, desert tortoises, gila monsters, kangaroo rats, squirrels, cottontail rabbits, and mule deer.

CULTURAL HISTORY

The Anasazi Indians inhabited the canyon for 800 years, between A.D. 750 and 1250. They left petroglyphs, artifacts, and structural remnants along the canyon walls. On the wall south of the ranger station, there is a panel of pioneer settlers' names and dates.

The canyon was discovered by cowboys searching for lost cattle, and was named for early pioneers of the region, Lorenzo and Erastus Snow (not for the rare snowfalls of the area).

FORMATION

Snow Canyon is composed of 170-million-year-old Navajo sandstone with more recent lava flows, which in many places flowed southward over the sandstone walls. The canyon ranges in elevation from 2,600 to 3,500 feet (792 to 1,067 m), with walls 500 to 700 feet (152 to 213 m) high, offering excellent one- and two-pitch routes.

MILE MARKER LOG—SNOW CANYON DRIVE

This log uses mile marker signs along Utah 300 as reference points.

12–11: Lava Caves Trailhead/West camp trail (right). The Lava Caves offer deep lava tubes to explore and are a recommended side trip. The trail is 1.5 miles (2.4 km) round-trip.

11–10: In the canyon is a picnic area on the left with tables, rest rooms, drinking water, and trash pickup. A ranger station is beyond the picnic area on the left, then the Shivwits Campground with thirty-six sites, including hookups and tent sites, modern rest rooms, showers, a sewage disposal station, drinking water, a group area, and volleyball.

10–9: Hidden Piñon Trail (right), then the Petrified Dune Trail (right). Hidden

Photo: Bill Hatcher

John Middendorf climbing a free route in Snow Canyon.

Piñon Trail is a 1.5-mile (2.4 km) round-trip trail introducing native plants and geology. Petrified Dune Trail begins at an area of soft red sand and leads quickly to an overlook of West Canyon.

DIVERSIONS

TUACAHN CENTER FOR THE ARTS

At its south end, Snow Canyon Drive intersects with Center Street (right) and Snow Canyon Parkway (left) at a sign for the Tuacahn Amphitheatre and Center for the Arts. Tuacahn, which translates to Canyon of the Gods, is the home of Utah's first charter high school for the performing arts.

From the intersection, the center is 1.7 miles (2.7 km) up the signed Tuacahn Drive. Well-known plays are performed live throughout the season. From November 24 through December 31, Tuacahn presents a Festival of Lights show, with hayrides and ice-skating under the stars.

Discounts are available for groups, local residents, senior citizens, college students, and AAA members. For further information, write to Tuacahn, P.O. Box 1996, St. George, UT 84771, or call (800) SHOW-UTAH (746-9882).

ZION CANYON IMAX

The Zion Canyon *Treasure of the Gods* is a dramatic thirty-seven-minute movie shown on a six-story-high screen. It is the story of the native legends and history of Zion Canyon. The production begins with Coronado in 1540, then early Mormon pioneers, and finally modern tourism, including mountain biking and climbing with Nancy Feagin and Doug Heinrich. Shown at the IMAX Theatre in Springdale near the entrance to Zion Canyon, it's a must-see production. For further information call (435) 772-2400, or visit on-line at www.zion canyontheatre.com.

UTAH SHAKESPEAREAN FESTIVAL

This internationally known, Tony-Award-winning theater celebrated its thirty-ninth summer and fall seasons in June and September 2000. For information call (800) PLAYTIX (752-9849), or visit on-line at www.bard.org.

QUAIL CREEK STATE PARK

Quail Creek State Park contains a 590-acre reservoir surrounded by barren red rock hills. The reservoir was created in 1985 to provide irrigation and culinary water to the St. George area. Most of the water in the reservoir comes from the Virgin River, pumped in through a buried pipeline; some water is from Quail Creek. The reservoir is contained by two dams: the Main Dam, an earthfill embankment dam, and the South Dam, a roller-compacted concrete dam, constructed to replace the original earthfill dam that failed in the early hours of New Year's Day 1989.

The area is a popular destination for fishing, boating, sailing, windsurfing, scuba diving, swimming, waterskiing, Jet Skiing, camping, and picnicking. The reservoir is located 15 miles (24 km) northeast of St. George and is known as one of Utah's best fisheries for largemouth bass. Other fish include rainbow trout, bluegills, and catfish. The park, at an elevation of 3,300 feet (1,006 m), boasts the warmest water in the state during the summer.

The campground on the southwest shore of the reservoir includes twenty-three developed campsites, each with a paved parking pad, fire pit, grill, and covered picnic table. Other facilities include modern rest rooms, swimming beaches, a concrete boat launching ramp, loading docks, and a fish cleaning station.

The park is open year-round. From St. George, exit Interstate 15 at the Hurricane exit 16, drive east 2.6 miles (4 km) on Utah 9, then north 2 miles (3.2 km) to the park. Or take the Leeds exit 23 and drive the frontage road south 3.4 miles (5.4 km), then turn left, and drive 1.5 miles (2.4 km) to the park. For further information write Quail Creek State Park, P.O. Box 1943, St. George, UT 84771-1943, or call (801) 879-2378 or (800) 233-3770.

FREMONT INDIAN STATE PARK

The Anasazi Indian culture settled mainly east of the Colorado River, the Fremont culture west of the river. Both inhabited the areas from approximately A.D. 700 to 1300. The Fremont Culture, first identified from sites found in 1928 along the Fremont River at Capitol Reef National Park, was named after Captain John

C. Fremont of the U.S. Corps of Topographical Engineers. Fremont passed through the area in the 1850s while searching for a shorter transcontinental railway route. During his journey, he mapped and surveyed parts of Utah, one of the last land masses to be explored in the United States. His name was given to the river by Major John Wesley Powell during his 1870s descent down the Colorado River.

Clear Creek Canyon has more than 500 rock art canvases and archaeological sites. It is also the location of the largest known Fremont Indian village, known as Five Finger Ridge Village. It contained more than 100 separate structures and housed up to 300 people. Unfortunately, this special place was destroyed by the construction of Interstate 70, another sacrifice to our gas-guzzling culture. So we can now view several tons of cultural heritage in the modern museum at the state park, like viewing wild animals in a well-designed zoo rather than in the original natural setting!

Special events taking place at the Fremont Indian State Park include monthly art shows from March through October; Primitive Technology Workshops in pottery making and other skills in June, July, and September; an annual Easter egg hunt in April (considered one of the better Easter egg hunts in the state), and a nondenominational Easter Sunday sunrise service on the front lawn of the visitor center. In April the annual Mountain Man Rendezvous is held behind Five Fingers Ridge; the annual San Rafael Trapping Party Mountain Man Rendezvous includes hawk throws, powder shoots, blanket trading, and 1800s camping. June 3 is free park day. June 17 is the date of the annual Atlatl Contest, considered the best of its kind in the United States, and the International World Atlatl Championship Tournament takes place in July. Annual Modern History Day is held in December.

If approaching St. George over Interstate 70 from the east, Fremont Indian State Park is a worthwhile stop. From Interstate 70, drive 20 miles (32 km) southwest from Richfield and take exit 17, then follow signs to the park. For further information write Fremont Indian State Park, 11550 West Clear Creek Canyon Road, Richfield, UT 84766, call (435) 527-4631, or visit on-line at www.nr.state.ut.us./parks/www1/frem.htm.

The desert is not more paintable than the Alps. Both are too big.

—John C. Van Dyke, *The Desert,* 1901

Index of Routes and Formations

Page numbers of illustrated routes and formations are set in **bold** type.

D

E

F

Q

R

S

Eric Bjørnstad—A Climbing Life

Photo: Joe Slansky

Eric Bjørnstad is perhaps best known as a pioneer of desert towers during the incredible early years when those phenomenal spires were first being climbed. Indeed, many of us climbing his routes today would shudder at the idea of doing them in the 1960s and early 1970s with the available gear and lack of information. Certainly, Eric's name is indelibly etched in the rich lore of desert climbing. But a broader look also reveals a life of great variety and interest, both within and outside the climbing world.

From the start, Eric engaged in a wide range of endeavors. Raised in California, his early passions included poetry writing, chess, speed typing, and classical music—playing both piano and oboe. He also sought physical challenges such as boxing, in which he excelled. Eric began camping early, with numerous trips to the High Sierra, and like many climbers then and now, a great love of high places was kindled.

Eric's first job was as a gandy dancer on the narrow-gauge railroad near Lone Pine, California. This began a working life of incredible variety; over the years he worked as a draftsman, piano salesman, photo processor, gardener, bartender, dump truck driver, tree topper, and handyman at a sorority (where he also lived), to mention only a few. His life apart from work was no less interesting. He married three times (to a Hungarian beauty queen, an art student, and the daughter of a major American business mogul), divorced three times, and fathered four children (David, Heather, Mara, and Eigerwand). He practiced Theravada Buddhism in Berkeley in the 1950s; partied with the likes of Alan Watts, Jack Kerouac, and Lawrence Ferlinghetti; and took up spelunking. In the late 1950s, he moved to Seattle and began a long career in alpine mountaineering. He amassed an impressive list of climbs and first ascents: Zodiac Wall, the first grade VI on the Squamish Chief, the North Face of Mount Howser in the Bugaboos, first winter ascent of Mount Robson, first ascent of the North Face of Mount Slesse, seventh ascent of Liberty Ridge on Mount Rainier, Mount Seattle in the St. Elias Range in Alaska, second ascent of the West Peak of the Moose's Tooth, and many others. He also taught climbing for the Seattle Mountaineers, served on the Seattle Mountain Rescue team for eight years, and represented American climbers durring the Seattle World's Fair French-American climbing week. It was also during this time that Eric began to write about climbing, in both magazines and books. He co-authored *Climber's Guide to Leavenworth Climbing Areas* with

Fred Beckey and wrote the Pitoncraft chapter for the second edition of the classic text *Mountaineering, Freedom of the Hills.*

From the 1960s on, Eric moved often and lived in cities across the country. He added weaving and three-dimensional stained glass to his professional repertoire, as well as the proprietorship of six restaurant-coffeehouses. He also developed a passion for climbing in the mysterious landscape of the Southwest desert. The routes that he and other desert pioneers established on these spooky towers tested the limits of existing equipment and techniques as well as their nerves. First ascents in the 1960s included Echo Tower in the Fisher Towers, the Beckey Buttress on Shiprock (20 days), Middle Sister and Jacobs Ladder in Monument Valley, Chinle Spire, and the 574th overall ascent of Devil's Tower when he and Fred Beckey put up the popular El Matador Route.

During these years, Eric climbed with such well-known figures as Ed Cooper, Alex Bertulis, Don Claunch, Harvey T. Carter, Yvon Chouinard, and Galen Rowell. He also developed an intense relationship with Fred Beckey—the two would share many first ascents over the years.

In 1970 he opened his famous Teahouse Tamarisk (24-page menu). In 1975 he began a ten-year period as a researcher investigating the effects of air pollution on lung health for the Harvard School of Public Health, which kept him traveling extensively. He returned to the desert time and again during this period, establishing first ascents such as Eagle Rock Spire in Monument Valley (another 16-day marathon), and Zeus and Moses in Canyonlands. He also did the fifth ascent of the incredible Totem Pole in Monument Valley, during the making of the film The Eiger Sanction.

In 1985 Eric finally returned to live in Moab and made the 600th ascent of Castleton Tower and the first ascent of the 1,000-foot El Piñon Blanca in Mexico, and participated in the first ascents of such well-known climbs as Zenyatta Entrada in Arches. He also undertook the phenomenal researching and writing task of authoring *Desert Rock*, the only comprehensive guide to the sandstone climbs of the Colorado Plateau.

Eric now gives private tours in little-known regions of the Colorado Plateau, drives four-wheel commercial tours, produces and sells Desert Glass Light Catchers—etched glass window hangings of Anasazi rock art—and is completing an expanded five-volume guide to technical rock climbs on the sandstone walls of the Southwest desert. Eric has truly lived a climbing life—in the high mountains, on rock walls, and in the desert Southwest. He has lived a well-rounded life as well, full of rich and enviable experiences. He loves the company of climbers, and will spend hours telling and listening to stories or pressing for information. His home is like a climbing museum. Yet, just as easily, he will revel in an opera or classical orchestral piece, or spend an evening preparing a fine dinner.

These guides are a tribute to Eric's life as a climber—and to his love for this desert land.

Jeff Widen